W9-BKJ-368

FAMOUS VERDI OPERAS

BY THE SAME AUTHOR

Autobiography
Opening Bars
Second Movement

Music
The Toscanini Legacy
Great Opera Houses
Glyndebourne: a History of the Festival Opera
Famous Mozart Operas
Famous Puccini Operas

Travel
Out of Season

Comedy
The Art of Coarse Cricket
The Art of Coarse Travel
The Art of Coarse Gardening (in preparation)

WITH CHARMIAN HUGHES

Travel
Eating in France
Eating in Italy (in preparation)

FAMOUS
VERDI OPERAS

An analytical guide for the opera-goer
and armchair listener

SPIKE HUGHES

With 469 musical illustrations

ROBERT HALE · LONDON

© *Spike Hughes 1968*
First published in Great Britain 1968

Robert Hale Limited
63 Old Brompton Road
London, S.W.7

SBN 7091 0205 4

PRINTED IN GREAT BRITAIN BY
EBENEZER BAYLIS AND SON, LIMITED
THE TRINITY PRESS, WORCESTER, AND LONDON

To
MY WIFE

Oh! come è dolce il mormorare insieme:
te ne rammenti?

Otello, Act I

CONTENTS

GIUSEPPE VERDI

Born: Le Roncole, near Busseto, 10th October, 1813
Died: Milan, 27th January, 1901

VERDI TODAY

As I come to write this study of the last of the three composers whose operas continue to dominate the international repertoire I realize that in my own lifetime the position of each one of them has undergone a significant and far-reaching change. Mozart, always respected, is now popular and much better understood; Puccini, always popular, is now more generally respected. In spite of the success of *Idomeneo* at Glyndebourne, however, the public has shown little eagerness to hear any other of Mozart's nineteen operas outside the five which were the subject of my earlier volume; nor has it been anxious to make closer acquaintance with the three Puccini works not discussed in *Famous Puccini Operas*. On the other hand, Verdi is not only enjoying unprecedented popularity and universal respect, but his unfamiliar operas are performed with increasing frequency to satisfy the public's curiosity and confirm its belief that there is very much more to Verdi than is to be found in his five or six most popular works.

As a consequence, in little more than a generation the change in Verdi's position in the musical world has been spectacular. Until shortly after the First German War public experience of Verdi was limited, even in Italy, to *Rigoletto*, *Il trovatore*, *La traviata*, *Aida* and not much else. Even the Requiem, now one of the fixtures and fittings of our concert halls, was an uncertain draw at the box office— at any rate in this country, which has always been a little shocked by Verdi's theatrical treatment of a theatrical subject. As for *Otello* and *Falstaff*—they were known to be masterpieces but were box-office poison so far as the "ordinary" Verdi public was concerned.

The great Verdi revival of our times can be said to have started with Toscanini's return to La Scala in 1921 and to have been developed with what has been called the Verdi Renaissance in Germany in the later 1920s. To speak of a Verdi "revival" or "renaissance" is a little misleading, of course, for it implies that the composer had hitherto been neglected in the sense that the recently revived operas of Rossini, Bellini and Donizetti had been neglected.

In fact, as everyone knows, Verdi has always been a popular composer—in the end perhaps the most popular, widely-known and universally loved composer who ever lived. At no time in the past 100 years has any ordinarily experienced opera-goer been able to say he had not heard at least two Verdi operas, whereas for a generation or more it has been all too easy to go through life in the opera house without hearing a note more of Rossini than *The Barber of Seville*, and nothing at all by Bellini or Donizetti.

Perhaps instead of a Verdi "revival" it would be more accurate to speak of the growth of the public's inquisitiveness about a composer to whom it was already devoted, the development of a healthy desire to learn more about a composer whose very success at the box office with three or four unfailing attractions had for so long paradoxically barred the way to a wider acquaintance with his work.

How and why this inquisitiveness and public demand for closer enquiry into Verdi's output came about is no longer relevant at this date. It may have been started by Toscanini's revelation of the unsuspected truth and beauty of music too long taken for granted (his *Trovatore* and *Traviata* were classic instances of this); it may have been a natural reaction to an overlong domination of musical life by Wagner and Wagnerism.*

In the course of a professional life of remarkable length and intensity Verdi wrote twenty-six operas. His first, *Oberto, Conte di San Bonifacio*, was performed in 1839, his last, *Falstaff*, in 1893—the one when Donizetti still had eleven more operas to write, the other when Puccini had already written three. *Falstaff*, indeed, went the rounds of the world's opera houses in the seasons immediately following its original production, hand-in-hand, as it were, with Puccini's *Manon Lescaut* which had been produced in Turin eight days before the première of *Falstaff* at La Scala—a happy coincidence linking two generations of opera.

It is not my intention in this study, however, to survey the whole of Verdi's output, although I admit in planning this book it was difficult to know where to draw the line between what were obviously Famous Verdi Operas and what were not. As time goes on we read more and hear more of Verdi and so more of his operas can be included in the category suggested by the title of this book. Not so very long ago nearly two-thirds of the operas I have included in this study were little more than names to most people, operas which were the vague sources of an aria or a duet on the radio, of an over-

* It is interesting to note that after their second unsuccessful world war the Germans have again reacted against the exaggerated nationalism that prompted them to start it. In a recent couple of seasons in Munich, the former capital city of the National-Socialist movement, there were 118 performances of operas by Verdi as against sixty by Wagner—nearly twice as many.

ture or ballet music at a concert. But today I think they can all be fairly described as "famous"; they are most of them available in two or more versions on gramophone records, and all are familiar features of the modern international repertoire.

In my attempt to keep this volume within reasonable bounds I have inevitably had to leave out operas which many readers will consider should have been included. Where, they may well ask, are *Luisa Miller* and *Ernani*, for instance? One of the reasons I left out these two operas was that when I drew up the plan of this book neither work was in the current repertoire of any European opera house at all. On the other hand, the Verdi operas that *were* performed during the season in question throw an interesting light on the changed status of the composer since pre-war days. Of the operas I have included *Nabucco* was performed in thirteen opera houses; *Macbeth* in five; *Il trovatore* in seventeen; *La traviata* in thirty-seven; *Rigoletto* in twenty-four; *Simon Boccanegra* in four; *Un ballo in maschera* in twenty-four; *La forza del destino* in sixteen; *Don Carlos* in eleven; *Aida* in twenty-six; *Otello* in eighteen; and *Falstaff* in twelve. The number of performances of *Nabucco* was particularly interesting—eight more than *Macbeth*, nine more than *Simon Boccanegra*, two more than *Don Carlos*, one more than *Falstaff*—for it showed that the opera could now qualify as a Famous Verdi Opera from practical experience instead of merely from hearsay.

The romantic story of the success of *Nabucco* and how the Lament of the Jews in exile aroused the national spirit of the Italians during the long Austrian occupation of their country was a tale learned by all lovers of Verdi at their mother's knee; as an opera, on the other hand, we felt it could probably have little more than academic interest now that it had lost its fortuitous topicality. This is an illusion which is immediately dispelled by a first hearing of the opera in the theatre, where *Nabucco* comes to life with great fire and vigour.

Where one has had in the past to take for granted the musical times and circumstances on which *Nabucco* made its first great impact, we now have a fair idea of the conditions and standards of Italian operatic life as Verdi encountered them in the early 1840s. This is largely due to the increased popularity and influence of Verdi himself whose music since the war has dragged in its wake a flourishing revival of the music of the three composers who dominated the Italian music scene at the start of his career—namely, Rossini, Bellini and Donizetti.

Italian opera as Verdi found it had been shaped by these three composers and each had his peculiar influence on the young Verdi. Rossini, who had retired, had developed the orchestra's role in opera and restricted singers by firm disciplinary measures to perform what he had written and not what they thought he ought to have

written. Bellini had a strong melodic influence which is very marked
in the early Verdi, not just in the long *cantilena* passages, but also,
less fortunately, in some of the trivial martial tunes.

The longest lasting influence, however, was that of Donizetti, and
in the end perhaps the most important. Not only was the Sextet in
Lucia di Lammermoor the obvious model for the Quartet in *Rigoletto*,
but there is no doubt that Verdi learned much of his dramatic tech-
nique and feeling for the theatre from Donizetti—particularly from
works like *Anna Bolena*, *Maria Stuarda* and *Lucrezia Borgia*.

Today, for the first time in the twentieth century, perhaps even
for the first time ever, it is no longer necessary to go into the library
to study the music of Verdi. The three distinct periods into which
the composer's working life was divided can be studied at first hand
in the theatre; the gaps in our knowledge—particularly of the early
operas and the "difficult" operas of Verdi's middle period, like
Simon Boccanegra and *Don Carlos*—have been filled and we now have
a panoramic view of his unique development as an artist covering
more than fifty years, from *Nabucco* in 1842 to *Falstaff* in 1893.

Like all great opera composers Verdi's treatment of the orchestra
was highly personal, original and, since it was always subservient
to the action, too often taken for granted. As one soon discovers by
attentive listening Verdi was no exception to the general rule that
more orchestral history is made in the opera house than in the concert hall. As in my studies of Mozart and Puccini I have designed
this book with the student of orchestration particularly in mind, and
I have made an index of Verdi's orchestration on page 543. This I
hope will prove a helpful supplement for those who have access only
to the vocal scores of the operas which inevitably can give no hint
of the colour, invention and splendid variety of Verdi's orchestral
language.

NOTE

I have included two Appendices in this book. The first, Appendix A, is intended as what I called in *Famous Mozart Operas* and *Famous Puccini Operas* an "Index of Contexts". Its purpose is to enable the reader who is listening to an excerpt from a Verdi opera, either as an item on the radio or as part of a "recital" on an LP record, or who just simply wants to refresh his memory, to refer quickly to the dramatic situation in the opera from which it comes. Thus, if the item concerned is "Questa o quella" the reader need do no more than look it up in Appendix A under *Rigoletto* to learn that its context is to be found on page 92.

Appendix B is a personal offering to those who may be interested in such things and to any editor preparing a complete collection of Verdi's letters—a transcription and translation of two of the composer's letters in my possession which, as far as I know, have not appeared in print before.

NOTE

I have included two Appendices in this book. The first, Appendix A, is intended as what I called in *Famous Verdi Operas* and *Famous Puccini Operas* an "Index of Contexts". Its purpose is to enable the reader who is listening to an excerpt from a Verdi opera, either as an item on the radio or as part of a "recital" on an LP record, or who just simply wants to refresh his memory, to refer quickly to the dramatic situation in the opera from which it comes. Thus, if the item concerned is "Questa o quella" the reader need do no more than look it up in Appendix A under *Rigoletto* to learn that its context is to be found on page 92.

Appendix B is a personal offering to those who may be interested in such things and to any editor preparing a complete collection of Verdi's letters—a transcription and translation of two of the composer's letters in my possession which, as far as I know, have not appeared in print before.

The Author Wishes to Thank

The Decca Record Company and Rare Records Ltd (Cetra) whose practical assistance and co-operation were invaluable throughout the preparation of this book;

The Glyndebourne Festival Opera for the loan of their full score of *Macbeth*;

Messrs G. Ricordi and Company for permission to quote from their copyright scores of *Otello* and *Falstaff*, and for the loan—to take home and live with—of the full scores of *Nabucco*, *Simon Boccanegra*, *La forza del destino* and *Don Carlos*;

Signorina Gabriella Carrara-Verdi for letting him look at Verdi's letters, books and scores in the villa at Sant'Agata;

His friend Sir William Walton, who gave him a fascinatingly annotated volume of the complete works of Shakespeare in Italian;

His friend Gwyn Morris, of the BBC's Italian Service, for his constant help in solving tricky problems of translation;

His wife Charmian, for her patience and her Index.

NABUCCO

Opera in four parts. Libretto by Temistocle Solera. First performed at La Scala, Milan, on 9th March, 1842. First performance in England: Her Majesty's Theatre, London, 3rd March, 1846 (as *Nino*). First performance in the United States: Astor Opera House, New York, 4th April, 1848.

IT WAS with *Nabucodonosor*—or *Nabucco*, as it has been more conveniently called since its earliest days—that Verdi considered his artistic career could truly be said to have begun. *Nabucco* was Verdi's third opera. His first, *Oberto, Conte di San Bonifacio* (1839) had had a moderate success of fourteen performances at La Scala. His second, the comic opera *Un giorno di regno*, had been a disastrous failure and was withdrawn from the Scala schedule for 1840 after a single performance. The story of how Verdi, stricken by the tragic loss of his young wife and both his children, bitterly resolved after the fiasco of his comic opera never to compose again, came to write *Nabucco* and to set the whole of Italy aflame with excitement is one of the most stirring stories in the history of music. Verdi has left his own personal account of how Bartolomeo Merelli, the impresario of La Scala, virtually bludgeoned him into reading Solera's libretto (written for Nicolai, composer of *The Merry Wives of Windsor*, who refused it); how when he returned home to his lodgings he threw the book down on the table, where it fell open at the words of the Hebrews' Chorus "Va, pensiero, sull'ali dorate"; how he put the book away out of sight but could not sleep for thinking about it; and how, after reading and re-reading it during the night, he took it back to Merelli only to be forcibly bundled out of the impresario's office and told he *must* compose it. "What could I do?" said Verdi.

The sensational success of *Nabucco* at its first performance was more than just a musical one, of course. By accident, or perhaps unconscious design, Verdi's setting of the Hebrews' lament for their homeland, had dramatized what the Italian people themselves felt as an oppressed and captive people. In all its sixty-two years of existence La Scala had never known what it was to bear anything but a foreign coat of arms on its prospectus (Milan itself had been occupied by one foreign power or another for 136 years) and Verdi and his opera came almost as a sign from heaven—the man and the music that Italy had been waiting for.

It does not need an unusually highly-developed historical sense, however, to perceive that although the political circumstances of the time undoubtedly favoured *Nabucco* and what appeared as its "message", Verdi's music must have made a tremendous impact in its own right. There is in this opera an element of youthful strength and energy which was entirely new in Italian music. Even those passages most strongly influenced by Bellini and Donizetti—the accompaniments especially—bear the unmistakable imprint of a vigorous personality which has injected the most commonplace rhythms with a new vitality. The orchestration, too, is distinctive, though perhaps in a rather negative way, for there is no doubt that while much of it is very individual it is not always very pleasant. Although *Nabucco* was Verdi's third opera his experience in the theatre had not yet enabled him to throw off the noisy brassy habits he had acquired writing overtures and marches for the town band at Busseto. But with all its faults it is a score in which, above all, the dramatic possibilities of orchestral dynamics are understood and exploited with imagination and, at times, with considerable originality. It is a young man's work, rough and awkward in its manner, but with many unmistakable pointers to the Verdi that was to come and as such a fascinating subject which, I think, justifies more than just a passing reference in this volume.

CHARACTERS IN ORDER OF SINGING*

ZACCARIA, *High Priest of the Hebrews* . . *Bass*

ISMAELE, *nephew of Zedekiah, King of Jerusalem* . *Tenor*

FENENA, *daughter of Nabucco* . . . . *Soprano*

ABIGAILLE, *a slave, supposed elder daughter of Nabucco* . . . . *Soprano*

ANNA, *sister of Zaccaria* . . . *Soprano*

NABUCCO, *King of Babylon* . . . . *Baritone*

HIGH PRIEST OF BAAL . . . . *Bass*

ABDALLO, *an old officer in Nabucco's service* . *Tenor*

Babylonian soldiers, Hebrew soldiers, Levites, Hebrew Virgins, Babylonian women, Babylonian Magi and Dignitaries, people, etc.

Scene: Jerusalem and Babylon   Time: Biblical

* The characters' names are given here as they appear in the Italian original. I hope I may be forgiven if I nevertheless refer to some of them henceforward by the names we know most of them by in England—and have known them since we were children. Nobody ever brought up in an English nursery can fail to recall with affection the verse which began:

> Nebuchadnezzar, the King of the Jews,
> Sold his wife for a pair of shoes.
> When the shoes began to wear,
> Nebuchadnezzar began to swear.

—and certainly none of us, having had Nebuchadnezzar's full name indelibly imprinted on our memories, has ever had need to shorten it to "Nabucco".

PART I

Scene : Inside the Temple of Solomon.

The action of *Nabucco*, it will be noticed is not divided into acts but into parts, each of which has a title. The practice of giving titles to each section like this was a characteristically romantic habit and one frequently affecting Verdi's operas until as late as *Il trovatore* (1853), although the operas were not always necessarily only in "parts"; the old-fashioned division into "acts" occurs from time to time. The idea of calling an "act" a "part" has never been properly explained; one can only presume that to the romantic librettist an "act" was too theatrical to be worthy of the Art of Literature in which the normal term of division was a Part.

Part I of *Nabucco* is preceded by an overture, said to have been written by Verdi in a Milan café on the suggestion of his brother-in-law when rehearsals for the opera had already begun. It is a rousing piece constructed of themes from the opera that follows which Verdi develops skilfully and with the brassy *brio* so characteristic of the score. Indeed, as though to prepare one gently for the typical tonal climate of *Nabucco* the overture begins with an introductory passage —*piano* and *maestoso*—for three trombones and tuba or ophicleide. Also, perhaps to indicate a little of the predominant part played by the chorus in the course of the opera, three of the four themes used in the overture are taken from subsequent choral passages. The second of these is the famous "Va, pensiero" which, to say the least, comes in for some rather odd treatment in the overture. Instead of the long flowing 4-in-a-bar tune heard in the opera, we have a curious, halting 3/8 version with a quaintly decorated melodic line and some unexpected flourishes in the solo trumpet (surely it ought to be a cornet?) which plays a very brass-band-like role in the orchestration. Few tunes which make so powerful an effect in the action can ever have made so undistinguished an impression as "Va, pensiero" in the instrumental form we hear before the curtain rises. Some instinct must obviously have prevented Verdi from giving the tune all he'd got, as it were, until the time and the place in the drama were right for it.

A stormy, brassy introduction raises the curtain on the first of the fine choral scenes in which this opera abounds. The Hebrews have come to the Temple to lament their defeat by Nebuchadnezzar, though the term "lament" does not fully describe the feeling of urgency and fear that hints unmistakably at things to come forty years later in the opening pages of *Otello*. This initial full-chorus passage is followed by a first and impressive indication of Verdi's understanding of the dramatic effect of the unison chorus. The bass voices of the Levite priests in a slow and solemn passage accompanied largely by trumpets and trombones playing *legato* clearly echoed in Verdi's memory when he came to the Priests in *Aida*. The Levites are not so malevolent as their Egyptian counterparts, but they are still inclined to push people around a bit. Their unison contribution to this first scene is an admonition to the other members of the crowd to pray. The praying is in fact done by the Hebrew Virgins, in a pleasant lyrical sequence for a three-part chorus of sopranos (there isn't much of a tune to it, but there is plenty of gentle orchestral atmosphere), which develops into a full choral ensemble notable for some very striking and imaginative contrasts of dynamics —*ff* followed by *pp* and the like—and ending with loud, reiterated cries of the word "stranier", which must certainly have had its effect on the first-night audience at La Scala. To expel the "stranier", or foreigner, was of course the burthen of Garibaldi's Hymn written in 1858 by Luigi Mercantini (words) and A. Olivieri (music), and at the time of *Nabucco* the word was almost as rabble-rousing in the theatre as any mention of "patria", which was to play such an explosive part in the fortunes of this opera.

Zaccharias, the High Priest, enters bringing with him Fenena, Nebuchadnezzar's daughter, as hostage, and in a short declamatory and brass-punctuated passage urges the Hebrews to have faith in the Lord. The High Priest's encouragement is continued in a Cavatina—Andante maestoso and *grandioso*—in which he reminds the crowd of the help they have received from Jehovah in former times of danger, to a tune which begins:

Ex *1*

A small-scale ensemble develops from this not-too-distinguished phrase, the chorus echoing Zaccharias in unison from time to time with both orchestral accompaniment and the melodic line of the voice parts influenced by the 12/8 which Verdi delighted to mix with 4/4 in his ensembles all his life, from *Nabucco* to *Aida* and *Otello* and the final fugue in *Falstaff*. The accompaniment, with its imposing trombones and the woodwind in a sequence of figures in thirds and sixths played *leggermente*, is typical of the Verdi of this period. Indeed, the woodwind figure is virtually repeated by the strings later in the same opera—in the final chorus of "Va, pensiero". This long lyrical movement for Zaccharias and the chorus is interrupted by the excited entrance of Ismael, who announces that Nebuchadnezzar and his army are approaching. Zaccharias places Fenena in the care of Ismael and in a final cabaletta leads the crowd away to repeated and—in 1842—inevitably rousing cries evoking Jehovah to bring "morte allo stranier".

A martial and diminuendo orchestral epilogue takes Zaccharias and the chorus out of sight, leaving Ismael alone with Fenena. We learn from them that Ismael had been Judah's ambassador to Babylon and that when he was thrown into prison (so much for diplomatic immunity in those days) Fenena had rescued him and they had fallen in love. Ismael promises to save Fenena from her captivity by the Jews, but the scene is interrupted by the sudden arrival of Abigail, sword in hand, at the head of Babylonian soldiers disguised as Hebrews, who announces the capture of the Temple. Ismael and Fenena are understandably surprised and disconcerted to see Abigail; as Ismael tells us in his short scene with Fenena, she is violently jealous and during his stay in Babylon had pursued him with a "furious love" which made Fenena's action in liberating him even more commendably defiant and courageous.

Abigail makes her mark as a character immediately on her entrance. She is a strong dramatic figure who expresses herself in a voice which ranges in the course of the opera over two octaves and a semitone—from the B natural below middle C to C'''. She is expected to combine coloratura with an energetic declamatory style and at one point to take the sudden drop from her top to her bottom C cleanly in her stride. Abigail's first words are angry and threatening, as she swears that the tomb shall be the lovers' nuptial bed. Her mood changes, however, and *sotto voce* she tells Ismael she loves him and will save him and his people if he will love her. From Abigail's wheedling Andante a trio develops, Ismael refusing her offer and Fenena, a Babylonian, significantly invoking the protection of the God of Israel for Ismael. It is a successful little scene, with the considerable lyrical beauty of Fenena's vocal line contrasting happily with the rather florid dramatic manner of Abigail.

The crowd—Hebrew women (with Zaccharias's sister Anna among the sopranos), old men and Levites, followed by disarmed Hebrew soldiers—enter the Temple *precipitosamente*, their panic at the approach of Nebuchadnezzar expressed Allegro agitatissimo

with a rapid triplet figure in the orchestra accompanying an exceedingly dramatic sequence of reiterated chromatic phrases.
Zaccharias enters hurriedly crying that the enemy is at the Temple
gates. Abigail, who has been in the background during this choral
scene, comes forward with her soldiers and cries, "Viva Nabucco!".
More Babylonian soldiers invade the Temple—in their own uniforms this time and not disguised as Hebrews, like Abigail's band of
Fifth Columnists. An inappropriate march accompanies their entrance and prepares us, as the soldiers fill the stage, for the cere-
monial arrival on horseback of Nebuchadnezzar.* The tune of the
march is worth quoting, I think, as characteristic of what was virtually a congenital Italian inability to write a dignified march until
Verdi himself produced one in *Aida*. The arrival of the Babylonian
soldiers begins with the brassily-scored—

Ex 2

—which has as its cadence into the dominant halfway point a
phrase that sounds even more than the first one as though it came
from a Rossini overture, piccolo and all:

Ex 3

Nebuchadnezzar and his horse are halted at the entrance of the
Temple by Zaccharias, who holds a dagger at Fenena and threatens
to kill her if the King desecrates the Temple. Nebuchadnezzar replies with taunts at the Jews and their religion and starts off the
first of the many characteristic large-scale, principals-and-chorus
ensembles we shall encounter in the course of this study.

The immature Verdi had naturally not yet developed those great
powers of musical characterization which in his later operas are

* In view of the Italians' insatiable passion for real live horses on the opera stage
I have often wondered if in Italy horses undergo some special training for what
must be a life's work in the theatre, similar to the training the horses of London's
mounted police are put through to accustom them to the city's traffic. The din of
Piccadilly Circus that has to be tolerated by a London police horse must surely be
nothing compared to carrying a soprano in full cry on your back in the last act of
The Girl of the Golden West.

among the wonders of all music, but there is already apparent in this scene more than a hint of the operatic child who was father to the man. Abigail, with her fury and cries of vengeance (she is instructed to sing "con ferocia"), and Nebuchadnezzar, with his threats of drowning the Jews in a sea of blood, are most clearly differentiated from the rest by their very individual contributions to the ensemble, echoing or imitating each other in phrases which have a character of their own. Fenena appeals to her father for mercy, while the others call on Jehovah to save them, the chorus punctuating the broad main tune which alternates between 3/4 and 9/8 with short *pp* and staccato phrases. The formula familiar to all who know their Verdi is already plainly recognizable.

The action resumes with Nebuchadnezzar commanding the Hebrews to bow down before him. Zaccharias repeats his warning and is about to stab Fenena when Ismael rushes forward and seizes the dagger from him; Fenena throws herself into her father's arms.

Nebuchadnezzar "with ferocious joy" fires the Temple and the Hebrews are taken into captivity. This all happens in the course of a final Presto which is worthy of a Rossini comic opera, developing from an orchestral figure repeated for bars on end—

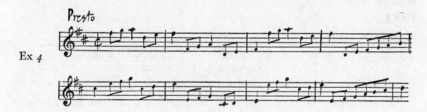

Ex 4

and leading to an equally Rossinian crescendo based on the third of the three themes on which the overture is constructed:

Ex 5

The curtain falls with everybody and everything singing and playing as loud and as fast as they can.

PART II

THE UNBELIEVER

Scene 1 : Apartments in the Royal Palace of Babylon.

Abigail is discovered alone, and as usual is in a rather ugly frame of mind. This time she has found a document which proves her to have been born a slave and not the King's daughter, as everybody has hitherto supposed. This humiliating discovery determines her to bring ruin on everybody—on Fenena, who is acting as Regent while Nebuchadnezzar is away at the wars, on Nebuchadnezzar, even on herself if necessary, to prevent her secret being divulged.

Her fierce declamation gives way to an unexpectedly tender little episode in which she sings wistfully of her love for Ismael to a tune which leaves no doubt about Verdi's admiration for the long cantilena of Bellini:

Ex 6A

Abigail's reverie is interrupted—or rather, since she has already delivered herself of an elaborate final cadenza, is abruptly followed—by the entrance of the High Priest of Babylon come to announce that Fenena is setting the Hebrews free and to ask Abigail to take matters in hand. The High Priest and a chorus of his followers, in a tenor-and-bass unison to the tune which in the Overture immediately precedes Ex 5, proclaim Abigail queen, telling her that they have already spread the rumour that the King has been killed in battle. Abigail, in the vigorous cabaletta which follows, gives a first hint of the heroic quality of Verdi melodies to come, as she resolves to mount the throne and avenge herself on her enemies:

Ex 6B

The curtain falls with everybody crying vendetta.

Scene 2 : A room in the Royal Palace which leads at the back into other rooms. On the right, a door leading to a gallery; on the left, another door communicating with the Regent's apartments. It is evening. The room is lit by a lamp.

A solo violoncello, accompanied by others divided into several parts, plays a slow and solemn tune to bring in Zaccharias and a Levite bearing the tablet of Hebrew law in preparation for the excommunication of Ismael. Zaccharias praises the Lord in a Prayer that is an impressive and justly admired bass aria to be sung, the composer indicates, *tutto sotto voce* :

Ex 7

The accompaniment is supported throughout by the divided violoncellos who introduced the scene. It is a rich and effective sound. At the end of his aria Zaccharias enters Fenena's apartments with the Levite.

A chorus of Levites now set on Ismael, cursing him for his treachery. In a furious unison of basses, full of sudden dramatic *pp* and *ff*, they assail him to the first quick staccato tune of the Overture :

Ex 8

Ismael cries out pitifully in his torment which is relieved by the sudden appearance of Anna, Zaccharias's sister, who proclaims that Ismael has saved a Hebrew, not a Gentile. Fenena has been converted to the Jewish faith. This, at least, is what we are expected to deduce from Anna's very bald declaration: "O brothers, pardon him! He has saved a Jewess!" The universal relief felt at this turn of events (Zaccharias corroborates his sister's words) is short lived, however. The ancient Abdallo enters excitedly, to the same kind of agitated triplets that accompanied the Hebrews' panic in the Temple, to relate that Nebuchadnezzar is reported to be dead and that Abigail and the Priests are on their way to take the crown from Fenena. Abigail storms in, with the High Priest beside her shouting

"Glory to Abigail!" and "Death to the Hebrews!", and is just going
to wrench the crown from Fenena when Nebuchadnezzar suddenly
appears, snatches the crown and places it on his own head. The four
dramatic pauses (each seven beats long) which occur after the King's
entrance and may puzzle the listener who knows the opera only
from records, are to allow for the expression of "terrore generale" at
these points.

The *ff* excitement in the orchestra dies down and Nebuchadnezzar
sets another ensemble in motion. This time, however, it is a rather
incongruous affair with music that sounds for all the world as if it
belonged to a typical Rossini "Ensemble of Stupefaction". Indeed,
the opening phrase of the principal theme will strike a ready chord
in the minds of those who remember the beginning of the great
comic duet between Dandini and Don Magnifico, "Un segreto
d'importanza", in *La Cenerentola*.

Nevertheless, in spite of this possible incongruity, which was one
of Verdi's most notable failings in his early operas, the ensemble
works up to an impressive climax without achieving anything in the
way of individual characterization comparable to the big ensemble
in Part I, although there is considerable distinction in the writing for
the chorus which contrasts effectively with the principals.

With some brassy interjections from the orchestra Nebuchadnezzar
commands all to kneel and worship him. Zaccharias, Fenena and
the Hebrews refuse, as Zaccharias warns the King against such
blasphemous pride. Nebuchadnezzar ignores the Hebrew Priest's
warning and as he proclaims himself God, is struck down by lightning. The crowd's hushed unison whisper of amazement and awe is
a dramatic and unexpected touch; one somehow anticipated an
inevitable *ff* cry of "Orror!" or the like.

The King is sent hopelessly mad by the shock, declaring that he
is persecuted and pleading pathetically for help from his daughter.
(Nobody seems to notice that he significantly speaks of only one
daughter. Abigail, it should be remembered, is still publicly believed
to be one of Nebuchadnezzar's daughters.)

The scene ends with Abigail picking up the crown which was
struck from Nebuchadnezzar's head, and to Zaccharias's declaration
that heaven has punished the blasphemer, replies: "But the glory of
Babylon lives on!"

PART III

THE PROPHECY*

Scene 1 : The Hanging Gardens.

Abigail is on the throne. The Magi and Dignitaries of Babylon are seated at her feet, while the High Priest and his followers stand near the altar from which rises the golden statue of Baal. Part III begins with a stealthy reprise of the march quoted in Ex 2. This is followed by an opening chorus of Babylonian women, people and soldiers who have little of any distinction to sing, and for the most part provide conventionally staccato punctuations of Verdi's townband tune in the orchestra.

The High Priest demands that the captive Jews, including Fenena, shall be put to death. Abigail feigns surprise at his request, but whatever she intended to say next is interrupted by the appearance of the ragged, dishevelled figure of the mad Nebuchadnezzar. Abigail dismisses the rest of the company and is left alone with the King.

The action of the rest of this scene takes place in the course of a lengthy duet between Abigail and Nebuchadnezzar. Abigail ignores the King's anger when he realizes that she is seated on his throne, and instead talks him into signing the death sentence of the Hebrews. She does this in a sequence which ranges from runs and trills to passages of powerful declamation, and which features from time to time an orchestral tune that one might be pardoned for believing was intended for a party scene in some other opera and had somehow strayed into *Nabucco*:

Ex 9

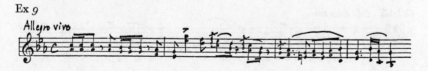

The effect of this, brilliantly scored with a predominant piccolo,

* The American translator and sub-editor of Carlo Gatti's well-known book on Verdi referred to this a little bewilderingly as "The Property". The original is "La profezia", not "La proprietà".

29

and the one non-choral theme quoted in the Overture, is understandably a little surprising when it is first encountered; but it sounds a shade less inappropriate when it accompanies Abigail's joy on getting Nebuchadnezzar's signature to the death warrant.

In a moment of clarity the King realizes he has signed the death sentence of his own daughter and when Abigail does nothing to hide her glee that Fenena is to die, he turns on her and shows her the document proving her slave birth. Abigail's answer is to snatch the paper and tear it up. There now follows a passage of two prolonged asides. First Nebuchadnezzar laments his fate as the shadow of the King he was; then Abigail rejoices in her day of glory, reflecting that her possession of power is worth more than the loss of a noble parent—not in any mood of exultation but in a lyrical tune which, while it is still in the manner of Bellini, already shows how Verdi was beginning to mould his melodic heritage to his own pattern.

Trumpets sound outside—the signal, Abigail explains, for the death of the Hebrews. (Evidently Nebuchadnezzar's signature was a mere formality, since everything seems to have been arranged for the massacre without Abigail having to move.) In desperation the King calls for his guards; they appear, but only to guard him as a prisoner. He pleads pathetically with Abigail, calling her Queen, and begging her to spare his daughter's life. Abigail retorts that his pleas leave her unmoved, and to convince us she makes her point to the tune of Ex 9.

The curtain falls on a loud and stirring coda.

Scene 2 : On the Banks of the Euphrates.

A short orchestral introduction brings us to the scene with which Verdi made musical and national history—the scene in which the spirit of "By the waters of Babylon" is translated into the captive Hebrews' chorus, "Va, pensiero, sull'ali dorate"—"Go, my thought, on golden wings":

Ex *10*

The appeal of this tune sung as Verdi wrote it seems to be universal and eternal. Anybody who has ever had occasion, as I have, to make use of it in the course of some radio or television programme knows that its broadcast will be followed by immediate, anxious and

numberless requests from the audience to be told what it is. Any disc
jockey could put it into the Top Ten without trouble or undue
plugging.

The dramatic impact of this simple and wonderfully moving
lament of the captive Hebrews for their homes and native hills is
unfailing and tremendous in the theatre, and it owes its emotional
effect as much as anything to what was a characteristic stroke of
genius by Verdi—the statement and reprise of the main part of the
tune by the mixed chorus in unison. By holding back all harmonization of the choral parts until the sudden *ff* of the middle section,
when the chorus is divided into six parts, Verdi gave the tune a simplicity and directness that can be almost unbearably moving. It
does not need much imagination to understand the sensation that
must have been caused among Italian audiences in Verdi's early
days by, for instance, the sudden crescendo to the words "Oh mia
patria . . ." as the last phrase of the complete tune begins.

It is a beautifully constructed tune, wavering characteristically
between the 4/4 and 12/8 which gave so many of Verdi's ensembles
their peculiar swing (there is no other word), and ending with a coda
that is not the least moving part of the whole episode.

When the last notes of "Va, pensiero" have died away *pp dim.*,
Zaccharias enters and rebukes the Hebrews for their pessimism and
lack of spirit. He tells them, to the kind of throbbing *pp* accompaniment by the brass in the orchestra that had not lost its novelty when
it occurred again in *Aida*, thirty years later, that the Lord has
promised their deliverance, and goes on to prophesy how the destruction of Babylon will leave nothing but a fatal silence broken
only by the sad *lamenti* of the owl when night falls. At the mention of
"lamenti" we have our first instance of one of Verdi's most characteristic expressions. Throughout his whole life, from *Nabucco* to
Falstaff, the suggestion of lamentation or tears was expressed either
by a plaintive rising semitone, or an equally plaintive falling semitone. At this point in *Nabucco* both forms occur eight times simultaneously, the rising semitone form in the oboe, the falling semitone
in the accented phrase of the violas:

Ex *11*

Zaccharias' simple and impressive prophecy ends on an optimistic note to the effect that not a stone of proud Babylon will be left standing. This is echoed with almost musical-comedy cheerfulness by the chorus, and the curtain falls.

PART IV

THE SHATTERED IDOL

Scene 1 : An apartment in the Royal Palace, as in Part II

Nebuchadnezzar, a prisoner in the Palace, is discovered asleep in a chair as the curtain rises. An orchestral prelude reminds us of three tunes we have already heard—the tune sung by the King when he was struck by lightning, the tune sung by Fenena and Ismael at the beginning of the ensemble in Part I (see page 22), and the march (Ex 2). The prelude ends with an agitato passage and Nebuchadnezzar awakens with a start from what we now know was a nightmare.

Nebuchadnezzar hears the crowd below clamouring for the death of Fenena, and looking through the window he sees her being led to her execution to the accompaniment of a funeral march for wind instruments. This funeral march in G minor is said to have been one of the many marches Verdi wrote for the town band of Busseto in his younger days and which was incorporated in *Nabucco* more or less unaltered. Certainly the scoring suggests this.

Unable to break out of his prison, Nebuchadnezzar falls on his knees and prays to the God of Judah to forgive his pride and blasphemy. His prayer is heard. The faithful Abdallo enters with the guard and Nebuchadnezzar, now recovered from his insanity, leads them off to rescue Fenena to rousing martial strains.

Scene 2 : The Hanging Gardens, as in Part II.

To the accompaniment of the funeral march Fenena and the Hebrews are led to the altar to be sacrificed by two *sacrifitori* who stand with axes either side of the High Priest of Baal. As Fenena reaches the middle of the stage she stops and kneels before Zaccharias,

Ex *12*

Andante

oh di-schiu-so è il fir-ma-men-to! Al Si-gnor lo spir-to a-ne-la...

2

who gives her consolation and encouragement in a solemn passage of recitative accompanied by trombones. Fenena answers with a prayer (Ex 12) which is quite lovely in its melodic simplicity and emotional effect.

Although the accompaniment is no more adventurous than Bellini, there is towards the end of this little aria one of the first of those unexpected harmonic twists which one finds in Verdi's lyric-soprano parts from Fenena to Desdemona and Nannetta in *Falstaff*. It is a moving conception altogether.

Preparations for the execution of Fenena and her companions are interrupted by the arrival of Nebuchadnezzar with drawn sword, followed by Abdallo and his soldiers. The King orders his guards to destroy the idol, but before they can do so it falls shattered to the ground of its own accord. Nebuchadnezzar bids the Hebrews rejoice and return to their homes; a new Temple shall rise dedicated to the glory of Jehovah. In the course of his praise of the Lord Nebuchadnezzar enumerates instances of the Almighty's omnipotence—his merciful restoration of sanity to the penitent unbeliever struck down with madness, and his punishment of the wicked Abigail, who has taken poison.

There follows a stirring unaccompanied hymn to Jehovah, sung by the seven assembled principals and the chorus. The dynamics vary from *ff* to sudden *pp*, the vocal forces from Fenena, Ismael, Nebuchadnezzar and Zaccharias in subdued moments as a quartet to tremendous outbursts with soloists and chorus in twelve parts. The interlude has great dramatic impact.

A plaintive oboe solo brings on Abigail, who is dying from the poison she has taken in remorse and despair. Her farewell is a moving and realistically disjointed affair in E minor, accompanied by a viola figure suggestive of the typical viola *lamento* shown in Ex 11. The key changes to the major and the flute becomes extremely busy with runs and arpeggios in the accompaniment. This is because the flute is the traditional romantic way to suggest that a character's mind is beginning to wander or that they are reflecting on heaven or the after life. In Abigail's case it is a bit of everything and the result is the first hint in a Verdi score of that "ethereal" orchestration whose problems intrigued him right up to the last scene of *Falstaff*. Praying for God's mercy Abigail falls to the ground and dies. Zaccharias, magnificently indifferent to Abigail's fate, brings down the curtain with a loud and solemn promise that in serving Jehovah, Nebuchadnezzar will be the King of Kings.

In spite of all I had read about its obvious shortcomings my first hearing of *Nabucco* on the stage was something I had always eagerly looked forward to. And when I did eventually hear it, performed by the Welsh National Opera at Sadler's Wells a few years ago, I was not disappointed. Certainly an opera in which the chorus plays one of the most important parts and, like the Devil, has all the best tunes, was an absolute "natural" for the Welsh chorus whose performance of "Va, pensiero" was magnificent. But then a Welsh choir can give a Verdi chorus what no other singers can give it—the fire and excitement that comes from that uniquely Welsh characteristic known as *hwyl*.

What came over in performance, however, was the extremely strong and peculiar atmosphere of Verdi's whole conception. The faults of the young composer, his lack of polish, his fierce brassy orchestration—so far from detracting from the quality of the opera became in fact almost virtues; for paradoxically they introduce a rough, barbaric element that is entirely in keeping with the Old Testament spirit of the story. Through the film left on the music here and there by Bellini and Donizetti there are clear signs of the new and vigorous personality of Verdi breaking through. The language may still be Bellini's, but the accent, the tone of voice and the thoughts behind the speech are unmistakably individual.

It is easy to find fault with *Nabucco*, easier still to laugh at some of the more ridiculously inappropriate tunes it contains, but it is a work that compels attention. It was Verdi's first determined step and when we realize what this step led to, the tremendous breadth of the steps that followed it, it is obvious that *Nabucco* cannot be dismissed as a work of mere historical interest. It is an opera full of life and vigour, and nowhere is this life and vigour more apparent than when it is heard and seen in the theatre. When I began this study of *Nabucco* I envisaged being able to deal with it in a few hundred words. I make no apology for finding I was unable to do anything of the sort.

MACBETH

Opera in four acts. Libretto by Francesco Maria Piave, with additions by Andrea Maffei. First performed at the Teatro della Pergola, Florence, on 14th March, 1847. Revised version performed at the Théâtre Lyrique, Paris, on 21st April, 1865. First performance in England: Glyndebourne Festival Opera, 21st May, 1938. First performance in the United States: Niblo's Garden, New York, 24th April, 1850.

FOR US, able to see Verdi's life's work in perspective, *Macbeth* has perhaps a special hold on our attention as the composer's first translation into opera of a play by the English dramatist who was to inspire his two last and greatest works—*Otello* and *Falstaff.*

Verdi's lifelong admiration for the man he referred to in his letters with engaging indifference as "Shacpeare" and "Shaspeare" was founded on a solid knowledge and instinctive understanding of his work dating from his earliest youth—a fact he was not slow to point out forcefully when he was accused, after the performance of the revised version of *Macbeth* in Paris in 1865, of not knowing Shakespeare. "He is one of my very special poets," retorted Verdi, "and I read and re-read him continually."

Macbeth was the first Shakespearian idea Verdi put into operatic practice, but it was by no means the first he had considered. Five operas and three years before *Macbeth* he had thought about *King Lear*, a subject which was to occur to him again and again during his lifetime. *Hamlet*, *The Tempest* and *Antony and Cleopatra* also came up for consideration in their time, though never with the regularity and tantalizing near-promise of fulfilment of *King Lear*.

Verdi's decision to compose *Macbeth* for Florence was dictated by a characteristic circumstance: the unavailability of a tenor to sing in either of the other two operas he was considering. One of these, based on Schiller's *Die Räuber* ("The Robbers"), became *I Masnadieri* in due course and the only opera Verdi ever wrote for London; the other, an adaptation of a play by the Austrian playwright, Grillparzer, never came to anything.

Once it had been chosen it was seen that *Macbeth* was a novel and unconventional subject entirely unlike anything Verdi had composed before. It had no love-interest; it was not filled with the romantic passion of *Ernani* (1844). And since it was composed for Florence, where there was freedom from political excitement and unrest, from the illogical and restrictive official interference which Verdi had encountered in the Austrian-occupied North of Italy, it did not suffer those grotesquely comic skirmishes with the Censorship that affected *I Lombardi alla prima Crociata* (1843).* Indeed, the whole nature of *Macbeth* seems to have been so strange to all concerned with its production at the Pergola that Verdi clearly had some difficulty explaining to them exactly who and what the opera was all about. The scene designer, for instance, had to be told by the composer in an urgent letter that "the period of Macbeth is much later than that of Ossian and the Roman Empire. Macbeth assassinated Duncan in 1040 and was himself killed in 1057. In England in 1039 there reigned 'Aroldo' called 'Harefoot', a king of Danish descent, who was succeeded in the same year by 'Ardicanuto', half-brother of 'Odoardo il confessore'." Verdi was a year out with one of his dates: Harold was in fact succeeded by Hardicanute in 1040, not 1039.

The composer's erudition, which would shame most of us in this country (how many English composers would be only a year out in the dates of even one of the reigning princes of Italy in the eleventh century?), not only put his contemporaries in their place, but was such that some of it has been over the heads of some of the Italians ever since. Verdi's reference to "Harefoot" has rarely appeared correctly in an Italian quotation of the letter. In the original Italian of Carlo Gatti's life of Verdi, revised in 1953, the sentence (which, like the rest of the passage, does not appear at all in the truncated American translation published in England) is quoted with a query: "In Inghilterra nel 1039 regnava Aroldo detto *Re di Lepre* (?) . . ." The author's question mark is not surprising for "Re di Lepre" ("King of Hare") is certainly a trifle puzzling. The answer obviously is that somebody has at some time misread the composer's handwriting. Verdi writing "Piè di Lepre" was correctly describing Harold I as "Harefoot".†

The composer's preoccupation with the production of *Macbeth* was comprehensive, and unusually intense and detailed. Having put everybody right on the question of the period of the action, he consulted London ("where they have played this tragedy continuously for two hundred years") on the best ways to manage Banquo's ghost; he raised a particular rumpus when the singer cast as Banquo objected to appearing as the Ghost who had nothing to sing. "All singers", Verdi insisted, "must be contracted to sing and to act. It would be a monstrous thing if another actor were to appear as

---

* See the author's *Great Opera Houses*, pp 105–6.

† In passing, I don't know why Gatti should still have been so bewildered as late as 1953. If he had consulted the *Copialettere*—the famous collection of Verdi's letters published in 1913—he would have found an editorial note explaining everything, and in particular that the king was known in England as "Hare-foat". But perhaps Signor Gatti was one of those thousands who, to the constant despair of authors, never read footnotes.

Banquo's ghost. Banquo must have the same face when he is dead as when he is alive." In all there were more than a hundred rehearsals supervised by the composer, and from the description of pre-production incidents and the general atmosphere of the opera's preparation which has been left by Marianna Barbieri-Nini, the original Lady Macbeth, it was an exceptionally strenuous time for all.* Verdi even made the unprecedented demand that the cast should actually wear their stage costumes and full make-up at the final and public dress rehearsal—an incident which gives us some idea of the haphazard conditions prevailing in opera production at the time.

As one might guess from these brief instances of his preoccupation with the details of the opera's production, the composer himself was responsible for the lay-out and prose draft of the libretto of *Macbeth*. Piave's contribution was comparatively small, being limited virtually to the supply of verses (with Andrea Maffei adding to, or amending, them in one or two cases) to fit what we would call nowadays Verdi's "treatment" of Shakespeare's play, which kept very much to the essentials of the plot; and though we encounter several passages which we know from the context to have been Shakespearian poetry at its most magnificent, very little of it survives after going through the double mangle of translation first into a foreign language, then into a different medium.

In the course of compressing the play to the dimensions of a practicable libretto characters naturally had to be jettisoned wholesale. Where the list of Shakespeare's *dramatis personae* shows more than twenty principals, the opera reduces the number to eight, of whom two—Duncan and Fleance—are seen but not heard. Duncan is limited to one son; Macduff is deprived of wife and child; Hecate makes a mute appearance, but then only if the ballet music added for the Paris revision of 1865 is included in the scene of the Apparitions. And the Porter, who provides the only comic relief in the play, is dispensed with altogether—along with Scottish noblemen like Ross, Lennox, Angus and the rest. To have included the Porter would have been quite impossible to one of Verdi's temperament, of course—at least, at the age when he wrote *Macbeth*. A more mature judgment might have sensed the musico-dramatic possibilities of a scene which in Shakespeare's play creates an unnerving suspense. The English listener to the opera, missing the few laughs (and the one or two home-truths on the disappointing effect of alcohol on desire) that the scene provides in the play will, I think, be compensated by the unconscious humour of several passages which unexpectedly and refreshingly off-set the gloomy tone of the work as a whole.

Although the first version of *Macbeth* came out at a time of political

* One of the more familiar episodes is related in *Great Opera Houses*, p 151.

unrest in many parts of occupied Italy, it was not an opera that suffered indignities at the hands of the Censor. On the other hand, that it roused the patriotic feelings of Italian audiences at the time goes without saying. The familiarly classic Scottish theme of *Macbeth*, which one might reasonably have considered incapable of political interpretation nevertheless caused nightly uproars at the Fenice in Venice whenever Antonio Palma, the Spanish tenor who sang the part of what many Italian writers have translated as "Macdubbo", came to the passage which begins:

> *La patria tradita*
> *piangendo c'invita;*
> *Fratelli gli oppressi*
> *corriamo a salvar.*

("Our country betrayed, invites us to weep; Brothers, let us hasten to save the oppressed . . .")

Only "the presence of Austrian bayonets", the annals of the Fenice report, prevented the audiences getting out of hand. (Those critics who complain that such trifling hold-ups as applause after an aria destroy the dramatic continuity etc. of an opera, should be glad they were not subjected to those early performances of *Macbeth* at the Fenice. At the fourth performance of the opera on New Year's Day, 1848, the second act was followed by a five-act ballet starring Fanny Cerrito. The performance of the opera was then resumed.)

Oddly enough, the only instance I can discover of official interference with the otherwise unimpeded progress of *Macbeth* happened in Russia where the first performance of the opera in St Petersburg in 1854 took place in an Italian version retitled *Sivardo il Sassone*. It is such a bewilderingly irrelevant title to encounter that one may be forgiven if, even after translating it as "Siward the Saxon" (or Sassenach), one is still no nearer knowing what it has to do with *Macbeth*. A moment's reflection, however, and it will be recalled that there are two people called Siward in Shakespeare's play. Old Siward, Earl of Northumberland and General of the English Forces, speaks a total of thirty incomplete lines of verse all told, which are spread about Scenes 4, 6 and 7 of the fifth and final act, when he asks questions that keep the audience in the picture about what has happened off-stage; his son, Young Siward, has seven lines in Act V, Scene 7, fights briefly with Macbeth, and is slain. Neither character appears, or is even mentioned in Verdi's opera, and both could be left out of Shakespeare's play and little harm done. Of all the bizarre changes suffered by Verdi's operas at the hands of Censors of all nations in their time, this was surely one of the richest and strangest. Even if one could discover why it was made (one can only guess that it was to distract attention in a shaky monarchy from a piece called after a regicide), there is still not the faintest clue to what music Old (or Young) Siward the Saxon was given to sing in the opera, at what point in the action he sang it, what words he sang it to, or—particularly—who wrote the music for it.

The fact that in the ten years following its first production at the Pergola in Florence *Macbeth* was heard in such widely distant countries as Spain, Poland, Cuba, Turkey, Brazil, Russia, the United States, Chile, Sweden and Portugal, does not suggest that it was altogether as unsuccessful as one has sometimes read, especially if one remembers that among the other products of this decade were three masterpieces, *Rigoletto*, *Il trovatore* and *La traviata*, which might understandably have been expected to distract attention from the earlier and less box-office-appealing proposition. As far as Verdi himself was concerned *Macbeth* occupied a special position among his early operas. It was undoubtedly a landmark in his own development, and perhaps because it was for so long his only completed Shakespearian opera (the plans for *King Lear* were continually falling through) he regarded it as an important experiment, sensing—if only subconsciously—that it was a firm step on the way that was to lead to *Otello*.

Certainly it must have been a deep-rooted conviction that *Macbeth* was no ordinary routine job that led Verdi, seventeen years after he had written it, to propose a revised version of the opera when his French publisher approached him in 1864 for something to follow a recent highly successful revival of *La traviata* in Paris. It is obvious, I think, that when the idea was first discussed Verdi considered *Macbeth* a good enough work to need no more revision than would be involved in the addition of a ballet to suit French taste. When it came to it, however, he discovered that seventeen years was a long time in a composer's life and that what had passed in 1847 sounded awkward and incongruous by the standards he had made for himself in the years between. The extent of the revision, which involved addition, subtraction, alteration and orchestral redecoration, will be discussed as it is encountered in the course of this study.

MM. Nuitter and Beaumont, the two French translators of the new *Macbeth* (for which Piave had provided new verses) are worth a passing mention, I think. As collaborators Charles Nuitter (an anagram of the surname of a lawyer called Truinet, who became archivist of the Paris Opera) and Alexandre Beaumont (*né* de Beaume), made the first French translations of *The Magic Flute*, Weber's *Abu Hassan*, *Preciosa* and *Oberon*. On his own Nuitter wrote five librettos for Offenbach, one called *Piccolino* for Ernest Guiraud, who composed the orchestrally accompanied recitatives universally used in *Carmen* when Bizet's opera is performed without spoken dialogue; and the scenarios of Delibes' *La Source* and *Coppélia*. With the

2*

help of others (not Beaumont) Nuitter also translated *La forza del destino, Aida, Rienzi, The Flying Dutchman, Tannhäuser, Lohengrin* and Bellini's *Capuleti ed i Montecchi*.

Those English-speaking readers whose experience of *Macbeth* includes acquaintance with the vocal score, the libretto in Italian, or synopses of the plot and the essays that go with them in the programmes of some Italian opera houses, will probably share my own strongly personal affection for the opera. There is, for us, something gently touching, for instance, in the Italians' incorrigible habit from Verdi's first draft onwards of referring to Lady Macbeth as plain "Lady", as though "Lady" were her Christian name and she was "Lady di Macbeth" like "Lucia di Lammermoor" or "Emilia di Liverpool"; or in the score's bewildering introduction of a character known as "Dama di Lady".

Though I have included in the list of the opera's characters the names by which Shakespeare's *dramatis personae* are known in Verdi's score, in analysing the opera itself I have purposely not referred to them by any but the names familiar to us from childhood, for I cannot imagine that the reader who hears a broadcast of *Macbeth* from La Scala will fail to associate the announcer's talk of "Duncano", "Banco" and "Fleanzio" with Duncan, Banquo and Fleance.

CHARACTERS IN ORDER OF SINGING

MACBETH	} *Generals in King Duncan's army*	*Baritone*
BANQUO (Banco)		*Bass*
LADY MACBETH, *wife of Macbeth* . . .		*Soprano*
DUNCAN (Duncano), *King of Scotland* . .		*Mute*
MACDUFF (Macdubbo), *Scottish Nobleman,*		
Thane of Fife (Signore di Fiff) . . .		*Tenor*
MALCOLM, *son of Duncan*		*Tenor*
GENTLEWOMAN (*Dama di Lady*) . .		*Mezzo-soprano*
FLEANCE (Fleanzio) *Banquo's son* . . .		*Mute*
A MURDERER		*Bass*
HECATE (Ecate), *Queen of the Night* . .		*Mute*
A HERALD		*Bass*
DOCTOR (Medico)		*Bass*

Witches, messengers, Scottish noblemen and exiles, murderers, English soldiers, lords and ladies, bards, spirits of the air, apparitions

Scene: Scotland and the borders of England and Scotland

Time: The eleventh century

ACT I

*Scene: A Heath.**

Before the curtain rises a short orchestral Prelude is heard which introduces three themes heard later in the opera. The first, played by oboe, clarinet and bassoon in unison, is associated with the Witches and is given a slightly sinister character by the register used by the oboe:

Ex *13*

A heavy, loud and solemn fanfare-like passage in the brass—two trumpets, four trombones and four horns—with all the depth and richness characteristic of Verdi's scoring in his early days, leads to a phrase played *pp* for a couple of bars by first and second violins which is used later to create an atmosphere of suspense in the Sleep-walking Scene:

Ex *14*

The stealth and quiet of this, however, last no more than the two bars the phrase consists of. It is loudly interrupted by a brassy tutti passage, which in turn leads to another quiet sequence—

Ex *15*

* The original Italian is *bosco*, meaning "wood" or "forest", but I have taken the liberty of reverting to Shakespeare's own description of a scene known to every schoolchild and reproduced by most scene designers.

45

—a broad, mournful tune (again *pp*), also heard later in the Sleep-walking Scene—and which, I may say, had already served Donizetti well in the mad scene of his *Anna Bolena* (1830).

After two more *fortissimo* interjections from the whole orchestra the Prelude dies away with a solo harp having the last whispered word.

To the sound of a stormy orchestral introduction the curtain rises on Verdi's opera to confront those who know their Shakespeare with an immediate surprise. There are at least eighteen Witches on the stage. This means, of course, that we are denied one of the most famous of all opening lines—"When shall we three meet again . . . ?" —and so have to begin the evening with the thunder and lightning of Act I, Scene 3 instead.

Verdi regarded the Witches as the most important characters in the opera after Lady Macbeth and Macbeth; he divided them into a three-part chorus calling them all sopranos and stipulating that there should be at least six singers in each group. Though there is no doubt, according to our ears, of the plurality of Witches, there is some inconsistency in the text. The third group of sopranos addresses the second group in the second person plural to ask where they have been. The second group, knowing a little Shakespeare, replies in a collective first person singular: "I have been killing swine". The third group then turns to the first group and addresses them in the second person singular, asking, "And thou?" The first group replies in the first person singular to tell in a Piave paraphrase of the sailor's wife who "had chestnuts in her lap".

The first group of Witches begin their narrative (carefully instructed by Verdi "not to forget that they are witches who are talking"), to a cackling kind of tune which is the Witches' musical idiom throughout most of the opera:

Ex *16*

There are passages later in the opera where they can be taken a little more seriously as supernatural figures than this quotation suggests, but for the most part the Witches behave like rather cheerful fairground fortune tellers, and Verdi has given them the music to go with it.

A drum-roll off stage tells the Witches of the approach of Macbeth, and they break out into another brilliant chorus, this time in the

major, in which Verdi makes typical use of sudden dynamic contrasts between *fff* and *pp*—a familiar and effective choral habit he
indulged in for many years. The chorus that greets the arrival of
Macbeth and Banquo includes a step or two of dancing by the
Witches who sing of themselves, almost in Shakespeare's words—

> The weird sisters, hand in hand,
> Posters of the sea and land,
> Thus do go about, about:

—to music which for brilliant orchestration and verve might have
done credit to Offenbach.

The musical mood and manner of the Witches changes suddenly.
Against a solemn background of woodwind and a solo trumpet they
hail Macbeth as future Thane of Glamis, Thane of Cawdor, and
King of Scotland; Banquo is greeted as "lesser than Macbeth and
greater . . .", the sire of future kings. Their prophecies at an end
for the moment the Witches sign off with cheers for Macbeth and
Banquo to one of the most unexpectedly perky phrases imaginable,
and disappear:

Ex *17*

For sheer surprise and incongruity this can be matched, in my
experience, only by the famous cadence sung by the Two Priests,
warning Tamino and Papageno in *The Magic Flute* against the wiles
of women and the fate of some poor fellow in the cautionary tale
whose lot was death and despair.*

Macbeth and Banquo are left alone meditating on the Witches'
prophecies when, to a loudly-scored martial tune in Verdi's liveliest
town-band vein, Messengers arrive (in lieu of Shakespeare's Thanes
of Ross and Angus, who have been cut out of the opera) and in
unison announce that the King has appointed Macbeth to succeed
the Thane of Cawdor who has been executed for treason. Banquo
shudders as he realizes that the Witches have spoken the truth.

A duet follows, begun by Macbeth to the Italian equivalent of the
words

> Two truths are told
> As happy prologues to the swelling act
> Of the imperial theme.

* See the author's *Famous Mozart Operas*, pp 218-19.

So far as the listener is concerned only one of the Witches' prophecies has been fulfilled at this point because the libretto has neglected to explain, as Shakespeare carefully does, how Macbeth became Thane of Glamis:

Ex 18

In this duet we see for the first time how unusually concerned with dramatic detail Verdi was in *Macbeth*. Macbeth is instructed to sing "aside, *sotto voce*, almost with terror", "con esclamazione", and—particularly—"cupo", a word which occurs more than any other in this score and gives a clue to the whole nature and intention of Verdi's music in *Macbeth*, for it means deep, pensive, sombre, obscure, bleak and dark. The last thing Verdi asked of his two principal characters in this opera was that they should have "beautiful" voices. Felice Varesi, the original Macbeth in Florence, was chosen by the composer because he suited the part "both as to figure and style of singing"; it did not matter that he tended to sing out of tune.

The duet develops with Macbeth and Banquo meditating independently in good Shakespearian asides, the one fighting against the thought of murder that obsesses him, the other uneasy about the power of "the instruments of darkness". The Messengers add a bass line (shared with great effect by the bass trombone) remarking that Macbeth doesn't seem terribly pleased to hear the news they have brought him. The sequence ends quietly with a slow general exit.

The Witches return and end the scene telling us, in a vigorous 6/8 chorus to another gipsy-like tune with a hint of the tarantella about it and reinforced by plenty of piccolo and solo trumpet, that they will be meeting Macbeth again when next they hear a roll of thunder —a faint echo at last of the words of Shakespeare's Act I, Scene 1.

Scene 2 : A Hall in Macbeth's Castle.

After an ominous and *agitato* orchestral introduction which, as Francis Toye once said, might almost have come out of the first movement of Beethoven's "Pathétique" Sonata, Lady Macbeth enters reading a letter. She reads it aloud in a normal speaking voice. The age-old operatic convention, particularly familiar to those who know *The Barber of Seville* and *Don Pasquale*, for instance, that the contents of any letter read for the benefit of the audience should be imparted in this way, is one which Verdi observed until as late as

La traviata—at least, in the purely spoken form. In fact, he adhered rigidly to the principle to the end of his life, using the nearest musical equivalent to express the spoken "quote"—that is, a monotone—in both *Don Carlos* and *Falstaff* when letters are read out loud.*

The letter Lady Macbeth reads is a shortened version of the one with which she makes her entrance in Act I, Scene 5 of the play— Macbeth's account of his meeting with the Witches and their prophecy that he shall be King.

The first phrases that Lady Macbeth sings establish her character firmly and immediately, and give a first indication of the declamatory style which gives the opera so much of its dramatic character. It is a testing start for any singer to be faced with an angry flourish that includes a high C before the part is sixteen bars old, and it is typical of a role which is one of the most difficult in the entire Verdi repertoire. Not only is the range demanded of the voice considerable—from low B flat to top D flat—but the composer stipulated that the quality of the voice should be "rough, hoarse and gloomy . . . with something diabolical about it". It was no use having a stupendous voice that was clear and powerful, he said, adding, "I should like Lady Macbeth not to sing at all". Lady Macbeth's cavatina on her first entrance needs some singing nevertheless:

Ex *19*

In a long stirring tune which builds up infectiously (at the point one wants to join in oneself the violoncellos inevitably come in with the tune too) Lady Macbeth echoes the sentiments rather than the exact words about Macbeth being "too full o' the milk of human kindness". There is still more than a trace of Bellini's influence in the construction of this cavatina, but it is an influence which Verdi adapts to his own good purpose, especially in the effective variety of dynamics. Orchestrally Verdi still tended to indulge in rather raucous doubling of the voice part by a solo trumpet in this scene, but it was a habit it took the former town-bandmaster some time to shake off.

A servant enters to announce that Duncan is coming to stay the

* It is interesting to note that in spite of the long-established—and one would have thought generally accepted—operatic habit of reading, instead of singing, the contents of a letter, the critic of the *Gazzetta musicale di Milano* in 1847 should have objected strongly to Lady Macbeth speaking the words, considering it a mistake and contrary to "commonsense and reason".

night as guest in Macbeth's castle. When the servant has gone Lady Macbeth whispers, "Duncano sarà qui? Qui? Qui la notte?" ("Duncan is coming here? Here? Here tonight?"). Verdi punctuates the lines with great damatic effect—the first two with a tense *pp* string tremolo, the third with an excited tutti as Lady Macbeth realizes the opportunity the King's visit will afford. In an energetic cabaletta (usually cut down by half in performance) Lady Macbeth invokes the spirits of hell to help her, almost, but not quite, in Shakespeare's words:

> Come, you spirits
> That tend on mortal thoughts! Unsex me here,
> And fill me from the crown to the toe top full
> Of direct cruelty.

Macbeth enters and is greeted by his wife with the quaint vocative "Caudore!" In a short passage of recitative, accompanied by some solemn chords for trumpets and trombones, two familiar Shakespeare sequences are concentrated into a few lines. Macbeth says: "The King will be here in a little", and Lady Macbeth asks: "And leaves?"

"Tomorrow."

"O never shall sun that morrow see." (Shakespeare.)

"What do you say?"

"Don't you understand?"

"I understand, I understand."

"Is all well?"

"And if the stroke should fail?" (Near-Shakespeare.)

"It will not fail—if you do not shrink."

This sort of telescoping of the original *Macbeth* is one of the recurrent, if inevitable, frustrations of the opera libretto. We lose Macbeth's great monologue "If it were done, when 'tis done . . .", while Lady Macbeth's determined "But screw your courage to the sticking place, And we'll not fail . . ." is inexcusably replaced by Piave's insipid line quoted above. It is the character of Macbeth that loses more in this instance, for while Lady Macbeth is musically drawn so firmly that for the most part the literary quality of the words she sings are comparatively unimportant, we learn nothing of Macbeth's vacillation which so stimulates Lady Macbeth to ruthless determination. The other thing, of course, about the half-dozen lines of which the scene consists in the opera, is that the listener unfamiliar with the Shakespearian situation might be pardoned if he considered Macbeth and his wife were talking double-talk. Such dialogue as "What do you say?—Don't you understand? —Yes, I understand . . ." hardly lets the audience into the picture at all. Husband and wife might be nudging each other in the ribs and winking for all we learn of their real intentions.

In the distance backstage music is heard to accompany the approach of Duncan and his followers. Macbeth and Lady Macbeth leave the scene to welcome their guests.

Shakespeare's stage directions for the arrival of the King at the castle ask for "Hautboys and torches". Verdi and Piave translate "Hautboys" as "musica villereccia" or "rustic music". I don't know what kind of musical staff composer and librettist imagined Macbeth maintained in a fairly sizable Inverness-shire castle, but it surely cannot have been quite so rustic as the music played by the *banda* suggests. When *Macbeth* was finally staged at Covent Garden in 1960 at least one critic was ecstatic about his discovery of the masterly irony of Verdi's commonplace 6/8 march—how appropriately trivial it was as an accompaniment to a trivial occasion etc. In practice, however, the band music—approaching, reaching its *fortissimo* on the stage and then receding to a distant and ingeniously fading *pp*—is a pretty piffling tune at best. For us in the twentieth century its principal charm is the similarity of its repeated "middle" to the third theme of Sousa's "Liberty Bell". It is not very impressive as a flourish for royalty.

Lest it should be thought that it is only a sophisticated posterity in all its superciliousness that has regarded this particular Verdi march as ridiculous it should be pointed out that contemporary critics of *Macbeth* considered this scene musically quite as ludicrous as we do. Alessandro Gagliardi, writing from Florence in 1847 for the French *Revue et Gazette Musicale de Paris*, deplored "la vulgarité de la musique villageoise executée par des instruments militaires". It is just possible, of course, that Signor Gagliardi was missing some subtlety exclusively apparent to commentators of our own time; but somehow I doubt it.

The procession accompanying the King—Banquo, Macduff, Malcolm, Macbeth, Lady Macbeth and followers—moves across the stage. Macbeth returns to the scene, telling a servant in Shakespeare's words, "Go bid thy mistress, when my drink is ready, She strike upon the bell." At this point in the score (the section is headed "Gran Scena e Duetto") Verdi adds the instruction: "The whole of this duet must be performed by the singers *sotto voce* and *cupa*, with the exception of a few phrases marked *a voce spiegata* ['spread', or 'unfolded'—in other words, louder]." It is also at this point that we have the cor anglais making its appearance in the Italian orchestra pit for the first time as an elegiac, instead of a pastoral, instrument.

In the space of a bare eight unpoetic bars of declamation Macbeth covers the opening stanzas of "Is this a dagger which I see before me . . . ?" and we have dark and gloomy hints of lines like "And on thy blade and dudgeon gouts of blood, Which was not so before . . ." The tempo changes all the time—a few bars Largo,

followed by an agitated Allegro. As Macbeth sings ". . . Now o'er
the one half-world Nature seems dead" and paraphrases Shakespeare's lines about the wolf that "with Tarquin's ravishing strides,
towards his design Moves like a ghost", Verdi introduces one of the
most original and mournful of all orchestral noises—the cor anglais
playing a tune with a clarinet doubling it an octave lower. It is a
peculiarly melancholy sound which, when I first had occasion to
use it, I thought I was filching from Sibelius. I had not yet seen the
full score of *Macbeth*.

The scene ends as the bell strikes—

> . . . the bell invites me.
> Hear it not, Duncan; for it is a knell
> That summons thee to heaven or to hell.

Macbeth goes into the King's apartment.

Lady Macbeth enters in an atmosphere of silence and suspense
which Verdi knew so well how to create in music. She hears a
distant lament, a phrase played twice in unison, *pp lamentoso*, by cor
anglais with bassoon and violoncellos an octave lower. "Peace! It
was the owl that shrieked . . ." Macbeth returns, staggering and
panic-stricken, with a dagger in his hand. "Con voce suffocata e
lento," he gasps that the deed is done—"Tutto è finito". We now
come to the duet which the two original principals maintained
Verdi made them rehearse what seemed like a hundred and fifty
times—"Fatal mia donna!" ("O fateful wife"):

Ex 20

The words of this duet, in which the cor anglais again plays an
important part, are taken sometimes phrase-for-phrase from Act II,
Scene 2—beginning with Macbeth's "Didst thou not hear a noise?",
and continuing with his description of the murder and

> But wherefore could I not pronounce "Amen"?
> I had most need of blessing, and "Amen"
> Stuck in my throat.

Lady Macbeth's comments on her husband's fears sometimes bear
some relation to Shakespeare's original, but tend to be telescoped
into repeated cries of "Folly! Mere folly that will vanish at the
break of day."

The duet movement dies away and to a grimly effective wind

accompaniment, to which unison trombones contribute some awesome sounds, Macbeth tells of the voice he heard cry, "Glamis hath murder'd sleep!"

At this point Piave (at Verdi's suggestion?) adds some things for Lady Macbeth to say that Shakespeare never thought of. "But tell me," she asks her husband, "did you not hear another voice that said, 'You are proud, Macbeth, but lack courage—Glamis, you hesitate and stop in the midst of your task—Cawdor, you are a vain weakling . . .'?'" Macbeth does not answer, but broods on his deed. After this unexpectedly lyrical episode, which towards the end includes two very characteristic and surprising harmonic twists, the tempo changes to an agitated 6/8 Allegro. Lady Macbeth tells her husband to take back the dagger. He has not the courage to do it. "Give me the dagger," cries Lady Macbeth, and snatching it from Macbeth's hand she goes into the King's room to "smear the sleepy grooms with blood".

There are three loud knocks at the gate of the castle, underlined *ff* in the orchestra as they are in *Don Giovanni*. The noise frightens Macbeth and he looks at his hands—

> What hands are here! . . .
> Will all great Neptune's ocean wash this blood
> Clean from my hand? . . .

Lady Macbeth returns. "My hands are of your colour . . . A little water clears us of this deed." The knocking is repeated and in a short Presto passage Lady Macbeth leads her husband away from the scene of the murder. The scene ends with an effective fade-out—on a solo flute in its lower register.

This first act duet was what Verdi called "re-kneaded" for the Paris production of 1865, though he did not include its revision among the major items to be done when he discussed the prospects and implications of a new *Macbeth* with his French publishers. Whatever later alterations Verdi may have made in its detail, however, there is little doubt that the general conception of this "Gran Scena e Duetto" did not change much over the years. Verdi considered this scene and the later Sleepwalking Scene as the two most important in the Florence *Macbeth*, and in spite of later revisions and additions to the opera it has lost none of its original dramatic power or effective characterization. Even in this one scene we see the development of Lady Macbeth as a character, dominant, ambitious, fearless in her obsession and, so far, still undisturbed by her conscience. Considering that Piave and Verdi allowed him little room to move in, as it were, Macbeth also makes his musical mark as a character. That he does not move us so much as in the play is due, of course, to his being denied all but the most fleeting hint of the great poetry in which the part abounds. We can know little of his apprehension if we do not hear all of "Is this a dagger . . . ?", or of the terror he feels after the murder if we are deprived of the relentless building up of the "Sleep no more!" speech. But of that all-important operatic ingredient, atmosphere, there is plenty in this scene. Verdi may not have given us the words of the drama, but he gave us the music.

The knocking, we now discover, was Macduff demanding entrance to the castle. He is accompanied by Banquo (in place of Shakespeare's Lennox) and has come in answer to the King's request to call him early. He enters the King's apartment. Banquo, left alone, reflects, after Lennox's manner, that "the night has been unruly . . . lamentings heard i' the air; strange screams of death . . . the obscure bird clamour'd the livelong night."—

Ex 21

It is a soliloquy remarkable less for its tune than for its accompaniment, and particularly for the imaginative use by Verdi of the sinister qualities of the oboe. The score of *Macbeth* abounds in astonishingly effective oboe passages; in some the lowest register of the instrument is exploited to give a cor-anglais-like mournfulness, in others a single sustained note makes an oddly dramatic point. In this short tune of Banquo's the "lamentings heard i' the air" are evoked by a sad reiterated G played in unison across two octaves by the solo oboe and two clarinets. It is an unusual and simple form of the *lamento* that recurred in Verdi's music from *Nabucco* to the last music he ever wrote—the Stabat Mater of the *Four Sacred Pieces*.

Banquo's interlude is brought to an abrupt close by the frenzied return of Macduff, who has discovered Duncan's murder but is unable to say what he has seen—"Do not bid me speak . . ." Banquo hurries into the King's room while Macduff rouses the household. Macbeth, Lady Macbeth, Malcolm, "Dama di Lady" and servants hurry on to the scene as Banquo returns to say that the King has been murdered.

There is a moment's horror-struck pause and in a tremendous *fff* passage, much of it in a shattering unison, the assembled company calls on the Jaws of Hell to consume the unknown and accursed assassin. It is a phrase which ends with Lady Macbeth's Gentlewoman sharing a high C with her mistress which, considering the part is rated in Ricordi's vocal score as a mezzo-soprano, shows the kind of range even the small-part singers are expected to have in this opera.

There now follows, unaccompanied except for a few important taps from the timpani to keep the sextet of principals and the chorus on course, an ensemble twenty-seven bars long in which the aid of God is sought (as a change from the Jaws of Hell) to bring the assassin to justice. It is an effective sequence, with frequent typical dynamic switches from *ff* to *ppp* and leading into a *grandioso* finale.

The reader familiar with Shakespeare will note an important divergence from the original in this situation. In the play Lady Macbeth faints at this stage of the action and is carried off. In the opera, because she is badly needed as prima donna, she is as full of life as any of them and in—literally—facing the music might conceivably be regarded as less of a suspect than her obviously feigned vapours suggest she might be in the play.

The *grandioso* finale starts off in a way that has been well and wittily described by Philip Hope-Wallace as a cross between "Va, pensiero" and "Mack the Knife" from Kurt Weill's *Dreigroschenoper*. It is a wonderfully rousing sound filled with the peculiar excitement Verdi knew instinctively how to generate in his early days by the well-timed alternation of unison and harmonized versions of a stirring vocal tune:

Ex 22

The tune is doubled by very audible solo trumpet and solo trombone, in addition to the violoncellos, first violins *divisi* in octaves, and woodwind, including piccolo, all playing it as confidently as possible to produce imposing orchestral support to an ensemble entirely devoid of any attempt at individual musical characterization of any of the principals. It is just a nice big tune which is built up until it has reached an appropriate degree of intensity when it gives way to an urgent and *strepitoso* final Allegro to bring down the curtain.

ACT II

Scene 1 : A room in the Castle.

The curtain rises to an exact orchestral echo of Macbeth's entrance after the murder of Duncan. The mournful notes to which he sang "Tutto è finito" are played by trumpets and trombones in unison octaves and lead to the orchestra playing the first dozen bars of "Fatal mia donna" (Ex 20).

Macbeth, who is now King, enters lost in thought, followed by Lady Macbeth. In a recitative ingeniously based on Scenes 1 and 2 of Shakespeare's Act III (with lines spoken by Lady Macbeth in Scene 2 answered by lines spoken by Macbeth in Scene 1) Lady Macbeth tells her husband to forget the past and to be thankful that Malcolm, by fleeing to England, will be suspected of his father's murder. Macbeth replies gloomily that the Witches prophesied Banquo would be the father of kings; and Banquo still lives; and Banquo's son. "But they are not immortal."

"No," says Lady Macbeth quietly, "they are not immortal." Macbeth decides to murder Banquo and he leaves the scene with a determined, if oblique, reference to Shakespeare's "Banquo, thy soul's flight, If it find heaven, must find it out tonight"—a line, it will be remembered which ends Act III, Scene 1 and spoken only after Macbeth had had his conference with the two murderers.

The whole of this first scene of the second act of the opera as we know it today dates from the Paris production of 1865, though up to this point there has been nothing that might not have been written for the Florence performance of 1847. As Macbeth leaves the scene, however, we are jerked rather suddenly into the future with a strangely Wagnerian phrase—

—which will probably worry those who know Verdi in general and not *Macbeth* in particular by its familiarity. It is, in fact, an unexpected anticipation of the phrase heard as Radames is brought

56

before Amneris in the first scene of Act IV of *Aida*, composed six
years after the Paris *Macbeth*:

Ex 24

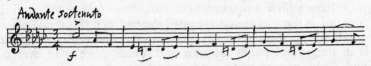

The two passages are not only very similar in time, harmony and
tune, but also particularly so in their orchestration. In both cases
the melody is played tremolo by the strings doubling a prominent
couple of oboes in unison, with a cor anglais added in *Aida*. The
game of spotting anticipations of Verdi-to-come in *Macbeth* can be
a little confusing at any time, of course; many things which one may
think forestall *Rigoletto*, for instance, turn out in fact to have been
added to the opera in Paris, fourteen years after *Rigoletto* was written.
It is even more perplexing to encounter the 1865 score in turn anticipating the shape of things to come even later.

The "forward-looking" orchestral introduction in question leads
to Lady Macbeth's big aria, "La luce langue"—which begins as a
soliloquy on the approach of night that will draw a veil over another
crime:

Ex 25

Though there is no exact equivalent for this aria to be found in
Shakespeare it is just possible that Verdi got the idea from Macbeth's lines in Act III, Scene 2:

> Come, seeling night,
> Scarf up the tender eye of the pitiful day
> . . . Light thickens, and the crow
> Makes wing to the rooky wood;

Lady Macbeth's first lyrical mood does not last long. She becomes determined and declamatory as she reflects on the necessity of
"this night's great fatal business" lapsing suddenly into a hushed and
uncanny phrase that modulates from B to B flat, to G sharp minor,
from B again to G major and back to B—"The dead have no wish
to rule; for them a requiem, eternity!" It is a sinister little sequence

evoking an atmosphere of evil that foreshadows the dark brooding of Iago.

Lady Macbeth's scene ends with a brilliant Allegro vivo in which she exults in the royal prospect before her. The cabaletta starts on a high G sharp which is marked to be sung "con trasporto", and that is more or less the way things are until the end. But this is no ordinary frenzied, whipped-up show-off finale to a prima donna's big *scena*. It is in these final pages that we find Verdi more than ever concerned with interpretation and expression marks—the strings to play their tremolo *il più piano possibile*, while the singer uses a *voce pianissima e un po' oscillante*; Lady Macbeth instructed to stress the word "mio" when she anticipates the ecstatic moment when "the sceptre will be mine" ("O scettro, alfin sei mio"). With its final, subtly varied and built-up display of excitement (and pleasure) at the imminent removal of the last obstacle to Macbeth's undisturbed enjoyment of the crown, it is a dramatic finish and interesting less for the vocal effectiveness of the whole than for the remarkably powerful musical picture that is drawn of the character of Lady Macbeth.

Scene 2 : A park. In the distance, Macbeth's castle.

A short and stealthy orchestral introduction introduces us to Shakespeare's Three Murderers who, like his Three Witches, have increased and multiplied themselves in the service of grand opera and are now a four-part male chorus. The murderers check on each other's identity and unite in a charming and quite incongruous chorus of conspiracy. At least, the dramatic context and the words suggest that it is a conspiracy. The musical evidence, on the other hand, is not so convincing:

Ex 26

Except for some sinister little punctuations from the timpani much of this chorus is unaccompanied, an exercise in extremely effective choral writing marked *sotto voce ed assai staccato*, which only the words reassure us is not a chorus of footmen strayed in from a Rossini or Donizetti comedy. To make sure we have not forgotten their bloody intentions the murderers end their opening chorus with some *ff* cries of "Trema, Banco!" (roughly, "Look out, Banquo!"), but in a moment revert to their first would-be conspiratorial mood. The reprise is accompanied by more of the orchestra this time, making much imaginative use of piccolo, horns and bass trombone playing *pianissimo* and very staccato. The passage will be noticeable to many English listeners who will recognize the familiar opening strains of the late Eric Coates's "Calling All Workers" signature tune of the BBC's near-everlasting "Music While You Work" in the figure which runs almost incessantly through the sequence:

Ex 27

Once again the Murderers warn Banquo at the top of their voices to look out, and leave the scene assuring us that they will wait in the silence they and the orchestra have only just that moment shattered with their threats. The music dies away with some more interjections by the timpani and ends with the flute taking over a diminuendo reminder of the ostinato of Ex 27.

Banquo enters with Fleance and after a gloomy recitative sings with awful presentiment of the evil the dark night holds:

Ex 28

Of the three meditations on night and nightfall we have so far heard in this act ("La luce langue" and the Murderers' chorus are the other two) this is the most oppressively mournful, for Verdi has dressed the music in grimly sombre colours, the elegiac tone of the oboe in its lowest register adding a plaintive overtone to the tune played in unison by clarinet, violins and violoncellos against a throbbing funereal background of four trombones. The originality of this orchestration is rather spoilt when the tune spreads out into a broad E major, and a solo trumpet doubling the melody sticks out like a sore thumb; but Verdi was still at the age when he did that sort of thing and the number was not one affected by the Paris revision.

Banquo and Fleance disappear in the park in an atmosphere of suspense neatly created by a short *ppp* orchestral epilogue to the aria. From the distance Banquo cries out in mortal agony to his son to fly.

Fleance runs across the scene pursued by one of the murderers and the music fades away.

Scene 3 : The Banqueting Hall in the Castle.

Macbeth and his wife are entertaining Macduff and others to a banquet with typical Allegro brillante party music to go with it— festive, cheerfully scored, thoroughly unelegant, unaristocratic, small-town stuff as out of place in Forres (where the scene should properly be laid) as it is in the Paris of *La traviata* where it seems to have moved on to after its appearance in *Macbeth*:

Ex *29*

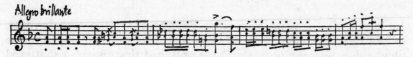

Macbeth bids his guests welcome and asks Lady Macbeth to propose a toast in their honour. She does so in a Brindisi, which is a pleasant bit of *exotisme* to encounter in eleventh-century Scotland, but not so dragged in as one might think, for there is in fact a toast in this scene in Shakespeare's play, although it does not occur at the beginning of the scene as this Brindisi does and in any case it is given by Macbeth:

Ex *30*

In spite of its cheerful brilliance the Brindisi, with its trills and runs and grace notes that make temporary nonsense of Verdi's wish that Lady Macbeth should "not sing at all", is a pretty commonplace set-piece, and one has fair warning of its quality when its first eight bars are used as an orchestral introduction with the tune played— inevitably—by a trumpet and sticking out like a cornet solo at a band contest.

Yet in a curious way, though the Brindisi never suggests for a moment that its singer is an aristocrat or that the chorus of guests at a royal Scottish banquet who repeat the last eight bars every time Lady Macbeth has finished are anything but peasants from the composer's native Po Valley, there is an air of half-heartedness about the whole thing. That, at least, is the feeling I get *in the theatre*, and which I never experienced from merely studying the score. The jauntiness of the tune with its broken-up, staccato phrases, creates an ironic atmosphere and gives the impression that Lady Macbeth is putting a good face on things and anxiously watching the clock as though she expected something to happen.

The first thing that does happen is the appearance at the door of one of the murderers. Macbeth leaves the table to talk to him and hears that Banquo has been dealt with, but that the son escaped. The conversation takes place against a *ppp* instrumental reprise of the Brindisi, with some intriguingly altered harmonies. The text comes roughly from Shakespeare, but unfortunately tells us all we really need know before the Murderer can get to the picturesque goryness of ". . . safe in a ditch he bides, With twenty trenched gashes in his head".

The Murderer leaves and the party music (Ex 29) starts up again. On his way back to the table Macbeth tells his wife significantly that Banquo will not be coming to the banquet. "I will sit in his vacant place," says Macbeth. As he goes to sit down he finds the seat occupied by Banquo's ghost, which is visible, of course, only to him (and, depending on the producer, perhaps to the audience as well). In terror Macbeth falls to the floor and in Shakespeare's words cries out to his guests: "Which of you have done this?" and then to the Ghost:

> Thou canst not say I did it: never shake
> Thy gory locks at me.

Lady Macbeth reassures her guests: "Sit, worthy friends; my lord is often thus", and turning to Macbeth whispers, "Are you a man?" Macbeth replies in a broad and dramatic tune to which trombones supply a persistent *pp* staccato accompaniment, and in words to the effect of, "Ay, and a bold one, that dare look on that Which might appal the devil." He sees the Ghost again and addresses it:

> If thou canst nod, speak too,
> If charnel-houses and our graves must send
> Those we bury back, our monuments shall be the maws of kites.

Those, at least, are Shakespeare's words. Piave reduces them a little prosaically to, "Since you can shake your locks, O phantom, can the grave return the dead?"

Banquo's ghost disappears.* Lady Macbeth reproaches her husband under her breath again. Macbeth calms down again, and in an unexpectedly lyrical passage asks his wife to repeat the toast. In the play it is here that Macbeth proposes the toast of the absent Banquo

---

* Verdi described in detail, from information received from London, how the Ghost should look—with wounds visible on his neck, his hair disarranged and his spectral body in ashen-grey veiling.

(the only toast, as we know, which is drunk in the banquet scene). An older, more experienced Verdi might have had Macbeth sing a verse of the Brindisi and so pointed some of Shakespeare's original irony; as it is, Lady Macbeth sings it with the final couplet altered this time to ask the company to empty their glasses to Banquo, "the flower of warriors".

The Ghost reappears. Terrified, Macbeth cries out, "Avaunt and quit my sight! Let the earth hide thee!" Macbeth's behaviour disturbs the guests increasingly as Piave's text keeps to most of the sense but none of the poetry of Shakespeare's magnificent scene. Verdi works up the excitement to a climax and at the end we have something of the awful fear of the original, "Hence, horrible shadow! Unreal mockery, hence!"

The Ghost disappears once more, and "with joy" Macbeth declares that he lives again, a phrase he sings broadly in a cadence which takes us firmly from the key of D flat to the E major of what now becomes the second-act finale of the opera.

The ensemble which builds up from this point will make those who already know their *Traviata* second-act finale feel very much at home, for the affinity between the two movements is remarkably close. It happens that, unlike some of the other "forward-looking" moments in *Macbeth*, this finale was already in the earlier Florence version, so it is not a case of prophecy-after-the-event, as it were.

When we come to *La traviata* we shall see that, like this one in *Macbeth*, the second-act finale is also marked Largo and builds from an initial phrase by a solo baritone voice; that it is in 12/8 time on a 4/4 base; that it rises to a series of climaxes and drops to a *ppp* whisper, leaving dramatic gaps between phrases when both voices and orchestra are silent. The similarities are endless, even to the final cadences in which Macbeth is heard muttering away in one opera and Alfredo in the other.

Against a typical chuck-chuck accompaniment Macbeth starts the ensemble—

Ex 31

It will have blood, they say; blood will have blood;
  . . . I will tomorrow—
And betimes I will—to the weird sisters:
More they shall speak; for now I am bent to know,
By the worst means, the worst.

Piave's Italian equivalent of these lines suffices Macbeth for the rest of the finale, which settles down into a stirring ensemble immediately he has finished his solo delivery. The movement grows out of a brief figure (marked "A" in the quotation below), which expands slowly into an infectious kind of phrase with a distinct flavour of an Italian street organ about it at times, thanks to the lavish use of the piccolo:

Ex 32

While Macbeth goes on thinking his thoughts about the Witches, Lady Macbeth's part in the ensemble is concentrated on telling her husband that the dead do not come back, Macduff gives voice to his growing suspicions; and "Dama di Lady" and the chorus tell us they are convinced the country has become a den of criminals. The power of music in opera to present four or more viewpoints simultaneously is well known and unique, of course, and Verdi was an unsurpassed master of it. In this particular ensemble again, as in the first-act finale of *Nabucco*, although his two "villains" express different thoughts in different words their affinity as characters is emphasized by the music they sing, which links them together in little runs, by echo and imitation of pointedly characteristic phrases. It is an ingenious and effective way of suggesting who is on whose side in the situation.

ACT III

Scene: A dark cavern. In the centre, a boiling cauldron. Thunder and lightning.

The third act, the most extensively revised of the four for the 1865 production, opens with a brassy passage which is briefly interrupted by a *pp* orchestra echo of the Witches' theme heard at the beginning of the opera (Ex 13). The Witches begin their chanting ("Thrice the brinded cat hath mew'd" etc.) to this theme and in a few moments the cauldron boils. The Witches divide into their three separate groups of six sopranos and in turn throw the familiar ingredients of toad, viper, Tartar's lips, finger of birth-strangled babe and (some of) the rest of Shakespeare's superb catalogue into their hellish brew. Though the items they sing about are gruesome and revolting enough the tune they intone as they stir the pot is quite grotesque in its incongruity, and worth quoting in full:

Ex *33*

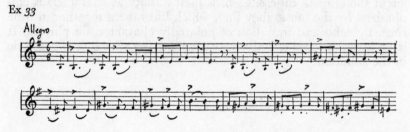

The third group of Witches, who start it off, sing the tune in E minor; the second takes it over in G major; the first follows in B minor. When, in the play, the three Witches have brewed their concoction and Hecate has congratulated them on it, Shakespeare adds the stage direction: "Music and a song, 'Black Spirits' etc.". Piave or Verdi with considerable wit, took this song title as the first line of their Witches' final incantation, a spirited ensemble affair starting in E minor and ending up *brillante* in an increasingly frenzied E major.

The Witches' cauldron scene at an end we come in the score to the ballet music interpolated for the Paris production. It is a lengthy sequence usually omitted from performance of the opera and—at the moment of writing—rather curiously not to be found in the record catalogues, although it is performed from time to time on the radio.

The idea of including a ballet at all clearly went against the grain with Verdi, but having accepted it he did his best to see that it had something to do with the drama. The ballet begins with the arrival of "spirits, devils and witches" who dance round the cauldron; after a while they stop dancing and invoke Hecate. With the appearance of Hecate, "goddess of the night and witchcraft", all stand "religiously posed, contemplating the goddess with awe". So far so good. The scenario now asks "Ecate" to perform some remarkable feats of dumb show, beginning with "she tells the witches that she understands their activities and why they have summoned her". Hecate next "examines everything attentively" and announces that "King Macbeth is coming to ask about his destiny and that they [the Witches] must satisfy him. If the Apparitions affect him too much, the spirits of the air must be evoked to bring him round again and give him renewed strength . . . but the ruin that awaits him must not be delayed." The assembled company "stand respectfully receiving the decrees of the goddess". Then, amid thunder and lightning, "Ecate" disappears, leaving the dancers to bring the ballet to an end with a waltz danced round the cauldron. (Purists and pedants are sure to object to a waltz for eleventh-century Scottish witches. But what else should they dance? A minuet?)

As I have never seen the ballet included in a performance of *Macbeth* I have no idea how successful a Hecate can be in conveying in pantomime all the information the scenario expects of her, but at least it shows a commendable willingness on the part of the composer to relate it in some way to the rest of the story.* Except for some remarkable orchestration (particularly for bass clarinet and brass) and the bright and charming waltz finale the music is not very distinguished.

Normal action is resumed with the entry of Macbeth. He demands that the Witches should show him the future, and for the first time in the opera the Witches' music has a convincing element of eeriness about it. A loud and sinister fanfare-like passage of four bars in which four horns and four trombones thump out repeated B flats in unison, precedes the Witches' evocation of the first of the Apparitions. There is a roll of thunder and there arises a warrior's head, wearing a helmet. The Witches, now in solemn unison, interrupt Macbeth when he wants to question the Apparition. "It knows your thought," they tell him. "Be silent and listen." The Apparition speaks against a *pp* accompaniment of slow and solemn chords from trumpets and

---

* A note in the orchestral score during the waltz reads: "In this *pp* of the orchestra it would be best to suspend the dance and in its place to have pantomime, or limit the dancing to two or three couples"—which, to me at any rate, suggests that the corps de ballet of the Théâtre Lyrique in 1865 were no lighter on their feet than their present-day descendants at the Opéra (see *Great Opera Houses*, p 305).

3

trombones—an interesting throwback to *Don Giovanni* with its eighteenth-century convention of associating trombones with the supernatural: "Macbeth! Macbeth! Macbeth! Beware Macduff!"

The first Apparition vanishes and the orchestral tutti which co-incides with his disappearance is notable for including a loud stroke on a tam-tam (or gong) played behind the scenes. Since the gong is not an instrument one associates with Verdi in the ordinary way I imagine its inclusion in the 1865 score of *Macbeth* was due to local influence, for the use of the gong had long been to French taste as a means of creating an atmosphere of horror and high drama. In normal theatrical acoustic conditions Verdi's back-stage gong is not likely to make much of an impression on the listener, for it is well and truly covered by a *ff* tutti on each of the three occasions it occurs during the scene of the Apparitions.

A roll of thunder and a second apparition appears—a bloody child whose prophecy is sung by a soprano to ominous *pp* and *fp* chords of trumpets and trombones once more:

> Be bloody, bold and resolute; laugh to scorn
> The power of man, for none of woman born
> Shall harm Macbeth.

On hearing this Macbeth cries, "Then live Macduff! . . ." but swiftly changes his mind and in a passage of unexpected Iago-like ferocity swears to kill Macduff. The third Apparition rises—"a Child crowned with a tree in his hand" and accompanied by the sustained chords of trumpets and trombones prophesies:

> Macbeth shall never vanquish'd be until
> Great Birnam wood to high Dunsinane hill
> Shall come against him.

Macbeth is overjoyed:

> That will never be:
> Who can impress the forest, bid the tree
> Unfix his earth-bound root?

—and rejoices in a brief passage very characteristic of the later Verdi in its vigour and harmony. He turns to the Witches to ask if Banquo's son will ever rule in his place. They tell him not to ask. Angrily Macbeth demands to know and raises his sword. The cauldron sinks into the earth.

From below the ground comes the sound of bagpipes—according to Verdi's score. Shakespeare, for his part, considered all Scottish music could be lumped together under the generic "Hautboys", which is all he calls for at this point of the play. To imitate the sound of bagpipes Verdi also uses "Hautboys"—but only two oboes in a subterranean orchestra which otherwise consists of six clarinets, two bassoons and a double bassoon. The sound of "bagpipes" is the signal for the "show of Eight Kings" whose appearance begins with the following:

Ex 34

The appearance and disappearance of each of the Kings is accompanied by this unusual wind band which Verdi instructed should be played under the stage, just below an open trap, so that the sound could penetrate the theatre, "but in a mysterious manner and as if at a distance". Each sequence is punctuated by the distraught outbursts of Macbeth and some most effective sudden contrasts between the pit orchestra and the muffled sound from below the stage. It is an eerie sequence made more dramatic by the absence of any change of tempo.

The scene moves steadily and inexorably to its climax—the appearance of Banquo with a looking glass in his hand as the eighth and last in the Show of Eight Kings.*

With the appearance of Banquo the steady tempo breaks and the "bagpipes" are heard no more. Macbeth raves and storms, drawing his sword to destroy the spectres which he realizes cannot be killed for they are not yet alive. "Will they live?" he asks the Witches. "They will live," they reply. Macbeth falls senseless to the ground. The Witches call on the spirits of the air to restore the King to his senses and interpreting Shakespeare's directions, "Music. The Witches dance and then vanish with Hecate", there follows a sequence of song and dance which is usually cut in performance. And rightly cut, I think, for although it dates from 1865 it is a trivial movement which lets us down badly and it is hard to believe (see Ex 35) that it was written at the same time as the magnificent dramatic

Ex 35

* Verdi seems to have tripped up here. Shakespeare's directions are "A Show of Eight Kings; the last with a glass in his hand; Banquo's Ghost following." In the opera the seventh king is followed by "the eighth, Banquo, with a looking glass in his hand". Banquo, of course, was not one of the future kings of Scotland and is present only in his capacity of the sire of kings.

music of the previous scene. We are back in the first-act mood of the Witches with a tune which I have quoted to show that the listener is not missing much by the omission of the scene—except perhaps a faint echo of the Murderers' chorus.

Macbeth recovers consciousness. Unless he is dispensed with, a Herald (of all people to meet in a cavern) announces the arrival of the Queen; otherwise Lady Macbeth enters alone—an episode which is not found in Shakespeare (Macbeth and his wife never meet again after the Banquet Scene) but which gives Verdi the opportunity to deal quickly with some of the bits of plot that are still left over at this stage in the opera.

Macbeth tells his wife what has been happening, what he heard from the Three Apparitions—that he must beware Macduff, that none of woman born shall harm him until Birnam Wood shall move. He goes on to tell her that Banquo's descendants shall reign in Scotland. This rouses Lady Macbeth to fury and in a violent and stirring duet, written entirely new for the Paris production, and much of it coloured by the dramatic declamation encountered later in *Aida*, she unites with her husband to vow the ruthless destruction of all that stands in their way. Banquo's tribe shall be exterminated; Macduff's castle shall be burnt to the ground, his wife and children killed. (The decision to murder Macduff's family was a secret which in the play Macbeth shared only with his hired assassins and Lennox. Its transposition to this scene in the opera is in practice extremely effective, for it is something more for Macbeth to be bloody, bold and resolute about as his wife inspires him to recover his courage.)

"Let there be vengeance!" is the theme of a scene which, while it does not exist in Shakespeare, fortunately exists in Verdi as an exciting finale to the act. It is not a long scene at all; it builds to its climax rapidly and simply from a phrase started by Macbeth:

Ex 36

It is echoed by Lady Macbeth, sometimes at a distance of a bar, sometimes of two bars. There is a short interlude marked *pppp* and to be sung by Macbeth and "Lady" *con voce repressa*, which suddenly creates tremendous and unexpected tension by being sung in the major and creating a kind of clenched-teeth air of determination, as well as an air of whispered conspiracy, that is helped by a few bars of imaginative scoring for flute and bassoon before the final cries of "Vendetta!" are unleashed.

It is a fine finish to what, with very few reservations, is a fine act.

ACT IV

Scene 1 : A deserted place on the border of Scotland and England. In the distance the forest of Birnam.

The first scene of this final act is an ingenious solution of several dramatic problems that must have faced Piave and Verdi in adapting Shakespeare's play. It was achieved by changing the running order of the original and putting into the setting of Shakespeare's Act V, Scene 4 (the Sleepwalking Scene, Act V, Scene 1, in the play, has yet to come in Verdi's opera) some skilfully adapted poetic ideas from Act IV, Scene 3. The first of these is the chorus of Scottish refugees which begins the act and is based on words used by Malcolm when, as an exile in England, he refers to "my poor country" where,

> . . . each new morn
> New widows howl, new orphans cry, new sorrows
> Strike heaven on the face. . . .

The scene of the Scottish refugees dates entirely from the 1865 score and is one of the most striking elegiac passages in all Verdi. It opens with a short and intensely melancholy orchestral introduction beginning with a passage of unexpectedly stark brass writing which dies away from a dramatic and arresting *ff* to a plaintive oboe note immediately recognizable in Verdi's music as an expression of lamentation. All his life Verdi expressed tears and sorrow in music by variants of one of the three following characteristic devices:

In this scene in *Macbeth* he uses all three, two of them simultaneously at one point. The oboe, heard playing form "A" shown in Ex 37, leaves us in no doubt of the emotional nature of what is to come. The choral movement itself begins with whispered monotone repetitions of the words "Patria oppressa!"—a strange pre-echo, as it were, of the A minor opening of Verdi's Requiem Mass. The key is the same and there is much of the same atmosphere in the two short passages of four- and five-part choral writing—the first

69

accompanied by wind alone, the second by strings—which serve as a prelude to the Lament of the Scottish Exiles proper.

Marked to sound *come un lamento* ("like a lament") the flute in its low register and the first violins play as a kind of two-bar vamp-till-ready the figure "B" in Ex 37. This continues with a solo oboe added to play figure "C" when a group of sopranos sings *tristissimo* and in unison to the words spoken above by Malcolm:

The two "lament" figures continue unceasingly as a second and third group of sopranos are added and eventually the whole chorus is engaged to build a semi-climax and die away again. The second half of the scene consists of a straightforward reprise of the tune of Ex 38 sung by sopranos and tenors in octaves, but punctuated by a short simple rhythmic figure intended to suggest the tolling of a bell:

It is sung first by the basses, supported by timpani, bass drum, and four trombones in unison, and echoed by sopranos, trumpet and two horns. It is an impressive *ostinato* that contributes a great deal to an episode which owes much of its moving quality to fine and imaginative scoring—such as the melancholy doubling of the tune by the violas and a sustained *pp* E by flute and piccolo. The Lament ends with two unison whispers of "Patria mia!" and a sudden shattering *ff* exclamation of the same words before a final dying sigh of "O Patria!"

My knowledge of the original chorus which this 1865 number replaced is limited to reports from usually reliable sources that it was a straightforward affair marked *cantabile e melanconico*, perhaps intended (Francis Toye suggested) as a kind of sequel to "Va, pensiero . . ." As a means of rousing patriotic feelings in occupied Italy in the early days of the opera, however, it does not seem to have had anything like the same effect as the *Nabucco* chorus. As I have already mentioned, the inflammable material in *Macbeth* was in the Malcolm-Macduff duet later in this scene. There was no mention of "Austrian bayonets" having to keep order at the Fenice on account of the chorus.

The new Scottish Exiles' chorus is no less moving for having been written in the comparative political peace and quiet of a free and united Italy, and there is no doubt that although it was deprived by circumstances of the rabble-rousing power of "Va, pensiero . . ." it is nevertheless a conception of unusual beauty and affecting nostalgia.

Macduff enters and in a recitative that takes its text from Shakespeare's Act IV, Scene 3, tells us that his wife and children have been murdered by Macbeth. He reproaches himself for escaping to England and leaving his family unprotected and helpless, in an aria to be sung *con espressione melanconica*—"Ah, la paterna mano" ("This father's hand was not there to shield you, my dear ones . . .")

Ex 40

Except for some retouching of the orchestration (which features a solo violoncello, as well as some stirring bars of violins and violoncellos in unison with the voice) this aria is more or less as it was in the Florence production—a tuneful and effective piece which, in a magnificent recording by Caruso, was for many of us not only our first introduction to Verdi's *Macbeth* but virtually our first inkling that Verdi had ever written an opera of that name at all.

For those unacquainted with the words of the aria it should be explained that the final twelve bars (including the cadenza) of a thirty-bar tune are a repeated Italian form of Macduff's oath to kill Macbeth ". . . if he 'scape, Heaven forgive him too!" (Malcolm's reply to this, if you remember, was "This tune goes manly . . ."—a fair comment, I think, in the case of this aria which has a peculiar virility as well as charm of its own.)

A drum is heard and Malcolm enters leading "many English soldiers" to a very military noise from the orchestra—first, a staccato woodwind-and-strings affair, and then a full blast tutti. It is an entrance that will never fail to delight those of us able to enjoy the purely private joke of recognizing a perilous—and fitting—likeness between the tune they march to and a bawdy British Army song called "The One-Eyed Reilly":

Ex 41

The text of the libretto now switches back and forth between Shakespeare's Act V, Scene 4 and Act IV, Scene 3, as Malcolm bids every soldier cut a bough from the wood of Birnam "and bear't before him", and in the next breath, encouraging him to be revenged on Macbeth, is answered by the bereaved Macduff: "He has no children."

The scene ends with Malcolm and Macduff brandishing their swords and, *con entusiasmo*, calling for the liberation of their betrayed and unhappy country to a naïve, rather Bellini-like tune:

Ex 42

The chorus joins in, the tempo quickens and after endless typical reiteration of half a dozen words from the text everybody storms off to rescue the *oppressi*.

Scene 2: A hall in Macbeth's castle, as in Act I. Night.

As I have pointed out, in Shakespeare the Sleepwalking Scene we are now coming to is the first scene of Act V, three scenes earlier in the running order than the Birnam Wood episode we have just had. Only the incorrigible purist, however, would deny that for the sake of the whole dramatic progress of Verdi's opera the placing of the Sleepwalking Scene at this point was absolutely essential. And above all, of course, a logical, practical theatrical step to take. It would have been demanding too much of both audience and singer, after the exciting and strenuous finale of Act III, to start Act IV with a long and exacting scene like the "Gran scena del sonnambulismo". In its present position the scene not only enables the singer to enjoy the important, purely physical advantage of a rest of an interval between the acts and a whole scene before she has to go on again, but the hushed atmosphere the composer intends to create is thrown into relief by the strong contrast with the noisy patriotic scene we have just heard; and, apart from anything else, it delays the disappearance from the action of the most important character in the opera.

The *gran scena* begins with a long orchestral introduction which rarely rises above *pianissimo* and creates a peculiarly hushed, uneasy atmosphere. The material comes mainly from the prelude to Act I, the themes of Exx 14 and 15 now played by muted strings and the whole coloured by frequent and imaginative use of the cor anglais whose elegiac quality is exploited with remarkable effect throughout the whole of this scene. The same two themes are heard again, when the curtain rises, punctuating the *sempre sotto voce* discussion in recitative by the Doctor and the Gentlewoman, who wait expectantly, as in the play, for the appearance of Lady Macbeth. Their conversation continues, following Shakespeare closely, as Lady Macbeth enters, walking in her sleep, and carrying a light. She puts the light down and rubs her hands together as though washing them.

From the orchestra comes the first sound of an accompanying figure which persists almost to the end of the big aria which Lady Macbeth now sings, the short rising phrase in the bass played by violas and violoncellos in unison, the wailing, descending semitone by the cor anglais reinforced later by the clarinet an octave lower to produce once more the unusual mournful sound I referred to on page 52 :

Like so much in *Macbeth* the "tune" of the Sleepwalking Aria does not lend itself to obvious quotation. So much of it is in near-monotone, or in broken phrases which add up to a whole, as it were, but do not mean much individually out of their context. There is nevertheless a certain melodic continuity about it firmly based on the inevitable progress of an inspired orchestral accompaniment. More than perhaps any other scene in the opera this needs to be *heard*, or at least to be studied in the orchestral score, for the vocal score gives little indication of the effectiveness of the music in performance or how well, in spite of its two short but dated cadenzas, this survival from the original version of 1847 fits in with Verdi's later and more mature interpolations.

The action and the text of the scene are taken faithfully from Shakespeare's. From "Out, damned spot! out, I say!" and "I tell you yet again, Banquo's buried; he cannot come out on's grave" to "What's done cannot be undone. To bed, to bed, to bed", there is little that is omitted. Paradoxically, Verdi has succeeded in expressing the poetry of Shakespeare perhaps more faithfully in this scene than anywhere else in *Macbeth*—paradoxically because in the play this is the only scene, apart from that with the Porter, which is written in prose. In prose, that is, until Lady Macbeth's exit, when the Doctor has his moving little speech in verse, bidding the Gentlewoman look after her mistress. The Doctor's epilogue has no place in Verdi's opera, but its pathos and sympathy are movingly implicit in Verdi's own brief, telling orchestral postlude.

3*

Lady Macbeth's departure from the scene and from the opera involves her in a notorious arpeggio up to a high D flat to be sung, Verdi says, as a "fil di voce"—a thread of voice. Some sopranos, we are assured, manage the top note unaided; others, we know, have had their last off-stage hurdle jumped by an anonymous off-stage soprano who, not having been involved in the rest of the prima donna's exhausting experience, contributes a fresh top D flat indistinguishable by the audience from what they imagine the prima donna's top D flat would sound like. As for gramophone recordings of the "Gran Scena del sonnambulismo"—who can possibly tell what splicings and editings and electronic cookery have gone on since the invention of tape?

Scene 3 : A hall in Macbeth's castle.

Macbeth is alone and in recitative echoes the Witches' prophecy— 'no man that's born of woman Shall e'er have power upon thee"— to reassure himself that he has nothing to fear from "the boy Malcolm" advancing at the head of his English army. Macbeth's optimism fades suddenly :

> . . . My way of life
> Is fall'n into the sear, the yellow leaf;

and in an aria, to be sung now *con espressione*, now *con dolore*, he paraphrases the remorse and sadness of the soliloquy in the play :

> And that which should accompany old age,
> As honour, love, obedience, troops of friends,
> I must not look to have; but in their stead,
> Curses, not loud but deep, mouth-honour, breath,
> Which the poor heart would fain deny, and dare not.

Ex 44

In its whole atmosphere—final cadenza and all—this is unmistakably an aria from the first version of *Macbeth*. Baritones no doubt look forward to it, and like the late Leonard Warren in the RCA recording, enjoy taking an unauthorized top A flat in the cadenza and so destroy what little pathos there is in the aria. It is a typical early-Verdi episode and if it is an infectious tune it is not altogether due to the melody's unmistakable similarity to that of a song made famous by Miss Marlene Dietrich. Indeed, at Glyndebourne it is traditionally known as "See what the Boys in the Backroom will have". It is a good tune anyway. The only thing the matter with it is that it was written too soon in Verdi's career, when he was not yet ready to make the most of the poetry and the situation Shakespeare offered him—particularly the poetry. The rest of the act from this point onwards is new.

Almost as a literal note-for-note echo of the lament Lady Macbeth heard when Macbeth had gone to kill Duncan in Act I, "a cry of women within" is heard off stage—"Ella è morta"—"She is dead". The oboe replies mournfully with the semitone grace note of its typical lament ("A" in Ex 37) coming from above instead of below. The Gentlewoman enters to tell Macbeth the Queen is dead. "Life!" says Macbeth *con indifferenza*, "—a tale Told by an idiot, full of sound and fury, Signifying nothing".

Macbeth's words are sung to a phrase which creates another remarkable pre-echo—at least, to my mind—and that is of the last scene in *Otello*. Macbeth's four nearly identical phrases—

Ex 45

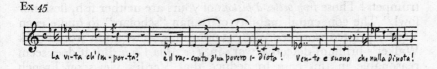

La vi-ta ch'im-por-ta?   è il rac-conto d'un povero i- diota !   Ven-to e suono che nulla biuota!

—seem to me to have much in common with Otello's contemplation of the dead body of Desdemona:

Ex 46

Come sei pal-li-da! e. stanca, e muta,

That *Macbeth* should provide a blue-print for a memorable moment in *Otello* has no great critical significance, of course; nevertheless this score of Verdi's, with its first and second thoughts separated by a gap of nearly twenty years, presents many intriguing instances of the composer's tentative sowing of ideas that did not come to full flower until his final period, and as such I feel they are worth a passing glance in a study of this kind.

Macbeth's soldiers enter crying that Birnam Wood is on the move. Macbeth calls for his arms; and with a flourish of off-stage trumpets the movement headed "Battle" in the score begins, while the scene changes to the battlefield. In the background of an open plain surrounded by hillocks and wood, the English soldiers advance slowly forward, each man carrying the bough of a tree in front of him.

Verdi's Battle Music written for the 1865 version is an original and arresting conception in the form of a fugue, and it evidently intrigued the composer considerably. He wrote to his French publisher Léon Escudier: "You'll laugh when you hear that for the battle I have written a fugue!!! A fugue? I, who detest all this sort of thing that stinks of school and which I haven't touched for nearly thirty years!!!! But I assure you that in this case it is the right musical form. The ebb and flow of subjects and counter-subjects, the clash of the dissonances, the general uproar, etc., etc., can express a battle very well. Only one thing I want and that is to have it played by key trumpets [*trombe a macchina*] like we have in Italy, which are so clear and penetrating. Your valve trumpets [*trompettes à pistons*] are too feeble and limp for this. For the rest, the orchestra will have fun. . . ."* From the words "Only one thing I want" to "too feeble and limp for this" this letter differs from the more familiar and more often quoted version included in the *Copialettere* of 1913 and in Franco Abbiati's four-volume study of Verdi published in 1959, where the letter reads: "If only we had our rich piercing trumpets! Those *trompettes à pistons* of yours are neither fish, flesh nor fowl." The congenital inability of Italian "scholars" to quote even Verdi's printed words correctly is notorious, as we know from Frank Walker's brilliant detective work in *The Man Verdi*. But it does seem reasonable in this case to deduce that Verdi's views on French trumpets were not altogether favourable.

The fugue is a superbly vigorous affair, and one can well understand Verdi's insistence that the brass should sound right if an unusual and ingenious movement, in which trumpets and trombones play such an important part, is to come off:

Ex 47

Unfortunately there seems to have developed recently an international conspiracy to mess about with Verdi's Battle Fugue. According to the score it accompanies the following seven incidents: (1) entrance of Macduff, who orders his soldiers to throw down their

---

* This letter is quoted in the original Italian 1953 edition of Gatti's book on Verdi (not, of course, in the ridiculously emaciated Anglo-American edition).

boughs, take up their arms and follow him; (2) exit of Macduff, Malcolm and soldiers; (3) entrance of Macbeth pursued by Macduff; (4) Macbeth's warning to Macduff that he bears "a charmed life which must not yield to one of woman born"; (5) Macduff's reply that he was "from his mother's womb untimely ripp'd"; (6) exit of Macbeth and Macduff fighting; (7) entrance of chorus of *agitatissime* Scottish women who bewail the unhappy day, pray for the salvation of their children, and as the battle and the music die down mutter, "The tumult ceases".

In both the 1965 Decca and 1960 RCA recordings the fugue is cut to pieces—as it was also in the production of the opera finally staged at Covent Garden in 1960, when, 113 years after the Florence première and ninety-nine after it was first scheduled at the Royal Opera House, you might have thought they could have got it right. The complete movement consists of 126 bars; the two recordings reduce it to fewer than seventy, which makes fairly good nonsense of Verdi's expressed intentions in writing a strict fugue in the first place.

The worst damage is caused by the total omission in both recordings of the entire gradually *diminuendo* coda Verdi carefully wrote to describe the ending of the battle (in addition to this—episode (7)—the RCA record cuts episodes (1) and (2) as well). This cut destroys the continuity of the fugue, depriving it of much of its shape and excitement, and ruins the "dying fall" of the whole scene in a senseless and unforgivable manner.

Those whose knowledge of *Macbeth* is derived from the RCA recording and the Metropolitan Opera production on which it is based, may perhaps feel that they are being compensated for the mutilation of the Battle Fugue by the unexpected performance at this point in the opera of a scene which is not to be found in any of the usual full or vocal scores of the work. Its absence from such places is not surprising, for it is a soliloquy by the dying Macbeth which Verdi wrote as an extremely conventional operatic ending for the first version of the opera and carefully cut out of the second. Its inclusion in the RCA recording is explained, if not necessarily excused, by the accident of the Metropolitan Opera House having borrowed the full score of *Macbeth* belonging to Glyndebourne, where the scene was used in the early production of the opera by Fritz Busch and Carl Ebert—not to conclude the opera, but to give us a last long look at Macbeth before the finale proper. The music of this scene, inserted in the score between the end of the Battle Fugue and the Hymn of Victory (that is, at the foot of p 289 of Ricordi's current vocal score), is in manuscript. There are no stage directions attached to it, but the RCA libretto tells us that after Macbeth has cried "Cielo!" on learning that Macduff was not born of woman, "they brandish swords and fight furiously. Macbeth falls. Macduff rushes off." Macbeth, as "little by little he manages to raise himself from the ground", then sings a short, not very tuneful passage punctuated by thumping funereal brass figures, in which—very much out of character—he is distinctly sorry for himself.

There is little doubt, I think, that Verdi's second thoughts on this question were right. And, of course, he has Shakespeare on his side, for except when Macduff returns with his severed head, we do not see Macbeth again in the play after his defiant exit line: "And damn'd be him that first cries, 'Hold enough!'" The fighting and Macbeth's death at the hand of Macduff take place off stage. For my part, in spite of the historical bonus supplied by RCA for those who are interested in such things, I prefer the 1865 version as Verdi left it, and which is now observed by Glyndebourne—with the fugue in full and no dying Macbeth.*

As the noise of battle dies away—in the score, at any rate—male voices off stage are heard triumphantly crying, "Vittoria!"; the cry is echoed by the Scottish women (forbidden by gramophone companies and others to sing where they should during the fugue), who are now on stage. Malcolm enters, followed by English soldiers leading in Macbeth's followers as prisoners. Macduff, accompanied by other soldiers and countryfolk, kneels before Malcolm and proclaims him King.

Having decided that Macbeth's death should be changed for the Paris production Verdi wrote, "I cannot do anything there but a 'Hymn of Victory'. Macbeth and Lady Macbeth are no longer on the stage and in their absence there is little to be done with the secondary characters." So he wrote the Hymn of Victory which rounds off the opera in much the same terms as Malcolm's final speech rounds off the play.

It must be said, however, that Verdi's Hymn of Victory is no ordinary C-major-maestoso affair. It starts off in A minor with open fifths on each beat in the accompaniment at the top and bottom of

---

* In the 1847 version (I was shown the vocal score at Sant'Agata) Macbeth's death on the stage is the last scene of the opera, followed only by a dozen or so rapid bars in which Macduff proclaims the liberation of Scotland and the chorus hails Malcolm as King before the curtain falls. It is a tidy ending and avoids all those problems of what to do about Macbeth's body which inevitably arise when the death scene is interpolated in the 1865 version, where, because no musical provision was made by Verdi in the score for its disposal, the corpse has to be left lying unattended while the final Hymn of Victory is performed. The fact is that what suited the composer in the 1847 production did not suit him in 1865 and that is why Verdi cut the scene altogether. At least, that is what he obviously hoped; unfortunately he had reckoned without the zeal of the twentieth-century opera producer.

the orchestra—"Macbeth ov'è . . ?" ("Where is Macbeth, where is the usurper?"):

Ex 48

It is sung *con entusiasmo* by tenors and basses, an oddly catchy kind of marching song which makes one or two rather reluctant excursions into C major.

The Scottish women, in the gentleness of their nature, introduce a tenderer note with a prayer of thanks to God who had set them free—"Salgan mie grazie a te"—

Ex 49

The restfulness of this hint of the gentler choral moments of *Aida* is disturbed first by Macduff and Malcolm in a hearty unison, and a moment afterwards we are back *ff* in the relentless rhythm of Ex 48. The conflict between major and minor, between the legato prayers of the women and the robust and vindictive rejoicing of the men continues and is resolved only in the last four bars, when a cadence is formed out of the tune of "Salgan mie grazie a te" and the curtain falls.

One way and another Verdi's *Macbeth* has a peculiar excitement of its own. It is uneven; it is ridiculous in places; but it leaves me, at any rate, constantly anxious to know what happens next—with the Witches in particular a constant source of delight to look forward to.

In the circumstances it is obviously unreasonable to expect *Macbeth* to be a masterpiece. However well one gets to know the music the sudden jarring changes of style always seem to happen without preparation or warning—perhaps because the score contains so much that is fascinating and absorbing that one is never ready for the passages that are not. What is amazing in the end is that through the murk created by inconsistency of style, moments of unbelievable (but comic) banality, and the disrupting effect of half a dozen changes of scene (by which I mean the occasions in the course of the evening when one has to sit impatiently in the dark with nothing going on even in the orchestra), the figure of Lady Macbeth emerges with three-dimensional clarity, a character whose psychological development and gradual tragic disintegration are shown with such remarkable skill and continuity that it is hard to believe the Sleep-walking Scene was not in fact written after "La luce langue"—so logically and naturally does the *Gran Scena del Sonnambulismo* of 1847 follow on as the dramatic consequence of the scene written in 1865.

The characterization of Macbeth, on the other hand, is not as complete and rounded to my mind as it should be. His musical status in the opera is second to that of Lady Macbeth which, of course, is in keeping with his dramatic status in the play. There are nevertheless several facets of his character which are not shown and which, even if they were shown in detail, would still not disturb the dramatic equilibrium of the whole. As I have already suggested, we learn little of his vacillating nature, and certainly nothing of his re-spect, and even affection, for Duncan which, if there were anywhere a hint of the great "If it were done when 'tis done" speech, would arouse a little sympathy for the Macbeths' first victim, For all we are told in the opera Duncan might have deserved everything he got.

Verdi expresses Macbeth's terror, his superstititious belief in the Witches' prophecies, his tormented conscience, but we see nothing of the great physical courage with which Shakespeare endowed him in the last scenes of the play; nor, for this very reason, do we have any feeling of the inevitability of events, of the odds inexorably mounting up against him. Macbeth's death, indeed, is oddly sudden and casual and the inclusion of the Busch-Ebert-Metropolitan death scene does nothing to alter this impression.

And yet the libretto is not without its ingenuities; there are moments of neat compression and telescoping which keep commend-ably to the spirit, if not to the letter, of Shakespeare's dramatic plan. But since it was the dramatist not the poet that drew Verdi to Shakespeare it is perhaps hardly surprising that it is the poetic element which is most conspicuously missing from the opera of *Macbeth*. There is more feeling for poetry in the later additions to the opera than in the first version, particularly in "La luce langue" and the scene of the Apparitions; but for the most part it is noticeably the gloom and horror of the action that moved Verdi, not the pecu-liar splendour and beauty of the verse in which the play is written.

With all the opera's faults, however, it is always unmistakably the voice of Verdi that we hear in *Macbeth*—whether the voice is speak-ing in the accents of 1847 or 1865. And if, as it does in me, the opera inspires a special kind of affection unlike anything one feels for any other Verdi opera, I think it is because it has a unique quality of *enthusiasm* about it. Verdi was so obviously instinctively excited by the whole idea of a *Macbeth* opera right from the start.

Perhaps it has to rate as a failure, or at best as an interesting experiment which, owing to numerous disconcerting circumstances, Verdi was unable to complete satisfactorily. But once having studied *Macbeth* even in the higgledy-piggledy state in which it has come down to us, it is difficult to think of any composer more naturally qualified to have made an opera of this play of Shakespeare's, or who has shown more clearly how peculiarly the subject seemed to "belong" to him, than Verdi.

RIGOLETTO

Opera (described in the original score as a "melodrama") in three acts* by Francesco Maria Piave, based on Victor Hugo's *Le Roi s'amuse*. First performed at the Teatro la Fenice, Venice, on 11th March, 1851. First performance in England: Covent Garden, 14th May, 1853. First performance in the United States: Academy of Music, New York, 19th February, 1855.

THE genesis of *Rigoletto*, Verdi's fifteenth opera and the first of that remarkable trio of works—*Rigoletto*, *Il trovatore* and *La traviata*—written one after the other in less than three years, was attended by more than its fair quota of those hazards created by what Verdi's wife described as "that gloomy thing called the Censorship". But while in the course of the composer's adventures with the authorities there were certainly many laughable and inconsistent instances of official interference and proscription it cannot truthfully be said that any of them denied us a masterpiece. Indeed, in the case of *Rigoletto* the Censor himself contributed materially to the creation of one.

In March 1850, when Verdi accepted the offer of the Fenice theatre to write a new opera for the following year, Venice was once more in Austrian hands. In March 1848 the Austrians had been driven out and for fifteen months the population enjoyed a precarious independence as a Republic. Owing to the "circostanze politiche" attached to life in a besieged city there had been no opera season during that time and it was not until the Austrians returned in July 1849 that operatic performances were resumed at the Fenice and the Venetians went back to what had become their normal existence since the first Austrians had arrived in 1815—life under a Military Government, and strict censorship of the arts, particularly in the theatre.

Verdi's first idea for an opera for the Fenice was one on the subject of a Spanish play by Antonio García Gutiérrez called *El Trovador*, but it seems that Piave, who had written the libretto of *Macbeth* and three other Verdi operas, was unable to lay hands on a copy. Next he thought of setting *Kean*, a play by Dumas *père*, but finally settled with enthusiasm for making an opera out of Victor Hugo's *Le Roi s'amuse*.

* The custom of dividing the opera into four acts still persists both in the theatre and in the recording studio where they often refer to Act I, Scene 2 as Act II, the original Act II as Act III, and the final Act III as Act IV. I have kept to the original form in this study as I am sure the intelligent reader will be able to make his own adjustments easily enough.

Verdi's choice of subject was accepted by the theatre, but without any great enthusiasm. Hugo's play had created such a scandal in Paris twenty years before, when it shocked the public so deeply that it had had to be withdrawn after a single performance. It was considered obscene and immoral, and there is no doubt that vice triumphed over virtue whichever way the story was looked at. The more the management of the Fenice considered the project the more doubtful they grew of its wisdom. Verdi refused to be diverted from his object. "The likelihood of *Le Roi s'amuse* not being allowed places me in a gravely embarrassing position," he wrote to the President of the theatre. "I was assured by Piave that there would be no obstacle to the subject, and accepting his word for it I have settled down to study and meditate on it profoundly, and the general musical idea and colouring are already fixed in my mind. Indeed, I can say that the main and hardest part of the work has already been done. If I were compelled to start on another subject now I would not have enough time to devote the necessary study to it, and I would not be able to write an opera satisfactory to my own conscience."

Piave completed his libretto, now re-titled by the composer *La maledizione* ("The Curse"), and in due course it was submitted to the Censorship who had already heard of the "unfavourable reception accorded to Victor Hugo's drama because of the *dissolutezza* with which it is filled". With this kind of prejudice to stimulate him it was not surprising that the Military Governor of Venice turned the idea down flat, a decision conveyed to the President of the Fenice in the following terms, only part of which I have ever seen published in English and which I will try to reproduce as nearly as possible in the flowery style of the original:

Imperial and Royal Central Direction of Public Order
To the Presidency of the Gran Teatro la Fenice
Venice 21 Nov. 1850
(Letter dispatched on 1 Dec)
His Excellency the Military Governor Cavalier de Gorzkowski . . . has commanded me to inform the above-mentioned Noble Presidency that he deplores that the poet Piave and the celebrated Maestro Verdi should not have chosen another field in which to display their talents, in preference to that of the revolting immorality and obscene triviality of the libretto entitled *La maledizione* the production of which the above-mentioned Presidency wishes to put on the stage of the Fenice.

His already-mentioned Excellency has therefore thought it right to prohibit its performance absolutely and desires that at the same time I should warn the above-mentioned Presidency to abstain from pursuing the matter any further. I am returning the manuscript sent to me with your esteemed accompanying letter of the 20th instant No 18.

The Imperial and Royal Central Director
Martello

Although the revolting *immoralità* and obscene *trivialità* of the subject may have been the loudly proclaimed reasons for the Censorship's outright ban on the libretto, it was obviously the political implications of *La maledizione* which most concerned the authorities. Victor Hugo's François I was a libertine and the whole thing showed royalty in an exceedingly poor light.

Carlo Martello, however, for all that he was Chief of Police (which is all that "Central Director of Public Order" meant in the end) was a man of taste, culture and initiative. He was also an admirer of Verdi's music, and no sooner had he passed on the Military Governor's edict than he suggested that the libretto could be saved if it was modified in accordance with his proposals. The first of these was that Piave should re-submit the libretto under the title *Il Duca di Vendôme*, thus eliminating a libertine king from the story and in his place putting a nondescript Duke (of a Dukedom which was in fact created out of a baronetcy by François I himself). This was one of the first "modifications" that did not at all impress Verdi.

There is in the archives of the Fenice a letter from Verdi to the President of the theatre written on the composer's receipt of the libretto proposed by the Chief of Police. One does not need to have read Martello's original suggestions for making the subject acceptable to the demands of the Military Governor: their nature can be only too clearly inferred from Verdi's forceful rejection of the entire proposition:

President Marzari

Busseto 14 December 1850
In replying immediately to your letter of the 11th, I have had very little time to examine the new libretto: but I have nevertheless seen enough of it to know that in this form it lacks character, meaning, and finally the dramatic points have become most tepid [*freddissimi*]. If it was necessary to change the names, then the locality ought to have been changed also, so that then it would be a prince or duke of another country—a Pier Luigi Farnese, for instance; or else place the action before the time of Louis XI when France was not a united kingdom, and have a Duke of Burgundy or Normandy etc., etc. In any case an absolute ruler. In the fifth scene of Act I the courtiers' anger at Triboletto [the Italian form of Hugo's jester, Triboulet] has no sense. The old man's curse, so terrible and sublime in the original, becomes ridiculous because the motive that forces him to utter the curse no longer has any meaning and he no longer addresses the King *così arditamente*. Without this curse what object or sense does the drama have? The Duke becomes a nonentity; it is absolutely essential that the Duke should be a libertine; without this it is impossible to justify Triboletto's fear that his daughter will emerge from her hiding place [in Act II], and the drama itself is impossible. Why ever should the Duke go to a remote inn alone in the last act without an invitation or an amorous

assignation? I do not understand why the sack should be cut out: what did the sack matter to the police? Are they afraid it might give people ideas? . . .

If the sack is taken away it is improbable that Triboletto would talk for half an hour to the body without a flash of lightning showing that it was his daughter's. Finally, I note that Triboletto is not to be ugly or a hunchback!! For what reason? A hunchback who sings! And why not? Will it be effective? I do not know; but if I do not know, then neither does the person who suggested these changes. In my view the idea of this character, with his ridiculous and deformed exterior, and his inner love and passion, is superb. I chose this subject precisely on account of these original and characteristic qualities, and if they are removed I can no longer write the music. If I am told that what I have written will do just as well for this drama I will answer that I do not understand such reasoning and will tell you frankly that my music, whether it is good or bad, is never fortuitous and that I always try to give it a definite character. In short, an original and powerful drama has been turned into something extremely commonplace and weak.

I am most sorry that the Presidency should not have answered my last letter. I can do no more than repeat what I said on that occasion: that my conscience as an artist will not allow me to set this libretto to music.

On 23rd December Marzari was able to reply to Verdi:

While your letter of the 14th inst. caused me grave embarrassment, I could not fail to recognize the justice of some of your observations. I therefore made them the theme of renewed representations to the Public Order Authority and I have finally agreed with the said Signor Central Director of Public Order that, time and place being changed as you yourself agreed, the libretto shall be allowed to retain the colour and characteristics of the original that you wish.

The character replacing François, who can be, to suit your convenience, a Pier Luigi Farnese, or perhaps better a Medici or a Duke of Burgundy or Normandy, is allowed to appear as a libertine and absolute ruler of his state. The jester can be deformed, as you asked. There is no objection to the sack, and all that is asked is that the abduction of the jester's daughter be decorously and unsensationally staged.

Although, as we can see from this letter, Verdi had won all his points, the final form of the libretto as we now know it was the result of Carlo Martello taking personal charge of things. He gave the opera its title. "Le Roi s'amuse" was clearly disrespectful to royalty, "La maledizione" was offensive to the God-fearing, and "Il Duca di Vendôme", although he had originally agreed to it, shifted the emphasis too much on to the behaviour of a member of the ruling classes, Better to call it after the jester; and from the French verb "rigoler", to make fun, Martello concocted the name "Rigoletto".

The names of one or two of the minor characters were also

changed to avoid the use of those borne by existing families: Castiglione (who had started life as Victor Hugo's Saint-Vallier) became
Monterone, and Cepriano was changed to Ceprano. Finally, and for
the same reason, the Duke was to be shown in the *dramatis personae*
only as "the Duke of Mantua", with the family name Gonzaga
omitted, for in addition to giving the opera its name, Martello
shifted the action from France to Mantua. This, as we shall see,
resulted in two quaint anomalies in the score: one was the retention
in Act I of a Périgourdine, a rough country dance hardly appropriate to the ducal court of Mantua; the other was the announcement by Sparafucile (literally "shoot-gun", Martello's masterly renaming of Hugo's assassin) that he comes from Burgundy—a possible but improbable story in a plot laid as far from his home as
Mantua.

Of all the changes made by Martello, his setting of the scene of
Rigoletto in Mantua has always appeared to me the most intriguing.
The obvious explanation and justified purpose of this was to replace
royalty by an unimportant princeling in a small Italian town. A
harmless enough amendment which satisfied the Austrian Military
Governor, and would strike most people even now as harmless until
it is remembered that Martello was, after all, first and foremost an
Italian, who not only resented having to take orders from an occu-
pying power, but was imbued with that peculiarly Latin spirit of
non-conformism which was the strength of the Partisan and Resis-
tance movements during the last war. It is hard to believe, at least,
that the Venetians were altogether ignorant of the real reasons for
the Censorship troubles suffered by *Rigoletto* and that the significance
of the name of the Duke of Mantua was lost on them. "Duke of
Mantua"—and also, incidentally, of Burgundy—was one of the
titles held by the Holy Roman Emperor, and the last Holy Roman
Emperor, though he abdicated in 1806, had died as recently as fifteen
years before the question of *Rigoletto* had arisen. He was therefore not
only remembered by the older people of Venice, but the very sound
of the title of Duke of Mantua must have had only one association
for them. Finally, the name of the last Duke and Emperor had been
—Francis I.

It has long seemed to me that Carlo Martello's sweeping alterations and highly practical suggestion which, in the light of the subsequent effect of *Rigoletto*, amounted to something approaching genius,
were more than innocent substitution of politically acceptable for
politically unacceptable details; that they were in fact the means by
which this immortal policeman perpetrated one of the subtlest de-
ceptions in the history of artistic censorship in pulling what one
would like to think was surely a cunning fast one over the Austrians.

The opera as it was finally staged with the approval of all the officials concerned is the opera as we know it today. But in the years following the première in Venice performances in other highly nervous political or moral centres like Rome, Bologna, Naples and Palermo, the work underwent some quite startling transformations at the hands of local Censors. In Rome and Bologna the title was changed to *Viscardello*, while in Naples the text was drastically altered, the scene removed to Scotland (then the most remote site known to opera), and the whole thing called *Clara di Pert*, only to be renamed *Lionello* when the opera was performed there again five years later. The most important incidents in the action, of course, were never immune from bureaucratic interference. Monterone's Curse and Gilda's abduction would be left out altogether, and in Palermo the poor girl, instead of being killed by Sparafucile, stabbed herself with a dagger snatched from the assassin.

When one considers what happened to an already officially-approved *Rigoletto* once the other Censorships laid their hands on it, one can't help feeling that we owe a considerable debt to Carlo Martello for giving us the opera as it is. Certainly Verdi was not wholly ungrateful when he remarked to Piave: "They'll never believe we had a policeman for a collaborator."*

---

* Gatti and Abbiati attribute these words to Verdi; the monograph *Verdi and the Fenice* published by the Fenice in 1951 tells us they were said by Piave. I have accepted the verdict of the 2-1 majority. Either way it doesn't affect the obvious truth of the words.

CHARACTERS IN ORDER OF SINGING

THE DUKE OF MANTUA	*Tenor*
BORSA, *a courtier*	*Tenor*
COUNTESS CEPRANO	*Mezzo-soprano*
RIGOLETTO, *court jester to the Duke* . . .	*Baritone*
MARULLO, *a courtier*	*Baritone*
COUNT CEPRANO, *Nobleman*	*Bass*
COUNT MONTERONE, *Nobleman* . . .	*Baritone*
SPARAFUCILE, *a professional cut-throat* . .	*Bass*
GILDA, *Rigoletto's daughter*	*Soprano*
GIOVANNA, *her companion* . . .	*Mezzo-soprano*
A PAGE	*Mezzo-soprano*
A COURT USHER	*Baritone*
MADDALENA, *Sparafucile's sister* . . .	*Contralto*

Courtiers, ladies, pages, guards

Scene: Mantua and the vicinity   Time: The sixteenth century

ACT I

Scene 1 : A large room in the Ducal palace at Mantua, with doors leading off into other rooms, all of them brilliantly lit.

Before the curtain rises there is a short and arresting orchestral prelude of thirty-four bars based on a solemn, ominous fanfare-like phrase of repeated C's by the brass which is associated throughout the opera with the Curse—*la maledizione*—placed on Rigoletto:

Ex 50

It is a sombre and evocative introduction to the grim drama which follows.

As the curtain goes up, the mood changes at once. The scene shows a crowded room in the palace where the Duke is having a party. A band is playing in the background and a crowd of lords and ladies in *gran costume* can be seen in the rooms at the back where dancing is visible. The stage-band music, one need hardly mention, is on the same level of taste and sophistication as the characteristic small-town *banda* music we have already encountered in Verdi's operas. But although as dance music (even without the bass drum Verdi indicates should be omitted) it is hardly appropriate to a court with the cultural record of Mantua, it has an odd kind of elation and spurious gaiety about it, contrasting most effectively with the gloom of the orchestral prelude, which is created by this sort of tune:

Ex 51

The Duke enters with Borsa, one of his courtiers, and in a conversational way refers to a young girl he is always seeing in church.

She lives, he says, in a back street, and a mysterious man goes into the house every night. Her lover perhaps, suggests Borsa. The Duke says he doesn't know. No sooner has he confessed his love for the unknown townsgirl than a number of ladies of the court pass by with their escorts and the Duke is telling his companion that Count Ceprano's wife, who is among them, is the most beautiful of all. Borsa advises the Duke to be discreet in case the Countess's husband should overhear. The Duke shrugs his shoulders, and proclaims that as far as he is concerned such matters are all the same to him—so long as the wives are pretty.

This aspect of his philosophy the Duke expresses in the aria "Questa o quella" ("This woman or that . . ."). Strictly speaking this is not an aria; it is labelled a *ballata*, a "dance song", and serves as introductory music for the dancers in the background, but the Duke has the tune:

Ex 52

Questa o quel-la—— per me pari so-no a quan-t'al - tre d'in-tor-no—— d'intorno mi ve-do

"Questa o quella" is, of course, more than just a tune with a chuck-chuck string accompaniment. It is a brilliant lightning sketch of the Duke's whole character. The voice, according to Verdi's instructions, is to sing *con eleganza*. The phrase is almost redundant, for the only word that can describe the whole character of this little *ballata* is "elegant". It has an elegant, aristocratic light-heartedness which in the course of a couple of bars tells us that the Duke is a charming, irresponsible, reckless, fatalistic young man who is always likely to fall on his feet whatever kind of scrape he has to get out of.

The orchestral coda of "Questa o quella" leads straight into a minuet played by another stage band, this time consisting of violins, violas and double basses. The absence of violoncellos can probably be explained by the fact that they are the only instruments in the orchestra (apart from the harp) which cannot be played standing up, and there was no doubt some good and practical reason why Verdi wanted to keep his musicians relatively mobile and not clutter the stage with chairs and the like.

The music of the minuet is more than a little reminiscent of the Celebrated Minuet from Mozart's *Don Giovanni*—an admirable model, of course, but a little puzzling to encounter in *Rigoletto* because Verdi was well known to have had more than enough of

Mozart's opera when he was young. One can only suppose that it was an unconscious association of ideas by Verdi that led him to choose the same sort of dance music for the dissolute Duke who had so much in common with Don Giovanni.

As the minuet begins the Countess Ceprano is waylaid by the Duke as she prepares to leave the party—her husband's wish, she explains. The Duke pays her an elaborate compliment, kisses her hand and leads her away while Count Ceprano is left angrily watching.

The town-band combination returns with the tune of Ex 51 as Rigoletto, the Duke's ugly hunchbacked court jester, enters and jokingly asks Ceprano what is the matter. The Count makes an impatient gesture and goes off after the Duke. The courtiers laugh and remark that the Duke seems to be enjoying himself. Rigoletto observes that there is nothing new in that—gambling, drinking, feasting, dancing, fighting—it's all the same; and in the words of Lady Macfarren's classic English translation, "Today he's for pastime besieging the Countess, while we watch the husband and laugh at his woes." Rigoletto laughs and leaves the scene.

The *banda* music gives way to the string orchestra once more and we are treated to what the score calls a "Perigordino"—in other words, the brisk 6/8 Périgourdine of little musical distinction which was left over from the pre-Martello version of the opera in its original French setting and which nobody remembered to re-title.

This irrelevant interlude is succeeded by the *banda* playing the only tune it seems to know, and the appearance of Marullo, a courtier who arrives, greatly excited, to tell his friends that Rigoletto has a mistress. Reaction to this is cut short by the arrival of the Duke and Rigoletto. The Duke complains that Ceprano is a nuisance; then abduct the Countess, suggests Rigoletto, throw the Count in jail, banish him, or cut his head off. Ceprano overhears Rigoletto's mockery and draws his sword. The Duke restrains him and taking Rigoletto to one side tells his jester that he always takes his jokes too far; he will get himself into trouble one day. Rigoletto boasts that he fears no one; he has the Duke's protection.

The pit orchestra joins the stage band and a rather confused ensemble is developed from the *banda's* persistent tune. It is confused because a considerable amount of plotting goes on between Ceprano and the courtiers while the Duke and Rigoletto repeat their couple of lines of conversation, and it is not at all easy to make out what is going on. In effect, Ceprano enlists the help of the courtiers, all of whom have suffered from Rigoletto's malicious wit at some time or other, and it is arranged that they will meet, armed, at his house the next night. After a series of four-note phrases to the words "sì, vendetta!" from chorus and principals the assembled company are joined down stage by the corps de ballet who have been dancing in

the background, and sing loudly that everything is festive and joyful
in a world of "voluptuous delights" (or so one English version
tells us).

The expression of pleasant communal sentiments is abruptly disturbed by the sudden entrance of Count Monterone, who denounces
the Duke for his crimes. (It is obviously common knowledge that
Monterone's daughter has been seduced by the Duke, for the
courtiers are astounded by the audacity of Monterone's accusation,
not the reason for it.) Rigoletto, exercising his prerogative as court
jester, replies on behalf of his master; with mock gravity he forgives
the Count for intruding and asks him why he keeps coming at all
hours to protest about his daughter's honour.* In the course of Rigoletto's short passage of irony the strings of the orchestra punctuate
the lines with unison phrases characterized by a rhythmic perkiness
which Verdi must mean us to associate with Rigoletto, the professional jester:

Ex 53

The only other time in the opera we encounter this kind of
scherzando figure is when Rigoletto is playing the jester again in
Act II.

Monterone's anger rises at Rigoletto's mockery and in a superb
declamatory passage, in which Verdi alternates moments of tremendously dramatic tutti with long tense sequences of reiterated
semiquavers in the strings, he curses the Duke and Rigoletto. The
Duke, unperturbed by Monterone's words, orders his arrest and the
old man, as he is about to be led away, turns to the jester to pronounce his final malediction against one who mocks a father's sorrow.
Rigoletto is horrified by Monterone's curse, which leaves him
cowed with terror and apprehension and unable to speak, while
the Duke and courtiers, in a wonderfully effective unison marked
sotto voce assai, warn Monterone of the anger he is bringing on his
head:

---

* The point of this line would have been clearer if Verdi had been able to include more of Hugo's original. In *Le Roi s'amuse* Monterone's daughter is Diana de
Poitiers and had been callously married off by her father to a hunchback in a
marriage of convenience, so that the jester's sarcasm is not so inhumanly cruel as
it appears to be in its operatic context.

Ex 54

This phrase, accompanied by a *ppp* string tremolo and the tune
doubled by bassoon, violoncellos and basses, builds to a climax with
Rigoletto crying "Orrore!" to himself and the rest abusing the
unfortunate Monterone, who is led away between two halbardiers.
The curtain falls as the courtiers follow the Duke into another room
to resume their festivities and "voluptuous delights".

Scene 2 : The deserted end of a blind alley. On the left, a modest house with
a courtyard surrounded by a wall. In the courtyard there is a large and tall tree
and a marble seat; a door in the wall opens out on to the street; at the top of
the wall there is a practicable terrace supported by arches, The door on the first
floor opens on to the terrace, which is reached by a flight of steps. On the left
of the street is the highest wall of the garden and a side of Ceprano's palace.
It is night.*

The curtain rises to a magnificent and original passage of musical
scene-painting, instantaneous in its evocation of darkness and
gloom. Rigoletto enters, alone, wrapped in a cloak, and on his way
home from the Duke's palace. His entrance is accompanied by the
unusual orchestral combination which is the feature of the start of
this scene; two clarinets, two bassoons, four violas divided in two
parts, a solo violoncello, the remainder of the violoncellos, and
double basses whose instruments are required to have the low C of a
fifth string, which was comparatively rare at the time *Rigoletto* was
written.

Rigoletto sings one phrase to himself: "Quel vecchio maledivami!"—"The old man cursed me!" It is a gloomy, monotone
echoing the opening bars of the opera, but with the harsh brass
chords toned down so that the theme of The Curse is heard in the
sombre, understated colouring of clarinets, bassoons, violas, violoncellos and basses, all in their deepest registers.

Having set his scene in a masterly manner, Verdi now embarks on
one of the most daring and effective passages of orchestration ever
heard in the opera house. He gives a tune to another, muted, solo
violoncello (the principal) and a muted solo double bass in unison
octaves, keeping as an orchestral background that same sinister
darkness of tone—two clarinets, two bassoons, four violas, a solo

* Often called Act II.

violoncello, the remaining violoncellos and double basses—which accompanied Rigoletto's entrance, but with a bass drum added to emphasize the *ppp* off-beat rhythm of the accompaniment. It is an astonishing sound:

This theme continues through a remarkable scene of operatic dialogue between Rigoletto and Sparafucile, the professional cutthroat, who has followed him and now enters, carrying a long sword beneath his cloak. Sparafucile sidles up to Rigoletto and offers his services. He specializes, he says, in disposing of rivals.

"And you have one," he tells Rigoletto.

"Who?" asks the jester.

"You have a mistress in there . . ." replies Sparafucile, indicating the house.

Rigoletto is astonished to hear this, but quickly pulls himself together and out of curiosity enquires how much it would cost him to be rid of such a rival. Sparafucile, who knows more of what is going on in this part of Mantua than he has told us so far, replies that in this case he would want the top price—half the agreed amount in advance and the balance on completion. In answer to Rigoletto's further—and ostensibly academic—questions, Sparafucile explains his methods: sometimes the victim is dealt with in the city, sometimes in his own house where his sister, Maddalena, pretty and buxom, is an irresistible bait. Can he be of service to Rigoletto? Not yet, Rigoletto replies, but asks the assassin's name. Sparafucile tells him. A foreigner? asks Rigoletto. From Burgundy, says the assassin. This rather anomalous reply, as I suggested earlier, was clearly left over, with the Périgourdine in Scene 1, from the pre-censored libretto of the opera when the action was laid in France and the character's roughneck geographical origin had some significance.

As Sparafucile turns to go, Rigoletto asks him where he can be found if needed. Sparafucile replies that he is always at this spot in the evening. He takes his leave, repeating his name a couple of times and with a long low F brings this extraordinarily dramatic and original scene to a close. All told the scene lasts less than four minutes; but it is a little masterpiece of musical characterization achieved by uniquely simple and imaginative vocal and instrumental means.

Rigoletto, left alone, reflects that he and Sparafucile have much in common. "Pari siamo" ("We are the same"), says Rigoletto. "I use my tongue; he uses the dagger. I am the man who laughs; he is the one who kills." Rigoletto's train of thought is interrupted as Monterone's curse comes to his mind: "Qual vecchio maledivami!" It is a distant echo of the monotone we heard earlier, the ominous chords once more coloured by the sombre *pp* of clarinets, bassoons, violas, violoncellos and basses in their low registers. Rigoletto resumes his reflections, railing in a powerful declamatory phrase against the life he has to lead—the Duke he has to entertain, the courtiers who have made him what he is.

The mood of anger and bitterness is dispelled suddenly by a *dolce* four-bar phrase by a solo flute. Rigoletto opens the door into the courtyard of his house and as he enters, he echoes the flute tune with the words "But here I change into another man". Again, without warning, Monterone's curse rings in his ears and fades into silence. For a moment Rigoletto is alarmed by the thought that keeps haunting him, but dismisses it all as mere folly. The character of the music changes completely as his thoughts turn to his daughter Gilda, who comes out of the house and throws herself in her father's arms:

Ex 56

This bright and cheerful theme provides the background of the joyful reunion of father and daughter in which they express their love for each other. Rigoletto, who sighs involuntarily as he asks what other happiness he has besides Gilda, is a mystery to his daughter. She does not know he is the Duke's jester, nor does she know anything about her family or even her father's real name. When she asks him, all Rigoletto replies is that she has no family, and what does it matter what his real name is.

"Then if you won't tell me about yourself . . ." begins Gilda. Rigoletto interrupts here. "Don't ever go out." Gilda replies that she goes to church, that is all. Good, says Rigoletto. Gilda continues: "If you won't tell me about yourself, at least tell me something about my mother."

Rigoletto replies to music which reveals an entirely new side to his character, that tenderness which Verdi had in mind when he described "this character, so deformed and ridiculous outside, so full of love and passion within . . ."—"Deh non parlare al misero del suo

4

perduto bene" ("Do not speak to a miserable wretch of his past happiness").

Ex 57

Vittorio Gui once suggested that Verdi's own tragic experience in early life as the father of two children, a daughter and a son, who died before they were two years old, had a long-lasting subconscious effect on the composer's treatment and characterization of unhappy, and usually widowed, fathers in his operas. Certainly, there is to be found in Verdi's music a recurrent strain of pathos peculiar to those characters who are fathers—and especially fathers with daughters. One has only to think of the fathers in *Simon Boccanegra* and *Aida*, as well as *Rigoletto*, to realize that the composer always seemed to keep something particularly touching in reserve with which to express paternal love—with the exception of the Marchese di Calatrava in *La forza del destino*, who curses his daughter with his dying breath.

The relationship between fathers and sons in Verdi's opera, on the other hand, is generally not very sympathetic. In *La traviata* Germont and Alfredo are hardly on the best of terms, and in the end it was only Germont's plea for his young daughter that touches our hearts; while in *Don Carlos* father and son are on even worse terms. The new psycho-analytical school of critics will doubtless be able to sort this out by attributing it all to the fact that not only was Verdi's firstborn a girl, but that, unlike other composers, he also had a mother.

Gilda reacts sympathetically to her father's sad memories of her mother, "that angel" who married him and loved him in spite of his deformity and poverty. In the short duet that develops Gilda tries to comfort Rigoletto, who still will not tell her his name or his history.

The music changes from the excitement of the duet's climax—in which Rigoletto tells Gilda that country, family, and the entire universe are centred in her—to a gentle *dolce* string passage for Gilda to ask her father for a little more freedom. She has been in Mantua for three months and has never once in that time seen more of the city than the nearest church. Rigoletto refuses his daughter's request firmly, reflecting in an aside that she might be followed and stolen from him—to dishonour a jester's daughter would be a great joke. He calls for the duenna, Giovanna, and questions her: does anybody ever see him coming to the house? No. Is the door to the street always kept locked? Yes. Nevertheless, Rigoletto urges the duenna to take even stronger precautions to prevent Gilda's existence becoming known: "Ah! veglia, o donna, questo fiore . . ." ("Watch over this flower . . .")

Ex 58

This phrase, too, develops into a tender duet between Rigoletto and Gilda but is roughly interrupted by a noise outside in the street. Rigoletto opens the garden gate and goes out into the street to investigate. While he is outside the Duke, disguised as a poor student, slips through the gate and hides behind a tree, throwing Giovanna a purse of money to keep her quiet.

Rigoletto returns and continues his questioning of Giovanna, a brief conversation which enables the Duke to identify Rigoletto as the father of the young lady he has come to see. The duet between father and daughter is resumed. Rigoletto's recapitulation of the tune of Ex 58 being decorated by an obbligato for Gilda, the tune of which is doubled in the same register by the oboe—an uncharacteristic lapse on Verdi's part in the use of an instrument nearly always liable to smudge a vocal line if it is used in this way.

In the final section of the duet the two singers repeat the words they have been singing to a different tune and *più mosso*. It is a section from which six bars are habitually and inexplicably cut. Their omission, which according to the metronome marking the score saves no more than twelve seconds altogether, is one of these puzzling "traditions" which have crept into the performance of Verdi's operas, and which in this case is not observed for any of the more familiar theatrical reasons—technical difficulty, lack of time, or downright dullness. It is obviously a foolish habit that, once started, has been continued not only without question, but in all probability without most singers and conductors even knowing what it is they are cutting.

In fact it is a charming little passage of three bars played twice with the sort of unusual harmonic sequence very typical of this particular Verdi opera, as I think the following reduction of the score will show:

Ex 59

Father and daughter bid each other farewell, and embrace; Rigoletto leaves, closing the gate behind him.

Gilda, left alone with Giovanna, is rather ashamed of the way she has deceived her father, not telling him of the young man. "Why should you tell him?" retorts the duenna. "You don't dislike the young man, do you?" Gilda sighs, and in a phrase which is never heard again in *Rigoletto*, but plays a leading and unforgettable part in *La traviata*, two operas later, she confesses that the young man is handsome and that she loves him:

Giovanna says she thinks the young man is wealthy and noble. Gilda replies that she has no desire for riches or rank, and with a delicately scored accompaniment for piccolo and flute (who sustain a rhythmic and unison D for twelve bars), oboes, clarinets and pizzicato strings, she muses on the youth who, day and night, waking or dreaming, fills her thoughts and inspires her with the constant longing to tell him how much she loves him.

The words are taken out of her mouth by the young man himself—the Duke, who appears suddenly from his hiding place, signals Giovanna to leave and completes the phrase Gilda has started: "t'a . . ." sings Gilda—"t'amo . . ." interrupts the Duke. It is a simple trick which Verdi uses most neatly and effectively.

Gilda panics and calls for Giovanna—in vain, of course, for the purseful of money has already taken care of her—and after some ardent declaration of his love by the Duke, she relaxes to enjoy the love scene which begins with the tenor's superbly seductive little aria, sung to a minimum of accompaniment—string "chuck-chucks" and occasional chords for woodwind—"È il sol dell'anima, la vita è amore" ("Love is the sun of the soul, its voice the beating of our hearts . . ."):

The tune of "È il sol dell'anima", once it has been sung right through by the Duke, is then divided between him and Gilda. While Gilda, reflecting rapturously that this is the voice she has dreamed of, adds her own characteristic embellishments, the Duke continues with the tune and the duet proceeds to a fascinatingly simple and original orchestral accompaniment, marked down to *pp*, and making a striking effect of violins and violas in their upper register, their hushed repeated six-notes-to-the-bar played *pp leggerissimo*. It is one of the many orchestral passages in Verdi which we often tend to take for granted, and whose very familiarity makes us forget that we are listening to what was a brand-new sound in its day and is still a remarkable and highly personal one more than a century later.

The duet ends with a cadenza for the two singers and the action is resumed by Gilda asking the young man to tell her his name. His immediate answer is delayed by the arrival in the street outside of Count Ceprano and Borsa. Ceprano says, "This is the place." Borsa answers, "All right," and the two leave together. The Duke, after a moment's thought, tells Gilda that he is Gualtier Maldè, a poor student.

Giovanna, who has been acting as look-out, enters the courtyard hurriedly to announce that there is a disturbance outside in the street. Gilda thinks it is her father returning and, after a farewell duet, sends her lover out of the side door, escorted by Giovanna. The farewell duet, it may be said, is almost a parody of operatic procedure in times of haste and crisis, with a text that seems to consist of endless repetitions of the one word "addio". The lovers do, in fact, sing other words in their urgent and musically undistinguished leave-taking but we are left in no doubt that the principal matter under discussion is a passionate good-bye.

Gilda, left alone, meditates on the name of Gualtier Maldè while a solo flute takes us gently from the D flat major of the farewell duet to the E major of Gilda's first solo scene, the aria "Caro nome . . ." ("Dear name which first awakened my heart") :

This aria is probably more misunderstood by prima donnas than any other in the repertoire. Its consequent vulnerability to maltreatment is due to the use of coloratura to express simplicity of character —an original and fatal inspiration on Verdi's part which did not take into account the fact that while most prima donnas are mentally simple to the point of inanity, there is scarcely one of them who does not consider she knows more about Gilda than the composer, and will finish the aria on a rising arpeggio to a high E he neglected (obviously in a moment of mental aberration) to write. One has only to hear Lina Pagliughi, in the classic Cetra recording of the

opera, resist the temptation to surpass her colleagues in this final
display (which she could have done with the greatest of ease) and
keep to the straightforward long diminuendo trill in the register that
Verdi wanted, to recognize yet another reason why she was by far
the finest Gilda of her generation.

There is a peculiar dreamlike quality of innocence and unreality
in "Caro nome" which is emphasized by the extremely sparing and
original orchestration. The strings are restricted to a minimum of
off-beat harmonic support played *pp*, with a solo violin occasionally
contributing distant repeated semiquavers on one note. For the rest,
the more remarkable features of an accompaniment of chamber-
music proportions and ingenuity are provided by woodwind treated
with a magical lightness of touch and producing such entirely unexpected and exquisite little passages as—

Ex 63

The coda of "Caro nome" is one of the most wonderfully effective
moments in the whole opera and it is created by quite ludicrously
simple means. As Gilda takes a lantern and climbs up the stairs to
the terrace, repeating the name "Gualtier Maldè", a flute, an oboe,
a clarinet, violins and violas, all *pianissimo*, play the opening phrase
of the aria in a syncopated form against an ostinato quaver E by
bassoon, violoncellos and basses on the beat:

Ex 64

When Gilda reaches the terrace she echoes the eight-bar phrase
just heard in the orchestra, but singing the words "Caro nome che il
mio cor festi primo palpitar" in a long, drowsy legato phrase instead
of as at the beginning of the aria (Ex 62). The orchestral accompaniment to Gilda's final bars, which get fainter as she enters the house,
is reduced to two solo violins playing a *ppp* tremolo high up in
octaves, with the violoncellos sustaining a similar tremolo along

with them, timpani added in support of the basses' steady pizzicato
and the unusual sound of a couple of phrases in which the solo flute
in its low register plays in unison with the bassoon. The orchestral
postlude dies away to the sound of timpani and a sustained E (*ppp*)
by flute and bassoon in unison once more.

To be honest, one cannot give as much of one's musical attention
to the remarkable coda of "Caro nome" in the theatre or on records
as one would like (or as one can by undisturbed study of the score)
because no sooner has Gilda reached the terrace than she is spotted
by Borsa, Ceprano, Marullo and a chorus of masked and armed
courtiers who have crept stealthily on to the scene and comment to
each other on the beauty of Rigoletto's *amante*.

Rigoletto, absorbed and wondering what has brought him back,
his mind still echoing with Monterone's curse, returns in the darkness and bumps into Borsa. Most of the action which immediately
follows takes place to this theme, first heard with its sudden variations of dynamics, in the strings:

Ex 65

When Borsa recognizes Rigoletto, Ceprano is all for killing the
jester at once, but he is persuaded that to do so would spoil the joke.
(Obviously some plotting we have not heard about has gone on
since the first scene in Act I. Then, it will be remembered, there
had been no talk of abducting the young woman, thought by
Marullo to be Rigoletto's mistress—which, we should know, is the
object of the present operation. The only meeting mentioned in
Act I was that convened by the angry Ceprano, who rallied his
friends to arm themselves and meet him the following night—that is,
at the time of this scene—with the sole implied aim of assassinating
Rigoletto.)

Marullo identifies himself and tells Rigoletto that they are planning to abduct the Countess Ceprano from the palace which, as we
know, is next door to his own house. Rigoletto is relieved to hear
this, and takes an immediate interest in a scheme which, after all,
he had himself suggested to the Duke. How can they enter Ceprano's
house, he asks. Marullo quickly takes the key from Ceprano and
hands it to Rigoletto, who can feel the Count's crest on it and is thus
reassured of the genuineness of an escapade he now asks to join. We
are masked, Marullo tells him. Then give me a mask, says Rigoletto.
Marullo puts a mask on Rigoletto's face, at the same time fastening

it by a band round his eyes which in the darkness he does not realize
is blindfolding him. As Marullo tells him to hold on firmly to a
ladder placed against the wall of the terrace, Rigoletto remarks
how densely dark it is. Marullo, in an aside to his companions, tells
them that the bandage will make Rigoletto deaf as well as blind.

There now follows a wonderfully conspiratorial chorus, sung *sotto
voce* with sudden bursts of a high-spirited *forte* on the occasional
single note, in which the chorus bid each other (often at the top of
their voices) make as little noise as possible in the execution of a plot
which will bring so much laughter at court in the morning—the
abduction of the jester's mistress:

Ex 66

This cheerful anticipation of joys to come is, of course, quite
appropriate in its context. The conspirators are not engaged in anything more serious than a practical joke with perhaps a little pro-
curing on the Duke's unwitting behalf thrown in. But remembering
the ludicrously inappropriate music for the murderers' chorus in
Macbeth one cannot help reflecting that if the *Rigoletto* conspirators
had been killers they might well have had to conspire to something
very like the same music.

While this delightful and skilfully contrived chorus is sung one or
two of the conspirators climb to the terrace, force a window, enter it
and reappear at the street door, which they open from the inside.
At this point the rest of their companions cease their joyful singing
(at the end of a superbly effective diminuendo), go into the house
and return with Gilda, who is gagged with a handkerchief. As she is
dragged across the stage and out of sight she drops a scarf. From the
distance she shouts to her father for help, but Rigoletto does not
hear her. Instead, he wonders if the abduction is over yet. Putting
his hands to his face he discovers he is blindfolded. He snatches off
the bandage and mask and by the light of a lantern that has been
left behind recognizes the scarf and sees the open door. He rushes
into the house and drags out Giovanna, whom he stares at in a
stupor. The stage directions continue: He tears his hair; he tries to
cry out but cannot; finally after several efforts he exclaims—"Ah!
la maledizione!"

The curtain falls as Rigoletto collapses in a faint.

ACT II

Scene : A salon in the Duke's palace. There is a large door facing the audience up stage centre, smaller doors on the left and right of the stage. The room is furnished with a velvet covered table, handsome chairs and other furniture.

A short, busy orchestral introduction for strings heralds the entrance of the Duke, who is alone and (the score says) "agitatissimo". As the curtain rises we note that in addition to other stage props and in accordance with the stage directions there hang beside the lateral doors "the full-length portraits, on the left, of the Duke, and on the right, of his wife"—the first intimation we have had that the Duke is married and the only visible part taken by his Duchess in the opera.

The Duke is *agitatissimo* because, after leaving Gilda in Act I, Scene 2, he had been back to her house and found her gone. In his opening recitative the Duke is vexed and bewildered and angrily swears to be revenged. In the aria that follows he sings a very different tune, lamenting the tears the loved one must be shedding and wishing he were there to comfort her. In English this elegant, effective and highly singable aria is known as "Each tear that falls" (*The Victor Book of Operas*), "Art thou weeping in loneliness" (Lady Macfarren), "Fair maid, each tear of mine that flows" (Kobbé's *Complete Opera Book*) or—begging to differ on at least one important point—"Dear maid, each tear of thine that falls" (Ricordi's English libretto, 1945). In Italian it is "Parmi veder le lagrime":

Ex 67

The accompaniment to this aria is even more economically scored than the accompaniment to "Caro nome". It is limited to strings, whose only activity is to reproduce what Bernard Shaw first called Verdi's "big guitar" in the orchestra, and seven woodwind instruments of whom no more than five ever play at one time. Even in the four bars which constitute the climax of the aria, the vocal line is doubled only by a solo flute, a solo oboe and a solo bassoon, in place of the *cantabile* support of strings in octaves that one expects. "Parmi veder le lagrime" is not one of Verdi's most inspired tunes, but it introduces a welcome note of comparative relaxation and repose.

The mood is quickly dispelled, however, by the arrival of the courtiers—Borsa, Marullo, Ceprano and the chorus—who are bursting to tell the Duke how they carried off Rigoletto's mistress. They tell their story, largely in unison, to an admirably unsophisticated tune whose healthy vulgarity is underlined by a healthily vulgar solo trumpet in the orchestra which sticks out ostentatiously above the other instruments doubling the melody:

Ex 68

With its characteristic dynamic contrasts of sudden fortissimos and pianissimos this is another of those Verdi tunes one cannot bring oneself to say anything harsh about. It is just a thoroughly lovable, enjoyable tune by the composer of the most lovable, enjoyable tunes ever written, and that is all there is to be said about it. Whatever its musical status, however, this male voice chorus plays its part in the action, for it tells the Duke what has happened to Gilda. When they have finished their story, he asks them where they have hidden their captive and is told that she is here in the palace.

It is at the point of the Duke's question and the courtiers' answer that performances and recordings of *Rigoletto* tend to diverge considerably from the original score. In some recordings the important question and answer are included; in others the question and answer are cut altogether, which means that for the action to make any sense the Duke has to guess the answer to the question he never asks aloud.

While there is a certain lack of unanimity among the so-called "complete" recordings in the matter of the Duke's enquiries after Gilda, there is even less when it comes to the music Verdi intended should follow the answer. This is a short scene for the Duke, a cabaletta in which he joyfully proclaims that love calls him and he must fly to Her: "Possente amor mi chiama":*

Ex 69

* A cabaletta is the contrasting fast and noisy traditional follow-up, often after quite a considerable lapse of time, of the earlier lyrical section of an aria.

It will be seen from the above quotation, I think, that the Duke's cabaletta is music of no great distinction and its omission from most performances is not deeply mourned except by those who love the tenor who sings the Duke more than they love Verdi. While between them most recordings include enough of the scene to enable us to have some idea at home of what is usually cut in the theatre, and why, the Mcneil-Sutherland set (Decca–London 1962) gives us the whole scene, including the courtiers' contribution to the final build-up—namely, their expression of bewilderment at the Duke's sudden and unpredictable change of humour.

Whether he sings all, part or none of his cabaletta, however, the Duke rushes anxiously from the room to find Gilda. When he has gone, Rigoletto enters, with an assumed air of casual indifference, humming a tune whose jauntiness doesn't ring true—a forced, half-hearted form of that perkiness already associated in Ex 53 with Rigoletto's professional performance:

Ex 70

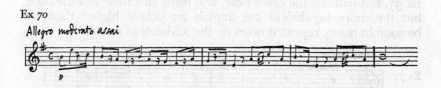

There is a subtle melancholy about the theme which gives great dramatic point to Rigoletto's anxiety as he looks around him for a clue to where Gilda must be hidden, and at the same time pretends to laugh at the courtiers' feeble jokes.

Rigoletto has still discovered nothing when the Duchess's page enters asking for the Duke; the Duchess wishes to speak to her husband. Ceprano replies that the Duke is asleep; Borsa that the Duke has gone hunting. "Alone and without arms?" exclaims the page. The courtiers turn on him and ask him bluntly: doesn't he understand that the Duke cannot see anybody at present? Rigoletto, who has been listening carefully to the conversation, deduces from the unconvincing nature of the courtiers' replies that Gilda must be with the Duke. In a magnificently angry outburst he turns on the courtiers and demands that they tell him where—no, not his mistress, as they think—but his daughter is. Rigoletto tries to force his way through the centre door to the Duke's room, but is held back; in a passionate aria, which is swept along by a stormy figure for the violins in octaves, he curses the courtiers as "Cortigiani, vil razza dannata" ("Vile, damned race of courtiers . . ."):

With only an occasional woodwind chord in support, the violin figures generate a remarkable sense of desperate determination. Rigoletto again throws himself at the centre door, but is held back by the courtiers; he struggles for a while, then sinks exhausted to the ground. The tempo becomes *meno mosso* as Rigoletto, in tears, turns to Marullo and implores him to tell him where Gilda is hidden. Verdi introduces yet another variant of his familiar musical expression of tears at this point, not unlike the form (A) shown in Ex 37, but without the grace note, and using this time, not the oboe, but the more lugubrious cor anglais an octave higher than the bassoon in heavy repeated notes on the off-beats of the bar:

The reason why Rigoletto should appeal to Marullo is not made clear in the libretto as passed by the Venetian Censor—or at least, as it was finally cut down to suit the exigencies of Verdi's music. But in the original Victor Hugo play, Marullo was the Court poet, Clément Marot (1495–1544), and as such Not Quite a Gentleman, as it were; for this reason the jester felt that he was more easily approachable, more likely to understand one of his own social origin than the nobility of which the rest of the courtiers were made up.

Rigoletto's appeal is in vain. Marullo is silent. In a final heart-rending passage the old jester implores the courtiers to have pity on him, to give back to an old man the daughter who is everything in the world to him:

The orchestral accompaniment is again one of great economy and originality. The vocal line is accompanied by the cor anglais playing a sixth higher, with the strings—except for a florid and very difficult obbligato by a solo violoncello—doing no more than supplying a pizzicato chord two or three times a bar. It is a moving little scene and Verdi, having made the effect with the cor anglais, put the instrument away in its box and forgot about it for several years. Its brief and exclusive appearance in a passage taking up no more than twenty-eight bars of the entire opera is a typical instance of Verdi's admirable and frugal orchestral sense which caused him to use an instrument only when he needed it, not because it happened to be available.

The courtiers are spared the necessity of thinking what to say to Rigoletto by the sudden appearance of Gilda, who rushes out of the door on the left and throws herself in her father's arms. She is in tears, dishevelled, and wears the nightdress in which she was abducted from her father's house. Rigoletto turns to the courtiers, and ironically forgiving them for their "little joke", orders them out of the room. The courtiers leave to stealthy conspiratorial music, promising among themselves to watch what goes on from a distance, and Rigoletto is alone with his daughter.

After the noise and excitement of what has gone before the sudden change of mood to one of stillness and suspense is managed with consummate dramatic skill. "Speak," says Rigoletto, "we are alone." In a furtive aside Gilda asks heaven to give her courage to reply, and from the orchestra there comes the plaintive—and because we have not heard it in such close-up until now—unexpected sound of a solo oboe, playing the elegiac opening phrases for Gilda's confession— "Tutte le feste al tempio . . ." ("Every Sunday at church . . ."):

Ex 74

Gilda tells the story of her betrayal, of the poor student she used to see in church, and her abduction by—I cannot resist the quotation from an English libretto—"men ferocious and unlook'd-for". Piave was not able in his libretto to tell us anything about Gilda's discovery that the "poor student" and the Duke were one and the same person. The only hint of what was a tremendously dramatic situation in Victor Hugo's play, cut from the opera in the course of the general process of censorship, is the off-hand remark made by the Duke as he goes to find Gilda, that he will have to admit his identity.

Gilda's recital, with the sparse orchestral accompaniment typical of so many of the "numbers" of this opera, goes its mournful and affecting way, but ends—as she recalls how the "men ferocious and unlook'd-for" dragged her forcibly to her cruel fate—in a passage of showy near-coloratura which has always struck me as out of character at this point. With an emphatic orchestral ff in support, at least, there seems to be far too much determination and vindictiveness about:

Ex 75

Rigoletto, after a moment's bitter reflection, turns tenderly to Gilda and forgives her, and in the brief and movingly restrained duet that develops bids her weep on his breast—the mere mention of tears, of course, drawing from Verdi yet another heartbreaking figure to express them, this time from the first violins *divisi* in octaves:

Ex 76

The simplicity of means by which Verdi makes his touching effect in this little duet is remarkable, for the whole thing is based on little more than the repetition of a single phrase—

Ex 77

—which Rigoletto sings four times, and Gilda punctuates with pathetic phrases of gratitude to her father in whom "there speaks an angel of consolation". It is a moving sequence which, according to the score, never rises above *piano* in the voice part or *pianissimo* in the orchestra.

The scene is ended abruptly as a door opens and Count Mon-

terone is marched across the back of the stage between halbardiers
on his way, a Herald tells us, to prison—"ire al carcere Monteron
dee". My reason for quoting this line is that it is not found in that
form in the libretto printed in Italy in Italian and English by
Ricordi in 1945. In its place there is the quite fascinating variant,
"ire al carcere Castiglion dee". "Castiglione", it will be remembered,
was the name born by Monterone in the original libretto and
changed by Martello to avoid using the name of an existing family.
How on earth this pre-Censorship (and therefore never-performed)
line survived in the libretto, and so far as I know only in this version
of the libretto, is as intriguing a mystery as the presence on the very
same page of two lines of Piave's verse which, if they were ever set to
music, certainly do not appear in any score of the opera I have ever
seen. In this libretto the lines

> *Non dir . . . non più, mio angelo.*
> (*T'intendo, avverso ciel!*)

occur in Rigoletto's part between Gilda's "Nell'ansia più crudel"
(Ex 75) and the familiar "Solo per me l'infamia" which follows
three beats later. It is a very quaint affair altogether, and while we
have grown accustomed to finding the pre-Censorship Périgourdine
in all normal scores of *Rigoletto*, the sudden appearance in a modern
libretto of one line from the pre-Censorship text and two lines for
which there is no music, is puzzling and surprising indeed.

As he passes the Duke's portrait, Monterone halts before it and,
with the orchestra giving him *ff* support, exclaims in sombre tones
that his curse has left the Duke untouched. The old man goes on
his way.

Echoing the ominous repeated C's of Monterone's curse, Rigoletto
calls after him, "No, old man, you are mistaken. You will be
avenged!" and plunges straight into a violent musical oath—
"Sì, vendetta, tremenda vendetta" ("Yes, revenge, tremendous
revenge . . ."):

Ex 78

The tune, which has its more vulgar features rubbed in by being
doubled by a solo trumpet from time to time, is taken up by Gilda
by way of a simple, sudden but effective modulation to D flat. While
Rigoletto's thoughts are concentrated on revenge Gilda, frightened

by the "wild joy" in her father's eyes, begs him to spare the Duke. The duet builds to a climax, with Gilda singing one set of words and Rigoletto another, and the act ends with a loud orchestral reprise of the tune, with two unison trumpets at their brassiest, as father and daughter leave through the centre door together.

ACT III

Scene: The right bank of the River Mincio, near Mantua. On the left of the stage, its front facing the audience, is a two-storied, partly ruined house. Through an archway on the ground floor can be seen the interior of a rough country inn, and crudely-made stairs leading up to a loft with a couch in it. There is a balcony on the first floor. On the road side of the house there is a door leading into the inn, but the outside wall is so full of cracks and holes that it is easy to see from outside what is going on inside. The rest of the scene shows a deserted stretch of the Mincio which runs behind a half-ruined parapet; beyond the river is Mantua. It is night time.

The curtain rises on an atmosphere of quite awful foreboding created by a slow, short, and simple phrase played *pp* by strings. Sparafucile can be seen seated at a table inside the inn, polishing his leather belt and unable to hear anything of what goes on outside. In the road outside are Gilda and Rigoletto. In a passage of quiet recitative, thinly punctuated by an occasional string chord, father and daughter continue a conversation that seems to have started before the curtain rose. "And you love him?" asks Rigoletto. "Always," answers Gilda, and as Rigoletto speaks of his oath of vengeance she begs him to have pity on the Duke. Rigoletto leads his daughter to a hole in the wall, and hoping to cure her of her infatuation asks her what she sees. "A man," Gilda answers. "Wait a little," says Rigoletto. As she watches she is horrified to see the Duke enter the inn. He is dressed as a cavalry officer and orders a room and some wine from Sparafucile.

The Duke, left alone while Sparafucile goes to fetch the wine, sings what must be the best known of all operatic arias—"La donna è mobile qual piuma al vento" ("Woman is as capricious as a feather in the wind"):

Ex 79

One of the unforgettable experiences in the life of every opera-goer must surely be the time when they first hear this tune in its dramatic context. It is then that one realizes how, although it is intended to be no more than a "number" in the sense that Cherubino's "Voi che sapete" in *Figaro* is a "number", the tune is in fact a brilliant summary of the Duke's frivolous and cynical character. As far as the plot is concerned "La donna è mobile" is merely something he sings to amuse himself; he likes that kind of song: it suits his philosophy. Verdi's masterstroke was to make the Duke's song so personal an expression of his whole personality that it is almost as though the young man had written it himself.

And, indeed, this is what had originally happened, for the sentiment of the song had first been expressed by François I himself, in a quatrain which began

> *Souvent femme varie*
> *Bien fol est qui s'ye fie*

and ended:

> *Une femme souvent*
> *N'est qu'une plume au vent*

It does not take much to recognize that these two phrases—"Woman often changes; he is a fool who trusts her" and "A woman is often nothing but a feather in the wind"—are the whole basis of "La donna è mobile". The French words even fit the Italian tune, which is usually known in France as "Comme une plume au vent". That there should be this close resemblance of content and metre between François I's little lyric and Piave's is understandable enough, however, for Victor Hugo included the King's original in *Le roi s'amuse*.

Though purportedly historical accounts of the incident are a little mixed in their details, it is said that during the rehearsals of *Rigoletto* in Venice, Verdi kept "La donna è mobile" away from the tenor until the last possible moment and then instructed him not to whistle or hum it outside the theatre. (One version goes even further than the familiar eve-of-production story and suggests that Verdi did not bring the number into the theatre until the afternoon of the first performance.)

The object of all this was apparently to ensure that the song did not become the common property of every gondolier and lay-about in the city before the opera's production and so deprive the tune of its novelty and dramatic surprise at its first performance. This precaution is still taken, of course, by modern popular song publishers who go to great lengths to prevent the public performance of the hit tunes in a new "musical" until a specified release date.

Verdi's concern in the case of "La donna è mobile" was fully justified, for it is without doubt one of the most immediately infectious and easily remembered tunes ever written. For obvious theatrical reasons, however, it seems unlikely that the composer would, or could, have done more than insist that the cast in general and the tenor in particular should keep the tune to themselves. What threats he may have used to enforce this restraint we do not know. But to have omitted "La donna è mobile" from even the first "read-through" of *Rigoletto* would have been impossible without leaving the artists ignorant of the dramatic progress and climax of a work which has been variously described in Italian as "shekspiriano" or "scespiriano" in its conception.

"La donna è mobile" is not just the Duke's song; it is an essential part of the plot and, as we shall see in studying this final act, it has to be "sung against" by other characters in the action. Consequently the "last possible moment" so often talked about as the first opportunity at which the tenor was allowed to see the number, is very relative indeed. One cannot somehow see Verdi embarking on the production of *Rigoletto* with gaps—and what gaps!—in the last act to be filled only when the opera was on the eve of its première. There is no doubt that the number must have been re-hearsed and re-rehearsed with the rest of this superb last act as early and as often in the course of the opera's preparation as the composer could manage. It surely could not have been otherwise with a work about which Verdi said at the time to Varesi, his first Rigoletto: "I am happy with what I have done and I believe I shall never do anything better."

The wisdom of Verdi's preoccupation with preventing a premature "leak" of the Duke's tune was, as we know, proved at the first performance. The song was an immediate overnight hit. There is, however, a quaint and less obvious indication in the score itself of Verdi's confidence that "La donna è mobile" would be an all-time popular favourite. He knew, only too well, that it would be encored, not only at the Fenice but probably wherever and whenever it was at all tolerably sung thereafter. The song consists of two verses; at the end of the second it comes to a full stop and a *da capo* repetition is easily made from the point at which the audience will always applaud in any case and the continuity is interrupted. By a neat trick Verdi made it possible to avoid not only a first encore, but a second if need be. The orchestral reprise which follows the second verse starts off in exactly the same way as the original introduction, but instead of coming to the famous silent bar which is the warning cue for the Duke's song, the tune continues quietly in such a way that before the audience has realized it the music and the action have gone too far for the tenor to be able to start all over again. The real joy of that orchestral reprise is that it is impossible for the audience to tell whether they are going to hear the song again or not.

The orchestral epilogue, having begun with its loud and deceptive tutti reprise of the first eight bars of the tune dies down with the same passage played quietly first by an oboe and a clarinet in unison, then again by a solo bassoon. During all this Sparafucile returns with a bottle of wine and two glasses which he puts on the table; he knocks twice on the ceiling with the hilt of his long sword. At this signal his sister Maddalena comes down the stairs from the bedroom above—a smiling girl dressed in gipsy costume. The Duke goes to embrace her but she avoids him. While this skirmish is going on Sparafucile goes out into the road where he takes Rigoletto to one side and whispers: "There is your man. Is he to live or die?" Rigoletto gives no direct answer, but promises to complete negotiations with Sparafucile later. The assassin wanders off into the distance. Rigoletto and Gilda are left alone in the road.

Parenthetically it should be noted that somewhere, somehow some of the plot has got lost—or perhaps never existed. It is never explained how the Duke was enticed to Sparafucile's inn in the first place. The Duke is incognito and, as we shall see later, Sparafucile remains entirely ignorant of his identity right to the end. Who made the rendezvous, and how and when was it made? Did Rigoletto tell his master about Maddalena as a potentially attractive evening's diversion after Sparafucile had described his methods as a cut-throat in the second scene of Act I? Obviously it was all arranged off stage sometime earlier during the action, but it is a puzzling loose end to find in an otherwise admirable libretto.

With Sparafucile's departure we come to what appears in the score as "No 12. Quartetto", although the celebrated Quartet does not in fact occur until the scene is well under way. Inside the inn the Duke continues making what are best described as "passes" at Maddalena to the accompaniment of an orchestral figure of an admirably frivolous character—gay, brilliant and full of elation and trills. Maddalena laughs at him, teases him, says he is drunk; the Duke insists that he wants to marry her, using the same euphemistic "sposare" presumably as Don Giovanni uses the word in his attempted seduction of Zerlina in Mozart's opera.*

The goings-on between the Duke and Maddalena are seen by the horrified and bewildered Gilda. Rigoletto turns to her and asks whether she has not seen enough. She replies: "Traitor!"

We now come to one of the most amazing and fascinating achievements in the whole history of opera: Verdi's great Quartet for the Duke and Maddalena who are one side of the wall, Rigoletto and Gilda who are on the other. The power of music to portray the subtlety of human characters, to distinguish the individual from the crowd and to enable the listener to hear several points of view of a

* See *Famous Mozart Operas*, p 92.

situation at once was first understood and exploited by Mozart. But not even Mozart ever quite excelled the prodigious invention and clarity of characterization achieved by Verdi in this Quartet, where each of the four characters expresses a highly individual emotion, for the most part simultaneously with the other three, sharing neither words nor melody with them, but contributing an indispensable part to a concerted movement that is a supreme demonstration of all that is meant by "musical characterization" in opera.

After the long busy Allegro of his unsuccessful flirtation with Maddalena the Duke addresses her in a slow and seductive sixteen-bar tune of an inspired simplicity emphasized by a sparse string accompaniment of pizzicato strings and occasional woodwind punctuations—"Bella figlia dell'amore . . ." ("Beautiful daughter of love . . ."):

Ex 80

Maddalena laughs and with all the provoking coquetry at the command of a teasing and maddening flower-in-the-mouth gipsy girl, replies that she has heard stories like the Duke's before:

Gilda, hearing the Duke's urgent love-making, cries out in the first of many characteristically affecting phrases—"Ah così parlar d'amore . . ." ("He spoke to me of love like that . . ."):

Eventually Rigoletto joins in to tell Gilda that she is wasting her tears on one who she can see has deceived her. But Gilda is inconsolable and her heartbroken sobs grow louder and more desperate above the laughter and skittishness of Maddalena, the Duke and his tune, and the muttered threats of vengeance coming from Rigoletto.

A perfect movement, rich in invention and subtle changes of dynamics, comes to an end with a simple cadence that is rarely sung as the composer wrote it. It is a point of honour with nearly all who sing Gilda to finish on a D flat an octave higher than the one Verdi wrote for them, reaching it by way of an unauthorized high A flat instead of the unspectacular C'' that appears in the score. As one is unlikely in the ordinary course of opera-going ever to hear the final three bars the composer originally had in mind we may be more than usually grateful that Toscanini recorded this final act of *Rigoletto* to enable us to hear the full dramatic effect of Verdi's carefully unexhibitionistic original.*

When the Quartet is finished Rigoletto turns to Gilda and tells her to go back home, take some money, change into boy's clothes and make her way to Verona on horseback; he will follow her next day. Gilda departs.

There now falls on the scene one of the earliest of those uncanny silences which Verdi created in his operas by almost unanalysable musical means. To explain that the ominous stillness of this scene in *Rigoletto* is produced by nothing more elaborate than some open fifths in the lower strings and a sustained A on a solo oboe gives little indication of the fantastically evocative effect of this sound in the theatre. It is unmistakably the quiet before the storm.

While the Duke and Maddalena are instructed by the stage directions to continue talking, laughing and drinking together ("business" which, though it is silent, shows their relationship growing far more intimate than ever it did while they were singing at each other), Rigoletto having obviously made up his mind that Gilda cannot be cured of her infatuation, goes behind the house and returns with Sparafucile to whom he gives money.

In a recitative which, in order to give the vocal line a deliberate starkness, Verdi indicates must be sung without the grace notes customary in the opera of his time, Rigoletto advances Sparafucile half the agreed fee of twenty crowns to deal with the murder of the Duke. He will return at midnight, when the deed has been done, with the balance. Sparafucile says he will throw the body in the river. Rigoletto says no; he will do that himself. "Very well," says Sparafucile. "What is his name?" Rigoletto replies: "Perhaps you would like to know mine too. His name is Crime; mine is Punishment."

The jester leaves the scene. As Sparafucile goes towards the inn the first distant rumble of thunder is heard following the flash of

* RCA–Victor *Verdi and Toscanini*—Part 2.

lightning across the sky which is described vividly in the orchestra by a recurring and rapid zigzag phrase for flute and piccolo. The first sound of thunder is accompanied by the sighing of the wind in the trees—an impressionistic effect produced, not by the orchestra, but by a mournful chromatic humming which comes from tenor and bass voices backstage.

Meanwhile, with a clarinet quotation of Ex 80, our attention is drawn once more to the Duke. He makes to embrace Maddalena but she begs him to be patient a moment; her brother is coming. Sparafucile enters the inn to say it will rain in a few moments. This gives the Duke an admirable excuse for staying the night at the inn. Maddalena begs him to go, but Sparafucile encourages him to stay, explaining in a whisper to his sister that a fee of twenty crowns is involved. Sparafucile offers to take the Duke to see his room. The Duke accepts, and stopping to whisper a word in Maddalena's ear, follows Sparafucile upstairs.

We see the Duke enter the loft that he is to sleep in; he remarks on the open-air nature of the accommodation (the room opens straight out on to the balcony), but he does not complain. He says good night, and taking off his sword and hat lies down on the bed for a brief nap. He falls asleep singing "La donna è mobile". Or, at least, some of it, for this version of the song is in reality a duet between the Duke and a clarinet; as he grows more drowsy so more of the melody is heard coming from the orchestra pit until the tune fades away into silence.

Maddalena sits down at the table, while Sparafucile drinks what remains of the wine in the Duke's bottle. They sit in silence, thinking. The silence is broken by Maddalena, who now begins to show clearly that she is strongly attracted to the young man upstairs. In answer to her musings Sparafucile remarks laconically that he is worth twenty crowns, and sends his sister upstairs to bring down the Duke's sword as soon as he is asleep.

Gilda now returns, having changed into boy's clothes, boots and spurs. She goes towards the inn and through a crack in the wall sees Sparafucile rummaging for something in a cupboard. While he is busy doing this Maddalena returns with the Duke's sword, full of the beauty of the Young Apollo who is asleep. She loves him, she says, and he loves her. (This is the first public intimation that Maddalena's feelings for the Duke are at all serious. One can only infer that love must have blossomed in the course of the words spoken, but not heard by the audience, in the scene between the two of them that followed the Quartet.)

Sparafucile finally brings out a sack from the cupboard and throws it to his sister, saying it is to put the young Apollo's corpse in later on. Gilda overhears Maddalena trying to persuade Sparafucile to spare the Duke's life and earn the money by killing Rigoletto instead. The cut-throat grows most indignant at such an unprofessional suggestion. "Kill that hunchback? Do you think I'm a thief?" he asks. "Or a bandit, perhaps, that I'd treat a client like that who's already paid me?" Maddalena turns to go and warn the Duke, but Sparafucile holds her back. The storm which has gradually been growing during this episode becomes more intense as Sparafucile begins an exciting sequence with an offer to Maddalena to kill the first man who comes to the inn before midnight, and substitute his body for the Duke's—"Se pria ch'abbia il mezzo la notte toccato" ("If before midnight . . .") :

Ex *83*

Maddalena, to the same tune, replies that the likelihood of anybody turning up on a night like this is pretty remote. Gilda overhears this and the idea of sacrificing herself crosses her mind for the first time. The trio is interrupted for a moment as a clock strikes half-past eleven—five strokes on one bell, followed by two faster strokes on another. As far as I can hear only Toscanini allows both the two final strokes to be heard clearly. In the other recordings the second is swamped by an exaggerated crescendo in the orchestra thus causing great confusion to the listener who has heard what is apparently a quarter-past eleven strike, only to be told by Sparafucile a moment later that there is still half an hour to wait until midnight.

Performed in accordance with what Verdi wrote and what one should hear in the theatre (if not in the gramophone studio), the striking of half-past eleven in this manner will be readily understood by those who have travelled in Italy. To this day there are numberless old Italian clocks which keep to a kind of six-hour system, dividing the day into four six-hour periods, striking once at 1 a.m., 7 a.m., 1 p.m., and 7 p.m., twice at 2 a.m., 8 a.m., and 8 p.m. and so on. The quarters are preceded each time by the full striking of the hour in which they occur, followed by one, two or three clearly distinguished strokes either on a different bell, or at a different tempo, to mark the passage of the first, second and third quarter as the case may be.

Maddalena begins to weep as she realizes how little time is left and her tears decide Gilda to give her own life for her lover's. She knocks several times at the door of the inn while Sparafucile prepares to carry out this alteration of his original plan. Maddalena opens the door; and with a final prayer for the happiness of the man she loves and for the forgiveness of her father, Gilda goes inside.

What happens now is left to the imagination, for the stage directions state that "everything is hidden in silence and darkness". This instruction, however, must be regarded as applying only to the stage action; our last sight of Gilda coincides with the *ff* outbreak in the orchestra of the full force of the storm—an overwhelming dramatic stroke. Above all, this storm is *music*, not "effects"; it is the expression, not the imitation of a storm. Verdi has translated the fury and terror of the tempest into musical terms and in the diminuendo scale passages of the final fading-away we have a very clear anticipation of the end of the *Dies Irae* in the Requiem Mass written twenty years later. The storm dies down leaving only an occasional sound of distant thunder and pale, infrequent flashes of lightning.

Rigoletto emerges from the shadows to wait for midnight. A clock strikes six times. (How twelve strokes first came to be shown in most scores of *Rigoletto* can only be attributed to some ham-handed editing at some time. If the alleged anachronism of a clock striking twelve in sixteenth-century Italy is to be accepted, then at least 11.30 should not have been struck according to the six-hour system. One or the other, in fact, but not an inconsistent mixture of both. Unfortunately, where Verdi had the orchestra playing while 11.30 struck, all he originally indicated for midnight was the instruction "the clock strikes midnight" placed over an empty pause bar, so that there is nothing to stop an over-zealous stage manager striking twenty-four times if he feels like it. Most of the recordings I have heard favour the six-stroke tradition.)

As midnight strikes Rigoletto knocks at the door of the inn. Sparafucile opens it and throws a heavy sack at Rigoletto's feet. "Here is your man," he says, and offers to carry it and drop it into the river; but Rigoletto says he will do it himself. The assassin replies, "As you like", and taking the balance of the fee, informs Rigoletto of the best part of the river in which to dispose of the body, bids his client a formal goodnight, and retires.

Rigoletto is alone on the stage. He reflects with pleasure for a moment on the success of his revenge and begins to drag the sack towards the river. At that moment a voice is heard off-stage singing "La donna è mobile"; it is the Duke on his way home to Mantua, singing with a final, magnificent irony of the fickleness of woman.

Rigoletto, unable to believe his ears, feverishly opens the sack. A flash of lightning illuminates the body in it and he sees it is Gilda's. She is still alive and just able to speak. She knows she is dying and tells her father that it is for the man she still loves. With her last few breaths Gilda tells Rigoletto that when she joins her mother in heaven she will pray for him eternally—"Lassù in cielo" ("Up there in heaven, beside my mother . . ."):

Ex 84

Lasù in cie - lo, vi - ci - na al-la ma - dre...

The accompaniment to this has a peculiarly ethereal quality which Verdi achieved by what he called in later life "vaporous" scoring. In this instance the effect is made by a series of staccato arpeggios by a solo flute accompanied by two solo first violins in unison, two solo second violins in unison, and two solo violas in unison—a combination which is rarely satisfactory in practice, for it is almost impossible for two solo violins playing in unison to sound in tune.

I went into the question in some detail in *Famous Puccini Operas* (p 26) so I will not raise it again beyond reminding the student of orchestration that Beethoven was one of the few composers who recognized this peculiarity and in his string quartets, instead of doubling the first and second violins in unison passages, would have the second violin play in unison with the viola an octave lower.

Gilda's touching words to her father are followed by a heartbreaking cry of despair from Rigoletto to a tune which Verdi makes almost unbearably moving by doubling in the orchestra across two octaves from violoncellos to flute—"Non morir mio tesoro . . ." ("Do not die, my treasure . . ."):

Ex 85

Non mo - rir mio te - so - ro... pie - ta - de...

Gilda repeats her promise to pray for Rigoletto, and with a sad, unfinished cadence, dies in her farmer's arms. Monterone's curse has been fulfilled, and the curtain falls with Rigoletto prostrate over the body of his daughter.

With *Rigoletto* the smouldering fire of Verdi's genius burst into an intense and brilliant flame for the first time. It was not only a landmark in the composer's own development but in the history of opera itself; for not since Mozart had there appeared on the opera stage flesh-and-blood figures whose actions, thoughts and emotions were those of human beings, expressed in a musical language of great dramatic power. There is in *Rigoletto* scarcely a character that can be recognized in any way as a type; even the courtiers act with the mob conformity of their kind, ganging up in their hatred and fear of Rigoletto's sharp tongue and laughing immoderately at the thought of their comical practical jokes.

The great Quartet in the last act is rightly honoured and loved as a spectacular display of Verdi's genius for clear-cut musical characterization, but it must not be forgotten that the Duke, Gilda, Maddalena and Rigoletto are no less distinctively and unmistakably drawn on every other occasion they appear. The Quartet brings these four finely-drawn musical characters together and presents their individual emotions simultaneously. My only regret has always been that Verdi did not write a quintet at this point and include a part for that magnificent conception, Sparafucile.

There are, of course, weak spots in *Rigoletto*—deficiencies of style and taste such as the ball music in Act I, Scene 1, and the farewell duet between the Duke and Gilda in Act I, Scene 2—but they detract very little from the greatness of the whole; the balance is more than restored by a tremendous and perfect last act in which it is impossible to find a false note or imagine a single phrase that could be cut.

The greatness of *Rigoletto*, however, was not recognized nearly so whole-heartedly or as soon as one might think. Few landmarks in musical history have ever been immediately accepted—at least, by the critics—and *Rigoletto* was no exception to this hazard. From all accounts the public of every country in which it was performed took it immediately and permanently to their hearts, but to read contemporary, and even much later critical opinion one would hardly think so. In London after the Covent Garden première in 1853 the *Illustrated London News* was quicker than most to see that this was an unfamiliar Verdi—"We recognize in *Rigoletto* a higher order of beauty than struck us even in *Ernani* and the *Due Foscari*, and an abandonment at the same time, of his most palpable defects. *Rigoletto* cannot be ranked, however, as a masterpiece; it is full of plagiarisms and faults, and yet abounds with the most captivating music."

The *Athenaeum*, on the other hand, was appalled by "odd modulations being perpetually wrenched out of the vain hope of disguising the intrinsic meagreness of the ideas, and flutes being used for violins, or *vice versâ*, apparently not to charm the listener but to make him stare. . . .* The air of display for Gilda in the garden scene

---

* This is surely one of the most peculiar of all objections to *Rigoletto*. If only the critic had been more explicit and could have given us chapter and verse for Verdi's use of a flute where convention demanded a violin (and *vice versâ*). But he was certainly right in one thing: it is still a score to make the listener stare, though perhaps not in the way he meant.

. . . is as ineffective a mixture of commonplace and eccentricity as it ever fell to the lot of a *prima donna* to deliver."

The *Times* critic of the same period had even less patience with the opera and produced a series of memorable phrases which read like a theatrical press agent's nightmare: "The imitations and plagiarism from other composers are frequent. . . . In aiming at simplicity, Signor Verdi has hit frivolity. . . . He has very few ideas that can be pronounced original . . . *Rigoletto* is the most feeble opera of Signor Verdi with which we have the advantage to be acquainted. . . .The most uninspired . . . the barest . . . the most destitute of ingenious contrivance. . . . Analysis would be a loss of time and space."

I have deliberately quoted these words out of their context; *in* their context the criticism is even less favourable.

The contemporary English Press were not alone in their critical disapproval of *Rigoletto*. The French considered the score was "melodically poor and entirely lacking in concerted pieces". Indeed, the lack in *Rigoletto* of the conventional ensemble with principals and chorus on stage to bring at least one of the acts to a close was considered a grave defect by both French and English correspondents. It must certainly have come as rather a shock to find that Act I ended with Rigoletto on the stage alone, while Acts II and III ended with duets for Rigoletto and Gilda. It is by the objections to such departures from Verdi's previous habits, however, that we can see exactly how novel and unexpected *Rigoletto* must have been to its first audiences. The only trouble was that where the paying public was so enthralled by the drama that it did not notice Verdi's innovations, the critics were so obsessed by the innovations that they did not notice the drama. As late as 1873 one finds an American critic describing Gilda's "Caro nome" as "an empty, sentimental yawn" and complaining that "in the quartet of the last act, a noble dramatic opportunity, she ejects a chain of disconnected, unmusical sobs, as offensive as Violetta's consumptive cough".

And even in such comparatively recent times as my own boyhood in the early 1920s one might still read in the latest edition of Charles Annesley's famous *Standard Opera Glass* ("Containing the PLOTS and STORIES of 158 CELEBRATED OPERAS with critical and biographical remarks, dates, etc.") that in Germany *Rigoletto* had not met with the same favour as in Italy. This was due "in great part to its awful libretto which is a faithful copy of Hugo's drama, and developed in a truly dramatic manner. The subject is however rather disgusting."*

---

* The high moral tone of Annesley's classic is one of the reasons why, for more than forty years, I have cherished my copy of the first book on opera I ever possessed. Those who are unfortunate enough not to know *The Standard Opera Glass* can learn something of its unique style and outlook from the lengthy quotation in the chapter on *Così fan tutte* in *Famous Mozart Operas* (pp 187–8).

There can be few acknowledged masterpieces in the history of opera that have been subjected to such unfavourable scrutiny and censure for so long as *Rigoletto* in its time. For seventy years, from Gorzkowski's first thunderous condemnation of *La maledizione* to Charles Annesley's horrified belief that "the subject however is rather disgusting", Verdi's opera never ceased to worry police, priests and pedants. But it never worried the public, nor has it done so to this day. Wherever *Rigoletto* has been performed the public has been unswerving in its affection and admiration for an opera which had a peculiar place in the composer's own affections. It is only in the course of the last generation or less, however, that what is incorrectly called "informed opinion" has finally caught up with public opinion, deciding to relax and enjoy *Rigoletto*, and so recognize it at last for the work of genius that it is.

IL TROVATORE

(*The Troubadour*)

Drama in four parts, libretto by Salvatore Cammarano, based on the Spanish play *El Trovador* by Antonio García Gutiérrez, and completed after Cammarano's death by Leone Emanuele Bardare. First performed at the Teatro Apollo, Rome, on 19th January, 1853. First performance in England: Covent Garden, 10th May, 1855. First performance in the United States: Academy of Music, New York, 2nd May, 1855.

ALTHOUGH it was Piave who had first been sent off by Verdi in a vain search for a copy of the Spanish Play *El Trovador**** the job of adapting Gutiérrez's piece as the libretto of *Il trovatore* was eventually given to Salvatore Cammarano.†

In principle at least the choice was a good one, for Cammarano, who had already written the librettos of Verdi's *Alzira* (1845), *La battaglia di Legnano* (1849) and *Luisa Miller* (1849), was also, of course, the librettist of Donizetti's *Lucia di Lammermoor*—one of the most successful romantic librettos ever written and a clear indication that its author was just the man to deal with such an essentially romantic subject as *Il trovatore*.

In practice, however, the libretto of *Il trovatore* turned out to be what has generally been regarded as a masterpiece of complication and confusion—a state of affairs which did absolutely nothing to prevent the opera immediately becoming, and remaining, more popular than anything Verdi ever wrote. On the other hand, Cammarano's book is in reality not nearly so incomprehensible as the combined effect of a century of parody, burlesque and serious critical study of *Il trovatore* would have us believe. I have read an intelligible synopsis of the plot that was no more than 148 words long, though nothing will induce me to say where this miracle of non-copyright précis can be found; we all have our livings to earn as synopsis-writers since sleeve notes were first invented.

Whatever one may feel about the finished article, however, the making of the libretto of *Il trovatore* was certainly not without its own bewildering and intriguing features. For instance, in the course of a long and often quoted letter from Verdi to his librettist, in which the

* See p 83.

† Salvatore Cammarano (1801–1852), scene designer, librettist and poet, was a fascinating and unusual figure whose story, unfortunately, is too long to retell even briefly in these pages. The reader who is interested, however, will find more about him and his remarkably gifted and adventurous family in the chapter on the San Carlo Theatre, Naples, in my *Great Opera Houses* (pp 201–5).

composer set out in detail his alternative suggestions to a scenario
he had received from Cammarano, we read of duets in Part II between Azucena and a character called "Alfonso". It is obvious from
the context that Alfonso is the same as the Troubadour, but after
these two references in Verdi's break-down of Part II we never hear
of Alfonso again. From that point onwards in the letter he is either
"the Troubadour" or the not-yet-Italianized Manrique. If nobody,
so far as I know, has ever made any comment on the sudden appearance and equally sudden disappearance of the mysterious Alfonso,
it is perhaps because it has always been regarded as too characteristic
of the whole business of *Il trovatore* to be worth mentioning anyway.

Up to the time of *Rigoletto* Verdi had written his operas at the rate
of sixteen in eleven years. Now there was a gap of nearly two years
before the new work, *Il trovatore*, appeared. A number of factors
combined to delay Verdi's work on the opera: Cammarano's initial
slowness off the mark when he was first contracted by Verdi to prepare the libretto (the poet's vagueness and dilatory attitude to the
answering of letters must have maddened the efficient and business-
like composer); the death of his mother in June 1851; a journey to
Paris in January 1852 which, with other things, kept Verdi away
from Busseto and his composing for the best part of three months;
the serious illness of his father shortly after his return home; and the
sudden death in July 1852 of Cammarano in Naples, leaving the
libretto in an unfinished state just as Verdi had settled down to work
in peace. And through all these disturbances there ran another factor
that must surely have had some unconscious influence on the progress of the work—the absence for a long time of a definite deadline.
Verdi, for the first time since he wrote his first opera, was not what
he described as "wearing the noose of a contract" round his neck.
This did not prevent Verdi becoming impatient from time to time,
of course, but it hardly helped to discipline Cammarano who was
temperamentally inclined to stray from the point at the best of
times.

On Cammarano's death another, younger, Neapolitan poet,
Leone Emanuele Bardare, was given the job of completing the
libretto—a task that consisted of supplying one or two verses that
were missing in Act III and writing all those in Act IV. In addition
to his collaboration with Verdi in the later stages of *Il trovatore*, Bardare is assured another niche in operatic history, for it was he who
turned *Rigoletto* into *Clara di Pert* for the benefit of the Neapolitan
Censorship in 1853. Verdi grew very fond of Bardare and, perhaps on
the strength of the poet's re-dressing of *Rigoletto*, discussed with him
the project of re-writing, to suit the Censor, Cammarano's libretto of
La battaglia di Legnano retaining, the composer said, "all the enthusiasm for country and freedom, without ever talking about country

and freedom". The idea came to nothing, as it happened, but the fact that it was once seriously considered by the composer will no doubt add to the satisfaction of the Welsh National Opera whose "up-dating" of the opera as "The Battle" recently proved a success-ful experiment.

When it was finished *Il trovatore* was staged in Rome. Venice and Naples had both been considered earlier, but had been ruled out as neither could offer a singer capable of doing justice to the part of Azucena. Rome, on the other hand, was able to do so, and so was given the première. Verdi's preoccupation with the interpretation of this particular part shows clearly the importance he attached to the character of Azucena. The old gipsy woman does not just turn out to be the most important figure in the opera by accident. Azucena was always deliberately seen as the principal character of the opera and in one of his earliest letters to Cammarano the composer par-ticularly refers to the gipsy as the lead, "a singular character after whom I intend to call the opera".

It is difficult to believe that there can ever have been any censor-ship trouble over *Il trovatore*; but there was. Only this time, instead of political censorship, it was the Holy City itself that went to work on the opera. The Vatican did not approve of Leonora's suicide; she must not be seen to take poison or tell anybody about it. On the other hand, while the stage business of drinking poison from the ring was cut, the famous line that goes with it was not. Leonora sang, "M'avrai, ma fredda" ("You shall have me, but cold and dead") leaving the audience without the slightest clue to how she was supposed to die.

The use of religious words was also strictly forbidden, of course, and in the case of the Miserere scene the Censors' alternations made near-nonsense of things. The word "miserere" itself had to go, and in place of

> *Miserere di lei, bontà divina;*
> *Preda non sia dell'infernal soggiorno*

—("Have mercy on his soul, O divine grace, and save it from eternal damnation")—there were substituted the lines.

> *Ah pietade di lei chi s'avvicina*
> *Allo splendor dell'immortal soggiorno!*

—("Have pity on the soul that now approaches the splendour of immortality")—which meant, as somebody has since pointed out, that the prayers were pleading not for mercy on the soul of the miserable sinner faced with an "infernal sojourn", but for pity on one approaching the splendour of immortality. A novel and un-expected change of dogma, but on reflection quite in keeping with

5

the whole bewildering nature of a masterpiece which was a tremendous success from the first moment and which the Italians themselves were parodying in the popular back-street theatres of Naples
and Milan within a few weeks of the première. Verdi's publisher
Ricordi took an unamused view of this; Verdi himself enjoyed the
burlesques immensely.

CHARACTERS IN ORDER OF SINGING

FERRANDO, *Count di Luna's Captain of the Guard*.   *Bass*

INES, *Leonora's companion*   .   .   .   .   *Soprano*

LEONORA, *Lady-in-waiting to a Princess of Aragon*   *Soprano*

COUNT DI LUNA, *a young nobleman of Aragon* .   *Baritone*

MANRICO (The Troubadour), *a Biscayan chieftain*
   and reputed son of Azucena .   .   .   .   *Tenor*

AZUCENA, *a Biscayan gipsy* .   .   .   *Mezzo-soprano*

AN OLD GIPSY .   .   .   .   .   .   *Bass*

RUIZ, *one of Manrico's soldiers*.   .   .   .   *Tenor*

A MESSENGER .   .   .   .   .   .   *Tenor*

Companions of Leonora, followers of the Court, soldiers, gipsies

Scene: Biscay and Aragon   Time: The beginning of the
                                              sixteenth century

PART I

THE DUEL*

Scene 1 : The hall of the Castle of Aliaferia, the palatial and heavily fortified residence of the Court of Aragon. On one side of the stage there is a door leading to the apartments of the Count di Luna.

The curtain rises after a short orchestral prelude—three ominous crescendo rolls on timpani and bass drum, a loud arpeggio sequence in unison for the whole orchestra, a distant horn call, a *pianissimo* echo by strings in unison of the tutti, another faraway horn call, an equally distant trumpet figure on one note like a sinister fanfare. It is a simple and wonderfully evocative introduction to the dark and violent atmosphere of witchcraft and babies burned by gipsies which pervades the action of an opera that takes place almost entirely at night.

On the stage we see Ferrando, a group of sleepy retainers leaning against the doorway of the Count's apartments, and a platoon of armed soldiers walking up and down in the background. Ferrando rouses the retainers by shouting a warning that the Count will be passing that way soon to spend the long lonely hours of the night underneath Leonora's window, and to hear—no doubt—the nightly recital given by his unknown rival, the Troubadour.

The presence of all these guards and retainers is explained by the country being in a state of civil war, although it is not until well into the second scene of Act I that we are able to deduce anything of the kind. For the moment the company's principal concern is to keep awake, and in order to do so they ask Ferrando to tell them a story. Not just any old story, but one they have obviously heard before; they ask specifically for the story about the fate of Garcia, the infant brother of the Count di Luna.

While everybody on the stage may know the story backwards its repetition is very welcome to us in the audience, for without it the whole action of *Il trovatore* would be virtually meaningless. It

* In accordance with the best romantic tradition of Guitiérrez's original play each Part—not "Act"—of *Il Trovatore* is also given a sub-title indicating the theme of the action.

enables us to learn what has occurred a considerable time before the rise of the curtain.

Many years previously, an old gipsy woman had been discovered at dead of night watching the sleeping infant son of the Count di Luna, father of the Count in the opera. The nurse, sleeping by the cradle, had awakened and given the alarm. The gipsy was seized, in spite of her protests that she was only going to cast the baby's horoscope. After the incident, however, the child sickened and the gipsy was led away and burnt at the stake as a witch. As she died, the gipsy called on her daughter to avenge her. The daughter had already anticipated her mother's wishes; she stole the child and threw it into the embers of the fire by which her mother had perished.

Ferrando tells his story in a long scene lasting the remarkable time (for a subsidiary character) of nearly ten minutes—with, of course, occasional comments, expressions of astonishment and questions from the chorus who keep wanting to know more of the gory details.

The first part of Ferrando's narration is told in stanzas based on the tune:

Ferrando continues his story, relating how the old Count di Luna died and on his death-bed, believing that the infant was still alive, charged his surviving son never to give up the search for his brother. The gipsy's daughter, Ferrando continues, had not been seen from that day to this, but the spirit of her mother had been fairly troublesome from time to time after dark. This is confirmed by the chorus who recall in a wonderfully effective *pp* unison sequence accompanied by strings, also in unison, that she has appeared on the roof-tops as a hoopoe, two sorts of owl, and a raven:

Ex 87

Ferrando adds that once when she appeared as an owl she frightened one of the old Count's servants literally to death. "She looked at him with glowing eyes", he says, "and rent the air with shrieks! And at that moment midnight struck . . . !"

And at that moment, as Ferrando speaks, midnight strikes on the stage, throwing soldiers and retainers into a panic of superstitious

fear. And not surprisingly, I feel, for this striking of midnight is unlike any other I have heard in opera. In place of the slow and
solemn strokes one usually hears, midnight is announced on this
occasion with twelve very rapid and quite alarming high-pitched
strokes of a piercing urgency one associates more with fire engines
than striking clocks. It is a terrifying and dramatic moment.

A drum sounds behind the scenes; the chorus goes off after cursing
the witch and in its final cry introducing a momentary chord of A
major, a sudden and unexpected contrast to the minor key mood
which has prevailed so far and returns immediately as the retainers
run towards the door of the Count's apartments. The soldiers hurry
off to their posts at the back, and the curtain falls.

*Scene 2 : The gardens of the Palace. On the right, marble steps leading to the
apartments. It is late at night, with dense clouds covering the moon.*

Leonora is in the garden with Ines, who is growing a little impatient
with her mistress for hanging about so long. The Princess has called
for her, she says. Leonora takes no notice; she is afraid that another
night may pass without seeing Him. We soon learn who He is when
Ines obligingly asks Leonora about him and "the dangerous flame"
she nurtures. Leonora—as is very much the habit of this opera—
begins her story. She tells how she first met him at a tournament, an
unknown knight in black armour who carried all before him. But the
civil war broke out and she has not seen him since.

Up to this point the story has been told in a declamatory manner.
Now, as Leonora reflects how the unknown knight vanished like a
golden dream, there is a sequence of unexpected and evocative
scoring: seven bars of a solo flute, and a solo clarinet playing arpeggios, accompanied only by a *ppp* trill for the violins. It is a
moment which shows how early in his development Verdi anticipated the magical nocturne in *Falstaff*.

She never saw him again, says Leonora, until . . .

Ines, who it is hard to believe has not heard all this before (how
does she know about the "dangerous flame", for a start?), keeps the
audience in the picture, as they say, by asking what happened next.

Leonora gives a detailed account in her first big aria, "Tacea la
notte" ("The night was still"):

Ex *88*

Ta - cea la not-te pla - ci - da e bella in ciel se- re — no

She tells of hearing the voice of a troubadour floating across the still, moonlit air—"Dolce s'udiro a flebile gli accordi d'un liuto" ("a sweet voice and the sad chords of a lute"):

Ex 89

This, like the one already quoted in *Rigoletto* (Ex 60), is another almost note-for-note phrase that later came to play an important part in the music of *La traviata*, where it occurs with the same key signature, the same broad 6/8 time, almost the identical orchestration. But whereas in *Il trovatore* the phrase is merely an incident in an aria, the later development of the idea in *La traviata* is used, as we shall see, with tremendous effect.

It was obviously a phrase to which Verdi was very much attached, for he was not using it for the first time in *Il trovatore*. We find it occurring several times in the course of one of six songs with piano accompaniment which he wrote in 1838, a year before his first opera, *Oberto*. In the song called "In solitaria stanza" ("The lonely room") we have the same harmonies, the same triplet accompaniment, the same characteristic *crescendo-diminuendo*:

Ex 90

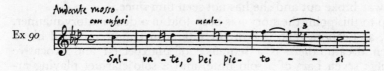

For all the similarity of tune, rhythm and dynamics, this original phrase has in fact emotionally less in common with its *Trovatore* form than with its descendant in *La traviata*, where, as in "In solitaria stanza", it is a plea for help.

Leonora continues her musings on the unknown Troubadour until she is interrupted once more by Ines who warns her this time (as all operatic companions do) that No Good Will Come of It, mark her words. And as all operatic sopranos with companions will, Leonora ignores the warning. Forget the Troubadour? The very thought of it sets Leonora off into an ecstatic and brilliant coloratura finale—

Ex 91

—insisting that if she cannot live for him then she will die for him—
"Di tale amor, che dirsi . . ." ("There are no words for such a
love . . ."):

What follows is a disappointingly conventional cabaletta—a word
which I have seen in an old Italian dictionary to mean "a pretty
simple air" but which is hardly apt in this case. It is a disappointing
sequence because in a way it undoes all the good of the earlier part
of Leonora's scene. When we first heard her talking about the
Troubadour we were listening to a woman in love; now we are
merely listening to a soprano. Our interest has shifted from the
character of Leonora to the voice of whatever singer happens to be
engaged for the part in the production. It is a cabaletta with all the
vocal and instrumental brilliance one would expect of a movement
primarily concerned with the display of virtuosity.

According to Verdi's score Ines should join in during the coda,
muttering gloomily as Leonora has her final vocal fling. In practice
Ines is not usually allowed to open her mouth at this point; if she
did she would hardly be heard over the noise of the prima donna in
full cry, anyway.

Her aria finished, Leonora enters the palace with Ines.

Count di Luna now enters, accompanied by one of those short and
characteristic passages for strings which Verdi used with such wonderful effect all his life to bring a character on to the stage. The
Count remarks on the stillness of the night—"Tace la notte"—
a phrase which is nearly always misprinted on English record labels
and in line-by-line librettos as "Tacea la notte", to start a lot of confusion in one's mind between this and the scene we've just heard.
Count di Luna stands beneath Leonora's window, where a light is
burning, and reflects on his love for her; he is just about to go up
the steps into the palace when the "sad chords of a lute" are heard
coming from a harp backstage.

Di Luna recognizes these bars as the introduction to the Troubadour's nightly serenade which begins a moment later with Manrico
singing "Deserto sulla terra" ("Alone on earth"), an oddly exotic
tune in which he describes his search for one kind heart to bless the
lonely Troubadour:

As the Troubadour finishes the second of the two short verses of
his serenade, Leonora rushes on to the stage from the palace; the
5*

Count seeing her approach, hides his face in his cloak, and to his great surprise, receives the full force of Leonora's embrace. Manrico, who is, of course, the primary reason for all Leonora's excitement, is not unnaturally put out by her behaviour and complains loudly from his hiding place in the bushes that she is unfaithful. A characteristic Allegro agitato starts up as Leonora recognizes the voice.

The moon comes out from behind the clouds to reveal the figure of the Troubadour who wears a helmet with the visor down. Leonora throws herself at his feet, explaining that it was dark, and protesting that everything she said to the Count was intended for the unknown singer.

The Troubadour embraces Leonora. The infuriated Count demands to know his rival's name. The Troubadour raises his visor and says he is Manrico. The Count recognizes him as a follower of the Pretender of Urgel, and realizes that he is face to face with an enemy.

"Well, what are you waiting for?" taunts Manrico. "Why don't you call out the guard?" The Count, however, is intent on a private, as distinct from a political, form of vengeance which he proposes to satisfy in a duel. He turns first on Leonora, then on Manrico in a vigorous tune which receives considerable support from a solo trumpet in the orchestra—"Di geloso amor sprezzato . . ." ("The fire of a jealous love burns within me . . ."):

Ex 93

Manrico defies the Count to do his worst while Leonora pleads with her lover to be reasonable, in one of those stirring, energetic soprano-and-tenor unisons so characteristic of Verdi at this period.

The Count, for his part, matches insult with insult and the scene ends with the men flourishing drawn swords, while Leonora falls to the ground in a dead faint. We do not know the result of the duel until some fifteen minutes after the beginning of the following scene.

PART II

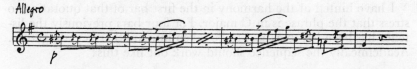

THE GIPSY

Scene 1 : A ruined house on the slopes of a mountain in Biscay. At the back, which is almost entirely open, a large fire is burning. Dawn is beginning to break. Azucena is seated by the fire ; Manrico is lying beside her on a mattress, enveloped in his cloak, his helmet at his feet, and staring motionless at the sword in his hand. A band of gipsies is scattered around.

The curtain rises on a loud and lively unison passage for the orchestra which, one is surprised to discover on closer examination, is not scored for the tutti one imagined, but for strings, woodwind and timpani only. The unison introduction leads to what experienced opera audiences in the nineteenth century immediately recognized as gipsy music—a sequence in which liberal use of grace notes and the triangle was made to create an atmosphere of the barbaric and exotic:

Ex 94

When the grace-notes-and-triangle method was first used to suggest gipsies and orientals in general I do not know. It is found as early as Gluck and Mozart and as late as Bizet's *Carmen*, while Berlioz was particularly struck by the effective use of the triangle made by Weber in the gipsy choruses of *Preciosa* where grace notes abound. At the beginning of this scene in *Il trovatore* it is used episodically with the opening orchestral unison as an accompaniment to whatever stage business the gipsies are called upon by the stage director to perform and to underline in sound the picture before our eyes. Between these exotic episodes the music is not noticeably gipsy in character, unless we have to rate as an exotic touch the trill expected of the male voice chorus in the stirring unison phrase with which they greet the dawn and prepare to start their day's work—

"Vedi! le fosche . . ." ("See how the clouds of night are vanishing . . .") :

Ex 95

With this phrase, as even those who have never seen or heard the whole of *Il trovatore* must surely suspect, it is only a matter of moments before the famous Anvil Chorus is in full swing. The men take up their hammers and with the basses striking the anvils on the beat, the tenors off the beat (Professor Walter Starkie says that anvil-beating is a traditional gipsy form of rhythmic accompaniment to singing), the chorus sails into one of the most exciting and certainly the most famous of all operatic choruses—"Chi del gitano i giorni abbella?" ("Who brightens the gipsy's day? The gipsy girl!") :

Ex 96

I have hinted at the harmony in the first bar of that quotation to stress that the phrase is in C major. For four bars previously the listener has been led to expect to be taken into another key altogether. Academically the sequence should work out like this :

Ex 97

Correct and logical, of course; but terribly dull, because it lacks the peculiar elation of Verdi's sudden and unexpected change to C major instead of the A major one expects. The effect is electric in the theatre where, for me at any rate, it never loses its power to surprise, even when Verdi repeats the process twice soon afterwards.

The Anvil Chorus, which began in E minor, moved to G major, and after threatening by way of E major to land up in A, finishes in

C with tenors and basses, unaccompanied, answering their own question with the enthusiastic cry that it is "la zingarella" who brightens their days for them.

There is no mention in the score of exactly what it is the hammerers are beating out on their anvils, but whatever it is it seems to be thirsty work. (The reason why gipsies have anvils is because they are traditionally tinkers by trade, of course.) Having ended their first Anvil Chorus the men lay down their hammers and ask their womenfolk for a drink. When they have been refreshed, they return to work with a reprise of the Anvil Chorus.

It was Verdi's principle in *Il trovatore*, above all his operas, that one good tune deserves another. No sooner is the Anvil Chorus finished than two introductory bars of "chuck-chucks" from the strings are enough to take us straight into an aria by Azucena, the old gipsy woman who, Manrico and the audience are led to suppose, is the Troubadour's mother.

The crackling of the fire reminds Azucena of the death of her mother at the stake, for we learn now that it was her mother who was the subject of Ferrando's story earlier on. As the gipsies gather round her to listen Azucena begins her grim reminiscence of the scene with "Stride la vampa!" ("The flames cry out"):

Ex 98

The orchestration of the accompaniment to Azucena's haunting recital is identical for each of the two stanzas and is a wonderful example of Verdi's astonishing economy of means. It is easy enough to dismiss this accompaniment as a typical passage showing Verdi's treatment of the orchestra as a "big guitar". A glance at the score (which is now happily available again in Ricordi's miniature edition) will provide the student with an object lesson in the art of omission, showing the certainty with which the composer knew when to have the first violins double the vocal line and when not to, when to support a melodic emphasis and when to let the voice tell the story on its own.

Azucena ends her song; it is followed in the score by an empty pause bar which the composer may have intended to have a dramatic effect, but which in practice is usually a cue for the applause Verdi considered should be specifically written into a score. Whatever happens at this point, however, the next music we hear is un-

expectedly original and dramatic. The gipsies are moved by the sadness of Azucena's song; she replies that it is no sadder than the
tragic story that inspired it. The gipsies make their comment in
unison, Azucena answers in the same sequence of notes—a dark and
gloomy passage supported by the strings in unison:

Azucena turns towards Manrico and in a monotone murmurs,
"Mi vendica . . . mi vendica!" ("Avenge me! Avenge me!")—a
phrase which comes to obsess Azucena as the very similar monotone
reflection on Monterone's curse obsesses Rigoletto.

There is a moment's pause. It is now almost broad daylight; the
gipsies pack up their hammers and tongs and in a rather subdued
mood move off down the mountain side, singing their Anvil Chorus,
but this time without anvil accompaniment. Their voices die away
in the distance, echoed by an effective *morendo* in the orchestra, and
Azucena and Manrico are left alone on the stage.

The Troubadour, who is intrigued by Azucena's story, begs her
to tell him more. And, since in *Il trovatore* everybody is always telling
stories of past experiences which it is essential the audience should
know if the plot is to make any sense at all, Azucena bursts into another superb narrative with "Condotta ell'era in ceppi" ("She was
led away in fetters"):

To the accompaniment of one of Verdi's characteristic weeping
figures (in this case oboe and first violins playing *sotto voce* the falling
semitone version shown as B in Ex 37), Azucena tells us with all its
gruesome details the full story of her mother's death, its drama and
horror emphasized by moments of imaginative use of timpani.

In the course of the old gipsy's narration we have the first indication in *Il trovatore* of the importance of "Stride la vampa!" (Ex 98) as
a recurrent theme. Verdi uses it only as a theme of association; it is
not "developed" in any way, or indeed used on any occasion except
in the same form, in the same key even, in which it is first heard.
The only change it undergoes is a change in orchestration to suit the

dramatic needs of the moment. On this occasion the tune is played *pianissimo* by the first violins against a whispered tremolo accompaniment by divided second violins who are joined after a few bars by violas playing tremolo, and provides an eerie background to Azucena's trance-like account of how the ghost of her mother appeared to her and bade her avenge her death. In an agitated final sequence Azucena describes how, in her frenzy, it was not the Count's child she had thrown into the fire but her own. The number ends with Azucena murmuring how she can still feel the horror of that moment; it is a sombre passage lying at the bottom of the singer's register with the tune doubled to great effect by violas, violoncellos, basses and bassoons in unison.

Azucena sinks back exhausted. Manrico, who has always imagined himself to be Azucena's son, is horrified at this sudden revelation. "Whose child am I then?" he cries.

Azucena, realizing that she has told him too much, reassures him that he is hers, of course; when she thinks of her mother's death, she explains, her mind tends to wander. "Haven't I always been a fond mother to you?" she asks.

Manrico agrees that she has always treated him like a son, and in a rapid recitative duologue we hear the details of one incident that illustrates Azucena's maternal concern for him—her rescue of him when he had been left for dead by Di Luna's army on the battlefield of Pelilla. This, of course, is the first we have heard of any battle, but it seems to have taken place *after* the duel which ended Part I and gave that act its title. The evidence for this supposition is that Azucena reproaches Manrico for having spared his enemy in a duel, thus allowing him to fight another day at Pelilla. After discussion of the battle we eventually get to the details of Manrico's duel with Di Luna which was not, as we had every right to believe, the last event of note before the rise of the curtain on Part II. It was obviously the last event but one.

When he is questioned by Azucena Manrico is unable to explain why he spared the Count's life. "Strana pietà!"—"What strange pity!"—is Azucena's simple and telling unaccompanied comment.

Manrico tells us the full story of what happened in the duel—"Mal reggendo all'aspro assalto" ("He could not last the bitter pace"):

Ex 101

He disarmed the Count, Manrico says, and in obedience to a

voice from heaven had spared him as he lay helpless on the ground.
Azucena tells Manrico that next time he must obey her command,
pointing out that heaven did not speak to the Count like that—"Ma
nell'alma dell'ingrato non parlò del ciel il detto":

Ex *102*

A duet gradually develops with Manrico promising to plunge his
sword into the Count's heart and Azucena urging him on. In the
course of this section there are several instances of Verdi's growing
and effective habit at this period of using the violoncellos to double
not the whole but a part of a vocal phrase, giving it a sudden
warmth and emphasis for no more than a few notes. The first time
this is heard is when the violoncellos play an octave below Azucena
for the first four notes of the third bar of Ex 102.

A short cadenza for the two singers ends the duet, and a distant
horn call is heard off-stage. Manrico answers by blowing on his
horn; he expects a message from his follower Ruiz. Azucena takes
no notice of this or of the short scene that follows. She sits in a brown
study of her own echoing only her mother's words "Mi vendica!"

A messenger arrives with a letter for Manrico, who reads it aloud
not in the spoken-voice convention followed by Lady Macbeth, but
in a near-monotone over a sustained chord in the strings. The letter
informs us that the town of Castellor has been captured, that Manrico is to take over its command and defence, and that Leonora,
having heard rumours of his death, is to retire to a convent that very
night.*

Manrico's cry at this last piece of news brings Azucena back to
life again and she asks what is happening. Manrico ignores her,
sends the messenger away to find a swift horse, and continues to talk
to himself in an agony of despair at the thought of losing Leonora.
Azucena concludes, with the peculiar insight of the near-lunatic,
that he is mad; she has every reason, from her point of view, to
believe that her diagnosis is correct, for without offering any explanation Manrico puts on his cloak and helmet and bids her farewell.
Azucena tells him firmly to wait a moment.

* We are never told what rumour Leonora based her fears upon. She had at
least two to believe—the first, that Manrico must have been killed in the duel as
the Count obviously survived and must have been seen around the Palace afterwards; the second, the story of the battle of Pelilla which the Count is also bound
to have spread around.

Another duet, the finale of this scene, is begun by Azucena ordering Manrico to stay; his wounds (whether received in battle or duel
we do not know) have left him in no fit state to embark on any more
adventures for the moment—"Perigliarti ancor languente":

To Azucena's swinging, agitated tune, Manrico retorts in a confident major key that unless he goes at once he will lose all that is
dear to him—"Un momento può involarmi" ("A single moment can
rob me of my beloved"):

The scene ends with Azucena begging Manrico to stay, and Manrico demanding that she should let him go. He is her own flesh and
blood, she says, now firmly reverting to her original story. Simultaneously Manrico cries desperately that surely she doesn't want to
see her own son dying of grief at her feet? He tears himself away,
and the curtain comes down with the music safely in G major, which
could be interpreted as a subtle indication that Manrico has
triumphed, but which was almost certainly intended by the composer as nothing of the sort.

*Scene 2 : The cloisters of a convent near Castellor. There are trees at the back
of the stage. It is night.*

With this scene we at last reach the point in the opera where nobody
tells anybody any more stories. From now on we can concentrate on
the plot as we see it before our eyes.

The curtain rises in a conspiratorial atmosphere created by the
strings of the orchestra playing a stealthy pizzicato to introduce the
Count, Ferrando and a company of their followers who enter
cautiously, their cloaks wrapped tightly round them. From a passage
of recitative we learn that Count di Luna has come to carry off
Leonora from the convent before she can take her vows. Ferrando
begs his master to be careful in the execution of his daring abduction
plan, but the Count brushes his objections aside. His rival is dead,

he says (thus confirming our suspicion that the battle of Pelilla came after the duel), and it will be only a matter of moments now before the final obstacle—the Church—will be overcome. And then——The Count sings rapturously of his love for Leonora and the radiance of her smile ("Il balen del suo sorriso") :

Ex *105*

While it is not unheard of for villains to sing love songs I cannot help feeling that the charm and beauty of this aria are just a little out of character. Unless, that is, we admit the truth of the saying that the Devil has all the best tunes. "Il balen del suo sorriso" is among the most seductive things Verdi ever wrote and it is an unfeeling listener whose view of the Count's character is not swayed a little by this aria.

Orchestrally the accompaniment of this number is interesting and unusual. In the first part, which is seventeen bars long, Verdi uses no violins at all. The arpeggios are supplied by a clarinet in its low register, the bass by double bass and violoncello pizzicato, the sustained harmonies by bassoons and horns from time to time but mostly by violas whose double-stopping was an orchestral practice very characteristic of Bellini, which Verdi inherited but used comparatively seldom after his early operas. Violins are not added until they join in the tune of a typical Verdi passage to be played "con espansione", and which forms the second half of the aria:

Ex *106*

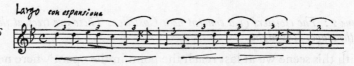

As the Count finishes his aria the convent bells ring four times to announce that the moment of Leonora's initiation is at hand. Di Luna and his followers hide themselves among the trees where the Count places himself so that he can watch the door through which Leonora will pass.

All this is performed to the accompaniment of a typical Verdi conspiracy sequence—the chorus throwing a *ppp* and *assai staccato* tune about between them in the manner we know so well from *Macbeth* and *Rigoletto*. The example in *Il trovatore* is neither so long

nor so famous as the choruses in the earlier operas; but it has a particular charm for us in the twentieth century: twice in the course of
eight bars we hear note-for-note the immortal opening phrase of
M. Maurice Chevalier's song "Valentine"—a song, we now recognize, with an unexceptionable pedigree.

Having got his conspirators safely behind the hedge Verdi now
throws all pretence of stealth and circumspection to the winds. The
Count, elated that His Hour is approaching, opens his lungs and
bursts into a loud and martial song with loud and martial assistance
from the orchestra, particularly the first trumpet, who doubles the
tune with much *brio*—"Per me ora fatale" ("My fateful hour is
come"):

Ex *107*

Per me o-ra fa-ta - le

As an interlude between paragraphs, as it were, of the Count's
thundering declaration, there is a reprise of the "Valentine" sequence
and we are dragged back to the hushed and dramatic reality of the
situation. But not for long. The Count has a second verse—or rather,
he repeats the whole of his first stirring twenty bars, words, music,
orchestration and all. This is followed once more by the chorus reminding us of the business in hand, but this time their whispers rise
in a not very gradual *crescendo* to a *fortissimo* tutti—at which point
they are telling us that they must hide themselves "in mystery in the
shadows". This *pp* to *ff* build-up is repeated and dramatic sanity is
restored only by a wonderfully effective *morendo* coda which makes
one think at the end of it that one has just heard one of Verdi's best
choral episodes. The scene is without doubt one of the most ludicrous
in all opera. Equally, it is such fun that it is a very toffee-nosed
listener who does not honestly enjoy every moment of it.

With the Count and his band finally hidden behind the trees there
is a moment's silence. Then, coming from off-stage we hear the
unaccompanied voices of nuns addressing Leonora, warning her
that life is but a shadow, and with the promise that in the convent
Heaven will open wide to her, bidding her take the veil. Against
this sombre religious background the Count, Ferrando and the
chorus of followers make their comments, emerging slowly, but not
too far, from the shadow of the trees.

Leonora enters accompanied by a group of women and a tearful
Ines (her tears are expressed by two melancholy phrases by a solo
clarinet), who is upset at the idea of having to leave her mistress.
In a simple and affecting *cantabile* passage Leonora reassures her

companion that it is all for the best, and that the world means nothing now that Manrico is dead. She turns towards the convent and is just about to enter when the Count jumps out from his hiding place and bars the way; but before he can do anything Manrico suddenly appears. The Troubadour's arrival, not surprisingly, causes a sensation. There is a general cry of astonishment and the music suddenly dies down to a *pianissimo* and a pause.

Verdi's dramatic sense at this point leads to an unexpected piece of music. Leonora is naturally excited, but she is also overjoyed and can hardly speak. So after her first cry of delight Leonora sings a breathless little tune, to be sung, nevertheless, with what the composer describes as "all joy"—"È deggio—e posso crederlo?" ("It is he—can I believe it?"):

Ex *108*

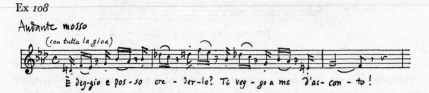

After her initial breathless excitement Leonora finds words to express herself in a great soaring phrase which she reaches by way of a passage that begins with a tune straight out of the Quartet in *Rigoletto*:

Ex *109*

Gilda, it will be remembered, broke up the first ten notes of that phrase. In Leonora's mouth it changes its character completely. Verdi shared with Mozart a peculiar gift of producing what one might almost call all-purpose themes from time to time; the notes are the same in each case, and yet in one opera they express a breaking heart, in the other the joy of a woman whose lover has come back from the dead.

Though *Rigoletto*, *Il trovatore* and *La traviata* are particularly rich in instances of Verdi's genius for making the same notes mean two different things, for creating two entirely different moods from superficially the same material, it was a characteristic feature of his work throughout his career and was found in its most astonishing form in his last two operas. *Otello* and *Falstaff*.

From Leonora's first phrases a typical and intricate ensemble builds up in which everybody states his or her point of view of the situation. Leonora reverts to her breathlessness once more, the Count is furious, Manrico has a long and lovely vocal line to himself, Ines and the chorus of nuns remark that heaven has rewarded Leonora for her faith. The ensemble comes to a temporary halt with the sudden entry of Manrico's followers who disarm the Count and his band, leaving Di Luna in a paroxysm of frustration.

For a moment there is a hushed reprise of Leonora's "Sei tu dal ciel disceso" (Ex 109) heard over *pp* tremolo strings. It rises to a rapid climax and the curtain falls after a conventional and noisy orchestral coda. In the score published in French for the Paris performance of the opera in 1857 Leonora sings the whole of the sequence in unison with the tenor, a practice which seems to have remained peculiar to the Paris edition, for there is no hint of it in the ordinary Italian editions I have seen. In a recent RCA recording, however, a compromise between the French and the Italian *Trovatore* was made and the tenor joined in with the "Sei tu dal ciel" in the third bar. It was an effective finish and not entirely contrary to the composer's wishes; but I imagine the number of times we are likely to hear it depends very much on finding a soprano amiable enough to share her stirring climax with anybody else.

As we have anticipated for some time, the act ends with Leonora having renounced all intentions of becoming a nun and swearing to follow Manrico to the ends of the earth.

PART III

Scene 1 : Count di Luna's camp outside Castellor, the towers of which are visible in the distance. On the right of the stage, with the flag of supreme commander flying over it, is the Count's tent. The Count's soldiers are occupied in various pursuits, on guard, playing dice, polishing their arms, or wandering back and forth across the stage.

The scene opens with an appropriately martial chorus in which the soldiers remark cynically that though they are enjoying a game of dice tonight they will face the sterner game of battle on the morrow:

Ex *110*

A band of archers arrives to reinforce the company; when they are all assembled Ferrando appears from the Count's tent to tell them of their supreme commander's order to attack Castellor, where Manrico and Leonora are besieged. Ferrando's words inspire the soldiers to another chorus, a determined piece with a town-band accompaniment, about honour, booty, waving banners and bugles sounding for battle:

Ex *111*

The chorus fades away in a characteristically effective *dim. e rall.* with the soldiers repeating the words "booty and honour"—which, one supposes, are their war aims in order of importance. The men disperse and resume their various activities.

For the performance of *Il trovatore* in French at the Paris Opera in 1857, when it was called *Le Trouvère*, Verdi added a ballet at this point in the action, a point which was reached musically, however, by means intriguingly different from the Italian score as we know it. The soldiers' chorus was in E, not F; it was nearly twenty bars shorter; the accompaniment was different in many important rhythmic and orchestral details, gaining added vigour in the process; some of the chorus writing was also adapted to enable Ferrando to enjoy one or two solo bars between hearty interjections like "Oui, courage!" Finally, any suggestion of the *dim. e rall.* ending was dispensed with altogether. The whole sequence was good and loud, and ended even louder.

The ballet music that followed consists of four numbers: "Pas de Bohémiens" (which included a Gitanilla), Seviliana, "La Bohémienne" and a final Galop. Some of it is good, some of it not so good, but it is unique among Verdi's ballet music in making use of themes from the opera itself. In all honesty, however, it must be admitted that the themes used in this way are not altogether dramatically appropriate. In the opening "Pas de Bohémiens" we hear an ingenious development of Ex 94 and a *ff* statement of Ex 96 played twice which is in fact in A major this time but which is still approached in an unobvious way—in this case from F sharp minor.

The dramatic inconsistency of this lies, of course, in both tunes being more or less the property of Azucena's gipsy band who would not, one feels, be entertaining Count di Luna's troops, even disguised as ballet dancers, especially in view of the turn taken by the plot when the action is resumed. One can only suppose that a gipsy ballet supplying the colourful interlude traditionally demanded by the Paris Opera, caused Verdi almost unconsciously to resort to the most easily accessible gipsy music he knew—his own. These two tunes, however, are the only themes from the opera to be heard in the ballet.

The Gitanilla turns out to be a robust bolero, well garnished with twiddly *espagnoleries*, but the "Seviliana" meanders about for some time in foreign tempos and time-signatures before finally getting to the characteristic and tuneful 3/4 its title leads one to expect. The Galop is a noisy and undistinguished finale which one wishes could have been written by Rossini or Offenbach.

The third movement, "La Bohémienne", is perhaps the most interesting of the four. Apart from offering some tunes which might almost be Spanish it includes two themes which may well strike the experienced opera-goer as familiar. The first has more than a suggestion about it of a recurrent phrase in the *Aida* ballet music:

The other is what one can only regard as a waltz version of the opening phrase of "Caro nome", with a minimum of decoration and alteration to disguise it:

Ex *113*

The ballet music to *Il trovatore* is indeed a charming and unusual interlude which Verdi rounds off neatly after the Galop with a coda to get the corps de ballet off the stage and to bring us back to the realities of the plot.

Count di Luna comes out of his tent and in a short and impatient passage of declamation reflects that Leonora is in the arms of his rival. His *dolce* cry of "Leonora!" suggests that he is all set for another aria when there is a disturbance off stage and Ferrando comes on to say that a spy has been found lurking near the camp. The "spy" is brought in. It is Azucena.

The old woman, her hands bound, is dragged before the Count and questioned closely; she replies that she was doing no harm; being a gipsy she was just wandering about, looking for the son who has deserted her: "Giorni poveri vivea" ("I was poor but contented . . ."):

Ex *114*

Azucena's tune goes from E minor to E major and brings from the orchestra another of those typical broad phrases in which this opera abounds and which are so often so effectively emphasized by the sudden sound of violoncellos doubling the tune an octave below the voice or first violins for a bar or two. In this case it is the violins and violoncellos who have the tune deriving from Di Luna's long flowing phrase in "Il balen del suo sorriso" (Ex 106)—a coincidence of no significance that I can see:

Ex *115*

Meanwhile Ferrando has done some thinking. Azucena has admitted that she comes from Biscay, and the Count has asked her whether she knew about his stolen brother. The gipsy shows some uneasiness when she realizes who the Count is, and in a moment of inspiration Ferrando recognizes her as the woman who threw the child on the fire by which her mother perished.

The Count at once orders his soldiers to bind Azucena more tightly. In desperation the old woman cries out for Manrico to come to her rescue, and she does so to a poignant phrase which, with slight variations, Verdi used again and again to express a woman's (and only a woman's) anguish until its final heart-breaking appearance in the last act of *Otello*:

Ex *116*

The scene ends with an energetic ensemble begun by Azucena, who vows that God will punish her malefactors, while the Count rejoices in an additional and unexpected opportunity for vengeance. He will not only kill his rival, but his rival's mother shall be burnt at the stake. The ensemble is remarkable for one or two imaginative dynamic contrasts in Azucena's part, some long and effective unison passages for the chorus, and the inevitable (but not incessant) doubling of the tune by a solo trumpet. The curtain falls with the Count feeling very pleased with himself as Azucena is led away to her death.

Scene 2: A room adjoining the chapel in Castellor, with a balcony in the background.

The curtain rises to an arresting unison phrase for strings which gives way to the sort of passage, *pp* and staccato, Verdi used so often and with such certainty to create an air of suspense. Leonora and Manrico, awaiting the Count's assault on the castle, are shortly to be married in the chapel. Ruiz is also present, but Manrico sends him away to inspect the defences and so is left alone with Leonora. He tells her that at daybreak he will go forth, to be victorious or to perish with her name on his lips. Manrico addresses Leonora without heroics of any kind, in a simple and moving aria which provides a

moment of lyrical repose all the more effective for being sandwiched
between two tumultuous outbursts of plot and the music to go with
them—"Ah sì, ben mio" (Ah yes, my love"):

Ex *117*

This aria has well been described in its time as almost Mozartian
in its simplicity, and indeed in the second part, in D flat, there twice
occurs a cadence which may be frequently heard note-for-note in
Mozart's works, trill and all. The more immediate model for "Ah sì,
ben mio", was not Mozart, however, but Bellini whose characteristically simple accompaniment of restful violin arpeggios and sustained viola harmonies is only now and then disturbed by such
unmistakably Verdian touches as the sudden unison of violoncellos
with the voice for a few notes at a time.

The sound of an organ comes from the chapel. In a quaint little
sequence of imitation and consecutive sixths Leonora and Manrico
reflect on the joys of their "chaste love", and walk hand in hand
towards the chapel for their wedding. They are interrupted, however, by the frenzied return of Ruiz with the news that the old gipsy
woman has been captured and that the Count's men are taking her
to be burnt at the stake. Manrico rushes to the balcony and sees for
himself: the pyre is already alight, and from his anguished cry at
what he sees, Leonora learns for the first time that he is Azucena's
son. Manrico sends Ruiz away to rally his soldiers and bursts into
"Di quella pira" ("The flames of the pyre burn my very fibre . . ."):

Ex *118*

That this famous cabaletta has never lost its power to stir and
excite the listener is largely because it has the *dramatic* justification
which Verdi increasingly sought for this convention. It is a stirring
tune at any time, of course, but it makes its greatest effect by virtue
of its context, and because it is in character. It is a superb expression
of the virility of the hero, of his determination to save the old gipsy
and so put his filial duty before even his love for Leonora, whose only
comment on the situation is to say between the first and second
verses of "Di quella pira" that it would be far better to be dead.

To talk of the "verses" of Manrico's cabaletta is misleading, of course, because he sings the same words and music both times to identically the same vigorous orchestral accompaniment. The only deviation from the letter of the first "verse" that is almost invariably made in the second is the way in which, the last time it occurs, the tenor sings the phrase:

Ex 119

It is a matter of pride, custom and the tenor's determination to display his masculinity and prowess that these two bars should be sung in this way:

Ex 120

It is usual to describe this sort of departure from the written part as a convention followed since "time immemorial". In this case, however, it happens that its origin is known and can be pinpointed in time to the first production of *Il trovatore* in Florence when Carlo Baucardé, the original Manrico at the Rome première, was suddenly inspired to introduce the famous high C and kept it in thereafter, though what Verdi's views were on this I do not know.

At any rate, for more than a century it has been a point of honour among all Manricos that they should sing that sustained top C— even though it means transposing the whole cabaletta down to B flat to get it.

Ruiz returns with the soldiers. There is a final rousing ensemble, in which Leonora takes no part, and after repeated trumpet calls and promises by his followers to give their lives for him, the curtain falls on Manrico leading his fully armed company away to do battle with the Count.

PART IV

THE EXECUTION

Scene 1 : A wing of the palace of Aliafera. In the corner is a tower with iron bars across the windows. It is a very dark night.

The gloom and pitch darkness of the scene is reflected in a sombre orchestral introduction for clarinets and bassoons, both featured in their lower registers.

The atmosphere of suspense and mystery is also reflected in the stage directions which stimulate our curiosity with "Two people come forward in cloaks", before telling us that "they are Leonora and Ruiz". Ruiz shows Leonora the tower in which Manrico is imprisoned. Exactly how Manrico came to be imprisoned is not explained. Indeed, it is only from Leonora's concern that we can deduce it is Manrico at all who is imprisoned, for Ruiz refers only to the "unfortunate one" ("l'infelice") who is in the tower. We can only presume that while his sortie from Castellor succeeded in distracting the attention of the Count and his army from the pyre lighted for Azucena, Manrico himself must have been captured in the attempt. At any rate, Manrico has been caught and the burning of Azucena (who, as far as we know, is still in custody) postponed.

Ruiz leaves and Leonora is left alone to brood on a desperate plan she has to save her lover. She gazes significantly at a ring she wears on her right hand (the significance of the ring is apparent later), and reflects that she is near Manrico and yet he does not know it. Leonora's little soliloquy is expressed in one of those near-recitatives which Verdi was now beginning to make as dramatically telling as his arias. The expected aria follows—"D'amor sull'ali rosee" ("Go, sad sighs, on rosy wings to comfort my love . . .") :

Ex *121*

The orchestral accompaniment of this aria (another in the F minor–A flat tonality which keeps cropping up in Leonora's solo scenes) is again quite astonishing in its simplicity, and deriving this time not only from Bellini but from Donizetti as well. From the one composer comes the typical economy of the string writing—the arpeggios in the second violins, the double-stopped harmonies in the violas; from the other, the familiar trick of closely following the vocal line with a flute playing a sixth above it. However, while the trimmings may have been supplied by Bellini and Donizetti, the meat of the aria is unmistakably Verdi and a wonderful lyrical beginning to what develops into a masterly fourth act.

A bell tolls; and from somewhere inside the Palace men's voices are heard singing the Miserere, the prayer for those about to die.* Eight bars of unaccompanied chorus lead us into what may be considered the Miserere proper—that astonishing ensemble which is perhaps the greatest passage in the whole opera.

In spite of its obvious derivation from the ensemble "Qual mesto gemito" in Rossini's *Semiramide* (where the key is the same and there is more than a hint of the same drumming accompaniment, at least for half of each bar), the Miserere impresses one as an entirely original conception. The most immediately striking feature of it all, of course, is the orchestral accompaniment with its thumping ostinato played *pp* by the entire orchestra—flutes and oboes in unison in their low register, trombones, tuba, bass drum and all:

Ex *122*

The instrumental "voicing" alone in this whole orchestral passage is worth careful study, for in spite of writing the three trombone parts in close clusters of chords in their middle register, and having the violoncellos in their low register play only a third above the double basses, Verdi avoids any suggestion of thickness in the texture in a miraculous manner. He achieves this, one imagines, because each note that is played in the orchestra lasts for so small a fraction of a second that it never has time to thicken. That is, if the passage is played as it is written.

Above the orchestral throbbing and the measured tolling of the

---

* It was because he had hesitated a whole month before deciding to use this one bell in *Il trovatore* that Verdi was said to have been so "scandalizzato" to learn that Puccini had used no fewer than thirteen bells in *Tosca*.

bell Leonora sings "Quel suon, quelle preci . . ." ("That sound! Those prayers!") :

Ex 123

Quel suon, quelle pre - ci sol-leu-ni, fu- ne - ste

It is a tune which not surprisingly has as its despairing cadence a variant in the minor of that sobbing anguish which we first heard Azucena sing in Ex 116. As Leonora finishes the whole mood and colour, but not the tempo, of the music changes with the voice of Manrico coming from the tower. Accompanied only by a harp the Troubadour sings his farewell to Leonora:

Ex 124A

Ah—— che la mor-te o- gno - ra

The chorus continues with its prayer, Leonora with her own tune, and Manrico with his. As the ensemble builds towards its climax the orchestra punctuates the singers less and less. The first two bars of Manrico's tune (Ex 124A) are developed as a kind of ground melody, Leonora protests that she will never forget her lover in a passionate and florid phrase which she sings four times—

Ex 124B

Di' te, di- te scordarmi!

—the bell (silent during Manrico's solo passages) tolls inexorably, and the movement finishes with the first *forte*—the first *forte* marked in the score, that is—since the end of the last act.

Immediately following on the Miserere there is a scene for Leonora, Ex 125, often omitted in performance, and usually cut from

Ex 125

Tu ve-drai che a-mo-re in ter-ra mai del mio non fu più for-te:

recordings, though Mmes Callas and Tebaldi included it in theirs—
"Tu vedrai che amore in terra" ("You will see that there is no love
on earth stronger than mine") :

It is a strangely simple little tune, to be sung *sottovoce ed agitato*,
which builds up to a rather flashy and unexpected coloratura finish.
Performed as written the whole episode is repeated word for word
and note for note, like "Di quella pira", with a grandstand coda
added. In practice, however, the routine is cut by half, and ideally
I think should be cut altogether. Coming immediately after the
Miserere it is inevitably an anticlimax which can be avoided only
by getting on with the plot as soon as possible.

The plot proceeds with the entry of the Count di Luna with some
of his followers who find the stage empty; Leonora has hidden herself at their approach. The Count reminds his men that although he
may be abusing the powers given him by the Prince of Aragon,
Manrico is to be hanged at dawn and Azucena is to be burnt at the
stake. The Count's men enter the tower and he stays behind to
remind us that he has not seen Leonora for some time. "Where are
you, cruel one?" he cries.

"Here", says Leonora, emerging from the shadows, The Count,
surprised at her sudden appearance in answer to what was almost a
rhetorical question, asks her what she is doing there, and she replies
that she has come to ask him to spare Manrico's life. The Count
laughs at what he considers a preposterous suggestion, and after a
short, busy to-and-fro sequence of pleas and refusals between
soprano and baritone, the tempo drops for Leonora to throw herself
at Di Luna's feet, promising that she will marry him if only he will
let the Troubadour go free —"Mira, di acerbe lagrime" ("A flood
of bitter tears flows at your feet") :

Ex *126*

Leonora's pleas, in the A flat we get to know so well in this opera,
are rejected by the Count, and what has developed into a duet is
brought to an end as Di Luna turns to leave. Leonora grabs hold of
him.

"What price are you willing to pay?" asks the Count.

"I give—myself!" she replies.

Leonora's offer has an immediate effect on Di Luna; his musical
share of the duet changes from furious intractability to a most joyful

anticipation of a dream finally come true. He goes towards the tower and whispers instructions in the ear of the warder. As he does this Leonora opens the phial of poison concealed in her ring and drinks from it, singing in a low-pitched and solemn monotone, "M'avrai, ma fredda" ("You shall have me, but cold and dead").

The Count turns to Leonora to assure her that Manrico will live. Raising her eyes "which are veiled in tears of joy" (the stage directions tells us) Leonora embarks on an elated cabaletta: "Vivrà! Contende il giubilo" ("He will live! I cannot speak for joy . . .!"):

Ex *127*

Allegro brillante

(Vi - vrà! Con - ten - de il giu - bi - lo   i det - ti a me, Si - gno - - re

This joyful outburst, with the piccolo adding an extra brilliance to the vocal runs and jumps, also develops into a duet. Sharing the same tune, often in unison, the Count and Leonora give vigorous and emphatic expression to their individual feelings of exultation. This does not, of course, result in the sort of characterization we have come to expect from Verdi after the Quartet in *Rigoletto*, but in a conventional way it makes an exciting enough curtain to the scene which ends with Leonora and the Count entering the tower together.

Scene 2 : A gloomy prison cell. On one side, a small barred window. There is a door at the back. A dim light hangs from the ceiling. Azucena is lying on a rough mattress, with Manrico seated beside her.

The scene opens with a simple and wonderfully evocative orchestral introduction consisting of no more than nine slow major chords scored for full orchestra (without percussion), but played *ppp* and creating a remarkable and immediate atmosphere of gloom and darkness.

The curtain rises on Azucena in a semi-delirious state of terror at the fate to which she is condemned. She rambles incoherently, weary and uncomprehending one moment, horror-stricken and raving the next. The opening bars of the scene is a vividly dramatic sequence which Verdi underlines with a masterly orchestral commentary—simple, imaginative and, in the sudden unison B flats across four octaves in the wind which he introduces against a falling string phrase, of quite arresting originality.

Azucena's hallucinations grow more and more real and she beseeches Manrico to save her from the flames. Mention of the fire is associated at once in Azucena's mind with the death of her mother, and Verdi reminds us of the earlier scene in which the old gipsy told us the whole story by a short and *pp* orchestral quotation of the theme of "Stride la vampa" (Ex 98). As she thinks of the fire Azucena's raving terror increases and she falls convulsed in Manrico's arms. Manrico lifts her to her feet and leads her to the rough bed to soothe her and beg her to try and get some sleep. The old woman lies down and quietly sings, to the softest of pizzicato accompaniments, that at last she is growing tired—"Sì, la stanchezza m'opprime":

In a contrasting major phrase Manrico bids his mother sleep, free of her troubled dreams—"Riposa, o madre":

Ex *129*

This phrase prepares the way for the most moving and lovely scene in the opera, when Azucena, "between sleeping and waking", thinks nostalgically of her native mountains—"Ai nostri monti" ("Let us return to our mountains"):

As Azucena sings Manrico continues his lullaby and the duet ends with the old gipsy falling asleep, exhausted.

Perhaps more than anything else in *Il trovatore* this duet defies analysis. Its restraint and heart-rending simplicity are as uniquely characteristic of Verdi's genius as the enhancement of the beauty and tenderness of the vocal line by an inspired economy of orchestral accompaniment—which, for all its economy, does not lack typically subtle touches like the delicate figure for muted first violins divided into three parts in the final bars of the duet.

6

With Azucena falling asleep with a series of yawning phrases at the end of her duet with Manrico, the action starts up again at once with the sudden appearance of Leonora. Manrico is overjoyed to see her but—literally—changes his tune when she explains that he is free to go; she will remain behind as the price of his freedom. Manrico rightly suspects that she has done a deal of some kind with the Count and he guesses what sort of terms the Count has laid down.

Manrico asks Leonora the price she has paid. She is silent, Manrico at once believes the worst and bursts out into a passionate phrase (well supported by a unison of trumpet and violoncellos) which dominates the duet that follows between tenor and soprano:

Ex *131*

"Ha quest'infame l'amor venduto"—"She has sold her love to this villain . . ." The duet is one of typical romantic misunderstanding, with Manrico sticking obstinately to his point of view and Leonora desperately trying to get him to see reason. As the argument continues Azucena wakes up and begins to sing her plaintive song about the mountains once more. Leonora and Manrico evidently do not hear this reprise of "Ai nostri monti" for they carry on with their misunderstandings throughout a scene which has now become a trio. With any luck, however, the two lovers will sing quietly enough to let us hear Verdi's effective use of the flute sustaining its low D *pp* for a couple of bars; it is an unexpected touch of orchestral colour.

As Azucena subsides once more into a state of half-sleep, Manrico begins to curse Leonora roundly for her infidelity in a throbbing movement in which the strings have an incessant and breathlessly urgent figure whose musical ancestor was the great sextet in Act II, Scene 2 of *Don Giovanni*. It is during this tensely dramatic passage that the poison Leonora has taken from her ring begins to work, and at last it dawns on Manrico that something unusual is happening when she collapses at his feet. Leonora is dying, her hands grow cold and in a last soaring phrase she explains that rather than live for another man she would die for Manrico—"Prima che d'altri vivere io volli tua morir!":

Ex *132*

Manrico begins to understand and in a frenzy of remorse reproaches himself for having been so stupid as to doubt Leonora. At
this point the Count enters the cell, and stopping in the doorway
remarks in a villainous aside that Leonora is obviously trying to
deceive him and die for the Troubadour. Another trio develops,
starting with Leonora's rising phrase (Ex 132). As she dies so the
same words—"Prima che d'altri vivere . . ."—are set to breathless
music, a series of short, disjointed, sobbing utterances which stand
out dramatically against the Count's cool, sinister summing up of
the situation and Manrico's desperate last-minute appeals to Leonora
for forgiveness.

Leonora dies. Within two bars the Count calls for his guards and
orders them to take Manrico off to his execution. As he is led away
Manrico cries farewell to his mother. Azucena awakes from her sleep
and implores the Count to listen to her before he does anything
more. The Count, in reply, takes Azucena to the window and says,
"Do you see?" Azucena sees only too well: she sees Manrico's
execution.

"He is dead," says the Count.

"He was your brother," Azucena tells him. And in a great dramatic phrase Azucena, finishing on the high B flat of one of the most
exacting and satisfying roles ever written for a mezzo-soprano, cries
triumphantly: "You are avenged, mother!" The curtain falls as the
Count exclaims: "And I still live!"

In the Paris version Verdi delayed the fall of the final curtain by a
highly theatrical device. When Manrico is led away the off-stage
chanting of the unaccompanied Miserere and the tolling of the bell
are heard once more. Azucena is awakened by this "chant de mort"
and cries out for her son. Manrico's voice is heard in the distance
invoking the blessing of heaven on his mother to the tune (sung
twice) of Leonora's passionate "Di te, di te scordarmi!" (Ex 124B);
the Troubadour's last thoughts, expressed to music from his own
part in the earlier Miserere, are for Leonora whom he is to join in
heaven.

The final moments are also different. A melodramatic side-drum
roll is heard as the Count takes Azucena to the window. The gipsy
has no time to implore the Count to listen to her; she sees Manrico
is dead and in a strangely off-hand manner tells the Count that Manrico is his brother. Di Luna cries, "Jour d'horreur!"; Azucena, instead of calling triumphantly on the spirit of her mother, announces
rather flatly that "Heaven has avenged my mother". The Count's
last words as the curtain falls, the ironic "And I still live!", are
omitted altogether; he merely exclaims, "O terreur!"

The end of the Paris Trovatore is one of the few second thoughts
Verdi had in his career which was not an improvement on the first.

The last Paris scene starts off most effectively; the repetition of the distant Miserere is good theatre, and it is pleasant to hear the Troubadour's voice once more, though why he should quote Leonora's tune when he's singing about his mother, and his own when he's singing about Leonora, isn't quite clear. But where the Paris coda falls down is in the final stages of the action, when both music and text are entirely lacking in the tremendous dramatic excitement and fire of the original.

For all that it has been called vulgar, unintelligible and ridiculous it is easy to understand as the curtain falls on its powerful and moving final act why *Il trovatore* has proved Verdi's most popular opera. The plot, as we can see, is frequently compressed to the point, if not of being unintelligible, at least of bewildering the inattentive listener.* But it was in fact this very compression, forced on Cammarano by the nature of the subject, which caused Verdi to be more lavish with his tunes than in any other opera he wrote.

Compared with *Rigoletto* there are remarkably few pages of dramatic dialogue in the score; principals and chorus play their parts in an unending sequence of slap-up tunes. Compared also with *Rigoletto* the characterization—with the exception of the superb figure of Azucena—is on the whole not nearly so careful or subtle; and in the *Trovatore* ensembles there is nothing faintly comparable to the masterly Quartet in the earlier opera. And yet the individual characters have unmistakable personality, if only because every note they sing is throbbing with the musical personality of a composer working at full blast, producing music in which drama and poetry, pathos and passion tumble over each other in an inspired way, and with such conviction, that the listener is swept along by the sheer force and vitality of it all. It is music full of colour and contrasts; there are moments, like the orchestral introduction to Part IV, for instance (to say nothing of the Miserere, of course), which are superb examples of technical subtlety and characteristic craftsmanship. Soprano, mezzo-soprano, tenor, baritone, chorus, all enjoy high spots which have a permanent place in the hit songs of all time, and no amount of learned quibbling about the inconsistencies

* The opera does not seem to have lost its power to confuse even today. As recently as November 1965, more than a century after its first appearance at Covent Garden, a critic on *The Times* (no less) was sent to the Royal Opera House to comment on some changes of cast in the current production of *Il trovatore*. Among the newcomers was the well-known English bass, Michael Langdon, in the part of Ferrando. The critic, bemused like thousands in their time, made up his mind that Ferrando must be the Count di Luna's first name and praised Mr Langdon (whose voice was not familiar to him) for his excellent singing of "Il balen del suo sorriso" and other items in fact being sung at the time by Mr Peter Glossop, the baritone.

or banality of the plot, or objections that the atmosphere of violence, witchcraft and babies burned by gipsies is unreal and ridiculous will ever move them from it. Verdi's genius in the theatre consisted of his almost unfailing power to suspend our disbelief. And in none of his operas had he greater need to do so, or was he more successful in doing so, than in *Il trovatore*.

LA TRAVIATA*

Opera in three acts (four scenes). Libretto by Francesco Maria Piave, based on the play
La Dame aux Camélias by Alexandre Dumas, the younger. First performed at the Teatro la
Fenice, Venice, on 6th March, 1853. First performance in England: Her Majesty's
Theatre, London, 24th May, 1856. First performance in the United States: Academy of
Music, New York, 3rd December, 1856.

"LA TRAVIATA last night was a fiasco. Is the fault mine or the
singers'? Time will judge."

In those few immortal words Verdi wrote to his friend Emanuele
Muzio to report and comment laconically on a spectacular, catas-
trophic failure without parallel in the history of opera, for *La traviata*
was not even redeemed by its second performance, like *Madam
Butterfly* and *The Barber of Seville*.

It is not at all certain exactly when Verdi first had the idea of
making an opera of Dumas' *Dame aux Camélias*. He is reported to
have seen the play in Paris soon after its first production there early
in 1852 and to have been greatly impressed by it. We know that he
signed a contract in May of the same year to write an opera for the
Fenice, but there was no mention of any specific opera in the agreement and indeed as long as three months later he was still apparently
contemplating several subjects, none of which was *La traviata*. It
seems not to have been until the end of October 1852 that Verdi
actually had a copy of Dumas' play in his hands, and as late as
January 1853 that Piave was still hard at work on the libretto.
Whether Verdi had already finished *Il trovatore* before he began to
write *La traviata*, or whether he worked on both operas at the same
time, one thing is quite certain: Verdi had a strong feeling while
composing the music that *La traviata* might prove a fiasco.

It was not just that the word "fiasco" kept cropping up whenever
the question of casting was discussed. At all costs, Verdi told Piave,
the part of Violetta must be taken by an "elegante"; otherwise "it
can be a fiasco, the goodwill and interest of the management will be
forfeited along with my reputation and a considerable sum invested

* I make no attempt to translate this title into English. The Italian verb
traviare means "to go, or lead, astray", and the nearest one can get to describing
a woman who is *traviata* would lead to something as awkward and ridiculous as
"The Erring One". To translate the title less precisely as "The Fallen Woman"
suggests a sordid melodramatic atmosphere which would be misleading and
foreign to the nature of the opera. I propose, therefore, to refer to it as *La traviata*,
the title by which it is universally known—except in Germany where the untrans-
latable is still sometimes translated as "Violetta".

by the publisher". It would be a fiasco, Verdi was convinced, if the part had to be sung by the Fenice's choice and not by any one of three sopranos he considered were better qualified.*

Verdi always seems to have known that he was on to something new and different. On New Year's Day 1853 he wrote: "I am doing *La Dame aux Camélias* for Venice which will perhaps be called *Traviata*. It is a contemporary subject. I can imagine another composer not wanting to do it—because of the manners and the period of the subject and a thousand other awkward reasons. I am doing it with every pleasure. Everybody cried out when I proposed putting a hunchback on the stage. All I can say is that I was happy to write *Rigoletto*."

There is a characteristic note of defiance in this letter which leaves little doubt of the great confidence Verdi had in his project—although doubtless modern psychologists would interpret it as a typical defence mechanism proving precisely the opposite and point to the failure of the opera as a clear indication that Verdi's subconscious lack of confidence was justified. How they would explain the opera's eventual success, of course, is another matter.

As Verdi said, however, time would judge; and it is now clear that while many things contributed to it the fiasco of *La traviata* was not Verdi's fault. One of the most notorious reasons long given for the opera's failure and still popular among the writers of record sleeve notes, was of course that the singers wore contemporary costume. This, however, proves to have been no more than a legend which I have myself helped to keep alive—until I looked closely at the original playbill for Sunday, 6th March, 1853, which states quite clearly that the action takes place in "Paris and its neighbourhood in about 1700". Furthermore, to show that this was not just a printer's frolic the *Gazzetta Previlegiata di Venezia*, in its notice of the opera on the following day, makes special reference to the action having been "put back to the time of Louis le Grand to allow grander and more lavish stage decorations".

I will confess that when I came to translate Verdi's New Year's Day letter quoted above I thought twice before using the word "manners" for the very ambiguous Italian *costumi*, which can mean "manners", "customs" or "costumes". The context of the letter gives one little assistance; Verdi could so easily have considered "costumes" to be one of the hazards of setting a subject he described significantly as "un sogetto dell'epoca". Whatever Verdi meant by the word in this case, however, there is no doubt that the question

---

* Verdi's own premonition of disaster was not lessened by the receipt of an anonymous letter from Venice which warned him that he would have a "fiasco completo" unless he changed the soprano and baritone. Verdi's only comment, when he wrote to Piave telling him this, was a resigned "I know, I know".

of the costumes for the first *Traviata* most certainly occupied the attention of all concerned, and one would like to know at what stage in the production the action was shifted to 1700 and—particularly—the real reason for it after Verdi's insistence on the importance of the contemporary element in the opera.

The same issue of the Venice *Gazzetta* leaves us in no doubt about the real reason for the opera's failure: the fault lay entirely with the singers. Fanny Salvini-Donatelli, as Violetta, sang well in the first act, which was by no means unsuccessful. Verdi was called to take a bow after the Prelude, after the Brindisi, and again after the Duet. In fact, the act was said to have had considerable *successo*. The rot set in during Act II, when Salvini-Donatelli's voice was just not up to the composer's demands, the tenor went hoarse, and Varesi, the baritone, sulked to show that he considered the part of Germont to be unworthy of a singer who had created the parts of Macbeth and Rigoletto.

But it was Act III that was the real disaster. No sooner did the Doctor on the stage remark that Violetta was dying of consumption and had only a few hours to live, than the house was in an uproar of laughter. Signora Salvini-Donatelli's figure was what the kinder Venetians euphemistically referred to as "troppo prosperosa". The audience's reception of the opera on the first night was repeated on the second and again at the third, though on this last occasion Verdi was given some personal applause at the end because, it was reported a little ambiguously, "the audience knew he was leaving Venice the following morning".

Nothing more was heard of *La traviata* until fourteen months later, when a certain Antonio Gallo, a music seller who was a passionate admirer of Verdi's and member of a family which owned two of the theatres in Venice, turned impresario with the sole intention of successfully reviving Verdi's opera. He presented it on 6th May, 1854, at the Teatro Gallo di San Benedetto and from that moment it was an immediate and universal success.

Verdi himself was not in Venice for the new production, and apart from a trivial correction of detail such as phrase marks here and there and an occasional transposition, nothing, he wrote, was otherwise changed, omitted, added, re-orchestrated, or in any way made to differ from what had been performed at the Fenice fourteen months previously. Verdi's only comment from Mandres near Paris, where he heard that virtually the same audience which had abused *La traviata* at the Fenice was now riotously acclaiming it at the San Benedetto, was to end one of his letters to a friend in Italy with: "Everything that was heard at the Fenice, is now being heard at the San Benedetto. Last time it was a fiasco; this time it is a furore. Draw your own conclusion!"

*6

CHARACTERS IN ORDER OF SINGING

VIOLETTA VALÉRY, *a courtesan** . . .	*Soprano*
FLORA BERVOIX, *her friend* . . .	*Mezzo-soprano*
THE MARQUIS D'OBIGNY	*Bass*
BARON DOUPHOL, *an admirer of Violetta's* .	*Baritone*
DR GRENVIL	*Bass*
GASTON, *Viscomte de Letorières* . .	*Tenor*
ALFREDO GERMONT, *Violetta's lover* . .	*Tenor*
ANNINA, *Violetta's maid*	*Soprano*
GIUSEPPE, *Violetta's manservant* . . .	*Tenor*
GIORGIO GERMONT, *Alfredo's father* . .	*Baritone*
A MESSENGER	*Bass*

Servants, guests in the houses of Violetta and Flora; gipsies; guests and dancers dressed as matadors and picadors, etc.

Scene: Paris and the neighbourhood   Time: 1852†

* I have called the characters by the names that appear in the score and have not followed the rather eccentric example of Covent Garden some years ago, when Violetta was made to revert to Dumas' original name of Marguérite, Alfredo to Armand, and so on down the cast list, as though Verdi had somehow been thwarted in his original intention to set Dumas' play and had been forced by an unfortunate set of circumstances beyond his control (such as censorship or loss of memory) to set Piave's libretto instead. In fairness to the strange whim of our Royal Opera House, it should be said that in Verdi's first sketches of the music the heroine appeared for purposes of identification as "Margherita". Alfredo, on the other hand, was never Armando; he was referred to merely as *il tenore*.

† The score still has "about 1700" for reasons already given on page 168 but as soon as 1852 was remote enough to be safely regarded as an historical period, *La traviata* became a costume opera and has remained so ever since. It would be interesting to know when productions of the opera were first regularly set in its proper period, for even towards the end of the nineteenth century performances of *La traviata* could present a remarkable spectacle with the tenor in tights, the heroine looking like Madame Récamier, and the elder Germont in a frock coat and knee breeches.

ACT I

Scene: A drawing room in Violetta's house. At the back, a door leading to another large room. There are two other lateral doors. On the left, a fireplace with a looking glass over the mantel. In the centre, a large and luxuriously laid dining table.

In the orchestral prelude heard before the rise of the curtain we encounter for the first time something of the new and peculiar intimacy and simplicity which give *La traviata* its unique charm and character. It is a prelude remarkable for the three qualities which may be said in effect to dominate the opera: pathos, tunefulness and restraint. Its instrumentation is of almost Mozartian proportions: one flute, one oboe, one clarinet; two bassoons, the second of which plays only twelve notes all told; three horns, with a fourth added for four repeated notes; and strings. Its forty-nine bars of Adagio consist of two themes, the second of them played twice. It begins *ppp* and ends *morendo*, rising three times to a *forte* to make a quick diminuendo in a bar or less.

The Prelude begins with a passage for sixteen violins (eight firsts, eight seconds) divided into four parts:

Ex *133*

It is an unforgettable sound which Verdi brings back with telling effect later in the opera. In the Prelude it serves to create a peculiar mood of tension and melancholy and leads quickly to the second theme:

Ex *134*

171

This tune, hinted at so clearly in *Rigoletto* (Ex 60) and which is also brought back at a superbly dramatic moment later in the opera, is played across two octaves in unison by first violins, violas and violoncellos against a simple chuck-chuck accompaniment by the rest of the small orchestra. Verdi leaves it in an unfinished state and then hands it over to the violoncellos to repeat. The repetition takes no more complicated a form than the violoncellos (reinforced by a clarinet and a bassoon in the same register) playing it for all they are worth, while the first violins add a simple staccato figure as a decorative countermelody on which a short *morendo* coda is eventually based.

It is a Prelude of great beauty and infinite appeal, forming with its companion piece, the Prelude to the third act of *La traviata*, an unique diptych of purely instrumental music unmatched by anything else in Verdi's output.

The curtain rises with an abrupt change of mood to some typical Verdi "party music"—an *Allegro brillantissimo e vivace* which makes up in vivacity and perky scoring what it lacks in elegance:

Ex *135*

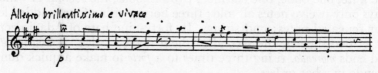

The initial statement of this tune retains some of the chamber-music dimensions of the Prelude in its instrumentation inasmuch as it is divided across three octaves between a flute, a piccolo, an oboe and a clarinet. The accompaniment, however, is pure small-town *banda*—an oompah figure provided by bassoons, timpani and a full brass section. The strings are silent until they join in to help with the last eight bars. Then, when the tune starts up again, there are long sequences in which the strings alone are heard and in purely chamber-orchestral proportions once more—two first violins, two seconds, two violas, a solo violoncello and a double bass. In what may be regarded as a kind of second subject the first violins share the tune with the solo violoncello an octave below them:

Ex *136*

All this forms the background to a party which is taking place in Violetta's house. Violetta is seated on a sofa chatting with her doctor,

Dr Grenvil. One group of her friends (the tenors in the chorus) curtly taxes another group (the basses in the chorus) with arriving late at the party. The basses answer this curious opening conversational gambit by saying they have been gambling at Flora's. This seems to explain everything, and Violetta rises to receive her guests —among them Baron Douphol, and Flora on the arm of the Marquis d'Obigny. A young man, Gaston de Letorières, joins the company bringing with him Alfredo, whom he introduces to Violetta as a great admirer of hers.

Violetta is politely touched to hear this, but turns away to invite her guests to be seated. The first party theme (Ex 135) starts up again as the guests sit down. Violetta sits between Alfredo and Gaston, Flora between the Marquis and the Baron. Conversation is resumed to the accompaniment of Ex 136, scored as before for a small group of strings, but this time with the two first violins playing the tune without help from the solo violoncello.

Gaston tells Violetta in an undertone that Alfredo is constantly thinking of her and called every day during her recent illness to ask after her. Violetta does not believe any of this, but when she turns to ask him Alfredo assures her it is true. All this tends to make the Baron bad tempered and when Gaston calls on him to propose a toast he sulks and shakes his head. Gaston turns to Alfredo who accepts after a gesture of feigned reluctance which is dispelled by Violetta's assurance that it would please her very much. This gives Alfredo his opportunity to launch off into the famous Brindisi— "Libiamo, libiamo ne' lieti calici" ("Let us drink with joyful glasses . . ."):

Ex *137*

Some commentators have been tempted to see a close affinity between this Brindisi and the one in *Macbeth* (Ex 30) on the ground that both pieces are marked Allegretto, are in B flat, and begin with an interval of a rising major sixth. But there, I should say, the resemblance ends, for the *Traviata* Brindisi is in 3/8 time (*Macbeth* is in 2/4) and its whole form, construction, atmosphere and character are entirely different.*

* If one is desperate to find an anticipation of the *Traviata* tune it is to be found not in *Macbeth*, but in a Brindisi written by Verdi for voice and piano in 1845. True, it is not in B flat, but in F; it does not begin with a rising sixth, but with a rising fourth. But it *is* marked Allegretto, and it *is* in 3/8—which is something, I suppose.

Alfredo's toast is replied to by Violetta, who is interrupted by a brief version of the first half of the tune sung suddenly in E flat by the rest of the company in unison. The key is quite ridiculously low for nearly everybody but basses and contraltos, but the violoncellos join in to reinforce the melody now played in unison by two trumpets as well as by first violins and woodwind across four octaves.

Violetta ignores the E flat interlude and continues with the "middle" of the tune in her original key and in some remarkable way finishes up in B flat as before. The Brindisi ends with a reprise in which Violetta and Alfredo sing mostly in unison against a wonderfully effective staccato three-in-a-bar sung *pianissimo* by the other principals and chorus. The orchestra, as so often when it is playing *pp* in Verdi, is used at full strength, with three unison trombones and *cimbasso* doubling the recurrent pizzicato figure in violoncellos and basses.*

From the next room comes the sound of a waltz, an Allegro brillante affair played with sparkle and vigour by the off-stage *banda*. Violetta is about to lead her guests to the dance through the centre door when, according to the stage directions, she suddenly turns pale—the first really broad hint we have been given that she is consumptive (we have heard one or two references to her "recent illness", but there has been no suggestion till now that it was a chronic condition). Violetta assures her anxious guests that she will be all right in a moment, but as she takes a few steps she is forced to stop again and sit down. She motions her guests to go on in and dance; she will be with them in a little. They all leave, except Alfredo. Violetta goes to the mirror on the wall and is perturbed to see how pale she is; as she turns away she is surprised to see Alfredo standing there. He tells her how necessary it is that her

* In *La traviata*, as in most Verdi scores until *Otello* (1887), the word *cimbasso* is used to describe the lowest instrument of the orchestral brass family. The origin of the word itself is most obscure and many modern Italians, at any rate, seem willing to settle for its being a generic term for such bass wind instruments (not necessarily brass) as have been used in the orchestra at one time or another, like the serpent, the ophicleide, the bombardon, or the bass trombone, and that when Verdi used the term it always meant the bass trombone. Apart from the fact that "cimbasso" appeared in Verdi's scores before the bass trombone was in anything like general orchestral use, when he did eventually use a bass trombone (in *Otello* and *Falstaff*, for instance) he always said so in the score. The most likely *cimbasso* at the time of *La traviata* was undoubtedly the ophicleide which is specifically indicated under its own name in the *Requiem* (1874), although it is possible that the bass trombone was already used in *Aida* three years earlier where no more than the usual *cimbasso* is shown in the score. The word *cimbasso* has never appeared in *Grove's Dictionary* until now, when the Fifth Edition states briefly that it is "the Italian small-bore tuba in B flat (see TUBA)", but adding in small type underneath "See also Ophicleide". And when we see also Ophicleide we find that the Italian names for the instrument are *oficleide* (more correctly *officleide*) and *cimbasso*. Which I think begins to throw a little light on the matter.

health should be taken care of. Violetta asks rather bitterly who
there is to take care of her. Alfredo replies that he will take care of
her; he loves her, and has loved her since first he saw her a year ago.
The musical perspective now changes. The waltz which has been
the background to this conversation stops—or at least we do not
hear it. It is obvious, since it has conveniently modulated to a key to
suit Alfredo's next phrase, that the waltz has not come to a full close.
It continues out of our earshot, probably deafening those of Violetta's guests unwise enough to dance too near the band, for there are
some passages scored for the *banda's* trumpets which must surely be
earsplitting at close quarters. But so far as we in the audience are
concerned the musical and dramatic emphasis shifts from background to foreground. Alfredo tells Violetta that he loves her, and
has loved her since the first moment he saw her—"Un dì felice":

Ex *138*

This first phrase is repeated and with a slight alteration (which
lands it in A minor), leads to a tune which takes on a special emotional significance on two later occasions in the opera:

Ex *139*

Violetta, recognizing the earnestness of Alfredo's declaration,
realizes the danger of the situation and begs him to leave her and
forget her. He must find somebody else and then it will be easy.
Violetta's pleas are made in an unexpectedly florid style which
might at first suggest to the listener unfamiliar with the opera that
Verdi was taking a retrograde step. The coloratura element in *La
traviata*, however, is not a return to the vocal conventions of Rossini,
Bellini and Donizetti, but, as we soon perceive, a skilfully devised
means of characterization. Violetta's whole philosophy is to enjoy
the pleasures and luxuries of life that are the rewards of her profession, and her *brillante* and decorative contributions to the duet
into which "Un dì felice" develops are superbly in character, their
light-heartedness and flippancy contrasting in a telling manner with
Alfredo's preoccupation with the cruelty and torment of love.

A joint cadenza, in which the characters ingeniously retain their musical identity, brings the scene to an end, and the music of the waltz is heard again in the next room as Gaston suddenly pops his head round the centre door and asks: "Well? What the devil are you doing?" ("Ebben? che diamin fate?"). Violetta replies that they were just playing the fool. "Good!" says Gaston. "Stay there!" And with those few words one of the most puzzling little scenes in all opera comes to an end and Gaston retires.

Dramatically, Gaston's appearance has no great significance that I can see; musically, on the other hand, it breaks up the duet between Violetta and Alfredo by opening the door and letting the waltz in again. The sentimental mood of the preceding scene is thus shattered, and Alfredo is brought down to earth. Violetta, against the prevailing repetition of the waltz, makes him promise to keep the bargain—no talk about love, just friendship. Alfredo is just leaving her when Violetta calls him back to give him a flower she takes from her bosom. "Keep this flower," she says, "and come back to me when it is faded."

"Heaven! Tomorrow——!" cries Alfredo.

"Well then, tomorrow," replies Violetta.

Fervently Alfredo declares his love once more—a declaration which Violetta makes him repeat before he kisses her hand and leaves, singing a distant farewell as the waltz comes to an end. The whole of this second waltz-sequence, though the vocal writing is declamatory and not very catchy, has about it a peculiar excitement generated by the rather breathless 3/4 time which is most effective and exhilarating.

Violetta's other guests, according to the stage directions, now return in tumulto—which can mean tumult, confusion or uproar— "flushed from wine and dancing". (The changes of complexion in which the stage directions of the libretto abound are at least more easily complied with by the chorus, who at this point can have added rouge while off stage, than by Violetta who must find it very difficult to turn suddenly pale to order.) The opening party music returns with the guests, its harmonies ingeniously altered to give a sense of winding-up. And it is a most ingenious winding-up chorus that now follows. In unison, but pianissimo, chorus and principals sing a bread-and-butter address to Violetta, thanking her for a lovely evening. The unison opening is followed by a rapid ensemble which the composer marks "pp and staccato, beginning ppp to make a crescendo". The crescendo follows in a manner worthy of Rossini and the guests depart in high and grateful spirits as dawn is breaking.

Violetta is left alone on the stage, deeply puzzled by the nature of her emotions. It is something new in her life to be in love and to be

truly loved in return. She asks herself whether Alfredo is the one
her soul, lost and lonely in the crowd, has so often imagined—"Ah
fors'è lui":

Ex 140

Violetta repeats the words and music of Alfredo's declaration of
love—"A quell'amor, quell'amor ch'è palpito" (Ex 139). In the
score all this, from "Ah fors'è lui", is repeated with different words
as a second verse, but in my experience, at any rate, it is always cut
in performance. And rightly so, I feel, for Verdi has made his point
and there is not need to labour it. The music subsides slowly leaving
Violetta reflecting on the mystery of the whole situation. Suddenly
she jumps to her feet, crying, "Folly! Folly! What sort of crazy
dream is this?"

In a moment the character of Violetta and her music changes. The
gloom and bewilderment of a moment before are dispersed at once
by the bright orchestral introduction which leads Violetta to her
famous cabaletta "Sempre libera . . ." ("I must always be free . . ."):

Ex 141

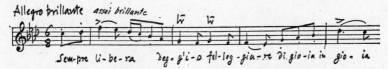

This cabaletta is unique in that the convention of the grandstand
coloratura finish is used by Verdi for a dramatic purpose. We are
not listening to a soprano showing off, but to the musical characterization of a human being expressing her let's-enjoy-ourselves-
while-we-may outlook on life quite brilliantly. We have already had
a glimpse of this side of Violetta's character in "Un dì felice"; in
this cabaletta her personality bursts into full bloom. A moment ago
she had been seriously in love, against her better nature, as it were;
now she has kicked over the traces and reverted to type as a woman
who lives life for what she can get out of it.

As Violetta finishes the first part of her cabaletta the voice of
Alfredo, accompanied by a harp off stage, is heard coming from beneath the balcony. He sings what has now almost become a theme-
song—or at least, a recurrent theme which we have come to associate

firmly with his love for Violetta—the tune now sung to the slightly altered words, "Amor, amor è palpito" (Ex 139).

The sound of Alfredo's voice has a momentary effect on Violetta; she is obviously moved by it. But before he has finished she has resumed her cries of "Folly!" with a tremendous coloratura flourish, and repeats her "Sempre libera".

Alfredo's voice is still heard off stage but Violetta ignores it, and as the cabaletta nears its climax her vocal runs and arabesques grow even more brilliant and abandoned.

The curtain falls on a vigorous coda in which virtually for the first time since Violetta began the scene all the woodwind in the orchestra are playing. Although all the brass seem to play at once when any brass play at all in this aria, some of the most brilliant and sparkling effects in the accompaniment and instrumental interludes are the result of that characteristic economy of means found so often in the score of *La traviata*. For long stretches in this final scene Verdi uses his woodwind on a chamber-music scale with a single flute, a piccolo, an oboe and a clarinet supporting the vocal line, sometimes in unison, sometimes in pairs. The orchestration of this whole finale is not the least important of the elements that contribute to the remarkably comprehensive portrait of Violetta and all the conflicts going on within her which so endeared her as a character to Verdi.

Scene 1 : The ground floor drawing room of a country house near Paris. At the back, facing the audience and between two french windows leading into the garden, is a fireplace. Above it, a clock and a looking glass. There are two doors facing each other on either side of the scene downstage. Two other doors, facing each other, lead to the first floor. The room is furnished with chairs, tables, books and writing materials.

The curtain rises on one of those rather breathless passages for strings which, like the one that begins Act II of *Rigoletto*, so often open a Verdi scene, serving no other purpose than to give a character time to get across the stage and settle down before telling us what is on his mind.

In this case it is Alfredo who enters, dressed in hunting clothes. He puts down his shotgun and tells us that he and Violetta have been living together for the past three months. She has given up everything for him and turned her back on her life of luxury and social gaiety. Continuing his soliloquy Alfredo declares in a short and warming lyrical passage that he is exuberantly happy—"De' miei bollenti spiriti . . ." ("My youthful ardour was tempered by the quiet smile of her love . . ."):

Ex *142*

The accompaniment is a simple throbbing figure for strings marked, according to my Ricordi score of 1914, to be played pizzicato. In Toscanini's and most other recordings of the opera the strings play these notes with the bow and in consequence it flows smoothly and urgently. In the 1954 Decca recording* it is played pizzicato, so that we can hear—if the instruction is in fact the composer's—how much less effective the passage sounds in its "official" form. What seems to me most likely to have happened, however, is

* The Tebaldi set Decca LXT 2992–4 and ACL 232–4 in Great Britain; London A 3412 in USA.

that the pizzicato was marked in the copy of the score from which my miniature edition was printed, by some conductor striving for effect or a change of routine. If, after more of Mr Denis Vaughan's researches, it does prove to have been Verdi who wanted the pizzicato, then I still don't think it is very good.

Annina, Violetta's maid, enters greatly agitated. She has just returned from Paris where, on her mistress's instructions, she has been to sell Violetta's jewellery and other personal belongings in order to meet the expenses of the house. Alfredo is horrified to hear this, and manages to drag out of Annina the information that a hundred louis are needed. He tells her he will go to Paris to raise the money, but that Violetta must know nothing about it.

Alfredo dismisses Annina, and in a vigorous and rather heroic cabaletta which has a distinct flavour of Manrico's "Di quella pira" about it, reproaches himself for his blindness to the situation and determines not to rest until he has put it right—"Oh mio rimorso! oh infamia!":

Ex *143*

It is a conventional enough cabaletta in all conscience, with its familiar thumping accompaniment; but there is undeniable excitement in the sudden thrilling entries of the violoncellos in unison support of the voice which make one regret that it is not included more often, at least in recordings. It is common practice in the theatre to omit it altogether. When this happens Alfredo goes off at once after his scene with Annina, leaving her alone on the stage to be joined by Violetta immediately afterwards.

As shown in the score Alfredo sends Annina out of the room and then—after the cabaletta—makes his own exit. Violetta then enters accompanied by Annina. The omission of the cabaletta entails the introduction of a bridge passage between Alfredo's exit and the entrance of Violetta, to get back into some sort of musical continuity. The provision of this link seems to be left to the conductor. Toscanini's brilliant unison passage for strings keeps the dramatic excitement from flagging; the interpolations supplied in other recordings are less stimulating.

By whatever means we have reached the scene Violetta has now entered, carrying a bunch of papers. She asks Annina where Alfredo is and is told that he has just gone to Paris but will be back before dark. (There is no doubt that, all puristic considerations apart, it is dramatically far more telling that Violetta should arrive to find Annina alone on the stage and be surprised not to find Alfredo there, than that she should ask Annina the question only when they both arrive in the drawing room having apparently walked downstairs together.) Violetta is puzzled by what Annina tells her, but turns to read a letter brought in by her manservant Giuseppe. The letter is from Flora inviting her to a party that evening. Violetta puts the letter aside saying that Flora will await her in vain. Giuseppe returns to say that a gentleman is waiting outside. Violetta asks that he should be shown in; she is expecting her lawyer.

It is no lawyer who enters, but Giorgio Germont, Alfredo's father. Violetta is understandably surprised when he introduces himself. He takes the chair she offers him and in an unexpectedly brusque manner repeats that he is indeed the father of the reckless boy whose life she is ruining. Violetta rises and with dignity reminds her caller that she is a woman in her own house; with his permission she will retire, more for his sake than for hers. Germont admires her spirit but persists with his theme that Alfredo is living beyond his means. Violetta, showing the old man some of the documents she had collected to show her lawyer, convinces him that so far from Alfredo keeping her, *she* is keeping Alfredo; that it is her money which keeps the household in what Germont describes as "tanto lusso"—so much luxury.

Germont has no doubt of Violetta's genuine love for Alfredo after this, but he does not hesitate to ask a sacrifice of her. He asks her to give up Alfredo for the sake of his daughter, Alfredo's sister, who is young and engaged to a young man who will not marry her unless her brother stops living with Violetta. The long sequence of dramatic declamation which began with Alfredo's exit now ends, and Germont sings "Pura siccome un angelo" ("Pure as an angel . . .")

Ex *144*

Germont's beautiful and simple appeal marks the beginning of a long and dramatic scene between him and Violetta, who is touched by the old man's plea and agrees readily to give up Alfredo—thinking that the separation will be for a little while only, until Germont's daughter is married. Germont, however, explains that there is no question of a temporary arrangement; it must be a permanent separation.

Violetta realizes that she is being asked to give up her entire happiness and in a passionate outburst tells Germont that she would prefer death to separation from Alfredo—"Non sapete quale affetto . . . ?" ("Do you not know what I feel . . . ?") :

Ex *145*

In the course of this breathless protest we hear from Violetta for the first time that she is suffering from a mortal disease and that she has not long to live. Germont is genuinely moved by her devotion but asks her to reflect on the consequences of her love. She is young now; but she and Alfredo will not always be young. What will happen when time and age have cooled the first fire of a passion not blessed by heaven?

Germont tells Violetta all this in simple musical terms and with a sincerity which makes him—for much of the opera, at least—one of the most endearing of operatic fathers—"Un dì, quando le veneri . . ." ("One day, when time has taken everything . . .") :

hardly! →

Ex *146*

This tune, with its typical quavering phrase in the second bar (a melodic peculiarity which keeps turning up in Germont's part), is supported by another wonderfully understated orchestral accompaniment. The vocal line is doubled by first violins *pp* in octaves with the characteristic group of demi-semi-quavers shown on the word "veneri" emphasized by flute and clarinet in octaves whenever they occur.

Violetta listens and murmurs, "It is true . . . it is true." Then, greatly affected by Germont's words, she pours her heart out in a passage of great pathos as she reflects to herself—"with extreme sorrow" as Verdi indicates—that life holds nothing for her : "Così alla misera" ("No hope remains") :

Ex *147*

Violetta's heartcry is not heard by Germont for it is intended as an aside (the words are in a long parenthesis); he continues to beseech her to make the sacrifice he asks of her. In tears Violetta turns to Germont and bids him tell his daughter that all will be well—"Dite alla giovane . . ." ("Tell the young girl . . ."):

Ex 148

Di-te al-la gio - va-ne   sì bel-la e pu - ra

This sequence, with its reticent string accompaniment and so characteristic of the dignity of the heroine of *La traviata*, develops into a duet in which Germont, greatly moved by Violetta's renunciation, assures her that he understands what she must be suffering and that her noble heart will triumph over everything. Germont introduces his own particular note of pathos to the duet with his "Piangi, piangi",—words which even if one does not understand Italian are at once explained by the music of Verdi's familiar expression of tears, intensified in this instance by the sudden addition of violoncellos in unison support of the voice:

Ex 149

Piangi,   piangi,   pian-gi, o   mise - ra

The scene is a masterly example of Verdi's unfailing instinct for clear-cut musical characterization. Violetta and Germont retain their individuality unmistakably in every bar of a duet that moves to a heart-breaking climax with a harmonic sequence of the greatest beauty and originality.

After a moment's silence Violetta turns to Germont. "Now tell me what to do," she says. He replies: "Tell him you no longer love him." Violetta answers that Alfredo wouldn't believe her; and if she left him he would follow. Violetta begs Germont to embrace her, and when he does so asks him to go into the garden and wait for his son. The old man turns to go, while Violetta sits down to write a letter. Germont hesitates, and suddenly overcome by Violetta's behaviour begs her to tell him what he can do for her.

In a tense and urgent phrase, with a characteristic four-in-a-bar *pianissimo* accompaniment by pizzicato strings, Violetta replies: tell Alfredo what she has done and why, and how she has suffered—

"Morrò! la mia memoria . . ." ("I shall die! Do not let him curse my memory"):

Ex *150*

Germont joins in once more, begging Violetta to believe that she has many happy years to live. Violetta beseeches the old man to leave; they embrace again and Germont goes into the garden.

Violetta now sits down and writes a letter. When she has finished it she rings for Annina who is surprised to see the address at which she is to deliver it. Violetta urges her to say nothing—from which we can only guess that the letter is an acceptance of Flora's invitation. Subsequent events do in fact bear out this theory, but it must be said that there is not a word in the libretto to suggest the exact nature of the letter.

Violetta begins to write another letter, this time to Alfredo; she hesitates, praying desperately for courage while a solo clarinet plays a plaintive four-bar phrase twice, the second time with a melancholy kind of decoration as though it were trying to keep its spirits up. Violetta finishes the letter and seals it, but hurriedly hides it away as Alfredo enters. Alfredo wants to know what she has been doing; she tells him she has been writing a letter—to him. But he cannot see it yet. Alfredo apologizes; he is distracted he says by the threatened arrival of his father who has written him a "severo scritto"—a severe letter. This gives Violetta an unexpected cue; greatly agitated she tells Alfredo that she must not be discovered by his father. She must leave at once; but before she goes she tells Alfredo how much she loves him, and how, if necessary, she will throw herself at the feet of his father who will not want to see them separated—"because", she cries, "you love me Alfredo, you love me—don't you?"

Alfredo replies that he loves her passionately. Violetta weeps at his reassurance and excuses her tears—she couldn't help them; with an effort she smiles at him, tells him she is happy and that she will always be there, close to him. Her false gaiety is echoed by a succession of restless trills in the orchestra which underline the breathless declaration of a woman who knows that none of this can happen and whose heart is on the verge of breaking. With a sudden crescendo the music rises to a great and burningly sincere outburst. The false, unfulfillable promises of a moment ago are forgotten in a tremendous cry from the heart as Violetta begs Alfredo: "Amami, Alfredo, amami quant'io t'amo . . ." ("Love me, Alfredo, love me as much as I love you . . .").

These words bring back the big tune from the Prelude to Act I (Ex 134). Violetta sings them ("con passione e forza") against a throbbing sustained orchestral accompaniment of quite surprisingly modest proportions. One of the greatest emotional moments in all opera, a sequence that can seem like the opening of the heavens themselves, proves on looking at the score to need no more from the orchestra than strings playing tremolo, sustained chords from two bassoons, four horns, and rolls by timpani and bass drum. There is a touch of genius, I think, in Verdi's sudden use of the bass drum whose purely percussive, tuneless quality adds a superbly dramatic sound to the first eight bars in which only Violetta has the tune. In the following eight bars the vocal line is doubled by flute, oboes, clarinets and a solo trumpet—the strings continuing their tremolo in the first position, supported by the roll of timpani and bass drum.

The melody of this sequence as Verdi wrote it is:

Ex *151*

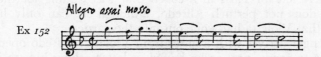

But you will be very lucky if you ever hear it sung like that. A bad and meaningless tradition has persisted for years which so alters the value of the notes in bars eleven to sixteen to make the passage sound roughly:

Ex *152*

As I wrote in my study of Toscanini's great recording of *La traviata** I do not know how or why this habit started, unless some bright person decided that since that was the way the passage was played in

* See *The Toscanini Legacy*, pp 219-35.

the Prelude to Act I Verdi must have made a mistake in not writing it to be played that way in Act II, Scene 1 as well. It was certainly not a practice countenanced by Verdi himself: many years after *La traviata* he was still writing the phrase in autograph albums exactly as it appears in the score and as I have quoted it in Ex 151.

Toscanini's restoration of the passage to its original form gives all of it that heart-breaking dignity which is so characteristic of Violetta throughout this whole scene. The half-time-value version reduces the passage to what is merely an hysterical snivel compared with the unbearable despair of the long and moving phrase with which Verdi intended Violetta to say her final and tragic farewell. The only sign of an uncontrolled emotional upset, the suggestion of Violetta breaking into tears—out of our sight and Alfredo's—is made by the few bars of agitated epilogue played by strings only as Violetta rushes from the scene; not before.

Conductors and singers, when accused of this regular distortion of the passage, have no convincing answer. They say it is the custom; or that the composer was asking too much to expect a singer to tackle this long phrase at the end of a difficult scene. They say anything, in fact, except admit they don't know a good tradition from a bad habit. The only singer of our time I have heard who does not double-up the tempo at this point is Maria Callas. But then one would expect it from one of the few of her profession who is not entirely bird-brained. Miss Callas is so set against the bad habits of her colleagues, indeed, that in her famous Cetra recording she errs in the other direction if anything. By dawdling on the top B flat she interrupts the rhythm of the phrase and almost undoes all the good of the honest adherence to the rest of the original note-values; but not quite. Toscanini's performance, however, is the true model for all time.

Alfredo, left alone, clearly does not understand the significance of Violetta's passionate outburst; he sits down to read a book, looks at the clock, and thinks perhaps it is too late for his father to come today. Violetta's servant Giuseppe enters to say that his mistress and Annina have left for Paris in a coach that was waiting for them; even this does not perturb Alfredo, although he can only have imagined that Violetta had gone out into the garden.

A messenger arrives with a letter from Violetta. Alfredo opens it and begins to read—not, as he hoped, a letter asking him to join her, but one which begins: 'Alfredo, by the time you read this . . .' Alfredo cries out and turns to fall into the arms of his father who has entered from the garden.

The elder Germont knows, of course, what has happened and tries to console his son by reminding him of their native Provence. While Alfredo sits at the table with his head in his hands Germont sings, "Di Provenza il mar, il suol . . ." ("The sea and earth of Provence . . ."):

Ex 153

Di Pro-ven-za il mar, il suol chi dal cor ti can-cel-lò?

Germont's aria, which aims to make Alfredo feel homesick, is one of the most popular numbers in *La traviata*. Musically, however, it is one of the least inspired passages in the opera; it is repetitive, un-interestingly orchestrated (the instrumentation and accompaniment of the two verses are identical); and not a little dull. Certainly it reaches nothing like the lyrical heights of the music Germont sings in his earlier scene with Violetta.

Alfredo is unmoved by his father's appeal. He is filled with jealousy, convinced that Violetta has gone off with Baron Douphol, and he will not listen to his father. Germont assures his son that he is not being reproved, only asked to forget the past—"No, non udrai rimproveri; copriam d'oblio il passato":

Ex 154

No, non ud-rai rim- pro-ve- ri; copriam d'oblio il pas - sa-to:

The group of four staccato semi-quavers so characteristic of Verdi's musical portrait of Germont occurs no fewer than seventeen times in the course of this short scene. It is virtually the only interest-ing point to be noted about this aria, however, which is usually com-pletely cut in performance.

The scene ends with Alfredo catching sight of Flora's invitation to Violetta. This confirms his worst suspicions; followed by his father, Alfredo rushes out of the house to go to the party and avenge himself on Violetta.

Scene 2 : A salon in Flora's house, which is richly furnished and brilliantly lighted. There is a door at the back and one on either side. To the right, down-stage, a gaming table ready for play ; on the left, a large table laden with flowers and refreshments. There are various chairs and a sofa.*

The curtain rises on Flora's party to the sound of some typical Verdi

---

* Italian opera houses still frequently describe this scene as Act III, in which case those hearing the opera for the first time must not expect the famous Act III Prelude at this point. This is played at the beginning of what the Italians call Act IV.

party music—Allegro brillante with the tune mostly in the wood-wind and plenty of piccolo. The hostess enters with the Marquis, the Doctor and other guests. In the course of conversation Flora announces that she has invited Violetta and Alfredo. "Haven't you heard the news?" asks the Marquis with surprise. "They have separated. She's coming here with the Baron."

This is certainly news to Flora and to the Doctor, who insists that he saw them only yesterday and they were perfectly happy. We hear no more on the subject, as the conversation is interrupted by the arrival of a company of Flora's female guests dressed up as gipsies. They tell us they are gipsies and can foretell the future; one group looks at Flora's palm, another at the Marquis'. This little charade is followed by the lively entrance of a chorus of male guests led by the untiring Gaston and dressed up as matadors and picadors. Having announced who and what they are from Madrid they tell a not-very-interesting story about a girl and a bullfighter in 3/8 time.

Neither of these party pieces inspires anything but pretty mediocre music. The most effective passage is the final 3/8 chorus when the men (who had obviously been invited to Violetta's party in Act I), remembering how effective that pp staccato sequence of the Brindisi had been, do much the same thing again now.

The entertainment has just come to an end when the atmosphere of the party is disturbed by the sudden arrival of Alfredo. He is alone, and the rumours that his affair with Violetta has come to an end are confirmed. Alfredo sits down at the card table and to a busy, excited theme the dramatic interest of the action revives:

Ex 155

This theme, introduced by clarinets, first violins and violas, is the musical pattern against which the scene now following is played. Gaston, who combines the position of entertainments manager with that of croupier, cuts the cards; Alfredo and others place their bets.

Ex 156

(Ah per-chè — ven-ni, in-cau-ta! Pie-tà, gran Dio, pietà gran Dio di me!)

Violetta enters on the arm of Baron Douphol. Flora greets them; the Baron remarks to Violetta that Alfredo is also present and forbids her to speak to him. In a moving, distraught aside Violetta laments that she has been so incautious as to come to the party and asks God to have pity on her (Ex 156).

This is the phrase, as I suggested on page 136, so clearly anticipated in *Il trovatore* and even earlier in the song "In solitaria stanza". But where in the earlier opera more or less the same notes served as a gentle expression of Leonora's love for the Troubadour, in this scene of *La traviata* they are filled with all the drama of a tense and moving situation—a wonderful example of Verdi's gift of being able to make the same musical idea mean two or three different things.

Violetta's despairing cry is heard three times in the course of this sequence, each time with a subtly different orchestration of the accompaniment. The first time the tune is doubled in the singer's register by an oboe with a solo bassoon an octave lower supported by first violins hinting at the melody with chuck-chucks—that is, on the second and third, fifth and sixth beats of the bar. The second time a clarinet is added to the oboe and the violoncellos join in with the bassoon; the first violins continue as before. The last time the off-beat figure is taken over by the second violins (still in the violoncello and bassoon register) while the first violins play the tune legato with oboe and clarinet. It is a simple process that increases the intensity of the accompaniment to match Violetta's growing anguish.

Meanwhile, Alfredo has been having fantastic luck at the card table, interspersing his bets with gratuitous insults directed at Violetta which, though she does not hear them, are overheard by the Baron. Douphol goes over to the table and takes a seat in the hope of winning back some of the money which Alfredo loudly announces he will use to buy back Violetta. Alfredo's luck still holds, however, but the game is interrupted by the announcement that supper is ready. Flora's guests troop off as the movement ends in a fading coda which leaves behind it a momentarily empty stage filled with a strange atmosphere of foreboding.

This gambling sequence is one of Verdi's most telling and ingenious scenes in which a remarkable air of tension is created by the simplest means. The busy figure in the orchestra, which is taken through some intriguing modulations and changes of instrumentation, scarcely rises above a whisper; even Violetta's unhappy outbursts do not interrupt the agitated flow of the music. Or, shall I say, should not? Because those bars in *Il trovatore* (Ex 89) are marked to be sung "con espansione" it has become common practice to slow up Violetta's three phrases, picking up the original tempo of the card music when she has finished. There is no authority for any such thing in Verdi's score, and Toscanini showed once and for all in his recording that when Violetta's three asides are kept rigidly *a tempo* the music has about it an indispensable nervous edginess which is lost if the tempo is ever relaxed.

Violetta returns to the empty room where she has asked Alfredo to join her. She begs him to leave the house at once; the Baron is angry and may kill him in a duel. Alfredo mockingly asks Violetta why she should worry about that. Violetta repeats her plea; Alfredo agrees to leave—on condition that she promises to follow him wherever he goes.

Violetta refuses; she has sworn not to see him. Sworn to whom? To Douphol? Violetta, with a supreme effort, replies, "Yes." "Then you love him?" cries Alfredo. Violetta answers, "Well, yes—I love him."

This bitter conversation takes place against a thumping, agitated figure in the strings which builds up to a climax as in a white-hot rage Alfredo goes to the doors of the upper room, flings them open and calls in the guests. He points to Violetta, who is leaning utterly humiliated against the table. "Do you know this woman? Do you know what she has done?" he cries.

In a short but vigorous passage Alfredo denounces Violetta— "Ogni suo aver tal femmina . . ." ("This woman would have squandered everything for love of me . . ."):

Ex *157*

It is a tight-lipped, vindictive denunciation, its brutality curiously underlined rather than weakened by the strict, unrelenting conventional rum-tum cabaletta rhythm of the accompaniment. Its climax is reached as Alfredo tells the guests, "I have called you in to witness that I have paid my debt!", and throws his winnings contemptuously at Violetta's feet.

Alfredo's action horrifies the assembled company and his fellow-guests turn on him in an angry unison with the full orchestra, telling

Ex *158*

him to leave at once. While the guests express their disgust at behaviour that has caused Violetta to faint in Flora's arms, the elder
Germont enters. His entrance silences the uproar and "with dignified fury" in the *grandioso* tones of Ex 158, he reproves and disowns
his son—"Dov'è mio figlio? più non lo vedo" ("Where is my son?
I do not see him"). Alfredo now begins to realize what he has
done—"Ah sì! che feci!":

Ex *159*

(Ah sì! che fe-ci!.. ne sento or-ro-re! Ge-losa smania delu-so a-more mi strazian l'alma

This brief, remorseful soliloquy leads into the final ensemble which
follows very closely the pattern of the second-act finale of *Macbeth**
where, it will be remembered, we found the same tempo, the same
characteristic 12/8 time on a 4/4 base, the sudden changes of dynamics from *ff* climaxes to *ppp* whispers, the same silent two-beat gaps
between phrases and the reiterated figure which keeps it all going.

Perhaps because of its obvious indebtedness to an ensemble
written seven operas earlier, this *Traviata* finale is sometimes considered rather disappointing. And certainly after the Quartet in
Rigoletto the characterization is not so careful or distinct as one would
expect. Chorus and principals comment on the general situation
according to what they think of things, but it is in words that they
express their individual point of view rather than in music. Once the
concerted movement gets going characters like Germont and Douphol who have plenty to say about things, are virtually swamped by
the sheer weight of the music as it were. Alfredo, for the most part,
is well defined, and Violetta revives for a moving solo passage—to
be sung, according to the composer's instructions, "with passion and
the weakest possible tone"—in which she tells Alfredo something of
the price she is paying—"Alfredo, Alfredo, di questo core . . ."
("You will never understand the love in my heart . . ."):

Ex *160*

Al-fre-do, Al-fre - do, Di ques-to co - re

This sequence, eighteen bars long altogether, is very much in
character, of course; but when it is over—which is much too soon

* See p 62.

—Violetta tends to become merely the principal soprano in a lovely
finale where hitherto she has been the principal character in the
drama. Because this ensemble has always been a favourite of mine
(it is surely one of the most infectiously tuneful concerted movements
in all Verdi), it is difficult to be sternly critical of it. It is just a wonderful noise and one must be unnaturally insensitive not to be swept
along by it. But there is little doubt I think that Verdi was more
absorbed in the music than in the drama when he allowed first
Alfredo and Germont, then Alfredo and Violetta to share a tune
like this between them in unison:

Ex *161*

At this stage in the action the three principal characters are
thinking very different thoughts, as we know from the words they
sing. They have nothing in common except possibly the anguish
caused by the whole situation; they should certainly not be expressing their individual thoughts by individual words to the same tune
—least of all in unison, for that implies at least some sort of
unanimity.

The general state of affairs at the height of the ensemble is that
Alfredo is ashamed of himself, the Baron speaks of punishing his
pride, Flora and her guests console Violetta, while Violetta herself
looks forward to the day when she will be able to tell Alfredo the
whole unhappy truth which Germont, for his part, regrets not being
able to tell at once.

The curtain falls with Germont leading his son away in disgrace,
and the rest of an embarrassed company dispersing in various
directions.

ACT III

Scene: Violetta's bedroom. At the back, a bed with half-drawn curtains; a closed window with inside shutters; beside the bed, a low table with a carafe of water, a glass, various medicines. In the centre, a dressing table with a sofa beside it; a little further away, another table with a night-light burning on it; several chairs and other pieces of furniture. The door is on the left; opposite it, a fireplace with a fire burning.

The curtain should rise at once, for what we have come to call formally the Prelude to Act III of *La traviata* is in fact the orchestral introduction to the number shown in the score as "No. 8, Scena ed Aria—Violetta", and intended by Verdi to reflect in music the sick-room scene we see on the stage.

Violetta is asleep in bed. Annina is dozing beside the fire. The overwhelming atmosphere of suspense and weariness created by the music is even more telling for our being able to see as well as hear what the music is about.

The first eight bars of this orchestral introduction are the same as those which open the Prelude to Act I, scored for eight first and eight second violins *divisi*, but this time a semitone higher and instructed to play *estremamente piano e assai legato*:

Ex *162*

The phrase leads straight into a long, exquisitely pathetic tune marked to be played "dolente" by all first violins in unison which begins:

Ex *163*

Once again we have the chamber-music orchestral proportions of the first act Prelude. The violins have the tune to themselves from start to finish, with a subdued minimum of accompaniment by strings and occasional woodwind (rarely more than one of each kind). It is the utter simplicity of the whole conception that makes this introduction almost unbearably moving—nowhere more so than in the coda with its characteristic weeping figure of falling semitones and the hushed dying away of the final trill, played first by all the first violins, then by four only, and finally by two.

As the orchestral introduction ends Violetta awakes, calling for Annina. "Were you asleep? You poor thing," says Violetta, as Annina rouses herself. Violetta's concern that she has disturbed Annina to fetch her a glass of water is a typical detail in the drawing of this most sympathetic of Verdi characters.

The duologue that ensues in recitative between mistress and servant is punctuated by the first and second short phrases from the opening (Ex 162) and the tearful coda of the prelude we have just heard. Annina goes to the window and opens the shutters; it is early morning and she sees Dr Grenvil coming through the garden towards the house. Violetta tries to get up from her bed and walk to the sofa in the middle of the room; but she is too weak and falls back. Annina helps her across the room, with the assistance of the Doctor who arrives at that moment.

Dr Grenvil feels his patient's pulse and asks how she has been. Violetta answers that she has gained great consolation from seeing a priest the evening before, and that she has slept well. The Doctor assures Violetta that it will not be long before she is convalescent; and shaking her by the hand he leaves. On his way out he tells Annina in confidence that her mistress has only a few hours to live.

Violetta asks Annina if today is a holiday. Annina replies that it is carnival and the whole of Paris is out in the streets. Indicating a drawer Violetta tells her she must take ten of the twenty louis it contains and give them to any poor people she can find; there are sure to be unhappy people even among the gay throngs outside.

Annina goes out. As soon as she is alone Violetta takes a letter from her bosom and reads it. She does not sing its contents to herself but reads it out loud "in a low speaking voice but in time" with the reprise of Alfredo's tune at the end of the first act, now played *pp* by

Ex 164

a solo first violin* against a tremolo accompaniment by one second
violin, two violas, a solo violoncello and another which supplies an
occasional pizzicato (see Ex 164).

"You kept your promise . . . The duel took place . . . The
Baron was wounded, but is recovering . . . Alfredo is abroad . . .
I told him myself of your sacrifice and he is returning to ask your
forgiveness . . . I also am coming . . . Take care of your health
. . . You deserve a happier future.—Giorgio Germont."

The device of reading instead of singing the contents of a letter in
opera was a long-standing tradition, of course (see page 48); and
where there was any music at all at such points it did not usually
amount to more than a chord sustained *ad lib* by the orchestra. In
this scene in *La traviata* the emotional effect of the reading is intensified by Verdi's dramatic quotation of a tune with strong associations played as a plaintive background by a string sextet.

When she has read the letter Violetta rises and looks at herself
in the mirror. She is pale; she tries to convince herself that the doctor
is right, that she is getting better; but in her own mind she is certain
there is no hope.

In one of the simplest and most moving of all Verdi arias Violetta
sings of her vanished dreams; she laments, above all, the absence of
Alfredo and cries that for her everything is finished. "Farewell", she
sings, "to those dreams of the past"—"Addio del passato":

Ex *165*

There are in fact two verses to this aria; the second is a note-for-
note replica of the first with different words, and is usually cut.
Rightly, I think, for I find one is harrowed enough by hearing it
once through.† The simplicity of means by which Verdi makes his
effect is remarkable and characteristic. An oboe echoes or anticipates the voice from time to time; the tune broadens into C major
with a minimum of accompaniment—a flute, an oboe, a clarinet
supporting the voice against the unobtrusive chuck-chucks of the
strings; the opening A minor phrase is transformed into the major
with that familiar and effective background of throbbing divided

---

* The score asks for two solo violins in unison, but the intonation is always safer
with one, which is how one hears it in Toscanini's recording, for instance.

† Those who want to hear it in full can do so by listening to Joan Sutherland's
Decca–London recording of the opera (1963).

strings we know from *Rigoletto* and *Il trovatore*. The aria ends, as it began, in the minor, and dies away with what the composer describes as a mere "thread of voice" coming from Violetta.

A sound of noisy singing and revelry breaks in on the silence of the scene as a rowdy carnival crowd passes by outside. It is a short *vivacissimo* sequence more remarkable for its high spirits than its musical quality and is accompanied off stage by a remarkable instrumental combination consisting of two piccolos, four clarinets, two horns, two trombones, tambourines and tabors (drums). The orchestration is most unusual and includes some startling glissando passages for the trombone.

This carnival chorus outside Violetta's window has been described as trite and uninteresting, but what company of noisy revellers is ever anything else? The very mediocrity of the interlude, with its unwittingly callous lack of concern for the woman dying before our eyes, creates a dramatic contrast which might have lost much of its effectiveness if the music had been on the same level as the rest of the act.

When the Bacchanal is over Annina enters full of suppressed excitement, asking her mistress anxiously if she is sure she is all right and to keep calm; she has a great surprise for her. A breathless figure in the orchestra builds up in a hectic crescendo as Violetta guesses that Alfredo must be outside. The door opens and the lovers rush into each other's arms.

In the same impetuous tempo Violetta and Alfredo sing a short duet—Alfredo asking forgiveness, Violetta crying ecstatically that all is forgiven, and that from now on neither man nor devil shall ever separate them. The excitement dies down and a quiet modulation brings us to another duet, which Alfredo, with one of Verdi's most graceful tunes, begins with "Parigi, o cara" ("We will leave Paris together") :

Ex *166*

Pa - ri - gi, o ca - ra noi la - sce - re - mo

Violetta echoes his words and the duet, which has all the yearning beauty of "Ai nostri monti", ends on a serenely happy note with a series of delicate staccato and *pp* passages for divided strings that echoes the end of the great duet in *Il trovatore*.

When the duet finishes Violetta suggests that she and Alfredo should go to church to give thanks for his return. But as she tries to get up and dress she falls back weakly into a chair. She declares it is nothing, and with trills in the orchestra supporting her own trills to prove it, she insists that she is better; she is strong and smiling. Violetta stands up to put on the cloak Annina holds for her, but she is too exhausted and collapses into the chair. Alfredo tells Annina to fetch the doctor. "Tell him", says Violetta, "that Alfredo has returned and that I want to live."

With a quick painful movement Violetta stands up and there is a new desperate force in her voice as she sings "Gran Dio! morir sì giovane"—("Great God, that I should die so young! . . ."):

Ex 167

This theme, with a firm four-in-a-bar pizzicato accompaniment, develops into a short duet which in practice is usually a very much shorter one than the composer intended. It is customary to limit this scene to Violetta's full sixteen bars which are followed by Alfredo's repetition of them, and then cut straight to the unison coda. This does away with two or three uninteresting and very conventional passages including a sequence in which Alfredo echoes Violetta and Violetta sings the words and music of all sixteen bars of the opening "Gran Dio" in full all over again, with some whispered words of sympathy from Alfredo. There is no doubt that the cut is an improvement.

After a final cadenza à deux Violetta collapses on the sofa. Germont and the Doctor arrive. Violetta embraces Alfredo's father who is shocked to see her so ill and in a condition for which he believes himself to be entirely responsible. She turns to Dr Grenvil and says, "Do you see? I die in the arms of all those I love best in the world."

Violetta opens a drawer in her dressing table and takes from it a medallion which she gives to Alfredo. In a monotone she tells him to take it; it is a portrait painted when she was younger which will help him to remember the one who loved him so much—"Prendi, quest'è l'immagine de' miei passati giorni". The whole orchestra, from flutes to bass drum, accompanies these lines *pianissimo* in a familiar elegiac rhythm:

Ex 168

Rhythm, dynamics and orchestration may be those of the Miserere in *Il trovatore* but in the context of *La traviata* the thumping ostinato of the earlier opera somehow loses its sinister Gothic character and adds a strangely pathetic emphasis to the words of a tired, dying woman.

The heavy, relentless figure continues spasmodically as Violetta tells Alfredo, in a gentle change of key for what is virtually the last episode in the opera, to show her portrait to the young girl whom he will one day marry:

"Tell her", Violetta says, "that it came from one who will be praying for her in heaven." As Violetta repeats these words a simple ensemble develops in which Alfredo, Annina, Germont and Dr Grenvil express their grief in their own ways. It is a subdued movement ended by the *pppp* tremolo of four violins. Played scarcely above a whisper by a small group of violins and violas we hear Alfredo's theme from the first act, the theme which accompanied Violetta's reading of Germont's letter earlier in this scene (Ex 164) now played in the higher key of A major.

In a quiet voice, half speaking, half singing, Violetta tells of a sudden feeling of life surging within her; her pulse begins to beat again, and she is regaining her strength. With a final ecstatic cry, "I am coming back to life! Oh joy! . . .", Violetta falls back dead. The curtain is brought down by a few dramatic bars during which the surviving characters are heard to lament Violetta's death (confirmed by Dr Grenvil's feeling her pulse). Toscanini included the voice parts in this coda; most other conductors do not. It doesn't matter much, either way. The curtain still falls on an unmistakable masterpiece.

There is no other opera by Verdi which has quite the peculiar charm and appeal of *La traviata*. The reason for this, I think, is that like the character of Violetta herself it has the unique quality of being life-size; emotions, dramatic situations are on such an intimate, everyday scale that we feel it could all happen to us. Some of this feeling of reality is obviously due to the origin of the subject, for we know that the Marguérite Gautier of Dumas' play was modelled on the real-life *demi-mondaine* Marie Duplessis. But it is in the end Verdi's music which brings Violetta so vividly to life as a figure in whom the characteristics of so many other Verdi heroines are uniquely combined. Something of the passion and tenderness of Amelia in *Un ballo in maschera*, the pathos and dignity of Desdemona, the devotion of Gilda and Aida, the charm and gaiety of Mistress Ford—these are all qualities that contribute to a peculiarly sympathetic and attractive character whom one regards with an affection one cherishes for no other heroine in opera.

Affection, indeed, is perhaps what one feels above all things for *La traviata* altogether. Certainly it is a work whose shortcomings one tends to overlook, turning a benevolent, uncritical, if not quite deaf, ear to musical lapses like the fancy dress party pieces, precisely because one loves the opera as a whole so much. In any case, even the weak musical sequences have their indispensable place in the dramatic development of *La traviata*. One could not cut the gipsies and the matadors, even if one wanted to, without destroying the atmosphere of frivolity which is essential to the continuity of the action. But even if one winces at the less satisfactory musical moments of *La traviata* as they occur and one's affection is not enough to forgive them altogether, one is surely made to forget them by yet another magnificent last act—the third in a row, and comparable to its immediate predecessors, the final scenes of *Rigoletto* and *Il trovatore*.

Abramo Basevi, an Italian critic writing only six years after the first production of *La traviata*, described Verdi's music to this opera as "chamber music". It is a happy phrase, not just in the technical sense that there is an unfamiliar instrumental intimacy from the very first notes of the Prelude to Act I (scored for a smaller orchestra than Wagner's *Siegfried Idyll*, for instance), but because everything in the drama and the music is scaled down to our size; in a curious and unmistakable way we are drawn into the action which takes place, not the other side of the footlights, but in the same room as ourselves. Unlike the murders and burnings, the suicides and angry vows of revenge of *Il trovatore*, the tears and laughter, the sadness and gaiety of *La traviata* are within the range of our own experience and so become real.

It is this peculiar reality and the rare tenderness pervading the music which more than anything give *La traviata* its unique quality and make Violetta perhaps the most lovable and touching of all Verdi's heroines.

SIMON BOCCANEGRA

Melodrama in a Prologue and three acts. Libretto by Francesco Maria Piave, based on a play by Antonio García Gutiérrez. First performed at the Teatro la Fenice, Venice, on 12th March, 1857. Revised version first performed at La Scala, Milan, on 24th March, 1881. First performance in England: Sadler's Wells Theatre, London, 27th October, 1948. First performance in the United States: Metropolitan Opera House, New York, 28th January, 1932.

As HAPPENED in the case of *Macbeth*, the strict chronological sequence of this study is inevitably disturbed when we come to *Simon Boccanegra*. Once again we have an opera written and performed at one stage of the composer's life and then thoroughly revised many years later to be performed in the form we know today. In the case of *Simon Boccanegra* the interval between first and second thoughts was even longer than it had been with *Macbeth*. The first version of *Simon Boccanegra* is separated from *La traviata* only by *I vespri siciliani*, composed for the Paris Opera as *Les Vêpres Siciliennes* and produced there in 1855. The second version of *Simon Boccanegra* belongs to a period a quarter of a century later when Verdi, then aged sixty-eight, had all the experience of *Un ballo in maschera*, *La forza del destino*, *Don Carlos*, *Aida* and the Requiem behind him. There were only *Otello* and *Falstaff* to come. It was a revision, in other words, made by the composer at the height of his powers.

The original *Simon Boccanegra* was written under a contract agreed in 1856 with the management of the Teatro la Fenice who, in spite of the notorious fiasco of *La traviata* at their theatre three years before, were nevertheless willing to commission another opera from Verdi. How Verdi came to choose the subject of his fifth Fenice opera is not clear. One can only suppose that he unearthed Gutiérrez's play *Simon Boccanegra* in the same way that he came across the same author's *El Trovador*—in the course of that incessant, untiring, pig-like routing for dramatic truffles which is every great opera composer's instinct. Gutiérrez, it seems, was for some time Spanish consul in Genoa and his dramatic treatment of a famous episode in Genoese history obviously struck a bell with Verdi, who made his winter quarters for nearly fifty years in the city where streets and piazzas bear names made familiar by this opera—Boccanegra, Adorno, Fieschi, Grimaldi. (The British Consulate, if ever you need it in Genoa, is in the via Fieschi.)

By an ironical coincidence the pattern of the genesis of *Simon Boccanegra* was curiously like that of *Macbeth*. In both cases Verdi

7*

made a detailed prose draft of the libretto before passing it over to Piave to put into verse.* In both cases when Piave had finished his work Verdi called in another writer to add new verses and touch up the old. With *Macbeth* it was Andrea Maffei (see p 39); with *Simon Boccanegra* it was Giuseppe Montanelli, a Tuscan poet and politician whom Verdi had met in exile in Paris. In both cases only Piave was credited as librettist on the title-page. Even the revised version of *Simon Boccanegra*, which appeared five years after his death and was the work of another man, bears only Piave's name.

When *Simon Boccanegra* was finally performed in Venice in 1851 it was a failure—the second consecutive Verdi opera to flop at the Fenice. Verdi was characteristically calm about it. The morning after the première he wrote to Vincenzo Torelli, the director of the San Carlo Theatre, Naples: "*Boccanegra* was as big a fiasco as *La traviata*. I thought I had written something passable, but it seems I was wrong."

Although it was initially a failure, whereas *Macbeth* had done comparatively well in its original version, *Simon Boccanegra* inspired in Verdi much the same sort of affection as the earlier opera had done. Whether it was due to a sentimental attachment to the opera's Genoese setting, to the feeling that he had not originally made his dramatic points clear to the public, or both, Verdi after some hesitation agreed when in 1880 his publisher Giulio Ricordi suggested he should revise *Simon Boccanegra*. At that time Verdi had written nothing since the Requiem in 1874, and though he was considering seriously in private Boito's plans for an Othello opera he deliberately gave the impression in public that he had had enough. The first objection he raised to Ricordi's suggestion was not only that it would involve considerable re-working of the score, amounting in many cases to long stretches of brand-new music, but that the text of the whole of the second act needed completely rewriting, and who would do that? Ricordi replied that he had just the man for the job, and enrolled Boito who may well have been reluctant to act as rewrite man on a pretty hopeless assignment, but who undertook it nevertheless out of regard for Verdi and in doing so strengthened the unique association which gave us *Otello* and *Falstaff*.

* The prose draft of *Simon Boccanegra* involved Verdi in yet another ludicrous skirmish with the Austrian Censor in Venice, when it was submitted for his approval. The Censor demanded to see the verses of the libretto before he would pass it. When he heard this Verdi wrote to the unhappy Piave, who had been the middle man in all the trouble over *Rigoletto*: "What does it matter if it is in prose or verse? What I sent is not a synopsis but the libretto the Censorship has to approve. . . . I am contracted to write an opera for the Carneval season at the Teatro la Fenice and this time, for the sake of novelty, I am setting a prose libretto to music!"

CHARACTERS IN ORDER OF SINGING

PROLOGUE

PAOLO ALBIANI, *a Genoese goldsmith* . . Baritone
PIETRO, *a Genoese citizen* . . . . Baritone
SIMON BOCCANEGRA, *Corsair in the service of*
the Genoese republic . . . . . Baritone
JACOPO FIESCO, *a Genoese noble* . . . Bass

Sailors, workmen, Fiesco's servants etc.

THE OPERA

MARIA BOCCANEGRA, *daughter of Simon*
Boccanegra, but known as Amelia Grimaldi . Soprano
GABRIELE ADORNO, *a Genoese noble* . . Tenor
PIETRO, *a courtier* . . . . . Baritone
JACOPO FIESCO, *under the name of Andrea* . Bass
SIMON BOCCANEGRA, *first Doge of the Republic*
of Genoa . . . . Baritone
PAOLO ALBIANI, *his favourite courtier* . . Baritone
A SERVANT OF AMELIA . . . . Soprano
CAPTAIN OF THE ARCHERS . . . Tenor

Soldiers, sailors, citizens, senators, members of the Doge's household, courtiers, etc.

Scene: Genoa and the neighbourhood   Time: The middle of
the fourteenth century

PROLOGUE

Scene: A piazza in Genoa. In the background, the church of San Lorenzo. On the right, the palace of the Fieschi, with a large balcony; on the wall, flanking the balcony, is a figure of the Madonna with a light burning before it. On the left there are other houses. Several streets lead into the square. It is night.

Since in the ordinary way of opera-going the listener is more likely to have heard *Aida* and *Otello* before getting a chance to hear *Simon Boccanegra* (which was not produced at Covent Garden, for instance, until 1965) the idiom of the short orchestral introduction for strings which precedes the rise of the curtain on the Prologue will be familiar enough. The introduction is built around a dark and gloomy sort of theme which Verdi characteristically carries over to punctuate the dialogue of the scene that follows:

Ex *170*

Verdi in his later operas made an effective practice of beginning a scene with a couple of characters who, like those in Shakespeare's plays, enter continuing a conversation that has obviously been going on for some time off stage. Act I of *Aida* and Act III of *Otello* both begin in this way and, like this sequence in *Simon Boccanegra*, it is largely done to a smooth-running string accompaniment.

The two characters discovered in earnest and conspiratorial conversation as the curtain rises on *Simon Boccanegra* are Paolo Albiani and his friend Pietro. Paolo is the leader of the Plebeian party whose political feud with the Patricians is the background of the story. Paolo and Pietro are planning to overthrow their aristocratic opponents and elect a Plebeian as ruler. In the conversation that begins the scene they are discussing the material advantages that would follow this move—not in the familiar recitative of the Verdi operas we have encountered so far (although some of the melodic line of the old recitative is still discernible), but in a finely developed and dramatic declamatory style.

Paolo and Pietro agree to nominate Simon Boccanegra, the Corsair who has kept Genoa's seas clear of African pirates, and Pietro goes off to organize the people's vote. The election is to take place at dawn—which leaves little time for canvassing or anything in the way of a campaign, for Boccanegra himself has heard nothing about any of this yet. Paolo has sent for him, however, and on his arrival he has everything explained to him. Boccanegra is at first all against standing for election, but is persuaded by Paolo of the power that is held by the man who is to be elected the first Doge of the Genoese Republic. As Doge, Boccanegra is reminded, he will be able at last to marry the patrician Fiesco's daughter Maria, whom he loves and by whom he has had an illegitimate child. Boccanegra asks Paolo what he knows of Maria. He replies, pointing to the Fieschi's palace, that she is kept a prisoner by her father—"but who could deny her to the Doge?" adds Paolo. Boccanegra consents to stand as candidate and leaves the scene.

As Boccanegra leaves Paolo withdraws to one side by the Fieschi's palace. Sailors and workmen, followed by Pietro, gradually fill the piazza in a stealthily conspiratorial manner. The crowd comes on to a hushed orchestral sequence which is a long way removed from the familiar conspiracy-music we knew so well from our earlier Verdi. This has a new lightness of tread, with its pizzicato rising on the dominant and tonic notes only of the chord through the violoncellos, the violas to the violins. It is nothing to look at on paper but in performance this simple string and woodwind passage creates a remarkable atmosphere of whispered plot-hatching. Pietro, *sempre a mezzavoce*, tells his sailors and workmen something of the valiant character of the "man of the people" he is asking them to vote for at dawn. The chorus, as good electors should, ask one or two questions, which Pietro answers satisfactorily while the orchestral background continues to give a "pre-echo", as it were, of two operas Verdi had yet to write—*Otello* and *Falstaff*. The purely instrumental quality of the sequence looks forward very clearly to the bonfire scene in the first act of *Otello*, and there is what may well be the first try-out of a purely rhythmic pattern which was to become very characteristic of Verdi's last two operas. Its melodic properties are not very distinguished in this case but its rhythm is unmistakably the shape of much that was to come:

Ex *171*

The chorus asks its questions in unison, which is not at all like any election meeting I've ever been to—at least, not until the speaker refuses to answer. The chorus breaks out into a four-part chord for the first time when, in answer to their question, they hear the name of the man they are to vote for. It is Paolo, not Pietro, who answers them. Coming out of the shadows he cries, "Simone Boccanegra!" The chorus, *ff*, echoes with surprise, "Simone!" and then, *subito sottovoce*, whispers in unison, "il Corsaro!"

The four bars taken up by this episode are very typical of the changes a quarter of a century's experience caused Verdi to make in the score of *Simon Boccanegra*. The dramatic impact of the crowd's whispered, shocked reception of the news that a former freebooter is to be the new Doge is incomparably more subtle and effective than in the original version where the chorus had bellowed out the words "il Corsaro!" *sempre ff*.

Paolo is asked what the Fieschi will do; he replies that they will say nothing, and gathering the crowd round him he points to the Fieschi's palace and prepares to address them "con mistero". His actions are accompanied by a theme played in unison by the strings which plays a small part later in the opera as a phrase associated with Jacopo Fiesco himself:

Paolo now embarks on a little address to the chorus in which he reminds them of the beautiful girl who weeps in the "sombre dwelling" which is the "evil lair of the Fieschi"—"L'atra magion vedete?" ("Do you see the sombre dwelling?") :

The topic is obviously not new to the chorus, for they contribute their own details to the narrative; one can only suppose that the scene is intended to keep the audience informed about things. And if one is inevitably reminded of Ferrando's storytelling at the beginning of *Il trovatore* then that is hardly surprising either, of course, since both operas were based on plays by Gutiérrez who was much given to this familiar theatrical device.

The scene between Paolo and his co-operative audience is a relic of the original version of the opera and is distinguished by an accompaniment of some effective string writing (the strings in both new and old versions play a considerable part in the Prologue) and the dramatic use of unison and dynamic contrasts in the choral passages.

The company is busy reflecting in hushed tones on the horrors of the whole set-up when a light suddenly appears in the palace. Paolo sends the crowd away, bidding them make the sign of the cross against evil spirits and reminding them to vote for Boccanegra in the morning. The crowd promise to do so and disperse into the night to the sounds of an effectively simple orchestral postlude which dies away with the open fifth of E–B held by flute and oboe.

Loud and solemn sustained unison notes in the strings punctuated by *pp* chords in the brass accompany Jacopo Fiesco as he comes out of the palace. He turns to look at it and bidding farewell to the building that has become the cold tomb of his dying daughter, curses the man who seduced her.

Fiesco now sings what, thanks to its frequent inclusion in LP recitals by bass singers, is virtually the only single number from *Simon Boccanegra* that ever finds its way into the record catalogues— the moving lament, "Il lacerato spirito" ("A father's broken heart"):

Ex *174*

Those who know this number only as an excerpt from the opera can have little idea of its poignant effect in its proper context. It is by no means just a pleasingly tuneful bass solo accompanied in its first stages by sombre brass chords and drum beats, as they might suppose. The gaps between Fiesco's phrases are filled, not by the plaintive woodwind chords one hears when the aria is sung in its concert form, but by the off-stage voices of women crying that Maria is dead. Verdi sets the words "è morta!" in four parts to one of his typical weeping phrases (in this case the familiar falling semitone) sung with an initial *forte* that dies down quickly to *piano*. The women's cries, an effect obviously derived from the single off-stage unison "è morta!" which announced the death of Lady Macbeth (see p 75), alternate with repeated unison *pp* mutterings of "Miserere!" by tenors and basses (also off stage) sometimes to a monotone, sometimes echoing the tearful phrase of the women. The orchestral accompaniment to this scene is of the utmost simplicity, played only by tremolo strings.

A sequence of great pathos, which belongs entirely to the first version of the opera, ends with a lengthy affecting orchestral coda during which various people—a priest, mourners and others—come out of the palace and walk sadly across the piazza, leaving Fiesco alone in the shadows. The coda itself consists of little more than the strings, still tremolo, playing this phrase twice:

Ex 175

The monotonous effect of a passing bell is added by a single note on a trumpet, played on the second beat of each bar until the postlude dies away with the violoncellos' echo of the women's tears and the men's "Miserere".

Boccanegra returns in an exultant mood. His name is on all lips, and soon, he says to himself, he will be able to marry Maria. Fiesco comes out of the shadow and recognizing Boccanegra asks him in a powerful, angry phrase what has brought him there, the man on whose head he has invoked the vengeance of God—"Qual cieco fato . . . ?":

Ex 176

The ferocity of this opening is underlined by the violoncellos and bassoons playing the tune in unison with the voice and adding an angry trill on the D in the third bar which makes one think of Iago's "Credo" in *Otello* at once. In fact, however, the whole of the magnificent scene between the two men which now follows dates from the original *Simon Boccanegra*, though clearly some of the details of the accompaniments were later revisions—particularly, I should say, a recurrent string figure which is heard in the early part of this scene and is heard again, slightly altered in the minor, not only here but much later in the opera—

Ex 177

In this case the figure is heard as Boccanegra throws himself at Fiesco's feet and begs forgiveness. Fiesco retorts that it is too late. Boccanegra, abandoning his fine declamatory manner for a moment, launches out in a rather martial, early-Verdi eight bars with an early-Verdi accompaniment, to proclaim how he had hoped to be worthy of Maria and had "snatched the laurels of victory from the altar of love". Fiesco is immovable. In despair Boccanegra offers his life in retribution, baring his breast and bidding Fiesco stab him. Fiesco draws back proudly. He is no assassin. "Kill me," pleads Boccanegra to an agitated version of Ex 177 in E minor, "and at least your anger will be buried with me." After a long pause Fiesco agrees to forgive Boccanegra on one condition: he must hand over the child born to him and Maria.

Fiesco makes his demand in an unexpectedly gentle and touching passage which is accompanied, as so often in this opera, mainly by strings—"Se concedermi vorrai":

Ex *178*

Boccanegra replies that his is unable to bring the child to Fiesco. He explains that the old woman to whom the child has been entrusted has been murdered and the child herself has never been seen since. Boccanegra tells his story in a simple little 3/8 tune beginning in F minor—"Del mar sul lido":

Ex *179*

Although this starts out as if it were going to be a formal aria, after an abrupt transition from A flat to E major all thoughts of recapitulation and the like are forgotten when Fiesco tells Boccanegra that if he cannot find the child there can be no peace between them. Fiesco ignores Boccanegra's pleas, and, turning his back on him, goes back into the shadows to watch. The unhappy Boccanegra decides he must see Maria whatever happens. He knocks at the door of the Fiesco palace, but there is no answer; finding the door open he goes inside and after a moment appears on the balcony. There is nothing but silence and darkness in the deserted palace. Boccanegra takes the lantern from the wall beside the statue of the Virgin and goes into the house once more. His anguished cry of "Maria!" as he discovers her body is heard inside the palace, and Fiesco remarks grimly that the hour of punishment has sounded. A moment later Boccanegra staggers out into the piazza. Voices in the distance are heard crying jubilantly, "Boccanegra!" As he stands heart-broken and dazed Boccanegra is triumphantly hailed as the first Doge of Genoa by the crowds that pour excitedly into the piazza. It is a situation of first-rate dramatic irony. Unfortunately, Verdi did not quite write the music to go with it. The scene ends to the sounds of a *banda* tune (plenty of piccolo) that is almost too banal to be true—

Ex *180*

In theory perhaps the contrast of this ludicrous quick step and Boccanegra's grief ought to point the irony of the situation with tremendous effect, but in practice nothing of the kind happens. It is just a plain, hopeless anticlimax which not even the loud ringing of bells as the curtain falls can save.

ACT I

PART ONE

Scene: The garden of the Grimaldi Palace outside Genoa. On the left is the palace; in the background, a distant view of the sea. Dawn is just breaking.

According to a note in the score, a period of twenty-five years has elapsed since the action of the Prologue. This is obviously a clerical error on the part of Gutiérrez or Piave, for if history is followed faithfully this would mean that Act I began the year after Simon Boccanegra's death—he was elected Doge in 1339, abdicated in 1344, re-elected in 1356, and died of poisoning in 1363.

However, Verdi was not setting a history book to music; perhaps if he had been some of the typical Gutiérrez confusion and obscurity that begins to cloud the opera from now on might have been avoided.

Before the curtain rises on the first scene of Act I there is a short orchestral prelude which Verdi wrote for the second version of the opera. It is an evocative passage of "mood music", full of muted violin trills and bird noises which feature the piccolo and include a couple of convincing but—orthithologically—undefined calls by oboe and clarinet. It is all *pp* and very much in the treble clef, with nothing the violoncellos play in their few little seven-note cantabile phrases that goes below the range of the violin.

As the curtain rises Amelia is seen gazing out to sea. At least, Amelia is the name the young lady goes by in the opera, even after she is discovered to be what the audience has already been told on the programme—Maria, natural daughter of Simon Boccanegra.

Amelia reflects on the dawn, the sky, the sea; on the "black, cruel night" long ago when her old nurse died; on how, though she lives in the splendours of the Grimaldi palace, she will never forget the humble abode in which she was brought up; on how her only joy is her love for the young man whose song she is waiting to hear. Amelia tells us all this in "Come in quest'ora bruna" ("How, in the morning haze . . .") :

Ex *181*

It is not a very distinguished aria, but it has an effective rustling strings and woodwind accompaniment scored with the same imaginative lightness of touch as the brief orchestral prelude played before the rise of the curtain. Its most unexpected moment is the bare fifths for wind which accompany Amelia's recollection of her nurse's dying words—"Ti guardi il ciel!" ("Heaven protect you!").

As soon as Amelia has finished the second "verse", which is scored with astonishing skill for the whole orchestra playing *ppp*, the voice of Gabriele is heard in the distance with an off-stage harp accompaniment, singing an aubade. The song seems to consist of only eight bars which, after an interval filled with excited cries of anticipation from Amelia, Gabriele repeats as he comes nearer. For a moment we are back in the musical world of *Il trovatore*.

Amelia greets her lover passionately, though not without asking him why he is late. Gabriele apologizes; he was delayed by business that will lead to great things. Amelia's mood becomes anxious at once. Why does he meet and conspire with Andrea and the others at night? She knows it will all lead to trouble and bring Gabriele to the gallows. Gabriele implores her not to speak so loud; walls have ears. Amelia points across the sea to Genoa where Gabriele's enemies are in power and begs him to give up his plotting and planning—"Vieni a mirar la cerula marina tremolante" ("Come, look at the blue shimmering sea . . ."). Amelia sings the opening phrase in a monotone against a simple 3/8 string figure in an accompaniment that flutters and chirrups rather than shimmers. She pleads with her lover in all the colourful metaphors of the original libretto of *Simon Boccanegra* to steer his thoughts to "the port of love"—

Ex 182

This phrase, with its first four bars which were to prove such an ever-present help in trouble to the composer of the familiar waltz called "Die lustige Brüder", is followed by sixteen bars for Gabriele interpolated in the 1881 revision and bringing a new melodic elegance to the duet that is very striking. Gabriele's gentle contribution takes us into the dominant for a moment, but Verdi returns to the tune of Ex 182, sung this time by Gabriele, echoed by Amelia and leading to an entrancing cadence that ends with one of those sudden surprising harmonic twists which were so characteristic of the composer—in this case a sequence progressing directly from G, to E flat (*ff*), E (*ppp*), D⁷ to G. It is a ravishing end to a charming duet.

A servant announces that a messenger from the Doge wishes to see Amelia. The messenger is Pietro, who enters to say that the Doge wishes Amelia to receive him. Amelia says he will be welcome, and Pietro leaves. She tells the anxious Gabriele that the Doge is coming to ask her to marry his favourite, Paolo. The only way out is for Gabriele to marry her at once; he must go and find Andrea quickly. In a short Allegro brillante duet of little musical distinction the lovers swear eternal fidelity in frequent and excited unison. Amelia goes into the palace. Gabriele turns to leave the garden and meets Andrea.

Andrea, of course, is Fiesco in disguise and although he is referred to by his assumed name in the action (only Gabriele knows his true identity), in the score and stage instructions he still goes by the same name as in the Prologue. As Andrea, Fiesco seems to stand *in loco parentis* for Amelia, though it is not quite clear how he came to do so nor how long ago. Gabriele asks Fiesco to consent to his marriage to Amelia, but Fiesco warns him that things are not what they seem. For a start, Amelia is not a Grimaldi. In a passage of admirable declamatory narration Fiesco relates how the real Grimaldi child died in a convent in Pisa—or, as the original Italian so poetically puts it, "among consecrated virgins in Pisa". A foundling was brought up in her place and given the name of Amelia Grimaldi in order to prevent the property of the real exiled Grimaldis being confiscated by the vindictive new Doge. (Why, once they were thought to have passed into the possession of a female Grimaldi these properties should have been less liable to confiscation is not explained. Perhaps as an ex-pirate Boccanegra had a professional sense of chivalry towards women.)

Gabriele is not in the least put out by all these revelations and asks for Amelia's hand. Fiesco gives his consent and blessing in a Sostenuto religioso in which Gabriele joins. It is a solemn passage preceded by a solemn brass introduction:

Ex *183*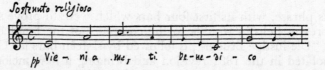

Although Gabriele contributes a couple of cadences which show it was written after the Requiem, Fiesco's benediction is sadly typical of the unimpressive music Verdi wrote when he set out to be deliberately "religious" in the theatre. When there was a dramatic justification for religious music, as in the Miserere in *Il trovatore*, or when he was inspired by the drama of a religious subject, such as the

Requiem and the Four Sacred Pieces he wrote in the last years of his life, it was another matter. At this point in *Simon Boccanegra* there is little dramatic reason that I can see why Fiesco should suddenly assume a clerical accent. You don't *have* to sound like a parson to wish a bridegroom luck.

In the first version of the opera there was a change of scene at this point. In the revised edition this is done away with. An off-stage fanfare announces the Doge's approach, and Fiesco and Gabriele leave; Amelia enters from the left accompanied by her attendants. Boccanegra comes in from the right with Paolo and a group of hunters. After a few words from the Doge about the serious situation in Genoa, Paolo, the hunters and Amelia's attendants leave him alone with Amelia.

Boccanegra (who is now always called the Doge in the stage directions and vocal score) tells Amelia that he has decided to pardon the two exiled Grimaldis whom he supposes to be her brothers. Having put her in a sympathetic frame of mind Boccanegra asks Amelia if she is really happy living a life of such seclusion at her age (Amelia must be at least twenty-six, if not more, which is quite an age for an unmarried lady in fourteenth-century Italy). Amelia replies that she is not lonely; she is in love with a noble-spirited man, but she is pestered by an evil suitor who obviously wants to marry her for the Grimaldi money. Most of this conversation takes place against a violin figure which the singers join when their vocal registers allow it:

Ex 184

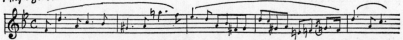

Boccanegra guesses correctly that Amelia's unwelcome suitor is Paolo. She then tells him that she is not a Grimaldi. She is an orphan brought up by a poor woman in Pisa—"Orfanella il tetto umile":

Ex 185

Or-fa - nel - la il tet -to u- mi-le m'acco- glie-a, d'u-na me- schi - na

In her sad narrative, prefaced by a plaintive anticipation of the tune by an oboe, and with a simple string accompaniment, Amelia tells how before she died the old woman had given her a locket containing the portrait of her mother. Amelia's words raise a faint, impossible hope in Boccanegra. He turns aside and prays to heaven that if he is dreaming he may die before he wakes up—"Ah! se la speme, o ciel clemente". Up to this point most of the music of this scene comes from the original version of *Simon Boccanegra*. From here on, however, much of the duet that develops is either new or the old one in an extensively revised and re-orchestrated form. The movements which began with Ex 185 ends with another of Verdi's characteristic and unexpected harmonic cadences.

Boccanegra asks Amelia to tell him more, and like his first series of questions and her answers to them, the conversation takes place to an agitated accompaniment in which the violins develop a phrase with much the same character as Ex 184. Boccanegra takes a miniature from his doublet. He compares it with Amelia's, and with a cry of joy recognizes her as his daughter Maria, whose mother, Maria Fiesco, died twenty-five years ago. Father and daughter embrace at a *ff* orchestral climax of a kind most unusual in Verdi which dies away slowly on a pedal C held for twelve bars taking us, by a rather Wagnerian process of a four-bar phrase played three times, from C major to the F major of the final pages of the duet.

As may be imagined, what follows now is not "about" anything very much. Father and daughter rejoice and look forward to joys to come in an effective and stirring duet begun by Boccanegra, to the accompaniment of a firm pizzicato and sustained woodwind chords, with the tune shown in Ex 186 to which I have added the exquisite little cadence (A) with which it ends and which plays a most moving part in the scene:

Ex *186*

At the end of their first passage together Amelia and Boccanegra sing the cadence (A) in unison with wonderful effect; at the end of a short, more animated interlude, they sing it in harmony, at which point the orchestra plays, as a brief postlude and *con espressione*, the beginning of Boccanegra's tune in Ex 186. The climax comes, behind a final couple of sustained notes by the singers, with the cadence (A) now played *fortissimo* by the orchestra.

The music dies down suddenly to *pp* as Amelia, to the sound of a series of harp arpeggios, goes slowly towards the Palace, watched "ecstatically" by her father. When she is out of sight Boccanegra sings—on a top F—the word "figlia" ("daughter") once more, and the final harp arpeggios die away.

Paolo enters hurriedly to ask Boccanegra how his suit is progressing. The Doge tells him bluntly that he must give up any idea of marrying Amelia, and leaves the scene. Paolo, bitterly angry at the Doge who owes his very crown to him, is joined by Pietro and together they decide to abduct Amelia and keep her prisoner in the house of a certain Lorenzino. They make their plans to some admirably busy conspiratorial music for strings which scarcely rises above *pp* and fades away on tip-toe. It is a beautifully neat curtain to a scene which has survived from the first edition of the opera but which I am sorry to say does not always survive in modern performances and recordings of the work.

PART TWO

Scene : The Council Chamber of the Doge's Palace.

With the exception of one sequence, the whole of this scene, both words and music, was written for the revised version of *Simon Boccanegra*. That the music is a product of Verdi's maturity is obvious from the first stormy bars the orchestra plays before the curtain rises, for it contains all that surprising vigour and dramatic ferocity which seemed to increase as the composer grew older. The whole musical atmosphere, indeed, inevitably reminds one of *Otello*—which, of course, is hardly surprising since Verdi was much preoccupied with plans for that opera at the time he was writing this new scene for *Simon Boccanegra*. Verdi, in other words, was speaking very much in the idiom of his last two operas.

The curtain rises to show Boccanegra seated on the Doge's throne. Twelve councillors representing the nobles sit on one side; on the other sit twelve councillors, among them Paolo and Pietro, representing the people. Also present are four sea-consuls, constables of militia and a Herald.

Boccanegra, having received a unanimous vote from both sides of the Chamber in favour of a proposed trade agreement with the King of Tartary, asks his councillors to vote on a more serious matter. "The voice which prophesied the glory and death of Rienzi is now raised against Genoa," says Boccanegra. "Here is a message from the hermit of Sorgues; he asks peace for Venice." The hermit of Sorgues—or as it appears in the score, the "romito di Sorga"—will be instantly identified (by those who know about such things) as the poet Petrarch who, however strongly we may think of him in the idyllic surroundings of Fontaine-de-Vaucluse, was obviously, as well

as oddly, associated in the mind of the author of this scene in *Simon
Boccanegra* with the unromantic little township of Sorgues (pop.
1966—10,578) five miles north of Avignon.

How quick the Italian public was—or for that matter, may still be—
in recognizing Petrarch as the Hermit of Sorgues I do not know, but
I doubt if it presented much of a problem to a people long accustomed to a maddening national literary failing—the habitual, desperate determination by Italian writers never to mention a proper
name if it can possibly be avoided by using a flowery synonymous
cliché instead. The Italian critic who can resist the temptation to
call Rossini "the Swan of Pesaro" or Verdi the "gran Bussetano",
to refer to Naples as "the Parthenopean capital" and its inhabitants
as "the devotees of San Gennaro", is not on the payroll of any
Italian newspaper I have ever encountered.

Paolo naturally recognizes at once that Boccanegra is talking
about Petrarch, and retorts that the poet should attend to his odes
to the "blonde *avignonnaise*"—who will be instantly identified (by
those who know about such things) as the Madonna Laura of the
Canzoni. Paolo's harshly sarcastic answer to Boccanegra has the
immediate and unanimous support of the councillors on both sides
of the Chamber, who demand war with Venice. Boccanegra tries to
reason with them: the Genoese and the Venetians are children of
the same fatherland.

"Our fatherland is Genoa!" comes the defiant unison reply.

The impressive declamatory style in which the dialogue has so far
been sung is interrupted at this point by a sudden agitated figure
for strings which is developed to play an important part in the
drama that follows:

Ex *187*

From a distance comes the murmuring of a crowd—a sustained
hum (Verdi indicates the notes to be sung *a bocca chiusa*) followed by
cries which are nearer each time. Paolo and Pietro go to the window
and report that a mob is fighting outside the Fieschi palace. Cries of
"Morte!" come from below. Boccanegra overhears Paolo asking
Pietro, "Is it he?" and immediately demands to know who "he" is.
His question is answered as he looks through the window and sees
Gabriele and another patrician fighting for their lives against an angry
crowd. The feud between the two factions has broken out again.

On Pietro's whispered advice Paolo, who realizes something must
have gone wrong with the abduction of Amelia, makes for the door,
but before he can reach it it is shut by the guards on the order of
Boccanegra who proclaims that anybody who leaves the Chamber
is a traitor. At the crowd's shouts from below of "Morte ai patrizi!"
("Death to the Patricians!") and "Viva il popolo!" the Patrician and
Plebeian councillors in the Chamber draw their swords. There is a
moment's pause in the musical excitement (still generated by the
figure of Ex 187) and the off-stage chorus is heard crying, clearly
and deliberately, "Morte al Doge!" (This is a really bewildering
switch in public opinion, for having shouted, "Viva il popolo!" the
popolo now shout for the death of the first People's Doge. Perhaps we
are concerned with the evils of the Cult of Personality, and anti-
Stalinism is not so new as we think.)

"With pride" Boccanegra echoes the crowd's words: "Death to
the Doge! Very well!" He sends a Herald to open the palace doors
and tell the mob, nobles and plebeians alike, that he has heard their
threats and is waiting for them. As the councillors sheathe their
swords on Boccanegra's command the crowd's threats and shouts
start up again with the return of the figure of Ex 187; but it is interrupted by the sound of a trumpet call in the orchestra which is
echoed by a trumpet outside. Boccanegra tells us it is the Herald's
trumpet and that he is speaking. We hear nothing but the musical
equivalent of a tense silence—a drum roll, *pp* drum beats, followed
by an empty bar. "All is silent," says Boccanegra. There is a joyous
shout of "Evviva il Doge!", to which Boccanegra adds the comment,
"the People have spoken".

Once more, and with even greater ferocity than before, the movement of Ex 187 is resumed in a superbly exciting passage for the
chorus who have entered to the sound of what continues for some
time to be almost a blue print of the storm music in *Otello*. The mob,
consisting of plebeian men, women and children all crying for blood,
drag in Gabriele and his co-belligerent, whom we now see to be
Fiesco. Boccanegra asks ironically if this is really the voice of the
people—which sounded like a hurricane in the distance, but near-to
is nothing more than the shrieks of women and children.*

Boccanegra asks Gabriele why he carries a sword. Gabriele replies
because he has killed Lorenzino, whom he discovered trying to
abduct Amelia. But Lorenzino, continues Gabriele, was not the real
culprit; before he died he said he had been forced to do it by a man
of high rank. Boccanegra asks Gabriele to tell him the name, but is

---

* Boccanegra's words at this point are accompanied by a fascinating orchestral
pre-echo of the passage that begins at fourteen bars before letter K in Act I of
Otello, though the role of strings and woodwind in that case are reversed in *Simon
Boccanegra*.

told "with tremendous irony" not to worry; Lorenzino died before he could reveal it.

"What do you mean?" exclaims Boccanegra.

Gabriele replies pointedly and "terribilmente" that Boccanegra is a man of high rank, and raising his sword he rushes towards the Doge. The crowd holds him back, but he struggles free and is about to strike Boccanegra when Amelia suddenly enters and throws herself between the two men. Her appearance quietens everybody down at once, and over a rather sinister six-note-phrase in the violoncellos and basses, she pleads with her father for her lover's life (the relationship between Amelia and Boccanegra is not known except to the audience, of course, and she still appears as "Amelia" instead of "Maria" in the score).

Boccanegra orders the guards not to harm Gabriele, then asks Amelia to tell him all about her adventure. Amelia's narrative which follows is the only passage in this act surviving from the original version of the opera, and even this has clearly been touched up— "Nell'ora soave" ("As I walked by the sea at dusk . . ."):

The mood of this opening phrase, with a lovely warm string accompaniment, does not last long however. Amelia tells us how she was walking by the sea when three ruffians seized her and took her on board a ship. She fainted; when she came to she found herself in Lorenzo's cabin (the diminutive "Lorenzino" obviously dates from the second version of the opera). When they hear this Amelia's listeners cry out "Lorenzo!" in astonishment although they have already heard from Gabriele himself how and why he killed him; indeed, the crowd called him an assassin for doing so and in no uncertain terms. Evidently the text at this point must be a left-over from the original libretto where, one can only suppose, Lorenzo's name had not been mentioned before. As most of this scene in the first *Simon Boccanegra* was taken up by an African ballet it is probable that there was no time to get Lorenzo's name in edgeways anyway.

Amelia eventually escaped, we learn, by the very simple ruse of threatening Lorenzo that the Doge would hear all about it if she was not released at once. The crowd comments *pp* that such a fiend fully deserved to die. But, Amelia continues, there is one even more evil who is still at large. She stares at Paolo who is half hidden behind a group of people.

"Who is it?" ask Gabriele and Boccanegra. The Plebeians draw their swords and answer the question with a threatening "A Patrician!" The nobles answer it in turn by accusing a Plebeian. An ugly situation is prevented once more by Boccanegra's intervention— "Plebe! Patrizi! Popolo dalla feroce storia!" ("Plebeians! Patricians! You people with a fierce history!"):

Ex 189

Boccanegra reproaches the crowd for their unending fratricidal quarrels, and in a broad, majestic passage in the major he appeals to them to restore peace to Genoa—"Piango su voi . . ." ("I weep for you . . ."):

Ex 190

The Doge's plea is the first stage in a superb ensemble, in which the crowd, Fiesco, Gabriele, Paolo, Pietro and Amelia all have different and important things to say. Amelia, who is the first of the principals to follow Boccanegra, pleads for peace with Fiesco; he, for his part, is preoccupied with the unhappy thought that his country should be in the power of a former pirate; Gabriele, in an aside, thanks heaven that Amelia is safe and loves him; Pietro beseeches Paolo to escape while he can, but Paolo refuses—he is too full of hate for the Doge. These are the different themes developed by the characters in an ensemble of singular beauty which is divided into three clear sections.

The second section (which follows Boccanegra's first long solo exposition) is distinguished by a quite lovely phrase from Amelia which ends, the second time it is heard, with the ravishing cadence—

Ex 191

The expected contrast comes immediately after this when Fiesco takes the whole thing into the minor (*più animato*) and—perhaps deliberately, perhaps by coincidence—reminds us of the tune of Ex 172. A throbbing accompaniment builds the ensemble to a momentary climax with Amelia, Gabriele and the strings towering in unison over the rest with a final repetition of Ex 191.

The dynamic range of this ensemble is most effectively limited; even at the climax I have just mentioned it does not rise above *forte*, and then not for long, for it is followed immediately by a quiet passage for the chorus which dies away to *ppp* as the principals sing their final phrases. As Verdi wrote them the last two bars of this ensemble are intended to be sung by Amelia unaccompanied, the singer finishing with a trill on an F sharp followed by a simple flourish and a final F sharp an octave lower. It seems, however, that the Italian conductor who is not just able, but actually willing, to prevent the orchestra as well as all Amelia's colleagues holding their final notes as a bonus background to what the composer imagined would be a soprano solo, has yet to be born. It is such an original idea of Verdi's on paper, it seems a pity nobody ever tries it out in practice.

After the ensemble has finished the term "Recitativo" appears in the score for the first and last time in this opera. It is a superfluous indication, for all that it leads to is a couple of bars of dramatic dialogue punctuated first by a single bottom C sharp for violoncello and bassoon, then by a bottom E for the same instruments, during which Gabriele offers Boccanegra his sword. The Doge refuses it; Gabriele will be kept prisoner for the night until the plot has been unravelled; all Boccanegra asks is Gabriele's word of honour. Gabriele gives it. Boccanegra, "con forza terribile", calls Paolo, who comes forward. From the orchestra comes a first hint of Iago's "Credo"—a shattering, brassbound unison across four octaves, with trills on every instrument in the pit:

Ex 192

Imperiously and with tremendous violence Boccanegra turns to Paolo and requests him, as custodian of the people's law, to help him. Boccanegra's words are punctuated by *ff tutti* unisons like Ex 192. There is a silent pause, and a solo bass clarinet plays *p* the first of five two-bar phrases closely based on Amelia's tune in Ex 191 which frame Boccanegra's words: "Here in this room", he tells Paolo, "a wretch is listening to me . . . I know his name . . ."

The tension is increased at these words by a string tremolo and violoncellos, violas and unison bassoons playing the first bar of Ex 192 three times in succession. The bass clarinet then takes over again and continues with its sinister, distorted variant of Amelia's "Pace" theme. "Before heaven and before me," continues Boccanegra to Paolo, "you are a witness. Let my sentence fall like thunder on the head of the criminal: 'He is accursed!' And you—repeat the oath!"

There is a moment's pause with a tense, dark, falling three-note chromatic phrase for bass clarinet heard sinisterly against a low-register tremolo of violoncellos and *divisi* double basses. Prostrate and terrified Paolo repeats the Doge's curse: "Sia maledetto!" The bass clarinet phrase, slightly altered in shape but not in its effect, is repeated relentlessly and *pp*. "Sia maledetto!" is cried *tutta forza* by chorus and the remaining principals (Pietro included, for he has no choice in the circumstances). Slowly everybody but Paolo moves away, muttering *pp* on a low unison C the words "Sia maledetto!", which grow more and more faint in the distance. Deep down in the orchestra, against a tremolo C and E, a low F sharp played by violoncellos and bass clarinet tolls like a death knell. In terror, Paolo flies from the room and the curtain falls with an echo, now loud and insistent in the brass, of the plaintive phrase with which the bass clarinet underlined Boccanegra's oblique denunciation of Paolo.

It is a superb ending to a scene of tremendous power and dramatic irony that rates among Verdi's finest achievements.

ACT II

Scene: An apartment in the Doge's Palace at Genoa. There are doors on either side of the scene. There is a view of the city from a balcony. On a table are a flask and a goblet. It is evening.

The curtain rises almost at once on Paolo telling Pietro to bring the two prisoners (Gabriele and Fiesco) from their cells. Pietro takes the key from Paolo and leaves. An ominous unison phrase from the brass—

Ex *193*

—reminds us of the curse pronounced to these notes by Boccanegra. It is characteristic of Verdi's musical powers of evocation that we immediately, almost subconsciously associate these four notes with the curse, although when they were heard in the previous scene they were sung only once by Boccanegra.

They were not "plugged", or even repeated to suggest they were of any thematic consequence. But there is no doubt of their significance when we hear them spotlit, as it were, by the orchestra in this scene, for they at once set Paolo brooding on the curse which he has laid on himself. In a fine, dramatic declamatory soliloquy, in which the rhythm but not the notes of Ex 193 are heard from time to time, Paolo vows to avenge himself on the Doge, who reviles him and yet owes his power to him. Paolo produces a phial and going to the table empties its contents into the goblet. This is according to the instructions in the score, though one would have thought it more sensible to pour the poison into the flask where it wouldn't notice, instead of into a goblet which the Doge would expect to find empty.*

A sinister little syncopated three-note chromatic phrase *pp* in octaves by the bassoon with the clarinet an octave lower against the dull thud of bass drum, violoncello and double bass pizzicatos, accompanies Paolo's movements and his description of the "slow and dreadful agony" that awaits his victim. This solo scene, which dates

* To have Paolo to be seen to poison the water was entirely Boito's idea. Piave merely mentioned it in passing.

entirely from the 1881 revision, is a kind of miniature "Credo" which has about it strong suggestions of the extraordinary quality of evil that permeates Verdi's portrait of Iago.

Pietro brings in Fiesco and Gabriele and the music reverts to the original version once more. To the accompaniment of an oddly graceful and relaxed tune for strings—

Ex 194

—Paolo offers Fiesco his freedom, if he will kill Boccanegra while he sleeps. Fiesco refuses indignantly; he is not a murderer. Paolo sends him back to his prison. Gabriele turns to follow him but is stopped by Paolo who tells him that Amelia is the Doge's mistress and is here in the palace. Does Gabriele want to spent the rest of his life in prison when he has only to kill Boccanegra to gain his freedom? Paolo goes out leaving Gabriele to think things over.

Gabriele, because it is that kind of opera plot, naturally believes every word Paolo has told him. Boccanegra who murdered his father has now seduced his mistress, and so called down a double vengeance on his head. In a fierce outburst of fury and jealousy Gabriele swears to be avenged—"Sento avvampar nell'anima furente gelosia!" ("Furious jealousy burns in my breast!"):

Ex 195

Gabriele's fury turns into despair and the fiercely vigorous chromatic string figure which gives the first part of the aria its impetus, subsides. He weeps (and the oboe weeps with him) when he realizes what he has been saying. In a gentle, sparsely-accompanied, but rather sub-standard lyrical episode Gabriele prays heaven to restore Amelia to him—"Cielo pietoso, rendila":

Ex 196

Largo

Cie - lo pieto - so, ren - ði - la   ren - ði - la a que - sto co - re

The whole form and atmosphere of this final section of Gabriele's *scena ed aria* could hardly be more characteristic of Verdi in the 1850s; nor indeed could Piave's (or Montanelli's?) verses, for we hear a clear echo of *La traviata* in Gabriele's words, "pura siccome l'angelo" (see p 181).

Amelia enters and Gabriele at once reproaches her for her infidelity. She protests her innocence, but says she cannot explain—yet —her relationship with the Doge (it is not quite clear why not, except that if she did it would spoil all Gutiérrez's fun and the show would end too soon). Gabriele asks her to reassure him that she loves him—"Parla, in tuo cor vergine la fede a me tu rendi":

Ex *197*

It is a simple kind of tune with a bare chuck-chuck accompaniment on the first and second, fourth and fifth beats of the bar. Amelia answers Gabriele's rather sad phrases with assurances in the more optimistic key of F sharp major that she loves him. The duet, which has no great distinction, ends with some effectively ethereal scoring but without Gabriele being really convinced of Amelia's innocence as the final cadence of the duet would lead one to suppose.

A trumpet sounds behind the scenes to announce the approach of the Doge. Amelia tells Gabriele to hide quickly as there is no escape; he will be executed. Gabriele retorts that he is not afraid. A short, hectic, and uninterestingly conventional duet passage follows in which Gabriele swears to himself to kill Boccanegra, while Amelia agitatedly pleads with him to have pity on her—a plea which obviously puzzles Gabriele as he has not been paying close attention. What Amelia means is that unless Gabriele hides he will be caught and executed, and if he is executed she will die with him; so please will he have pity on her.

Gabriele's only reaction to this is to ask absently, "Have pity on you?" and then to mutter repeatedly, "He shall die!" When he has said these words no fewer than seven times the duet comes to an end and Amelia manages to hide Gabriele outside on the balcony. It is a rather grotesque episode altogether, which comes dangerously near to parody at times.

A sombre four-bar unison phrase for strings in a low register brings in Boccanegra who enters slowly, reading a document. He looks up and sees there are tears in Amelia's eyes. He questions her and learns to his horror that she is in love with Gabriele Adorno, his sworn enemy, whose name as one of the Patrician conspirators appears on the document in his hand. Amelia begs her father to forgive Gabriele. He refuses. Amelia swears she will die with her lover. In a broad, simple phrase Boccanegra laments that no sooner has he found a daughter than he loses her again to an enemy. There is a brief pause and a *pp* echo of the busy string figure derived from Ex 177 in the Prologue (see p 209). Amelia's devotion clearly moves her father; after a moment's thought he suggests that if Gabriele would repent it might perhaps be possible to pardon him. Boccanegra sends Amelia away and he is left alone to reflect that if once again he is about to pardon a traitor it is because he feels punishment would be a sign of fear on his part.

He goes to the table, fills the goblet with water from the flask, and drinks. From the orchestra come sustained *ppp* chords played by the trombones, and the stealthy beat of pizzicato basses and drum rolls. A sudden *ff* chord in the trombones dies away to solemn *pp* chords that might have strayed from *Don Giovanni* (we are in fact in the same ominous key of D minor). "Even spring water", Boccanegra sings sadly, "tastes bitter to him who wears a crown." He grows drowsy and falls asleep as Verdi intensifies the air of silence and apprehension which has now come over the scene with a series of little three-note phrases played so quietly and *leggerissimo* by violins and violas that they are scarcely audible:

Ex *198*

Boccanegra is not dead, of course, for it will be remembered that Paolo picked on a slow-acting poison that would give him time to escape from Genoa. In his sleep Boccanegra murmurs his daughter's name—Amelia, who loves his enemy. From the orchestra comes an echo of the tune heard in the duet between father and daughter in Act I (Ex 186), played *dolcissimo* by flute, clarinet and oboe in unison while six first violins, divided into three parts, expand their groups of three semiquavers (Ex 198) into an uninterrupted, delicate figure of four semiquavers in their high register, which has something about it of the light-fingered string passage heard not long before the curtain falls on Act III, Scene 1 of *Falstaff*.

The context in the case of *Simon Boccanegra* could not be more widely removed from *Falstaff*, of course, for under cover of this violin passage, as it were, Gabriele enters stealthily from the balcony and

approaches the sleeping Doge. He looks down at the old man, and
after a moment's hesitation, draws his dagger to stab his father's
murderer. Amelia suddenly appears and once more throws herself
between Gabriele and her father. Boccanegra wakes with a start and
baring his breast defies Gabriele to stab him. Gabriele exclaims
that an Adorno's blood cries out for vengeance.

Boccanegra replies bitterly and sadly, in a majestic passage of
declamation, that Gabriele has amply avenged the father who suffered at his hands: "You have robbed me of my one treasure—my
daughter." Gabriele is thunderstruck when he learns of this relationship and in a misery of shame and self-reproach asks the forgiveness of Amelia and Boccanegra: "Perdon, perdon Amelia . . .":

Ex *199*

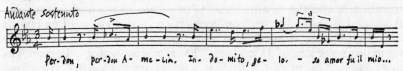

From this beginning a trio is gradually built up—Gabriele continuing in much the same desperate frame of mind throughout (and
at the words "dammi la morte" contributing each time a finely
virile phrase); the Doge wondering whether or not to spare his
enemy's life and reflecting that by doing so he might bring peace at
last to Genoa; and Amelia praying that her father's heart may be
filled with pity. The trio, which dates from the first version of the
opera, but was extensively revised and refurbished for the second,
is a characteristic and, at this stage of the opera, very welcome
episode. It is also, unfortunately, the last music of any merit we hear
in this act. Voices are heard in the distance; Amelia runs to the
window to see a warlike crowd approaching—at least, it is the
women among them who specifically shout for war: the men are
content merely to call for mobilization and a sense of duty:

Ex *200*

In the course of a long, martial choral sequence that is unaccompanied except for two off-stage side drums and a short flourish from
the orchestral brass for the chorus to check their intonation by, we
learn that the crowd are heading for the Doge's palace to "seize

that crowned demon". Boccanegra bids Gabriele join his friends. Gabriele refuses; he will never fight against the Doge again. Then go to them, says Boccanegra; take a message of peace so that tomorrow's dawn will not break on brotherly strife, and Amelia shall be his reward. The chorus rises to a climax; the orchestra joins in, Boccanegra and Gabriele cry, "To arms!" and Amelia exclaims, "Father!" The curtain falls on a typical and by no means unexciting or ineffective early-Verdi din.

ACT III

Scene : Inside the Doge's Palace a few hours later. Balcony windows at the back look out on a prospect of Genoa illuminated by numberless torches. Beyond is the sea.

At the climax of a short orchestral introduction, based on the chorus that ended the second act (Ex 200), shouts of "Evviva il Doge !" and "Vittoria !" are heard coming from behind the scenes. The curtain rises. The Captain of Archers leads in Fiesco, and giving him back his sword tells him he is free. Fiesco learns that his faction has been defeated; it is a sad and bitter moment of freedom.

Paolo is brought in, closely guarded. Fiesco is surprised to see him; where are they taking him? To the scaffold, replies Paolo; he had found himself by mistake among the rebels and had been captured; Boccanegra has condemned him to death, but he himself had already condemned Boccanegra to death. Paolo tells his brief story to a melancholy tune doubled an octave lower by the violoncellos whose lower register gives it a peculiarly sombre and pathetic character, enough indeed for the listener to feel a sudden sympathy for an otherwise unprepossessing figure :

Ex 201

Fiesco is horrified when he learns that Paolo has poisoned Boccanegra. "Perhaps", remarks Paolo, "he may even precede me to the grave." From inside the palace women's voices are heard singing a wedding hymn for the marriage of Amelia and Gabriele. The sound of it unnerves Paolo and he blurts out angrily that Gabriele Adorno is marrying the girl he abducted. Fiesco (who is also, we must not forget, "Andrea", Amelia's guardian) draws his sword and is about to kill Paolo, but replaces it—"the axe is waiting for you".

This short scene—from Paolo's confession to Fiesco sheathing his sword—takes place most effectively against the background of the unaccompanied wedding hymn. As the women's singing comes to an end Paolo is led away to his execution by the guards to the sound of Ex 201, played once more by violoncellos, but supported this time by clarinets, bassoons, two horns and violas.

Fiesco, left alone on the stage, reflects that Boccanegra's death by poisoning was not the kind of vengeance he wanted. He hears Boccanegra approaching and hides in a dark corner. The Captain of the Archers enters with a trumpeter. Their entrance is accompanied in the orchestra by a most unusual and solemn unison phrase for horns, which—because of the instrumentation—has an inescapable flavour about it of the opening of the third act of *Tosca*:

Ex 202

The trumpeter blows a short call, and the Captain goes out on to the balcony to address the crowd below. The Doge has proclaimed that, as a tribute to the brave dead, all illuminations in the city shall be extinguished and all sounds of rejoicing silenced. The Captain and trumpeter withdraw to a repetition of the unison horn theme (Ex. 202.)

Boccanegra enters, walking unsteadily as the effects of the poison begin to be felt. As he speaks of the fever that afflicts him and the fire that rushes through his veins his words are three times punctuated by a superbly expressive phrase scored for trombones and bassoons and strings, and rising by a semitone at each repetition:

Ex 203

Boccanegra struggles for breath, and as he breathes the cool fresh air from the sea he thinks sadly of the happy days of triumph and excitement he experienced as a sailor. In a simple and quite lovely twelve-bar phrase he sings of his yearning for the sea; it is a wonderfully nostalgic lyrical passage with the tune mostly in the violins and violoncellos over an insistent, bubbling little figure in the violas:

Ex 204

"The sea—the sea", repeats Boccanegra. "Why did I not find my grave in her bosom?"

Fiesco steps out of his hiding place and, addressing Boccanegra, says menacingly: "It would have been better for you!" Boccanegra calls for his guards, but there is no answer. Fiesco stands firmly before him, and in the course of warning the Doge of the end that approaches, reveals his true identity to the man who had thought him long since dead. Fiesco begins a scene that develops into a fine duet between the two men with a sinister chromatic phrase:

The whole of the duet that now follows—that is, the next fourteen pages or so in the vocal score—dates from the first version of the opera, though the orchestration has been touched up in places. The accompaniment of this first passage, however, which is distinguished by some unexpectedly melodramatic emphasis in the form of chromatic punctuations from the trombones and *cimbasso* in unison, seems to have its orchestral feet firmly planted in the earlier score; and indeed the familiar thumping of *pp* brass and drums we heard at dramatic moments in both *Il trovatore* and *La traviata*, is heard again when Boccanegra begins to recognize Fiesco.

The tempo of the music changes suddenly to a rapid one-in-a-bar 3/4 time as Fiesco impresses on Boccanegra that he has come "like a wraith" to avenge a long-standing outrage. This is a vigorous sequence, with the air of a rather sinister scherzo, in which Boccanegra joyfully reminds Fiesco of the conditions of forgiveness laid down twenty-five years before: they can at last be fulfilled, for Amelia Grimaldi is the child born to Boccanegra and Fiesco's daughter Maria. Fiesco weeps that he should have seen the truth so late; and his weeping is echoed in an orchestral passage by a combination in this case of two of Verdi's most characteristic expressions of tears—the one by a falling tone or semitone, the other by the rising semitone, both of them first encountered in *Macbeth* (Ex 37).

The tearful rising semitone is heard again, expressed in various instrumental forms—by the oboe, by divided violas—during the

Ex 206

course of the Largo sequence (Ex 206) which Fiesco begins with, "Piango, perchè mi parla in te del ciel la voce" ("I weep because in you the voice of heaven has spoken . . .").

There is immense pathos in the scene which develops between the old men—in the sadness of Fiesco, and the love shown him by Boccanegra because he is Maria's father. One broad and memorable phrase emerges, sung by Boccanegra, which deserves to be quoted here, for it plays an effective instrumental part in the drama a couple of pages further on:

When they have finished their duet together with a formal two-part cadence, Fiesco tells Boccanegra that a traitor has poisoned him; and the ominous thumping of the funereal orchestral *tutti* we have already heard returns. Boccanegra takes the news calmly; he already feels the touch of death on him. He sees Amelia coming and begs Fiesco (who refers to her as "Maria") to tell her nothing. To the tune of the phrase in Ex 207, Boccanegra says he wishes to bless her once more. He sinks into a chair and the tune of Ex 207 is heard twice again, played softly by the violoncellos now in the key of A flat, on their lowest, most resonant string. During this *ppp* orchestral postlude Amelia and Gabriele enter, followed by ladies, gentlemen, senators, and pages bearing torches.

Both Amelia and Gabriele are understandably surprised to see Fiesco. Boccanegra explains to his daughter, slowly and deliberately, who Fiesco is. He continues to talk to her in the same grave mood, and calling her "Maria" for the first time tells her that he is dying. Like a funeral knell two bassoons, four horns and the brass bass repeat a sombre C for ten bars on the first beat of a two-in-a-bar Moderato. The same sad stillness continues while Boccanegra thanks heaven that he may die in her arms. Maria, as she is now referred to in the stage direction of the score—but not in the vocal part, where she is still Amelia—kneels before her father with Gabriele. Boccanegra struggles slowly to his feet and raises his hands to bless his daughter and son-in-law. Boccanegra's blessing (like Fiesco's earlier on) is rather more ecclesiastical in style than one would have thought necessary, and not even its accompaniment of *pp* divided violins with its inevitable suggestion of the last scene of *La traviata*, does much to secularize it, as it were. The harmonies are disappointingly simple and respectable and have none of the emotional effect of the famous *Traviata* passages. To me, at any rate,

8*

it is the only occasion in the whole opera when Boccanegra is musically out of character.

However, it is not long before the blessing is superseded by the first notes of what is obviously going to lead to a big ensemble. Amelia pleads with her father not to die; love will loosen the icy grip of death—"No, non morrai, l'amore vinca di morte il gelo":

Ex *208*

Slowly, with a brief four-bar interruption of its progress by a few words of Boccanegra's blessing, the expected ensemble builds up, with Fiesco grieving in a solemn monotone that earthly joy is an illusion, Boccanegra beseeching his daughter to hold him to her heart, and Amelia and Gabriele making a tremendously dramatic impact at intervals with what is one of the oustanding musical features of the movement—a unison phrase to the words "Non morrai": "You will not die".

The chorus joins in softly to mourn the passing of the Doge at the point where a characteristically throbbing accompaniment of quaver triplets begins to work up from *pppp* to a series of typical climaxes, to end suddenly on a general *ppp*.

There is a long pause. Boccanegra calls his Senators round him and proclaims Gabriele Adorno his successor. He asks Fiesco to see that his wish is carried out. Then he turns to his daughter, and in a feeble voice says, "Maria . . ." Muted and *ppp* divided strings echo the ethereal sound of Boccanegra's blessing. He tries to speak but his strength fails him. He places his hands once more on the heads of Amelia and Gabriele to bless them, and dies. In the musical silence created by the divided strings sustaining a high chord of A flat, Fiesco walks over to the balcony and addresses the crowd in the piazza below: "Citizens of Genoa, acclaim your Doge, Gabriele Adorno!" From the crowd comes the cry: "No! Boccanegra!"

"He is dead," replies Fiesco solemnly. "Pray for the peace of his soul."

Fiesco sings these words in the course of a superbly dramatic *ppp* cadence of the chords of D[7], G minor, E flat[7], A flat. Inside the Palace the crowd kneels and on the bare fifths of A flat and E flat murmurs, "Pace per lui! Pace per lui!" A bell tolls as the same open fifths are sustained in the orchestra until, in the last two bars, a C natural is added to make the final major chords on which the curtain falls.

It is understandable, I think, in view of what we know of the original opera, that *Simon Boccanegra* should have been a failure at its first Venice performance. It may well have been as "cold and gloomy" as Verdi said it was, but it must also, I believe, have been a little too experimental for the public of its time. It was not the Verdi they knew; it was sometimes not even the Verdi the composer himself knew. There are passages in the first *Simon Boccanegra* which look ahead in an astonishing manner. For instance, the impressive declamatory style of the fine duet in the Prologue between Fiesco and Boccanegra shortly after "Il lacerato spirito" (also from 1857), fitted perfectly into the later version with only a few changes of detail. Its presence in the Venetian edition can only have contributed to the unpopularity of an opera whose principal fault (apart from the unintelligibility of the libretto) was the lack of those lyrical highspots which Italian audiences of the time had reason to expect. Verdi's preoccupation with the development of a declamatory style —more musical than recitative, more mobile than the aria—designed to suit the peculiar dramatic grimness of the action, led to much music that was very different from anything that had been heard in any of the earlier operas.

By the time he came to revise *Simon Boccanegra*, Verdi had perfected that highly personal declamatory idiom which gives his later operas their peculiar strength and fluency, and the grim drama that the comparatively immature composer was trying—not always successfully—to express in the 1850s, suddenly came to life in the experienced hands of the mature and articulate artist of the 1880s.

Virtually all Verdi's major revisions and additions to *Simon Boccanegra* were concerned with the essentially dramatic situations. The lyrical aspect of the subject was barely touched on; it had been a weak point in the first version; it was still of secondary importance in the second, for with the exception of an effective passage added for Gabriele in the duet with Amelia in Act I, and the restrained and moving climax of Boccanegra's duet with his daughter later in the same scene, the lyrical passages were for the most part taken over intact from the original score.

Those who know *Simon Boccanegra* only from the vocal score or from records will certainly think it an uneven sort of work, even though the figure of Boccanegra himself is a superbly consistent and dominating figure. But as with so much of Verdi that seems below standard in the study—like *Macbeth*, for instance—*Simon Boccanegra* is another matter altogether in the theatre, where it bursts into life as a work of great character and above all, with an overwhelming atmosphere of its own. While it certainly adds to one's enjoyment of *La Bohème* to have been to Paris in one's time, it is not essential to know the topographical setting of an opera to enjoy it (if it were, one wouldn't get very far with *The Magic Flute*, for example). It is certainly not essential with *Simon Boccanegra*. But perhaps more than with any other opera of Verdi's, familiarity with the purely physical background of *Simon Boccanegra* gives the work a special fascination. There is in the wonderful Council Chamber scene, and in the final moments of the third act, a stark Gothic quality about the music and the drama which is peculiar to this opera. Those who know the city will recognize it as an unmistakable characteristic of Genoa to this day; those who do not will sense it none the less, for it is an element that colours every bar of a work containing some of the most magnificent, dramatic pages Verdi ever wrote.

UN BALLO IN MASCHERA

(*A Masked Ball*)

Melodrama in three acts. Libretto by Antonio Somma, based on the play *Gustave III*, by Eugène Scribe. First performed at the Teatro Apollo, Rome, on 17th February, 1859. First performance in England: Lyceum Theatre, London, 15th June, 1861. First performance in the United States: Academy of Music, New York, 11th February, 1861.

OF ALL Verdi's adventures with "that dark and gloomy thing called the Censorship" perhaps the most frustrating and celebrated were those associated with *Un ballo in maschera*.

After the production of *Simon Boccanegra* in March 1857, Verdi was approached by the Fenice for yet another opera, but he declined the opportunity to write what would have been his sixth work for the same theatre. Apart from anything else he had already in February finally signed a contract drawn up in May 1856 to write an opera for the San Carlo, Naples. This was to have been *King Lear*, a subject which, as we know, had fascinated the composer since 1843 (that is, before the composition of *Macbeth*) and was to come up again and again as a project until 1865 and even later. The idea of *Lear* indeed, is said to have been raised at the time of the Rome première of *Falstaff* in 1893 when Verdi, touched by the reception he had been given, jokingly said to Boito that he needed a new libretto. Boito, who had heard the widespread rumours in Rome that Verdi still hoped to write *King Lear*, took the old man's remark seriously enough to draft out a brief scenario, compose some verses and outline one scene. On this final occasion *Lear* did not materialize because Verdi reluctantly had to admit that at eighty he was really too old.

At the time of the San Carlo contract, however, *King Lear*, with a libretto by Antonio Somma, was abandoned because Verdi was dissatisfied with the singers available. The San Carlo management pleaded with him to continue with *Lear*, even if there was no satisfactory Cordelia. "Sometime or other, you will come across a better Cordelia," they told him, "but you will never have a better baritone, tenor or bass." Verdi was not to be persuaded. Instead, he considered Victor Hugo's *Ruy Blas*, and another play by Gutiérrez, *El Tesorero del Rey Don Pedro* ("The Treasurer of King Pedro"); and hesitated promisingly for a moment over *Gustave III*, Scribe's play of the assassination of the King of Sweden in 1792, but discarded that subject too.

As he was unable to think of anything completely new to qualify as the *prima assoluta* expected of him Verdi tried to bargain with the San Carlo, offering them a newly and extensively revised and refurbished version of *La battaglia di Legnano* (1849), *Aroldo* (which, having started its career in 1850 as *Stiffelio*, had been "refurbished" with remarkably little success to open a new theatre at Rimini in August 1857), and the recently performed *Simon Boccanegra*, as well as a promise of *King Lear* for the following year if a suitable cast would be collected.

None of these proposals—perhaps understandably—was acceptable to the San Carlo. Verdi thereupon agreed to set Scribe's *Gustave III*, commissioned Somma to adapt a text which had already been used as the libretto of Auber's *Gustave III, ou Le Bal Masqué* in Paris in 1833, and adapted by Cammarano as the libretto of *Il reggente* by the Neapolitan composer Mercadante in Turin in 1843. A prose version of the libretto was submitted for censorship to the authorities; it was not approved owing to the time, place and characters of the action. It was suggested, however, that these were failings that could easily be remedied.

We have Verdi's own account of how in November 1857 he received a letter from the Censorship with their suggestions and how he acted on them:

"1. 'The Sovereign to be changed into a Duke'—I made him the Duke of Pomerania.

"2. 'Celtic region and a period which justifies superstitions, belief in the witch, and the invocation of spirits unrelated to Christian beliefs'—The region is Celtic [?]. In the second half of the 17th century people believed in witches. Lucifer is mentioned and Lucifer is pagan.

"3. 'The librettist to use any Northern place except Sweden and Norway'—Stettin is in the North and is not in Sweden or Norway.

"4. 'The protagonist's love must be always noble and ardent, yet, from the beginning, filled with remorse because of his close friendship with the husband of the woman he loves'—His love is always noble and ardent, yet filled with remorse. From the early scenes he says, 'L'anima mia il rimorso dilacera e rode' ['Remorse tears and gnaws at my soul'].

"5. 'His enemies must hate for reasons of inheritance, such as the usurpation (real or imaginary) of property'—His enemies seek his death because he has seized the heriditary castle of one of them and murdered the brother of another.

"6. 'The festivity must conform with the customs and legends of the place selected'—The festivity is a ball; in the North they dance, and a great deal (*e molto*).

"7. 'No firearms'—The assassin uses a dagger."

This confirms very clearly what Frank Walker, whose sadly early death occurred while I was writing this chapter, pointed out in the first of the three volumes on *Un ballo in maschera* published by the Istituto di Studi Verdiani of Parma: that "contrary to what one reads in all the biographies, Verdi was kept informed of these developments", agreed to Somma's alterations as well as to the renaming of the work *Una vendetta in domino*.

The familiar story, it may be remembered, was that Verdi had never known anything of any objection by the Censor; that when he had sent the prose draft to Vincenzo Torelli, secretary of the San Carlo, for submission to the Censorship in October 1857 and had heard nothing more, he had presumed all was well and had gone ahead with the composition; that he learned for the first time only on his arrival in Naples in January 1858 that the libretto had been rejected outright three months previously. Torelli's excuse for this, we were told, was that he had not wanted to interrupt the Maestro's flow of inspiration by discussing such trivial and easily-disposed-of objections.

When, therefore, he arrived in Naples on the 14th January, 1858, Verdi had completed the music to a libretto already altered to meet the Censor's demands; there remained to be finished only the orchestration, which he usually left until rehearsals for a new work were under way, and to complete what Verdi can have regarded as only a simple formality—the submission of the full versified libretto to the Censor.

Unfortunately, Verdi arrived in Naples the very day after the attempted assassination on leaving the Paris Opera of Napoleon III by an Italian, Felice Orsini; he found the city understandably in an uproar of excitement and official panic at the news, and the Censorship scarcely in a mood to countenance operas about assassinations and conspiracies.

On receiving the versified libretto the Censor at once began to raise objections—or, as he put it, to propose "modifications". The "modifications", Verdi reported to Somma, included:

1. To make the protagonist a simple gentleman, doing away altogether with the idea of a ruling sovereign;
2. To make the wife a sister;
3. To modify the witch's scene, transferring it to a period when people believed in witches;
4. To eliminate the ball;
5. To have the murder take place off stage;
6. To eliminate the scene where lots are drawn.

These suggested "modifications" were only the beginning, however. By the time the Censorship had finished they presented Verdi with what was virtually a brand-new libretto. This was an anonymous monstrosity, said to have been devised by a local hack called

Domenico Bolognese and entitled "Adelia degli Adimari", which Verdi refused pointblank to have anything to do with.

This libretto changed the scene to Florence, the period to the fourteenth century, the page boy Oscar into a strapping young soldier, abolished all wearing of masks, but in permitting "Adelia" to wear a veil in the final scene (no longer a ball but an inanimate sort of reception) made her the most conspicuous figure on the stage, and so made as much nonsense of the action as the hack's verses made of the music. These, it may be said, were only a few of the officially-approved features of the libretto now being offered to Verdi; there were many others just as ridiculous and typically lunatic.

Verdi's refusal to discuss any question of adapting his music to what he said might just as well be called "Adelia degli animali" for all the title meant, led the San Carlo to bring a legal action against him for breach of contract. Verdi lodged a counterclaim from which it is as clear as ever that he had made the alterations demanded by the Censor in November 1857.

The dispute, which was preceded by angry threats from the President of the San Carlo to imprison the composer, was eventually settled out of court with an agreement that Verdi would return to Naples to stage *Simon Boccanegra* in the autumn of 1858.

Meanwhile, remembering that not only Scribe's original play of *Gustave III*, but another on the same subject by an Italian called Dal Testa had been allowed by the Roman Censors Verdi took his opera off to Rome. Ricordi had told him that La Scala wanted to do it, but Verdi refused as he particularly wanted it performed "practically under the city gates of Naples, so as to show them that the Rome Censor allowed the libretto".

The Rome Censor however, did not allow the libretto—at least, not as it stood. True to inconsistent type he refused to accept the argument that because *Gustave III* had been permitted as a stage play it could therefore be permitted as an opera libretto. It seems to me that what in fact the Roman Censor was shown was not the original Somma-Verdi *Gustavo III*, but the libretto of *Una vendetta in domino* as altered to the specifications of the Neapolitan authorities in November 1857.

Although they were clearly calculated to plague Somma (who, in spite of having long ago insisted that his name should be taken off the libretto had nevertheless loyally continued to work with Verdi) the alterations demanded by the Roman Censorship did very little structural damage to the fabric, for one of the first changes we hear about is the reduction of Gustave, Duke of Pomerania, to the rank of Count of "Göthemburg"—a puzzling conceit indeed, as the nearest approach to anything of this name is Gothenburg or Gottenburg, which are both Germanic forms of Göteborg, the second city of

Sweden, and so land us right back in the country everybody first thought of and was trying at all costs to avoid.

Somma did what was required of him, though not without letting it be known how irritated he was by trivial and apparently nonsensical "modifications" by the ecclesiastical authorities of so-called "heretical" words—"infamous gallows", for instance, had to be altered to "infamous groves".* Verdi, on the other hand, seemed to find the authorities almost reasonable and made no unfavourable comments when he had to report to Somma that, while the Censorship had finally approved the subject and situations, they wanted the action to be set outside Europe. "What do you think", Verdi asked his librettist, "of North America at the time of the English domination? If not America, some other place. The Caucasus perhaps?"

The action was transferred, as Verdi suggested, to North America —to Boston, Massachusetts, in the late seventeenth century. The protagonist, after declining from King to Duke to Count, was promoted again to become Duke of Surrey, Governor of Boston. It was only a temporary promotion, however, for the Censor objected to a Duke as being too nearly a sovereign. Somma, remembering that it was the Censors who had invented the character of the Count of "Göthemburg", decided that an Englishman of equivalent rank would probably be permissible and created Riccardo, Count (or Earl) of Warwick—a title which appears in the most recent full-length Italian biography of Verdi as "Warvick", in my Ricordi score as "Warwich", and throughout the original Italian and most of the American translation of Carlo Gatti's biography as "Norwich".

Finally, after the names of one or two of the characters had been (more or less) anglicized, and Verdi had quietly persuaded the authorities to modify some of the more drastic alterations they had demanded in the verses and dialogue, the opera was retitled *Un ballo in maschera*, thus differing only in the choice of indefinite instead of definite article from Scribe's original sub-title, "Le Bal Masqué". After all the trouble everybody had been through it is satisfying to report that *Un ballo in maschera* was a considerable success on its first performance, and that in the form in which it was originally performed in Rome it has remained to this day one of Verdi's most popular operas.

In spite of recent tendencies to the contrary I propose to refer in my analysis to the characters by the names under which they appear in the score, the libretto, most public performances and in all the gramophone recordings I have encountered so far.

* There may just have been a political reason behind this. The original phrase was "colonne infami" (literally "infamous columns"); the Colonnas (or "colonne") were an old and influential Roman family and it is quite possible that a Colonna was a Cardinal or a Papal Count or something at the time.

CHARACTERS IN ORDER OF SINGING

SAMUEL } *conspirators, enemies of the Governor* . Bass
TOM } . Bass
OSCAR, *a Page in the service of*. . . *Soprano*
RICCARDO, *Earl of Warwick, Governor of Boston* *Tenor*
RENATO, *a Creole, his secretary* . . . *Baritone*
A JUDGE . . . . *Tenor*
ULRICA, *a Negro fortune-teller*. . . . *Contralto*
SILVANO, *a sailor*. . . . . . Bass
A SERVANT of AMELIA . . . . *Tenor*
AMELIA, *Renato's wife*. . . . . *Soprano*

Delegates, officials, sailors, guards, men, women and children of the populace, gentlemen, followers of Samuel and Tom, servants, masked guests and dancers

Scene: Boston, Massachusetts, and its neighbourhood

Time: End of the seventeenth century

ACT I

Scene 1: A room in the Governor's house. A door at the back leads to his private apartments.

A shortish orchestral prelude before the rise of the curtain introduces three themes, two of which play a considerable part at various points later in the opera. The first, a rather lugubrious and hymn-like affair, is scored for clarinets in their low register, bassoons, divided violas and violoncellos, and eventually violins on their G strings, and is punctuated by a little unison woodwind figure first heard in the six kind of vamp-till-ready opening bars of the Prelude:

Ex 209

This mood is dispelled by a short fugato for strings on a theme starting *assai piano e staccato* in the violoncellos and basses and evoking an unmistakable atmosphere of stealth and conspiracy:

Ex 210

The key changes to D. The third theme which, like that in Ex 210 is heard again later in the opera, is introduced by flute and oboe in unison in their lower registers an octave higher than the clarinet, and decorated by repeated violin harmonics in the rhythm of the woodwind figure of Ex 209:

Ex 211

243

The violins take this up in A major on their G strings. The theme is briefly developed between strings and woodwind, the conspirators' theme (Ex 210) makes a short reappearance to build a climax, and the Prelude fades away in a typical "dying fall" coda in which the first half of the seventh bar of Ex 211 is played *dolcissimo* by flute and piccolo in octaves and echoed first by oboe and clarinet an octave lower, then by the bassoon an octave below that.

The curtain rises on a crowd of deputies, gentlemen, citizens and officials, together with Samuel, Tom and their followers, all awaiting an audience of the Governor. The music accompanying the scene explains in a compressed form the significance of the first two themes (Ex 209 and 210) we heard in the Prelude. To the tune of the first, in the same key and accompanied by the same scoring as in the Prelude, Officials and Gentlemen express in hushed tones their loyal wishes that the Governor may rest in peace and enjoy happy dreams —for all the world, it sounds, as though they were just putting him to bed instead of waiting for him to get up.

As in the Prelude the rather sanctimonious mood of the first tune is disturbed by the deliberate tread of Ex 210. This time no fugato develops but we note that the theme is sung in unison by Samuel, Tom and their followers, who talk in a menacing, typically conspiratorial way of the punishment that awaits the hated Governor for his misdeeds. While the conspirators continue their muttering the courtiers repeat their loyal sentiments and the opening chorus dies away in a coda almost identical with that which ended the orchestral Prelude.

Oscar the Page enters to announce the arrival of the Governor, Riccardo, Earl of Warwick. Riccardo greets the waiting crowd to a perky accompaniment of strings with occasional support from flute and piccolo which is very characteristic of the new element of gaiety and lightness that Verdi brings to the score of *Un ballo in maschera*. In the dialogue which is carried on in a freely moving declamatory style Oscar asks Riccardo to look at the list of guests for the forthcoming ball. Riccardo sees Amelia's name among those invited and in a lengthy lyrical aside to the tune of Ex 211 reflects on the joy of seeing and hearing her again—"La rivedrà nell'estasi".

As Riccardo develops his soliloquy the conspirators revert to their muttering and decide that the time is not yet ripe and the place obviously not the best for their plan. The Officials and Gentlemen reaffirm their loyalty and belief in the Governor's wisdom and generosity. As the company retires Riccardo takes Oscar to one side and tells him to wait outside with the others until he sends for him. The general exit is accompanied in the orchestra by a direct reference to the first fugato (Ex 210) combined with one or two hesitant, slightly distorted echoes of the opening phrase of Riccardo's "La rivedrà nell'estasi" (Ex 211).

Renato, Riccardo's friend and adviser and Amelia's husband, enters and remarks on the Governor's moody, distracted air. Riccardo confesses that "a secret, bitter care" weighs him down. Renato replies that he knows his friend's secret—a remark which throws Riccardo into a state of horror, dispelled only when Renato goes on to say that the secret he has discovered is of a plot to assassinate the Governor. This is a great relief to Riccardo, who treats the information most casually, refusing to let Renato tell him the names of those in the plot. Renato sings loyally of his concern for Riccardo's safety in a short, pleasant, but not very inspired aria, with a bolero-like accompaniment and a cadenza that are an unexpected throwback to the composer's earlier days—"Alla vita che t'arride" ("Your life, so full of hope and joy"):

Ex 212

Oscar announces the arrival of the Chief Justice, who enters to an unexpectedly sprightly theme which Verdi develops and toys with in the instrumental background to the ensuing dialogue:

Ex 213

The Judge hands some papers to Riccardo who learns to his astonishment that he is expected to authorize the banishment of a Negro fortune-teller called Ulrica. Oscar stands up for her; she is a very popular fortune-teller. The Judge insists that her cave is a den of criminal intrigue. Riccardo asks the opinion of Oscar, who describes the fortune-teller and her skill in a charming and brilliant aria—"Volta la terrea fronte alle stelle" ("When she lifts her dark face to the stars, how her eyes shine . . ."):

Ex 214

The quality of light-heartedness, hinted at earlier in the scene between Oscar and Riccardo and in the sparkling woodwind unison derived from the Judge's music and immediately preceding this aria of Oscar's, now blossoms fully for the first time in the opera.

It is not entirely true, I think, to say that the element of frivolous gaiety in this music is altogether unlike anything encountered in Verdi before, for it is certainly to be found in the characterization of the Duke in *Rigoletto* and of Violetta in *La traviata*. The main difference between the musical portrait of the Page and that of the earlier characters seems to be to me the orchestral framework in which it is set—and, of course, the consistent gaiety of his music. Even the Duke of Mantua has moments of seriousness and depression. Oscar's light-heartedness is emphasized by a peculiarly brilliant and vivacious orchestral language, in which the piccolo plays an important and characteristically jaunty part to support the singer in such typical passages as the second section of the aria below:

Ex *215*

If Oscar's music in generally considered to hint at the Verdi of *Falstaff*, then so does the use of the piccolo in *Un ballo in maschera*, where we find the instrument stretching its limbs, as it were, in preparation for the almost *concertante* part it eventually takes in *Falstaff*.

Oscar sings another verse—different words to an identical orchestral accompaniment. The Judge repeats his demand for the fortune-teller's banishment. Riccardo refuses to accept it; instead he calls the company back and proposes that everybody should go to Ulrica's cave in disguise. He himself will go disguised as a fisherman. Riccardo, catching something of his Page's outlook on life, is delighted by the whole idea which he regards as an admirable joke. Renato, on the other hand, is apprehensive, and the conspirators, while sneering at his fears, decide among themselves that an opportunity for revenge might well present itself on this outing.

The bright mood of Oscar's aria continues quietly in the orchestra during this dialogue and bursts out again when Riccardo launches

into a cheerful appeal to everybody to follow him and enjoy the fun
of the fortune-teller:

Ex 216

There are ominous, no-good-will-come-of-it warnings from
Renato, but they do little to disturb the gaiety and momentum of
the music, least of all Oscar's *brillante*, piccolo-spiced contribution in
which he decides he will definitely have his fortune told.

Riccardo fixes the time for the rendezvous at three o'clock, and a
cheerful miniature finale is built up on a polka-like tune which
seems to have strayed in from a Strauss or Offenbach operetta:

Ex 217

Riccardo's high spirits carry everybody along with them (even
Samuel and Tom may be discerned singing the same words as the
rest of them) and the curtain falls on an orchestral reprise of Riccardo's call to pleasure.

*Scene 2 : The fortune-teller's hovel. On the left is a fireplace ; the fire is alight
and the magic cauldron steams on a tripod. On the same side is a dark recess.
On the right, a staircase that winds up under the roof and leads to a small
secret door. At the back is the main entrance with a window at the side of it.
In the centre there is a rough table ; hanging from the roof and walls are the
instruments and general paraphernalia needed by the fortune-teller.*

The curtain rises, after three short, shattering tutti chords, on a magnificently sinister *misterioso* orchestral sequence achieved by those
immediately effective, simple means which Verdi handled with
such mastery all his life. In this case the atmosphere is created by the
violoncellos on their open C string, two clarinets in unison in the low
register, and violins and violas in octaves:

Ex 218

Another *ff* chord breaks this musical silence, which is restored by a short *pp sotto voce* passage for double basses and violoncellos in thirds, with violins and violas in thirds an octave higher. Though it does no more than suggest the tone-colour of a passage a few bars later, it is nevertheless worth quoting as an example of the richness of Verdi's orchestral invention in the score of *Un ballo in maschera*:

Ex *219*

All this accompanies Ulrica's "business" with the smoking cauldron which is watched by a fascinated crowd of women and girls. The idea of Ex 219 grows into a brief *ff* climax, helped along by a sinister repeated trumpet figure. As though the sudden din had been made by some of the crowd on the stage instead of by the orchestra, the chorus of women—suddenly very reminiscent of the Witches in *Macbeth*—whispers "Hush!", and in a monotone unison over the tense "silence" of Ex 218, tells us that the Devil is about to speak to Ulrica. The music dies away in a couple of *pp* chords for the full orchestra and some faint drumbeats. All this has been a magnificently effective introduction to Ulrica's invocation proper which now follows ("Invocazione" is the heading in the score at the beginning of this second scene of Act I).

"As though inspired" Ulrica calls on the king of the underworld to make haste—"Re dell'abisso, affrettati":

Ex *220*

The orchestral accompaniment to the broad and dramatic vocal line is distinguished by a quite remarkable restraint as well as a wealth of imaginative detail. The opening bars of Ulrica's tune are accompanied by violins and violas doubling the vocal line (the violins in the same register as the singer, the violas an octave lower), with a semiquaver figure in the low register of the violoncellos to suggest the harmony, and a *pp* punctuation of empty beats by timpani. Woodwind are gradually added—the flute in its lower register, the bassoon at one point near the top of its compass in unison with the oboe. The sinister repeated C's of a solo trumpet are doubled an octave lower by the bassoon, and we hear an echo, in a different instrumentation, of Ex 218.

The first part of Ulrica's Invocation comes to an end without the Devil appearing. Instead, to the accompaniment of an impudent little 6/8 tune for piccolo, flute, oboe, and two clarinets (Allegro brillante, of course), Riccardo enters disguised as a fisherman and pushes his way through the crowd, announcing that he is the first to arrive. He is smartly pushed back into place by the chorus of women and girls whose indignant two-part rebuke makes them sound more like Verdi's *Macbeth* Witches than ever.

Riccardo retires laughing. The scene gets darker and suspense is built up by a powerful orchestral crescendo to a *ff* tutti, which drops immediately to *pp* as Ulrica, in an exalted mood, proclaims that she feels the Devil's embrace. The music takes on an oddly martial quality at this point, as a result of the four steady beats to the bar supplied by horns, trombones, tuba, timpani, strings and second bassoon. Six solo instruments—piccolo, flute, clarinet, bassoon and trumpet play the tune of Ex 220—but in the major and in unison across four octaves. The marching movement merges into a highly dramatic and originally-orchestrated section which includes a superbly effective passage for Ulrica when, against a relentlessly repeated *ppp* C from the trumpets, her vocal line at the words "nulla, più nulla ascondersi al guardo mio potrà" ("Nothing can now be hidden from my sight") is doubled by a flute in the singer's register, by clarinet and bassoon an octave lower, and by the violoncellos an octave lower still on their bottom string. An even lower octave is added by the double basses who double the tune below the violoncellos when the climax approaches. It is a remarkable passage of scoring.

According to the stage instructions in my 1914 orchestral score of the opera, when she has finished her Invocation, Ulrica strikes the ground and disappears to the cries of "Evviva!" from the chorus of women and girls. From below ground Ulrica tells them to be silent.

With a change of tempo to the now almost inevitable Allegro brillante, Silvano enters. He tells us briefly in the sing-song metre of the theme in Act II of *Simon Boccanegra* (Ex 194) that he is a sailor who has been in the Governor's service for fifteen years and has come to ask Ulrica if the future holds anything for him. The fortune-teller reappears, accompanied by the sombre reiteration of eighteen E's and twelve C sharps played in octaves by trumpet and trombone. She tells Silvano that he will shortly receive money and a commission. While Ulrica is speaking Riccardo takes a piece of paper, writes on it quickly and slips it with some money into the unsuspecting Silvano's pocket. Silvano feels in his pocket for money to pay

Ulrica for her encouraging prediction and discovers Riccardo's paper and money. On the paper is written: "Riccardo to his dear Silvano, officer." The sailor is delighted; and the crowd is so impressed by the speedy fulfilment of her prophecy that they hail Ulrica as "our immortal Sibyl".

There is a knock at the small secret door. Ulrica opens it and a servant enters. In the characteristic monotone conventionally used by heralds and messengers in early nineteenth-century operas he announces that his mistress is waiting outside and wishes to consult the fortune-teller. Riccardo recognizes him as Amelia's servant and hides when Ulrica, proclaiming that she wishes to have a private conference with Satan, sends the crowd away. The crowd's exit music is typically neat and lightfingered and one is a little surprised to discover that Oscar is not among those present; it certainly sounds as if he ought to be.

Amelia enters *agitatissima* to a sympathetically agitated tune in the strings:

Ex 221

The 3/8 time and general shape and breathlessness of this tune are a clear blue print of the theme which plays a principal part in the overture and action of *La forza del destino*. As we hear it in *Un ballo in maschera* it underlines Amelia's urgent plea to Ulrica for some means of curing her of her love for Riccardo (who overhears this confession and is delighted to hear that Amelia loves him). Ulrica's answer is a gentle *cantabile* description of what Amelia must do. She must go to the outskirts of the city where the gallows stands, and at midnight pluck the herb which grows at its foot and whose magic drops will soothe her troubled heart. The words of Ulrica's directions give a gloomy and sinister picture of the scene Amerlia has to visit, but the tune they are sung to is oddly lyrical and has the kind of string accompaniment which becomes increasingly characteristic of Verdi's style as it developed in later years:

Ex 222

To the anticipation-hunter the third and fourth bars will bring particular joy as an unmistakable forecast of Iago's "Era la notte" in *Otello* nearly thirty years later. The orchestration, too, is almost identical.

Amelia is horrified by Ulrica's words and she and the music revert to their earlier *agitato* mood. Riccardo in his hiding place overhears her decision to carry out Ulrica's instructions and determines that she shall not go alone. Amelia prays to God for strength to purge her heart and cool her flaming passion in a tune which Verdi uses later as an effective instrumental theme:

Ex 223

From Amelia's statement of the tune over a *ppp* string tremolo a short trio builds up. Amelia reiterates her prayer, Ulrica bids her keep her courage up and Riccardo expresses his love and determination to follow Amelia to the very abyss to be with her. It is a simple and telling scene.

On the four occasions that the three singers and orchestra rise to *ff* the instrumentation, which at a quick glance and a first inattentive hearing one presumes to be a normal tutti, is remarkable for the omission of flutes, trumpets and trombones, but the inclusion of whatever brass bass is used nowadays as *cimbasso*. Twice, when the highest note is Amelia's top G sharp, the *ff* orchestral support is kept to a register well below it (the highest note in the orchestra is a B from the oboe, a sixth lower than Amelia); and twice, when the climax of the vocal line is no higher than Amelia's C or C sharp above middle C, the orchestra is kept strictly to the singer's register. It is an intriguingly unconventional orchestral sequence.

The sound of voices outside demanding to be let in brings the trio to an end and Amelia leaves hurriedly by the secret door. Ulrica goes to the main entrance and opens it to let in Samuel, Tom and their followers, Oscar, and various officers and gentlemen of the Governor's staff disguised "bizzarramente" according to the score.

Riccardo comes out of his hiding place and mingles with them. A brassy passage of entrance-music accompanies the new arrivals who call noisily on Ulrica to foretell the future. Ulrica doesn't answer, even when Riccardo makes a personal application to have his fortune told. Her negative reaction is perhaps explained by the words "Scena e Canzone" over the music which lets in the Governor's entourage. At any rate, she makes no audible comment until

Riccardo has sung his Canzone. This proves to be a cheerful ditty in which Riccardo, in his character of fisherman, sings defiantly of death and fate and bids Ulrica tell him the worse—"Dì tu se fedele" ("Tell me if the sea is faithful") :

Ex 224

Riccardo's true character comes through his fisherman's disguise in an elegant, slightly Neapolitan song with a brilliant "middle" to it—marked *leggero pp e staccato assai* and coloured by the chirpy eloquence of the piccolo which distinguishes the score of this opera. Riccardo sings two verses of his Canzone with the chorus each time echoing his final phrase in a hearty vocal and orchestral unison.

Ulrica rebukes Riccardo for his flippant attitude to a serious matter, but takes his hand and begins to tell his fortune. A trumpet and two trombones in octaves repeat a sombrely monotonous series of A flats as Ulrica, also in a monotone, looks at Riccardo's palm and reads it. It is the hand of a nobleman, she says, who has lived under the influence of Mars. An oboe, clarinet and bassoon take over the gloomy trumpet-and-trombone ostinato, adding their own sinister variations to it as Ulrica suddenly pushes Riccardo's hand away from her and refuses to read it any more. Everybody including Riccardo, insists on her finishing. Ulrica hesitates and then speaks: Riccardo will shortly die, at the hand of a friend.

The fortune-teller's words are heard with horror expressed first in a *ff* outcry, then in hushed, awestruck tones ending *pp* on the basses' low F—a note doubled and given added awesomeness by the bassoons and trombones in unison.

For a moment there is an apprehensive silence broken only by the thud of timpani and bass drum. Then suddenly the atmosphere changes with a skittish little three-bar introduction for woodwind, and Riccardo looks around him and remarks (*con eleganza*) that Ulrica's prophecy is either a joke or madness, and laughs at his companions' credulity—"È scherzo od è follia" :

Ex 225

Inevitably the piccolo joins in to add sparkle to the *leggerissimo* accompaniment begun by the strings. Riccardo's opening phrase marks the start of a really admirable ensemble. The next voice to be heard is Ulrica, who turns to Samuel and Tom and warns them not to laugh. The conspirators are gravely disquieted by what she says and they mutter away among themselves about Ulrica, whose words are barbed and whose glance is like lightning.

In Verdi's characterization of the conspirators in this ensemble we encounter an entirely new element for the first time. Samuel and Tom not only have their own distinctive vocal line, but they are followed about by their own distinctive instruments. The tune of their mutterings and grumblings is doubled by a solo bassoon (always staccato), by violas and violoncellos. This use of particular instruments to give added colour and individuality to a character is something Verdi developed with increasing skill in his later operas and brought to its highest point in *Falstaff*. On its rather tentative first appearance in *Un ballo in maschera* this form of instrumental characterization succeeds admirably in suggesting the conspirators' obviously nervous and half-hearted laughter.

Oscar is the one character who is perturbed by the whole situation —a little surprisingly, considering the impression of carefree gaiety made so far. But he is genuinely affected nevertheless by Ulrica's prophecy of his master's fate, and he is moved to show his concern in a series of warm, broad phrases:

Ex 226

The ensemble reaches a conventional half-way mark and starts up again to develop in a typically dexterous manner (with a brief reminder of the conspirators' bassoon) and ends in a deft, instrumental signing-off in the vein of Riccardo's opening phrase.

If its emotional and dramatic content is understandably not so intense as that of the *Rigoletto* quartet, Verdi's technical skill and distinctive characterization in this ensemble are every bit as ingenious and effective. Riccardo's frivolousness, Oscar's disquiet, Ulrica's solemn reiterated warnings, the uneasy laughter of Samuel and Tom are clearly and unmistakably defined in the course of a masterly little sequence.

The action is resumed with Riccardo asking Ulrica who the assassin will be. She replies: the first man who shakes Riccardo by the hand. Riccardo gaily offers his hand to his companions, but

254 FAMOUS VERDI OPERAS

although there is nothing in the music to suggest any sinister reaction to Ulrica's prophecy none of them will accept it. At this moment Renato suddenly appears; Riccardo hurries to greet him and clasps him by the hand. This is a great relief to Samuel and Tom, who have been pretty nervous all along of their plot being discovered, while the rest of the company recognizes the folly of Ulrica's prophecy. Renato, Riccardo points out, is his closest and most trusted friend, and he goes on to reproach Ulrica for her deficient second-sight: she did not know his identity or the fact that she had been threatened with banishment. Riccardo throws her a purse. The fortune-teller, thanking him for his magnanimity, reminds him nevertheless that he must beware of treachery.

Voices crying, "Viva Riccardo!" are heard outside, and a crowd bursts in headed by Silvano, who leads them in a hymn in praise of the Governor, "O Figlio d'Inghilterra amor di questa terra!" ("Son of England, idol of our land!")* The main eight-bar theme of his hymn has the dreadful banality of one of Bellini's march tunes; Verdi scores it for half a town *banda*—bassoons, horns, trumpets, trombones, tuba and drums. It is succeeded by another eight-bar tune sung *con entusiasmo* by Oscar and Riccardo which has the rhythmic pattern, but little of the elegance of Oscar's sweeping phrases in Ex 226. A subdued interlude follows to a sparse and *pp* woodwind accompaniment: Ulrica and Renato full of forebodings, the conspirators annoyed by the crowd's display of loyalty to their popular ruler. Samuel, Tom and their followers express themselves in their familiar staccato manner—a characteristic which is also adopted significantly by Renato whose eventual role in the drama is thus hinted at.

But not for long; the suggestion of stealth and secrecy is brusquely swamped by a *ff* outburst in which the Oscar-Riccardo tune is played as a counter-melody to the march-like strains of "O Figlio d'Inghilterra"—Ulrica joining Oscar, Riccardo, woodwind, violins and violoncellos in a melodic battle with the rest of the company, horns and brass. The tempo quickens to *più mosso* and a noisy coda develops with loud fanfares from the brass, and the curtain falls. In the excitement and bustle of these final pages, the student of orchestration may be intrigued by one detail: the timpani player, his instruments tuned to A and E, persists on a couple of occasions with a lone E natural while the rest of the orchestra play a chord of A flat major. Today with rapid mechanical tuning the player can conscientiously

---

* Those who still possess the recording of *Un ballo in maschera* made by Gigli, Caniglia, Barbieri and Bechi during the war will note that the Italian censorship of this opera did not end in 1859. Mussolini's mob altered "Figlio d'Inghilterra" to "Figlio della patria".

tune his E natural to E flat, but if he doesn't he will be demonstrating what Verdi knew well enough: that with all that din going on a semitone one way or the other in the timpani isn't going to be very noticeable. Or if it is, the wrong note can always be blamed on the double basses.

ACT II

Scene : A lonely place at the foot of a steep hill in the neighbourhood of Boston. On the left, at the back, the two white pillars of the gallows. The scene is lit by the light of a misty moon.

As with the last act of *La traviata* the curtain rises immediately and the orchestral Prelude begins—in this case on a vigorous and agitated tutti:

Ex 227

The question of the phrasing of the first six notes of Ex 227 has recently been the subject of some learned Italian controversy owing to the discrepancies between the 1914 and the 1959 editions of the score. In the earlier edition a slur appeared over each group of three notes; in the later, the slur was over the first two notes only of each group. The phrase as it appears in my example is taken from Verdi's own manuscript—or at least, from as much of it as was reproduced in Francis Toye's classic book on Verdi and which anybody else could have consulted before arguing the irrelevant toss between the 1914 and 1959 editions.

The stormy mood of the opening gives way to a solo flute, accompanied by *pp* tremolo strings, playing the tune of Ex 223 *dolcissimo* and *espressivo* in D major, as Amelia, come to pluck the magic herb Ulrica told her about, appears high up on the hillside. She kneels and prays, and the tune is repeated *cantabile* by violins and violoncellos across two octaves. This short lyrical interlude is brought to an end by a noisy and dramatic tutti which accompanies Amelia as she rises and slowly descends the hill.

This brings us to another point in the score which has been causing learned headaches. In this case it is not a matter of phrase marks but

Ex 228

of actual notes in the tune which begins the anxious, rather plaintive coda of this orchestral prelude.

Ex 228 shows how the phrase appears in the 1959 edition. In the 1914 score the note I have marked * is shown as E instead of F. In the Toscanini and Gigli recordings, both made after 1914 but before 1959, the phrase is played as shown above. The Cetra recording, however, made during the same period, sticks to the E of the 1914 edition, while the Decca–London recording, made after the 1959 score also—and surprisingly—favours the 1914 E. There is little doubt to my mind that the F is the right note, and not the E. One has only to look at the variation of the tune that begins in the second half of the fourth bar of Ex 228 to see that the series of suspensions is on the basic melodic sequence of B flat, A, G, F, G, F, E, D, and not—as it ought to be, if the 1914 version were logically followed—on B flat, A, G, E, G, F, E, D.

In a long and dramatic declamatory passage Amelia expresses all the terror and apprehension she feels in her eerie, sinister surroundings. She plucks up her courage, however, and makes as if to approach the gallows, but hesitates and wonders what will remain for her when she has plucked the herb and rid herself of her love for Riccardo—"Ma dall'arido stelo divulsa, come avrò di mia mano quell'erba" ("But when I have plucked the herb from its withered stem . . ."):

Ex 229

The cor anglais plays an effectively mournful part in Amelia's melancholy and skilfully constructed opening Andante. This section of the aria consists of a fifteen-bar phrase played twice through. The first time it consists of three bars of unaccompanied cor anglais followed by twelve bars sung by Amelia to a reticent string accompaniment punctuated by occasional comment from the cor anglais. The second time it consists of three bars of cor anglais (unaccompanied but for two pizzicato string chords) followed by the cor anglais playing the first six bars of Amelia's tune which she herself takes over at the end of the sixth bar and finishes. During what might be called the "middle"—that is, the six-bar passage of cor anglais tune—Amelia weeps, but her sobs are heard mostly in the orchestra where the breathless off-beat semiquavers in the violins are an effective variant of the sighing semitones of Verdi's traditional expression of tears.

9

Midnight strikes in the familiar six-stroke form we heard in *Rigoletto* (see p 121), and the terrified Amelia imagines she sees a head staring at her from the ground. Her horror is expressed in a stormy change of tempo, which leaves her hypnotized by what she sees and repeating ("con voce soffocata") that she is transfixed—a sinister, dramatic moment which Verdi emphasizes with a hushed and effective low-register unison of bassoons, trombones and tuba. (Verdi's use of trombones in such moments becomes increasingly fascinating and individual as one studies each succeeding opera—not least for his ability to give the music a sombre quality without ever making the music sound "fat" as his German contemporaries so often did.)

Amelia falls on her knees to pray; the tempo changes to the opening Andante and the cor anglais returns with the phrase:

Ex 230

In the score these three bars are cued into the oboe part with Verdi's instruction that "for greater safety in performance these three bars may be played by the oboe, the rest by the cor anglais".

It is on this phrase, with the A and G in the second bar turned into dotted quaver and semiquaver, that Amelia's brief prayer is based, the coda of which, at the word "miserere", echoes the familiar thumping rhythm of the *Trovatore* scene a couple of times. On this occasion, however, the *pp* instrumentation is limited to unison bassoons, trombones, tuba, timpani and bass drum.

Riccardo enters suddenly and in an agitated, breathless passage tells Amelia passionately how much he loves her. She begs him to have pity on her; she is the wife of his closest friend. Riccardo tells her of the remorse that gnaws at his soul and pours out his love for her in a lyrical passage accompanied to begin with by strings (without double basses) which has about it more than a hint of the uniquely beautiful string-writing later found in *Otello*—"Non sai tu che se l'anima mia il rimorso dilacera e rode" ("Do you not know that if remorse tears and gnaws at my soul . . ."):

Ex 231

There is in Riccardo's long opening passage a quality of tenderness which is virtually making its first appearance in Verdi's tenor

roles, and which is encountered ever more frequently from this
opera onwards. Amelia is the one who disturbs the mood when,
after offering a prayer to heaven in a sudden ravishing change of
key from F to D flat, she once more reminds Riccardo that she is
the wife of his best friend. Riccardo pleads with her to say at least
that she loves him. Amelia hesitates, and then admits that she does
—"but", she begs him, "save me from my heart". Amelia's words
are heard in a *pp* coda in which the tenderness characteristic of so
much of this scene is expressed in a beautiful and moving passage
for violoncellos:

Ex 232

Riccardo greets Amelia's confession excitedly and then, *a mezza
voce dolcissimo*, sings to her of the ecstasy in his heart—"Oh, qual
soave brivido"—a tune which is accompanied, in addition to energetic quaver-triplets in the harp, by an unusual *ppp* and *leggerissimo*
string figure which I have indicated below:

Ex 233

The full startling effect of this string accompaniment is very
seldom achieved in practice, but when it can be made to come off
(as Toscanini made it so superlatively) it creates an original impression of Riccardo's excitement and rapture. A kind of despairing
rapture, indeed, is the dominant emotion in the duet which develops
from Riccardo's long opening tune. Amelia repeats the melody, but
the palpitating string figure gives way to a legato accompaniment
(still with the harp arpeggios) by flute and two clarinets. The duet
builds to a climax as Riccardo once more asks Amelia whether she
loves him. This time she does not hesitate, although she still pleads
with her lover to save her from herself, and the whole orchestra

plays *tutta forza* the lyrical tune of Ex 232, adding a particularly stirring one-bar phrase heard later in Riccardo's "Non sai tu che se l'anima mia" than the quotation in Ex 231 shows.

From the E major in which the duet temporarily dies away, we return to Riccardo and, without ceremony, to the C major of a repetition of his "Qual soave brivido". The same *leggerissimo* string figure is also repeated, although this time Riccardo is joined by Amelia whose desperate mood continues—much of it expressed, it must be said, in the same optimistic tune and with the same *entusiasmo* as her lover. The duet ends with conventional *brio* and a note in the score that the moon grows increasingly bright all the time.

The lovers are interrupted by the sudden appearance of Renato. Amelia quickly covers her face with her veil. Renato tells Riccardo that he has come to warn him against the conspirators who have heard of his rendezvous with a woman and are already on their way to kill him.

In a scene of some confusion, but of exciting and dramatic music, first Renato implores Riccardo to escape, giving him his cloak to disguise himself in and showing him a path that will be safe. Next, Riccardo grasps Amelia's hand in the darkness and tells her to save herself; then, in a whispered reply, she entreats him to save *his* life. While Renato goes to one side to see if the conspirators are approaching, Riccardo and Amelia each start arguing to persuade the other to escape. Amelia wins her point, then, in a vigorous and far-from-whispered aside proclaims that if she is able to save Riccardo her soul will no longer fear the cruel fate to which it is condemned.

It is a stirring passage, remarkable in the orchestra for Verdi's comparatively rare use at this period of the *cimbasso* unattended by trombones. Riccardo agrees to go, but before he leaves he makes Renato promise to escort the unknown lady back to the gates of the city without ever speaking to her or looking at her face.

Renato promises, and his oath is rounded off by a sudden and arresting *ff* roll on the timpani, which dies away quickly as, according to the synopsis given away with a recent recording of the opera, "Amelia's fearful ear now detects the approach of the assassins". Amelia repeats her desperate entreaties to Riccardo, this time (*sotto voce* and *agitatissima*) in a precipitate Presto assai which begins for all the world—as Frances Toye reminded us—like a Gilbert and Sullivan patter song—"Odi tu come fremono cupi per quest'aure gli accenti di morte?" ("Do you hear the words of death . . . ?"):

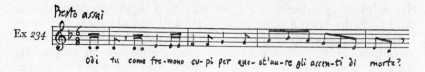

Ex 234

Presto assai

Odi tu come fre-mono cu-pi per que-st'au-re gli accen-ti di morte?

The excitement of the scene which now develops is generated by
what is little more than a two-part invention of tremendous vigour, a
tune that hurtles along with half the orchestra playing it in unison
with Amelia, and half (including once again the *cimbasso* independent of its trombones) punctuating it with a breathless two-note
figure of a semitone sometimes rising, sometimes falling. So long as
it is heard while Amelia is singing it would be tempting to regard
these semitone figures as yet another variant of Verdi's ways of expressing tears; but since it also occurs when the tune is repeated by
Renato, who is keeping a lookout in the background and makes
another and untearful personal appeal to Riccardo to escape, one
can only suppose that in this context it is an expression of urgency
and not of weeping.

After a brief, strictly *a tempo* interlude contributed by Riccardo the
tune starts up again, sung initially by Amelia and Renato in unison
and then, without alteration of the original melodic and harmonic
structure or its straightforward diphonic character, built up into an
exciting trio with a neat and effectively theatrical coda to accompany
Riccardo's exit.

Renato and Amelia are about to move off when Samuel, Tom
and the other conspirators are heard approaching, very much on
the warpath, to the unaccompanied and characteristic strains of the
first ten notes of Ex 210. The orchestra then introduces another of
those stealthy staccato phrases which follow the conspirators around
in this opera—a *pp* sequence played three times by first and second
violins, with a flute and oboe joining in the second and third times
it is heard:

Ex 235

The mood of secrecy and stealth is roughly broken by Renato's
cry of "Who goes there?" in a voice which is instantly recognized as
not being the Governor's. Renato's presence with a veiled woman
in such an unprepossessing rendezvous naturally intrigues the conspirators, and Tom, feeling cheated of the evening's entertainment
he had expected, insists that at least he should be allowed to know
who the Mystery Woman might be. He makes a move to tear off
Amelia's veil but Renato draws his sword and threatens to kill anybody who lays hands on her. Amelia, fearing bloodshed and by now
in a thoroughly confused and desperate state, lifts the veil herself and
creates what can best be described as a sensation all round.

Samuel is the first to recover his senses; and he rejoices in what
strikes him as the superbly humorous situation—as he rather bawdily

puts it—of a husband romping in the dew with his own wife as
though he was on his honeymoon. Samuel's comments are made to a
tune marked to be played by the violins *con eleganza*, which has
about it something of the light-hearted cynicism of some of Rigoletto's music. It is cynical, but behind the cynicism there is also
something of the embarrassment of Rigoletto's "La-ra-la-ra" (see
p 107) which suggests that perhaps everything isn't quite so funny
and straightforward as it seems. The instrumental decoration of the
tune with grace notes and trills adds a wonderful touch of awkward
jauntiness to Samuel's "Ve', se di notte":

Ex 236

The humour of the situation begins to appeal to Tom as well, who
joins Samuel in laughing at the sensation and gossip it is going to
start in town. There is nothing full-throated or good-natured about
their laughter; it is a malicious chuckle, emphasized once more by
the acid *staccato assai*, and reminding us, by the characteristic
rhythm of "E che baccano sul caso strano", that we are still in the
sinister company of conspirators whose sworn object is murder:

Ex 237

Renato now begins to rage at what he not unnaturally considers
Riccardo's shabby behaviour, while Amelia laments her fate in one
or two poignant phrases addressed to herself. The points of view of
husband and wife merge with the laughter of Samuel, Tom and
their confederates and a short, admirably characterized ensemble
develops. As it ends Renato goes over to Samuel and Tom and asks
them *risolutamente* to come and see him in the morning. They are a
little puzzled by the request but agree to do so. They go on their way
as stealthily as they came, accompanied successively by the tunes of
Exx 235, 236 and 237, and laughing among themselves.

Renato, left alone with Amelia, reminds her that he has given his
oath to accompany her back to the city gates and leads her away. In
the distance the laughter of the conspirators grows fainter and fainter,
and the act ends on a witty and wonderfully effective curtain.

ACT III

Scene 1 : The study in Renato's house. The walls are lined with books, and on the mantelshelf are two bronze vases. At the back there is a magnificent full-length portrait of Riccardo ; in the centre is a table.

A ferocious brass unison fanfare, Allegro agitatissimo e presto, raises the curtain and prepares us for the sight of a storming, angry Renato who enters, drawn sword in hand, dragging in Amelia. He puts down his sword and closing the door tells his wife that her prayers are in vain; she must die. Amelia, admitting that circumstances are against her, nevertheless protests her innocence. Renato, whose brutal determination is underlined in the orchestra by the brass bass teamed up with the bassoons in the absence of trombones, repeats his call for blood. Amelia resigns herself to her fate; but begs, as a last favour, to be allowed to see her child: "Morrò, ma prima in grazia" ("I shall die, but first let me embrace my son"):

Ex 238

This tender and moving aria is introduced by a solo violoncello who continues to contribute a simple lyrical obbligato which greatly adds to the pathos of the scene.

Without looking at Amelia, Renato points to the door. She can see her son in there, he says—in darkness where her blushes and his shame will not be seen. As soon as Amelia has left, Renato realizes that it is not on his wife that his vengeance should fall but on Riccardo. He gazes fixedly at the portrait of his friend that hangs on the wall, proclaiming that it is Riccardo's blood that must wipe out the injury he has suffered. A tense and arresting orchestral introduction—

Ex 239

—sets the mood of vindictiveness of the first half of the aria that follows, in which the string figure and the ominous tones of trumpet and trombone are a prominent feature of the accompaniment. Still gazing at the portrait Renato accuses Riccardo—"It was you, who defiled that soul, that was my heart's delight" ("Eri tu che macchiavi quell'anima . . .") :

Ex 240

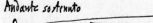

Bitterly and angrily Renato reproaches the man who has repaid the loyalty of his best friend in such a way. Renato's bitterness and anger give way to a sudden, unexpected melancholy as he remembers the days of happiness with Amelia, which are now gone for ever, leaving nothing but hatred and death in his widowed heart. The change of mood is brought about by a gentle transition from the ferocious opening D minor to the peaceful relative major key of F. The change of orchestral colouring at the end of this first part of the aria, however, is abrupt and striking. Harp arpeggios and a solo flute, later joined by a colleague a third lower, play as an introduction the opening tune of the second part of Renato's aria—"O dolcezze perdute!" ("Oh lost delight . . .") :

Ex 241

It is a lyrical passage of unusual poignancy created, as so often in Verdi, by the simplest means—like the characteristic harmonic twists in the coda, and the featherweight orchestral accompaniment featuring harp, flute and *ppp* tremolo strings, that hovers over Renato's final heartbroken phrases.

From violoncellos and basses there now come the unmistakable conspiratorial sounds (*ppp staccato assai*) associated with Samuel and Tom, who enter as the strings develop a short fugato in the manner we first heard in the Prelude to the opera.

Renato surprises them by saying that he knows all about their conspiracy; he has proof in the papers lying on the table. But they need not be alarmed; so far from telling the Governor anything about their plot, he wants to take part in it; and to show his good faith he offers his son as hostage—to the accompaniment, it must be observed, of an oddly frivolous kind of figure played by first violins and violas in octaves:

Ex 242

Samuel and Tom accept Renato's pledge, and in determined martial tones the conspirators and their new recruit resolve that vengeance shall fall swiftly and terribly on Riccardo's head. Renato is the first to proclaim their intention—"Dunque l'onta di tutti sol una" ("Then shame of one by the shame of all . . ."):

Ex 243

If this stirring, pleasantly vulgar episode seems a little familiar it is because the time, the key, the tempo, the accompaniment and the instrumentation combine to provide a clear and powerful "pre-echo" of "Ora e per sempre addio, sante memorie" in Act II of *Otello* (see Ex 405). The same key of A flat, the same thumping four-in-a-bar accompaniment of harp and pizzicato double basses divided into four parts are common to both passages—except that in *Otello* a triplet quaver figure punctuates the march rhythm from time to time.

Samuel and Tom repeat Renato's tune, which is reinforced in the orchestra by a typical early-Verdi solo trumpet with trombones and tuba adding weight to the harp-and-basses four-in-a-bar.

After a resolute unison the three men begin to dispute who shall have the privilege of killing Riccardo. Renato stakes his claim first, as a reward, one gathers, for his co-operation in the conspiracy. Samuel replies that it is *his* right, the Governor stole his ancestral home from him. Tom asks what part *he* is to be allowed to play—whose brother Riccardo killed ten years ago. This discussion, which takes place to the tune of Ex 242, is brought to an end by Renato who says that chance alone must decide. He goes to the mantelshelf and taking down one of the bronze vases places it on the table.

9*

Samuel writes their three names on three pieces of paper and drops them into the vase.

These dramatic movements are matched by the orchestra with a passage of fine dramatic suspense. Over a sustained tremolo by violas and basses, with sinister intermittent rumbles by *ppp* unison bassoons, trombones and tuba and whispered chromatic runs by violins and violoncellos, a solo trumpet is heard ominously and distantly playing:

Ex 244

The use of a solo trumpet in the mounting tension of this long sequence is one of Verdi's most masterly strokes as an orchestrator. It may be because one is instinctively afraid the player is going to crack, or it may be because the instrument is being cast slightly out of its familiar noisy character, but there is always a peculiarly tense quality about a really exposed slow trumpet solo in the orchestra. In this instance the characteristic clarity of the instrument has a kind of calculated ruthlessness which creates an astonishing atmosphere of suspense and foreboding. Just how dead right Verdi's instrumentation of this passage is becomes apparent immediately one tries to imagine it played on any other instrument in the orchestra. It is an uncannily brilliant stroke of instrumental casting.

Amelia enters to say that Oscar has arrived with an invitation from the Earl. Renato tells her that Oscar must wait, but she herself must stay in the room. Amelia is at once filled with agitated premonitions which she expresses in a short, breathless passage that takes her up to a top B flat and down again. Renato meanwhile reassures Samuel and Tom that his wife knows nothing of their plot. He then turns to Amelia and takes her towards the table. He points to the vase and tells her that it contains three names; her innocent hand must draw one from it. These words are delivered *sotto voce* and with an "accento terribile", against a sustained *pp* chord for one trumpet, the three trombones and tuba, which is twice disturbed by a shattering and terrifyingly unexpected *fff* ratatatat from the timpani, which the same instrument echoes *ppp*.

Amelia goes slowly to the table and with a trembling hand draws from the vase a slip of paper which she hands to her husband, who passes it on to Samuel. Her action is accompanied by another astonishingly dramatic passage of orchestration. The frivolous tune of Ex 242 is played *ff* in the minor and stretched out in such a way

that it sounds curiously like a distorted form of the trumpet solo of
Ex 244. It is scored for the lowest register of two clarinets in unison
with the two bassoons and the violoncellos, against a sustained *ff* roll
for timpani and bass drum and a harmonic background provided by
a vigorous tremolo on the violas, and on the double basses who are
divided into no fewer than three parts. Trumpets and trombones
interject a couple of thunderous C's which lead to a sudden *ppp* and a
strongly distorted echo of Ex 244 played by a bassoon and violoncellos—a point in the score marked with a star as the cue on which
Amelia extracts the slip of paper from the vase.

Samuel reads the name on the paper and announces (*con dolore*)
that it is Renato's. Renato is overjoyed at his good fortune and in
unison with Samuel and Tom launches out into an exultant reprise
of Ex 243, this time with words to the effect that the traitor who
boasted of America's woes shall atone for them. Amelia adds her
cries of dismay when she realizes what is happening.

Renato goes to the door to let in the Earl's messenger. Oscar
enters, accompanied by a sprightly passage for strings played *ppp con
eleganza*, and turning to Amelia tells her that she and her husband
are invited to a *splendissimo* masked ball that evening, an invitation
which Renato accepts eagerly once he has made sure that the Earl
will be present—a circumstance which also appeals to Samuel and
Tom. Oscar greets Renato's acceptance with delight in a sparkling
passage in which he is accompanied by his now inseparable companion, the piccolo—"Ah! di che fulgor, che musiche esulteran le
soglie . . ." ("Ah, what splendour and music we shall enjoy"):

Ex 245

This is the beginning of a finely characterized ensemble in which
Oscar continues on his cheerful way, Amelia sings the tune of his
"Ah! di che fulgor" in the minor to words expressing the misery of
her position, Renato mutters away to himself about the joyful prospect before him, and Samuel and Tom rejoice in the opportunities
offered for revenge—that *vendetta in domino* which was the original
pre-Censorship title of Verdi's opera.

For all Amelia's repeated efforts to drag the movement into B flat
minor, it ends obstinately and with some exciting unison passages
for Amelia and Oscar in the major, leading into a coda based on
Oscar's opening phrase (now played *ppp sotto voce* by strings—no

basses), during which Amelia desperately tries to think of a way of
warning Riccardo without betraying her husband, and Renato and
his confederates decide that they will each wear a blue garment with
a red sash knotted at the left and that the password will be "death".

The scene ends with a few final bars of ensemble in which the conspirators cry "Morte!", Amelia repeats her desperate desire to warn
Riccardo, and Oscar assures her (for the second time) that she will
be Queen of the Ball.

*Scene 2 : A luxurious room in Riccardo's house. A table with writing materials ;
at the back, a great curtain which separates the study from the ballroom.*

The curtain rises with a passage for strings only, the first violins
playing the tune of Ex 211.

Riccardo is alone at his desk, and having decided that honour and
duty demand an end to his assocation with Amelia, is preparing to
write an order sending Renato and his wife back to England. Riccardo writes, but realizing that it means he will never see Amelia
again, lets the pen drop from his hand as he is about to sign the order.
He finally signs it and places the document in his tunic. Filled with
despair Riccardo swears that though he is forced to lose her for ever
he will always love Amelia—"Ma se m'è forza perderti":

Ex 246

This is a short and attractive aria with a "middle" distinguished
by some imaginative scoring to match those passages which Riccardo
is instructed to sing "cupo" (or darkly)—clarinets, bassoons and
violas in thirds—and a sudden ravishing modulation from D flat
into the C major in which the aria ends.

The sound of music is heard through the curtains at the back of
the stage—obviously the usual small-town *banda* which is to supply
some characteristic small-town bourgeois dance music at an otherwise elegant and aristocratic function:

Ex 247

Allegro vivissimo

This time, however, Verdi makes use of a neat technical trick. Instead of having his band play incessantly while characters on the stage are engaged in conversation we are intended to hear, he leaves silent gaps in the back-stage music. This has the effect of bringing the dialogue into close-up, as it were, and giving the impression that the background music is still going on all the time but is temporarily out of focus.

The first of these dialogue close-ups is of Oscar, who enters with a note for the Earl. It is from an unknown woman warning him that an attempt is to be made on his life. Riccardo decides to ignore the whole thing; he would be thought a coward if he stayed away from the ball. He dismisses the idea from his mind and thinks only of seeing Amelia again during the evening—a reflection Riccardo makes in a sudden and satisfying warm echo of what can now be regarded as the love theme of the opera—the tune of Ex 211.

The curtains at the back of Riccardo's study part and reveal:

Scene 3: A large and luxurious ballroom, brilliantly lit and richly hung. Gay music introduces the dancing and as the curtains open a crowd of guests is seen. Most of them are masked, a few of them are wearing dominos, others are in evening dress without masks. Among those dancing are one or two young Creoles. The guests look for their friends, avoid them, greet them, pursue them. Negro servants are in attendance, and everything is magnificent and gay.

With occasional help from the orchestra in the pit, the *banda* and chorus make a joyful noise to the tune (now in B flat) of Ex 247. The chorus falls silent, however, and the *banda* grows more subdued, with a new and more sedate sequence in the relative minor key of G minor, when Samuel, Tom and their followers enter, dressed in blue dominos with red sashes. Renato, similarly disguised, enters slowly a moment later. The *banda* is now directed in the score to reduce its numbers so as not to disturb the speakers—in other words, to allow us to hear the conspirators identify each other and exchange passwords. The only hitch in their plans at this stage is the absence of Riccardo, or—if he is present—of any clue to what he is wearing. For a few bars the *banda* is augmented "to obtain a *mezzo forte*" while the conspirators disperse among the crowd. Renato, however, is closely followed by Oscar who quickly sees through his disguise. (The *banda* is still in the background but is now a smaller group once more.) In retaliation Renato pulls off Oscar's mask and reproaches him for enjoying himself at the ball while his master is asleep. Oscar answers that the Earl is here at the ball; but he refuses to tell Renato how to recognize him. Renato continues to pester the Page, but Oscar laughs at him and, with the *banda* laying aside its instruments

for the first time, sings a teasing song at him—"Saper vorreste di che
si veste . . ." ("You'd like to know what he's wearing . . .") :

Ex 248

Sa- per vor-re-ste di che si ve-ste

This is Oscar at his gayest and most charming again, full of high-
spirited, mocking tra-la-las and the piccolo following him around
like a spotlight. He sings a couple of verses, when a crowd of masked
guests and dancing couples invade the scene and separate him from
Renato. The *banda* strikes up again with help from the pit orchestra
and the chorus repeats the jolly and appreciative sentiments it expressed when the scene began. This time, however, the crowd doesn't
stay so long and Renato and Oscar are able to make contact again
very quickly. The musical routine is very much the same as it was
in the earlier sequence, with the stage band reduced in size whenever
there is any important dialogue to be heard.

By insisting that he has important business to discuss with the
Earl, Renato finally persuades Oscar to tell him how he is disguised :
he is wearing a black coat with a rose-coloured ribbon on his breast.
Renato tries to ask one more question, but Oscar disappears in the
crowd who return with Ex 247, now becoming something of a plug-
number. This time, however, it leads into an unmistakable coda
which grows louder and faster and, after a couple of *pp* to *ff* crescendos leading to false climaxes, comes to a rowdy and brilliant
conclusion. From the moment the coda begins the *banda* is directed
to omit the bass drum—a direction one can only regard as a con-
siderate thought by the composer for the musician concerned who,
however hard he might hit it, would hardly make the instrument
heard with all the noise already being created by his counterpart
(plus cymbals) in the orchestra pit.

My score of the opera is a little sparing with stage directions at
this point, for although it is obvious that Renato should now go off
in search of his confederates, and that the crowd, with nothing more
to sing, should disperse once more, all that is definitely stated is that
Riccardo enters, pensive and dressed in a black domino with a pink
ribbon, and is followed by Amelia in a white domino.

With Riccardo's entrance the music changes in character abruptly:

Ex 249

From the wings comes dance music played by a small orchestra of "four or six first violins and two seconds", two violas, two violoncellos and two basses.

This is usually described as a mazurka, although the Germans have melodramatically christened it the *Todesmenuett*—or Minuet of Death. Whatever else it may be, with its simple chuck-chuck accompaniment, it most certainly isn't a minuet, even though Verdi does not commit himself one way or the other beyond writing the tune in 3/4 time and marking it Assai moderato.

Disguising her voice and speaking *sotto voce*, Amelia begs Riccardo to leave; his life is in danger. She continues her entreaties but Riccardo refuses to move, even when her sobs give away her identity. The dance music, which has been played all through this sequence, now modulates to D flat and repeats the tune with a pit orchestral accompaniment provided by a solo quintet of violins, viola, violoncello and double bass who do little more than add their chuck-chucks to those coming from the off-stage band. Amelia, telling Riccardo that she loves him, begs him desperately on her knees to leave before it is too late. Riccardo replies that since she loves him his fate doesn't matter, and against the dance band's endless mechanical repetition of its rather modest repertoire, there emerges the counterpoint of "Sin che tu m'ami, Amelia":

Ex 250

Riccardo is supported from time to time by a solo flute in its lower register playing a third above his vocal line; this, and an occasional sustained note for a bassoon, are the only decoration of an austerely simple instrumentation. The dance band is pushed into the background with the out-of-focus effect of the earlier dialogue between Oscar and Renato (see p 269) as Amelia's pleas become more intense and the tempo inevitably grows urgent. As she completes her long phrase, however, the dance band is heard for a bar on its own, going its imperturbable way.

At the end of what has developed into a short duet the tune of Ex 249 returns, still in D flat and played by a stage orchestra which has been reduced to a string quintet. The strings of the pit orchestra limit their support now to a quaver on the first beat of the bar and a plaintive, sighing four-note figure on the G string played once a bar for thirty-one bars by the first violins. This is the musical background against which Amelia and Riccardo say their heart-breaking

last farewell when Amelia learns that she and her husband are to
return to England the next day. During the last few bars of this duet
Renato has entered unseen, and at their final "addio" rushes for-
ward and stabs the Earl. Amelia's horrified cries for help bring in
Oscar and a crowd of guests, officials and soldiers who tear off
Renato's mask and noisily demand his death as a traitor. Samuel and
Tom also appear, but remain in the background.

The company's angry outburst is silenced by what can only be a
gesture, implicit but not indicated in the score, from Riccardo, and
from the wings comes once more the sound of the string band still
unconcernedly playing the familar tune of Ex 249. They play it now
for the eleventh time, back in its original key of F, with all that unswerving devotion to duty and stoical indifference to the hazards of
their calling which has for so long been a credit to the dance band
profession.

In a faint voice against this relentless background Riccardo
orders the crowd to release Renato. He takes the document from his
bosom and tells Renato to come closer and listen. The off-stage band
reaches its final cadence and fades out.

Two solo violins *divisi** and the sombre low notes of a clarinet
introduce a new elegiac air to the music as Riccardo, in a near-
monotone, swears to Renato that Amelia is innocent:

Ex *251*

Riccardo changes from his tense, dramatic utterance to a flowing
lyrical phrase as he speaks of his love for Amelia and how he respected her purity—"io che amai la tua consorte" ("I who loved
your wife . . .") :

Ex *252*

io che a- mai la tua con- sor - te, ri -spet - ta -to ho il suo can-dor.

The mournful violin phrase is heard again when Riccardo gives
Renato the document he has signed and tells him that he was to
return to England with Amelia to take up a new post. Then, as

* The score asks for four solo violins divided in two parts, but in practice and for
familiar acoustical reasons the passage is usually played by two solo violins.

though he had side-tracked himself, Riccardo sings about Amelia once more to the tune of Ex 252, assuring Renato again that although he loved his wife she was innocent.

Amelia, Oscar and Renato express their individual feelings of sadness and remorse in a brief trio passage ending with a poignant anticipation by Renato of the last moments of *Otello*, and rounded off by Riccardo in a noble phrase forgiving all those who may have been involved in the conspiracy against him.

There follows a short hymn-like passage of ensemble rising from a *ppp sotto voce* with only harp and tremolo violas and violoncellos as accompaniment, to a *ff* climax in which Samuel and Tom also join to praise Riccardo's "great and generous heart". With a great final effort, and to the accompaniment of the tears of those who watch, Riccardo bids farewell to his "children" and his beloved America. His voice fails him in the middle of a word and with a whispered "Addio!" he dies. The curtain falls on the survivors expressing their horror ("Notte d'orror!") in the corny kind of conclusion that was apparently inevitable at a stage in Verdi's career when there were still nearly thirty years to go before he learnt the art of leaving the assembled company speechless in the face of tragedy and bloodshed. The death of Riccardo is an effective scene; it could have been better if the surviving principals and chorus could have found no words to express their grief and dismay.

Whatever else one may feel about *Un ballo in maschera* there is little doubt, I think, that it has a charm and fascination peculiarly its own. It has moments of distressing banality; equally it has moments of tremendous dramatic power and originality. The dance music in the last scene of Act III, for instance, is unbelievably trivial, but it is this very quality which heightens its effect as a dramatic device, providing an unchanging, ironic background to the tragic events taking place out of sight of the musicians who play it so unconcernedly. But above all, *Un ballo in maschera* is a score full of far greater musical variety and orchestral invention than anything Verdi had written before. The gaiety and wit of Oscar, the quaint sardonic humour of the conspirators, the light-hearted but not libidinous charm and sex-appeal of Riccardo are all elements which were not only new but were to play an increasingly important part from now on in Verdi's development as a composer. In short, to use a critical cliché of our time, *Un ballo in maschera* is very "forward-looking"; and it is important, I think, to recognize that many of what we regard as the more astonishing technical and idiomatic features of *Otello* and *Falstaff* have their origin in the works of Verdi's "middle" period and did not, as it were, spring Minerva-like, fully armed from the head of their creator.

The question of the final form of the libretto of *Un ballo in maschera* seems to have worried everybody but Verdi. As in the case of *Rigoletto* once he had resigned himself to the Censor's mutilation of the original conception of the opera he left things as they were. When Italy had gained her independence and the Censorship which had dealt with *Rigoletto* and *Un ballo in maschera* no longer applied, it was neither of these operas that Verdi revised, but *Simon Boccanegra, La forza del destino* and *Don Carlos*. The truth is, I suspect, that so long as the characters, situations and general emotional conflicts presented by the story were acceptable to him and were what the Italians call "musicabile", Verdi was not greatly concerned whether the scene of his opera was laid in Boston or Bangkok. He certainly can never have considered he was writing a documentary opera or anything like it, and to try to turn it into one, as the Swedes have done, seems to me to make absolute nonsense of Verdi's music.

The Swedish Royal Opera, it will be remembered, not only restored the opera to its Swedish setting but altered the character of Riccardo to suit the historical fact (or allegation) that Gustav III was a mincing homosexual, whose page was his mignon, and whose affair with Amelia was (to quote the hand-out issued by Covent Garden in 1960 to explain all these facts of life) "a great lark, a romantic exercise". If Verdi ever knew any of this he made a very poor job of portraying it in music; Riccardo has only to open his mouth to make the whole Swedish conception of the character a preposterous fantasy.

There are, admittedly, some puzzling aspects of the opera as Verdi left it. Why on earth, for instance, should Renato be described in the cast list as a Creole? One can only imagine—colour prejudice being what it is—to make him more quickly recognizable as a villain. Otherwise, there is no justification or even mention of it to be found in the libretto, so far as I can see; and certainly no suggestion of it in the music. Renato, indeed, so far from being as black as he is painted, ends up with more than a little of one's sympathy, the victim of a tragedy that is as much his as it is Riccardo's or Amelia's.

There have also been recent productions of *Un ballo in maschera* which, while not going to the Swedes' extreme of emasculating the hero, have nevertheless reverted to the original Swedish setting and some of the Scribe names. This has meant that the conspirators instead of being known (to the delight of so many Anglo-Saxons) as Samuel and Tom, have been given (to the delight of so many Anglo-Saxons) the quaint names of Count Ribbing and Count Horn. The fact one has to face, I fear, is that Verdi's music is far more appropriate to the plebeian figures of Samuel and Tom than to the aristocratic characters who usurp their position in modern adaptations of the opera.

Even in the early stages of the libretto the two conspirators seem to have been commoners at the court of the King, Duke or whomever. When the project was still called *Una vendetta in domino* they appeared as Ermanno and Manuel; in *Adelia degli Adimari* they were Donato and Lando; later they became Mazeppa and Ivan, while in the 1880s Bernard Shaw reported that Covent Garden had rechristened them Armando and Angri.

For all their amateur status as assassins Samuel and Tom are fundamentally the same class as the anonymous professional murderers in *Macbeth* and no fancy titles will disguise the fact. By comparison Sparafucile in *Rigoletto* has breeding and a distinctive natural nobility, and one would be far more ready to believe that *he* had been robbed of an ancestral castle by a despotic ruler than that Samuel had ever been. But if the conspiratorial music to which they do most of their plotting and planning does not raise them above the social level of the rest of Verdi's cloak-and-dagger figures, Samuel, Tom and their confederates differ from their prototypes in one important respect. As Francis Toye said of them, they have learnt to laugh.

Laughter, indeed, is the most strikingly unexpected and distinctive characteristic of an opera basically concerned with death and destruction, which is not commonly regarded in the opera house as a laughing matter. There is the spontaneous high-spirited laughter of Oscar, the incredulous, slightly embarrased laughter of Riccardo's "È scherzo od è follia", the cynical chuckling of the conspirators. The women, on the other hand, do not contribute any laughter; but then they have absolutely nothing to laugh about.*

What has always seemed to me to be an admirable solution to the question of the opera's topographical and historical setting was suggested by the form of the programme (though not of the production) of *Un ballo in maschera* on an occasion at Covent Garden before the war. In accordance with the custom of the house the names of the characters and interpreters were given quite baldly: "Riccardo . . . Dino Borgioli"—"Amelia . . . Eva Turner". If we wanted to know more about them we turned to the synopsis where we read that Riccardo was simply "the Governor". There was no hint of his being the Earl of "Warwich", any more than there was of Amelia's husband being a Creole. Samuel and Tom (who are never addressed by name in the opera, anyway) were Italianized as Samuele and Tomaso; and there was no mention of Boston as the scene of the action. That, we were told, took place in Naples in the seventeenth century.

* One really cannot regard Oscar as a woman, any more than one can think of Cherubino as a woman. Verdi, like Mozart, wrote a boy's music. The fact that a woman has to be cast in the part is entirely the management's bad luck.

There has long been a great deal of haughty laughter at the idea, said to have been started by Mario, of setting the scene in Naples and turning Riccardo into the Spanish Duke of Olivares. But it is far more sensible than it sounds. Naples was ruled by Spanish viceroys from 1503 to 1707, and the viceregal court is an obvious and uncomplicated setting for the plot; for apart from many other things, it would avoid the absurd notion of posting a Creole to England in the seventeenth century. Samuele and Tomaso, as they would now be, would still be a problem; even calling them Don S and Don T would still never make musical grandees of them. But there is little doubt, I think, that the whole colour and ambience of Naples is far better suited to Verdi's score than the prim surroundings of Puritan New England, or the historically authenticated Swedish royal court where the King was a queen.

I cannot remember how, or even whether, the text of *Un ballo in maschera* was changed at Covent Garden in 1937 to fit in with the Neapolitan setting. In any case, anyone who wanted to adapt the words in this instance would find it easy enough. Mussolini has already given us "patria" for "Inghilterra", and where "patria" is not specific enough as an alternative, "Spagna" will certainly serve instead. America is mentioned by name twice in the course of the opera: by the conspirators in the first scene of Act III and by Riccardo in his dying breath. There should not be much trouble here either. "Napoli" or "Italia" can both be substituted with the smallest structural alteration to the rhythm of Verdi's notes. While the scene-designer should relish the opportunity seventeenth-century Spanish-occupied Naples offers to dress the whole thing like a Velasquez, no doubt there would still be headaches for the producer. But since the modern producer has virtually usurped the functions and position of the conductor in the opera house, I for one will shed no tears over his difficulties.

Finally, there is a certain neat justice in placing the action of *Un ballo in maschera* in Naples, for it was there that the whole opera started in the first place.

LA FORZA DEL DESTINO

(*The Force of Destiny*)

Melodrama in four acts. Libretto by Francesco Maria Piave, based on the Spanish play *Don Álvaro, or La Fuerza del Sino*, by Ángel Pérez de Saavedra, Duke of Rivas. First performed at the Imperial Theatre, St Petersburg, on 10th November, 1862. First performance in England: Her Majesty's Theatre, London, 22nd June, 1867. First performance in the United States: Academy of Music, New York, 24th February, 1865. Revised version first performed at La Scala, Milan, 20th February, 1869.

AFTER the launching of *Un ballo in maschera* in 1859 Verdi had every intention of retiring from active musical life. He had written no fewer than twenty operas in seventeen consecutive years of unceasing composition and the final two years of struggle and frustration caused by *Un ballo in maschera* had left him tired and exhausted. At the end of 1860, however, the comparative peace of what has been called his "intermezzo politico" was disturbed by a letter from Russia.* It came from the tenor Enrico Tamberlik, then engaged at the Imperial Opera at St Petersburg, who wrote in that gushing, highly-scented prose which seems to affect all Italians as soon as they get a pen in their hand.

"I have heard", Tamberlik told Verdi, "that it would perhaps not be impossible to induce you to add another jewel to the splendid crown of your operas, whose sequence you threaten to bring to an end. Hardly had this ray of hope shone on me than I spoke to the Director of the Imperial Theatres, Signor Sabouroff, who immediately authorized me to invite you as warmly as I was able to save a spark of your genius for the theatre of St Petersburg. To the invitation of Signor Sabouroff and the prayers of the population I could not resist introducing a sentiment of noble egoism by adding mine to the supplications of the others. . . ."

Tamberlik's letter, which included one or two less flowery passages assuring the composer of complete freedom in all matters of subject, librettist, production conditions and rights in the opera, had its effect; and in due course Verdi signed a contract. As the new opera would involve them in a journey to Russia, Giuseppina Verdi made sure that every provision was made in St Petersburg for her

* The story of Verdi's unexpected career as a member of the first Italian Parliament is unfortunately a little too much beside the point to tell in the context of what is intended as an essentially musical study. The inquisitive reader, however, will find more about it in the chapter on Turin in my *Great Opera Houses*, pp 285–90.

husband's comfort. She was particularly anxious that he should be properly fed, and in her letters to a friend there arranged for the dispatch to Russia of Italian rice, *pasta*, cheese, salami and "such other things as are either not to be found in Russia or are prohibitively expensive there". Giuseppina then added a list of wine Verdi would require for his stay of three months in the Russian capital:

> 100 small bottles of Bordeaux as table wine,
> 20 bottles of Bordeaux *fino*,
> 20 bottles of Champagne.

That the Verdis should have been concerned about what they were to eat in Russia is understandable. The inability of the Italians to stomach anything but the food *mamma* makes is exceeded only by the Chinese. What is encouraging to note, on the other hand, is Verdi's extremely un-Italian insistence that his wine should be French—a taste which may or may not have been due to his being born in French-occupied territory.

In spite of Tamberlik's promise that he should have freedom of choice in the subject of the new opera Verdi's first proposal was turned down flat—perhaps not surprisingly. The story of Victor Hugo's *Ruy Blas* was hardly likely to appeal to the Imperial authorities since its hero (according to a nineteenth-century American synopsis I have) "is a lackey who rises to power, loves the queen, enjoys a terrible revenge on his former master, Don Salluste, who endeavours to degrade her, and kills himself to save her honour".

Verdi then decided on a Spanish play called *Don Álvaro*, the subtitle of which, *La Fuerza del Sino*, served as the title of the opera *La forza del destino*.* The question of *La forza del destino* was something Verdi had considered—or at any rate been aware of—as long before as 1852, when his friend Cesare De Sanctis had written to him: "I asked you to let me know what subject you were working on for Venice, but you haven't told me. Is it *Faust*, or *Kean*, or *Pagliaccio*, *Forza del destino*, *Gusmano il buono*? I hope it is none of these: we are always condemned to seeing your librettos turned down by the Censor and so I can't ever enjoy your music. . . ."

(I cannot throw any light on *Pagliaccio*, but I am interested to see *Faust* mentioned in De Sanctis' list because as late as 1880 Verdi, in a letter written in French which I have in my possession, was thanking a friend for having sent him a French translation of Goethe's

---

* Ángel de Saavedra, Duke of Rivas, poet, historian, politician and diplomatist, and the author of *Don Álvaro*, was born in Cordova in 1791. He was twice exiled from Spain for his liberal opinions, living in Malta, in France (he wrote *Don Álvaro* at Tours), and in England. He died in Madrid in 1865, where *Don Álvaro* was described as "immense as the life of man", and attaining "a vast amplitude like the dramas of Shakespeare and Schiller".

play. How seriously Verdi considered it as a possible operatic subject I do not know; but since *Faust* has attracted such widely different composers as Berlioz, Spohr, Bertin—who was a woman—Gounod, Boito and Busoni in its time, its endless possibilities may well have crossed his mind even at that time in his life.*)

The next we hear of *La forza del destino* is in 1856 when Verdi's friend and pupil Emanuele Muzio wrote to tell Tito Ricordi, the publisher, that Verdi had rejected the idea of *La forza del destino* for no other reason than that he didn't want to set it to music; after *Il trovatore* he did not want to treat a subject that was "perhaps dangerous".

By the time Verdi was in touch with Piave in 1861 about the libretto Giuseppina was able to say to a friend that *La forza del destino* "had pleased" for years; which makes one think that the subject was discussed and contemplated by the composer more often than the available documentary evidence suggests.

The first performance of *La forza del destino*, originally scheduled for early 1862 in St Petersburg, had to be postponed owing to the illness of one of the singers, but eventually took place in November of that year. During the next five years performances followed in Rome, Madrid, New York, Vienna, Buenos Aires and London. The opera as we know it today, however, is the revised version made by Verdi with the libretto altered by Antonio Ghislanzoni for the first production of the opera at La Scala in 1869.

* See Appendix B.

CHARACTERS IN ORDER OF SINGING

THE MARQUIS OF CALATRAVA . . . *Bass*
DONNA LEONORA, *his daughter* . . . *Soprano*
CURRA, *Leonora's maid* . . . . *Mezzo-soprano*
DON ALVARO . . . . . . *Tenor*
A VILLAGE MAYOR . . . . . *Bass*
DON CARLO DI VARGAS, *Leonora's brother* . *Baritone*
MASTRO TRABUCO, *muleteer and pedlar* . *Tenore brillante*
PREZIOSILLA, *a young gipsy* . . . *Mezzo-soprano*
FRA MELITONE ⎫ . . *Baritono brillante*
THE FATHER SUPERIOR ⎬ *Franciscans* . *Bass*
(Il Padre guardiano) ⎭
A SPANISH ARMY SURGEON . . . *Tenor*

Muleteers, Spanish and Italian peasants, soldiers and *vivandières*, orderlies, Italian recruits, Franciscan monks, beggars, tavern host and hostess, tavern servants, drummers, trumpeters, mountebanks, hawkers and pedlars of all kinds

Scene: Spain and Italy   Time: Towards the middle
                                    of the eighteenth century

ACT I

SEVILLE

Scene: The house of the Marquis of Calatrava in Seville. A room hung with damask, family portraits and coats of arms, and decorated in the style of the eighteenth century, though in rather poor condition. At the back, two windows; the one on the left is shut, the other on the right is open and practicable, and through it can be seen a clear moonlit sky and the tops of trees. Between the windows is a large closed cupboard containing clothes, linen, etc. etc. Each of the lateral walls has two doors. The first, on the right of the spectator, is communal; the second leads to Curra's room. On the left at the back is the Marquis' apartment, nearer the proscenium is Leonora's. Centre, a little to the left, is a small table covered by a damask cloth, on which there are a guitar, vases of flowers, two silver candelabras with shaded lights burning in them— the room's only illumination. There is an armchair beside the table; between the two doors on the left, a piece of furniture with a clock on it; above another piece of furniture, hanging on the left hand wall, is a full-length portrait of the Marquis. There is a parapet outside the room.

The opening scene, which is introduced in the score with probably the longest and most redundantly detailed stage directions in all Verdi, was originally preceded by an orchestral prelude. For the Scala revision of 1869, however, this was extended and elaborated into the full-length Overture which is today the best known of the handful of Verdi orchestral pieces heard in the concert hall.

It is a stirring affair which, though it leaves a rather brassy impression behind it, is in fact as full of lyrical contrast as the tunes from the opera which provide the thematic material. Three powerful unison E's played twice by the brass begin the overture and remind one instinctively of the statue's arrival in *Don Giovanni*; but though Verdi had no intention of evoking the supernatural as Mozart had, they nevertheless create a portentous atmosphere which is intensified by the agitated theme associated with the *Destino* of the title:

Ex 253

This theme is never sung in the opera, but occurs solely as an instrumental theme usually played, as here in the Overture, by violins and violoncellos in octaves punctuated *pp* by bassoons and trombones in their lower register. In the Overture, however, Verdi makes a great deal of it, developing it in its own right as well as using it as a recurrent figure which throws an ominous shadow across the other themes. The first to be coloured in this way is the melancholy tune scored for flute, oboe and clarinet in unison which turns up again when it is sung by Alvaro in the last act:

Ex 254

This tune is stated simply in full and leads to another theme, the lovely soaring tune associated later on with Leonora, which starts out played *ppp* by violins in octaves before being propelled by a grim ostinato of bassoons and violoncellos, eventually reinforced by a trombone, double basses and tuba, into a stormy development of the phrase marked "A" in Ex 253:

Ex 255

Another lyrical interlude follows, this time foreshadowing a duet between Leonora and the Father Superior in Act II. The theme is presented by a solo clarinet accompanied by *two* harps—a phenomenon peculiar to the Overture, for elsewhere in the opera only one harp is written for:

Ex 256

The twenty peaceful bars of this episode are followed by another turbulent passage in which phrase "A" of Ex 253 goes through some stirring treatment. This is temporarily interrupted by an unexpected and rather solemn fourteen-bar sequence for brass which, since it seems to have no obvious thematic connection with anything heard so far in the Overture, or indeed with anything in the opera either, may well be some sort of relic of the original Prelude. At any rate, it is a brief and not distracting diversion from the otherwise unwavering straight line of this overture which reaches a brilliant grandstand finish by way of some effective crescendos and some ingenious combining of themes.

As the curtain rises on the scene described at such length on page 281 there is a sinister *pp* echo of the ominous E's which began the Overture, played this time by a solo flute with the clarinet an octave lower on the lowest note of its register and producing that peculiarly hollow sound Verdi used to such dramatic effect all through his career from *Macbeth* to *Otello*. These first six notes for flute and clarinet, however, are the last we hear of any instrument but strings for some time, for the action of *La forza del destino* begins with another of those characteristic opening sequences of four-part string writing with which Verdi was uniquely able to create the illusion that a conversation, now reaching its most interesting point, had been going on for some time before the curtain rises. In this case the audience sees the Marquis of Calatrava, a light in his hand, saying goodnight to his daughter Leonora, who seems preoccupied. Curra, Leonora's maid, enters from the left. The Marquis remarks that the window on to the balcony is open, and closes it. He is obviously concerned that his daughter should be so distracted, but even the unusually tender and gentle music in which he addresses her fails to make her confide her troubles in him—for reasons that become clear, of course, when he has said his affectionate goodnight and Curra has locked the door behind him.

Curra returns quickly, opens the balcony window and taking a bag from the cupboard fills it with linen and clothes in preparation for what we soon learn is to be Leonora's midnight elopement with Don Alvaro. Leonora, in tears, is full of remorse and indecision about having to leave her father and homeland. Curra, with that impatience which has characterized all nurses, confidantes and personal maids in opera since Monteverdi first wrote the part of Arnalta in *L'incoronazione di Poppea* in 1642, goads her mistress into making up her mind by bluntly doubting her love for Alvaro. Leonora protests her love strongly, though not without letting us know how unhappy and "condemned to endless tears" she is likely to be. She begins her moving lament in a monotone punctuated by occasional rising arpeggios played by a solo violoncello.

The middle section of this short aria Leonora is instructed to sing "col massimo dolore" and her tears are emphasized by the typically plaintive sound of the oboe associated with weeping in *Nabucco* (see Ex 11). This scene may well be all that is known of the music for Verdi's projected opera of *King Lear*, where in the drafted libretto there occurred a cavatina for Cordelia which included the words:

Me pellegrina ed orfana
Lungi dal cile natio

and

Non ho per te che lacrime
Dolce Inghilterra, addio

These words, with very little alteration, are the same as those on which Leonora's aria is based. Where in *Lear* Cordelia says, "Exiled and orphaned, far from my native sky", Leonora sings, "Exiled and orphaned, far from my paternal home":

Ex 257

Cordelia's words of farewell are, "I have nought for thee but tears, dear England, adieu!"—Leonora's, "I leave thee, alas, with tears. O my dear country, adieu!":

Ex 258

If, in fact, the music for Leonora's phrases was not originally conceived for Cordelia at least we would not be far out in supposing that if Verdi had set Cordelia's cavatina he would probably have written music for it like Leonora's.*

It is a moving scene, but it leaves Curra untouched and she begs her mistress impatiently to help her pack. Leonora at once becomes apprehensive. Supposing Alvaro doesn't come? It is already past midnight. No, he will not come. These last words—"Ah no, più non verrà!"—are rather surprisingly marked in both vocal and full scores to be sung "con gioia"—surely one of the most puzzling directions in all opera; if it is a misprint, what is it a misprint for? Possibly for "noia"? At least Leonora might more reasonably sing with what my dictionary translates as "weariness, ennui, annoyance . . ." than with joy. Leonora's fears (or elations) are set at

* In his prose draft of the libretto for *King Lear*, Verdi alters the names of the three daughters from Cordelia to Delia, Goneril to Nerilla, and Regan to Rosana. In general Italian translators of Shakespeare's play go no further in their Italianization than Gonerilla and Regana. Cordelia stays the same.

rest, however, by the sound of galloping horses (a 6/8 Allegro vivo
building up from *pp* strings in unison to *ff*) and Curra's remark,
after her mistress has run to the window, that it was always impossible that Alvaro should not arrive. This belief is confirmed. In a
passage of the unusually detailed stage instructions which are found
in this score, we read that Don Alvaro "without a cloak, and wearing
a shirt with full sleeves and a light green waistcoat over it, a snood
on his head, booted and spurred, enters by the terrace window and
throws himself into the arms of Leonora".

Don Alvaro makes an immediate impression as a man of action
and enthusiasm and there is a convincing urgency about the music
in which he expresses his excitement and happiness that at last the
hour of elopement has come. Leonora falters once more, however; it
is nearly daybreak, she says. Alvaro's reply is a gentle lyrical reassurance that pure love triumphs over all opposition—a sixteen-bar
phrase ending in the dominant of the G flat major which has made
a sudden appearance in what is otherwise a scene in B flat—"Ma
d'amor sì puro e santo" ("But from a love so pure and sacred"):

Ex *259*

The tempo reverts to its first eagerness as Alvaro turns to business,
ordering Curra to throw the clothes she is packing over the balcony.
Leonora tells Curra not to; Alvaro tells Curra she must, and turning
to Leonora implores her to follow him and leave her prison for ever.
Leonora, in a manner that would drive less determined lovers to
drink, confesses to Alvaro that she cannot make up her mind. Alvaro,
instead of throwing what would be a justifiable tantrum, once more
makes a purely lyrical approach to her irresolution, telling her in a
gentle tune that horses are waiting and a priest is ready to marry
them—"Pronti destrieri di già ne attendono":

Ex *260*

Even this fails to make up Leonora's mind. It is too late, she says;
they must wait until tomorrow. And in a tearful sequence in which
her weeping is matched in the orchestra by both the rising- and

falling-semitone expression of tears, Leonora tells her lover that she wants to see her father once more, at the same time reassuring Alvaro that her heart is full of joy and that she loves him.

This is finally a little too much for Alvaro. "Your heart is full of joy—and tears. Your hand is as cold as the tomb. I understand everything, signora"; and he goes on to say that if that's the way she feels about it then he will free her from her vows. He quite understands if she regrets . . . Leonora interrupts him with a magnificent phrase, swearing that her heart and her life are his; and with her mind now apparently made up, she launches into an enthusiastic declaration of her love and resolution—"Ah! seguirti fino agl'ultimi confini della terra" ("I will follow you to the ends of the earth . . .") :

Ex 261

Ah! se -guir-ti fi-no a-gl'ul-ti-mi con-fi-ni del-la ter-ra;

This phrase is the start of what becomes a conventionally rousing duet of no great musical distinction. When Leonora has sung her first sixteen bars they are repeated with words of similar sentiment by Alvaro. Phrases are echoed, imitated and tossed from soprano to tenor and back again as first one and then the other sings, "Andiam, andiam", in a sequence that comes dangerously close to parody. The singers are on the point of their final cadence when they are brought up short by the sound of doors opening and closing on the left of the stage. Curra cries that there are people coming up the stairs. The lovers, with a final "Let's go!", complete their cadence and hurry towards the balcony.

It seems to be too late, however. Leonora points to her room and tells Alvaro to hide in it. He refuses; he draws his pistol, declaring that he will defend her. Leonora implores him to put it away; does he want to use it against her father? Replacing the pistol, Alvaro replies: No—against himself.

After several blows the door on the left at the back opens violently and the Marquis of Calatrava enters in a fury, sword in hand, and followed by two servants with lights. The music changes at once to the "destiny" theme (Ex 253) which is developed to accompany all the fast-moving action of the remainder of the scene. The Marquis denounces Alvaro as a vile seducer, and his daughter as infamous. Alvaro protests that he alone is responsible; and baring his chest he urges the Marquis to kill him.

The Marquis refuses; Alvaro deserves no more than death at the hands of the common executioner, and he orders his servants to arrest him. Alvaro draws his pistol and threatens to shoot the servants if they move: he then turns to the Marquis once more and asks him to strike him down. The Marquis again refuses. Alvaro protests that Leonora is innocent and "as pure as the angels"—a favourite expression of Piave's first heard in *La traviata*, then in *Simon Boccanegra*, and now used for the third time with "pura siccome un angelo" modified to the plural "pura siccome gli angeli". Don Alvaro ends his plea, proclaiming that he stands unarmed before the Marquis, and as a sign of good faith throws his pistol away. As the pistol hits the ground, however, it explodes and fatally wounds the Marquis. Before he dies in the arms of his servants, he curses Leonora. The curtain falls as his body is borne away and Don Alvaro takes the grief-stricken Leonora towards the balcony.

ACT II

THE VILLAGE OF HORNACHUELOS AND THE NEIGHBOURHOOD

Scene 1 : The large kitchen on the ground floor of an inn. On the left, a door to the street ; at the back, a window and a large sideboard with plates, etc. etc. On the right at the back, a fire burns in a big fireplace in which there are various pots and pans. Nearer the proscenium there is a short stairway leading to another room, with a practicable door. On one side, a large table set for a meal and lit by a lamp hanging over it. The Host and Hostess (which are silent roles) are busy preparing supper. The village Mayor is seated near the fire ; a Student sits near the table. Trabuco sits on his pack saddle among a group of muleteers. Two peasant men, two peasant women, the waitress and a muleteer dance the Seguidilla. There is a second table with wine, glasses, flasks and a bottle of brandy.

The curtain rises to the sound of the six unison E's that started the Overture, but if the listener expects to hear the familiar strain of Ex 253 following them he will be disappointed. Nor are they followed, as one might be led to expect from the stage directions, by the slightest suggestion in the music of a seguidilla. The corps de ballet of muleteers and peasants may well be going through the steps of the dance on the stage, but they do so with absolutely no musical encouragement from Verdi in the pit, where instead of an exotic Spanish tune in triple time, we have a delicate, lightly-scored 2/4 which provides something for the dancers to dance to and a background for some of the ensuing dialogue:

Ex 262

It is just possible, of course, that the mention of a seguidilla in the stage directions is a relic of the first version of *La forza del destino* and that what we now hear in its place dates from the revised version of 1869, but so far I have seen no evidence of this.

During the performance of whatever it is that Ex 262 is supposed to be the assembled company sit down to eat when the Hostess brings in a large tureen of soup. The Student, who the listener had better know at once, is Leonora's brother Don Carlo di Vargas in disguise, tells us in an aside that he is searching in vain for his sister and her seducer. This is the first indication of his identity the audience is given, for as we have seen, the stage directions mention merely the inclusion among those present of "a Student" who has never been mentioned before, who does not appear in the list of characters in the opera, and whose part in the vocal score is referred to throughout the whole of this scene as "Studente", becoming "Don Carlo" only on his appearance in Act III, when, as it happens, he is once more masquerading under a false name.

The second indication of his identity comes a moment or two later when, after Don Carlo in his capacity as Student and Latin scholar has said grace, Leonora makes a brief and timid appearance at the door of the room on the right of the stage and crying, "What do I see! My brother!" hurriedly disappears again.

The number of dancers has meanwhile dwindled to a single couple who nobly continue while everybody else is eating. The dancing, the supper, and Don Carlo's question to Trabuco about the identity of a young man who came to the inn with the muleteer, are interrupted however by the entrance (*saltellando*—or tripping) of Preziosilla. She is evidently a popular figure, for the men all ask her to sit next to them at the table. Preziosilla ignores these invitations and comes to the point at once: Italy has been attacked by the Austrians and she is asking for recruits to the Italian army. (The libretto in fact refers to the "eternal scourge of Italy" as Germans—probably, one imagines, because *Tedeschi* is a more singable, if less historically correct word than *Austriachi*. My 1944 vocal score, on the other hand, for obvious reasons mentions no names, only "the enemy".) Having aroused the chorus's enthusiasm and extracted from them a unanimous promise to go off and join the Italian army, Preziosilla sings a song in praise of war. She addresses her hearers individually, enumerating the attractions of army life and the prospects of promotion like a recruiting poster, and rounding off her points with the slogan, "War is beautiful! Long live war!" ("È bella la guerra! . . . Evviva la guerra!"):

Ex 263

These rousing sentiments (which must rate among the most

10

fatuous lines in any Italian libretto) are echoed with spirit by the
chorus, Don Carlo and the Mayor. When Preziosilla has finished
her song, Don Carlo asks her to tell his fortune. She predicts terrible
misfortunes ahead, adding that she does not believe he is a student.
To set his fears at rest, she assures Don Carlo she will not say a word
to anybody, and she does so in a passage which suggests she is a full
sister of Oscar, the page in *Un ballo in maschera*:

Ex 264

Not only has the accompaniment the sparkle and brilliance of the
earlier opera, but Preziosilla's final tra-las are sung to a phrase
almost identical with the first two bars of the second-time bar in
Ex 215. She soon returns to her hurray-for-war motive, however,
which the chorus echo and bring to an end with a noisy coda.

From outside comes the distant sound of pilgrims singing on their
way to the jubilee celebrations of the local Franciscan monastery.
As the singing comes nearer the crowd in the inn falls on its knees in
prayer, and an effective passage follows which hovers most intriguingly between major and minor—the pilgrims in the minor,
except for a final major chord at the end of each of their three-bar
phrases, the crowd in the major. Leonora appears at the door once
more and adds her prayer to the rest: to be saved from her brother.
A short and typical 12/8 ensemble builds up which leads to everybody singing words we hear rather often in this opera: "Pietà,
Signor" ("Pity, O Lord!"). The scene ends with a return to the
major-minor conflict of the pilgrims' chorus off stage as a wonderfully effective coda. Leonora goes back to her room closing the door
behind her, and the rest of the company return to their places at table.

Don Carlo, in a hearty mood, proposes everybody's health; his
good wishes are reciprocated and while the company presumably
settles down to an evening's drinking, he turns to Trabuco to question him further about the young stranger who came with him to the
inn. Trabuco protests it is none of his business and refuses to confirm
any of Don Carlo's suspicions. Carlo turns to the Mayor, but as he
also proves unhelpful he tackles Trabuco once more. This time the
muleteer says he considers all this questioning an insufferable bore,
picks up his saddle and leaves, saying that he is off to the stables to
sleep with his mules who don't know any Latin and have no university degree. Trabuco's indignant exit is greeted by general laughter
which dies away in a wonderful diminuendo.

The whole of this short scene is in the cheerful conversational style Verdi was beginning to develop with this opera and perfected in *Falstaff*. The music flows in an easy-going 2/4, with the main melodic interest in the lightly-scored and tuneful figures in the orchestra.

Don Carlo, who plays the Student as an incorrigible undergraduate at heart, now suggests that they should go and paint whiskers and a moustache on the face of the beardless stranger, but the Mayor puts his foot down and remarks that since the Student is so inquisitive why doesn't he tell them something about himself? This is obviously the opportunity Don Carlo has been waiting for, and he embarks on his Ballad, "Son Pereda, son ricco d'onore" ("I am Pereda, and I am rich in honours") :

Ex *265*

In the course of his narration to this tune which, in spite of the direction that it should be sung *con eleganza*, is one of Verdi's least elegant conceptions, Don Carlo tells us that he is Pereda, a B.A. of Salamanca University. He gave up his studies a year ago, he says, when he went with his friend Vargas in pursuit of his sister and her foreign lover who had killed the old Marquis, Vargas' father, and had fled from Seville. "We followed them to Cadiz", Don Carlo's story continues, "but could not find the bloody lovers." At Cadiz they were told that the sister had been killed in a fight between the followers of her father and of her lover. The murderer ("the damned seducer") was believed to have fled to South America and Vargas had followed in search of him. The ballad comes to a conventional end with the chorus echoing the tune of Don Carlo's last four bars to appreciative words on the gruesome nature of the story and the generous nature of its teller.

Preziosilla, with her gipsy second sight, doesn't believe a word of it, but contents herself with laughing at Don Carlo in the same tra-la-ing way as she did earlier (Ex 264). The Mayor looks at the clock and says it is time to go home. The company agrees and a general goodnight is said in a charming passage started by Don Carlo:

Ex *266*

It is answered by the chorus in a ravishingly effective unison, repeated by Don Carlo and finished off by Preziosilla whose phrase includes a couple of optional high notes which are not usually taken when the passage is first heard.

The company is in no great hurry to leave, however, and the "seguidilla" starts up again at the back of the scene. The tune of Ex 262 is mixed this time with a quotation by Carlo of the opening strains of his Ballad and a reprise of Preziosilla's high-spirited tra-la's. The orchestration of all this is wonderfully deft and gives a hint or two of things to come much later in Verdi's career—notably the "Fuoco di gioia" passage in the first act of *Otello*. After a repetition of the "Buona notte" quoted above, which most Preziosillas round off with the higher notes this time, and an orchestral version of the cadence of her tra-la tune as a coda, the curtain falls.

Scene 2 : A small level place on a steep mountainside. On the right there are precipices and crags ; facing, the façade of the Church of the Madonna of the Angels ; on the left is the Monastery gate in the middle of which is a small window ; at one side there is a bell pull. Over the gate is a small overhanging turret. Beyond the church there are high mountains and the village of Hornachuelos. The wide door of the church is closed, but above it there is a semicircular window through which lights can be seen shining inside. Midscene, a little to the left, is a rough weatherbeaten cross raised on four steps. The scene is lit by a bright moon.

Leonora enters, exhausted from climbing the rocks on the right of the scene. She is still dressed as a man, in a cloak with wide sleeves, a broad hat and boots. Her agitated state of mind is underlined by the familiar *Allegro agitato e presto* of Ex 253 which punctuates her sighs of relief at having reached safety. We learn from her that the story she overheard her brother telling at the inn is the first indication that Don Alvaro is alive and had not, as she thought, been killed in the fight that obviously took place soon after the curtain fell on Act I. Instead, she is now convinced that Alvaro has deserted her—though, to be fair, he would have had his work cut out to find her, miles from where he last saw her and disguised as a man.

In the depths of despair Leonora prays to the Virgin to purge her heart of all thoughts of her faithless lover. Leonora's prayer—"Madre, pietosa Vergine" ("Blessed Virgin, full of pity")—is one of the high spots of the opera, including as it does one of the broad tunes already trailed in the Overture. The opening passage is marked to be sung "come un lamento" and its elegiac quality is stressed in the orchestra by a figure for flute and clarinet in octaves, which I have indicated in the following example. The instruments, both in their low register, are instructed to play "sotto voce, come un lamento":

Ex 267

The gloomy minor of this first part of the aria gives way to the major and the wonderful soaring phrase first heard in the Overture —Ex 255. Leonora (*con passione*) prays to God not to abandon her but to have pity—"pietà di me Signor". When Leonora has completed the phrase for the first time she hears the monks singing matins to an organ accompaniment behind the scenes, and the sound brings her great comfort. But she relapses into her mood of fear and anguish, and repeating the tune of Ex 255 beseeches God once more not to forsake her but to pity her. The aria comes to a climax with a final *animando* of this theme, now with considerable orchestral support behind it for the first time, and dies away in a coda full of pathos as Leonora repeats "pietà, Signor".

Leonora rings the monastery bell. The little window in the door is opened by Fra Melitone, the porter, who shines a lantern through the grille in Leonora's face and startles her. Melitone asks who she is; she replies that she wants to see the Father Superior; Father Cleto has sent her. Mention of Father Cleto's name ("that holy man") impresses Melitone and he tells Leonora to come in. She replies that she cannot, which strikes Melitone as odd; perhaps she's excommunicated. Anyway, he'll see what he can do and bumbles off.

When she is alone again Leonora reflects on her plight. Suppose she is denied refuge? She calms down and prays to the Virgin for help, while a solo clarinet plays *con espressione* the long tune of Ex 255 with the coda that Leonora sang to end "Madre, pietosa Vergine".

The Father Superior (called the "Padre Guardiano" in Franciscan monasteries) enters and hearing that what Leonora wishes to say is secret sends Melitone away. Melitone mutters, "Always secrets! Only the holy ones are allowed to know them. The rest of us are just so many cabbages . . ."—a line with which Verdi gives us our first glimpse of the musical character of Melitone:

Ex 268

The Father Superior asks him what he is mumbling about. Melitone replies blandly that he said the door was heavy and made a lot of noise; he goes into the monastery, closing the door behind him.

Leonora reveals to the Father Superior that she is a woman and begs him to save her from damnation. At first the Father Superior is doubtful if he can help, but when she refers to a letter sent by Father Cleto he recognizes her as Leonora di Vargas and bids her kneel before the Cross where Heaven will comfort her. Leonora kneels down and kisses the Cross; turning to the Father Superior she tells him that she feels more at peace—"Più tranquilla l'alma sento":

Ex 269

Leonora's tune is doubled in the same register by flute, oboe and clarinet—an effective passage of orchestration which needs a little adjustment in modern times, however, inasmuch as the lowest note on the flute is no longer the B natural it was in Verdi's day, but the C a semitone higher. In practice the flute plays the B an octave higher or leaves it out altogether. There do exist some flutes with this low B natural, but while the B is impressive enough it seems that the rest of the notes on the instrument are excruciatingly out of tune.

The scene that now takes place between Leonora and the Father Superior is in its earlier stages a skilful blend of declamatory and lyrical vocal writing, in which the theme quoted above (Ex 269) is used from time to time. Leonora beseeches the Father Superior to be allowed to end her days in expiation of her sins in a hermit's cave Father Cleto has told her about. The Father Superior advises her to reflect before taking any such serious step and suggests she should enter a convent. Leonora firmly rejects the idea and tells the monk that if he turns her away she will wander in the hills until the wild beasts put an end to her sufferings. "This is my haven," she says, "would you deprive me of my refuge?"

Leonora's firm resolve convinces the Father Superior and he gives way, praising the omnipotence of the Almighty in a curiously martial 3/4 tune accompanied by a firm three-beats-a-bar from bassoons, horns, trombones, tuba and pizzicato strings:

Ex 270

Poco più mosso

In spite of the rather defiant character of the Father Superior's prayer (and its accompaniment) the duet sequence it develops into becomes gradually much gentler, and the episode dies away with a low F sung by the bass and a very Aida-like cadence from Leonora who has continued to sing of her haven and refuge. The Father Superior agrees to Leonora's request. She shall live dressed in monk's clothes as a hermit in the cave; he alone will know who she is and will leave food for her beside a nearby spring once a week. The Father Superior then summons Melitone, whose approach is heralded by a recognizable instrumental version of the last five indignant bars of Ex 268, and tells him to call the monks to prayer. Turning to Leonora he bids her make ready to receive the holy sacrament before going alone to the hermitage at dawn. The scene ends with a short duet which Leonora, rejoicing in the prospect of the new life before her, begins to the tune of Ex 256 first heard in the Overture but now, for some reason, with the melody altered in the third and fourth bars. At the end of the duet Leonora and the Father Superior go into a room beside the gate.

What is generally known as Scene 3 now begins, although as no change of scenery is involved both action and music can continue without a break. Some recordings, however, start a separate band at this point.

The stage directions run as follows:

Scene 3: The big doors of the church open. Straight ahead one can see the illuminated high altar. The organ plays. On both sides of the chancel the monks, holding lighted candles, are formed in a procession. They are followed by the Father Superior who walks ahead of Leonora, now in a monk's habit, leading her out of the church. As the monks group themselves around the scene, Leonora prostrates herself before the Father Superior who solemnly stretches out his hand over her head, and chants:

In the score these stage directions appear at the head of the music and it is several pages before we know exactly what it is the Father Superior chants, as there are forty-seven bars of organ and orchestra to come first which accompany the silent action described above. The organ voluntary which begins the scene I must admit does not strike me as a very inspired piece, and though it creates an appropriately ecclesiastical atmosphere I find it is always a relief when the orchestra comes in with the tune of Ex 255. This is shown in the score to be played to a *pp* accompaniment of tremolo strings by two muted violins, but in practice it is played by one unmuted—for the usual acoustic reasons (see p 122). The organ interrupts for four further bars as Leonora prostrates herself before the Father Superior and the silent action comes to an end with a repetition of Ex 255,

still played by a solo violin, but this time with the cadence sung by
Leonora at the end of "Madre, pietosa Vergine".

The Father Superior announces to the assembled monks that a
repentant soul has come to beg shelter, and is to occupy the hermit's
cave. Nobody may approach the refuge, or try to discover the hermit's identity. Whoever dares to disobey this command shall be
accursed. These simple instructions and their acceptance by the
monks are set to some imposing music for bass and an all-male
chorus. To the throbbing 12/8 accompaniment of a rigidly 4/4
vocal line—a characteristic feature of so many Verdi ensembles—
the Father Superior and the monks unite in a movement of great
dramatic power. The choral passages, ranging from *pp* to *tutta forza*,
are all in unison, and point clearly in the direction of the Priests in
Aida.

The Father Superior turns to Leonora, and bidding her rise tells
her that there is a bell in the cave which she may ring in a moment of
extreme danger, or when in the hour of her death she needs the Last
Sacrament; otherwise she will never see a human being again. The
monks, now singing *pp* and *sotto voce* in three and four parts, pray
to the Virgin of the Angels to protect Leonora—"La Vergine degli
angeli" :

Ex 271

Leonora joins in, at first alone, with the harp playing a prominent
part in the restrained and economical orchestral accompaniment,
then with the chorus. It is a short movement of unusual simplicity
and great beauty bringing the act to a quiet and moving end on a
final *morendo* chord played by strings, trombones, tuba and bassoons,
as Leonora kisses the Father Superior's hand and goes alone towards
her hermitage. The Father Superior stretches out his arms towards
her in benediction, and the curtain falls. It is an impressive finish.

ACT III

IN ITALY NEAR VELLETRI

Scene 1 : A wood on a very dark night.

The curtain rises after a vigorous tutti—a noisy 6/8 kind of fanfare mostly in unison—to show Don Alvaro in the uniform of a Spanish captain of the King's Grenadiers. He enters slowly from the back. Voices can be heard coming from back-stage on the right—an unaccompanied sequence for male chorus who, to judge by the solo voices heard, are soldiers playing cards. Exactly what game they are playing I do not know, but for the benefit of those who might, the only clue seems to be in the following brief dialogue which is heard between the hearty choral passages:

Bass : An ace on the right.
Tenor : I've won.
Bass : A three on the right.
Tenor : Five on the left.
Bass : I lose.

The game is quickly over, however, or at least we hear no more of it, because our attention is now focused on the figure of Don Alvaro by a long slow passage for solo clarinet derived from Ex 259:

Ex 272

The clarinet continues in this melancholy strain for nearly three minutes, embroidering the tune like a Bellini prima donna but without for a moment threatening to destroy the mood of weariness and sadness it sets out to create. "Sorrowfully, but with force" Alvaro tells us in a declamatory passage punctuated by the solo clarinet's opening theme that life is hell for the unhappy, and goes on to bewail the fate that robbed him of Leonora and all happiness

10*   297

in a single night. He then reflects on what can only be described as the Chapter of Accidents which have brought him to his present unhappy state—how his father hoped to free his ancient South American country from the Spanish yoke and gain its crown by marrying the last of the Incas; how Alvaro himself was born in prison and raised in the wilderness; and how he has survived only by keeping his royal lineage a secret. The lugubrious nature of this recital is emphasized by the part played by bassoon arpeggios in the accompaniment to what may be regarded, in the language of popular songs, as the "verse" to the "chorus" that follows.

In the "chorus" Alvaro calls on Leonora, whom he believes dead, to look down from Heaven and have pity on his suffering—"O tu che in seno agli angeli" ("You who are among the angels"):

Ex 273

This obviously rather difficult, but immensely effective aria is typical of the wealth of melodic and harmonic invention to be found in *La forza del destino*. With a simple accompaniment the tune wanders effortlessly and unselfconsciously through various unexpected keys, landing securely in A flat with a final reappearance of the solo clarinet in the two-bar instrumental postlude to make sure that the instrument which began the scene so effectively shall not be forgotten.

The sounds of a quarrel are suddenly heard coming from behind the scenes. Alvaro rushes off in the direction of the shouting; the clash of swords is heard, and several officers run from right to left across the stage in a state of disorder. A moment later Alvaro returns with Don Carlo, now in the role of soldier instead of student, who has got into a brawl with the gambling school— behaviour which Alvaro finds frankly puzzling in an officer and a gentleman.

Don Carlo explains that he arrived only yesterday with orders from the general, and asking the name of the man who saved his life introduces himself (with an aside for the audience's benefit that his rescuer must not know his real name) as Don Felice de Bornos, adjutant to the "Duce"—who, we suppose, must be the general already mentioned. Alvaro replies that he is Don Federico Herreros, Captain of the Grenadiers—whom Don Carlo immediately recognizes as the army's bravest soldier. In a solemn Andante maestoso, singing in thirds and sixths punctuated by brass unisons and rumbling "Miserere" chords, Don Alvaro and Don Carlo clasp right hands and swear eternal friendship in the familar tenor-and-baritone key of A flat Verdi so often used on these occasions.

Two, four, and finally six trumpets are heard off stage left, calling the soldiers to arms, and with final expressions of esteem for each other's prowess and courage, Don Alvaro and Don Carlo hurry away together.

The scene changes at once, without a break in the music.

Scene 2 : It is morning in the room of a high officer of the Spanish army in Italy not far from Velletri. At the back are two doors, the one on the left leading to a bedroom, the other is communal. On the left near the proscenium is a window. The sounds of the nearby battle are audible.

The musical sounds of the nearby battle include effective use of single piercing trumpet notes off stage in the course of an orchestral sequence which bears distinct rhythmic likeness to the call to arms in Act II of *Simon Boccanegra* (see p 228) :

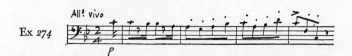

Ex 274

While the battle is going on a military Surgeon and several order-lies enter through the communal door and run to the window, where the Surgeon gives us a running commentary on what he sees of the battle through his telescope. It is an exciting enough account we get, for the battle seems to ebb and flow most rapidly. In the space of a few stirring bars of battle music we hear that "Herreros" has fallen wounded, that his men ("valiant Grenadiers") have been pushed back, that the adjutant [Carlo] has rallied them and is leading them in a charge, that the Germans/Austrians/Enemy (according to whether we translate the original "Tedeschi" as Germans, Austrians or follow the 1944 score with Enemy) are in retreat and the battle has been won. The orderlies greet the news as a Spanish victory or cry, "Viva Italia!" according to their nationality and the scene ends in fanfares and shouts of "Vittoria!" The noise subsides and after a simple, halting elegiac sequence for strings, a solo clarinet and a solo bassoon, the seriously wounded Alvaro is brought in on a stretcher by four Grenadiers. On one side of him is the Surgeon (who must have gone out to meet him, though there is no indication of this in the score), and on the other Don Carlo, who is very sad and covered in dust. A soldier places a case on a small table. The stretcher is put down in the middle of the stage.*

In a sombre silent atmosphere Don Carlo urges the Surgeon to do his best to save Alvaro's life. At length Alvaro opens his eyes and asks where he is. Don Carlo replies that he is with his friend and that he has been awarded the Order of Calatrava for his bravery. The mention of the name Calatrava has an immediate effect on Alvaro which is not lost on Don Carlo who, however, makes no further comment. He turns to the Surgeon and asks him to leave them together. The Surgeon retires to the background and Don Alvaro makes a sign for Don Carlo to come closer. There follows a *duettino*, long one of the most popular and effective in the tenor-and-baritone repertoire, in which nevertheless the tenor has the major share of the jam.

Alvaro asks Don Carlo to swear he will carry out a vow he has made. Don Carlo must take the key he finds round Don Alvaro's neck, open the box which is on the table and take from it a sealed envelope which must be burnt in the event of Alvaro's death as it contains a secret that must die with him. Don Carlo swears he will do as Alvaro asks—"Solenne in quest'ora" ("In this solemn hour") :

Ex 275

This scene may be labelled a modest *duettino* but it is of far greater dramatic intensity than the description suggests, and it makes its initial effect by characteristically simple means—a persistent three-note pizzicato bass, a few sustained woodwind chords, a couple of bars in which the plaintive quality of two bassoons in thirds is superbly exploited. It is an impressive and moving opening in which Don Carlo's promise (though we must suspect his motives by now) has a sincere ring to it.

---

* Those who may have followed the opera only from the elaborately produced libretto given away with the 1960 RCA–Victor records may well wonder how a table came to be in the middle of a wood near Velletri. This is because in addition to referring to the Father Superior as "Father Guardiano" or "Guardiano" as though "Guardiano" were the monk's Christian name, this version of the libretto fails to mention that the scene is supposed to change on the exit of Alvaro and Carlo at the end of the Scene 1. All we are told at that point is, "They run off. The Surgeon and several orderlies enter." So they do, but not in the same surroundings as the tenor and baritone have just left.

With a change from C minor to C major, Alvaro, convinced that Don Carlo will keep his oath, says that he will now die happy—"Or muoio tranquillo":

Ex 276

Or muo - io tran-quil-lo... Vi strin-go   al cor mi - o

Don Carlo embraces his friend "with great emotion" and tells him to have faith in Heaven. The reprise of the nine bars in which the two men express these sentiments is accompanied by a suggestion of what Verdi later came to call his "vaporous" orchestration—achieved here by *pp* staccato arpeggios for two flutes and clarinet. Alvaro and Carlo bid each other farewell and the Surgeon and orderlies carry the wounded man into the bedroom.

When he is alone Don Carlo reflects on the brave but mysterious Alvaro whose reaction to the name of Calatrava makes him wonder whether he is not the "cursed Indian" he is looking for. Don Carlo goes to break the seal of the envelope entrusted to him, but remembers his oath and throws it down—"Urna fatale del mio destino, va, t'allontana, mi tenti invano . . ." ("Get away from me, O fatal urn of my destiny, you tempt me in vain . . ."):

Ex 277

Ur-na fa- ta-le del mio de - sti- no, va, t'al-lon-ta-na mi ten - ti in-va- no

There is a sombre beauty about this aria which is very characteristic of so much of the music in this opera, and which has a final cantabile section as infectiously singable as similar baritone passages in "Il balen del suo sorriso" in *Il trovatore* (Ex 106) or "Non morir, mio tesoro pietade" in the last pages of *Rigoletto* (Ex 85).

As he is forbidden by his oath to open the envelope Don Carlo looks through the box for some other clue, and finds a locket; having never made any promises to Don Alvaro about a locket (which has no seal on it to be broken anyway) he opens it and finds a portrait of Leonora. When the Surgeon enters to say that Alvaro's life had been saved Carlo's excitement and pleasure know no bounds. He will now be able to kill his father's murderer with his own hands, and he rejoices at the prospect in a short exultant cabaletta—"Egli è salvo!

oh gioia immensa che m'innondi il cor, ti sento!" ("He is saved! Oh what joy I feel in my heart!"):

Ex 278

It is a finish to the scene more remarkable for its spirit and vigour than for any unusual musical interest—except for the rather negative one of some high piping woodwind triplets which seem to have strayed into the orchestra from a fairground steam-organ—but it brings down the curtain with a determined flourish as Don Carlo strides away with murder in his heart.

Scene 3: A military camp near Velletri. In the foreground on the left is a secondhand dealer's booth; on the right is another where food, drinks and fruit are sold. Scattered here and there are soldiers' tents, pedlars' barrows, etc. etc. It is night and the scene is deserted.

The curtain rises on a superbly evocative orchestral sound of sustained open fifths played by piccolo, flute, oboes and horns, which reminds one immediately and inevitably of the opening of Act III of *La Bohème*. With this rather unearthly sound held over long *pp legatissimo* quaver phrases played by violas and violoncellos in octaves, Verdi creates by new means an astonishing atmosphere of darkness and stealth. It is in this atmosphere that a night patrol of tenors and basses enters cautiously to look round the camp and to comment in chorus on the stillness of the scene:

Ex 279

The patrol's captivating little tune, with its wrong-footed accents on the weak syllables of words, is accompanied by clarinets and bassoons and later repeated in instrumental form by piccolo, flute, oboes and horns. The whole of this scene, which was written for the 1869 revised version of the opera, is a little gem of orchestration and subtle harmonic invention which, in the liquid, flowing viola and violoncello parts particularly anticipates the colour and atmosphere

of some of the most characteristic moments in *Falstaff*. The music
dies away as the patrol moves off into the distance, and the open
fifths now limited to the oboes with the piccolo on a high harmonic-
like G, are left suspended *ppp* as violas and violoncellos sign off with
another long legato phrase in quavers.

Dawn now begins to break slowly and Alvaro comes on thought-
fully with the solo clarinet echoing his gloomy mood with the theme
of Ex 272. Don Carlo enters and asks if Alvaro's wound is healed
and whether he is well enough to fight a duel. Don Carlo's questions
and Don Alvaro's puzzled answers are set to an oddly gentle lyrical
passage for strings which reminds one inevitably of the deceptive
charm of some of the scenes between Otello and Iago:

Ex 280

The charm is deceptive because it is obviously intended as a lull
before a storm, which breaks in this case when Don Carlo asks,
"Didn't Don Alvaro the Indian send you a message?" and challenges
him to fight. Alvaro, though appalled that the man he considerd his
friend should have broken his word, refuses to accept the challenge,
and when Don Carlo reveals his own identity, protests that he was
innocent of the death of the Marquis and the seduction of Leonora.
He goes on to tell him that after he had recovered from the wounds
he received on the night the Marquis died, he had searched for
Leonora for a year; then he learned she was dead. Don Carlo calls
him a liar; Leonora is not dead, but is a fugitive. This news is
greeted rapturously by Don Alvaro, who begs Don Carlo to join
him in searching for her. "She is alive," replies Don Carlo, "but in a
short while she will be dead"—words which he pronounces to one
of the most arresting and harmonically surprising phrases in the
whole opera, or indeed in any opera Verdi had written up to this
time:

Ex 281

Not the least unusual feature of these two bars is the orchestration which, since the vocal score can give no idea of it, I have tried to indicate—the unison trombones, and the descending chromatic part for horns and trumpet.

The agitation and drama that has filled the duet up to this point is now relaxed a little as Don Alvaro repeats his plea to Don Carlo that they should search for Leonora together and points out that there can be no objection to their marriage since, like the Vargas family, he too is of noble birth:

Ex 282

No, d'un i-me-ne il vin-co-le strin-ga fra noi la spe - me;

Don Carlo remains unmoved by Alvaro's appeal. How can he call a man brother who has taken everything from him and continues to deny that he is guilty? Alvaro, angered by Carlo's reiterated determination to kill Leonora, at last loses patience and swears that her brother shall die first. The two men draw their swords and begin to fight furiously, but the duel is interrupted by the arrival of the camp patrol who separate the contestants, arrest Don Carlo and take him away.

Don Alvaro, left alone, throws down his sword in disgust. To a series of solemn woodwind chords, he announces that he will enter a monastery, for only there will he be able to find peace; he leaves the scene.

The sun is now shining brightly. Reveille is sounded by a roll of four side drums behind the scenes and a fanfare in octaves of trumpets and trombones in the orchestra (which sound for all the world as if they were going to break into the "March of the Wooden Soldiers" any moment). The scene grows gradually more animated as Spanish and Italian soldiers of all ranks emerge from their tents, cleaning their muskets, swords and uniforms. Some younger soldiers play dice on the drumheads. *Vivandières* sell drinks, bread, fruit, etc. Preziosilla, standing on top of a stall, is telling fortunes. The scene, according to the stage directions, is "animatissima".

A chorus of *vivandières* and soldiers announce in a hearty tune in Verdi's best small-town *banda* manner that the military life is the one for them—let tomorrow look after itself, etc. Preziosilla, turning first to the women, then to the soldiers, offers to tell everybody's fortune in a *brillante* strophic song with an accompaniment featuring two piccolos in a way that would suggest that Bizet perhaps learnt something from the scoring of *La forza del destino*—except that

Verdi's opera was not heard in Paris until 1876, a year after the first performance of *Carmen*:

Ex 283

Preziosilla finishes her song with a brilliant run that takes her up to a top C if she can get it, with an alternative run that doesn't if she can't. After some mutual toasting by the soldiers to the union of Spain and Italy and to the health of "our hero, Don Federico Herreros" coupled with the name of "his noble friend Don Felice de Bornos", Trabuco, whom we last knew as a muleteer, enters in his new profession of pedlar to the forces. He comes out of the booth on the left, carrying a tray of cheap goods which he offers for sale in a melancholy song—"A buon mercato, chi vuol comprare . . ." ("Who wants a bargain?") :

Ex 284

Trabuco's stock seems to consist only of scissors, pins and scented soap, but he is also in the market to buy things from the soldiers—an offer which makes a more instant appeal, and leads to some lively bargaining over the price the pedlar will give for an assortment of rings, watches and necklaces. The dialogue to this sequence is carried on in a near-monotone while the orchestra plays *con eleganza* a series of rather skittish Donizetti-like phrases:

Ex 285

Business is inevitably concluded to Trabuco's advantage and satisfaction and he wanders off with his tray to the other side of the camp, singing his mournful little song, which is oddly Russian in character.

The depressing minor mood of Trabuco's advertising jingle is continued by a group of peasants leading children by the hand and tearfully asking for bread. (The peasants, according to the score, are "four or six first basses with whom the children can also sing".) The atmosphere, with the help of a plaintive oboe, becomes increasingly Russian when a very fearful and homesick group of new and very young recruits (their voices are still contralto) come in to lament the cruel way they have been torn from their mothers.

Cheerfulness breaks in, however, when with the return of the orchestra's tune in Ex 285, the *vivandières* raise the recruits' spirits by giving them a drink and promising to love them like sisters. Preziosilla also mixes with the recruits and teases them for being such babies. The theme of Ex 285 is developed with some cheerful orchestration (piccolo and violas frequently sharing a jaunty unison ostinato at a distance of three octaves from each other) as Preziosilla and the *vivandières* take the recruits firmly and brazenly by the arm and a *vivacissima* general dance starts up. "In a short time", the stage directions state, "the confusion and tumult reach their height."

The nature of the general dance is not specified in the stage directions, but in the score it is a tarantella, to which the chorus, mostly in unison, contributes another medley of those bright philosophical thoughts that it seems to express at the shake of a baton in this opera. Having sung "Evviva la guerra!" at the top of its lungs in Act II, it now cries, "Viva la pazzia!" or long life to madness. Both scenes throw a sinister light on mob psychology.

As the tarantella, and the shouts of "Viva la pazzia!" reach their climax (the whole movement is perhaps significantly in a minor key), Brother Melitone enters and is caught up in the "vortex of the dance", so that for a moment he is whirled around by the *vivandières*.

Melitone finally manages to free himself and starts to preach an indignant sermon. In the first few lines we learn that contrary to our suspicions, Melitone was not posted to the Italian battlefront by the librettist, but has come from Spain to treat the wounded and beg alms. And what does he find but a camp full of infidel Turks instead of Christians.

It is difficult to quote from the music of Meletone's sermon as it is in effect an extended passage of what one might call "buffo declamation" in which the words are more important than the notes and there is little in the way of a tune or theme to get hold of. The most prominent musical feature, indeed, is a reiterated figure started off by Melitone's mention of the world as a vale of tears—tears expressed in the familiar form of the rising semitone, but in this case most unusually scored across four octaves, from double bass to piccolo. The theme of Melitone's sermon is entirely admonitory and is delivered in a series of simple puns, almost none of which—with the exception of the preacher's allegation that his hearers are more interested in bottles (*bottiglie*) than battles (*battaglie*)—is readily translatable into English.

Though this scene still has its roots firmly fixed in the soil of *opera buffa* the figure of the bluff and blustery friar nevertheless emerges clearly as an earthy, real-life character entirely different from any other so far encountered in Verdi's operas. As Francis Toye once said, Melitone has the plebeian humour of Leporello, not the gay and elegant wit of Oscar in *Un ballo in maschera*; so that it is therefore quite in character that his famous sermon should end in his being chased from the scene by his exasperated audience of equally plebeian soldiers.

Preziosilla now comes forward again and rebukes the soldiers for making war on a monk. She calls after them, but as they do not hear her she picks up a drum and goes through the motions and noises of playing it. At the sound of her first "rat-a-plan" the soldiers rush up and gather round her, followed by the whole of the rest of the crowd who also enter at the double.

There now follows the famous "Rataplan" chorus which is unaccompanied except for two side drums on the stage and a few bars of orchestral assistance to keep the chorus up to pitch during the three verses of martial encouragement sung by Preziosilla to a tune that is little more than a bugle call. The chorus supply a constant onomatopoeic background, varying the sound of their imaginary drums from "rat-a-plan" to "pim-pum-pum" and exploiting sudden changes of dynamics from *ff* to *pp* with the utmost effect. It is a scene patently modelled on the rataplan chorus for Bois-Rose and the Huguenot soldiers in Act III of Meyerbeer's *Les Huguenots*, and a deliberate technical *tour de force*. With the entire company pretending to fire a musket on the final unison and *fortissimo* "pim" it is one of the few frankly theatrical passages in Verdi which has no deeper purpose than to bring the house down as the curtain falls. It rarely fails in its object.

The third scene of Act III of *La forza del destino* is not at all today what it was when the opera was first performed. Originally the scene began with the trumpets-and-drums arrival of the crowd described on page 304 and continued from there until the end of the "Rataplan" chorus when everybody ran off leaving the stage clear for the resumption of the plot after a fairly generous *divertissement*. The remainder of the scene consisted of an aria for Don Alvaro ("Miserere di me, pietà Signore"), and his duet with Don Carlo which ended with the two men continuing their duel off stage and Alvaro returning to tell us that once more he had spilt the blood of a Vargas—though whether Don Carlo was killed or only wounded in this duel the audience were not to know until later in the opera, of course.

In the belief, however, that there was altogether too much emphasis on bloodshed in the action Verdi and Ghislanzoni made drastic
changes for the revised version of 1869, thereby shifting the whole
dramatic and musical centre of gravity in an alarming way, and
leaving us, as the scene is now, with an anticlimax of quite remarkable dimensions. The introduction of the night patrol at the very
start of the scene is a welcome musical addition and has a dramatic
use when, in order to establish in front of the audience's eyes that
Don Carlo is not killed or even wounded by Alvaro, the patrol reappears to separate the combatants and arrest Don Carlo. It could
still be used for both these purposes without losing its point if—as
was done in Germany in the years of the Verdi revival there in the
1920s—the patrol's opening chorus were to be followed by the crowd
scenes which end in the "Rataplan" number.

The second half of the scene could then begin and the plot be
resumed with Alvaro's entrance, continued with the duet and duel
and the intervention of the patrol and end with Don Alvaro's
announcement that he is to enter a monastery—a piece of information of considerable importance to the plot and which, Verdi
realized, was infinitely preferable to the vagueness of Alvaro's
original curtain line about spilling Vargas blood again.

Any fears that a re-arrangement of the running order of this
scene would have any awkward effect on the key-sequence of the
music are easily allayed. As the scene is played at present the C
major of the patrol is followed by E minor at Don Alvaro's entrance,
which leads by way of the duet, the duel and the patrol's re-appear-
ance, to E major when the crowd enters. The curtain falls on C
major. In the running order I have laid out above the patrol's C
major would be followed by the crowd's E major (instead of Alvaro's
E minor); and the "Rataplan" ends in C and would therefore be
followed (as the patrol's C major is at present) with the E minor of
Alvaro's entrance. All that needs doing is to splice in a couple of *ff*
orchestral bars of E major from almost any other Verdi score to
bring down the curtain on Don Alvaro's exit.

I am not by nature in favour of messing about with a composer's
work, but there is no doubt that the German re-arrangement of this
scene was a great improvement both musically and dramatically on
the 1869 revision; one is rightly brought up to respect composers'
second thoughts, but it is surprising how often—as in the case of the
last scene of Act II of *La forza del destino*—they are not necessarily
better.

But even as it appears in the score today, the scene is preferable I
think to the form encountered in a couple of "complete" recordings
of the opera. These both began with the night patrol and continued
with the crowd scene, but the patrol was never heard of again be-

cause Don Alvaro, Don Carlo, their duet, their duel and everything about them were cut from the performance altogether. As a result we were left with a whole scene consisting entirely of music and action which are quite nonsensically irrelevant to the story. It seems a great pity that the record companies, who are unaffected by the more inconvenient restrictions of time and space and union rules suffered by the opera house, have so far given no thought to the question of re-revising Act III, Scene 3 of *La forza del destino* and so restoring its original musical and dramatic balance.

ACT IV

IN THE NEIGHBOURHOOD OF HORNACHUELOS

Scene 1 : Inside the monastery of the Madonna of the Angels. A simple arcade encloses a small courtyard planted with orange trees, oleanders and jasmine. On the left of the spectator is the door to the street; on the right, another door with a sign over it reading CLAUSURA [the name given to a secluded enclosure in a monastery]. *The Father Superior is walking about solemnly reading his breviary. From the left enter a company of beggars of all ages, carrying in the hands roughly-made bowls, pots and plates.*

The curtain rises to a dignified seven-bar phrase for strings which ends in a cadence extraordinarily reminiscent of the more solemn moments in *The Magic Flute* and in any case intended, one imagines, to create a similarly solemn and religious atmosphere.

Contrary to what these few bars may have led us to expect, however, we do not hear from the Father Superior. He continues to read his breviary while first the old men (basses), then the younger (tenors), and finally the women among the beggars ask for charity and then, in a united crescendo of angry impatience, point out that they have been waiting for an hour and must be on their way—the only operatic instance I know of that typical umbrage always taken by those who, like citizens of welfare states, consider their "right" to something for nothing is not being properly respected.

Brother Melitone, wearing a large white apron and helped by another lay-brother, enters from the right carrying a big cooking pot with two handles. They put it down in the centre of the stage, and the lay-brother departs. With some justification Melitone turns to the beggars and asks them indignantly if they think they're in a tavern. The only answer he gets is a repetition of impatient shouts for

Ex 286

Allegro vivo

food. Melitone starts to ladle out soup from the pot to protests from the beggars that the other fellow is getting too much, and to the accompaniment of the theme in the orchestra shown in Ex 286.

There is some effective scoring in the four bars that are repeated for clarinets and violas in unison with bassoon and violoncellos an octave lower. The tune starting after the second-time bar, however, plays a busier part in the course of the arguments Melitone has with the beggars, and is ingeniously developed. Melitone's principal disputes are with those who complain about the quality of the food, and with a woman who asks for four ladlefuls because she has six children. Why has she got six children? asks Melitone. She wouldn't have them if she spent her nights reciting her rosary and the Miserere. The Father Superior interrupts gently and when Melitone remarks with reason that the fecundity of the poor is appalling, bids him be charitable. The beggars continue to try Melitone's patience with repeated cries for more soup, and the women among them point out that Father Raffaele was much more charitable.

Melitone retorts that that may be so, but after a week Father Raffaele had had enough of soup and beggars and unloaded the job on to him—"Sì, sì, ma in otto giorni":

Ex 287

Allegro vivo

si, sì, ma in ot-to giorni, a-vutone abba-stanza ?i pove-ri e mi-ne-stra, re-stò nella sua stanza

With this tune, which is again something that might have come from a Donizetti comic opera, Melitone grows increasingly furious with the beggars, and in spite of the Father Superior's reminders that charity is a duty towards the poor, he abuses them roundly as rogues and vagabonds.

The reply of the beggars is to bring up the subject of Father Raffaele again, who was an angel and a saint, they insist in a reiterated phrase on one note that torments Melitone almost beyond endurance and is sung against an orchestral figure based on that rhythm of the last bar of Ex 286 which was to become such a noticeable feature of both *Otello* and *Falstaff*.

Melitone's temper reaches breaking point, and kicking over the pot he tells them to take all that's left and get out. He's had enough of them:

Ex 288

Allegro vivo

Il re-sto a voi pren-de-te-vi, non vo-glio più pa-role non voglio più pa-ro - - le non voglio più pa-ro - - le

A trumpet which from time to time prominently doubles the vocal line is one of the features of a brilliant and delicate orchestral accompaniment to a passage which adds further detail to the well-rounded musical portrait of Melitone. It is in this sequence too that we first encounter the use of that distinctive breadth of musical phrase which was to be so characteristic of much of the comedy in *Falstaff* thirty years later, and which is anticipated in the sudden expansiveness in the midst of a lot of conventional patter, of a passage like Melitone's "pezzenti più di Lazzaro, sacchi di pravità" ("Worse beggars than Lazarus! Sacks of wickedness!"):

Ex 289

Accompanied by strings in unison, the four *rallentando* bars are a good example of the use of understatement as a means of emphasis, and add still more to the characterization of Melitone.

The beggars counter the monk's insults with renewed and insistent praise of Father Raffaele as angel and saint in a crescendo that culminates in Melitone lashing with the apron he has taken off and driving everybody (except the Father Superior) out of the courtyard. His final excited shouts of "Via di qua!" are doubled by a loud tutti unison from the orchestra, trombones, tuba and all.

Melitone takes a handkerchief out of his sleeve and mops his brow with it, declaring that he really hasn't enough patience for that sort of thing. The Father Superior calms him down, telling him not to be too upset if the beggars don't like him as much as they like Father Raffaele. Melitone replies that Raffaele is his friend, but he has rather odd ways—talks to himself, and has a strange look in his eyes. Only yesterday, Melitone goes on, he had remarked jokingly that Raffaele looked like a mulatto and Raffaele had glared at him and clenched his fist. And then there was the time when lightning struck the belfry and Raffaele had gone out into the storm and Melitone had shouted at him, "You look like a wild Indian!" and his blood had frozen at the yell Raffaele had let out. Why is he so strange? asks Melitone. The Father Superior replies that disillusionment with the world, his penances and fastings have disturbed Raffaele's mind—"Del mondo i disinganni":

Ex 290

Andante mosso

Da' mou-do i — di - sin - gau - ni, l'as-si - dua — peu - ni - ten - za

A feature of the string accompaniment to this dignified tune are the unusual harmonies, which I have tried to indicate above. Melitone is much impressed by what he hears, and in his own *buffo* way repeats the Father Superior's words more or less verbatim. It is an effective little duet of great charm, ending with a low F for the Father Superior and a characteristic final patter phrase from Melitone.

The bell at the front door rings loudly and, telling Melitone to answer it, the Father Superior leaves. The visitor is Don Carlo who asks to see Father Raffaele ("Another one!" mutters Melitone in disgust). It seems there are two Father Raffaeles in the monastery—one is fat and as deaf as a mole, the other is skinny, dark and with eyes . . .("Heaven, what eyes!") . . . Which does he wish to see? Don Carlo replies: the one from hell. This seems to be sufficient identification for Melitone, who shambles away, grumbling like the Porter in Shakespeare's *Macbeth*, to fetch Don Alvaro (alias Father Raffaele), to see the visitor who gives no name but says merely that he is a gentleman.

While he is waiting Don Carlo reflects with satisfaction on the prospect of being able to take his revenge. Alvaro, in monk's habit, enters but does not immediately recognize Don Carlo; when he does, he is surprised to see him alive—which suggests that the words in the libretto at this point were not altered in the 1869 revision to conform with our knowledge that Don Carlo was not even wounded, let alone killed in the duel which ended with his arrest in Act III, Scene 3. Carlo expresses his ferocious joy at having found Alvaro at last in a phrase which I quote less for its tune than for its unusual accompaniment for bassoons, divided violoncellos, tuba and basses:

Ex 291

Sostenuto

col san - gue sol can-cel - la si l'im-fa - min ù il de-lit - to

Don Carlo, realizing that such things are not usually found in monasteries, tells Alvaro that he has brought two swords with him for their duel. Alvaro protests that he has made amends for his faults by becoming a monk, and though Carlo taunts him with cowardice, he refuses to fight.

To the melancholy tune of Ex 254, which was heard in the Overture, Alvaro begs Carlo to be merciful and leave him alone. In the fine, powerful duet that develops Alvaro once more declares that both he and Leonora are innocent, while Don Carlo, turning Ex 254 into the major, repeats his refusal to be placated in any way: Alvaro must pick up his sword and fight. Still Alvaro refuses to fight, and prostrates himself at Carlo's feet in a phrase that takes him to a low B flat (a note few tenors can sing with much conviction).

The spectacle of Alvaro humiliating himself before him makes Don Carlo angrier than ever and he now resorts to personal abuse: Don Alvaro is of low birth, he is a mulatto. This stings Alvaro into action; snatching a sword from Don Carlo's hand (to a series of fiercely dramatic brass chords) he is about to leave the scene to fight when with a last attempt at self-control he holds back. Flute, oboe and clarinet in unison once more play the tune of Ex 254; the devil shall not triumph, says Alvaro, and throws the weapon to the ground, It is only when Don Carlo deliberately strikes him across the face that Don Alvaro is finally provoked to pick up the sword again and accept the challenge. In a noisy, quarrelsome coda the two men cry, "Morte!" at each other, and the curtain falls as they leave hurriedly together.

Scene 2 : A valley among inaccessible rocks, traversed by a stream. At the back, on the audience's left, is a grotto with a practicable door, and above it a bell which can be rung from within. It is sunset. The scene slowly darkens, and a full moon rises.

Leonora, pale and wan, comes out of the grotto in a state of great agitation, which is reflected in the orchestra by the reappearance of the *agitato* theme of the Overture (Ex 253), and prays to God for peace.

There are few moments in any of Verdi's operas where the sudden change of tempo is so arrestingly dramatic as the change from this *agitato* to the Andante of Leonora's first heartbreaking "Pace . . .". Verdi classes this number quite simply in the score as "Melodia", and there could be no better description of one of the most ravishingly simple and beautiful scenes he ever wrote:

Ex *292*

Pa- ce, pa- ce, Pa-ce mio Dio pace mio Di - o!

What has been justifiably described as the Mozartian simplicity of this aria is instinctively matched by the simplicity of the orchestral accompaniment, which for long stretches consists of little more than a harp and a quartet of woodwind. Even at the modest but dramatically moving climax of the first half of the number, when Leonora cries in despair at the "fatalità" which has torn her from Alvaro, the number of instruments in the accompaniment is not increased. The tempo grows a little more urgent as the *agitato* theme of the Overture (Ex 253) returns and the violins are heard for the first time since the introduction playing the theme in a way that doesn't seem to scan. This is because where in the 3/8 of the Overture the group of three semiquavers is played only twice before the phrase marked "A", in Leonora's 4/4 it is played three times.

The agitated tempo subsides after a moment and Leonora finishes her aria with a short unaccompanied cadence (it is too restrained to be considered a cadenza). She crosses to a rock where provisions have been left by the Father Superior. As she picks them up Leonora hears the clash of swords; she returns quickly to her grotto and locks herself in.

The voice of Don Carlo is heard off stage crying for a confessor. Alvaro, drawn sword in hand, enters filled with agonized remorse that once again he has shed the blood of a Vargas. Don Carlo's voice is heard again in the distance; Don Alvaro throws his sword down and then, seeing the grotto, runs across to it to beat on the door and ask the supposed hermit to come out and give the dying Don Carlo absolution. Running through this short sequence is a plaintive little phrase, first heard on the oboe against a throbbing quaver accompaniment, which in various forms plays an important part as the scene develops:

Ex 293

Leonora replies from within that what Don Alvaro asks is impossible. Alvaro beats on the door still more loudly. In desperation Leonora rings the bell for help and comes through the door to call on Heaven to punish those who have invaded her retreat.

The lovers recognize each other, but as Leonora goes towards him Alvaro tells her not to touch him: his hands are dripping with blood. With the phrase of Ex 293 building up in a contracted form Alvaro explains what has happened—how he had done everything to avoid a fight with the man who lies dying, how he had passed his days in a monastery, but had been tracked down and finally provoked into a duel. When Leonora asks who the man was, Alvaro tells her it was her brother. She rushes away towards the woods where Don Carlo lies dying. The hollow sound of a long note in the clarinet's lowest register creates the dark and sinister mood in which Don Alvaro bitterly reflects that he should find Leonora alive at the very moment that he has killed her brother.

There is a sudden shriek and Leonora staggers in wounded, supported by the Father Superior who has come in answer to the ringing of the hermit's bell for help. Leonora is dying; Don Carlo had recognized his sister, but even in his last moments would not forgive her and had stabbed her. Leonora's brief story is told in a monotone accompanied by one of the most dramatically simple orchestral passages in any of Verdi's operas:

Ex *294*

The sustained unison G's are played by piccolo, flute, two oboes and two clarinets, against the thumping of brass, strings and bass drum in the first two bars; the figure in the *ppp* bars is played by strings only. These four bars are played exactly as they are four times consecutively (except for a C flat in place of the C natural in the last bar of all); it is a passage of tremendous dramatic effect which Don Alvaro concludes with a curse on the vengeance of fate.

The Father Superior bids him not to curse fate, but instead to humble himself before God, who is just and holy—"Non imprecare, umiliati a Lui . . .":

Ex *295*

With this lovely tune the final trio of the opera begins. While the Father Superior urges Don Alvaro to kneel, Leonora promises him God's forgiveness. She will die happy, she tells him, for in Heaven love is sacred—"Lieta poss'io precederti":

Ex *296*

There is an essential innocence about this tune which is very typical of the music Verdi wrote for his more harshly-treated heroines and particularly reminiscent in this case, I think, of the dying Gilda in *Rigoletto*. The simplicity of the melody is matched by the simplicity of the accompaniment—a harp playing chuck-chucks with occasional sustained chords in the woodwind. After a short and agitated interjection by Don Alvaro, in which he laments the prospect of survival alone, Leonora repeats her "Lieta poss'io precederti", while the Father Superior sings the first ten notes of Ex 295 in the major to words in admiration of her suffering. This time Leonora rounds off the four bars quoted in Ex 296 with a cadence in which she bids farewell to Alvaro; she will be waiting for him in heaven:

Ex 297

Alvaro repeats the phrase after her, beseeching her not to leave him; the trio comes to a climax with the lovers in a *ff* unison in the third bar, which dies down at once to *pp*. Flutes, oboes, a clarinet and a bassoon play the bar marked "A" in Ex 295 as a six-bar ostinato that becomes faster and faster and ends abruptly as Leonora dies. "She is dead!" cries Alvaro. In a monotone of five E flats (which few singers are disciplined enough to keep to without substituting E naturals on the second and fourth notes of the phrase to give it "expression") the Father Superor replies: "She is gone to God."

The curtain falls slowly on an echo—*estremamente piano*—of the first three bars of Ex 297, played by divided strings with clear single notes on the harp, which fades away in a *ppp morendo* tremolo.

The beauty of this last scene was bought at the expense of considerable revision of the original dramatic plan. We have seen how Verdi, feeling there was too much emphasis on blood and thunder, altered the running order and completely upset the dramatic balance of Act III, Scene 3 with an irrelevant variety show. He evidently felt similarly squeamish about the end of the last act, where in the revised version of 1869 the killing of Don Carlo and consequently the stabbing of Leonora both take place out of our sight, while the suicide of Don Alvaro never happens at all. In Piave's libretto, which followed Rivas' *Don Álvaro* closely at this point, duel and stabbing both took place in full view of the audience and after a short scene with him Leonora dies forgiving her brother's trespasses. Don Alvaro is then joined by the Father Superior and the rest of the monks (heard singing the Miserere as they approach) who are surprised to discover that the unknown hermit was a woman. They address Don Alvaro by his monastic name, but standing on a high rock he snaps back at them: "Imbeciles! Father Raffaele is not here—I am a messenger from Hell!" With a final curse on humanity he climbs higher up the rocks and throws himself over a precipice.

In view of the superb musical quality of the trio which now ends the opera and the dramatic music accompanying Leonora's entry after she has been stabbed, there is obviously nothing much that can be done about this last scene at this date. Except—as I remember was done at the performance I saw in Berlin in 1928—to have Don Alvaro and Don Carlo fight at the back of the stage where the audience could see them until Don Carlo is driven into the wings to beg for a confessor, stab Leonora, and die.

The most usual criticism of *La forza del destino* is that it is too full of coincidences to be convincing. This is due largely, I think, to the misleading title of the opera which is not an exact equivalent of the original Spanish *La Fuerza del Sino*. "Sino" is better translated as "fatalità"—a word which, when it is sung so emphatically by Leonora in the last act (in the "middle" section of "Pace . . .") gives an important, if rather belated, clue to the underlying theme of the opera: the power of "fatality" in the sense of what the dictionary defines as a "predestined liability to disaster". Looked at in this way it is clear that Don Alvaro is just downright unlucky from beginning to end. Besides, is the shooting of the Marquis by what has been ridiculed as a "ballistically inconceivable accident" really so improbable? I recall a famous English murder trial of the 1930s when the defence of a woman charged with shooting her lover was that the pistol was accidentally discharged when it fell to the floor during a struggle. If the jury was able to accept this defence and acquit the prisoner in an age when firearms are fitted with numberless safety devices, why should not a comparatively primitive eighteenth-century pistol thrown on the floor explode and kill a bystander? The news columns of the daily papers are filled with reports of accidents in which "inconceivable" coincidences play quite as alarming a part as they do in Verdi's opera.

Whether the plot of *La forza del destino* is altogether credible or not, the music remains some of the most enjoyable Verdi ever wrote, rivalling the score of *Un ballo in maschera* in its variety and emotional range and *Il trovatore* in its endless succession of tunes. Their unusual tunefulness, of course, is not the only thing *Il trovatore* and *La forza del destino* have in common. Apart from the Spanish settings, the monks, the gipsies, heroines called Leonora, the blood feuds, both operas have a peculiar power to inspire the sort of affection in the listener which causes him to overlook the many obvious dramatic shortcomings. And this is particularly the case, I feel, with *La forza del destino*, where the reluctance of the librettist to let even the audience know who's who and why, is typical of the sort of thing which is forgiven because it is at once forgotten in one's enjoyment of the intensely personal charm, invention, and vigour of exceptionally lovable music.

DON CARLOS

Opera in five acts. Libretto by François Joseph Méry and Camille du Locle based on the play by Schiller. First performed at the Paris Opera, on 11th March, 1867. First performance in England: Covent Garden, 4th June, 1867 (in Italian). First performance in the United States: Academy of Music, New York, 12th April, 1877. Revised version reduced to four acts by Verdi and Antonio Ghislanzoni, first performed at La Scala, Milan, 10th January, 1884.

THE IDEA of composing an opera for Paris on the subject of Schiller's *Don Carlos* was first suggested to Verdi in 1850 by Alphonse Royer and Gustave Vaëz, the librettists who had turned his *Lombardi alla prima crociata* (1843) into *Jérusalem* (1847) for the Paris Opera. The play, they recommended, could be used as "a simple point of departure" and would surely appeal to Verdi who had already gone to Schiller for *I masnadieri* (1847), based on *Die Räuber* ("The Robbers"), and *Luisa Miller* (1849), taken from *Kabale und Liebe* ("Intrigue and Love"). Verdi had also, though they forgot to mention it, used Schiller's Joan of Arc play, *Die Jungfrau von Orleans*, as the basis of *Giovanna d'Arco* (1845). *Don Carlos*, they continued, was a much larger and more poetic canvas; it had the *grande passion* that the composer needed.

What MM. Royer and Vaëz called "Fiesque" was also a beautiful subject, they said. "But love plays a smaller part in it than in *Don Carlos*." ("Fiesque" was the French way of describing Schiller's *Die Verschwörung des Fiesco zu Genua: republikanisches Trauerspiel*— "The conspiracy of Fiesco at Genoa: a Republican Tragedy"— which was once mistakenly thought to have inspired Verdi's *Simon Boccanegra*.)

Verdi did nothing about any of this, however. He was badly put out because the librettists' letter had been written on behalf of the Director of the Paris Opera, and he felt that M. Nestor Roqueplan might have had the courtesy to write to him himself; in any case Verdi was preoccupied with other things at the time, among them first thoughts on a new opera (it turned out to be *Rigoletto*) for La Fenice in Venice. When, four years later, Verdi did eventually write his first "original" for Paris the subject was not *Don Carlos* but Scribe's *Sicilian Vespers*. In the years that followed *Les Vêpres Siciliennes*, or as it is now better known, *I vespri siciliani*, Verdi was approached from time to time by the Paris Opera —on one occasion with the proposal that he should consider Gustave Flaubert's *Salammbô*. It was only when he was in Paris in 1865 to discuss the first French performance of *La forza del destino* that he suddenly dropped that particular project and contracted to write *Don Carlos* for the theatre he called "la Grande Boutique". The libretto was begun by François Joseph Méry, who died, aged sixty-seven, soon after starting on it, and completed by Camille du Locle, son-in-law and secretary of the Director of the Paris Opera.

Since it was commissioned by the Paris Opera *Don Carlos* not unnaturally conformed to the Grand Opera conventions and traditions of the theatre; it was in five acts with a ballet and was staged in the lavish and spectacular manner expected by the Opera public, and according to the formula popularized by Meyerbeer and invented by Rossini (who pronounced, on the evidence of *Don Carlos*, that Verdi was "the only man alive capable of writing Grand Opera").

It was obviously something of an unwieldy work from the start, for Verdi sanctioned several substantial cuts at the second performance which, however, he didn't wait to attend.* The Paris production of *Don Carlos* was not a success. At best it could be regarded as a *succès d'estime* inasmuch as it received good notices. Nevertheless in its five-acts-with-ballet-form the opera was heard in countries as widely separated as Russia, the United States, Poland and Argentina during the following nine years.

Verdi gave *Don Carlos* no further thought until after the performance at La Scala of the revised version of *Simon Boccanegra* in 1881, when the prospect of a production in Vienna ("where the porters shut all the front doors at ten o'clock and everybody settles down to eat and drink beer and *Gateaux*") prompted him to make drastic and not altogether happy alterations. In collaboration once more with Ghislanzoni, who had worked on the revision of *La forza del destino* and was by now, of course, known as the librettist of *Aida*, Verdi reduced *Don Carlos* to four acts.

The first act of the Paris original was discarded entirely, all that remained of it being Don Carlos' aria ("Io la vidi") which was transplanted in a slightly altered form to what had been the second act and was now the first, and a theme from a duet for Elisabeth and Don Carlos which, in the new four-act version, is heard only during the last act when it reminds the listener of nothing he remembers having heard before. The ballet was dropped, and there were many other changes which will be discussed in the course of this chapter.

The revised version in four acts, first performed at La Scala in

* Writing to Giulio Ricordi in 1868 Verdi tells of an interesting custom observed at the Paris Opera at the time which I do not think is generally known: "At the Opéra, as you know, the composer's name is not mentioned on the first night's programme even of a new opera. If the public wants to hiss, they hiss only a piece of paper. That is good; the only good thing there is at the Opéra." Verdi suggested that the same system of anonymity should be observed at a proposed performance of *La forza del destino* at La Scala.

1884, has for many years been the form in which Verdi's opera has been most frequently performed. There is, however, a third version of *Don Carlos* which was made in 1887. It is in five acts once more, but without the ballet; the original first act has been restored and the remaining four acts incorporate most of the revisions made for the Scala production of 1884. I say "most", because with the reinstatement of the first act, Don Carlos' "Io la vidi" is back in its original context and has no place in what now becomes Act II again.

It is this version which I have used as the basis of this study of *Don Carlos* and which is being used more and more frequently in the theatre—both Covent Garden and La Scala have recently adopted it to everybody's satisfaction in preference to the truncated four-act version of 1884. The English Decca company, confirming its praiseworthy belief in the duty of the gramophone to provide what is often impracticable in the opera house, issued in 1966 a *really complete* recording of the five-act *Don Carlos*—a genuine, uncut presentation of all the music found in the Ricordi score of the "third version" which dates from 1887, and which is never, so far as I know, performed without cuts in the theatre.

To those who know the opera only from the existing four-act recordings or vocal score the analysis of Act I, the Fontainebleau scene, will, I trust, be of some interest—if only because a little knowledge of the earlier part of the story may make those musical allusions to it in the last act the more poignant.

Although librettos, recordings and vocal scores now usually refer to the opera as "Don Carlo" I have retained the original *Don Carlos*, not only because that was the form Verdi himself used, even when discussing the purely Italian 1884 revision, but because I believe the Spanish (French and German) form of the name comes more easily to us. Equally, nobody with schoolboy memories of English history can possibly start thinking of Philip II of Spain as "Filippo" at this date. As for Elisabeth de Valois—she was French, and even if the process of anglicization strips her name of the acute accent on its initial "E", I still think Elisabeth is a prettier name than "Elisabetta".

CHARACTERS IN ORDER OF SINGING

DON CARLOS, *Infante of Spain* . . . *Tenor*
TEBALDO, *Page to Elisabeth* . . . . *Soprano*
ELISABETH DE VALOIS . . . . *Soprano*
THE COUNT OF LERMA, *Spanish Ambassador* . *Tenor*
A MONK . . . . *Bass*
RODRIGO, *Marquis of Posa* . . . . *Baritone*
PRINCESS EBOLI,
    Lady-in-waiting to Elisabeth . . . *Mezzo-soprano*
KING PHILIP II of SPAIN (Filippo) . . *Bass*
A ROYAL HERALD . . . . . *Tenor*
A VOICE FROM HEAVEN . . . . *Soprano*
THE GRAND INQUISITOR . . . . *Bass*

Flemish deputies, Inquisitors, ladies and gentlemen of the French and Spanish Courts, woodmen, people, pages, guards of Henry II of France and King Philip, monks, servants and officials of the Holy Inquisition, soldiers, magistrates, deputies from the Spanish provinces, hunters, etc. etc.

Scene: France and Spain   Time: About 1560

ACT I

Scene : *The Forest of Fontainebleau in winter. On the right, large rocks form a kind of cave. At the back, the royal palace can be seen in the distance.*

Before the curtain rises the sound of hunting horns is heard coming from back-stage; two B flat horns are shown in the score to be played on the right, and three in E flat on the left of the stage. As the curtain goes up the orchestra takes over in a brief tutti which lets us hear something of the largest orchestra we have so far encountered in Verdi's operas. The less usual features of the instrumentation include three flutes (the third doubling piccolo), no fewer than four bassoons, two cornets in addition to two trumpets (this was also a feature of the score of *I vespri siciliani*, Verdi's other Paris opera), four timpani, and in due course a cor anglais, a double bassoon, and a harmonium. For the first time in any of the Verdi scores discussed in this study the brass bass, instead of appearing non-committally in the score as the *cimbasso*, is specifically indicated as an ophicleide which was, of course, the instrument always used at the Paris Opera.

On the stage a few woodmen are cutting wood, their wives are seated by a large fire. Elisabeth de Valois enters on a horse led by her page Tebaldo. There is a large company of hunters, some of whose fellows are heard singing a short and hearty hunting phrase off stage on the right accompanied by the B flat horns, while others answer off stage on the left with the E flat horns in attendance. Elisabeth crosses the scene throwing money to the woodmen as she goes. Don Carlos appears on the left, hiding himself among the trees. The woodmen watch the Princess as she rides away, then picking up their tools they leave by paths in the background. These actions are accompanied by a united outburst of huntsmen's chorus and horns and in a gradual and effective diminuendo the music dies away with a brief echo of the horn call coming from the right and answered an octave lower on the left.

Don Carlos emerges from his hiding place. In defiance of his father's opposition he has come from Spain to catch a sight of the Princess who has been chosen as his bride and whom he has never met. In the short *scena* of near-recitative in which Don Carlos tells us this, a solo clarinet plays a distinctive and versatile part and gives the first indication in this score of Verdi's growing preoccupation with the individual characteristics of woodwind instruments—a

325

preoccupation which was to have astonishing results in the three operas which followed and which one imagines was greatly affected by his personal experience of this unique aspect of French orchestral playing.

The *scena* is followed by a *Romanza*—Don Carlos' "Io la vidi e al suo sorriso" ("I saw her and at her smile the sun shone on me . . .") :

Ex *298*

Andante un poco mosso

Io la vi - dia al su - o sor-ri-so scin-til-lar... mi parve il so - le

The romance is a tuneful and straightforward expression of Don Carlos' love for the Princess he has just caught sight of for the first time, with an orchestral accompaniment featuring several passages for woodwind only.

Don Carlos hurries away in the direction that Elisabeth went, but stops uncertainly and listens. From the far distance comes the faint sound of hunting horns—a disjointed couple of phrases, followed by a silence created by the simple and unfailing means of a *pp* timpani roll. It is now getting dark, and in the depths of the forest Tebaldo is heard calling; the Princess and her page have lost their way. As they appear through the trees, Don Carlos quickly hides himself for a moment so that the audience may hear what the situation is; he then comes forward and kneeling before Elisabeth, tells her that he is Spanish and a member of the Ambassador's suite. In the background Tebaldo announces that he can see the lights of the Palace of Fontainebleau and will take the Princess back. Elisabeth sends him away; she is not frightened; as Don Carlos' fiancée she has every faith in Spanish honour. Tebaldo bows and goes, leaving Don Carlos, with hand on sword, standing *dignatosamente* on Elisabeth's right.

The scene which follows is introduced by a tender and graceful phrase for strings :

Ex *299*

Allegro assai moderato

During this instrumental episode the stage directions in the libretto tell us that "Elisabeth sits down on a rock and looks up at

Don Carlos who is standing before her. Their eyes meet and Don Carlos, as if involuntarily, kneels before Elisabeth."* Elisabeth is surprised by this action but "Don Carlos picks up a few small branches off the ground and revives the fire [left smouldering by the woodmen's wives]," explaining as the flames rise that when soldiers light a fire at night in wartime and it burns brightly it means victory or love. Elisabeth makes no comment but asks questions which Don Carlos answers: peace between France and Spain is to be signed that night and one of the conditions is that Elisabeth, daughter of Henry II of France, shall marry Don Carlos, Infante of Spain. The Princess is apprehensive about leaving her home and family to live in a foreign country—will the Infante love her as much as she means to love him? Don Carlos swears to her that the Infante will devote his life to her and love her. Don Carlos' assurances are so ardent that Elisabeth asks anxiously who he is. Don Carlos replies that he is a messenger from the Prince and has brought a bejewelled envelope for her which contains a portrait of his "master". Elisabeth opens it nervously and at once recognizes the man before her as Don Carlos himself, who falls at her feet and tells her he loves her.

The dialogue of the *scena* which ends at this point, is set to a series of tuneful or dramatic phrases which merge from one into another and are typical of the style of what may be called "plot music" Verdi was now beginning to develop to supersede the traditional recitative altogether, although the indication "Recit^{vo}" did not disappear from his scores entirely even in *Falstaff*.

There now follows a duet, which begins with Elisabeth reflecting on the love she feels—"Di qual amor—di quanto ardor quest'alma è piena":

This lovely opening tune, accompanied here by little more than a clarinet arpeggio and some pizzicato chords, returns as a motif in the course of the 1884 four-act version of *Don Carlos*, but of course can make little of the effect Verdi originally intended since it has no associations for the listener deprived of the Fontainebleau scene.

There is a sound of six cannon shots, the signal that peace has

* I am quoting from a copy of the libretto of the original five-act Paris version translated into Italian in 1869, which I bought off a barrow in Catania and is more detailed in its stage directions than the vocal scores of either 1884 or 1887 or the full score which combines both forms.

come; and there is growing excitement in the lovers' voices as the brilliant lights in the windows of Fontainebleau can be seen through the trees in the distance. Don Carlos takes Elisabeth in his arms and together they rejoice in the happiness they have found in the dark forest. In unison they sing the long fifteen-bar tune of Ex 300 and the duet ends—a little conventionally, after the unison sequence which was still not such a frequent occurrence in Verdi's operas— with a joint cadenza for two voices, mostly in sixths.

Tebaldo enters with pages carrying torches. The pages remain at the back, while Tebaldo comes forward alone towards Elisabeth. He prostrates himself and kissing the hem of her skirt greets her as Queen, the betrothed of Philip the king. Elisabeth protests that she is betrothed to the Infante. Tebaldo replies that her father, King Henry, has decided she shall marry the King of Spain, and be Queen. Elisabeth and Don Carlos are stunned by the news, which she receives with a single despairing cry, and he with an incredulous muttered monotone backed by ppp chords in the lower register of the trombones and brass bass, and a hollow low F reiterated by two clarinets in unison. Trombones and tuba, playing pp with the four bassoons and horns, also punctuate in dramatic fashion the short, tensely agitated passage that follows when the lovers, with some effective unison singing against an unusual harmonic sequence, see the destruction of their short-lived happiness by a fate crueller than death itself.

In the distance a crowd is heard approaching, expressing in a long unaccompanied choral sequence a number of appropriately joyful sentiments wishing glory and honour to the Princess who will be Queen of Spain. The tune to all this is frankly pretty footling:

Ex *301*

As the singing draws nearer an orchestral accompaniment is gradually added until everything is going full blast on the arrival of the Count of Lerma (the Spanish Ambassador), the Countess d'Aremberg (a mute character who proves to be Elisabeth's companion but is difficult to identify among those present), the Princess's ladies-in-waiting, pages bearing a litter, and the large crowd we have heard singing. The Ambassador makes a formal announcement of the information we have learned from Tebaldo, adding that while King Philip leaves the Princess every liberty of choice he hopes that she will give him her hand in marriage.

Elisabeth says nothing until a chorus of women, singing in a short, rather poignant unison, beseech her to accept the Spanish King's proposal and so bring peace at last. In a "dying voice" the Princess answers simply: yes. The crowd invokes God's blessing on the Princess in a solemn seven-part choral passage, while the distracted lovers express their despair and misery in long unison passages together. Some of these passages are a little optimistically written in the middle of the singers' voices to be sung against chorus and orchestra in a ff performance of Ex 301, now put up an octave so that there is virtually no chance of Elisabeth and Don Carlos being heard over it. From time to time, however, there are gaps in the choral sections through which they can be heard, though it is at these points that cuts are usually made.

With ff flourishes from cornets and trumpets Elisabeth, led by the Count of Lerma, enters the litter; the procession moves off; the crowd follows with cries of "Gloria, o Regina! Gloria, onor!" and Don Carlos is left alone, "desolate, his head in his hands, leaning against the rock where Elisabeth had sat".

The tune of Ex 301 is now taken over and made to sound a little less trivial by gentle treatment, first by woodwind, then by horns, trumpets, trombones, tuba and the four bassoons with a staccato figure in the lower reaches of the violoncellos. The voices of the chorus grow fainter in the distance with one last reprise of Ex 301 in its original register, unaccompanied once more except for a series of short pp timpani rolls, while Don Carlos, "con disperazione" and in a near-monotone, mourns the loss of the happiness which has vanished for ever with a beautiful dream.

The act ends with a gradual dying away of a motif based on the first four notes of Ex 301 and ingeniously treated harmonically and instrumentally.

ACT II (I)*

PART ONE

Scene : The Cloisters of the monastery of San Giusto.† On the right, a lighted chapel in which the tomb of Charles V can be seen behind a gilded grille. On the left, a door leading to the exterior. At the back, the inside door of the Cloisters. The garden has high cypresses. It is dawn.

There is a short prelude before the rise of the curtain; it is a solemn passage played by four horns, much of it in unison. It is of no thematic significance, but creates a magnificently sombre atmosphere which is emphasized by the addition in the cadence of three trombones, four bassoons and tuba.

The curtain rises with the monks chanting in the chapel—a distant, rather sinister sound, hovering between minor and major, in which they reflect gloomily that the great Charles is now turned to ashes and stands trembling before his Maker. The air of pessimism is maintained by a Monk who adds a solo reflection on the deceased Emperor's shortcomings—remarking on his immense pride, his ambition to conquer the world—gloomy words accompanied by a typically gloomy and "dark" orchestral background of violas, violoncellos, bassoons and tuba.

The monks resume their minor-major chanting punctuated on a couple of occasions this time by the same sort of bare *pp* chord for woodwind (piccolo, flute, oboes, bassoons) and horns which was so effective in *La forza del destino*, Act III, Scene 3 (see p 302). In this case the bassoon makes a perfect chord of F sharp major by contributing the necessary A sharp, but it is the only A sharp in the

* Figures in brackets refer to the Acts in the four-act version of 1884.

† The name "San Giusto", found in both Italian and English versions of the opera, is obviously a corruption of "San Jerónimo de Yuste", the monastery near Plasencia where the Emperor Charles V retired after he had resigned the Spanish throne in favour of his son Philip II in 1556. Charles lived in a building which was specially constructed for him and which he occupied from 1557 until his death there, aged fifty-eight, in 1558. He lived at Yuste in considerable state with a large retinue and—according to my Baedeker of 1913—"he gave free rein to his taste for mechanical pursuits, made a large collection of clocks and watches, and spent much of his time with Giovanni Turriano ('Juanelo'), an ingenious engineer and mechanician of Cremona".

chord and the suggestion of the bare fifths of F sharp and C sharp is
still very strong in the two and a half octaves above it. Once more the
peculiar character of the sound comes from Verdi's use of the distinctive quality of sustained notes on the piccolo played *pianissimo*—a
practice he followed with increasing effect in his later operas.

In a final broad and dignified tune the Monk asks forgiveness for
Charles' sins and praises the Lord, while the accompanying chorus,
although reluctant to abandon altogether its pessimistic dust-and-
ashes references to the Emperor, now chants in an uncompromisingly
major tonality.

During all this dawn has been breaking slowly, and Don Carlos,
pale and distraught, has been moving silently in the Cloisters. He
stops to listen and uncovers his head. A bell rings; the monks—with
the exception of the bass soloist who stays behind to pray before the
tomb of Charles V—leave the chapel, cross the scene and disappear
into the interior of the monastery while the orchestra echoes a couple
of phrases from the Monk's last long tune as a postlude which dies
away in an unexpectedly charming cadence played by the cornet
and second violins.

At this point in the four-act version of 1884 we have a lengthy
interpolation made necessary not only by Verdi's understandable
anxiety not to lose Don Carlos' aria as a result of the elimination of
the Fontainebleau scene, but also, of course, because having been
deprived of that scene we have to be what is known as "put in the
picture". Don Carlos, *molto agitato*, tells us how he has lost Elisabeth
twice over—to his King and father. There is a *pp* reminder of Ex 300
in the orchestra, which will be lost on the listener who has never
heard the love duet in the original Act I, but which serves to set Don
Carlos reflecting on the day when he and Elisabeth were alone and
happy in the forest of Fontainebleau. These memories of the "sweet
soil of France" give Don Carlos the cue to sing his aria "Io la vidi"
in a revised form—in B flat instead of C, and with alteration to both
words and melody already apparent in the opening bars:

Ex 302

Io la vi-di e'il suo sor-ri-so nuo-vo un cièl a-pri-va a me!

In spite of the similarity between the opening phrases of this and
the tune as it appears in Ex 298, Don Carlos' aria this time is in another mood altogether. In the Fontainebleau scene Don Carlos was
singing an untroubled love song, full of anticipation of joys to come;
here he is mourning the loss of everything he held most dear. Not

unnaturally words and music have been changed to fit the 1884 situation, and have introduced a note of austerity to the aria; the tune, where it is not completely different, has been simplified and shorn of the decoration which was a feature of the earlier version. Even allowing for the difference in the emotions expressed it is an interesting example of Verdi's melodic development over a period of sixteen years or so.

With the end of Don Carlos' aria the four-act version of 1884 and the five-act version of 1887 follow the same course. In the 1887 score the bars between the orchestral postlude to the monks' chanting (p 330) and the point in the action we have now reached, consist of a brief recitative by Don Carlos on his entrance informing us that he is vainly seeking peace in the monastery of San Giusto where his grandfather Charles V had finished his days. He seeks peace in vain, Don Carlos says, because the image of Elisabeth, who has been taken from him, is constantly present. In the four-act version we are never told, either now or later on, exactly why Don Carlos is in a monastery at all.

Don Carlos has reached the bottom of page 11 of the 1884 vocal score, and the top of page 64 of the 1887 edition, when the Monk who remained behind when the others went inside the monastery, rises from his knees and approaches him. In solemn tones, accompanied by the four bassoons, the three trombones and tuba, the Monk proclaims that the sorrows of the world follow one into the Cloister; only in heaven can the heart find peace.

Don Carlos draws back in terror at the sound of the Monk's voice, imagining that it is Charles V himself he hears and sees wearing armour under his monk's habit. The Monk walks slowly and gravely past Don Carlos and into the monastery where his voice is heard chanting again and fades into the distance.

Rodrigo, Marquis of Posa, arrives and is embraced joyfully by Don Carlos who is delighted to see his dearest friend again. Rodrigo tells him that he—Carlos—is urgently needed to free the oppressed Flemish people from the tyranny of Philip. The look of anguish on his friend's face, however, makes Rodrigo wonder what is the matter, and when Don Carlos remains silent, he begs him to tell him why he is so unhappy. Don Carlos confesses that he loves Elisabeth. Rodrigo's natural surprise at this is at once interpreted by Carlos as disapproval; but Rodrigo reassures him of his love and loyalty. The sequence of dialogue which begins with Rodrigo's concern at his friend's sorrow is set by Verdi to one of those passages of music— so characteristic of the "conversation" music of his last operas—in which the variety and subtlety of vocal inflexion are underlined by an easy-flowing, beautifully scored orchestral background. Don Carlos' hesitation in confessing his love for Elisabeth, for instance, is expressed not by any exaggerated rubato or pauses for emphasis, but by spacing the words, and the music that comments on them, in such a way that the basic 6/8 rhythm and Allegro tempo of the sequence are not interrupted.

As I have already mentioned, Verdi still included passages marked "Recitativo" in *Don Carlos*, but they no longer conform to the formula of recitative as we know it from his earlier operas. Instead, we find the text being treated with increasing melodic and harmonic freedom and the accompaniment with a greater variety of instrumental colour. Where the conventional setting of words to passages on one note is still heard it has the effect not of a return to *recitativo secco* but of focusing attention on the words. This is what happens, at any rate, when Rodrigo reverts to recitative after the tuneful 6/8 passage of dialogue and asks Carlos whether the King knows anything about his secret. On being told that he doesn't, Rodrigo suggests that his friend should ask for the Governorship of Flanders, where he may forget his private sorrows and learn how to become a king in a country of oppressed people.

A bell sounds, the signal that the gates of the monastery are opening and, Rodrigo explains, Philip and the Queen will shortly arrive. In a solemn near-monotone passage which ends in a four-bar phrase accompanied *pp* by the imposing sound of all the bassoons, horns, cornets, trumpets, trombones, and the tuba, Rodrigo bids Don Carlos pray for strength.

There now follows a typical passage in that vein Verdi seemed to reserve affectionately for duets between tenor and baritones who have reached agreement on some important point or other—either to fight each other, or to be loyal to each other—in each case until death do them part. Don Carlos and Rodrigo combine in their duet to swear eternal friendship—"Dio, che nell'alma infondere":

Ex *303*

The best that can be said about this tune is that its banality is rather touching—in the same way that the sentimentality of an old comrades' reunion is touching in its unabashed sincerity. Nevertheless, there is little in opera quite so corny as the singers' unaccompanied, free-tempo unison on "Ah!" leading to the return of Ex 303 at the end of the eight-bar "middle"—unless it be the identical phrase sung by Elisabeth and Don Carlos in the Fontainebleau scene as a lead-in to the *ff* tutti when the chorus sings the tune of

Ex 301 an octave up on its arrival on the scene as described on page 329.

Don Carlos and Rodrigo bring their duet to a noisy conclusion as King Philip, leading Elisabeth by the hand, enters with the monks. Rodrigo, bidding his friend have courage, moves away from Don Carlos who bows to the King "sombrely and suspiciously", trying to restrain his emotion. Elisabeth is surprised and moved to see Don Carlos again. The King and Queen walk towards the tomb of Charles V, where Philip kneels bareheaded for a moment; he rises and leaves with the Queen.

Inside the monastery the monks are heard chanting their minor-major phrases once more, which are punctuated by Don Carlos' cries of anguish at the loss of Elisabeth, and by the "bare fifths" chords of F sharp major described on page 330, this time with the three trombones and tuba added to give extra F sharps four and five octaves below the piccolo. Don Carlos' mood changes from despair to enthusiasm as he and Rodrigo repeat their resolve to live and die together and with their dying breath to cry: Liberty! Their determination is expressed with the orchestra playing the tune of Ex 303 softly (oboes and clarinets in thirds, divided violins and bassoons in thirds an octave lower), and the curtain falls as they leave together to a *ff tutti* reprise of the same tune by the orchestra.

The effect of the orchestral reprise was so powerful in the early days of the opera in Italy that it was regularly encored on its own.

PART TWO

Scene : A pleasant garden at the gates of the Cloisters of San Giusto. There are a fountain, stone seats, groups of orange, pine and mastic trees. On the horizon, the mountains of Estremadura. In the background, on the right, is the door of the monastery which is reached by a flight of steps.

The curtain rises on a chorus of various ladies of the Queen's suite, who are seated round the fountain; pages stand beside them.

In the interest of brightening up the opera for the sake of the Paris Opera, Verdi doesn't bother us with the plot for some time after the curtain rises on this scene. A page tunes a mandoline (which is purely a prop to be seen and not heard, as there is no provision for the instrument in the score), and after a bright and slightly exotic orchestral introduction, in which piccolo and triangle have prominent parts they do not relinquish for some time, the women's three-part chorus sings gently of the trees and the shade of their peaceful surroundings.

The accompaniment to this is more interesting than the singing, and includes further effective passages of scoring for the piccolo's sustained notes played *piano* in octaves with the oboe, as well as an early example of an effect for violins which Verdi was beginning to try out. For instance, in a sequence of eight quavers in a 4/4 bar the first violins would play a quaver with the bow on each of the main beats of the bar, while the same notes would be echoed pizzicato by the second violins as off-beats on the quaver following—that is, on the second, fourth, sixth and eighth quavers of the bar. Verdi certainly did not overdo this device once he'd discovered it, for in fact the only other instance I know of it occurs in a slightly more complicated form in the first act of *Otello*, where it is used most skilfully and with great effect.

At the end of the chorus's first number Tebaldo enters with Princess Eboli, the Queen's lady-in-waiting, and since the Page is a kind of Oscar *manqué* the orchestral accompaniment to his observations on the trees, flowers and general ambience of San Giusto immediately acquires a lightness and sparkle created by piccolo and strings launching out on a series of *leggero* figures. (Verdi obviously had Oscar somewhere at the back of his mind in writing the part of Tebaldo, but it is plain that the character was too unimportant to warrant more than a superficial suggestion of general cheerfulness and good nature.) The accompaniment to Tebaldo's few words develops a series of trills played by piccolo and first violins which is carried over into the accompaniment of a repetition of the women's opening choral passage, now sung to different words on the same subject and supported by Tebaldo.

Eboli now proposes to sing; her suggestion is greeted with general enthusiasm, and asking Tebaldo to accompany her on the mandoline (why not a guitar in Spain?), announces that she will sing the familiar Saracen "Song of the Veil" (*Canzone del Velo*). A *fortissimo* orchestral introduction in the rhythm of the seguidilla (at least, it is more of a seguidilla than the one described as such in *La forza del destino*) prefaces Eboli's ballad—"Nei giardin del bello Saracin ortello" ("In the gardens of a beautiful Moorish palace . . ."):

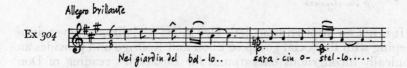

The flattened seventh indicated above is characteristic of Verdi's careful exoticism in a song which makes a brave attempt in a couple of cadenzas to imitate the chesty arabesque decoration of flamenco singing (Verdi marks his reiterated four-note flourish "come un mormorio"—"like a murmur"). The song itself is the story of how

King Mohammed makes love to a veiled woman only to discover
that it is the Queen. Boccaccio might have made something of the
situation but as it appears here it is a pretty pointless story which, if
it is not funny, is at least clean.

The narrative is restricted to two verses, followed each time by a
4/4 refrain sung mostly in thirds by Tebaldo and Eboli (the Page
taking the higher part) in which all pretty maidens are recommended to weave veils while the sun shines and wear them at night
to attract their man. The refrain is repeated each time by the
women's chorus.

The diversion at an end, the action is resumed by the entrance of
Elisabeth who comes out of the monastery in a melancholy mood.
Even when she remarks on the happy song she has just heard, she
reflects that happiness is something she herself no longer knows.
Rodrigo appears at the back of the scene. Tebaldo goes over and
talks to him and then announces him to the Queen.

Rodrigo comes forward, bows to Elisabeth, and giving her a letter
from her mother in France at the same time slips into her hand a
note which he begs her in an urgent whisper to read. Elisabeth, sus-
pecting at once that it is from Don Carlos, stands motionless and confused for a moment while Rodrigo goes over to Eboli. There follows
now a longish passage of small-talk between Rodrigo and Eboli,
who discuss the latest news from France (the text is plastered with
tactful references to the brilliance and beauty to be found at Court
in that "gentle and courtly land"). Their dialogue takes place to a
rather self-consciously "elegant" orchestral accompaniment which
features the first violins in a kind of imperfectly remembered paraphrase of the similarly "elegant" mazurka in the last scene of *Un
ballo in maschera*:

Ex *305*

It is not an inspired tune, let's face it. Its triviality, however, is in
keeping with the social gossip of Eboli and Rodrigo and provides an
ironically incongruous background for Elisabeth's reading of Don
Carlos' letter—read, it will be noted, in the traditional monotone
of operatic letter-reading which Verdi did not altogether forsake
even in *Falstaff*. The letter runs: "By all the memories that bind us,
and in the name of the past so dear to me, trust this man, I beg you
—Carlos." Elisabeth turns to Rodrigo to thank him and bid him
ask a favour of her. Rodrigo accepts, but not for himself. Elisabeth

guesses what is coming and apprehensively asks whom the favour is for.

Rodrigo replies: for Carlos, who lives a life of sadness and loneliness in the monastery; if Elisabeth will see him he will recover the hope and contentment he has lost—"Carlo, ch'è sol—il nostro amore vive nel duol":

Ex 306

Rodrigo's Romanza, which demands but rarely gets a trill from the singer in his cadence of the first eight-bar phrase, has a second verse with another lot of words to the same tune and a different accompaniment largely based on the rhythm of Ex 305.

The second verse is usually cut in public performance, however, and with it the troubled asides of Elisabeth and Eboli in the short agitated interlude between the first and second verses. Eboli's aside is of some importance: she is in love with Don Carlos and it crosses her mind that the agitation she has so often noticed in Don Carlos when he has been in the presence of the Queen may perhaps be the result of his undeclared love for herself. The omission of the second verse also means that neither the audience nor Elisabeth is told that one of Don Carlos' greatest sorrows is the hostility of his father towards him.

In practice, though we are denied Rodrigo's second verse, we still get something of the two women's reactions—Elisabeth's fear that to see Don Carlos again will be to die, and Eboli's bewilderment that Don Carlos should conceal his love for her. But as they both tend to sing at once the effect is a little confusing for the listener. The Queen finally makes up her mind and "with dignity and resolution" sends Tebaldo with a message to say that she is ready to see her son (step-son, that is) again.

Rodrigo takes Eboli by the hand and talking to her *sotto voce* leads her into the background to a reprise of the violin tune of Ex 305, now decorated by a busy viola figure.

There now follows a "Gran Scena e Duetto", introduced by an unusually detailed set of stage directions. "Don Carlos is brought in by Tebaldo. Rodrigo speaks in a low voice to Tebaldo who goes into the monastery. Don Carlos approaches Elisabeth slowly and bows without raising his eyes. Elisabeth, restraining her emotion with difficulty, motions Don Carlos to come nearer. Rodrigo and

Eboli make signs to the ladies-in-waiting, withdraw and disappear among the trees. The Countess d'Aremberg [who has been playing her mute part since the curtain rose] and two ladies are left standing alone, at some distance, perplexed by the way they are obliged to behave. After a while the Countess and the ladies go from bush to bush plucking flowers and withdraw."

Rodrigo's busy stage management has now left Don Carlos and Elisabeth alone. Carlos greets her formally and begs her to use her influence with the King to send him to Flanders. As his manner grows more urgent Elisabeth is obviously moved, but carefully addresses Don Carlos as "my son". When Carlos protests vehemently that she should speak to him in this way Elisabeth tries to leave, but Don Carlos holds her back, asking her to have pity and calling on heaven to grant him one single day of happiness. Elisabeth promises to speak to Philip, and if the King heeds her Don Carlos will be able to leave for Flanders the very next day. (There is a puzzling and rather irrelevant piece of stage action at this point, when Rodrigo and Eboli—who, we were given to think, had left the scene—now reappear, cross the back of the stage deep in conversation and then leave. Their entrance is marked to coincide with the beginning of Elisabeth's lines about talking to the King, their departure with the end of the phrase, eight bars later.)

Elisabeth makes a gesture of farewell to Don Carlos and tries once more to leave, but Don Carlos pleads with her in anguished tones (matched in the orchestra by a weeping figure for flute and oboe) for one word of compassion and understanding. Elisabeth, greatly moved, asks him why he accuses her of indifference; it is duty that makes her silent.

Don Carlos understands; and in music of great lyrical beauty consoles himself with the thought that though he has lost Elisabeth at least he can hear her voice. The passage beginning with Don Carlos' words, "Perduto ben, mio sol tesor" is one of the outstanding moments in the opera—an exquisitely tender tune accompanied by three flutes and a clarinet, with the first flute doubling the melody and the clarinet playing arpeggios:

Ex 307

These six bars—which may well sound faintly familiar, since they are hinted at in *Simon Boccanegra* (Ex 208)—are repeated with just enough variation to ensure a full close in the key of B flat. Elisabeth

repeats the complete twelve-bar phrase note for note, except for the
addition of a very Pucciniesque grace note at the end—but to different words and to a different accompaniment. Her words reassure
Don Carlos as she bids him goodbye that she still loves him; the
accompaniment continues to feature the three flutes, but they are
now heard an octave higher with some effective violin harmonics
and a cor anglais added.

Don Carlos is overjoyed at her words, but in his exaltation falls in
a dead faint.* Don Carlos' loss of consciousness is very well handled
by Verdi who avoids all suggestion of hysteria, but instead has him
collapse muttering incoherently that he wants to die of love at
Elisabeth's feet.

Elisabeth believes that he is dying, and prays anxiously for Don
Carlos, "killed by sorrow, dying of love", who was "destined for
her by heaven". Don Carlos recovers consciousness but remains
delirious. In spite of his delirium Don Carlos recognizes Elisabeth,
seated beside him as she had been when they met in the forest:

Ex 308

The orchestra in this short passage is again most imaginatively
used; the cor anglais supports the vocal line, while harmonics in the
violins, single notes on the harp, and the three flutes used *pp* give a
subtle whispered quality to the orchestral sound. Don Carlos declares his love with increasing fervour, but on coming to himself
suddenly grows gloomy, with thoughts of death expressed against
sombre wind chords and the ominous rumble of timpani. Suddenly,
Carlos' mood changes and proclaiming passionately that though the
earth and heavens should open up and destroy him, he will still love
her, he takes Elisabeth in his arms.

It is a brief, determined outburst with a couple of arrestingly
dramatic interjections of unison C's by the entire wind section of the
orchestra from flutes to tuba adding a note of defiance. Elisabeth
struggles free and with fierce sarcasm turns on Don Carlos telling
him to hurry and kill his father and then, covered with his blood,
lead his mother to the altar. "Go and kill your father—go!" she
repeats. Horrified, Carlos rushes away in despair, crying that he is
accursed. In one of those simple and lovely cadences Verdi reserved

* The experienced opera-goer will accept this as everyday operatic behaviour,
of course, but it seems that in real life Don Carlos was in fact an epileptic. The
libretto makes no mention of this, however.

for his sopranos, Elisabeth kneels and exclaims that God has watched over them:

Ex 309

So ends a "Gran Scena e Duetto" of great emotional variety, in which tenderness and despair, restraint and fervour, joy and poignancy are superbly expressed in music full of dramatic contrast and melodic and orchestral invention.

Tebaldo enters hurriedly to announce the King. Philip, who is followed by a crowd which includes Rodrigo, Eboli, the Countess d'Aremberg, pages, and a chorus of ladies and gentlemen of the court, enters and demands angrily why, contrary to his express orders, he finds the Queen unattended. Who was the lady-in-waiting responsible? Countess d'Aremberg steps forward silently from the crowd and stands before the King, who orders her to return to France immediately. When the Countess collapses in tears, the chorus murmur their surprise at the insult to the Queen.

Elisabeth bids her companion not to weep. She may be banished from Spain but not from her heart, which will follow her to their native country—"Non pianger, mia compagna":

Ex 310

This is a moving and simple aria consisting of two sections—an eight-bar phrase in the minor followed by a ten-bar phrase in the major. It is introduced by the cor anglais which continues to play a prominent part in the accompaniment where Verdi's characteristic expression of tears by the rising semitone is intensified in the F minor passage by the addition of a series of C's played by two flutes in octaves as a syncopated ostinato through the entire eight-bar phrase. The F major section features a solo flute in a sequence of staccato arpeggio figures.

In the score the same routine is repeated for what one might call the second "verse" of the aria, in which Elisabeth gives the Countess d'Aremberg a ring as a last token of her affection, bidding her to keep silent about the insult for which, Elisabeth says, she is still blushing, and not to talk of the Queen's tears and sorrow. This part of the aria is often cut in the theatre, of course, which means that we come sooner to the coda in which Rodrigo and the chorus express their sympathy for Elisabeth, while Philip confesses in an aside that he is now almost inclined to believe in his wife's sincerity. The cor anglais has a final word in a four-bar orchestral epilogue during which Elisabeth takes a tearful leave of the Countess and goes out supported by Eboli. The chorus follows.

As Rodrigo is about to leave, Philip calls him back. Why, asks the King, has he never asked for an audience or a favour of any kind; he is a loyal and distinguished subject, is there no reward he can give him? Rodrigo replies that there is nothing he wants; to serve Spain is its own reward. Philip continues to press him; Rodrigo repeats that there is nothing he wants for himself; but after a moment's hesitation he admits there is a favour he would like to ask on behalf of others.

He then tells the King that he has just returned from Flanders where tyranny and persecution have turned a once happy country into one of blood and tears. Rodrigo's passionate account of the horrors he has seen is delivered in the fluent dramatic style of setting the dialogue which Verdi was now adopting to an increasing extent. Quotation becomes not so much difficult as unprofitable; the music is an endless succession of tuneful phrases, some long, some short, all of them subjected to a more ambitious harmonic and orchestral treatment than ever before in Verdi's operas. In Rodrigo's story of the misery and desolation of Flanders, we still hear the familiar imitation of weeping by the oboe, but it emerges from a more complex and technically advanced orchestral accompaniment than we have heard hitherto.

The agitation and urgency of Rodrigo's narration gives way for a moment to a more lyrical mood when he thanks God that he is able to tell the King about Flanders and to appeal to him in person. The seven-bar phrase in which Rodrigo does this is worth quoting, I think, as an example of the kind of tune encountered in this form of musical dialogue which Verdi was content to use only once and forget before passing on to something quite different:

Ex 311

Philip's answer to Rodrigo's appeal is that bloodshed and the suppression of heresy alone can ensure peace in the world. Look at Spain, he says, where the people are faithful to God and loyal to their King; he will give the same peace to Flanders.

Rodrigo, appalled by the King's words, retorts that peace like that is the peace of the graveyard. This angry line is emphasized by three ferocious *ff* bars in which trombones and tuba are heard growling away in their lower register, finally fading to leave a sinister *ppp* of open fifths in the low register of the clarinets as background to Rodrigo's warning to the King to beware that history does not say of him: "He was a Nero."

Rodrigo goes on: is this the sort of peace Philip wants to give the world—where every priest is a hangman, and every soldier an assassin and a bandit? In a long and exciting passage Rodrigo urges the King to save the world by giving it liberty.

Philip reacts calmly to Rodrigo's forceful words, telling him that he dreams strange dreams; he would think differently, he says, if he knew human nature as a king knows it. The orchestral sequence of what Francis Toye called "vacillating triplets" which precedes and accompanies Philip's words is worth studying as an intriguing and skilful experiment in harmony and orchestration. The orchestration in particular has a wonderfully elusive, understated quality. Philip goes on to reassure Rodrigo that he has nothing to fear from him; but he must beware of the Grand Inquisitor.

The King now changes the subject and confides in Rodrigo that his life is filled with anxiety and sorrow; he is unhappy as a father, even unhappier as a husband. He is disturbed about the Queen and Don Carlos, and adds *con esplosione di dolore*, that there is nothing on earth so precious as what his son has taken from him. Philip's first words in this sequence are sung *sotto voce* to this phrase:

Ex 312

The notes in the first bar are accompanied only by violins and violas in octaves. When Philip has confided his fear and suspicions to Rodrigo Verdi makes ingenious use of the same notes played staccato and *pp* by the violins as a figure running behind Philip's next words—which are to tell Rodrigo to watch Elisabeth and Don Carlos. Rodrigo is also told that he may have privileged access to the Queen at all times, an opportunity which he greets joyously with "an unexpected dawn appears in the sky".

What has so far been a conversation between two characters now changes into a duet for the final moments of the scene. Both men talk to themselves, often at the same time; Rodrigo rejoices in his good fortune and Philip repeats the hope that peace will soon come to him.

There is a pause in which the King warns Rodrigo once more to beware of the Grand Inquisitor; his words are punctuated this time by a couple of *pianissimo* chords played by the entire wind, brass and strings in the orchestra with remarkably ominous effect. Philip extends his hand, Rodrigo kneels and kisses it, and the curtain falls *rapidamente*.

As the nature of much of the music suggests, the greater part of the long and dramatic scene between Philip and Rodrigo dates from the revision of the opera for La Scala in 1884. But the differences between this and the Paris original are not only musical. The whole of the scene from the point where Philip holds up Spain as a model of the peace he proposes to give to Flanders to the end of the act is new. In the 1869 libretto Rodrigo repeats his plea for liberty in Flanders and throws himself at the King's feet. Philip, in an aside, remarks on the novelty of such talk and admits he is surprised; nobody so near the throne has ever spoken in that way before, nobody has ever revealed to him that thing "unknown to Kings, which has the name of Truth!" He raises Rodrigo off his knees and tells him he is too young yet to try and frighten with such spectres the old King who owns half the world. Philip dismisses Rodrigo, telling him to keep clear of the Grand Inquisitor if he can. As Rodrigo leaves the King calls him back, telling him to stay; he likes his proud spirit and wants to open his heart to him. There follows a short duet passage in which the King beseeches Rodrigo to bring peace to his sorrowing heart, and Rodrigo soliloquizes with satisfaction that things now look more hopeful. Philip turns to the Count of Lerma, who has meanwhile arrived on the scene with a group of courtiers, and orders that Rodrigo is to be allowed access to him "at all hours".

It will be seen from this brief account of the Paris version that the changes made by Verdi and Ghislanzoni for Milan were not only extensive but also a considerable improvement. The character of Rodrigo is more rounded, we learn far more of the King's suspicions about Elisabeth and Don Carlos (we can only guess the reason for his "sorrowing heart" in the Paris duet), and we end with the more ironically dramatic situation of Rodrigo being given privileged access, not to the King, but to the Queen.

ACT III (II)

PART ONE

Scene : A grove in the Queen's Gardens in Madrid. At the back under a leafy arch is a statue with a fountain. It is a moonlight night.

It was in this scene that the action in the original Paris version was interrupted for the ballet. The curtain rose on what was clearly a *festa* of some kind; the stage was filled with *elegantissime* ladies in masks attended by gentlemen, and an off-stage chorus, accompanied only by castanets and tambourine, sang an imitative song about mandolines. The Queen and Eboli then arrived with their attendants, but the Queen, feeling tired, decided to retire, giving Eboli her mantilla, necklace and mask to wear in her place. Eboli then sang a song about the brief hour she would enjoy as a queen, how grandees would bow to her, and how before the night was ended she would "intoxicate Don Carlos with love". Summoning a page Eboli quickly wrote a note and sent him off with it. The scene then changed for the ballet.

In order to give some idea of what an opera written for Paris involved for Verdi the following is the argument of the ballet. I have tried to preserve some of the flowery language in which it was written.

"LA PEREGRINA"

(The Rare One)

"Inside a magic grotto, made of mother of pearl and coral, several marvellous Ocean Pearls are hidden from all profane eyes, guarded by the jealous Waves.

"A Fisherman approaches this grotto which is forbidden to mortals. Dazzled by so much magnificence he thinks he is dreaming, and the Pearls coquettishly show off all their seductive beauty before him.

"Suddenly the Queen of the Waters appears, who wants to punish the audacious Fisherman by throwing him into the depths; the pleas of the Pearls fail to assuage her anger.

"A Page arrives, carrying the arms and colours of Philip II, and declares that by order of the King of Spain the Fisherman must look at the bottom of the sea for the most beautiful Pearl. Hardly has the

344

dreaded name of Philip been pronounced than the Queen of the Waters bows with respect and offers the Fisherman all the riches of her kingdom. But none of the pearls is worthy of Philip: the beauty of all the pearls must be combined in one. The Pearls divest themselves of their necklaces and place them in a golden shell from which emerges *La Peregrina*, the most beautiful jewel in the Crown of Spain.

"This pearl, which has no equal except the famous pearl of Cleopatra, is impersonated by the Queen. Princess Eboli, wearing Elisabeth's mantilla and mask, appears on a dazzling car; the sounds of the Spanish hymn are heard, the Pearls kneel, and the Ladies and Gentlemen taking part in the *festa* also kneel to render homage to their Queen."

The music to this typically Paris-Opera ballet production (which could be put on for a run at the Folies-Bergère any time at all) consisted of five numbers; Introduction, Andante and Waltz, Variations, Pantomime (*azione mimica*) and Hymn, *Galop finale*. When it was finished the scene reverted to the Queen's Gardens described above.

Verdi and Ghislanzoni decided that no harm could possibly be done to the course of the drama if the whole of the ballet and the scene before it were jettisoned. In its place Verdi wrote a short and very lovely orchestral prelude based on the theme of the second version of Don Carlos' aria, "Io la vidi" (Ex 302). It is full of exquisite scoring, mostly for strings, the violins divided in four parts, solo violoncellos in their high register and a couple of bars at the end in which legato phrases played pp on the piccolo contribute their peculiar gossamer quality to the creation of the moonlit atmosphere of the scene that follows. The last eight bars of the Prelude, indeed. with their rich changing harmonies on a pedal note sustained by violoncellos and basses, are among Verdi's happiest harmonic inspirations.

The curtain rises on the scene already described on page 344. Don Carlos is alone, reading in the traditional monotone an unsigned letter of assignation near the fountain in the Queen's Gardens at midnight. If we know what happened in the opening scene which was cut out in the revision we will know that the letter is from Princess Eboli; otherwise, seeing how Don Carlos rejoices over it, we can only suppose it to be from Elisabeth.

Eboli enters, her face covered by a veil, and Don Carlos immediately believes her to be the Queen. If, according to the action of the original libretto, Eboli appears wearing the Queen's mantilla, necklace and mask, then Don Carlos' mistake is easily explained; as it is, of course, he may be regarded as the victim of wishful thinking. After all, whom would he expect or hope to see but the Queen?

In an excited, ardent *mezza voce* Don Carlos greets the supposed

Elisabeth with a fervour which, believing she is the cause of it, fills
Eboli with "supreme joy", and she grows more ecstatic as Don Carlos' protestations become more passionate. Eboli takes off her mask,
and Don Carlos in an aside expresses deep dismay at discovering
that it is not the Queen. His sudden cold silence puzzles the Princess;
what spectre, she asks, has come between them?

It is obvious at this point that we had better forget all we know
from the Paris original about Eboli being dressed like the Queen.
Otherwise, while we know that Eboli believes Don Carlos is in love
with her, if she goes to meet him deliberately looking like the Queen
in order to deceive him, why should she ever imagine that Don
Carlos is making love to *her*? If the situation is to be at all credible
we must presume that Don Carlos, not knowing either the Queen's
or Eboli's handwriting and so believing, as well as hoping, that the
letter he received was from Elisabeth, genuinely thinks he is making
love to the Queen, and that Eboli, veiled but not disguised, and
knowing nothing of the Elisabeth-Don Carlos relationship, just as
genuinely thinks Don Carlos is at last confessing his love for her.

Eboli tells Don Carlos *con passione* of the perils that threaten him—
"Ignoto forse, ignoto ancora . . ." ("Perhaps you do not know . . .") :

When Don Carlos replies that he is only too well aware of the
dangers ahead of him, Eboli assures him that she can save him. An
oddly lyrical colloquy develops considering that only Eboli is in any
sort of lyrical mood. But it is not a mood that lasts long. Don Carlos
excuses himself: they have both of them only been dreaming—a
strange dream in a night filled with the scent of flowers. Eboli now
realizes that all the passionate words she has heard were intended
for somebody else; fiercely she accuses Don Carlos: "You love the
Queen!"

In the Paris version of the opera, where she wears the Queen's
clothes, Eboli's conclusion is reached logically enough, if a little
slowly. In the 1884 revision, where she has no circumstantial evidence, it is no more than a wild guess, which turns out to be correct,
however, as she deduces from Don Carlos' immediate consternation.

Rodrigo enters suddenly and tells Eboli to take no notice of his
friend's words; he is delirious and mad. Eboli, in whom the fury of
the woman scorned is now rising with a vengeance, retorts that she
knows the truth; Rodrigo may be the King's confidant, but he will

find her a formidable, powerful enemy. In a menacing *mezza voce* to
Rodrigo, Eboli repeats her threats of vengeance—"Al mio furor
sfuggite invano" ("You will not escape my fury . . .."):

Ex 314

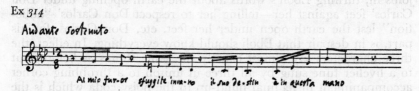

This agitated muttering of Eboli's is the start of a trio composed,
it must be admitted, to a remarkably limited set of words. Eboli
says little more in an extremely busy part than repeat her opening
lines with an occasional reference to her "wounded heart"; Rodrigo
is restricted to two lines in which he endlessly asserts that the anger
of God who protects the innocent will fall upon her; while Don
Carlos, in the few broad phrases of the whole episode, is just generally very sorry for himself and the stain he has brought on his
mother's name (the only mention in the opera, incidentally, of
Carlos' other parent, Maria, daughter of John III of Portugal, who
was Philip's first wife and who died after giving birth to Don Carlos).

Musically it is not an outstandingly inspired trio, but the characters are well defined and there is some effective orchestration, notably the use of the three trombones and tuba to support the bass
line in a passage of *ppp* legato low-register unison.

In a brief outburst of bitter irony ("con ironia amara") Eboli
refers scornfully to the Queen—"and I used to tremble before her!
This saint, with her mask of heavenly virtue, who has drained the
cup of love!" Rodrigo draws his dagger and threatens to kill her,
but Don Carlos holds him back. After taunting Rodrigo and daring
him to stab her Eboli turns on Don Carlos and with renewed fury
tells him to beware of her vengeance—in a short while the earth
will open under his feet:

Ex 315

Eboli's vigorous and menacing eight-bar phrase is unaccompanied except for woodwind octaves in unison with the voice on the first notes of the second, fourth, sixth and eighth bars. Rodrigo then joins in, turning Eboli's words about the earth opening under Don Carlos' feet against her—telling her to respect Don Carlos' "affliction" lest the earth open under her feet, etc. Don Carlos, for his part, is in despair that Eboli should know everything. In effect, the three characters say almost exactly the same things as before, but to a livelier tune sung by all three in unison to a throbbing cornet accompaniment in its final build-up to the noisy coda which is the cue for Eboli's stormy exit.

Left alone with Don Carlos, Rodrigo begs him urgently to give him any confidential, compromising documents he may have. Don Carlos hesitates to hand over anything to the man who is now the King's confidant, but Rodrigo reassures him of his loyalty and Don Carlos gives him what he calls "these important papers". The two reaffirm their affection for each other with a short, characteristic tenor-and-baritone cadenza in thirds and sixths. They embrace and the scene ends with another loud orchestral reprise of the "loyalty" theme of Ex 303.

PART TWO

Scene: A large square in front of the church of Our Lady of Atocha in Madrid.* The church is on the right of the scene and is approached by wide steps. On the left, a palace. In the background, another flight of steps leading down to a lower square where the top of a funeral pyre is visible. Large buildings and distant hills form the horizon.

A loud and brassy orchestral introduction, with bells proclaiming a *festa* begins a scene which Verdi for the first time in his life describes as a "Gran Finale"—a term he used only once again, in the similarly Super-Spectacular surroundings of *Aida*. The square is filled with a large crowd who are controlled with difficulty by a company of halberdiers and sing exultantly of the glories of King and country.

Ex 316

* "Atocha", it appears, is a Spanish word for esparto grass which grew where the original Eremita de Atocha was built. The church referred to in this scene was a sixteenth-century enlargement of the hermitage. The present-day Basilica de Nuestra Señora de Atocha dates from 1890.

The crowd rejoices to a tune of some banality, which seems to have been the origin of a number older readers may well remember featured by Paul Whiteman in the very early musical film *The King of Jazz* and called "A Bench in the Park" (Ex 316).

The gaudy sounds of popular rejoicing gave way abruptly to a funeral march of monks who cross the scene leading to the stake those who have been condemned by the Inquisition. It is a passage of sinisterly "dark" music remarkable for its unusually effective and original orchestration:

Ex *317*

I have tried to suggest something of the instrumentation in the above quotation from a passage which comes off most admirably, especially in such details as the unison phrases played by a solo bassoon, with the violoncellos' pizzicato doubling the bowed notes of two solo double basses, and the ominous impact of the three unison trombones on their low G sharp.

The monks (all basses) chant in a menacing, near-monotone unison that the day of terror and reckoning has dawned. But, they add magnanimously, there is hope of salvation if the sinner is willing to repent in his last hour. The monks still keep to their monotone in what may be called the trio of the funeral march, even though the key changes to G major and the violoncellos in the orchestra are given a *cantabile espressivo* tune to play in their upper register:

Ex *318*

The grim cortège passes out of sight and the crowd resumes its rejoicing with a short development, through various keys, of the tune of Ex 316, ending with increasingly jubilant cries of "Honour to the King!"

A *banda* on the stage is now heard with a fanfare, shared with the pit orchestra, to start the march which is the signal for the grand procession to emerge from the palace. The company includes State officials, the entire court, deputies from all the provinces of the empire, and the grandees of Spain. Rodrigo is among the grandees, the Queen among her ladies. Tebaldo carries Elisabeth's train. Pages, ladies, courtiers, royal heralds are in attendance.

This imposing procession is accompanied first by the stage band playing a cantabile tune of quite enchantingly unceremonial fatuousness in Verdi's best small-town-*banda* manner. The tune is worth quoting, I think, to show how even at this late stage the composer of *Don Carlos* (who was now fifty-three) still had a long way to go to achieve anything of the dignity of the marches in *Aida*:

Ex *319*

Not even the abrupt change of key from A major to C major when the pit orchestra takes over does anything to improve the social status of the tune, and it comes as a relief when the conventional cuts are observed in this march sequence and the chorus, *banda* and orchestra open their lungs in a hearty reprise, with a *più animato* coda, of Ex 316.*

The procession draws up before the steps of the church. A Herald comes forward and standing before the closed door of the church demands in an unaccompanied eight-bar phrase that it shall be opened to reveal the King to his people. The crowd, bareheaded, echoes the Herald's words and music in six-part harmony, also unaccompanied. The doors of the church open and Philip, wearing his crown, can be seen approaching beneath a canopy borne by monks. The action is accompanied by what can best be described as some neo-Gregorian chords in the orchestra, which create an appropriately imposing and quasi-religious atmosphere and are decorated by a fanfare of unison arpeggio figures from the *banda*. The King, against a solemn background of two clarinets and four bassoons, repeats the oath he took when he first wore his crown: to put all heretics to death by fire and sword. The crowd cries glory to Philip and the

---

* It is reported that on the first night of *Don Carlos* at the Paris Opera the stage band played disastrously out of tune. It performed under the direction of no less a musical figure than M. Adolphe Sax himself, thus doubtlessly confirming the unfavourable opinion Verdi had already expressed a couple of years earlier (see p 76) of the unreliability of the instruments constructed by the inventor of the saxophone.

Almighty and then kneels in silence.* Philip descends the steps of
the church and is about to take Elisabeth's hand and continue his
progress when six Flemish Deputies, led in by Don Carlos, suddenly
appear and throw themselves at Philip's feet—an action which
causes both the Queen and Rodrigo to wonder what the Infante is
up to.

In unison the Deputies (all basses) plead with the King to give the
Flemish people freedom from their oppression—"No, l'ora estrema
ancora non suonò" ("The last hour has not yet sounded"):

Ex 320

The scoring matches the dark and plaintive unison of the six
basses. Violas and violoncellos double the voice part in the same
register (that is, an octave lower than shown in the example above),
the four bassoons, also in unison, keep up a staccato arpeggio figure,
while oboe and horn provide a characteristic weeping figure as an
ostinato. Philip rejects the Deputies' pleas; they are rebels who are
unfaithful to God and King. He orders the guards to take them
away; the six monks echo his words in a unison phrase emphasized
by trombones, bassoons and tuba in octaves. The reaction of the rest
of the company—Elisabeth, her Page, Don Carlos, Rodrigo and the
populace—is more sympathetic. They beg the King to be merciful
and have pity on Flanders. They continue their pleading as a big
ensemble builds up with King and monks alone muttering vengeance. The movement reaches a halfway mark with a phrase sung
only by Elisabeth, Tebaldo, Don Carlos and Rodrigo, and accompanied mostly by woodwind, which is of great beauty and harmonic originality. The tune of Ex 319 sung by the Deputies is resumed, and once more an ensemble develops increasingly dominated by the King's iron resolve. Elisabeth and Don Carlos join in
an unaccompanied unison phrase with the Deputies in a last desperate plea for mercy, but in vain.

The tempo changes to a vigorous 6/8 and Don Carlos, telling his
father that he is tired of leading an inactive and pointless life, asks
to be allowed to govern Brabant and Flanders. Philip refuses flatly

* It was at this point, I seem to remember, that the ballet was introduced when
Don Carlos was performed to inaugurate the new opera house at Geneva a few
years ago, thus making quite a day of it for the citizens of Madrid who in the
ordinary way are offered no more than a human barbecue for their entertainment
in this scene.

to place in his son's hands a weapon that could be turned against himself. To everybody's horror Don Carlos draws his sword, vowing that he will save the Flemish people. The King orders his guards and courtiers to disarm his son, but the Grandees draw back as Don Carlos continues to defy them. The King himself, in a white rage, grabs the sword of his Captain of the Guard who is standing next to him, but Rodrigo steps forward and commands Don Carlos to hand him over his sword. The dumbfounded Don Carlos gives up his sword, to a distant echo of the "loyalty" theme played *piano* and *dolce* by two clarinets in the register shown in Ex 303, with a solo flute sustaining the G below them on the third and fourth beats of each bar to sound like a faint trumpet call. The suggestion of tense silence created by these few bars is masterly.

Rodrigo kneels before the King and gives him Don Carlos' sword. Philip rewards him with a Dukedom, and without more ado, proceeds to the *festa*; leading Elisabeth by the hand and followed by the Court he takes his place on the tribune from which to watch the *auto-da-fé*—or more correctly, since the scene is Spain—the *auto-de-fé*.

Orchestra, *banda* and chorus unite in a joyful reprise of Ex 315, which is followed by a repetition of the funeral march (Ex 316) with the same orchestration and the menacing near-monotones of the six monks. This time, however, instead of the "trio" being in the relative major of the minor (that is, the G major shown in Ex 318) it is heard in E major sung by a soprano Voice from Heaven ("very distant"), accompanied by harp and harmonium.

The unexpected and unjustifiable introduction of the supernatural into an otherwise intensely realistic story of love, politics and religion was obviously one of the penalties Verdi had to pay for writing *Don Carlos* for the Paris Opera, and I do not doubt for a minute that it stopped the show. Nevertheless, it is a disturbing—not to say ridiculous—element in a work which has otherwise been dramatically fairly consistent so far (though we may well ask, on reflection, why Eboli is not present with the rest of the court in this scene).

The celestial voice sings to those about to die: "Fly towards heaven, fly, unhappy souls; hasten to enjoy the peace of the Lord!" —words which may or may not have brought much comfort to the unfortunate wretches able to hear the Voice over the crackling of the flames they perished by.

There is a final repeat of the funeral march theme, this time in the major—perhaps to express the monks' satisfaction with their day's work. The Voice from Heaven dies away in trills rising to a top B, accompanied once more by harp and harmonium; Philip and the monks cry, "Glory to Heaven"; the crowd echoes them; and as the flames of the pyre grow increasingly bright, the curtain falls.

The general effect of the *auto-de-fé* scene is impressive, for the whole, which leaves the impression of one long and varied ensemble, is far more than the sum of the parts. Such trivial things as the march played by the *banda*, the opening chorus, and the Celestial Voice (we are lucky it isn't a choir, which it could well have been), are in the end absorbed by the magnificent sweep of the whole thing and obliterated by the memory of such fine passages as the funeral march, the principal ensemble movement, and above all, of the growing stature of the musical character of King Philip, who dominates the opera increasingly with each successive appearance.

ACT IV (III)

PART ONE

Scene : The King's study in Madrid.

A sad and moving orchestral introduction precedes the rise of the curtain, creating a mood of oppressive weariness by such an inspired simplicity of means as to be almost ridiculous. It begins with three slow unison A's, which, with their grace notes, at once suggest the tears Verdi first expressed with an oboe in *Nabucco* (see Ex 11, p 31). But because they are more generously scored (for strings, four horns and four bassoons across two octaves downwards from the A below middle C), they acquire a heavy-hearted masculine character. The phrase is repeated and it is followed by a sequence for an unaccompanied solo violoncello, a plaintive figure by muted first violins, the solo violoncello again, unaccompanied at first, then accompanied by the violin figure; the mournful A's are played by a horn from time to time during this, and that is all.

The second half of the violoncello's eight bars of soliloquy (one instinctively uses the theatrical term) consist of the phrase:

Ex 321

This is followed, when it is first heard, by a poignant, whispered figure played *pp* by muted violins:

Ex 322

As the curtain goes up the solo violoncello is heard on its own once more, to be joined shortly by the violins with Ex 322 as an accompaniment to a cantabile passage in which the tune of Ex 321 is extended for a further four bars.

Like the prelude to the last act of *La traviata* this instrumental introduction is a sublimely simple and affecting musical picture of silence and gloom.

The King is discovered deep in thought, leaning against a table strewn with papers, where two lighted candles are nearly burnt out. It is dawn.

Philip, "as though dreaming", laments the failure of his marriage to Elisabeth, his opening words—"Ella giammai m'amò" ("She never loved me . . .")—punctuated by the plaintive weeping figure which is now played by a flute. Philip remembers how sadly Elisabeth looked at his white hairs when she arrived from France— a reflection made to the accompaniment of the extended violoncello tune with the violin figures that ended the orchestral introduction. This time, however, all the violoncellos play the passage, muted.*

Philip, coming out of his reverie, is surprised to see that day is breaking, and laments wearily that he cannot sleep. The melancholy unison A's of the introduction are thinned down to a plaintive solo echo by the oboe two octaves higher, which, with a series of mournful four-note figures played by two horns, is a recurrent feature of the accompaniment of what follows—"Dormirò sol nel manto mio regal" ("I shall sleep only when my day is done . . ."):

Ex 323

What is perhaps the most magnificent solo scene for bass voice in all Verdi is another wonderful instance of a supreme effect achieved by the simplest means. Although it is described broadly as a *scena*, the main vocal part of an episode that lasts more than ten minutes is almost classically formal. The opening section "A" in D minor is followed by section "B", a broad lyrical phrase in B flat major; a short *parlato* interlude leads back to the opening section "A". The lyrical tune of section "B" is repeated, played this time in the orchestra only by bassoons, violoncellos and double basses in unison in the

---

* Although contrary to Verdi's instructions I have heard the entire unmuted solo part played by all the violoncellos with mutes, and I must admit it is unusually moving. Perhaps this is because with a solo instrument one is instinctively anxious about the player's performance, his individual progress over the hurdles of tone and intonation; whereas one somehow relaxes automatically in the belief that there is safety in numbers when the whole section tackles the part.

key of D major. The aria ends in this key with the opening and closing phrases of Philip's introductory "Ella giammai m'amò" condensed in a masterly way to give the scene a coda of great pathos.

When Verdi was in Madrid for the first performance there of *La forza del destino* in 1863 and saw the Escurial for the first time, he wrote that it was "severe, terrible, like the brutal sovereign who built it". With this picture of Philip II established in his mind it is not surprising that when Verdi came to write *Don Carlos* he should have drawn with such strength and certainty the character of the King as absolute monarch, as the ruthless bigot who did not hesitate to throw his own son into prison.

Equally it was typical of his genius and humanity that Verdi should have found an unexpected and sympathetic side of the King's character, and in this superb monologue should have distinguished so miraculously between Philip the man and Philip the king, revealing all the loneliness of a human being, who though he has power and riches, is loved by no one. From the first mournful notes of the introduction to this first scene of Act IV the whole centre of dramatic gravity of the opera is in danger of shifting, and one suddenly finds oneself watching with anxiety and compassion the progress of a character who has all at once become the subject of a tragedy himself, where before he had merely seemed to be the cause of tragedy in others.

Philip lapses once more into silence, but is disturbed by the arrival of the Grand Inquisitor, an old man of ninety, who is blind, and walks with the support of two Dominican monks. The Grand Inquisitor, who has been sent for by the King, enters to a five-bar phrase which is heard to magnificent effect during the scene which now begins:

Ex *324*

The unusual instrumentation of this is most ominously in the mood of that "severity" Verdi found in the Escurial—the tune is played by bassoon and violoncellos with double basses and double bassoon an octave lower, the sinister thumps of the bass drum is echoed by a rumble of timpani and three trombones add their syncopated punctuation.

The opening of the dialogue between the Grand Inquisitor and the King follows a symmetrical musical pattern. The bass tune of Ex 324 and its accompaniment is taken through a series of cadences: twice into A flat, as in the quotation, then into D flat, E flat minor, F minor, and finally into F major. Interspersed between these passages there is from time to time a series of remarkable chord progressions in four minims played by the three trombones, tuba and bassoons. (After the second playing of the phrase shown in Ex 324 the syncopated trombone punctuations are taken over in a higher register by the trumpets, cornets and horns.)

The symmetry of all this is followed very closely in the dialogue; Philip's words are accompanied by the legato phrases of Ex 324, while—except once—the Grand Inquisitor speaks only against the solemn background of the measured chord changes of trombones, tuba and bassoons.

Philip asks the Grand Inquisitor for advice. Don Carlos is a rebel. Shall he be allowed to escape, or shall he be put to death? If he executes his own son will the Church absolve him? The Grand Inquisitor replies that God sacrificed his son to redeem mankind. Philip hesitates: must the voice of nature and love not be heard? Everything must be silent to maintain the Faith, is the reply.

As the King has no more to ask him, the Grand Inquisitor now speaks at length, and for the first time since his entrance we hear violins and violas again in the orchestra. They do not in effect bring any great brightness to the music, but they permit the introduction of a more lively tempo. The Inquisitor warns Philip that Don Carlos' treason is a "futile game" compared with the threat presented to the Faith by Rodrigo, the King's friend and trusted companion:

Ex 325

The old man's fury rises, backed by fierce hammer-blow unisons from the brass. Philip replies that Rodrigo is loyal, the only man in the Court who has brought him comfort. The King sings these words in a near-monotone to one of the most remarkable passages of orchestral accompaniment in the whole work. It consists of no more than a descending scale of F major played four notes to the bar by the strings starting at F *in alt* (F''') and finishing on the C below middle C, while oboe and piccolo in octaves move slowly upwards from the same high F to the C above it. It is all played _pp_, an almost naïvely unconcerned and elementary essay in the writing of contrary motion in two parts.

The Inquisitor is unmoved. What need has a King of a lesser man's friendship? Philip angrily tells the old man to say no more—"Tais-toi, prêtre!" ("Be silent, priest!" were the words in the original French which are said to have upset the Empress Eugénie and her clericalist obsessions so much, and in consequence to have affected the success of _Don Carlos_ in Paris.)

The Grand Inquisitor continues unperturbed; he reproves the King for harbouring dangerous thoughts and wanting, with his "feeble hand", to break the sacred yoke of Holy Church. In an oddly gentle _pp_ passage accompanied only by woodwind, the Inquisitor bids Philip return to his duty; to those who have hope and are penitent the Church offers complete forgiveness. "Give me the Marquis of Posa," he demands.

Philip refuses. In a voice of granite the Grand Inquisitor tells him that but for this meeting in the Palace he himself might have been called before the Inquisition the next day. Supported by _ff_ chords played by trombones, tuba and bassoons, the King retorts that he has suffered enough of the priest's cruel words.

Angrily "con forza", the Grand Inquisitor asks Philip if he wants to destroy the work of years like a madman. Then with a sudden quietness the old man asks why he is there. What does the King want of him? As he turns to go, the heavy opening theme (Ex 324) returns in its original orchestration; Philip hopes there will be peace between them.

"Peace?" echoes the Inquisitor, continuing on his way.

"You must forget everything that has passed here," replies the King.

As he goes through the door the Grand Inquisitor says: "Perhaps." In a noble cadence in the major over two octaves from his high to his low F, Philip remarks: "So the throne must always bow to the altar!"

While musically the impressive opening and closing passages may have obvious roots in the baritone-bass duologue between Rigoletto and Sparafucile (see p 96, Ex 55), where we find very similar characteristics of melody, rhythm, unusual orchestral colouring and even of key, this tremendous scene in _Don Carlos_ remains a _tour de force_ without parallel. Anything dramatically less absorbing or musically less promising than a scene in which two basses argue religion and politics is surely hard to imagine, but the way it turns out it proves to be entirely fascinating. The two characters are so superbly differentiated, their music so individual, that the monotony one might fear from two similar voices is avoided altogether, and even in the "blind" conditions of listening imposed by the gramophone there is no question of confusing one with the other.

Above all, Verdi avoids any suggestion of monotony in the instrumental colouring of the music, even though he aims throughout the scene at the expression of that peculiar *severità* he sensed as common to the Escurial and its founder.

Action and music now become suddenly *agitato* as Elisabeth enters, and throws herself at the King's feet demanding justice: somebody has stolen her jewel case containing not only her jewellery but all her most treasured possessions as well. The original Paris stage directions tell us that Elisabeth pulls herself up abruptly, "frightened by the terrible expression on the face of the King". Modern editions are content to direct merely that the King rises slowly, goes over to the table and takes from it a casket which he gives to the Queen: "This is what you were looking for. Open it!" he says. The Queen refuses. Philip takes the box and breaking it open discovers inside it the portrait of Don Carlos. Elisabeth is silent, but admits at length that she keeps it with her jewellery. "And you dare confess that to me?" storms the King.

Elisabeth reminds him that he knows perfectly well she was engaged to marry Don Carlos, and swears that she is innocent. Philip grows increasingly angry; she thinks he is weak, but he warns her his weakness can turn to fury. In despair Elisabeth asks what she has done. Retorting that she has perjured herself, the King threatens her with death if she has deceived him. The Queen asks him for pity. Brutally Philip exclaims: "Pity for an adulterous wife!" Elisabeth faints.

The King opens the doors at the back and calls for help for the Queen. Eboli enters, and although the audience has no idea what she is talking about, she exclaims in an aside as she sees the Queen lying on the floor: "Heavens! Whatever have I done?" Rodrigo also enters and without further ceremony reproaches the King for his lack of self-control. Philip does not reply but initiates a quartet with an aside in which he curses the demon that has sown "fatal suspicion" in his mind of the woman whose proud bearing has now convinced him that she is innocent. For some reason the words of Philip's first acceptance of Elisabeth's innocence are not sung to a tune but are muttered *parlante e mezzavoce* while in the orchestra violoncellos and a solo bassoon play this:

Ex 326

What is puzzling is that while Philip does not join the orchestra in this phrase the first time (when surely the words ought to be "planted"), he does do so on two of the remaining three occasions in the quartet when he comes to the same words again. Meanwhile, Eboli had started her own aside, lamenting that she has lost the Queen through an "infernal crime" we are still very much in the dark about. Eboli's opening phrases are followed by Rodrigo's determination, also expressed in an aside, that the hour has struck for a man to die for Spain and the country's happiness.

As one may guess from the look of Ex 326 one of Verdi's characteristic 12/8 movements in 4/4 time is now under way. It becomes a quartet when Elisabeth recovers consciousness and in a plaintive passage accompanied only by the three flutes (with a clarinet added in due course as a bass instrument), she sings unhappily of being a stranger in a foreign land. Four lines of verse are allocated to each of the four characters and it suffices them for the duration of an effective, if rather conventional, quartet with its feet pointing less to Verdi's future than sticking firmly in the past glories of Act II of *La traviata*, where Alfredo's "Ah sì che feci!" (Ex 159) is an easily recognizable blueprint for Rodrigo's opening phrase in this quartet—as, indeed, it can also be considered for Eboli's first words in the trio with Don Carlos and Rodrigo quoted in Ex 314.

At the end of the quartet, Philip departs after a moment's hesitation; Rodrigo follows him "in a resolute manner" and Eboli is left alone with the Queen. Throwing herself at Elisabeth's feet, Eboli pleads desperately for forgiveness. The Queen is understandably puzzled, until Eboli confesses that it was she who stole the casket and accused her of infidelity. Eboli explains the mixture of love, the jealousy, the anger, and hatred which turned her heart against the Queen. She loved Don Carlos, she says, but he spurned her. Elisabeth is surprised to hear this and tells Eboli to rise. She remains kneeling; there is something else she must confess.

An atmosphere of sudden tension is created by a simple syncopated figure played *pp* by flutes in their low register and supported by strings; Eboli admits that she has been seduced by the King; the very thing she had accused the Queen of doing, she has done herself.

For a moment Elisabeth says nothing. It is left for the orchestra to comment with an astonishing *fortissimo* two-bar phrase consisting of nothing more original than a chromatic descent from middle C to the G sharp below it and back again, but coloured by such unusual instrumentation that the effect is quite startling. The "tune"—that is, the chromatic fall and rise—is played only by the violins doubled two octaves lower by the double basses. Violoncellos, violas, bassoons and tuba (no trombones), flutes, oboes, clarinets and four horns combine in a penetrating and sinister passage of sustained unison C's from middle C down over two octaves. The chromatic phrase is played three times, the second time *pianissimo*, the third still more quietly with the orchestration limited to strings and timpani only.

Elisabeth speaks, with her sentences punctuated by *ppp* and then—so the score says—*ppppp* playing of the chromatic phrase, shorn of its initial C this time, by violins with the double basses still two octaves below them, and only a solo horn sustaining first an E flat, then a G flat, against them. It is a superbly effective passage of "suspense" orchestration.

In a monotone Elisabeth tells Eboli to give back the cross she is wearing and warns her to leave the Palace at daybreak. "You may choose between exile and a nunnery," she says. The Queen leaves. In the Paris libretto Elisabeth added the words, "May you be happy", which were cut in the revised version—a pity, I think, for they are surely very much in character.

Left alone, Eboli rises to her feet and in despair cries that she will never see the Queen again. Three vigorously brassy bars follow to serve as introduction to her famous aria, in which she curses the fatal gift of beauty given her by heaven—"O don fatale" ("O fatal, cruel gift, which heaven bestowed on me in its anger") :

Ex 327

O don fa-ta-le, o don cru-del che in suo fu-ror mi fece il cie . . . lo!

There must be very few of us who can honestly say that when we first heard of this aria we were not convinced, in view of the opera's title and our ignorance of both text and context, that the singer must be addressing Fatal Don Carlos himself. Silly perhaps, but understandable. If, however, instead of the fancy poeticizing of the version we know today, the words of the original translation had been adhered to, this distressing confusion might have been avoided: in the Italian libretto of 1869 Eboli sings simply and unambiguously, "Dono fatale, dono crudel".

Heard in its context and in full knowledge of what it's all about this aria of Eboli's is a masterly portrait of a woman in the grip of bewildering, contrasted emotions. First there is the anger of the opening phrases, with the tearful despair and hopelessness of a short passage which serves as an interlude before, in an even more intense and dramatic outburst, she curses her beauty once more. Next there comes the long and movingly reticent lyrical section in which, full of

12*

remorse for the wrong she has done to the Queen, she decides that only in a convent will she be able to hide her anguish from the world:

Ex 328

Molto meno

O — mia Re - gi - na, io t'im - mo - la - i

Finally, as a noisy and energetic coda to the scene, there is Eboli's sudden realization that Don Carlos is to die tomorrow and that she must save him. Accompanied by some pretty blatant scoring for cornets, Eboli continues to proclaim her determination to save Don Carlos and the curtain falls on a rousing, sure-fire flourish to re-assure us that the Verdi who wrote the two great scenes for basses earlier in the act, could still bring the house down with the best of them.

PART TWO

Scene: A dark underground prison where Don Carlos is captive. A few pieces of Palace furniture have been hurriedly moved in. At the back there is an iron grille which separates the prison from a courtyard above it where guards are seen walking to and fro. A staircase leads into the courtyard from the higher floors of the building.

Don Carlos is discovered seated with his head in his hands, lost in thought. A leaden, mournful phrase for strings, ponderously accented and monotonous, gives way for a moment to an echo on a solo oboe of the theme of the duet in Act I (Ex 300), but returns when Rodrigo enters. He talks in an undertone to some officials who leave immediately. He looks sadly at Don Carlos, who is startled to see him. Rodrigo's presence is a great comfort to Don Carlos, who is still tortured by his love for Elisabeth; the purpose of his visit, however, is to tell Don Carlos that he has come to say goodbye—"Per me giunto è il dì supremo" ("For me the supreme day has come"):

Ex 329

Andante sostenuto

Per me giun- to è d dì su - pre-mo, no, mai più ci ri - - ve - drem

Don Carlos is puzzled by his friend's talk of dying for him. Rodrigo explains quickly: he and not Don Carlos is to lead the Flemish rebellion in future; the details of the plot, given to him by Carlos, have been discovered in his possession and there is a price on his head.

While this conversation has been going on two men have come down the steps into the prison. One of them is dressed in the costume of the Inquisition; the other is armed with an arquebus. They stop for a moment and point out Don Carlos and Rodrigo to each other.

Rodrigo continues: Don Carlos must on no account tell the King anything. He must wait and fulfil his destiny in Flanders when he succeeds to the crown, and bring a new Golden Age to the country. "You must reign," says Rodrigo, "and I shall die for you."

The man with the arquebus fires at Rodrigo who falls mortally wounded, murmuring that the King has taken his revenge. As Rodrigo lies in Carlos' arms there comes from the orchestra a poignant sound created by the unlikely means of two cornets in thirds, their phrases punctuated by the tearful interjection of a solo bassoon, and the anxious rumble of timpani:

Ex 330

Against this oddly elegiac background Rodrigo tells Don Carlos that his "mother"—that is, Elisabeth—will be waiting to see him tomorrow at San Giusto. Taking Don Carlos' hand in his Rodrigo tells him that he dies happy in the knowledge that Spain will have him as saviour—"Io morrò, ma lieto in core":

Ex 331

The accompaniment to this tune brings the harp into prominence with busy arpeggios that suggest only too clearly that we are in the midst of a death scene. A neat and effective modulation into A major brings back a distant reminder of what, in other theatrical surroundings, might be called the "plug number", but which we recognize as the theme of loyalty between Rodrigo and Don Carlos— the tune of Ex 303 played by piccolo and flute, with two oboes an octave below them, and the rum-ti-tum rhythm of the accompaniment divided between bass drum, bassoons and *pp* trombones.

Rodrigo begs Don Carlos not to forget him and with one or two slight variations in the latter part of the melody, repeats the words and music of Ex 331, which this time acquires a rather oppressively celestial tinkle by the addition of trills for flute and piccolo throughout its entire eight bars. With a final prayer to Don Carlos to save Flanders, Rodrigo dies.

I cannot help feeling that his death scene would have been more telling if, instead of giving us a second helping of the baritone tune, Verdi had had Rodrigo die to the very effective and moving echo of the "loyalty theme". Rodrigo could just as well have said all he wanted to say about Flanders at that point and the very "ham" death-agony cadenza we now get would not have been necessary. We learn nothing from the reprise of Ex 331 that we do not already know and the negligible decoration of the tune with six quavers hardly justifies the repetition in full of a not-very-distinguished passage. It strikes me, indeed, that a neat and unobjectionable cut can be made from the end of the "loyalty" episode to the crashing chords marking the moment of Rodrigo's death in the score. Whether any baritone would ever agree to this is another matter, of course; there would inevitably be much righteous—and suspiciously uncharacteristic—indignation about the sanctity of what the composer wrote. It could be an enjoyably ironic situation nevertheless.

In all public performances and all recordings except the exemplary 1966 Decca version, the act comes to an end with the death of Rodrigo, and in doing so follows a practice which has been common, if not commendable, for many years in productions of the opera. It is also, in fact, a practice once approved by Verdi himself as one of the modifications he sanctioned after the Paris first night, and in the Ricordi libretto of 1869 there is a note stating that "Act IV ends with the death of Rodrigo", although the text of the remainder of the scene is still printed in full.

While Verdi certainly suggested this cut among several others for the second performance of *Don Carlos* in Paris (which he did not attend), it was plainly never his intention that it should be a permanent feature of the opera. But it just as obviously developed into a bad habit which he was still trying to stamp out when preparing the revised version of 1884, for we find him writing to Ricordi to insist that the opera be performed intact "as I have now adjusted it —without cuts, without omissions, without transpositions of key, and continuously, without interruption of any kind. I demand this *con rigore* as all baritones want to finish the act with their aria. The Finale I wrote lasts two minutes. It is necessary and must be performed *coûte que coûte* [cost what it may]".

Apart from anything else there is still the question of the plot to be considered and to end the act with Rodrigo's death has as irritating an effect on the audience's understanding of what's going on as the frequent omission in public performances of Elisabeth's reference to her engagement to Don Carlos in the first scene of this act.

As Don Carlos throws himself on Rodrigo's dead body the King, accompanied by Grandees, enters to give his son his sword back. Don Carlos (*con desolazione*) accuses his father of killing his friend: "I am your son no more!" Philip is deeply moved by the sight of Rodrigo's body; he bares his head, realizing that his worst fears have come true, and murmuring sorrowfully that he has lost a man who is irreplaceable.

An alarm is sounded and from outside comes the clamour of a crowd approaching the prison, shouting death and destruction. The Count of Lerma enters to announce that the people have rebelled and are asking for the Infante Don Carlos. Philip, to the consternation of his followers, orders the iron gates of the prison to be opened. The crowd pours in *furiosamente*, and continues to hurl threats in a *vivacissimo* 6/8 which is exciting and, without being outstandingly good music, is mainly interesting as a rough draft of the choral writing in a similar vein in Act I of *Otello*.

Hidden in the crowd is Eboli in disguise, who goes over to Don Carlos and during a lull of two beats when nobody else is singing, urges him to escape. Her words are almost interrupted by Philip, who addresses the crowd and demands to know what they want. They reply that they want the Infante; the King points to where Don Carlos is standing. At that moment the Grand Inquisitor appears at the back of the scene, and in thunderous tones emphasized by blasts from unison brass, commands the crowd to prostrate themselves before the King whom God protects. His rising crescendo, which is joined by Philip in its last bar, comes to a sudden *ppp* when the awestruck crowd falls on its knees and asks forgiveness. The curtain falls with brass flourishes as the Grand Inquisitor and Philip move slowly towards each other.

It is clear from the original libretto that the scene following Rodrigo's death was in serious need, if not of total elimination, at least of the pretty drastic pruning it received when Verdi revised his opera for Milan. In the Paris version Philip does not merely arrive on the scene and hand back Don Carlos his sword; he explains with magnanimity why he was mistaken. Don Carlos is far more violent and bitter in his language, telling his father to choose a son more like himself from among his gang of murderers. At these words Philip turns to go, but is held back *con violenza* by Carlos who tells his father in passionate terms how Rodrigo gave his life for him.

Philip is moved by the sight of Rodrigo's body, but while he remarks on the presentiment he had had of his death, does not (as in the later libretto) make any comment on the loss of a trusted friend. At the sound of the rioting crowds, the Count of Lerma comes in with a detailed account of the rebels' intentions, which is followed by a stage direction saying that Rodrigo's body is removed from the scene and that Don Carlos follows it.

Elisabeth, greatly agitated, now enters crying that the King must be saved—she assures her husband that her heart trembles for him and they must fly together. Philip orders the iron gates to be opened, and while the crowd continues in its angry mood Eboli appears on the steps in the background, followed by Don Carlos who is dragged away by the mob. The King now faces the rebels and baring his breast asks them what they are waiting for. Why don't they strike their old King down and put Carlos on the throne? At this point the Grand Inquisitor appears and the scene continues in its familiar form.

It will be seen from this brief account of the original action that Verdi's second thoughts were well advised. Not only was a shocking amount of dramatic time being wasted on unnecessary words and elaborations but the introduction into the scene of Elisabeth, with a couple of agitated lines, was surely a stroke of quite startling irrelevance, although doubtless it provided another instance—if one needs one—of her remarkable sense of duty towards her husband. The elimination of Elisabeth from this episode is something of a personal relief, I must confess, for I would inevitably have worried about her being able to keep her appointment with Don Carlos the following evening. The scene of the rendezvous, the monastery of "San Giusto", otherwise San Jerónimo de Yuste, was all of 150 miles from Madrid. As it is, I am still a little concerned about Don Carlos getting there in time.

ACT V (IV)

Scene: The Cloisters of the monastery of San Giusto as in Act II (I). It is a moonlit night.

Before the curtain goes up we hear an instrumental version of the minor-major chant of the monks heard in the monastery scene of Act II. It is played by trombones, horns and tuba, fortified by the four bassoons when the dynamics rise from *pp* to *f*.

When the curtain rises Elisabeth enters slowly, deep in thought, and goes towards the tomb of Charles V where she kneels. Her entrance is accompanied by a series of short, tense phrases played each time with an urgent crescendo by first and second violins and violoncellos in unison across two octaves to punctuate the minor-major brass passages. The string phrases are finally released into a passionate tune which might have been written by Mascagni:

Ex 332

The Allegro agitato tune subsides to allow a *pp* echo—played three times—of the first bar quoted above, and what has in fact turned into an orchestral prelude nearly three minutes long ends with one of those impassioned, unaccompanied passages from the top to the bottom register of the violins (plenty of tone on the G string) which became much more typical of his Italian successors than of Verdi himself.

Elisabeth invokes the spirit of Charles V in a broad and impressive unaccompanied passage punctuated by deep *pp* unison C sharps by the bassoons, trombones and tuba—

Ex 333

—which leads into a lyrical passage of exceptional beauty in which she beseeches him, "if they still weep in heaven, weep for my sorrow and carry my tears to the throne of the Lord" ("s'ancor si piange in cielo, piangi sul mio dolore"):

Ex 334

A slightly more restrained form of the first tune quoted in Ex 332 acts as a brief coda to this moving passage of only twelve bars. The word "Recitativo" now appears in the score—somewhat surprisingly, for there is little to suggest the conventional recitative in Elisabeth's few breathless words punctuated by stealthy, apprehensive string phrases. Elisabeth is determined that when she says goodbye to Don Carlos it shall be for ever; he must forget her and follow his destiny as the liberator of Flanders. She promised Rodrigo to "watch over his days"; as for herself, her day has already turned to evening. There is a *lungo silenzio*, then a solo flute, accompanied by the other flutes and a clarinet, revives memories of France for Elisabeth with an echo of the love-duet theme in Act I (Ex 300) now quoted more fully than hitherto in the four-act (1884) version. Elisabeth thinks back on the happy days in Fontainebleau, where she swore eternal love and eternity lasted only a day.

This comparatively lengthy quotation from the love duet is entirely in the woodwind of the orchestra, where it provides a melodic background to a dramatically unmelodic vocal part. Elisabeth continues to let the orchestra have the tune; first, against a shimmering string tremolo and a flute-oboe-clarinet unison of the tune Don Carlos sang in his delirium in Act II, Part Two (Ex 308), when she asks that tonight when Don Carlos comes their love should be sung only by the rocks, the brooks, the fountains and the trees; then again when she bids an agitated, tearful farewell to her dreams and illusions to a chromatic figure that very clearly anticipates one of Amneris' themes in *Aida* (see p 386, Ex 342). Only for a moment does she join with the orchestra in the *allegro agitato* tune of the introduction to the act (Ex 332), before returning to her breathless farewells and a final sombre expression of her desire for the peace of the tomb.

Elisabeth returns to the opening mood of her soliloquy and invokes Charles V once more. This time, however, she sings all eight bars of her commanding phrase of Ex 333—"Tu che le vanità conoscesti del mondo"—to the sole throbbing semiquaver *ppp* accom-

paniment of two cornets (*a 2*) and three trombones, whose brass
monopoly is disturbed only by one rapid chromatic run-up for
strings. This original and effective passage is followed by a reprise of
Elisabeth's lyrical F sharp major tune (Ex 334), coming to a close with
its 12/8 accompaniment prominently featuring divided violins and
the three flutes, who together produce a sound very reminiscent of
the airy fluttering of the orchestra in Amelia's aria at the beginning
of the first act of *Simon Boccanegra* (see p 212).

Don Carlos enters, to be told at once by Elisabeth that she com-
mends him to heaven in his mission, but he must go and forget. He
replies that he wants to be strong, but when love is broken it can kill
sooner than death itself. Elisabeth tells him to think of Rodrigo;
he didn't sacrifice himself for foolish ideas. Mention of Rodrigo
changes Don Carlos' mood at once and *con entusiasmo* he declares his
intention of raising a monument to his friend in Flanders finer
than a king's; and in an exquisite phrase Elisabeth adds *dolcissimo*
a simple wish that the flowers of paradise may smile on him. This
lovely, gentle four-bar cadence to the resolute declamatory passage
before it, brings a lyrical quality into the music again which blossoms for a moment with the haunting theme for three flutes from the
"Gran Scena e Duetto" in Act II, Part Two (Ex 307) played *ppp*
with a scarcely audible pizzicato accompaniment by first violins.
Don Carlos is reflective and silent for a moment, but his dream
vanishes and his thoughts return to Flanders once more. With
mounting enthusiasm he tells Elisabeth of his determination to
liberate Flanders or die in the attempt—a passage which develops
from the dreamy three-flutes theme in a strangely Wagnerian
manner. At least, the urgent propulsion of a one-bar phrase upwards a semitone or a tone at a time is familiarly Wagnerian. The
one-bar phrase itself, on the other hand, is familiarly Verdian, for it
is almost note-for-note the same as the little tune that occurs so
often in the *Ingemisco* of his Requiem.

Don Carlos' enthusiasm inspires Elisabeth, who embarks on a
"Marziale" section in which she sings (*con entusiasmo*) of the sacred
flame of heroism, the love that makes man into a God, etc.:

Ex 335

As some may have suspected from a glance at the vocal score of
the opera and from experience of Verdi's methods, the four-square
military beat of this *marziale* is supplied by the harp, and only the

harp (the melody line is played *pp* by cornets and trumpets with an occasional *ff tutti* crash and a chord for woodwind). For some reason to Verdi the harp playing four-beats-in-a-bar was one of the most martial of instruments and obviously associated in his mind with resolution, for we encounter it frequently, if not always in moments of prospective military action, at any rate when some form of civil commotion (such as murder) is being unanimously agreed upon. It is an odd role for such a normally gentle and romantic instrument to be called on to play.

While she continues to urge him on and not to delay in his task Don Carlos seconds Elisabeth's resolution, as it were, in an equally *marziale* manner, proclaiming that honour has proved stronger than love and that he can now embrace her without passion or regret.

In the theatre the *marziale* is usually cut altogether and to do so is certainly a service to Verdi—one which he might indeed have done for himself when he came to revise *Don Carlos* in 1884, for it really is a pretty dreadful piece of music to find in a work that was revised when the composer was at the height of his powers. For many years the *marziale* was thought to have been added by Verdi at the time of the revision and in consequence was not surprisingly considered by Francis Toye in 1931 as "a definitely bad afterthought". The passage, however, dates from the original Paris version; this was noted by Frank Walker, though not until the Supplementary Volume to the Fifth Edition of *Grove's Dictionary*, where he mentions it among the additions and corrections to his main article on Verdi in Volume VIII. It is also to be found in my 1869 Italian libretto, in the translation by Achille de Lauzières which must have served as a handy crib when the time came for Ghislanzoni, whose "revision" of the text often consisted of little more than paraphrasing the original by picking on a more poetic synonym—like substituting "sali" (mount or ascend) for "monta" (ascend or mount), "a people who are dying" for "a people who mourn".

Whatever the fate of the *marziale* the passage which follows Don Carlos' embrace of Elisabeth is always included in the theatre. This is a moving little scene, full of tears in the orchestra shed by the oboe and violins for Elisabeth, by bassoons and violoncellos for Don Carlos. But there are real tears as Don Carlos in a calm *parlato* tells Elisabeth that everything is now over and takes his hand from hers. She weeps, she says, the tears that women weep for heroes. In the affecting context of the music it is as lame and unconvincing an explanation as the old one about getting a piece of grit in your eye.

Gradually the tears go out of the music and in a calm and solemn voice Elisabeth comforts Carlos with the assurance that in heaven they will find a better world, where all they have longed for on earth will come true—"Ma lassù ci vedremo in un mondo migliore . . .":

Ex 336

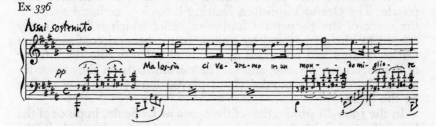

The accompaniment, with its gentle, placid figure played by strings and clarinet, has a peculiar unhurried tranquillity about it that reflects the mood of resignation expressed first by Elisabeth, and then by Don Carlos who echoes her opening phrase. The duet which develops has a rare reticence and calm and is among the most beautiful things Verdi ever wrote. Neither voice is marked to rise above *pp* (much of what is sung is shown as *ppppp*), except for a momentary *ff* unison climax which is built up from Elisabeth's lyrical reference to the day which for them will have no morrow:

Ex 337

From the eventual *ff* the music drops immediately to *ppppp*; two plaintive phrases from the oboe suggest something of the tears behind their words as Elisabeth and Carlos say their last farewells to each other—as mother and son: "Farewell for ever!"

"Yes, forever!" The words come from Philip, who enters, followed by the Grand Inquisitor, monks, and guards of the Inquisition, and grabs Elisabeth by the arm. "I demand a double sacrifice. I shall do my duty. But you?" he asks, turning to the Grand Inquisitor.

The old man replies: "The Inquisition will do its duty", and he motions his guards to seize Don Carlos.

Drawing his sword, Don Carlos keeps his adversaries at bay and retreats towards the tomb of Charles V. The grille of the chancel opens and the Monk, who was in the earlier scene in the monastery, appears and in commanding tones sings as before that earthly sorrows follow mankind even into the Cloister, and only in heaven will the conflict of the human heart be stilled. The Monk's solemn words are accompanied by the three trombones and the ophicleide, an instrument whose colourful name does not occur again in the Verdi scores studied in this book.

The Monk, not to put too fine a point on it, is something of a puzzle. The Grand Inquisitor, hearing his voice, exclaims that it is the voice of the Emperor Charles—a belief which is immediately echoed by the guards and by Philip. In the general confusion Don Carlos escapes and is carried in a state of collapse into the interior of the monastery by the Monk. The curtain falls on the minor-to-major chords of the monks' chant played loudly and *assai marcato* by the brass.

In the 1960–61 production of the opera at La Scala, in place of the big orchestral finish the monks were heard chanting distantly in the chapel off stage (the same words and music as in the earlier scene), and the curtain falls on a quiet *religioso* coda. This complete deviation from anything found in the two scores of *Don Carlos* commonly in use—the five-act version of 1887 and the four-act of 1884—is explained by the Scala authorities, just to confuse everybody, having decided to end the opera as it had ended in the version played in Milan in 1869.

None of this, however, makes it any clearer who or what the Monk is supposed to be who whisks Don Carlos off into the monastery. In the scores of the familiar five-act and four-act revised versions we read quite simply in the bald unequivocal stage direction that when the Monk sings, "It is Charles V wearing his royal mantle and crown". The next relevant stage direction also reads quite simply: "Charles V pulls the bewildered Don Carlos into the Cloister". The first version of the opera, on the other hand, contains no specific mention of Charles V in the libretto at all. All we read is that the Monk appears, takes Don Carlos in his arms, covers him with his cloak and in due course drags him inside the monastery to safety. It is only the Grand Inquisitor, the King and their followers who seem to think the Monk is Charles V.

As for what we in the audience are supposed to believe it is obvious that our guess is as good as Philip's. One of the points Verdi made in a letter to the librettist Du Locle while at work on the final scene, was that the action should be very rapid after the appearance of Charles, "so that Philip has no time to wonder how or why Charles V appears, whether he is a ghost, or alive, etc. etc." The quickness of the action may also have been intended to forestall awkward questions by the audience as well, of course, but unfortunately our interest in the opera does not end with the fall of the final curtain. From the way Verdi wrote about Charles V to his librettist, however, it looks very much as though he meant the figure to be real, the Emperor-Monk himself, no less.

If we are to believe this then we must subscribe to the familiar theory that Charles V lived several years longer at "San Giusto" than is officially recorded. At the time of the opera's action he would have been only sixty or so, and it was not until eight years later that his body was moved to the Escurial and the outside world had any proof of his death.

If we are not expected to believe in a real Charles V, are we to believe it to be a ghost, as some commentators think? We have already been asked to swallow the Voice from Heaven at the end of the *auto-de-fé* scene, so why not another demand on our belief in the supernatural?

Finally, there is the theory that it is only the Monk dressed up after all. If so, how did he manage to scare the wits out of Don Carlos in the first monastery scene when he isn't dressed up, but only making a noise like Charles V? Or was the "Monk" Charles' ghost all along? Or—but the truth is that in the end the whole business of the final scene is so idiotic and ridiculous that we believe none of it and are grateful that it is so rapidly over and done with in a couple of pages of score.

The real mystery, however, is not who helps Don Carlos to escape but why on earth Verdi thought this sort of ending was needed in the first place. It is not as though he was ignorant of the ending of Schiller's play, where Philip hands over his only son to the Inquisition. The situation in fact actually occurs in the Paris libretto of the opera when Philip delivers up his son to the Grand Inquisitor as a traitor, "the unworthy son that God gave me", and explains exactly why he does so. But instead of making it the climax of the work Verdi abandoned the idea, allowing Don Carlos to escape from the Inquisition's grasp and be rescued in the ludicrous manner we know only too well. To reflect on what music Verdi could have written as a final ensemble is a heart-breaking pastime. The words are all there in the libretto for the mere polishing—the individual points of view of Elisabeth, Don Carlos, Philip, the Grand Inquisitor, guards and monks. And even if running-time had not permitted a final ensemble, the bare drama of Philip handing over his son would have made a magnificent curtain that needed no more than a few bars of further musical comment.

One can only think that perhaps Verdi was bored or tired by the time he came to the final scene, and so agreed to anything that would save time and trouble. The Monk's passages and the off-stage chorus's chanting had only to be lifted from the earlier scene and a few bars of dramatic "climax" music spliced in and the job was done.

It can surely *only* have been for some practical professional reason like this that *Don Carlos* was made to suffer such a puzzling and banal curtain. Or did Verdi suddenly feel, after all his years of operatic death and damnation, that a (semi-) happy ending was wanted? Or was it just his personal view of the fatuousness of the Paris Opera and all its works that made him deliberately write what he considered a "French" finale to show what the Parisian public and the impossible "Grande Boutique" would put up with?

The true explanation of one of the most striking lapses of artistic judgment in history has still to be found, it seems.

The trouble with *Don Carlos* is that even after all Verdi's drastic cuts and alterations it still obstinately remained a *grand opéra*. As Camille Bellaigue put it in his attractive little study of the composer: if Verdi did not make sacrifices on the altar of French art of the time, at least he made *quelques politesses*; and the effect of those *politesses* was extensive. Not only did they make Verdi forsake that brevity which, Bellaigue said, he "loved above everything, but in no other work of Verdi's does the superb quality of so much of the music have to fight so desperately for recognition or struggle so hard to escape from the stranglehold of an alien form, as in *Don Carlos*".

Of all the conventions and traditions of French *grand opéra* the worst was undoubtedly that insistence on inordinate length which led to the creation of what the Italians have described as "mastodonti musicali". (It has always been a bit of a mystery that the French, with their carefully exploited reputation for being all that is witty and most penetratingly logical, should have developed this form of opera to quite such lengths—and lengths is just the word, of course.) It was not merely the irrelevancies, such as the interminable ballets and repetitious songs introduced to create local colour that took up so much valuable time, but the incurable megalomaniac nature of *grand opéra*, with its huge sets, its changes of scene, its spectacular crowd sequences, and above all the absence of artistic discipline to keep the whole thing within reasonable limits of time and good taste—inherent defects which no composer ever completely overcame. It is almost as though by its very nature *grand opéra* prevented the composition of music that was good from beginning to end of the work. It is significant, anyway, that there does not exist a single *grand opéra*, whether by Rossini, Meyerbeer or Verdi, that does not have to be cut and is not the better for it. And I do not think it is the fault of the composers but of a medium which somehow depends on the second-rate and flashy for its very existence (if the rules of the game are to be observed).

Because even in its final revised form *Don Carlos* is an unwieldy and uneven work, a great deal of the blame for this has been put on Meyerbeer. It is true that the political theme running through the story is basically the conflict of Catholics and Protestants, as in *Les Huguenots*; that the idea of the Grand Inquisitor appearing on the stage first occurred in Act I of *L'Africaine*, where the eight Portuguese bishops, all basses, singing in unison, may well have been the model for the all-bass unison of the six Flemish deputies in *Don Carlos*. But while we may blame Meyerbeer for having set the standard and pattern of *grand opéra* which Verdi was obliged to follow if he wrote for the Paris Opera, it is not quite fair to blame him for any of the purely musical shortcomings of *Don Carlos*. Verdi was quite capable of writing bad music on his own without any help from Meyerbeer or anybody else.

What is unfortunate about *Don Carlos* is that even in its most carefully cut and edited form so much poor music has to be left in for the sake of the action, or the general situation—like the chorus that ends Act I (Ex 301), the crowd's opening and closing chorus in the *auto-de-fé* scene (Ex 316), the dreadful *banda* tune for the procession in the same scene (Ex 319), or the *marziale* in the final scene which is often cut in practice when it leaves something of a gap in our knowledge of Elisabeth. Or music has to be kept in for the sake of a singer—like Eboli's "Song of the Veil", which I must confess I find an unattractive item and which is, of course, quite irrelevant. Equally, we must admit that some of the finest musical moments are the result of thoroughly effective grand-operatic ideas, like the funeral march of the heretics to the stake (Ex 317).

As we know it today *Don Carlos* is still a long-winded work; it is also quite fantastically absorbing, for in no other Verdi opera does one encounter such a variety of sharply contrasted human emotions or such mastery in their characterization. Not one of the principal characters seems to stand still, as it were—except the Inquisitor, of course, whose whole function and position is one of rock-like immovability. But the others are developing all the time, revealing first one side of their nature, then another, as each in turn is overtaken by those spectacular misfortunes which seem to have been particularly prevalent in Verdi's operas with a Spanish setting.

Elisabeth, as one gets to know the opera better, emerges as one of the most sympathetic of Verdi's heroines. She is a figure of dignity and charm whom the classic conflict between Love and Duty seems to hit more cruelly than it does Don Carlos or Philip, who enjoys all the rapture and promise of young love, only to have it brutally snatched away from her, and so not only loses the man she loves but is condemned to an unhappy political marriage which her upbringing and sense of duty make her accept silently and without question.

In her three duets with Don Carlos we can trace the development of Elisabeth's character from the youthful warmth and elation of the Fontainebleau scene, through the mixture and dramatic contrast of emotions ranging from tenderness, anxiety and sorrow, to bitter sarcasm in Act II, to the poignant resignation of the last scene—a many-sided study which is among the finest and most complete in Verdi's gallery of human portraits. It is in these duets, too, that we learn about Don Carlos—his ardour, his feeling of frustration, the suggestion of epilepsy, and finally his resolution and strength of character.

Princess Eboli, in spite of some of her over-melodramatic moments, is an intensely human being, confused, jealous, unreasonable, her love turning to hate and, like Amneris after her, perversely set on destroying what she loves—but so blindly that she is genuinely surprised when her revenge on Don Carlos harms the Queen, whom she adores.

As Verdi himself admitted, Rodrigo is an anachronism "inasmuch as he holds essentially modern humanitarian ideas at the time of Philip II, who, if he had met anybody like this, would have crushed him and certainly wouldn't have warned him to beware the Inquisitor". As a musical character Rodrigo is for the most part little more than the conventional Tenor's Friend that so many baritones have to be in operatic life; except, of course, in the fine dialogue with Philip which dates from the revision of 1884 and brings him magnificently to life.

The character of Philip is one of Verdi's most inspired and impressive conceptions—*severo*, *terribile* and *feroce*, but also, because of his loneliness and circumstances which involve him in a conflict between his love as a father and his duty as a King, a figure who can move us to pity, and who in the end is perhaps the most tragic character of them all, because he could have altered the whole course of events, but did not.

There is no denying that *Don Carlos* is long-winded; that it is uneven; that it is grim and gloomy; equally, there is surely no other opera by Verdi in which shortcomings of detail, dramatic misjudgments, or misguided conformity to an unsympathetic and alien pattern, so signally fail to detract from the power and beauty of the music, or to blur the originality and colour of the complex and individual characterization.

AIDA

Opera in four acts (seven scenes). Libretto by Antonio Ghislanzoni. First performed at the Opera House, Cairo, on 24th December, 1871. First performance in England: Covent Garden, 22nd June, 1876. First performance in the United States: Academy of Music, New York, 26th November, 1873.

THE STORY that *Aida* was performed either at the opening of the Suez Canal, the opening of the new Cairo Opera House, or both, is still oddly prevalent. The fifth and latest edition of *Grove's Dictionary of Music and Musicians* (Vol. II, p 895) states that Cairo's opera house "opened with Verdi's *Aida* (1871), specially composed for it". The passage in *Grove* is corrected in the Supplementary Volume where on page 120 it says that "Verdi's *Aida* was commissioned for its inauguration (1871), but the house was actually opened with Meyerbeer's *Huguenots*". This is still not right; for although *Aida* was commissioned for the new theatre and was produced there in 1871 it was never intended for its inauguration. The Cairo Opera House opened on 1st November, 1869, with *Rigoletto*; the first performance there of *Les Huguenots* was some time in 1870; and the Suez Canal was opened on 16th November, 1869.

The first contact Verdi seems to have had with Egypt was in the summer of 1869 when, Frank Walker relates in *The Man Verdi*, he was approached—unsuccessfully—by Draneht Bey, Director of the Khedive's Theatres, to write a festive "hymn" of some kind for the opening of the new opera house. What happened next is recounted in a letter written by Verdi to his publisher Giulio Ricordi in June 1870: "At the end of last year [1869] I was invited to write an opera for a very distant country. I answered No. When I was in Paris [during March and April 1870] Du Locle was instructed to talk to me again and to offer me a large sum. Again I answered No. A month later he sent me a printed *précis*, telling me that it had been done by an important personage (which I do not believe), that it seemed good to him, and please would I read it. I found it excellent and answered that I would set it to music on certain conditions, etc. etc. Three days afterwards I received a telegram: 'accepted' . . ."

Verdi may appear to have been a little over-cautious in not giving his publisher any indication of the subject of the opera or where the "Distant Country" might be, but perhaps it was understandable: Ricordi was the soul of indiscretion with the Press when he smelt a news story and to have told him more would inevitably have resulted in precisely the sort of publicity that Verdi detested.

Verdi turned down the invitation from "a Distant Country" twice in the course of about six months: the first time, as he recalled, at the end of 1869; the second time in March or April 1870 in Paris when Du Locle's instructions to talk to Verdi *again* suggest that perhaps he made the original approach as well.

In the period between rejecting and finally accepting the invitation, however, Verdi was in constant touch with Du Locle in the hope of finding a suitable subject for the Paris Opera or the Opéra-Comique. There was *Froufrou*, a five-act comedy by Meilhac and Halévy; there were *Piccolino* and *Patrie!* by Sardou; there were thoughts about Molière's *Tartuffe*, and a glance at *Acté et Néron* by Alexandre Dumas *père*. The most likely project during this time was the libretto of *Nerone* by Arrigo Boito which, Verdi wrote to Du Locle, "I still believe . . . could be a subject for a grand opera, and naturally done in my own manner—which would be impossible at the Opéra, but *possibilissimo* here [in Italy] . . ." The idea of *Nerone* was dropped, however, and as is well known Boito eventually set it himself, although it was not performed until six years after his death, when after considerable revision and tidying up Toscanini staged it at La Scala in 1924.

Du Locle kept on at Verdi to write something for Paris and he did not give up even when the composer, in a long letter discussing the manners and moods of the Paris public, insisted that "the conclusion of all this is that I am not a composer for Paris". Nevertheless, the truth was that while he regularly turned down Du Locle's suggestions Verdi still encouraged him to go on looking for a suitable subject. Thus when Du Locle made his famous approach with the Distant Country project during Verdi's stay in Paris in the early spring of 1870, the composer's firm rejection was characteristically accompanied by a request that Du Locle should find him a copy of a comedy by the contemporary Spanish playwright Adelardo Lopez de Ayala, which Verdi thought would do admirably for the Opéra-Comique.

Du Locle, who was by now director of the Opéra-Comique and therefore more anxious than ever to get an opera out of Verdi, posted off a copy of the Ayala play to the composer in Italy, but cunningly included in the parcel a privately printed four-page *programma*—the synopsis of the opera for a very Distant Country.

In due course Verdi wrote back that he had read the Lopez de Ayala play but that it was unsuitable—"one neither cries nor laughs". He had also, he said, read the *programma Egiziano*. "It is well done," he wrote, "the *mis en scène* is splendid, and it contains one or two situations which, if they aren't entirely new, are certainly fine. But who did it? It shows a very expert, experienced hand that knows the theatre very well. Let me know the financial conditions in Egypt, and then we will decide."

Du Locle replied: "The Egyptian libretto is the work of the Khedive and Mariette Bey, the famous antiquary; nobody else has had a hand in it. . . ." Verdi's encouraging reaction to the *programma Egiziano* must have come as a great relief to Du Locle, for not long before Mariette had written to him, ending his letter with the postscript: "One last word. If M. Verdi doesn't accept, H.E. [the Khedive] begs you to knock on another door . . . ! Gounod and even Wagner are being considered. If the latter wanted to, he could do something really *grandioso*." Although Du Locle credits the Khedive, Ismail Pasha, with co-authorship of the four-page opera synopsis, it was a pretty honorary kind of post, for when, on a visit to Rome in 1880 there was some public dispute about the libretto of *Aida*, Du Locle stated categorically in the local French language newspaper that "the first idea of the poem belongs to Mariette Bey, the celebrated Egyptologist".

Even if Auguste-Edouard Mariette (b. Boulogne 1821–d. Cairo 1881) had not earned immortality by his invention of the story of *Aida*, he would still be remembered in his own right, as it were, for his work as an Egyptologist. He went to Egypt in 1850 to look for Coptic manuscripts, but was sidetracked by monuments showing above the ground on the site of Memphis. He set about digging and under the sand discovered the temple of Serapis and the tombs of the Apis bulls. Mariette's researches were described as "the most important and the rarest ever made in Egypt", and included, among others, the clearing of "the celebrated colossus of the Sphinx" to satisfy himself that "this gigantic monument had been sculptured as it stood from a natural rock".

Mariette was eventually given the title of Bey and worked full time for the Khedive, though not always as an Egyptologist. Once Verdi had accepted Ismail Pasha's commission Mariette was involved in the opera to a far greater extent than his initial contribution would have suggested. The genesis of the libretto of *Aida* was like nothing so much as that of a modern film script. In the beginning there was Mariette's story. Then came Du Locle's "treatment"— which turned the synopsis into a detailed scenario in French prose. Finally there was the "shooting script"—in which the French prose was turned into Italian verse by Antonio Ghislanzoni.

But while there was nothing startlingly new in this method as such (Verdi himself had, after all, made the prose treatment of *Macbeth* for Piave to make into a shooting script), never before had the composer taken such an actively creative part in the construction of the libretto as he did with *Aida*. It was not just a matter of making helpful suggestions; right from the first discussions of Mariette's synopsis with Du Locle Verdi weighed in with numerous important changes, not the least of them being the final scene of the opera, which was entirely his own conception. When Ghislanzoni started on the libretto proper Verdi's contributions were increasingly detailed and frequent. He had things to say about the psychology of the characters and the chorus; he added dances, off-stage choruses, invented opportunities for some of the most effective lyrical sequences in the opera; he made changes in the metre of the words, and had Ghislanzoni rewrite the third act—this after having approved of his work in the first place. Verdi's correspondence with Ghislanzoni about *Aida* is preserved in the famous *Coppialettere*—the collection of the copies Verdi made in five fat, rough exercise books of letters he wrote, which was published in 1913. The letters to Ghislanzoni take up just on forty pages of a volume which has maddeningly been so long out of print that if you are lucky enough to find a copy today it will cost you all of £10. It is astonishing and frustrating that even now, after all the Verdi literature of the past thirty-five years, there should still exist no English edition of the *Coppialettere* to which the reader can be referred; for while the letters in general have been handsomely quoted in their time, the *Aida* letters need far longer and more detailed quotation than is remotely possible in a study like this if they are to give a comprehensive idea of the composer's share in the words he set to music.

Verdi was also frequently in touch with Mariette, checking with him the distance from Memphis to Thebes, the number of priestesses permissible in the consecration scene; learning that the ancient Egyptians didn't have iron or steel, only gold, silver and brass; discussing a dozen other points to avoid anachronism or that might add to the theatrical effectiveness of the opera.

The first performance of *Aida* at the Cairo Opera House was fixed for January 1871. In July 1870, however, the Franco-Prussian war broke out and all work was suspended on the scenery and costumes being made in Paris under the supervision of Mariette, who not only designed them but had also conducted earlier negotiations with Verdi, and in fact signed the contract on behalf of the Khedive. When the siege of Paris began in September Mariette was shut up in the French capital—if not incommunicado, at least in the frustrating position of not being able to make any closer contact with the outside world than was permitted by post carried by balloons launched from the roof of Charles Garnier's still unfinished Théâtre National de l'Opéra. Du Locle was also caught up in Paris, but managed to maintain what was inevitably a rather one-sided correspondence with Verdi by "ballon monté".

The siege of Paris was finally raised in January 1871, and *Aida* was produced on 24th December, 1871, in the Khedive's sumptuous red, white and gold theatre, built largely of wood and for all its elegance and comfort, having a capacity audience of only 700.* The Cairo stage, on the other hand, seems to have been large enough to have done *Aida* proud, for no fewer than 300 people were on the stage for the finale of the second act, including Arab trumpeters and a local *banda*. The opera was conducted by Giovanni Bottesini, the great double bass player—a colourful and endearing figure whose career in the late 1880s as director of the opera in Parma is among the Teatro Regio's most treasured episodes.†

The success of *Aida* was tremendous and immediate, and although thanks to their twenty years' start there may have been more performances over the years of *Rigoletto* and *Il trovatore*, it remains probably the most popular and appealing of all Verdi's operas. It has been translated into twenty languages, and has been sung in Italian in Yokohama, in Russian in Shanghai, as well as in Croatian, Hebrew and Lithuanian. The only language it never seems to have been sung in is the Arabic of the country which commissioned its composition. But perhaps this is because the voice of the male Arab is considerably higher than that of the typical Italian soprano Verdi obviously had in mind.

* Hamish Wilson, designer of the first Glyndebourne productions before the war, who was working in Cairo recently, tells me that it is the limited seating accommodation which has finally led to the closing of the Cairo Opera House. A newer and larger building is to take its place on another site. Meanwhile, the Khedive's theatre, with its accommodation for more than a hundred fewer spectators than Glyndebourne holds, is still used for rehearsals by various theatrical enterprises in the Egyptian capital.

† See *Great Opera Houses*, pp 136–7.

CHARACTERS IN ORDER OF SINGING

RAMFIS, *the High Priest* . . .	Bass
RADAMES, *Captain of the Guard* . . .	Tenor
AMNERIS, *Daughter of Pharaoh* . .	Mezzo-soprano
AIDA, *her Ethiopian slave*	Soprano
PHARAOH	Bass
A MESSENGER	Tenor
AMONASRO, *King of Ethiopia and Aida's father* .	Baritone

Priests, priestesses, ministers, captains, officials, Ethiopian slaves and prisoners, Egyptian soldiers, crowds, etc.

Scene: Memphis and Thebes   Time: In the days of the Pharaohs

ACT I

Scene 1 : A Hall in the Palace of the Pharaohs at Memphis. To the left and right are colonnades with statues and flowering shrubs. At the back, a great gateway through which can be seen the temples and palaces of Memphis, and the Pyramids.

An orchestral Prelude before the rise of the curtain introduces two of the most important themes from the opera that follows. The first, played *pianissimo* by muted violins, is associated with Aida:

Ex 338

This is expanded into a brief, exquisite passage for violins in four parts and violas, coloured by a couple of bars for flute and clarinet in their lowest register.

The second theme, which follows, was described by Verdi as the Song of the Priests:

Ex 339

This theme, which goes through some fiercely dramatic treatment in the course of the opera, is played here by muted violoncellos but is quickly built up into a *ff* conflict with the Aida theme—a simple and pointed musical suggestion of the principal conflict underlying the drama. The Priests' tune is thundered out by trombones, horns, violas and bassoon in unison, while Aida's theme is played, also *ff* and in unison, by violins and woodwind with occasional support from a trumpet. It should be pointed out here that the orchestra in *Aida* is much smaller than it was for *Don Carlos*, even though, as we shall see, *Aida* is every bit as much of a grand opera as the earlier work.

The main difference in the instrumentation is the absence of cornets, and the limitation of the bassoons to two. Verdi was also concerned about what form our old friend the *cimbasso* was to take in *Aida*. In discussing the orchestra for the first Scala performance (February 1872) he insisted on having a fourth trombone if possible; if the part could not be played easily, then the conductor Franco Faccio was to use one of "the usual ophicleides that go down to low B [flat]". One thing Verdi would not have was "that devil of a *bombardon*"—the bass tuba which, he said, never mixes with the rest of the brass. Verdi was by now obviously dead set against using the tuba for his brass bass; in both *Otello* and *Falstaff* it is indicated to be played by "fourth trombone".

The conflict between the two themes does not last long; there is a return to Aida's tune by strings *ppp*, a short build-up to a loud *ff* *tutti* bar and the Prelude ends on a long quiet cadence for the first violins, divided into two parts, which dies away in their high register to conclude a supremely simple and direct orchestral introduction.

Verdi, who had never heard the Prelude performed (he did not go to Cairo for the première), was apprehensive about the effect it might have in practice when he was preparing for the first Scala production. Just in case it didn't come off he wrote a longer, more conventional orchestral introduction (he called it an Overture) which ended with trombones and double basses "howling out" the Song of the Priests, with violins and woodwind "shrieking the jealousy of Amneris" (see Ex 342), and Aida's tune played *fortissimo* by the trumpets. The overture was tried out by the orchestra at a Scala rehearsal and quickly put away. "The piece might have succeeded", Verdi reported, "if the construction had not been so cumbersome; but the excellence of the orchestra only showed up more than ever the pretentious dullness of this co-called overture."

The curtain rises on a conversation between Ramfis and Radames, which, like the opening conversation of *Simon Boccanegra*, has the air of having been going on for some time. To a stately four-in-a-bar accompaniment of violoncellos divided into three parts Ramfis tells Radames of a rumour that the Ethiopians are threatening to invade the Nile valley; the goddess Isis has been consulted and she has advised the choice of a young soldier to lead the Egyptian armies. Ramfis leaves to tell Pharaoh of the goddess's instructions and departs, leaving behind him a violoncello arpeggio which ends in mid-air in its high register. (For some reason Du Locle repeatedly confused Ramfis and Radames with one another when he was working on the scenario of the opera, and it took him a long time to sort them out.)

Radames, left alone, wonders whether it is he whom Isis has in mind. His recitative reflections are punctuated by short vigorous fanfare-like phrases for trumpets and trombones, which underline his determination to free Aida from slavery and marry her, if his military ambitions are fulfilled.

The mood changes abruptly for Radames to sing of Aida's beauty in the *romanza* which is perhaps the loveliest of all Verdi's love songs —"Celeste Aida . . ." ("Heavenly Aida . . .") :

Ex *340*

Ce_ le _ ste A- i - da..... for - ma di - vi - na....

Like "Questa o quella" in *Rigoletto*, "Celeste Aida" is another of those tunes which are thrown away in the first few minutes of a Verdi opera and which, as they are never referred to again, the late-comer can never catch up with. The latecomer to *Aida* will not only miss a superb aria, of course, but also the first indication of the new and original orchestration which is so characteristic of the opera. The orchestral accompaniment to "Celeste Aida" has an almost chamber-music quality in which the flute in its low register plays a striking part. The flute, indeed, seems to colour the whole of *Aida* in the same way that the bassoon predominates in *Don Giovanni*, and the piccolo in *Falstaff*.

We also have in the accompaniment to Radames' *romanza* the first hints of what Verdi described as the "vaporous" orchestral effect he aimed at in the final scene of the opera. Here it is suggested by occasional whispered figures for six muted solo violins in three parts, indicated to play as a separate unit—*a parte*—while the rest of the violins play their conventional first and second parts.

As far as performance is concerned the final bars of "Celeste Aida" will always be a problem so long as tenors fear their manhood may be questioned if they do not belt out the final high B flat at the top of their lungs. If they sing it as Verdi wrote it, of course, their manhood might still be in question, but they would prove themselves to be better singers, for the bars concerned are shown to be sung *ppp dim.*, followed by *pp morendo*, thus making the high B flat quieter than *pp*.

The solution of this problem is only possible by those conductors who, like Toscanini, are able to keep tenors under control. In his recording of *Aida* Toscanini has the tenor sing his high B flat full out, and then repeat the words "vicino al sol" *pp* on the middle B flat an octave lower. This departure from the written bar was Verdi's own idea, first thought up for the benefit of Giuseppe Capponi, one of the earliest singers of the part, who had had to stand down from

13

the original Scala production on account of illness, and who was later tenor soloist at the first performance of the Requiem in 1874.

Verdi recommended the same procedure on another occasion when he angrily refused to allow Enrico Nicolini to transpose the aria down a semitone into A. It was this instance which Toscanini had in mind when he explained the modification in his recording of the opera.* "Transpose it down a semitone," Verdi wrote to Ghislanzoni, "and the whole *tessitura* would be that of a baritone and by leaving out the A's any baritone could sing it. I know very well that the two final bars of B flat transposed to A would sound fuller, rounder and easier, but is it worth the trouble of turning everything else upside down just for a one-note *effect*? I know also that it is hard to sing the B flat as it is written; but it was to remedy this that I myself added the three notes for Capponi."

Radames' daydream is interrupted by the entrance of Amneris accompanied by this ingratiating, rather slinky theme played by the first violins:

Ex 341

Amneris asks him why he has such a rapturous look on his face. Radames replies that he has hopes of being chosen by Isis to lead the Egyptian army into battle. Amneris is not completely convinced by this answer; she loves Radames passionately and as her love is not returned she is naturally suspicious. Amneris tells us this in a series of asides, while Radames—also in asides—is perturbed lest she should discover his love for Aida, her slave.

This scene is accompanied by a restless orchestral figure, originating in the strings, which is associated throughout the opera with Amneris' jealousy:

Ex 342

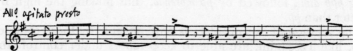

An agitated duet sequence develops in which Amneris and Radames continue to express their fears to themselves. The passage dies

* Great Britain: RCA–Victor RB 16021–3; U.S.A.: RCA–Victor LM 6132.

away with Amneris repeating the words "oh guai" ("oh woe !") on a
characteristic falling three-note phrase:

Ex 343

oh gua-i,   oh gua-i,   oh gua-i)

Aida enters, accompanied by her theme (Ex 338) played *dolce
espressivo* by a solo clarinet. The reaction of Radames and Aida on
meeting is plain enough to strengthen Amneris' suspicions. The
Princess addresses her slave in hypocritically affectionate terms,
asking Aida—whom she considers more of a sister than a servant—
why she is so agitated. Aida replies that she is appalled by the prospect of war between Egypt and her native Ethiopia.

"Are you speaking the truth?" asks Amneris. "Isn't there something else more serious disturbing you?" Aida is silent; she "lowers
her eyes and tries to hide her agitation". Looking at her, Amneris'
suspicions begin to grow into jealous fury and in "a dark voice", as
the jealousy theme returns, she mutters threats against her slave;
Radames continues his anxious prayer that he has not given himself
away, and Aida tells us that it is not only the fate of her country
that troubles her but her general unhappy state. The climax of this
short trio is reached with Aida and Radames, but not Amneris,
bewailing their misfortune in the "guai" phrase first heard in Ex
343—which suggests admirably that all three characters are in
despair. Indeed, I can think offhand of no other Verdi opera where
so early in the course of the drama three people are so deeply involved in a situation.

A powerful fanfare of trumpets, trombones and horns, punctuated
by a wonderfully effective series of *ff* unison trills in the strings (first
and second violins in their lower register), accompanies the arrival
of Pharaoh, preceded by his bodyguard and followed by Ramfis,
Ministers of State, priests and captains. Over what may best be
described by the neologistic musical term a "walking bass" of
pizzicato violoncellos and double basses, Pharaoh proclaims that
the gathering has been summoned to hear the official news of the
invasion given by a Messenger. In dramatic tones no longer tied to
the monotone of the conventional operatic herald, the Messenger
announces that Egypt has been invaded and Thebes is threatened
by an army led by King Amonasro.

The crowd receives the news with enthusiastic cries of "Guerra !";
Pharaoh goes on to declare that Isis has chosen Radames to lead the
Egyptian army. In two short asides Aida and Amneris react charac-
teristically to this: Aida with horror that her lover is to lead an

army against her father, the King of Ethiopia, and Amneris with pride to think that the man she loves has been given such a high honour.

Pharaoh now instructs Radames to go to the Temple of Vulcan to be invested with the arms and insignia of leadership. Then, in a sudden switch to A major where the reiterated C sharps in woodwind and brass would lead one to expect F sharp major, Pharaoh addresses his soldiers, bidding them rise and guard the sacred shores of the Nile with the stirring tune:

Ex 344

The harmonization of this familiar four-square tune is a superb example of how a composer of genius can use a series of common chords and make something entirely his own out of them. The tune could be harmonized in half a dozen different ways; they would all be academically unexceptionable; but none of them would have that peculiar Verdian flavour, described by H. C. Colles in the third volume of *The Growth of Music* as "just a matter of letting quite ordinary chords progress in a very uncommon way".

Ramfis continues with a "middle" to Pharaoh's tune, which is still accompanied only by strings; the "first eight" are then repeated by the chorus in unison with individual contributions from Pharaoh and Ramfis, and a vigorous orchestral accompaniment rather surprisingly limited by the omission of flutes, trumpets and trombones. These missing instruments return, however, to provide the *pp* four-in-a-bar wind-only background when, with a striking change of key, Radames takes over the tune in C major. Singing *grandioso*, he proclaims his blind enthusiasm for the task ahead of him, while the unhappy Aida, in a passionate aside, reveals the full extent of the great emotional conflict in which she is inextricably involved—"per chi piango? per chi prego?" ("For whom shall I weep? For whom shall I pray? What power binds me to him? I must love him, and he is an enemy, a foreigner!").

Amneris, to the tune of Ramfis' "middle" and faint military sounds from the orchestral trumpets, presents Radames with a banner. The scene ends with a Grand Reprise of Ex 344, with a cascade of unison scales for the violins, excited cries of "Guerra!", and Amneris bidding Radames to return a conqueror—"Ritorna vincitor!"—words echoed in unison by the whole company, who then move off to the ceremony to be held in the Temple of Vulcan.

Only Aida stays behind—horrified when she is alone to realize that she too had cried, "Ritorna vincitor!"

Away from its context the famous solo scene which follows often sounds as if Aida were supposed to be addressing the words "Ritorna vincitor!" to Radames, as a kind of pep-talk before he goes into battle. As one soon realizes in the theatre, there is nothing enthusiastic about the way Aida begins her *Scena e Romanza*. She echoes the words of the chorus in inverted commas, almost cynically, rebuking herself for ever having uttered them when they may mean the death of her father and her countrymen. In the course of this declamatory passage the tension is heightened by a curious orchestral throwback to the mournful chromatic humming of the tenors and basses during the storm music in the last act of *Rigoletto* (see p 119).

In an agitated and pathetic prayer Aida beseeches the gods to forgive her insane words, to restore her to her father and to destroy their oppressors:

Ex 345

L'in - sa - na pa - ro - la o Nu - mi, sper - de - te!

As she grows more fervent in her prayers to defeat the enemy (her urgency and determination are dramatically stressed by the perpetually syncopating string accompaniment), Aida suddenly realizes what she is saying. To the tune of Ex 338 and accompanied by a solo clarinet and a *pp* string tremolo, Aida asks in despair how she can forget the man she loves and pray for his death. Her confusion and anguish increase with a sequence of great pathos, sung *triste e dolce* against another restless syncopated string figure played *ppp*, and leads to one of the most beautiful and moving passages in all opera. In her final desperation Aida beseeches heaven to have pity on her in her suffering, and let her die—"Numi, pietà del mio soffrir":

Ex 346

Nu - mi, pie - tà del mio sof - frir! spe - me non v'ha pel mio do - lor...

The long, thirty-bar passage with which Aida ends this scene has a strange serenity about it which seems to look beyond the words of her prayer, as it were, to the granting of the prayer itself. The simplicity of these final bars, with their delicate, trembling string accompaniment and their hesitation between minor and major, creates a remarkable feeling of Aida's pathetic resignation to the only possible solution of her tragic dilemma.

The curtain falls as Aida leaves, and the music ends with a curious reminiscence of the rising violoncello arpeggio that ended suspended in mid-air when Ramfis left the stage earlier on.

Scene 2 : The interior of the Temple of Vulcan at Memphis. A mysterious light shines from above. A long line of columns stretches away into darkness ; statues of various deities are visible in the shadows. In the centre of the stage, on a platform covered with carpets, is an altar surmounted by sacred emblems. The smoke of incense rises from golden tripods.

Although it does not say so in the stage direction quoted above from my copy of the orchestral score, it is clear from what happens in the music as well as from the notes Verdi made in a copy of the libretto during the early stages of first producing the opera in Italy in 1872, that the curtain is not meant to go up on an empty stage at the start of what is called the *Gran scena della consecrazione*. From behind the scenes come the voices of Priestesses invoking the almighty Phthà. They are accompanied by the four-in-a-bar thrumming of "harps" (Verdi did not specify how many), played by other priestesses in the background somewhere behind the altar. During the invocation, Verdi insisted, "Priests as well as priestesses must remain absolutely motionless", adding that they must hold their hands on their chests, "but not crossed".

The tune of the invocation, sung mainly as a solo by a Grand Priestess, and which plays an effectively dramatic part at the end of the opera, is a first striking example of the peculiar exoticism Verdi invented for many of the scenes in *Aida* :

Ex *347*

Verdi consulted Mariette on many points while he was composing *Aida*, but at no time did he show any great curiosity about ancient Egyptian music. It wouldn't really have done him much good if he had anyway, for although he listened to the sound produced by some Egyptian flutes in the Florence museum (and disliked it intensely) what he heard was of course the *noise*, not the music, made by ancient Egyptians. In any case, Verdi had no need of anything remotely "authentic" with which to create local colour.

Where Mozart, in *Die Entführung aus dem Serail*, absorbed the superficial elements of "Turkish" music and made pure Mozart out of it; where Puccini, in *Madame Butterfly* and *Turandot*, absorbed genuine Japanese and Chinese tunes so thoroughly that they came out sounding like genuine Puccini, Verdi absorbed no foreign bodies whatever. In *Aida*, when he had to create an atmosphere that was entirely new and different from anything he had done before he just wrote an entirely new and different kind of music to do it with.

What Verdi himself called the responses to the Priestess's litany are made unaccompanied and *pp* by Ramfis and the Chorus of Priests who, since they are not shown in the score as singing off stage and as we know from Verdi's notes, must be on the stage when the curtain rises. There is nothing exotic about the Priests' music; it is very much the same sombre sound we heard from the monks in *Don Carlos* and *La forza del destino*.

The Priestesses-Priests routine, which is heard three times and creates a superb atmosphere of mysterious lights and smoking tripods, is followed by a Sacred Dance of the Priestesses—danced, of course, by the priestesses who have been standing silent and motionless with "their hands on their chests, but not crossed". The Sacred Dance is again in Verdi's most exotic manner and makes most effective and original use of three flutes. In the opening phrases the instruments are mostly in three parts, with a simple pizzicato accompaniment by strings:

Ex 348

The "middle" of the tune is for the three flutes in unison (again with pizzicato accompaniment)—a passage which is also heard again with considerable effect in the last scene of the opera, and which is typical of the general shape and colouring of so much of the deliberately exotic and evocative episodes in the score:

Ex 349

While the dance is in progress Radames enters. He is unarmed and goes to the altar where a silver veil is placed on his head. The dance comes to an end, and Ramfis begins the ceremony of investment, addressing Radames in solemn phrases declaimed against a solemn *pp* background of trumpets, trombones, tuba and bassoons, and repeated in a forceful unison by the Chorus of Priests.

Turning towards the altar Ramfis invokes the god's protection of Egypt—"Nume, custode e vindice" ("O god, protector and avenger of our sacred soil"). He does so in a "broad phrase" marked to be sung "larga la frase" and remarkable for the unexpected and arresting accompaniment of three trombones playing *pp* and from time to time in sequences of rather surprising consecutive fifths:

Ex 350

Ramfis' tune and sentiments are taken up by Radames and the chorus and built up towards a climax which is twice delayed by the sound of the Priestesses' distant off-stage singing of their hymn to the almighty Phthà with harps accompanying them as at the start of the scene (Ex 347). The male ensemble develops very briefly, but dies down to give way once more to the Priestesses who are now heard singing the first bars of their invocation *ppp* in octaves, punctuated by Radames and the Priests with a whispered *pppp* unison of the opening phrase for their invocation (Ex 350). After a long pause Radames and Ramfis sing "Immenso Fthà!"—*ff* in thirds, as though they were ending an heroic duet in any of Verdi's early operas, and the curtain falls with the same words echoed even louder by visible and invisible choruses.

Verdi's production notes and comments on Act I, Scene 2 made in the printed libretto are followed by a lengthy "N.B." in which he writes:

"Only at the last bar of the third Invocation do the dancers [*ballerine*] put their fans on the tripods and get ready to start the *danza sacra* at the sound of the three flutes in the orchestra . . . The dance must end so that the dancers are once more grouped around the four tripods.

"When the chorus approaches its *ff* the dancers take their fans and go noiselessly up stage to the front of the altar for the final group. On the last *forte* of the general 'Immenso Fthà!' the dancers round the altar all raise their fans to form one immense fan."

There was obviously something of the choreographer as well in Verdi.

ACT II

Scene 1 : A Hall in Amneris' apartment. Amneris is surrounded by women slaves who are dressing her in preparation for the triumphal feast. Scented vapours rise from tripods. Young Moorish slaves dance and wave feather fans.

Verdi, the choreographer of Act I, Scene 2, becomes Verdi the stage designer, with a touch of the stage carpenter about him, in his production notes on this scene, stipulating the exact measurements of the chair in which Amneris should be seated on top of "a large, very high rostrum about 1,60 metres [5 ft 2 in]".

The curtain rises immediately, and once more to the sound of a harp. This time the harp is in the orchestra and, with occasional *ppp* monotone interjections from a solo trumpet, assumes an almost military character with a vigorous and firmly proclaimed four-in-a-bar passage which serves as the instrumental introduction to the chorus of slaves who sing the praises of Radames while they attend to Amneris. (News of the Egyptian victory over the Ethiopians was obviously known before the rise of the curtain.)

Perhaps because of its heroic subject-matter this passage also has a strongly martial flavour. Harp and timpani keep up a square four-in-a-bar accompaniment (short, sharp quaver chords only in the harp) with more intermittent and *pp* D's from the solo trumpet. The brisk, rigid accompaniment and the shape of the opening phrase of the tune itself make one think involuntarily of the march in the last scene of *Macbeth* (Ex 48), a resemblance which exotic cadences do not altogether disguise:

Ex *351*

There is a sudden change of tonality and mood, though not of tempo, when the slaves decorate Amneris's hair with flowers and laurel, and with violins playing the tune and the harp playing an arpeggio figure in the accompaniment for the first time, sing the wonderfully melting phrase which begins:

Ex *352*

As the slaves sing about "hymns of glory sounding forth with songs of love", Amneris (to words which Verdi described as "voluptuous") thinks aloud of the man she loves, calling on him to return and fill her heart with joy in an exquisitely warm and lyrical cadence which rounds off with such tenderness the passage begun in a brisk march-like fashion—"Ah, vieni, vieni, amor mio . . ." ("Ah, come, come, my love . . .") :

Ex 353

These five bars, with the D sharp in the first bar, the G sharp in the fourth bar so neatly avoided in the third, are a superb example of those instinctive touches that made Verdi the unique melodist he was.

The whole episode is repeated with different words from the start of the tune in Ex 351 to Amneris' final aside, which leads directly into the Dance of the Little Moorish Slaves—a brief ballet put on for the entertainment of Amneris while her slaves continue with her toilet. The idea of having a miniature ballet of what he called "Moretti etiopi" ("little Ethiopian Negroes") was entirely Verdi's and was conceived to add colour and variety to a scene which has so far been lyrical and dramatically static, as well as allowing the stage "business" of the Princess's complicated toilet to be carried on in a leisurely manner. It is theatrically very effective and even if it held up the action (which it doesn't, because so far there has been no action in the scene to hold up), it would justify its inclusion as one of Verdi's most original and successful sequences of dance music. It is a movement of great charm and sparkle with some admirable writing for woodwind and a perky theme—

Ex 354

—which, rather surprisingly, proves to be quite manageable when played in unison and *ff* by trombones and tuba at the climax of the dance.

The ballet comes to an end and there is a reprise of the passage which began with Ex 352; the words are those heard originally, but this time Amneris' coda is accompanied *ppp* by the slaves' voices as well as *tremolando* strings.

Violas, violoncellos and a solo bassoon playing her theme in unison announce the approach of Aida. Amneris dismisses her slaves, and with superb hypocrisy expresses her concern for Aida's feelings: "Daughter of the vanquished; her grief is sacred to me."

Aida enters, carrying the crown; at the sight of her Amneris' doubts and suspicions are aroused again and she determines to learn the truth. "With simulated kindness" she tells Aida how her heart bleeds for her—"I am your friend—you shall have everything of me and live happily." Aida asks in anguished tones how she can be happy far from her native land and ignorant of the fate of her father and brothers. Amneris tries to calm her; time will heal the wounded heart—time and the strongest force of all: love.

At the mention of love Aida becomes agitated; the Princess notices this, and watching her intently, asks Aida to tell her what is on her mind: is she in love with somebody in the army perhaps? They are wheedling words set to a wheedling tune—"Ebben: qual nuovo fremito t'assal, gentil Aida?" ("Come, what new passion assails you, gentle Aida?"):

Ex 355

Poco più lento

Amneris traps Aida into confessing her love for Radames by saying that he has been killed. Aida's reaction to this news gives her away at once; Amneris turns on her, crying that she has found her out. Radames is not dead. With a cry of joy Aida falls on her knees and thanks the gods. "With intense fury" Amneris tells Aida that she also loves Radames—"Do you hear? I am your rival—Pharaoh's daughter!"

Aida rises from her knees and standing proudly before the Princess is on the point of proclaiming that she, too, is the daughter of a King; but she checks herself, falling at her mistress's feet to ask forgiveness—"Ah! pietà ti prenda del mio dolor . . ." ("Oh, have pity on my anguish . . ."):

Ex 356

Adagio

Ah! pietà ti pren-da del mio do- lor... è ve- ro... io l'a- mo d'immenso a - mor...

It is a passage of great pathos, accompanied only by two flutes, a clarinet (with a second added for a bar and a half) and a solo bassoon playing a mournful series of broken arpeggios. In the short duet that develops Aida appeals to Amneris for the clemency that a Princess in her powerful position can grant. Amneris remains unmoved by these pleas and threatens Aida with all the vengeance and fury that is in her heart.

The duet is interrupted by a distant fanfare and a chorus off stage singing the war hymns from Act I—"Su, del Nilo al sacro lido" (Ex 344). While this continues in the background Amneris intensifies her mental torture of Aida: when Pharaoh's daughter sits on the throne beside her father to welcome Radames, Aida shall bow down in the dust before the conquering hero. The off-stage music ceases for a moment. Aida renews her pleas for pity, but Amneris rejects them: "Follow me", she cries, "and we shall see whether you can compete with me as your rival or not."

Amneris sweeps out to the sound of the final couple of bars of the war hymn coming from behind the scenes. Aida is left alone, to sing her simple, moving prayer to the gods—"Numi, pietà del mio martir", that long pathetic phrase hovering between minor and major and accompanied by the scarcely audible, trembling strings which ended the first scene of the opera.

Scene 2 : One of the entrances to the city of Thebes. Downstage, a group of palm trees. On the right, the Temple of Ammon. On the left, a throne surmounted by a rich canopy. At the back, a triumphal arch. The scene is crowded with people.

Anyone professionally concerned with the staging of what is called "Gran Finale Secondo" of this opera, may be interested to know that where the score and libretto state that "the scene is crowded with people" Verdi himself, in his famous production notes, carefully indicated: "When the scene changes there are few people on the stage. The populace enters from different directions and in small groups." In other words, Verdi wanted the stage picture to build up gradually as the music is built up (from the opening fanfare for a stage *banda* which the printer of my score refers to as a "Panda") on the orchestral figure:

Ex 357

Verdi allows the crowd twenty bars of this Allegro maestoso in which to collect and arrange themselves before the entrance of the King, accompanied by his Ministers, the Priests, Captain, fan bearers, standard bearers, "etc. etc.". Amneris enters with Aida and slaves. The King takes his place on the throne with Amneris seated on his left, and the crowd, supported by the *banda*, breaks into the chorus "Gloria all'Egitto" ("Glory to Egypt"):

Ex 358

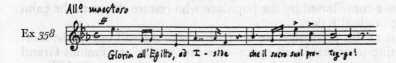

This is the tune which the Khedive, on first hearing it at the dress rehearsal of *Aida* in Cairo, is said to have adopted as the official Egyptian national anthem on the spot. A little later, however, Verdi appears to have written an instrumental march which served as a wordless national anthem for Egypt until the 1940s, when according to *Grove* the Arabic Music Institution put words to it (the British Army stationed in Egypt had, of course, already provided its own notorious set of words about King Farouk earlier in the war). From the few bars quoted in *Grove's* article on National Anthems it is hardly vintage Verdi:

Ex 359

Whatever may or may not have happened to it as a national anthem "Gloria all'Egitto" in the opera is only eight bars long altogether, and when it has been heard once Verdi reverts to the introductory march movement (Ex 357). This time, however, the crowd joins in the orchestra's tune and with many "glorias" and stirring expressions of loyalty a considerable choral din is generated. This is followed by what one might call the Trio of the march, a quiet, *cantabile* section for women's voices only—"S'intrecci il loto al lauro ..." ("The lotus and the laurel crown the victors' brow ..."):

Ex 360

With the tune of Ex 339 distorted into a tense and relentless march rhythm, Ramfis and the chorus of Priests urge the populace to give thanks to the gods for victory. The passage is in the form of a brief four-part *fugato* in which the parts are supported by the dark unison tones of double basses and bassoon, violas and clarinets, violoncellos and bassoon, second violins and unison oboes in their low register. This rather sinister atmosphere is dispelled by the final cadence contributed by the populace who restore things to the calm of the original E flat.

It is at this point that we hear what is to me still one of the most arresting moments in all opera—the first bars of the famous Grand March from *Aida* played in unison by long valveless so-called "Egyptian" trumpets on the stage:

Ex *361*

Even after all this time the opening phrase of this tune, played entirely on the open notes of three "natural" trumpets in A flat, never fails to surprise me and cause a slight *frisson* of excitement. The sudden modulation to A flat, the change to a completely new instrumental sound, the inspired simplicity of a tune that once heard is never forgotten—all these things combine to give the beginning of the Grand March a peculiar thrilling quality which it has never lost for me.

The three trumpeters, discreetly accompanied by the *banda*, march at the head of a contingent of victorious Egyptian troops who parade past Pharaoh. When the tune has been played right through in A flat, there is a sudden and startlingly effective modulation to the key of B major and the march is repeated by three trumpeters who enter playing on the open notes of natural instruments in B (accompanied this time by the orchestra, not the *banda*) and leading another company of troops who parade past the King.

Verdi had the trumpets played in this scene specially made in Milan for the Cairo première—"long, straight, in the ancient Egyptian form". With his eye on the visual effect of the instruments he was only sorry that, owing to their higher pitch, the B trumpets would have to be shorter than those in A flat. The question of the stage trumpets was something that intrigued Verdi right from the earliest days of *Aida*; and he went to great lengths to get them to sound, and particularly, to *look* right. The look was most important. Nothing by M. Sax would do at all. As far as the sound was concerned there was no difficulty; open notes are produced by the same method on a trumpet today as in Egyptian times. What is sad is that Verdi did not live to hear the trumpet found in the tomb of Tutankhamen, who lived in the fourteenth century B.C. A recording of this instrument played by a British soldier stationed in Egypt is in the BBC's archives. Unfortunately, it did not occur to anybody to ask the performer to let us hear how the *Aida* march would have sounded on a genuine 3,400-year-old Egyptian trumpet. Instead, Trooper Whatever-his-name-was treated posterity to his rendition of "Post Horn Galop".

When the B trumpets have played their version of the first twelve bars of the March the A flat trumpets take over again at the "middle four" and finish the tune in their key while the B trumpets, thanks to Verdi's ingenuity, are able to use their D sharp as the enharmonic E flat, and so contribute a colourful flourish to the climax.

The march tempo, which began the scene and has continued without interruption for about five and a half minutes, now gives way to a sequence of admirable ballet music as a group of dancers appear, carrying the spoils of the conquered Ethiopians.

The ballet music in *Aida*, is generally regarded as the most successful of all Verdi's essays in this form; and its success, I believe, is due to the fact that for the first time in writing a grand opera the composer was his own master. He did not have to conform to French taste and compose the kind of long, spectacular ballet that had held up the action in the Paris versions of *I vespri siciliani*, *Don Carlos*, *Macbeth* or *Il trovatore*. He was free to write what he considered was necessary and no more; consequently the *ballabile* in this particular scene, instead of being an endless string of waltzes, adagios, variations, *pas de deux* and final galops, is written all of a piece—at one tempo, in one time, and lasting a bare four and a half minutes which Verdi crammed full of attractive and vigorous tunes in his own highly individual "exotic" idiom, decked out in all the contrasting colours created by brilliant orchestration in which piccolo and triangle seem to work overtime.

The ballet ends and the original march tempo is resumed. The chorus sings the tune of "Gloria all'Egitto" to new words—"Vieni, o guerriero . . ." ("Come, O warrior . . .")—as the stage fills with soldiers, war chariots, sacred vessels and statues of the gods. This is the first stage in the great choral sequence which builds up mainly on the Priests' theme and the women's tune in Ex 360, and culminates in a tremendous climax of "glorias" to greet the arrival of Radames standing under a canopy carried by twelve officers.

Pharaoh, with stage fanfares punctuating his words, comes down from his throne to greet Radames as the saviour of Egypt and bid him accept the victor's crown at the hands of Amneris. Radames

kneels before Amneris and receives the crown—a short and simple
ceremony performed to an echo of the theme heard at Amneris'
first entrance in Act I (Ex 341). It is played *ppp sotto voce* by the first
violins with an arpeggio accompaniment by a solo clarinet in its low
register, and sustained *ppp* notes by flutes and piccolo.

Pharaoh turns to Radames and as a further reward offers to grant
him any wish he may make. Radames' first wish is to have the
prisoners of war brought in. This is the cue for Ramfis and the
Priests to urge the populace once more to give thanks to the gods
for victory. This time their march-theme is sung *ppp* and *legato* in
unison, to another superbly "dark" orchestral accompaniment
reminiscent of the grim funeral march in the *auto-de-fé* scene in *Don
Carlos*. Tuba and bass drum beat out the rhythm *pianissimo*; clarinets,
bassoon and violas in unison double the voice part; and the three
trombones in a low register growl out a sinister crescendo on sustained notes. It is to this grim passage that the Ethiopian prisoners
are led in by the guards; the last of the group to enter is Amonasro,
dressed in the uniform of an ordinary Ethiopian officer.

Aida recognizes her father and rushes forward to embrace him;
he implores her in a whisper not to give him away. In answer to the
King's question, Amonasro explains that he is Aida's father, and he
goes on to invent (in considerable detail) a full and convincing story
of how the King of Ethiopia is supposed to have died. He tells it in
a brief and extremely dramatic passage of narrative notable in its
early passages for its punctuation by a couple of short, sudden and
ferociously *fortissimo* two-note unison tuttis.

Amonasro then turns to Pharaoh to beg for clemency for himself
and his fellow-prisoners in one of Verdi's most moving phrases accompanied, when it is first heard, by some characteristically lovely
writing for divided strings—"Ma tu, Re, tu signore possente . . ."
("But you, O King, who are so powerful . . ."):

Ex 362

Ma tu, Re, tu si-gno-re pos-sen-te, a co-sto-ro ti vol-gi cle-men-te

One of Verdi's greatest ensembles is built up from this tune of
Amonasro's. Aida echoes her father's entreaties, repeating his
words and music to a *dolcissimo* accompaniment mainly of woodwind
and horns, while slaves and prisoners add their supplications in the
background. This lyrical atmosphere is sharply interrupted by another fierce unison outburst from Ramfis and the Priests who demand that the prisoners shall pay the full penalty and be put to

death, or else the gods will be offended. The people of Thebes, however, take the side of the prisoners and plead with the King for clemency.

Radames, who has been silent so far, watches Aida anxiously and in a passionate aside declares how her sorrow makes her more beautiful, how each tear she sheds increases his love for her. Amneris, who has been jealously watching Radames, is filled with the vengeance and fury of a woman scorned. A half-way climax is reached, and after a moment of repose created by a short unaccompanied phrase sung by Aida the ensemble is resumed *ppp* with a return to the tune of "Ma tu, Re . . .". This time the movement works up with an even greater intensity and comes to a full, formal and *fortissimo* close.

Radames now turns to Pharaoh and reminds him of his promise to grant his wishes. Pharaoh says the promise is still valid. "Well then," says Radames, "I ask for the life and liberty of the Ethiopian prisoners."

This immediately brings loud cries of "Death to the enemy!" from the Priests, which are answered by a soft unison plea for mercy from the Egyptian crowd. Ramfis protests that it would be folly to free the prisoners; they would go back to their own country and invade Egypt again as soon as they were ready. Radames points out in reply that since the King of Ethiopia is dead there can hardly be much likelihood of that.

By way of compromise Ramfis suggests that, if the prisoners go free, Aida's father should be kept as hostage. Pharaoh considers this a reasonable solution and agrees; then, turning to Radames, to whom the country owes everything, he gives him the hand of Amneris as a reward, with the further promise that he shall eventually reign over Egypt with her. Only Amneris, of the three characters most affected by the King's action, reacts musically to this news in any way. In a fierce aside she exclaims: "Now let the slave try and steal him from me if she dare!"

Before anybody else can say anything we are back with the solemn rhythm of "Gloria all'Egitto", accompanied by the *banda* and sung not only by the Egyptian crowd but also by the Ethiopian slaves and prisoners who put their own words of thanksgiving and relief to it. Ramfis and the Priests continue with a *cantabile* unison in praise of Isis—a swinging kind of tune which in due course proves to be an ingenious counter-melody to "Gloria all'Egitto" which the listener can continue to sing when Aida and Radames, appalled by the turn things have taken, come out in unison with yet another stirring counter-melody to "Gloria all'Egitto".

In a quiet moment before the final stage of the Gran Finale Secondo is reached Amonasro whispers to Aida to take heart—their country's day of revenge is near. Aida, however, is not comforted; she foresees nothing but tears and oblivion.

The scene ends in the grandiose manner one would expect: in an all-out reprise of that "Gloria all'Egitto" which Verdi said he began to think sounded like the Marseillaise after a while. Populace and prisoners sing their respective words to it as before, Aida and Radames unite in their counter-melody, Ramfis and the Priests in theirs; Amneris, instead of muttering vengeance, is able at last to rejoice in her prospects. As the tempo becomes *più mosso* there is a brief and unexpected reappearance of the Priests' tune in its original form (Ex 339), but this is soon lost in the general excitement and working-up towards the instrumental coda in which the familiar strains of the Grand March are heard in the orchestra for the first time, while the *banda* and the A flat Egyptian trumpets contribute a series of triple-tongued B flats from the stage. The accident of this coda being in the key of E flat unfortunately prevents the B natural trumpets taking part, although one would have thought some work might have been found for their D sharps in the final bars of reiterated chords of E flat. In these four last bars, however, all the instruments on the stage are silent.

ACT III

Scene: The banks of the Nile. Granite rocks overgrown with palm trees. On the summit of the rocks is the Temple of Isis, half hidden by foliage. It is a starry night illuminated by brilliant moonlight.

The shimmer and colour, almost the scent, of the hot stars-and-moonlight night scene on which the curtain rises is created by the orchestra in one of the most original instrumental passages in the whole history of music.

The means Verdi employed were so simple that analysis is virtually pointless. All we can learn is that the composer used muted violins and violas, and unmuted violoncellos to play the note G in a variety of ways and registers. The first violins play their G's in this way:

Ex 363

The second violins play theirs as the uppermost note in a *ppp* fingered tremolo D″–G″. The violas play their three G's—G, G′, G″—pizzicato in groups of three *ppp* quavers. The violoncellos are divided into two parts; one half plays the highest practical harmonic G on the instrument (which, as Sir Henry Wood used to say, "gives off" the same note as the high G on the first violins); the other half plays the harmonic G an octave lower. The violoncellos sustain their harmonics without a break, the violins and violas repeat their figures, bar-in, bar-out, with the exception of a couple of bars when, in the second violins' tremolo, the D″ changes to E″. Against this indescribable rustling, whispering background a solo flute burbles in a languid rhapsodic kind of way to produce a sound apparently coming out of nowhere.

Having attempted to analyse this astonishing orchestral episode I realize that this is perhaps the only passage of Verdi's orchestration discussed in this book from which the student can learn nothing. In other instances the details of Verdi's use of instruments can be of practical value to anybody concerned with orchestration. But here, having learnt exactly how Verdi produced the sound he did, the knowledge is of absolutely no use except to somebody who wants to write the orchestral introduction to the third act of *Aida*.

As the flute finishes its long exotic solo, the violins and violas stop playing too. The violoncellos still hold their high harmonics, however, as the sole accompaniment to the sound of Priests praying in an eerie unison to the goddess in the Temple of Isis. After a brief solo a Priestess joins in with the Priests. Like the Priestesses' chanting in Act I, Scene 2, the distant chorus in this scene is wonderfully evocative of a remote and mysterious world, and one feels that if the sacred music of Ancient Egypt didn't sound like this then it should have done. While the chorus is singing a boat draws up at the shore; Amneris lands from it, accompanied by Ramfis and followed by guards and several heavily-veiled women.

From a brief passage of dialogue, full of that easy tunefulness peculiar to the "conversation music" of Verdi's last operas, we learn that it is Amneris' wedding eve and that she is to spend the night in the Temple in prayer to the goddess Isis. As she enters the Temple with Ramfis and her attendants the night music for strings and flute that began the scene is heard again, this time with the off-stage voices of two Priestesses instead of one, with the male chorus.

Once this extraordinary sound has died away Verdi does not return to it. There is no need to, for in an uncanny way it seems to stay in our subconscious ear for the rest of the scene—an indelible musical picture that forms a permanent backcloth to the action which follows.

For a moment after Amneris' departure the stage is empty; three flutes in unison play Aida's theme in a low register, accompanied by a high sustained G by two solo violins and murmured *sotto voce* figure in the violas. The passage ends with the flutes' last phrase repeated three times in octaves—a sombre sound produced by the flutes in unison, with the violas an octave below them and the violoncellos an octave below that. Aida enters cautiously; she is heavily veiled and apprehensive. She has come to meet Radames, and is afraid of what he will say to her; if it is farewell, she will throw herself in the Nile to find peace, for she feels in her heart that she will never see her native country again.

The word "nostalgia" has been so misused in the past thirty years and more that one hesitates to use it in its correct sense to describe the aria now sung by Aida. "Nostalgia" has come to mean anything from sentimental regret for a youthful love affair evoked by hearing a tune by Cole Porter or Rodgers and Hart, to a yearning for the dead distant days when whisky cost less than £2 a bottle. It has long since ceased to mean the homesickness and longing expressed by Aida in the heart-breaking soliloquy, "Oh patria mia, . . . mai più, mai più ti rivedrò!" ("Oh my homeland, never more shall I see thee . . .”). This exquisite scene is introduced by a passage on the oboe:

This wistful little tune, with the sinuous exotic line that characterized the flutes in Ex 349, is accompanied for the most part only by two clarinets, and frames Aida's desperately unhappy opening words which are heard again in this aria as a kind of refrain (Verdi used the French word *refrain* to describe it). Aida thinks longingly of the blue skies and soft breezes, the green hills and scented shores of her native land in a passage (referred to by the composer always as the "idillio") of quite astonishing beauty and originality—"O cieli azzurri, o dolci aure native . . ." ("O azure skies and sweet breezes . . ."):

The C sharp in the bars quoted above is marked by the composer to be "sfumato"—to evaporate like smoke. It is a direction underlined by the highly original orchestra accompaniment, a shimmering, misty affair of three flutes, a solo clarinet, and a solo bassoon. Strings playing *ppp* fingered tremolos are added as Aida sings of her native hills and shores to the phrase which is the "refrain" of the aria:

The first "verse" of the aria ends, after a passage of considerable pathos coloured by a solo oboe and a solo bassoon (in an unexpectedly high and effective register), with another despairing and extended cry of "O patria mia, mai più ti rivedrò !"

A shortened version of the oboe introduction (Ex 364) leads to the second "verse", in which Aida sings of the cool valleys of her home that she will never see now that her dreams have been shattered. The

orchestral accompaniment differs slightly this time in that the woodwind parts in the opening phrases are now overlaid with a series
of plaintive, whispered figures of almost chamber-music quality
played by a solo violoncello, two violas, two first violins and the
normal complement of seconds. The melancholy "middle" provided by the oboe and the bassoon is heard again but now leads
quickly to a couple of bars involving Aida in a high C to be sung
dolce before she comes down in a slow arpeggio sequence to complete
the cadence. There is a quiet brief echo of the oboe's introduction to
the scene and with a final pathetic repetition of the words of the
"refrain", set to a long phrase descending from, and returning to, a
high A, Aida ends what is one of the most moving and original
lyrical scenes in all Verdi.

In a hushed orchestral postlude a solo clarinet plays to the end of
the third bar of Ex 366, accompanied by flutes and the rustle of
strings, but is cut short as Aida turns round at the sound of footsteps,
and is surprised to see, not Radames, whom she expected, but her
father Amonasro approaching. Amonasro has followed her to enlist
her help; he has a plan which will enable her not only to defeat
Amneris but also to save her country.

Amonasro does not go into details immediately; he approaches
the subject slowly and skilfully, reminding Aida of their native
forests and valleys where she will be able to spend the rest of her
days with her lover—"Rivedrai le foreste . . ." ("You will see the
forests again . . ."):

Ex 367

Aida is immediately transported by her father's words and repeats
them to herself, looking forward ecstatically to "one enchanted day
. . . one day, one hour of such joy and then to die!"

In a sombre tone of voice Amonasro reminds Aida how the
Egyptians had raped and pillaged, and how they had destroyed their
beautiful buildings and temples. Aida says certainly she remembers.
In a broad, *cantabile* phrase (Ex 368), accompanied by some lovely

Ex 368

scoring of the tune an octave above, and a tenth below, the voice which is left unmolested in its own register, Aida exclaims: "Deh! fate, o Numi, che per noi ritorni . . ." ("Grant, ye gods, that peaceful days will dawn again for us . . .").

This warm lyrical mood is interrupted for Amonasro to tell Aida that the Ethiopians have been mobilized again and Radames is to lead the Egyptians against them once more. Everything is ready, continues Amonasro, except for the definite information about which route the enemy is to take into Ethiopia. If this can be discovered, it will enable the Ethiopians to ambush the Egyptian army. Only one person can get this information: Aida. Horror-struck by her father's suggestion, Aida cries that she will never do this.

Amonasro turns savagely on his daughter, and in a vigorous 6/8 passage, in which his fury is matched by some ferocious trills and runs in the horns and trumpets and valve trombones, sarcastically bids the Egyptian armies invade the homeland—there is nothing to stop them. With ever-increasing anger he tells Aida of the spirits of the defeated Ethiopians who will haunt her, crying: "Through you our country dies!"

Dropping his voice and accompanied by the dark tones of bassoons, violas and violoncellos, Amonasro tells his daughter of the one spirit that stands apart from the rest to curse her—her mother. "In the utmost terror" Aida breaks down and begs her father for pity. "You are not my daughter. You are the slave of the Pharaohs!" Amonasro repulses her "with such violence", according to Verdi's production notes, that he throws her to the ground.

Aida, prostrate at his feet, begs her father not to curse her; she is his daughter and she will be worthy of her country. Aida's pleas are made to music of almost unbearable sadness—an elegiac minor passage beginning with a syncopated monotone *ostinato*, marked to be played *pppp* by the violins, through which a mournful tune gradually emerges, played in unison by bassoon, violas and violoncellos.*

The rather halting tune with which Aida gradually calms her father's fears merges into Amonasro's "Pensa che un popolo, vinto, straziato, per te soltanto risorger può" ("Remember that a defeated and tormented people can rise again only through you"):

* The tremendous emotional effect of the violins' repeated A flats has perhaps never been more clearly and dramatically realized—both in the sense of being understood and made real—than in Toscanini's astonishing recorded performance of the opera, where the passage is quite uncannily moving. (See *The Toscanini Legacy*, p 270.)

This phrase is famous, of course, for its great resemblance to the first four bars of the main lyrical theme in *La forza del destino* (Ex 255), but where the rhythmic pattern is identical in both cases, it will be noticed that Amonasro's tune goes its own way from the third bar onwards, the remainder of the eight-bar phrase being altogether different, as the listener to *Aida* will quickly hear.

Even with this slight change of mood and key, the syncopated violin figure still goes on; but now, after sixteen slow bars of 129 A flats, it rises step by step, a tone or a semitone at a time, in a gradual crescendo; the key reverts to the minor as Aida, with great pathos, exclaims in long, affecting phrases, "O my country, what you are costing me!" The music dies away with the sudden *ppp* that follows the crescendo; Amonasro whispers that Radames is approaching, and telling Aida to have courage, hides himself among the palm trees where he can hear everything.

Radames, after a few bars of muffled excitement in the orchestra, enters to a fine enthusiastic phrase—"Pur ti reveggo, mia dolce Aida" ("At last I see you again, beloved Aida"):

Ex 370

Aida's reception of her lover is rather lukewarm. She reminds him that he is betrothed to Amneris and that their position is hopeless. Radames' enthusiasm is not damped; he fervently declares his love again, in spite of Aida's insistence that everything is against them. Radames replies with the proposal of a plan he has made to solve all difficulties. Egypt is at war again, and when victory has been won he will ask Pharaoh for Aida's hand as his reward—a naïvely optimistic plan, surely, after being given Pharaoh's daughter with so much ceremony only a little while previously. Radames' talk of war is emphasized by the distant martial sound of trumpets, playing very softly against a background of pizzicato strings:

Ex 371

Allegro giusto

leggerissimo e staccato

"You will be the crown of all my glory and we will live happily for ever more," cries Radames, bursting out once more with the elation

of Ex 370. But Aida is not convinced by the plan, and with the
orchestra playing Amneris' "jealousy theme" (Ex 342) she tells
Radames how the Princess's vengeance is bound to fall on herself
and her father. The only thing for them to do is to fly from Egypt.
Radames is thunderstruck.

A lone plaintive oboe plays a rather pastoral tune in the background as Aida declares *sotto voce parlante* that they must flee to a
new land which is waiting to welcome them. The oboe introduction,
as it did earlier, leads to another outstanding lyrical passage; to the
striking accompaniment of three flutes (which I have indicated in
the quotation below) Aida gives a ravishing account of her native
land, of the ecstasy and happiness that can be found there in surroundings where the outside world can be forgotten—"Là, tra
foreste vergini . . ." ("There, in the virgin forests . . ."):

Ex 372

Radames, instead of being attracted by Aida's proposal, is scepti-
cal. How, he asks sadly, can he fly to a strange land, leaving behind
him the gods he has worshipped and turn his back on the scene of
his triumphs? How can he forget the country under whose skies he
first loved Aida? Radames asks his questions in the phrase:*

Ex 373

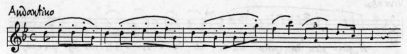

Once more Aida sings her seductive description of the virgin
forests—the same words, the same tune, but this time with some *pp*
string effects (pizzicato, tremolo) added to the three-flute accompaniment, and some disjointed repetition by Radames of the line
about forgetting the sky that witnessed their love. Aida does not
allow these comments to interrupt her but continues her lovely tune

* If, to those who have not heard *Aida* before, the first two bars of this tune
sound a little familiar, it may be because they were used some years ago as the
opening phrase of an American popular song called "I'll String Along With
You". The words ran something like "You may not be an angel, for angels are so
few . . . But until the day that one comes along, I'll string along with you." One
encounters Verdi in the strangest places.

to the end. Radames now repeats his question *con forza*, and what is surely one of the most fatuous questions ever asked by any operatic lover gets a straight answer. It is a fatuous question, of course, because nobody but a fool would go on so irrelevantly asking how he can possibly forget the place he first fell in love with his mistress when he has been offered the chance of spending the rest of his life with her elsewhere.

Firmly, in the mood and manner of Radames' first asking of the question (Ex 373), Aida tells her lover that under her native sky they can love freely and unconcerned and—since this is one of the questions that first worried Radames, though he has not mentioned it for some time—they can worship the same gods in the temples. Radames remains unconvinced, and the first part of a long and superbly lyrical scene comes to an end with him in as pessimistic a mood as ever, and Aida quietly trying to reassure him on the question of the gods. In a final arpeggio, ascending softly to a high B flat, she pleads with him to fly—"Fuggiam, fuggiam . . ."

Radames turns hesitantly to Aida. She tells him sharply to go; he doesn't love her. Let him go back to Amneris who is waiting for him at the altar, and leave her and her father to their fate. Like Amonasro's angry taunt that Aida was no better than an Egyptian slave, Aida's fierce words to Radames do the trick and the situation is at once transformed. In a flash Radames makes up his mind and exclaims with such *appassionata risoluzione* that one might think it was Aida, not him, who had been vacillating all along—"Sì, fuggiam da queste mura . . ." ("Yes, let us flee from these walls . . ."):

Ex *374*

In the accompaniment behind this passionate outburst there are some busy and effective eight-in-a-bar pizzicato passages for violas and violoncellos each divided into two groups. The first half of the bar is played by one group, the second half by the other—a thoroughly professional division of labour by a thoughtful composer who did not want to exhaust his players in a sequence which, if played by *tutti*, would inevitably have ended in a scramble.

The enthusiasm of Radames' acceptance of Aida's proposal is such that he, too, begins to talk of the endless desert that will be their bridal bed and the stars that will shine above them. Aida takes up the tune to paint a rosier picture of what lies ahead in the country "where the breeze is sweet-scented and the earth fragrant

with flowers". Cool valleys and green meadows, she says, will be
their bridal couch. The duet ends with the lovers singing the same
words to the same music in a brief coda based on a rather unexpected
return to the tune Radames sang so enthusiastically on his entrance
(Ex 370)—to suggest perhaps that optimism is in the air once more.

As the lovers turn away quickly to leave, Aida stops and asks
Radames which road they are going to take so as to avoid meeting
the Egyptian army. Radames replies that the Egyptians are planning to use the Napata Gorge—but not until tomorrow.

Amonasro steps from the shadows and echoes the words: "The
Napata Gorge". Horrified, Radames asks who it is has been listening, and receives the dramatic reply from Amonasro: "Aida's
father and King of Ethiopia!"

"You! Amonasro!" whispers Radames incredulously. "You!
The King?"—a short disjointed sentence broken by alternating *pp*
and *ff* comments by the strings. Radames cannot believe what he
has done is true; it is a dream. Aida and Amonasro try to calm him,
telling him to trust in Aida's love and he will gain a throne—words
that are sung to a quite beautiful phrase which Verdi uses twice and
then wantonly discards:

Ex 375

Radames is not to be consoled, however. He has betrayed his
country through his love for Aida, and throughout the short trio
which develops repeatedly proclaims his bitter feeling of shame with
"Io son disonorato!" ("I am dishonoured!"):

Ex 376

Aida continues to try to comfort her lover, while Amonasro
assures him that he is not a traitor; it was the will of Fate. Telling
him that all will be well Amonasro takes Radames by the arm and is
on the point of dragging him away when Amneris appears suddenly
from the temple and denounces Radames as a traitor.

Amonasro draws a dagger and rushes to stab Amneris, but
Radames steps between them, urging Aida and her father to escape.
At this moment Ramfis enters, and calling the guards from the
Temple tells them to follow Amonasro and Aida.

Amneris, Radames and Ramfis are left alone on the stage. Radames turns to Ramfis and says in a firm voice: "Priest, I am yours." The curtain falls.

It is perhaps inevitable that one should remember the Nile Scene more for the sheer magic of the opening and the lyrical beauty of Aida's "O patria mia" and "Là, tra foreste vergini" than for anything else, for these are among Verdi's most inspired moments. But it is also an act in which Verdi reaches great heights of characterization and dramatic tension. It is in this act that the conflict between Love and Duty increases in intensity. Radames has been involved in it all along; now it faces Aida as well, and she finds herself torn between her duty to her father and her country and her love for Radames, as Radames is torn between his love for Aida and his duty as a soldier.

Amonasro alone is free to pursue relentlessly his single goal—the defeat of his country's enemies. That there is a gentle side to his nature we heard in his dignified plea to Pharaoh in the second act. But it hardly shows through in his relationship with Aida in the Nile Scene. He is stern and harsh with her in his insistence that she shall help him in his task; and even his promises to her, made to the lovely tune of "Rivedrai le foreste" (Ex 367) are primarily a bribe. The fragrant forests are soon forgotten when Aida refuses to co-operate; he then denounces her as the slave of the Pharaohs. Amonasro, one of the most powerful of all Verdi's characterizations, may be Aida's father, but he shows little of the sincere paternal affection or concern for his daughter's happiness shown by Rigoletto (who is every bit as vindictive in his way as Amonasro) and Simon Boccanegra. Even when he takes a knife to kill Amneris Amonasro tells us it is because she is spoiling his plans; he is not attacking her to remove his daughter's rival.

From what we see of him Amonasro has dignity and tenacity; he is a man obsessed by the determination to avenge his country's defeat, and he concentrates on that object with a ferocious single-mindedness to the exclusion of all else. In less harassing circumstances he is probably a different man; as we know him he lacks genuine tenderness and does not arouse compassion.

ACT IV

Scene 1 : A Hall in the King's Palace. On the left, a great door leads to the underground Hall of Judgment. On the right, a passage leads to the prison in which Radames is confined.

The curtain rises with a brief descending passage for unison woodwind in octaves played by piccolo, two flutes, two clarinets (who all end up in their lowest register) and two bassoons. These seven bars, which are followed by a silent bar, have no thematic significance; but their unusual sound creates an unmistakable feeling of tension, and leads into a repetition of Amneris' "jealousy theme" (Ex 342) played *pp* by first violins only, accompanied *ppp* by a quaver figure on the flutes and sustained notes by the piccolo. Amneris' theme is developed briefly in the strings and the short instrumental introduction ends with the first few notes of the woodwind unison.

Amneris is discovered crouching mournfully by the door leading to the underground chamber. She is in a state of complete bewilderment; her rival has escaped. Radames is awaiting sentence as a traitor. "But he is not a traitor!" she cries. Then: "But he gave away the great secret of the war. He wanted to fly with *her*. They are all traitors! Death to them! Death to them!" She pulls herself up: "Oh, what am I saying?"

The urgency and bitterness goes out of her voice, and accompanied only by the strings playing the warm lyrical tune of what can be called her "love-for-Radames-theme" (Ex 341), Amneris sings *con passione* of the hopeless, insane love that is destroying her life. She wants to save him, but how? She calls the guards and orders them to bring in Radames.

Radames is brought in to the sound of the short, unexpectedly Wagnerian orchestral passage so clearly anticipated in the Paris revision of *Macbeth* (see p 56 and Ex 23 and 24), which is played *f* by two oboes, cor anglais and first violins tremolo in unison. The Wagnerian flavour of the episode in *Aida* is further emphasized by a couple of unaccompanied bars for bass clarinet which, like the cor anglais, is making its first appearance in this score.

Amneris beseeches Radames to save himself by pleading his case —"Già i sacerdoti adunansi . . ." ("The Priests are already sitting in judgment . . ."):

Ex 377

The bass clarinet, with a triplet arpeggio figure, plays a prominent part in the accompaniment to this, which also includes dramatic
_pp_ punctuation by trumpets and bass drum, and some effective
echoing of the voice by cor anglais. From E flat minor the key
changes to F sharp minor for Radames to take up Amneris' phrase,
and with virtually the same accompaniment, to tell her that his
conscience is clear. He admits he disclosed an important military
secret, but he denies that he did so with any treasonable intent.
"Then save yourself!" begs Amneris. "No," replied Radames. "Life
holds nothing for me and I would rather die."

Amneris, in a passionate declaration of her love for Radames offers to
give up her throne, her country, even life itself for his sake—"Ah! tu
dêi vivere! . . ." ("You must live, for my love you shall live . . .") :

Ex 378

Radames, echoing the first two bars of Amneris' phrase, retorts
that he has already given everything for the one he loves; dishonour
awaits him, and now Amneris wants him to live. In a few bars of
great bitterness, to the tune of Ex 377 (with the cor anglais now
playing a bigger part in an outstanding accompaniment), Radames
accuses Amneris not only of having caused him infinite misery, but
of having killed Aida—and in return she wants to offer him his life.

Aida is not dead, exclaims Amneris; Amonasro was killed, but
his daughter escaped. In a rather churchy phrase accompanied by
strings, Radames prays that Aida will reach her native country
safely, and that she will never learn that he died for her sake.

Amneris again offers to save Radames' life—on condition that he
never sees Aida again. Once more Radames refuses; he is ready to
die. Amneris' pleading now turns to fury; in a superbly angry outburst she declares her hatred of Radames, and calls with growing
intensity on heaven to avenge her tears—a climax which includes
an effective and unexpected trill for two trumpets. Radames remains

Ex 379

unmoved and in another phrase with a quaintly Wagnerian outline to
it (Ex 379), repeats that he looks forward to the joy that death will
give him.

The duet ends stormily with Amneris crying once more that
heaven will avenge her tears, and Radames proclaiming that he
does not fear human wrath; he fears only Amneris' pity. Amneris
collapses helplessly in a chair as Radames is led away by the guards
to a tremendous syncopated orchestral coda.

After a short silence there now follows what is called in the score
the Judgment Scene and which begins with the Priests' theme
(Ex 339) played only by muted double basses whose phrases are
punctuated at intervals by the sombre sound of long single notes
from three unison trombones *ppp* in their low register. Against this
grim background Amneris, alone and "in the greatest despair",
begins to realize what she has done and curses the insane jealousy
which has made her abandon Radames to the Priests.

Amneris' tearful and pathetic reflections are accompanied by the
Priests' theme which is repeated in unison with little variation by
muted violins and violoncellos and supported, in due course, by a
clarinet and a bassoon in the same register. The addition of a
steady percussive pattern of *pp* quavers played by bassoons, horn,
tuba and timpani, gives the music something of the character of a
funeral march—an impression strengthened by the appearance of
the Priests in procession, who cross the stage and enter the underground judgment chamber. Amneris sees them and bitterly calling
them the "ministers of death", covers her face with her hands to
avoid looking at "those white phantoms". The funeral march
rhythm is relaxed and with a final repetition of the Priests' theme by
muted violins in unison with a solo flute in its low register, the
movement ends in a string coda of startling harmonic originality,
in which Amneris once more reflects disconsolately that she herself is responsible for delivering Radames into the hands of the
Priests.

From the underground hall comes the voices of the Priests led by
Ramfis praying for heaven's guidance in a unison chant (without
time signature) sung by basses only. In despair Amneris calls on the
gods to have pity on her and save the innocent Radames.

Amneris' supplication is drowned by the Priests' theme, played
now in A minor *tutta forza* by the orchestra, as Radames is taken
across the scene by guards and disappears into the underground
Hall of Justice. The Priests' theme is played in a harsh, brutal form
almost in unison except for the addition of bare, repeated E's by
woodwind, horns and trumpets, supporting Amneris' cry of "Who
will save him?" as she catches sight of Radames, and repeated A's
from the Priests below ground which are doubled by four unison

trumpets and four unison trombones who, with a bass drum, are
also placed underground.

The scene which now follows is a superb piece of Theatre. Amneris is alone on the stage; from the depths she hears the voice of
Ramfis, intoning the name of Radames. In a monotone the High
Priest calls the name three times; the third time the rhythm of the
three syllables of "Radames" is repeated in unison octaves by the
trumpets and trombones underground. Ramfis charges Radames with
having betrayed his country's secrets to the enemy: "Defend yourself!" "Defend yourself!" echo the Priests.

There is no answer except the roll of the bass drum underground.
"He is silent," says Ramfis. "Traitor!" cry the Priests.

When Amneris, listening apprehensively to the trial conducted
below ground, hears the Priests' accusation she pours out her
anguish and despair in a phrase ending with that wonderfully
characteristic sobbing cadence heard in Azucena's "E tu non vieni"
(Ex 116), and the Miserere in *Il trovatore*, in Violetta's "Amami,
Alfredo!" (Ex 151) in *La traviata*—"Ah pietà! egli è innocente,
Numi pietà . . ." ("Have pity, he is innocent. Ye gods have
pity . . ."):

Ex 380

Ramfis indicts Radames twice more, charging him with deser-
tion from the army and with betraying his King, country and
honour. Each time Radames is silent; the drum rolls, the Priests
cry, "Traitor!" and Amneris sobs her moving, desperate, "Ah
pietà!"

The form of these two sequences follows the same routine as
the first, but the tension of the scene is imperceptibly increased
as each indictment, and its imitation by the trumpets and trombones underground, each response by the Priests and each outcry
by Amneris is raised by a semitone.

When, for the third time, Radames remains silent, Ramfis and the
Priests, in a powerful unison passage punctuated by great crashing
chords in the orchestra, pronounce him guilty and he is sentenced
to be buried alive. The two conventionally loud and dramatic orchestral bars that follow the Priests' last words have little musical
distinction, but the first of them is notable for the inclusion for the
second time in a Verdi score of a "tam-tam" or gong. It is given one

note to play on the heavily accented second beat of the bar. It is
an unexpected appearance.

Amneris, whose anger on hearing the sentence pronounced is
reflected in these two bars, flies into a range, cursing the Priests
whose lust for blood is never satisfied and who dare call themselves
Ministers of Heaven.

Ramfis and the Priests emerge from the Hall of Judgment, marching to a *ff* and subtly distorted version of the Priests' theme played in
unison by two clarinets, bassoon, four horns, violins, violas and
violoncellos. Double basses playing tremolo and divided in two
parts, bassoon, tuba, and a sustained low note played by three
unison trombones provide a sinister and disquieting harmonic
background to the tune. Monotonously the Priests repeat the one
word "Traitor!" Amneris turns on them in a fury to accuse them
of having outraged divine and human justice by their condemnation
of an innocent man. Her anger is superbly reflected in the ferocious
orchestral accompaniment which includes some more effectively-
used trills in the trumpets. The Priests answer: "He is a traitor and
shall die!"

To the same music Amneris addresses Ramfis, warning him that
she loved the man they have condemned and that the curses of her
broken heart will fall upon their heads. Unmoved, Ramfis and the
Priests inexorably repeat that Radames is a traitor and must die.

In a poignant passage Amneris repeats her accusation that the
Priests have outraged divine and human justice by condemning an
innocent man:

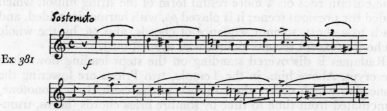

Ex 381

This warm, expansive phrase is doubled in an infectiously *cantabile*
manner, either an octave above, an octave below, or in the same
register as, the voice, by virtually every instrument in the orchestra
capable of playing a tune, including first and second horns. The
harmony is left to third and fourth horns, the second bassoon, tuba,
violas and divided double basses; in the second four bars piccolo
and trumpets support the tune and trombones are added to provide
richness to the harmony.

The music grows more excited as Amneris firmly denies the
Priests' repeated assertion of Radames' guilt. Amneris begs them to

14

have pity, but once again they answer, "Traitor!" As the Priests leave the scene, their sinister, unemotional repetition of the word "traditor" gradually growing fainter, Amneris rises to invoke the curse of Heaven on them and rushes wildly from the scene. The coda to which the curtain falls is astonishingly harsh and dramatic, consisting of virtually no more than the following phrase played three times by the strings in unison—

Ex 382

—while the rest of the orchestra alternates short, sharp unison A's on the first beat of the bar with sustained shakes and piercing trills from the woodwind helped by the trumpets.

The passage comes to an abrupt, shattering end, helped by another note on the tam-tam, which now holds its peace until it is heard again in the opening pages of *Otello*.

Scene 2 : The stage is divided into two floors. The upper floor represents the interior of the Temple of Vulcan, resplendent with gold and brilliant light. The lower floor is a crypt, with long arcades disappearing into the darkness. Colossal statues of Osiris, with crossed hands, support the pillars of the vault.

The curtain rises on a more restful form of the string unison which ended the previous scene; it is played *pp*, with harmonies added, and leads to a short, solemn sequence of chords, also *pp*, by the whole orchestra (except second violins, who are left out).

Radames is discovered standing on the steps leading down into the crypt. Above him, in the Temple, two Priests are lowering the stone slab which covers the entrance to the vault. In a monotone, punctuated from time to time by sombre brass chords (horns, trumpets, one trombone) and the tune of Ex 382, now played *pianissimo* and sometimes in an altered form, by strings in unison once more, Radames resigns himself to his fate in the dark vault which is to be his tomb. He reflects that he will never see Aida again and prays that she will live happily in ignorance of his fate.

As he utters these words Aida herself comes out of the shadows, making her entrance to a tense and rapid string figure (violins, violas and violoncellos only) which builds up in a fierce crescendo, as Radames gradually realizes, in "massima disperazione", who is with him in the tomb.

Aida explains how she had foreseen what was to happen to her

lover and had concealed herself in the vault so that she could die in
his arms. This short and moving narrative, ranging from "triste" to
"con passione" and a final "dolce allargando", is accompanied by
the repeated, *ppp* sound of minims played twice in a bar, on the
lowest D's of clarinet, bassoon, violas and violoncellos; the mournful
character of the passage is increased by the elegiac beats of a bass
drum and double bass pizzicato.*

The mournful hollow sound of the clarinet's bottom register is
not so clearly marked in this passage as it was in *Un ballo in maschera*,
La forza del destino, and *Don Carlos*, for it is partly obscured by the
violas whose doubling of the same note brings additional melancholy
to the music.

When Aida tells Radames of her intention to die with him, he
replies with a short and lovely tune full of sadness that she, who is
still so young and beautiful, should die for his sake: "Morir! sì pura
e bella . . ." ("To die, so innocent and beautiful . . ."):

Although Radames is instructed in the first bar to sing *con passione*,
his feelings are expressed in a passage of particular restraint and
lyrical beauty, against a simple background of pizzicato strings with
occasional support from two clarinets in thirds to underline the
melody marked by the composer to be sung successively "dolciss.
senza string.", "con espress." and "dim. con grazia dolciss. e
legato".

From A flat the music modulates in copybook fashion to D flat
and to the first of those passages of "vaporous" scoring which Verdi
was so anxious to hear about after the first orchestral rehearsal in
Cairo—the accompaniment to Aida's "Vedi? di morte l'angelo . . ."
("Do you see? The angel of death approaches us . . ."):

Ex 384

* In the small Ricordi orchestral score of 1913, which has served many interested
people for a long time, the clarinet part throughout this passage on page 424
should be played on a B flat clarinet, not a clarinet in C as shown in the score,
thus making the low E which is printed there sound the D the composer intended.
(The C clarinet does not normally go down to D; E is its lowest note.)

Aida is described in the score at this point as "vaneggiando"; in other words, she is delirious, and it is the peculiar light-headedness and unreality of what she sings that is so superbly reflected in the accompaniment.*

The "vaporous" quality Verdi aimed at is achieved by some original and effective *pp* writing for the strings. The first violins are muted and divided into altogether seven parts; "six or eight first violins" play legato quavers in a high register, the remaining six, divided into three parts, follow the line of Aida's melody, but each part is played in two different ways—the first player at each desk playing the notes with the bow while his partner plays pizzicato. For the rest, the remaining strings contribute a *pp* pizzicato and (second violins and violas) occasional bars of even quieter—*ppp*—tremolando; the notes played by the six divided first violins are doubled by a flute and two clarinets, the harp adds some simple and clearly audible arpeggios in the right hand, horns and bassoons play the odd quaver or sustained note. The first of Verdi's "vaporous" passages comes off with all the *effetto* he can have hoped for.

Aida's wanderings are interrupted by the grim reality of the voices of the Priestesses and Priests in the Temple. The Priestesses chant the invocation to Phthà which opened Act I, Scene 2, but on this occasion the off-stage harp, instead of playing un-arpeggioed chords (or whatever the English equivalent of a chord played *non arpeggiato* can be), spreads the open fifths of D flat and A flat across two and a half octaves in the steady four-in-a-bar already familiar from the earlier scene. The same open fifths are also sustained on "Ah" by four tenors and basses of the Priests for five bars as a background to the Priestesses—singing, as Aida laments, "our hymn of death".

---

* In a letter written on 10th December, 1871, to Bottesini in Cairo Verdi wrote: "I ask you warmly to give me news of the final duet when you have had two or three rehearsals with the orchestra. . . . Reading the score you will know that I have taken every care in this duet; but because it has what one might call a *vaporoso* quality, it could well happen that the effect isn't what I wanted. So tell me honestly the whole truth, so that the truth will be useful to me. Tell me only about the 3/4 in D flat (Aida's passage) and the duet in G flat. Tell me about the vocal and instrumental parts from the point of view of the *effect* . . ."

Verdi received no reply to his questions, so on thanking Bottesini for his telegram after the première, he raised the matter again in a letter of 27th December, 1871: "I was interested and I'm still interested to have exact and detailed news of the *effect* of the last piece. Please understand I am not referring to the merit of the music but only to its *effect*. If you haven't already written, write to me at length about this and tell me the whole truth. I want to know which were the orchestral effects, which the vocal, and above all the over-all effect, or alternatively what impression it made . . ."

I have been unable to trace the text of Bottesini's reply, but from a letter written by Verdi in January 1872 to thank him for "the observations of your last two letters, from which I shall profit", it seems that his answers had set the composer's mind at rest.

With a desperate effort Radames struggles to lift the stone away
from the entrance to the vault, and for a brief moment the hushed
near-silence is disturbed by a sudden *ff* phrase from the invocation
sung by Priests in unison with the Priestesses, and emphasized by a
couple of loud beats on the kettle drum and *fortissimo* open fifths
played by the orchestral harp and pizzicato strings.

Radames fails to move the stone; he sinks back, exhausted and
without hope, and the music dies down again; the three flutes in
unison play the sinuous, exotic tune of Ex 349 as Aida and Radames
recognize that everything on earth has come to an end for them.

Once more the music modulates in a discreet, copybook manner,
from D flat to G flat and to the final sequence of the opera—the
farewell sung by the doomed lovers to the world and its vale of
tears—"O terra, addio; addio; addio valle di pianti . . .":

Ex 385

O terra, od - dio; addi - o val - le di pian-ti...

This tune, sung first by Aida, is accompanied by the second
passage of the "vaporous" scoring Verdi was so anxious about. This
time even less seems to happen in the orchestra. To begin with the
second violins are left out altogether; instead, the first violins are
divided into two sections, and with the violoncellos produce a series
of whispered harmonics, sometimes sustained, sometimes played
tremolo. The violas and a solo double bass supply soft pizzicato notes
on the strong beats of the bar, the harp supplying chords on the
weak beats. There are occasional *ppp* held notes for the flute (on its
bottom D flat), the two clarinets, and an important part emerges
for a solo bassoon.

When Radames repeats the tune the second violins join in with
fingered tremolos, first violins and violoncellos adopt a new figure
for their series of harmonics an octave apart from each other, and
after a silence of four bars or so the woodwind repeat their delicate
and effective accompaniment to Radames' closing phrases.

The duet is interrupted for a moment by a loud unison from both
Priests and Priestesses, who sing the second bar of the original tune
(Ex 347) three times invoking "Immenso Fthà", accompanied by *ff*
octaves in both hands of the off-stage harpist, and a low D flat sustained in unison by the three flutes in the orchestra—a sinister
sound which carries as clearly as a trumpet.

The flutes revert once more to their exotic unison triplets (Ex 349)
as Amneris enters the Temple. She is dressed in deep mourning and
throws herself on the stone over the entrance to the vault, as Aida

and Radames repeat "O terra, addio" in unison. With a voice "suffocated by tears" Amneris prays in a monotone that Isis will grant peace to the man she has loved and sent to his death.

In the final twenty bars of *Aida* Verdi abandons his "vaporous" orchestration in favour of a more conventional but no less effective method of scoring.* First and second violins, each divided into two parts, have abandoned their mutes and with the violas play a series of straightforward tremolo passages which follow a remarkable two-bar pattern of subtle dynamic changes from *pp* to *f* to *ppp*. The full complement of woodwind and horns is frequently used in support, and all the double basses, instead of just one, now play the intermittent pizzicato notes. Only the violoncellos, with a series of harmonics, preserve anything of the score's earlier ethereal atmosphere.

As Aida and Radames end their long unison, the Priests and Priestesses are heard singing a couple of bars of their invocation in harmony for the first time, and while the off-stage harp provides its regular four-in-a-bar accompaniment, the orchestral harp can be heard playing single notes in unison first with the flute, then with the bassoon—an effect of orchestration which one would swear had not been invented until many years after *Aida* was written. With a final hint in the background of the three flutes' unison temple theme coming to a full close, Aida and Radames sing their last words. Aida falls lifeless in her lover's arms, and we come to what might be called the coda of the whole opera.

The first violins (who, like the seconds, have now replaced their mutes) echo the last phrase of "O terra, addio"; they play it *ppp* an octave higher than it was sung by Aida and against a whispered tremolo background of violas and divided second violins. Amneris intones her prayer to Isis—"Pace t'imploro—pace t'imploro—pace —pace—pace." The end of the opera comes with Amneris' final long-drawn "pace". In the background the Priests and Priestesses chant "Immenso Fthà!", the off-stage harp plucks four final chords, and the orchestra sustains a long *ppp* chord of G flat—strings, woodwind, horns, timpani, and a *tremolando* harp.

The unique character of the final curtain of *Aida* is in its way subtly typical of a work which is perhaps the most original of all Verdi's operas. It is not just the setting, the endless melodic invention or the splendidly vivid harmonic and instrumental colouring of

---

* I have analysed the earlier orchestration of this scene so closely because, unlike the opening of the Nile Scene, from which, as I suggested, the student of orchestration could learn little that would enable him to do more than reproduce exactly the sounds Verdi made, the "vaporous" passages are full of instructive details. The variety of writing for strings, and the telling simplicity of Verdi's treatment of the woodwind are masterly. These are pages from which all orchestrators may learn.

the music that are new and striking; there are to be heard in *Aida*
long stretches of a musical language which, while unmistakably
Verdi's own, is entirely peculiar to this opera. The Nile Scene, the
temple chants, the dance of the Priestesses are completely spontaneous musical creations, having neither precedent nor posterity;
they were invented exclusively for *Aida*, and it seemed that having
served their purpose they disappeared without trace from Verdi's
musical world.

Though its foundations may be considered to have been laid by
Rossini with his Paris operas, *Le Siège de Corinthe* (1826), *Moïse* (1827)
and *William Tell* (1829), Grand Opera developed into an essentially
French operatic form, the principal features of which were spectacular staging, endless irrelevant ballets and a general, appalling
musical and dramatic prolixity.

We have seen the results of Verdi's experience of what he called
"La Grande Boutique" in *Don Carlos*, which was insufferably long
as first written for Paris in 1867, awkward and unsatisfactory in its
truncated Italian four-act form of 1884, and most fully effective only
when in 1887 Verdi combined the best of the first two editions in a
third version in five acts. That Verdi had nothing against the
medium of Grand Opera, only against what the French made of it,
is clear enough in the letter to Du Locle quoted on page 378, in
which he discussed the possibilities of *Nerone* as a grand opera "done
in my own manner". The commission to write *Aida* for Cairo at last
enabled him to produce a Grand Opera in his own manner, allowing him to strip the original French model of its irrelevancies, and
impose on it the much-needed discipline of his own dramatic tempo
and sense of dramatic proportion.

When Verdi had finished nobody could say that *Aida* did not conform to the rules—it had a ballet, triumphal procession and a final
scene of great ingenuity which, if it wasn't blown sky-high like the
last scene of *Le Prophète*, was mechanically as well as dramatically a
highly original conception. *Aida* not only conformed to the rules but
proved to be the greatest and most successful Grand Opera of all,
from which not a bar needs to be cut, nor can be cut without up-
setting the musical and dramatic balance of the whole and depriving
listeners of rich musical experience.

Its appeal is uniquely universal. It can stupefy the senses produced
in the spectacular elephants-and-cast-of-thousands manner of the
Baths of Caracalla or the Verona Arena; it can touch the heart performed as it used to be at the Old Vic more than forty years ago,
when my local wine merchant was in the chorus and marched in
full black-face across the stage as a triumphant Egyptian warrior,
then dashed behind the backcloth, changed his headdress, and re-
appeared to march across the stage as an Ethiopian prisoner.

It is an opera on an heroic scale, of emotional conflicts which, though they appear to be larger than life, are none the less recognizably human. Radames and Aida may be involved in a conflict between Love and Duty worthy of the French classical drama (Mariette, after all, was a countryman of Racine and Corneille), but they suffer, and move us, as human beings. Amneris, the most human figure of all, suffers more than either of them, for her conflict is concerned only with a hopeless love and its consequences—jealousy, hatred and final remorse. Aida and Radames resolve their conflict and die happy; but Amneris survives and experiences all the agony of survival in a world without hope. She is not even spared the humiliation of believing she has lost Radames to her own slave, for she never learns Aida's true identity. Just as Amonasro, in Frank Walker's words, "almost bursts out of the frame of the picture", so Amneris emerges from the pages of *Aida* as one of Verdi's most brilliantly successful characterizations. Where Aida is one of those people to whom things happen, Amneris is constantly active—her moods changing swiftly and unpredictably from passion to bewilderment, from despair to frustration, from vindictiveness to deepest sorrow. She is a fascinatingly human figure.

OTELLO

(*Property of G. Ricordi and Co.*)

Opera in four acts after Shakespeare. Libretto by Arrigo Boito. First performed at La Scala, Milan, on 5th February, 1887. First performance in England: Lyceum Theatre, London, 5th July, 1889 (by a company from La Scala). First performance in the United States: Academy of Music, New York, 16th April, 1888.

"PASSING over *Montezuma* in five acts, which Verdi completed in 1878, and which was given for the first time at La Scala, Milan, we come to the master's next great Shakespearian setting—*Otello*."

These words, from Frederick J. Crowest's *Verdi : Man and Musician*, are surely the most intriguing in all Verdi literature. Apart from the idea of "passing over" any five-act opera Verdi might have written between *Aida* and *Otello* in so superbly casual a manner, it is a sentence full of puzzling features. What on earth made Crowest pick on Montezuma as a likely theme for this fictitious opera? In his time Verdi considered thirty or forty subjects which he never set to music; they ranged from *The Tempest* and *Tosca* to *Salammbô* and *Manon Lescaut*, but never once, so far as I can trace, was Montezuma mentioned in this connection. Why didn't Crowest show any curiosity about "Montezuma"? What was wrong with the work that it had not been performed in London by the time Crowest wrote his book— in 1897? Didn't he try to find a vocal score? Had the opera been entirely ignored by the foreign correspondents of the newspapers and musical journals that Crowest was unable to quote even the most fourth-hand account of it? The most astonishing aspect of the whole thing, of course, is that Crowest was not even faintly suspicious that "Montezuma" might not exist.

I have quoted this remarkable passage, however, not only because it is quaint and one of my favourite mysteries, but because it is very symptomatic of the lack of available hard and fast news concerning Verdi's activities as a composer after *Aida* and the Requiem (1874). His lifelong dislike of publicity increased as he approached old age, and his secretiveness inevitably led to endless speculation of the kind which was obviously at the bottom of the "Montezuma" legend.

The full story of how *Otello* came to be written is long and fascinating and has never been better told, in my opinion, than in the chapter "Boito and Verdi" of Frank Walker's *The Man Verdi*, where one may read in detail of the growth of a friendship between librettist

14*

and composer that developed into the greatest partnership of its kind in opera.

The gestation of *Otello* was slow and by no means smooth. After *Aida* and the Requiem Verdi had come to regard his career as a composer at an end, and it was not until the summer of 1879 that at a dinner party Giulio Ricordi had steered the conversation in a shrewdly offhand way round to the subject of Shakespeare, *Othello* and Boito, and had succeeded in reawakening Verdi's interest in the theatre. Boito took a first sketch of the libretto to Verdi three days later; the composer read it and "found it good". He told Boito to write the libretto: "It will come in handy for yourself, for me, or for somebody else." Towards the end of 1879, Boito had finished the libretto; Verdi liked it, bought it—and, according to his wife Giuseppina, put it away with the drafts of the *King Lear* project which had "slept profoundly and without disturbance for thirty years in its portfolio".

The libretto of *Otello* was not allowed to sleep profoundly or un-disturbed, however, for in spite of numerous time-consuming distractions during the five years which passed before Verdi, aged seventy, finally started on the actual composition of the opera, composer and librettist were in constant touch and continued to discuss, revise, change and add to the libretto throughout this whole period.

Among the "distractions" were a visit by Verdi to Paris for the first performance there of *Aida* in 1880, the revision of *Simon Boccanegra*, which gave Boito his first practical experience of close professional collaboration with Verdi, and the revision of *Don Carlos* for performance in its four-act form at La Scala in 1884. For much of this time what was known conspiratorially to Verdi, Ricordi and Boito by the code name of the "Chocolate Project" and to Giuseppina as "the African", was known as *Iago*—a title which, while its first purpose may have been to distinguish the opera from Rossini's *Otello*, nevertheless clearly pointed to where the musico-dramatic centre of gravity of the opera eventually lay.

The figure of Iago fascinated Verdi from the beginning and he expressed firm ideas of the character's physical appearance to his painter friend Domenico Morelli, when Morelli wanted to show him as "a small, malevolent-looking man". A character like that, insisted Verdi, would arouse everybody's suspicion and deceive no one. Iago must be a tall thin man, with thin lips, small eyes set close to his nose like a monkey's, a high, receding forehead with the back of his head well developed.

The working title of *Iago* was used for a couple of years or so, until in 1883 we find Verdi writing to Ricordi that he had "written nothing of this *Iago*—or better, *Otello*". Even so, it appears that "*Iago*" was still in circulation as late as the beginning of 1886 when Verdi, demanding that once and for all the opera should be referred to as *Otello* and not *Iago*, explained his reasons for the change. Iago, he said, was the Demon who set everything in motion, Otello was "the one who acts, who loves, who is jealous, who kills and kills himself". Furthermore, Verdi added, it appeared pure hypocrisy to him not to adopt the title of *Otello* for fear of comparison with Rossini's opera. "I would prefer", said Verdi, "people to say, 'He wanted to challenge a giant and failed', rather than, 'He wanted to hide himself behind the title of *Iago*'."

Not long after Verdi had begun to set Boito's libretto to music there occurred an event so nearly disastrous to the whole project that there might well have been no opéra, let alone any title to worry about. In March 1884, at a banquet in Naples following the success of his *Mefistofele* at the San Carlo, Boito said something in the course of conversation with his neighbour at table which was half-heard, entirely misunderstood and grossly misreported by an unscrupulous eavesdropping journalist in a local newspaper where he was quoted as saying that he had written the libretto of *Iago* against his will, but, having finished it, he regretted not being able to set it to music himself.

Verdi read the report and immediately took it to mean that his ability to write a satisfactory score was in question; he offered to return the libretto to Boito as a gift (it was, of course, Verdi's property) for him to set to music or not—as he pleased.

In a long and moving letter Boito explained to Verdi what had happened, and impressed on the composer why he and he alone must compose *Otello*. "My libretto", said Boito, "belongs to you by the sacrosanct right of conquest . . ."

Verdi accepted Boito's explanation of the Naples incident, and friendly relations were restored, but he refused to commit himself to going on with the music to *Otello*. He was too old, he told Boito— "My *years of service* are too many!!!! The public must not be able to say to me too evidently : '*Enough!*' " In a letter to Franco Faccio, Boito's intimate friend who was later to conduct the first performance of *Otello*, Verdi was even more emphatically discouraging: "According to you, then, I should really finish this *Otello*? But why? For whom? I don't care! And the public cares even less. . . ."

With Verdi in this thoroughly unco-operative and difficult state of mind the problem of getting him to resume work on *Otello* needed very careful handling. The turning point came when Boito, thanking Verdi for having understood the Neapolitan banquet affair, enclosed in his letter the words of Iago's Credo in Act II. Verdi, Boito recalled, had not been satisfied with a scene for Iago in the second act in double pentasyllabic lines, and that he had wanted something freer, less lyrical. Boito had proposed doing "a sort of *evil* Credo" and had now written one in a broken metre and unsymmetrical.

Verdi was delighted. "Most beautiful, this Creed; most powerful and wholly Shakespearian," he wrote to Boito, adding that meanwhile it would be well "to leave this Othello in peace for a bit, as he too is nervous, as we are—you perhaps more than I". Verdi's letter was written in May 1884 and concluded with an invitation to Boito: "If later on you come to Sant'Agata, as you have led me to hope, we can talk about it again, and by then, with the necessary calm . . ." Boito spent three days at Sant'Agata at the end of September; at the beginning of December Verdi wrote to him from Genoa saying that he had begun to compose again and asking for some extra lines for Iago and Emilia in the second-act quartet. The crisis was over.

Verdi finished the orchestration on 1st November 1886, when he was seventy-three years old. He wrote off to Giulio Ricordi: "I write to tell you that *Otello* is completely finished!! Positively finished!!! Finally!!!!!!!" and, not trusting the mail to Milan, arranged that he would hand over the manuscript in person to Garignani, Ricordi's chief copyist, whom he would meet at Fiorenzuola on the main line to Milan, a few miles from Sant'Agata. To Boito Verdi wrote the famous envoi: "It is finished. Here's a health to us . . . (and also to *Him*!!). Addio."

One or two small alterations still remained to be made, however, and the completed score was not finally in the copyists' hands until the week before Christmas. Seven and a half years had passed since the subject of *Otello* had first been so cunningly put into his head at Giulio Ricordi's dinner table, and Verdi was touchingly affected by what he felt was almost the loss of an old friend. "Poor Othello!" he wrote to Boito from Genoa, telling him that the last pages of the opera had been given to Garignani. "He won't come back here any more!!!"

Boito's feelings of pride and satisfaction as he consoled Verdi with the thought that a "great dream had become reality", must inevitably have been accompanied by a sense of inexpressible relief. No masterpiece in the history of art can ever have come so near to destruction in the course of its creation for such a comparatively trivial reason as *Otello*. It had been a perilous voyage all along, and if in the end the ship captained by Verdi was able to reach harbour safely it was due in an incalculable measure to the skill and patience of its pilot, Arrigo Boito.

CHARACTERS IN ORDER OF SINGING

MONTANO, *Otello's predecessor in the government
of Cyprus* . . . . . . *Bass*
CASSIO, *Otello's Lieutenant Captain* . . . *Tenor*
IAGO, *Otello's ancient* . . . . . *Baritone*
RODERIGO, *a Venetian gentleman* . . . *Tenor*
OTELLO, *a noble Moor, general in the service of the
Venetian State* . . . . . . *Tenor*
DESDEMONA, *his wife* . . . . . *Soprano*
EMILIA, *Iago's wife* . . . . *Mezzo-soprano*
A HERALD . . . . . . *Bass*
LODOVICO, *ambassador of the Venetian Republic* . *Bass*

Soldiers and sailors of the Venetian Republic, Venetian
ladies and gentleman, Cypriot men, women and children.
Greek, Dalmatian and Albanian soldiers, Island girls, an
innkeeper, four potmen at the inn, people

Scene: A seaport on the island of Cyprus
Time: End of the fifteenth century*

---

* Boito put the action of the original source of Shakespeare's play at "a little
before 1527", which would allow the costumes to be modelled on the paintings of
Carpaccio and Giovanni Bellini—a suggestion which might be followed by those
who have to design this opera.

ACT I

Scene : Outside the Castle. A tavern with an arbour. In the background, the Castle battlements and the sea. It is evening; a hurricane is blowing, with thunder and lightning.

The curtain rises at once on a stormy, *fortissimo* orchestral chord of the eleventh. (Those who play the guitar from the symbols printed on popular sheet music will recognize this at once as a chord of G minor seventh with a C in the bass.) The stage is filled with Cypriots and Venetians anxiously peering into the storm from the quayside for a sight of Otello's fleet returning from battle with the Turks. It is an arresting, unforgettable opening and the earliest instance I know (at least in the familiar repertoire) of an opera which dispenses altogether with all orchestral preliminaries. The storm makes its visual and audible impact simultaneously on the audience.

Verdi's treatment of the opening scene of *Otello* is among his greatest conceptions—a tremendous, surging Allegro agitato that drives relentlessly along like the first movement of a Beethoven symphony, its dynamics ranging from great shattering fortissimos to sudden, hushed, scarcely audible pianissimos and back again, and creating an unceasing tension and excitement.

The orchestra is a large one; in addition to the two cornets and four bassoons first heard in *Don Carlos*, Verdi includes two bass drums, three timpani, a gong ("tam-tam"), and a back-stage organ to provide a purely non-musical sound effect in the form of a deep and menacing cluster of the three notes C, C sharp and D sustained on pedals "in the registration of double basses and timpani" for 225 bars from the rise of the curtain. The term "cimbasso" disappears from the score entirely and the brass bass part is played throughout on a bass trombone which Verdi had specially constructed for the first performance. Although there is no specific indication to this effect in the score the three tenor trombone parts were originally intended to be played on valve instruments; Verdi expected them to play trills and rapid scale passages with the agility of the cornet and his use of these instruments in this opening sequence is masterly.

The initial orchestral outbursts to which the curtain rises subsides quickly into a sudden lull, with a sad, moaning phrase in the horns; by the light of a flash of lightning (represented by piccolo and flute arpeggios straight from the storm in *Rigoletto*), four tenors and

431

four basses in the crowd catch sight of a sail out to sea. The ship flies
the standard of the winged lion of St Mark. A distant trumpet is
heard behind the scenes (the one note played three times cannot
rate as a fanfare; it is surely what Shakespeare meant by a "tucket"),
a cannon is fired from the castle and we know that it is Otello's ship
that has been sighted.

The persistent Allegro agitato is now given an added urgency by a
rapid *ppp* triplet figure played *molto staccato* by the strings. The excitement builds up in a wonderfully dramatic running commentary.
Cassio, Montano, Iago, Roderigo, who are among those waiting
for Otello's safe return, add their eye-witness accounts to the
crowd's, describing the struggles of Otello's ship in the tempest. The
choral passages are magnificent, particularly in such phrases as the
basses' powerful cry of "Fende l'etra un torvo e cieco spirto di verti-
gine" ("A blind and threatening spirit of dizziness splits the air")
backed up by the four bassoons and three trombones in unison:

Ex *386*

At this point the previously all-male company is joined by a
crowd of Cypriot women who add their cries of horror to the general
turbulence. A startling modulation from E flat minor to E minor
produces a sudden lull and a series of melancholy phrases played by
the horns in unison which expresses the crowd's apprehension and
dismay. The horn parts are marked to be played "come un lamento", an instruction that has been a characteristic of Verdi's scores
ever since *Nabucco*. But where hitherto Verdi has nearly always expressed weeping by an oboe, a bassoon or strings, and the tears, even
when shed by a man, have usually had a slightly feminine accent,
at this point in *Otello* the instrumental colouring gives them an unmistakably masculine character; the horns sob in the register of the
male voice and the familiar plaintive rising semitone is played by
bassoons, violoncellos and double basses:

Ex *387*

The storm rises again suddenly with a series of quite terrifying

unison crotchets by cornets, trumpets and three trombones playing, first, seven F sharps, then seven B naturals a fourth higher, and finally seven E's a fourth above that. An effect of what might otherwise have been described as a sequence of twenty-one hammer-blows is transformed into one of twenty-one ferocious, searing whip strokes by the addition of three rising grace notes to each crotchet. The four horns, in unison with themselves, sometimes play in unison with the cornets and trumpets, sometimes a bare fourth below them. It is a superbly thrilling noise and well described by the chorus's excited reference to the "titanic trumpets sounding in the sky". These dramatic six bars lead up to another great outburst, the orchestra now sounding *tutta forza* and the chorus praying to God to save Otello's ship:

Ex 388

I have indicated in the third and fourth bars the cornet and trumpet parts which, doubled by trombones an octave lower, punctuate the chorus phrase with electrifying effect. A powerful climax is built up from this opening choral phrase, then once more the fury of the storm subsides momentarily. It will be noticed that unlike most storms in music Verdi's is not at full gale force all the time; the waves recede, and the wind drops to gather strength and strike more violently than ever. In the lull that follows the great choral outburst, Iago remarks that the mainsail of Otello's ship has been torn away and, turning to Roderigo, hopes that the ship will founder. In this vicious aside we have our first glimpse of the evil nature of Iago; it is a musical portrait drawn with consummate skill within the frame of a mere couple of rapid bars, and making its immediate effect by means which are easier to recognize (especially in Toscanini's immortal performance) than to analyse.* Iago's hopes are not fulfilled, however, and in a broad, peaceful cadence in E major like a sigh of relief, the populace exclaim that Otello is saved.

Excitement starts up again with a return to the rapid triplet figure in the strings while voices behind the scene shout instructions about lowering boats, making ropes fast, and the crowd on the stage rush to the quayside crying, "Evviva!". Otello, ascending the steps from the shore to the quay and followed by sailors and soldiers,

* The Toscanini recording in Great Britain is RCA–Victor RB 16093–5; in the U.S.A.: RCA–Victor LM–6107.

makes one of the most magnificent entrances in all opera to the noble phrase which I quote in full:

Ex 389

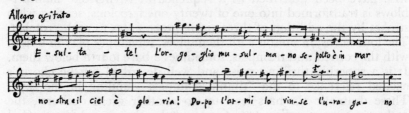

—"Rejoice! The Moslem's pride is buried in the sea; the glory is ours and Heaven's! After our arms, the storm defeated him!" This arresting passage is sung to sustained chords in the horns, and, punctuated by an occasional arpeggio and double-stopped f chords in the strings, is an exemplary instance of the striking declamatory style in which Verdi expresses the prose conversations, as distinct from the poetry, of *Otello*. It is not a "tune"; equally, it contains no trace of those features of traditional recitative still to be found in some of the declamatory passages of *Aida*. It is, in fact, essentially and continuously melodic and introduces into *Otello* a convincing essay by an inspired melodist in that "eternal melody" Wagner was always talking about.

Otello's words are greeted by "Evvivas" from the crowd and a sudden switch to a jubilant Allegro vivace 6/8 with trumpet and cornet flourishes to accompany Otello as he enters the fortress followed by Cassio, Montano and soldiers, amid cries of "Vittoria!" from the populace.

The storm, now much moderated, continues with occasional rolls of thunder and flashes of lightning, but its musical representation is more or less limited to the sustained pedal notes of the organ; the general fury and hubbub have subsided enough to enable us to hear the chorus reflecting joyfully and excitedly on the result of the battle in quite lengthily sustained pp passages:

Ex 390

The choral sequence built up from this phrase (with the tenors echoing the basses), and the orchestral accompaniment that goes with it have a lightness of touch which presents a most startling contrast with what has gone before. Verdi uses his woodwind in chamber-music proportions to give the movement something of a conspiratorial character that looks backwards to the courtiers of *Rigoletto* and forwards to the gaiety of the women in *Falstaff*. With its hushed, excited beginning and its ending in a climax of enthusiastic cries of "Vittoria!" this is one of the most intriguingly effective passages Verdi ever wrote.

After an exuberant final "Evviva!" the storm begins to die away; the organ notes get increasingly quieter, the piccolo's flashes of lightning grow feebler, the strings sign off with a neat little pizzicato phrase as the organ finally stops, and the scene ends with the chorus expressing its relief in a peaceful *morendo* chord of the same E major to which the music has constantly gravitated since the start of the opera.

In spite of the tremendous changes in Verdi's declamatory style to be found in *Otello* the sequence that now follows is marked "Recit." in the score. Iago turns to Roderigo, who is hopelessly in love with Otello's wife, Desdemona, and asks him what he is thinking about. Roderigo replies dejectedly that he is thinking of drowning himself. Iago tells him not to be despondent; it is only a matter of time before Desdemona finds Otello's "black kisses" repulsive. Iago protests his friendship for Roderigo, and breaking into a rather skittish little tune of six bars, promises him that Desdemona shall be his. The phrase ends with an abrupt downward leap of an octave in the orchestra (the higher note with a rising grace note attached to it) which is used frequently during the rest of this act as a kind of final gesture to give emphasis to what Iago has just said.

While Iago has been talking to Roderigo people have been moving about busily in the background, ascending the steps from the shore and taking arms and baggage into the castle. Townspeople have entered carrying branches, which have been stacked up into a large woodpile near the quay, while the rest of the crowd have gathered round, noisy and curious.

As Iago continues to talk to Roderigo, Cassio returns to join a group of soldiers. Iago points him out to Roderigo as the reason for his hatred of Otello. In spite of his long experience in battle Iago has been passed over by Otello in favour of Cassio, who has been promoted to captain. "Such was Otello's will", he exclaims sarcastically in a superbly evil and serpentine phrase doubled by violins and violas in octaves and ending in a fierce trill for singer and strings, "and I remain his Moorish excellency's ensign." At this point clouds of smoke, growing increasingly dense, begin to rise from the woodpile which has been set alight. Iago, taking Roderigo out of earshot, boasts that if he were Otello he would not want to have a Iago near him.

The bonfire bursts into flame, the tavern servants light up the arbour and the crowd sings the chorus which had to be repeated no fewer than three times at the Scala première—the famous "Fuoco di gioia!" ("Fire of rejoicing"). This episode is another of those pieces of music which are virtually impossible to describe or analyse, and pointless to quote from. It is a purely decorative interlude of no dramatic significance, which brings a moment of much-needed relaxation after the excitement and drama of what has gone before. "Fuoco di gioia" rates as a choral number, but its main interest is orchestral—a sparkling, crackling, filigreed scherzo movement full of the most intriguing and original scoring. It is a masterly lesson in woodwind writing, where every detail is clear and dead right (there are passages for the bassoon that might have been written by Mozart), in the highly imaginative and varied use of rapidly alternating bowed and pizzicato notes, and in the subtle colouring of the cymbals sometimes played *pp*, sometimes allowed to ring in a *piano* woodwind passage.

The choral writing, too, is wonderfully effective and includes many characteristic staccato passages as well as a series of rich low E's for the basses. The scene ends with a ravishing *pp* coda that dies away to nothing as the fire gradually goes out and complete calm succeeds the storm. It is an episode of great charm and originality which points the way unmistakably to so many of the magic moments in *Falstaff*.

During this interlude Iago, Roderigo, Cassio and some other soldiers have been sitting at a table drinking wine. Iago, knowing that Cassio has a weak head for liquor, insists on filling up his glass. Cassio protests that he has had enough, but lifts his glass and drinks a little when asked to drink a toast to the marriage of Otello and Desdemona. While Cassio grows increasingly eloquent in his praises of Desdemona Iago warns Roderigo that Cassio is his greatest rival, "a cunning seducer" who will get in his way. They must make Cassio drunk—"If he is drunk, he is lost!" Iago calls for more wine and fills three glasses again—one for himself, one for Roderigo, one for Cassio—to the accompaniment of an Allegro con brio 4/4 unison passage for strings, woodwind and horns, which cuts like a knife. The time changes to 6/8 and after a short two-in-a-bar vamp-till-ready supplied by four bassoons, violoncellos and double basses in octaves, Iago launches out into his famous Brindisi—

Ex *391*

—the drinking song Boito derives from Shakespeare's "And let me the canakin, clink, clink; . . ."

With the characteristic abrupt drop of an octave associated with Iago, now heard in the voice part as well, it is clear that this is to be no ordinary drinking song. As will be seen, it is very much part of the action and its whole nature is strongly influenced by the evil and cunning of Iago's personality. Iago's opening stanza (its tune is twelve bars long altogether) is answered by a similar four-line stanza sung by Cassio which, contained in a phrase of music only eight bars long, somehow makes the distinction between the two characters oddly sharp. Cassio's lines bring what one may call the "verse" of the song to an end in the A major, or the "chorus", Iago now sings to the general company, bidding everyone drink with him:

Ex 392

Chi al-l'e-sca ha mor-ro   del di- ti-ram- bo spaval-do e stram- bo be- va con me

Iago's "chorus" ends with a strikingly sinister cadence of three slithering chromatic runs in the words "beva con me" ("drink with me"), doubled by strings, a clarinet, bassoon and horn in unison. The refrain is repeated by the crowd and Roderigo; the chromatic cadence, however, is sung alone by Iago except for the third run in which he is joined by Roderigo. The orchestral accompaniment is fascinatingly vigorous and lively, with the cornets and trombones playing an important part in a sequence written for long stretches in two parts: tune and accompanying bass.

Cassio is observed to the satisfaction of Iago and Roderigo to be getting steadily drunk, but he is still capable of singing his part of the Brindisi when Iago comes to the second verse. The routine of Iago's refrain and its repetition by the chorus is followed once more. When Iago begins the third verse of the song, however, Cassio interrupts, coming in with his part nine bars too soon. This confuses Iago, who interrupts in turn, repeating the tune of his first line to the words of his second. Cassio knocks back another drink and goes blissfully on with his singing.

Iago cuts in again, this time in an attempt to get going with the tune of Ex 392, but Cassio interrupts, and in the confusion Iago repeats the notes of the first two bars of the refrain to the words of the third and fourth. Cassio by now is roaring and staggering about, and to the great delight of the crowd, tries to repeat the tune of Iago's "verse" (Ex 391) but can't remember it. He has another shot at it but fails again; as his speech thickens and he grows increasingly incoherent Iago urges Roderigo to pick a quarrel with Cassio. It is an admirable sequence of purely *musical* comedy which Verdi allows to speak for itself; so far from exaggerating the incident with any orchestral by-play he accompanies the last stages of Cassio's befuddledness by a simple rhythmic figure of stark open fifths and fourths in the woodwind and pizzicato strings. The laughter of the crowd gets louder and the Brindisi ends with everybody drinking to a loud orchestral unison coda with piercing trills in all those instruments capable of playing them, including horns, cornets and trumpets.

The Allegro con brio 6/8 of the Brindisi is continued with the entrance of Montano who has come to tell Cassio that the guard is waiting for his orders. Cassio is described in the score as "barcollando"—an expressive term which, used at sea, means pitching, rolling or heaving, or on land, wavering, reeling or staggering. Montano, shocked by Cassio's condition, is assured by Iago that it is a regular nightly occurrence. As Cassio starts to stagger away Roderigo laughs at him, and calls him a drunkard. Cassio hurls himself at Roderigo and the two men start fighting. Montano separates them by force; Cassio threatens to split his brains open if he interferes; Montano retorts that these are the words of a drunkard. Cassio draws his sword; Montano does likewise and a furious fight ensues. The crowd falls back in alarm.

The music to all this has been building up steadily from a rapid descending *leggero* figure in the violins, punctuated by low-register unison trills from the piccolo, two flutes and two oboes and supported by abrupt regular chords played *pp* by the four trombones. An intense crescendo leads to a loud tutti as the two men draw their swords; the dynamics, but not the rhythmic vigour of the music, subside for a moment to let us hear Iago tell Roderigo to hurry off to the harbour to spread confusion and horror among the population with cries of "Revolt! Revolt!" and the ringing of a tocsin. Roderigo runs off.

Iago turns to Cassio and Montano and tells them to stop fighting, but they ignore him. The music continues to grow in excitement and ferocity with powerful *ff* off-beat accents from the entire orchestra as the women in the crowd fly in terror from the scene, shouting for help, and the rest raise the alarm. A final tremendous unison sequence in the orchestra is cut off abruptly by the appearance of Otello followed by torchbearers. "Lower your swords!" he commands in a ringing phrase which, I must confess, I find more arresting than Shakespeare's original line at this point. There is something a little uncompelling, I feel, about, "What is the matter here?"

The fighting stops. Violins, violas and violoncellos in unison, with the double basses an octave lower, hammer out the phrase:

Ex 393

Those who know Toscanini's recording of *Otello* will not need reminding of the frightening quality of anger and authority he brought out in the performance of these six notes which Verdi uses in two or three altered forms to punctuate or emphasize Otello's angry questions and reproaches. "Am I among Saracens?" he asks. "Has the Turks' madness entered your veins that you tear one another to pieces?" Then quietly and sadly, Otello bids "Honest Iago" speak. There is a moment's silence. Haltingly, and accompanied by *ppp* pizzicato notes Iago answers (in words very close to Shakespeare's) that he does not know—everybody there was friends, civil and merry. "But on a sudden as if some evil planet had bewitched their senses, drawing their swords they fell upon one another furiously— would that my legs had been cut off ere they had borne me here."

Otello turns to Cassio: how did he come so far to forget himself? Cassio craves pardon, he cannot speak. And Montano? Otello sees he is wounded and grows angry again, his words matched once more by the violence of the biting six-note string phrase.

At this moment Desdemona appears; her rest has been disturbed by the uproar. In a final outburst of fury Otello deprives Cassio of his captaincy. Cassio drops his sword on the ground; Iago picks it up, and giving it to a soldier murmurs his delight at the outcome of events. The music now suddenly becomes peaceful, settling down to a lengthy sequence for strings in which the violoncellos play a throbbing pedal F for twelve bars while the first violins, after a couple of bars echoing the first subject of the finale of Mozart's Jupiter Symphony (Verdi uses the same theme again later in the opera), establishes a gentle rocking figure:

Ex 394

This subdued orchestral passage accompanies Otello's instructions to Iago to restore peace and quiet in the city. When Iago leaves, Otello orders Montano to be helped into the castle and "with an imperious gesture" tells the rest of the company to return home. The scene empties. Otello motions his torchbearers to re-enter the castle, and he is left alone with Desdemona. The music becomes increasingly tranquil and over another long pedal F (sustained in octaves by the double bass this time with some pulsating support from the horns), the dotted-crotchet-and-quaver rhythm of Ex 394 acquires a poignant accent on the quaver and is briefly developed, by flutes, clarinet, bassoon and strings, dying away to leave a solo muted violoncello to climb unaccompanied in the same rhythm to a high E flat.

The solo violoncello is joined by three others, also muted, in a simple lyrical passage of wonderful warmth and beauty which serves as the introduction to the loveliest duet Verdi ever wrote. It is a duet unlike any other in its whole concept. It cannot be described as a "love duet", for in opera most such duets are concerned with the enthusiastic expression of love newly discovered by an un-married couple who are usually comparative strangers to each other. Otello and Desdemona are husband and wife; the days of their courting and first careless rapture are far behind them and in their place there has developed a tenderness and understanding born of experience, maturity and happiness. Their scene together, in fact, is less of a duet than an intimate conversation. In the entire eight or nine minutes the episode lasts they sing together only twice —and on neither occasion for more than three bars.

It is the utterly unusual nature of this duologue that makes analysis so difficult. There are no "themes"; there is just a seemingly endless sequence of exquisite tunes which meander through one unlikely key after another in the most unexpected but unchallengeably logical manner. What on paper may appear as just a string of independent tunes is heard as a masterly display of the undisturbed continuity and sense of the inevitable that is the art of true composition.

The mood of tranquillity that now prevails after the tempest and turbulence of what has gone before is expressed superbly in the calm near-monotone of Otello's opening phrase, accompanied by the rich warmth of the four solo violoncellos—"Già nella notte densa, s'estingue ogni clamor" ("Now in the dark night all noise is stilled"):

Ex 395

The masculine sound of the violoncellos gives way to the more feminine softness of muted violins and violas, mostly in four parts, as Desdemona, answering in a long lyrical phrase that matches

Otello's, reflects on the hopes and trials and suffering that have led
to the happiness and love they now enjoy. "How sweet," says Desdemona, "to murmur together: 'Do you remember?'" These last
three words, sung "like a distant voice", conclude a passage that has
reached C major from G flat major, and are accompanied by a
long *ppp* chord of C major. This is a breathtaking moment created
by such a superb example of simple scoring that it should be contemplated in silent and humble meditation by composers of all ages
every night before they go to bed. Verdi uses two flutes and a piccolo
to play the triad C''–E''–G'', a harp with a rising *allargando morendo*
arpeggio across four octaves, two bassoons who double the low C
and G of the four solo violoncellos' two bottom open strings, and
first and second violins and violas each divided into two parts. One
of the greatest lessons to be learnt from the way this chord is scored is
what is left out. There is nothing, except the climbing harp arpeggio,
between the low G of the violoncellos and bassoons, and the G two
octaves higher of the violas. Perhaps the open, but silent, C and G
strings of the violas and the G strings of the violins vibrate in sympathy; perhaps it is the ear's imagination; but it is a chord that
sounds much fuller and richer than one is led to expect from what is
written down.

The duologue continues with the lovers recalling the events which
have led to their present happiness. Each of these sequences is a
complete melody in itself with an enchanting cadence, and distinguished in a remarkable way by its own highly characteristic orchestration. The strings which have predominated up to Desdemona's
distant, "Do you remember?" are replaced in the next phrase by
flutes, cor anglais, bass clarinet, bassoon, horns and a harp in its
lower register (violoncellos and basses supply a discreet pizzicato
twice a bar).

The calm simplicity of this passage is followed by the agitation of
Otello's memories of battle and the orchestra's hushed, *ppp* suggestion of martial rhythms from cornet, trumpet and timpani distantly
heard through restless string figures and rapid harp arpeggios
marked to sound "come un mormorio"—"like a murmur". The
music builds towards a climax for the first time, but it quickly dies
down for another long lyrical passage for Desdemona in which the
voice part is doubled by cor anglais, flute, and for a couple of bars,
a horn, in unison:

Ex *396*

Poi mi gui-da-vi ai fulgidi de-ser-ti al-l'ar-se a-re-ne, al tuo materno suol

Against this violins and violas keep up a gentle throbbing pp semi-quaver figure and the violoncellos play a series of sustained harmonics which sound in the same register as the first violins' notes.

Otello's reply brings yet another abrupt change of colour in the orchestra—sustained ppp C's and a pedal F in the strings, and a pleasant gentle burbling in the woodwind (the bass clarinet plays a particularly effective part in this). Desdemona's phrase which follows is only two bars long, a short bridge leading from D flat to F major, but even this brief passage is scored in such a way as to make it sharply different from sound of what has gone before.

At this point the music pauses for breath for a moment, the constant modulation ceases and gives way to a long passage that remains firmly in the key of F with a comparatively lengthy cadence to prove that it was no accident. Otello sings, with a necessary change of the personal pronouns from third to second person singular, the famous lines which Boito lifted from the first act (Scene 3, lines 167–8) of Shakespeare's play and interpolated in this duet:

> She lov'd me for the dangers I had pass'd,
> And I lov'd her that she did pity them.

Ex 397

For the first time in the duet a tune is repeated; Desdemona echoes what Otello has sung, in her turn altering the personal pronouns. And for the first time, too, we encounter in the libretto the familiar operatic convention of the bracketed, as-the-case-may-be alternative—"that $\left\{ \begin{matrix} \text{you} \\ \text{I} \end{matrix} \right\}$ did pity them"—when, for six notes that last less than three bars altogether, Verdi reverts to the traditional love-duet practice of having tenor and soprano, hero and heroine, sing simultaneously.

The orchestration of the twelve-bar passage which starts with Ex 397 is again highly characteristic—this time in the way in which first one, then another solo wind instrument is added to colour the ppp string tremolo, and then taken away to leave the full *dolcissimo* warmth of the strings alone to accompany the last moments of the moving cadence.

The range and variety of Verdi's orchestral invention in this duet becomes more and more remarkable as the music continues calmly and smoothly in a series of exquisite lyrical passages, each distinguished by its own characteristic instrumental colouring. The full, sympathetic sound of the unhurried rising bass-clarinet arpeggios in Otello's first lines after the episode of Ex 397, the dramatic contrast of the sudden *pp dolcissimo* strings with the preceding wind accompaniment to Otello's words at Desdemona's supremely simple and affecting *"Amen* risponda"—these are unforgettable moments of sheer sensuous beauty in a scene which abounds in such moments.

The climax of the duet is as original and affecting as the conception of the duet itself—a tune of magical loveliness, played *pp* by the orchestra, which Otello punctuates with the murmured words, "Un bacio—un bacio—ancora un bacio" ("A kiss—a kiss—one more kiss") :

Ex 398

Verdi uses this phrase three times in the course of the opera—now, and twice in the last act of the work when it has a heart-rending poignancy. It is a superb demonstration of the art of creating a tune with such tremendous initial impact that, once heard, it needs no plugging to ensure that we recognize it again three acts later.

The sky has now cleared, the moon has risen and Otello and Desdemona walk slowly towards the castle, clasped in each other's arms. Three measured, ascending harp arpeggios, high *ppp* notes held by violins and violas, and a flute and cor anglais whose long unison notes rise in semitones, slowly changing the harmony, lead to a chord of D flat that shimmers like moonlight on water. In a scene that has been remarkable for the prodigious invention of the orchestration this sudden burst of colour is a superlative touch, created by the most obvious means of shakes and trills in violins, violas, flutes, oboe and piccolo, and a swish of rapid harp arpeggios.

The chord is sustained long enough for Otello and Desdemona to hold a long note together—their second and final passage of conventional operatic procedure—before the orchestra dies away, leaving only a *ppp* trill in the first violins to accompany a return to the sound of the four solo violoncellos who echo, as a brief coda, the tune of Otello's first words, "Già nella notte densa" (Ex 395).

The curtain begins to fall slowly at the violoncellos' entry, the number of violins playing the *morendo* trill is reduced to two, and the act ends with the harp striking a descending succession of tonic and dominant octaves which fades slowly away to a resonant low D flat —a last word which the gramophone, if not the average theatre audience, allows one to hear undisturbed.

Boito's decision to eliminate the first act of Shakespeare's tragedy and begin the action of the opera at Act II was, without doubt, a master-stroke. It not only provided Verdi with a superb opportunity to make a tremendous initial impact, and exploit the great musical possibilities of the storm's progress as a means of heightening the excitement of the drama; it also cuts down the number of characters (Desdemona's father, Brabantio, and Bianca, are two who do not appear in the opera at all), and in doing so avoided one situation— the scene between Brabantio and Othello in Shakespeare's Act I, Scene 2—which would inevitably have been too reminiscent of that between Don Giovanni and the Commendatore at the start of Mozart's opera for Verdi's liking. (Verdi had a life-long aversion to *Don Giovanni*.)

Nevertheless Boito drew on Shakespeare's first act to a greater extent than is usually acknowledged, for in addition to the inspired inclusion in the love duet already discussed, there are several passages in the duologue between Iago and Roderigo in the opera which have been most neatly transferred from Shakespeare's first act. Some of these are important—such as Iago's account of how Cassio was promoted over him ("And I—God bless the mark!—his Moorship's ancient"—Act I, Scene 1), his admission to Roderigo, "I hate the Moor" (Act I, Scene 3), while from the famous, "Put money in thy purse" speech at the end of Act I, Scene 3, comes Iago's assurance to Roderigo that Desdemona will soon tire of her husband, and his promise that if "a frail vow . . . be not too hard for my wits and all the tribe of hell, thou shalt enjoy her".

Boito also made use of Shakespeare's first act to provide some of the details in the language of the libretto—lines such as Roderigo's melancholy, "I will incontinently drown myself" from Scene 3, and Iago's

> It is as sure as you are Roderigo,
> Were I the Moor, I would not be Iago:

find their way with little alteration into the first act of Verdi's opera.

Boito's libretto has long been admired as a masterpiece of condensation and of the art of knowing what to discard altogether without even trying to condense it, and his achievement in preserving, and sometimes even inventing, the essence of Shakespeare's tragedy

ranks as one of the few completely inspired and successful feats of
adaptation in the history of opera. What was equally remarkable,
however, was his judgment, in the midst of all the intense concentration of action the subject demanded, of the extent to which a
scene of such complete irrelevance as the "Fuoco di gioia" chorus
could be introduced without interfering with the progress of the
plot. Obviously Verdi would have opposed Boito's idea if it had
threatened to upset the dramatic and musical balance of the act;
but the rightness of the whole episode was never questioned. It was
as though Boito had instinctively foreseen that this moment of dramatic relaxation, suggested by no more than four words in the
Herald's proclamation in Shakespeare's Act II, Scene 2—"It is
Othello's pleasure, our noble and valiant general, that . . . every
man put himself into triumph; some to dance, some to make bonfires . . ."—would inspire a sequence that is one of the most fascinating and sensuously original pieces of music Verdi ever wrote,
and which fits miraculously as a piece of decoration into the design
of the whole.

ACT II

Scene: A Hall on the ground floor of the Castle. A glass partition divides the room from a large garden. A terrace.

Where in *Aida* Verdi gave some of his characters a distinct musical label in the form of a theme which was used from time to time throughout the opera, in *Otello* there are only two themes ever heard outside the act in which they originally occurred. The first is the love-theme at the end of Act I (Ex 398), played only once in the duet, and heard again twice in the last stages of the opera three acts later; the other is a theme encountered later on in this second act, heard for a second time in an elaborated form at the start of the third, and then never played again.

Otherwise, Verdi is content to think of a theme, develop it, and, when it has served its immediate dramatic purpose, discard it for good.

The second act begins with just a theme, introduced in a brief orchestral prelude before the curtain rises and used in a variety of ways in the background to the opening scene. It is first heard at the start of the prelude, played in unison by four bassoons and violoncellos, then by violas and clarinets:

Ex 399

This figure, which starts off so ferociously, is used in various forms—to sound wheedling and graceful, angry and impatient, and adding an unmistakable charm by its unpretentious contribution to the lovely lyrical phrase which, with its ravishing cadence, is heard repeatedly in these early stages of this scene:

Ex 400

After its fierce unison opening of bassoons and violoncellos, the orchestral prelude relaxes into a sinuous elegance to prepare us on the rise of the curtain for Iago, at his smoothest and most plausible, beseeching Cassio not to torment himself. If he will only trust him, says Iago, he will recover his lost commission and enjoy the favours of Monna Bianca once more. (Boito's very fleeting reference to Bianca presupposes a certain acquaintance on the part of the audience with Shakespeare's play. Those who have not read the play since their schooldays may need reminding that Bianca is Cassio's mistress, left behind in Venice when he was posted to Cyprus.) In a series of ingratiating phrases in which the graceful cadence of Ex 400 predominates, Iago tells Cassio that he must get Desdemona to intercede with Otello on his behalf and his pardon will be ensured. "She is the leader of our leader. He lives for her alone." Iago adds that Cassio's opportunity to talk to Desdemona will come shortly; she will be taking her customary walk in the garden with Iago's wife, Emilia.

Cassio moves away to stand and wait on the far side of the terrace; as Iago watches him go, there is an angry *ff* version of the first phrase of Ex 399, coloured by woodwind and horns in unison with the strings (the double basses joining in for the first time in this act). "I see your end already," growls Iago, darkly (*cupo*). "I am your evil genius who drives you on—just as I am driven on by the inexorable God in whom I believe". A tremendous unison, its character clearly hinted at in *Simon Boccanegra* (see Ex 192), is played *ff tutta forza* across five octaves by the whole orchestra to introduce Iago's famous Credo—"Credo in un Dio crudel":

Ex 401

Iago's declaration of his belief in a cruel God is surely one of the most powerful representations of evil ever expressed in music. And not a little of this quality, of course, comes from Verdi's underlining of the words with an inspired use of the orchestra—of harsh trills in the penetrating lower register of the two oboes, for instance, of short, incisive string phrases marked to be played *aspramente* (harshly or bitterly), one of which is heard over an astonishing and sinister cluster of notes in "close harmony" in the low registers of bassoons, double-stopped violoncellos and divided double basses.

In a magnificent series of declamatory passages Iago proclaims his faith in the ruthless God who has created man in his own vile image. Iago is evil because all human nature is evil; an honest man is a jesting buffoon whose tears, kisses, glances, sacrifices and honour are all lies. "I believe Man to be the plaything of an evil fate, from the germ of the cradle to the worm of the grave." At these last words —"al verme dell'avel"—the music subsides dramatically and we hear a harmonized version of the opening unison with the tune played legato an octave lower than shown in the quotation (Ex 401) and scored for strings, horns, bassoons, and clarinet. An original sequence of harmonies leads the phrase, not into the expected key of F minor, but into a sinisterly foreign chord of D minor in which the four trombones join with a sustained and ominous *ppp*: "After this huge mockery comes Death. And then?—and then?" Iago's questions are punctuated by another *pp* echo of Ex 401, again legato, but this time harmonized differently and for strings only.

Iago answers his own question in a low voice: "Death is a void", and as a triumphant Q.E.D. proclaims at—literally—the top of his voice: "Heaven is nothing but an ancient fable." A brassy orchestral flourish accompanies the forceful high F with which Iago ends his Creed and a brief coda leads quickly without interruption into the following scene.

That Boito, the composer of *Mefistofele*, should have introduced some Mephistophelean characteristics into his conception of Iago is perhaps not surprising, but it is unfair, I think, to insist that the Credo has about it more of the spirit of Goethe than Shakespeare. Verdi hailed it as "most powerful and wholly Shakespearian" and a study of what I have always regarded as Iago's "bad language" passages in Act I of Shakespeare's play certainly does not suggest that Boito's Credo is in any way out of character. The young man (Iago is only twenty-eight) whose coarse words, even if deliberately designed to provoke, caused Brabantio to call him a "profane wretch", and whose evil nature is clearly apparent from his final scene with Roderigo (Act I, Scene 3), was surely quite capable of the blasphemous philosophy of the Credo.

Whatever the source of Boito's inspiration, however, with Verdi's music Iago's soliloquy is a magnificently powerful study of the man after whom the opera was originally called.

The coda of the Credo dissolves into a soft, rather conspiratorial quaver-passage for strings as Desdemona can be seen walking in the garden with Emilia. Iago hurries to the terrace to tell Cassio of Desdemona's approach, Cassio goes towards Desdemona, bows and speaks to her. We hear a description of what is happening from Iago —a kind of running commentary that he keeps up to the accompaniment of the strings' almost incessant *leggero* eight-in-a-bar in which a solo bassoon joins to double and intensify the violoncello part.

Iago wonders how he can get Otello to see his wife and Cassio together—"They are talking . . . and she smiles and tilts her

pretty face—— One gleam of that smile would suffice me to ruin
Otello." Iago makes to leave quickly by the entrance on the right
side of the scene, but stops suddenly when he sees Otello approaching. He stands motionless on the terrace, looking fixedly towards
the garden where Cassio and Desdemona can be seen. Pretending
not to see Otello, Iago is heard to say, as if to himself, "I am grieved
by this." Otello overhears this and going up to Iago asks him what
he means. Iago replies: nothing; and then feigning surprise at seeing
Otello, adds that it was "merely an idle word". Otello asks Iago
whether it was Cassio who has just left Desdemona. "Cassio? No,"
answers Iago. "That man started guiltily when he saw you." Otello
says he thinks it was Cassio nevertheless.

The two men have now left the terrace; in the duologue that
follows Iago asks, with a convincing casualness, whether Cassio
knew Desdemona in the early days of Otello's love affair. "Yes,"
replies Otello. "Why do you ask?" "A vague thought," says Iago,
and goes on to ask whether Otello had confidence in Cassio. Otello
answers that Cassio used often to carry some present or token from
himself to his bride—"Don't you think him honest?" Imitating
Otello, Iago echoes, "honest?" "What are you hiding in your
heart?" Otello asks. Note for note Iago imitates him: "What am I
hiding in my heart?" In a fury Otello imitates the imitation and
exclaims: "By heaven, you echo my words! What monster is hidden
in the cloister of your mind?"

Otello tells Iago that he overheard him say, "I am grieved by this"
(Otello's quotation is of Iago's exact words and music). What was it
grieved him? He mentioned Cassio's name and frowned. What is it
all about? Let Iago speak out—and say the worst. Iago keeps up his
air of reticence and remarks that his thoughts are his own. Let
Otello beware of jealousy—the green-ey'd monster which, in Boito's
libretto, becomes "a dark hydra, malignant, blind, that poisons itself
with its own venom——" Iago's words are set to an astonishing
passage of music, the first four bars accompanied *pp* by the whole
orchestra in a superbly sinister sequence that breaks all the academic
laws about consecutive fifths and octaves, the second phrase by
unison violas and clarinet, bassoons and violoncellos in octaves:

Ex 402

Otello firmly refuses to accept vague suspicion as proof. Before doubt there must be enquiry; after doubt, proof; after proof, "Away at once with love and jealousy". Iago, becoming at once more frank in his manner, expresses pleasure at being free to speak more openly. There is no question yet of proof, but he warns Otello to watch Desdemona carefully—a single word can restore faith or confirm suspicion.

Iago's words are sung in a rapid near-monotone against an off-stage chorus singing in the garden and accompanied at this point only by bagpipes—a tonic and dominant ostinato on the notes E and B which Verdi indicates in the score may be played if necessary by two oboes; he also suggests that the mandolines and guitars which are included in the score a couple of pages later may be replaced by four harps—two for the mandolines, and two to play the guitar part "transposed an octave down etc."

The eight-bar phrase the chorus is heard singing ("very distantly") has a cadence of immense lyrical charm which I quote because it is used with great effect a little later in the scene:

Ex 403

During a brief interlude which features a six-bar series of semi-quavers played smoothly and *con eleganza* by the strings, Desdemona is seen to return to the garden through the large opening at the back. She is surrounded by women, children and Cypriot and Albanian sailors who come forward in turn to offer her flowers and other gifts. They sing, accompanying themselves, the stage directions tells us, "on the *guzla* (a kind of Mandola), others have small harps slung over their shoulders".* The chorus sing again the song we heard off stage, this time with help from the orchestra pit where tonic-and-dominant chords and an ostinato arpeggio figure in the first violins provide a background for the bagpipes, mandolines and guitars on the stage.

With a change of time to 6/8 the orchestra leaves the accompaniment entirely to the stage instruments. A chorus of children begin to strew lilies on the ground and tell us all about it in a unison tune sung against a rocking "rum-pum-pum" for adult chorus. The bari-

* There seems to be some confusion here. *Grove* describes a *guzla* as "a kind of rebab, a bowed instrument with one string only", and a Mandola as "an instrument of the lute class, with a rounded-back body and a short neck". Not that it really matters one way or the other; the instruments are seen but not heard.

tones in the chorus now come forward with their tune (doubled by guitars and bagpipes) to which they offer Desdemona necklaces of coral and pearls. It is then the turn of the women of the chorus, who strew leaves and flowers to an oddly melancholy minor tune supported by the earlier rocking rhythm.

The opening sequence is repeated with the pit orchestra joining in as before; it leads to an entrancing coda (with high tremolo B's in the violins and low pedal E's in the violoncellos and basses) started by Desdemona, who sings the whole of the phrase I have quoted in Ex 403 to words telling of her joy and love and hope. Otello, deeply moved by what he has heard, adds his own short lyrical contribution; the chorus gently wishes Desdemona and her husband a happy life in this place where Love so obviously reigns; and Iago mutters in an evil aside that he will shatter all these sweet harmonies. The high tremolo B's and the low pedal E's of the violoncellos and basses that have been held *ppp* through this coda, finally die away and an instrumental postlude follows when the first violins play an extended and beautiful legato sequence of semiquavers in which the tonic and dominant arpeggio figure that accompanied the chorus is transformed into a long tune.

During these six languid bars Desdemona kisses several of the children on the head; some of the women kiss the hem of her dress; she gives a purse to the sailors. The chorus leaves. Desdemona, followed by Emilia, enters the hall and goes towards Otello. She asks him to pardon Cassio—and immediately all the suspicions which had been dispelled by the beauty of the little choral episode, are violently aroused again.

Desdemona's gentle plea is rejected harshly by Otello with, "Not now!" Disturbed by her husband's agitation, Desdemona takes out her handkerchief to wipe his forehead but he snatches it from her and throws it on the ground, shouting at her to leave him alone. Emilia picks up the handkerchief while Desdemona sadly says to Otello: "If I have unwittingly offended you, grant me the sweet and glad word of pardon." Without causing any interruption in her delivery of it the second part of Desdemona's line—"dammi la dolce e lieta parola del perdono"—becomes the opening phrase of the quartet which begins with Desdemona's

Ex 404

dam-mi la dol-ce e lie-ta pa-ro-la del per-do-no

The quartet that develops from this is as characteristic of Verdi's four-points-of-view writing as one could wish—a long pleading vocal line from Desdemona, a bitter soliloquy from Otello who ignores his wife and wonders what it is that has led to this situation—perhaps he does not understand the subtle deceits of love, perhaps he has passed his prime, perhaps it is the colour of his skin. Iago and Emilia, for their part, carry on a private war ("I am your wife, not your slave") over Desdemona's handkerchief which Emilia refuses to surrender. Iago finally snatches it away from her and remarks with satisfaction in an aside that his plan is already beginning to work.

It is not a spectacular quartet, in the sense that it will ever stop the show like the quartet in *Rigoletto*, but the clear differentiation between the characters and the simultaneous presentation of three dramatic situations places it among Verdi's finest achievements in this form. It includes one remarkable passage of orchestration—a "dark" *ppp* sequence in which the two cornets and two trumpets play a long B flat and the four trombones play a series of three- and four-part chords in their low register. The two bars concerned are accompanied by the rather unusual instruction by the composer that "if it it not possible to obtain a *pianissimo* the trumpets and trombones are to be omitted. In small theatres it is better to omit them in any case."

The quartet ends with a short unaccompanied cadence in the earliest Verdi tradition, and a beautiful coda in which Desdemona repeats her opening words, but not the tune that went with them in Ex 404; that, with a slightly different second bar, is played by the first violins in octaves and echoed by the violoncellos.

Otello tells Desdemona to leave; he wishes to be alone. As Emilia turns to leave, too, Iago warns her under his breath to keep silent. The two women withdraw. Iago makes as if to leave by the door at the back, but remains. He looks at the handkerchief, then hides it in his doublet, telling us in an aside that it will be hidden in Cassio's dwelling. He watches Otello closely and notes with satisfaction that the poison is beginning to work when the Moor, exhausted, throws himself in a chair and cries out to himself at the thought of Desdemona's guilt.

Iago comes forward and in a casual, hearty manner bids Otello think no more of it. Otello turns on him in anger and despair, cursing him for having put suspicions in his mind where before there had been the contentment of ignorance. Otello's agitation increases in another of those superbly dramatic declamatory sequences in which the opera abounds. It comes to an abrupt end with Boito's adaptation of the famous "Farewell the tranquil mind" speech that cul-

Ex 405

minates in "Othello's occupation's gone"—"Ora e per sempre addio, sante memorie" (Ex 405).

If, to those hearing *Otello* for the first time, there is something vaguely familiar about this episode with its firm martial four-in-a-bar, it may well be because they have heard *Un ballo in maschera*, where we find in "Dunque l'onta di tutti sol una" (Ex 243), a number in the same key, with the same determined rhythm beaten out by a harp (two harps in *Otello*), and pizzicato double basses divided into four parts, which anticipates this later music in the most unmistakable manner. It is not just in the relentless thumping of harps and divided basses that the orchestra might still be accompanying Renato, Samuel and Tom; the typical punctuation by unison brass triplets, the *pp* double of harps and basses in due course by the trombones, the quasi-military flourishes of cornets and trumpets which emphasize that this is a farewell to arms—all are further clear reminders of an earlier style.

Iago's attempt to console Otello only makes matters worse. In a stormy sequence started off by a tremolo triplet figure which had made a restrained appearance in the violas and violoncellos in the first stages of "Ora e per sempre addio", Otello rages against Iago, swearing that unless he can produce proof of Desdemona's guilt he shall know the full force of his fury. To the sound of a terrifying orchestral tutti of unison octaves Otello seizes Iago by the throat and flings him to the ground. Iago rises, and in a calm voice informs Otello that he is no longer his ensign: "I want the world to be my witness that honesty is dangerous". Iago makes a pretence of leaving, but Otello calls him back and insists on proof—"I believe Desdemona is true and I believe she is not; I believe you honest and I believe you disloyal—I want proof! I want certainty!"

Iago asks him what kind of certainty he needs. "Perhaps," suggests Iago, his words sung *cupo* against an uncanny unison shake by two flutes, "perhaps you would like to see them embraced?"*

Since, as Shakespeare put it, "It were a tedious difficulty . . . to bring them to that prospect", Iago proposes that perhaps a reasonable certainty, a strong conjecture, would serve to convince Otello instead, and he describes a dream he says Cassio had—"Era la notte, Cassio dormia" ("It was night, Cassio was sleeping"):

Ex 406

Andantino
mezza voce

E-ra la not-te Cassio dor- mi-a, gli stavo ac- can-to

* This is Boito's rather euphemistic paraphrase, obviously more suitable for family audiences, of Shakespeare's much coarser original to be found in *Othello*, Act III, Scene 3, lines 396–7.

Boito keeps fairly close to Shakespeare's original "I lay with Cassio lately"—at least, in its essentials, for Iago does not tell us in the opera how he was kept awake, "troubled with a raging tooth", or refer to Cassio's rather alarming physical behaviour while dreaming (no doubt it was a question of family audiences again). On the other hand, Boito's Iago is a little more detailed in description of Cassio's tone of voice, of the "mournful tones" in which he is alleged to have said, "Sweet Desdemona, Let us be away, let us hide our loves!", of his anguished, "Cursed fate, that give thee to the Moor!"

Iago tells this tale in what is perhaps one of the most beautiful passages of music Verdi ever wrote; it has the deceptive simplicity of Mozart and by its very beauty and charm creates an effect of evil surely without parallel in opera.

The orchestration has the same inspired simplicity as the music of this scene. The writing for muted strings is exquisite and there are masterly little touches to be studied, such as the strong instrumental differentiation that underlines Verdi's musical differentiation between Iago's story and his direct quotation of Cassio's words. The monotone to which the phrase beginning, "Sweet Desdemona . . ." is sung is accompanied by a couple of four-part *ppp* chords which, scored for three flutes in their lower register with an oboe taking the top voice, have an oddly unreal effect. The wonderful downward chromatic slither with which this quotation ends (Verdi instructs Iago to sing *strisciando*—"creeping like a snake") is another imaginative moment superbly coloured by inventive orchestration—in this case the doubling of the woodwind's *strisciata* by the tremolo of four solo violins and a solo viola.

Iago's second imaginary quotation—"Cursed fate, that gave thee to the Moor!"—is sung entirely on one note, marked "cupo (sempre mezza voce)", and accompanied by dark low-register chords in clarinets, bassoon and horn. The two-bar string phrase which follows, and forms a brief interlude to make the transition from Cassio's dream to Iago's matter-of-fact account of how the dream faded into "blind lethargy", is one of the most ravishing moments in all opera. Just how ravishing a moment it can be, those who know Toscanini's performance of it will know well; his uncanny understanding of Verdi's intentions and his scrupulous observance of the unexpected accentuation of a startlingly original harmonic sequence made these few bars, and the coda it leads to, one of the most breathtaking experiences in his unforgettable recording of the opera.*

In his determination that "Era la notte" should not stop the show, Verdi makes Otello react immediately to what he has just heard and tread on Iago's last note with an agitated cry. Iago re-

* See *The Toscanini Legacy*, pp 287–8.

minds him cunningly that he was only talking about a dream; some further proof is needed—for instance, has Otello ever noticed Desdemona carrying a fine handkerchief embroidered with flowers? (Iago's words are sung to an exquisitely lyrical four-bar phrase accompanied by strings which contrasts unexpectedly with the forceful declamatory style of the rest of this conversation.) Otello replies that the handkerchief was the first pledge of love he gave Desdemona.

"Yesterday," Iago continues, "I saw that handkerchief in Cassio's hand."

In a thunderous outburst of rage Otello cries out: "O God give him a thousand lives! One is poor prey for my fury!" These words, neatly adapted from the original "O! that the slave had forty thousand lives;" are followed by others more closely translated from the same speech—"Look here, Iago; All my fond love thus do I blow to heaven: 'Tis gone" and, after a more prosaic rendering by Boito of "Swell, bosom, with thy fraught, For 'tis of aspics' tongues!", the final despairing, "O! blood, blood, blood!"

This is the cue for the short and stirring duet which ends the act. Otello kneels and in a solemn monotone begins his oath of revenge "by yond marble heaven". In the orchestra, clarinets, bassoons, bass clarinet and—an unusual choice—horns in low A, in an impressive unison play:

Ex 407

Here we have the perennial unchanging Verdi who, for all his great age and experience, still pulled out all the heroic stops that had served him for oath-swearing male duets since his earliest days. The orchestral accompaniment, although inevitably much fuller than in Verdi's earlier works, is by no means subtle. The steady three-in-a-bar of the specified 3/4 which from the very start becomes a firm 9/8, is punctuated by Verdi's traditional timpani and bass drum rumbles and bangs on the off-beats. What starts off as a fierce declaration of vengeance becomes an oath-swearing duet when, at the end of his declaration, Otello starts to rise off his knees, but is prevented by Iago who, kneeling beside him, swears to devote heart and soul to his service.

Iago sings his words to the tune quoted in Ex 407, which is now developed and built up *crescendo e stringendo* with the help of a spectacular rising chromatic run for three unison trombones in

semiquavers, before leading us to a return of Tempo I°. Raising
their hands to heaven as for a solemn oath Otello and Iago sing
the words of the opening stanza together—"Yes, I swear by yond
marble heaven, by the twisted lightning, by death and by the dark
destructive sea . . ."—Otello repeating his first monotone phrases,
Iago singing the same tune as before.

The music builds up once more, growing in excitement and intensity, and a two-bar phrase which, like the trumpet tune in the *Aida*
march, threatens to lead to an endless sequence of modulation onwards and upwards, is taken from C sharp major to F major, and
then, to one's great relief, left in peace.

The duet's climax comes when, after a false finish, one is surprised
to hear Otello and Iago indulging in a good old unaccompanied
tenor-and-baritone cadence—not cadenza—as together, a major
third apart, they invoke the God of Vengeance. The curtain falls on
an orchestral coda which, with its arresting succession of *pesante*
major chords (complete with consecutive fifths and octaves) in
the sequence A–G natural–F sharp–F natural–E major–A, quickly
drags us back into the musical atmosphere of Verdi's maturity.

The second act of *Otello* is in effect a continuous conflict between
Otello and Iago, with Iago, if not yet the victor, obviously the one
who will triumph in the end. Musically, of course, the act is dominated by Iago; the violence and drama of his tremendous Credo,
and the uncannily evil, subtle, beauty of "Era la notte", are highspots in an act without a weak bar in it—unless we except the musical and floral tribute to Desdemona, and even this has a naïve charm
and an air of innocence that contrasts strongly with the horror of the
inevitable unfolding of the drama.

Boito's libretto of this act is again a model of ingenious condensation, full of masterly touches and, in the case of the Credo, passages of inspired invention. Comparison with the original play
shows that most of the action and much of the language have been
retained with great skill. The opening scene between Iago and
Cassio is taken from Act III, Scene 1 of Shakespeare's tragedy; the
rest is based on Act III, Scene 3. Boito made one effective alteration
in the running order, however. In Shakespeare the scene in which
Desdemona asks Othello to pardon Cassio comes before the "green-
ey'd monster" scene between Iago and Othello. In the libretto the
Iago-Otello scene comes first; and then, after the islanders' choral
sequence has established a gentle lyrical mood, comes the scene
between Desdemona and Otello, to contrast dramatically with the
peacefulness of what has gone before in a way that can only be
achieved by music. The transposition of these two scenes was one of
Boito's happiest strokes.

ACT III

*Scene : The Great Hall of the Castle. On the right, a large portico which leads
to a smaller room ; at the back, a terrace.*

The act begins with a very short orchestral introduction based on
the "Jealousy" theme that begins at the fourth bar of Ex 402. This,
as I have already indicated, is the only theme, apart from the love-
theme at the end of Act I, to be heard again outside the act in which
it originally occurred. Verdi's reticence in this matter becomes more
astonishing the longer one thinks of it. Otello's jealousy not only increases in intensity as the story proceeds but is, of course, the very
root of the whole drama ; yet not once, after this introductory orchestral passage, does Verdi ever refer to the theme again. Otello's
jealousy propels the drama along with such force that we need no
leitmotif as a constant reminder—in case our attention might wander
—of what is going on. Only Wagner among Verdi's operatic contemporaries had the inventiveness to be able to dispense with
thematic labels of this kind, but unfortunately he seems to have
lacked the courage to try it out.

Verdi's orchestral prelude to the rise of the curtain on this act
lasts less than seventy seconds, but in that time he develops the
theme, first by strings (no double basses), then by a dramatic six-bar
passage in which the brass play a *ff* part, to create an oppressive
atmosphere of tragic tension and poignancy.

The curtain rises on Otello and Iago whose conversation is interrupted by the appearance of the Herald announcing, against a
ppp chord by horns, cornets, trumpets and trombones, that the galley
bringing the Venetian envoys to Cyprus has been sighted. The
Herald leaves and Otello, who doesn't seem to have been paying
much attention to the Herald, begs Iago to go on with what he was
saying—namely, his plan to get Cassio into a compromising conversation which Otello will overhear and so be convinced of his guilt.
As Desdemona approaches Iago leaves, turning back for a moment
to remind Otello not to forget the handkerchief.

Desdemona enters, and greets her husband to music of immense
charm and grace (Ex 408, p. 458).

To the same warm lyrical music Otello takes her hand and pays
ironical tribute to her chastity. Desdemona, deceived perhaps by the
dolcissimo quality of the music, does not notice the irony of Otello's
words and ends a passage of great beauty with the assurance to her

15*

husband that " 'twas that hand that gave away my heart". The
ravishing string phrase which began this little scene now serves as a
coda to round it off.

Ex *408*

Desdemona begins to speak of Cassio once more. Otello ignores
her words, and in great agitation tells her to mop his brow; he is
overcome with "a salt and sorry rheum". Desdemona offers her
handkerchief; Otello refuses it, demanding the handkerchief he
gave her. Her reply that she hasn't got it with her, brings a sinister
warning from Otello: misfortune will come to her if she has lost it
or given it away. The handkerchief has magical properties, woven
into it by a powerful enchantress.

Has she lost it? Desdemona says no; she will look for it later.
Otello insists that she produce it at once.

The music to this Allegro agitato dialogue is based on a figure in
the strings, heard for the most part *pp*—

Ex *409*

—which Verdi uses ingeniously to create the tension and fury of
Otello's mounting hysteria. Desdemona accuses her husband of
making all this fuss about a handkerchief to prevent her pleading for
Cassio. "This is a trick to put me from my suit", Desdemona protests
con eleganza and *con garbo* ("gracefully") to a tune whose richness in
both these qualities makes Desdemona's innocence unquestionable:

Ex *410*

Otello, deaf to his wife's pleading, repeats his demand for the handkerchief with ever-growing fury. He seizes her by the shoulder, and putting a hand under her chin, forces her to look at him and swear she is innocent and chaste. Desdemona looks at him firmly and swears it. Otello shouts at her that by protesting her innocence she has damned herself. She falls on her knees, terrified by the words she hears but does not understand; she speaks in a monotone punctuated by a grim *ppp* thumping of trombones, horns and bassoons in their low registers, like heartbeats heard in a strained silence.

In a passionate, tearful phrase, Desdemona begs her husband to look at her, and then in a broad, moving tune with a slow throbbing four-in-a-bar accompaniment prays to heaven for him with the "first tears" she has shed in her suffering:

This passage, with its rich-sounding but in fact wonderfully simple orchestral accompaniment, must be one of the few occasions when tears and weeping are mentioned in a Verdi opera and not expressed in one or other of the composer's typical *piangendo* phrases first heard in *Nabucco* and *Macbeth* (see Exx 11 and 37).

It is only in the agitated movement which follows, when Otello pushes Desdemona angrily away from him, that his own hysterical sobs are reflected in the music by a taut syncopated chromatic figure. Otello continues to insult his wife, accusing her of "the blackest of crimes" and calling her *vil cortigiana*—"vile whore". Desdemona continues to protest her innocence in vain. Suddenly Otello's mood changes from anger to calm irony. Returning to the grace and charm of Ex 408 he takes her hand and leads her to the door, apologizing that he should have thought so wrongly of her— "I took you for that cunning whore of Venice That married with Othello."

Otello pushes Desdemona out of the room; and there is a *ff* comment from the orchestra based on the agitated chromatic phrase of Ex 409 which dies down as Otello returns to the centre of the stage in deep dejection to reflect on his feelings of misery and shame in a magnificent soliloquy, "Dio, mi potevi scagliar tutti i mali della miseria, della vergogna . . . " The near-monotone of the voice is accompanied by an orchestral figure (in the first violins) which Verdi develops simply and with immensely pathetic effect:

Ex 412

Gradually Otello's anger rises again and he bursts out stormily proclaiming that Desdemona shall first confess her sin and then die. He is interrupted by the appearance of Iago, who tells him that Cassio is waiting near the entrance. If Otello will hide himself he will be able to overhear their conversation and so be convinced of Cassio's guilt. To the accompaniment of a series of terrifying *ff* G flats hammered out in the orchestra Otello hides behind a pillar on the terrace, and Iago goes to greet Cassio, addressing him as Captain and welcoming him with a charm of manner as captivating as it is evil, and expressed in the music by a superbly sensuous and ingratiating passage for strings with this tune on the G strings of the first violins:

Ex 413

Otello, from his hiding place, is unable to hear clearly the conversation that follows between Cassio and Iago, though he can see their expressions. Because he hears Desdemona's name mentioned at the beginning of the dialogue (Cassio says he had hoped to see her and learn how her plea for his reinstatement had fared) Otello imagines that his wife is the reason for Cassio's smiles and laughter. In fact, after this first reference to Desdemona Iago has cunningly steered the conversation (which takes place to some coyly skittish music) round to Cassio's love-affair with Bianca. Much of what Cassio says is inaudible to Otello (and to the audience), but Cassio's obviously happy mood is underlined by the elegance and gaiety of the scherzo-like music which now forms the background to the conversation—a sequence of exquisitely delicate orchestral writing on a chamber-music scale:

Ex 414

When Cassio begins to talk of his discovery of Desdemona's handkerchief at his lodging Iago leads him out of earshot of Otello whose
worst suspicion now becomes certainty. At this point Verdi reduces
the number of strings to four first, four second violins, two solo violas
and two solo violoncellos to allow us to hear a remarkable *pp* passage
for two flutes and a *pp* minor-third shake in the piccolo's low register
which accompanies them from time to time.

Making sure that Otello can hear what is going on Iago asks
Cassio to show him the handkerchief. Cassio takes it from his doublet
and Iago holds it behind his back for Otello to see and recognize with
a dramatic cry and a blood-curdling series of unison quavers and
trills in the orchestra.

The tempo changes and in an Allegro brillante 6/8 sequence,
accompanied *pianissimo* and *molto staccato* by strings (no double
basses) Iago describes the handkerchief to Cassio as a spider's web
that has entangled his heart and from which there is no escape:

Ex 415

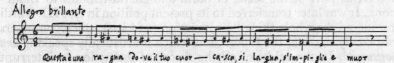

The movement started in this feather-light manner develops into
another, faster scherzo, this time with a brief lyrical Trio interlude of
great charm at a slightly slower tempo in which Cassio grows rapturous about the beauty and workmanship of the handkerchief he
has taken back from Iago. Cassio's *cantabile* solo is accompanied by
a striking passage of orchestration, the feature of which is a series of
pedal points sustained high in the violins and low in the other strings
against a captivating woodwind doubling and harmonization of the
vocal line. The whole scene—Iago's Allegro brillante and Cassio's
interlude—points unmistakably to the light touch and gaiety of
Falstaff, without for a moment being out of the character of *Otello*.

When the *Tempo primo* is resumed Otello joins in and immediately
the music's former brilliance is darkened by his frustrated comments, which the return to the major in the trio's final moments and
the orchestral coda fail to obliterate.

In the distance there is a sound of trumpets and a cannon shot;
the call is answered by trumpets in the Castle and echoed by a third
group from another point. Iago tells Cassio that the fanfare is to
announce the arrival of the galley from Venice and advises him to
leave before Otello appears. Cassio leaves hurriedly. Otello comes
out of his hiding place and comes to the point immediately: how
shall he kill Desdemona? Iago must give him some poison. Iago

replies that it would be better to "strangle her in her bed, even the
bed she hath contaminated", an idea which appeals to Otello, for
"the justice of it pleases". As for Cassio, continues Iago, "let me be
his undertaker". Otello rewards Iago by appointing him his Captain.

This short, dramatic conversation is carried on against a background of trumpet calls that grow louder and more brilliant, and the
"Evvivas" of the off-stage chorus of Cypriots greeting the arrival of
the Venetians. Iago suggests that in order to avoid suspicion Desdemona should appear before the Ambassador; Otello agrees and sends
Iago to fetch her. Otello goes towards the back of the Hall to receive
the visitors.

Provision is made at this point in the score to interrupt the exciting
trumpet flourishes and interpolate the *ballabile*—the ballet music
written for the production of the opera in Paris. Although the Paris
performance of *Otello* was not until October 1894, the question of the
ballet and its music was on Verdi's mind some months before the
Scala première in 1887. The first plan was to introduce the ballet in
Act II, as part of the scene of floral-and-choral-tributes to Desdemona. It was later transferred to its present position in Act III. Verdi
considered the whole thing "a concession (a *lâcheté*) which composers
mistakenly make to the Opéra, but which is artistically speaking *una
mostruosità*. In the midst of all the furore of the action to interrupt
with a ballet?!!!"

Verdi's earliest intention was to base the music on seventeenth-
century models and he asked Giulio Ricordi to find him Sarabandes,
Gavottes and Gigues—there were some in Corelli, he said, but they
were far too well done and had never been used for dancing.

By the time he had to think seriously about the *Otello* ballet once
more—in the summer of 1894—Verdi had changed his mind and
decided to have a characteristically "Cypriot" ballet. He pestered
Ricordi to find him "something Greek, Turkish and Venetian". As
Ricordi failed to find him anything suitable Verdi did his own re-
search and delivered a score consisting of Turkish Dance, Arab
Song, Invocation to Allah, Greek Song, Greek Dance, "La Muranese", and War Song.

"Your Doctors of Music have found nothing," he wrote to Ricordi,
when sending the finished score, "but I have found a Greek song
dating from 5000 years B.C.! If the world didn't exist at that time
then it's too bad for the world. Then I have found a *Muranese* composed two thousand years ago for a war between Venice and Murano
which the Muranesi won. It doesn't matter that Venice didn't yet
exist." (This at least leaves no doubt about the meaning of "La
Muranese", which I saw translated recently as "The Moorish
Girl".)

For the benefit of the ballet master of the Opéra, Verdi—already

experienced with *Aida* in the remote control of choreography—
drafted his own programme for the *Otello* ballet. (He also insisted
that the ballet master should see the full score of the music in good
time, and so know not to have lots of people dancing during the quiet
passages and only a few during the loud passages.)

The ballet, Verdi said, should last 5 minutes and 59 seconds. The
"programme" was as follows:

"As soon as the trumpets play at the beginning a group of Turkish slave
girls appear who dance reluctantly and with ill-humour (because they
are slaves). At the end of this first movement, hearing the *Arab Song*,
they grow more lively and end up by dancing wildly.

"At the *Invocation to Allah* all prostrate themselves on the ground. Just
then there appears among the columns a group of beautiful young
Greek girls, followed four bars later by another; the dancers come forward and at the thirteenth bar join in a dance that is quiet, aristocratic
and classical.

"There follows at once *La Muranese*. Allegro vivace 6/8 and a group of
Venetian men and girls come out from between the columns. followed
eight bars later by a second group. At the *fortissimo* in the eighteenth bar
they are downstage when they dance.

"After this *ff* there is a *leggerissimo* passage in F sharp which must be
danced as a *pas de deux*. The theme is repeated (in a louder orchestration) when all the Venetians dance. With the reprise of the first 6/8
theme I would be glad to see another group of Venetians come forward.

"The dance to the *War Song* should be performed by men only. On the
return to the first theme all the Venetians dance; then at the *più mosso*
Venetians, Turks, Greeks and everybody can join in—*Amen*."

The ballet music for the Paris *Otello*, composed a year and a half
after the first performance in February 1893 of *Falstaff*, was the last
music Verdi ever wrote for the stage. It is a vigorous piece of work, as
unmistakably by the composer of the *ballabili* in *Macbeth*, *Il trovatore*
and *I vespri siciliani* as it is by the composer of the *Aida* ballet. The
orchestration, in particular, ranges from the robust to the exquisite—
from the uninhibited use of cornets to play good vulgar tunes (as
well as a superbly effective sustained *pppp* trill leading into the *Arab
Song*), to the subtle colour of the passages for two harps in the *Greek
Dance* where the first harp doubles the tune of the first violins in the
same high register (the second harp doubles the second violins).

Just how drastic an interruption to the action the introduction of a
ballet into the third act of *Otello* must have been one may now know
from its inclusion in the 1961 Decca recording of the opera. The
result would be less of a *mostruosità* if the ballet music were clearly
marked as a separate band, thus making it easier for the listener to

skip clearly to the point in the record where the normal version is resumed. One thing is certain: it may be interesting to hear the ballet music in its reluctant context once, but not every time one wants to play the recording. It must be said in Decca's favour, however, that they did not go so far as to perform *Otello* altogether in its Paris form, for that would have meant observing the cuts and modifications made by Verdi for the Opéra later on in Act III in order to shorten the running time, lower some of the vocal hurdles facing the French ensemble, and reach the climax of the act without further delay. It is a pity, nevertheless, that the Paris ballet supplement is not detachable in this recording.

When the trumpet fanfares do not lead to the ballet they accompany Otello's reception of the Venetian envoys, and the entrance of Roderigo, the Herald, dignitaries of the Venetian Republic, Ladies, Gentlemen, soldiers, trumpeters, Iago with Desdemona and Emilia. The crowd renews its acclamations and ends them with the chorus sopranos on a high C.

Lodovico, the principal Venetian ambassador, hands Otello a dispatch from the Doge and Senate of Venice. While Otello is reading it Lodovico talks to Desdemona and Iago, and remarks that Cassio is not present. He is out of favour with Otello, says Iago; Desdemona adds that she believes Cassio will return to grace. Without looking up from his reading Otello snaps at Desdemona: "Are you certain?" "What do you say?" asks Desdemona. Lodovico intervenes telling Desdemona that Otello was reading; he was not talking to her.

When Iago says that perhaps Cassio will be restored to grace Desdemona replies that she hopes so, for she has a true affection for Cassio. Otello overhears her last remark and, still pretending to read, warns Desdemona in an undertone to hold her tongue; then, roused to a fury, he raises his arm to strike her, but is held back by Lodovico. Otello orders the Herald to fetch Cassio. Lodovico is horrified by what he has seen and asks Iago what has come over him—"is this the noble nature whom passion could not shake?" Iago replies: "He's that he is—I may not breathe my censure."

Cassio enters. Otello reads out the Doge's dispatch, dropping his voice to taunt Desdemona in a series of venomous asides—"how well you feign your weeping!"—"keep up your tears!' The Doge has ordered Otello to return to Venice forthwith, and to the fury of Iago, has appointed Cassio to be governor of Cyprus. Cassio, Otello observes to Iago, significantly shows no sign of elation at his appointment, while Desdemona's tears, he is now convinced, are because she is to return to Venice and so be parted from Cassio.

Lodovico begs Otello to comfort her; his answer is to throw Desdemona savagely to the ground, an action followed, as Lodovico

and Emilia lift her up, by a series of overpowering chords in the
orchestra:

Ex 416

A long ensemble follows, building up from a simple pizzicato
figure in the lower strings and another echo of the first subject of the
Jupiter finale already hinted at in the first bars of Ex 394.

Desdemona, whose misery is heart-rending, has the two big tunes
which dominate one of the most complicated concerted passages in
all Verdi's operas. The first is a superbly simple four-bar phrase for
which the third and fourth bars are no more than a slight elabora-
tion of the first two, and which is first heard with an exquisitely
delicate *pp* staccato accompaniment by woodwind:

Ex 417

The second tune is much longer and plays a bigger part in the
development of the movement:

Ex 418

The complicated nature of this ensemble, in which it was customary
a generation ago to make huge cuts of forty bars or more, springs
from the unusually large number of points-of-view expressed by the
principal characters in addition to the comments made by the
women of the chorus which, in turn, differ from those of the men.

Desdemona continues to lament her plight, which deeply touches Emilia; Cassio reflects that the honour conferred on him gives him no joy; Roderigo is unhappy that Desdemona is to leave Cyprus; Lodovico is appalled by Otello's behaviour. The women in the chorus are moved to pity, the men are horrified.

For some time Iago and Otello are silent; when at last Iago speaks it is to urge Otello to make haste in taking his revenge; he himself will take care of Cassio. Iago turns to Roderigo and tells him that if he is not to lose Desdemona he must quickly dispose of Cassio (an "accident" to Cassio would mean, of course, that Otello and Desdemona would not leave for Venice).

As the ensemble reaches its climax with a great *ff* repetition of Ex 418 (the last bar in a formidable unison) Otello turns on the crowd and shouts at them to go. When they hesitate he grows more violent. Behind the scenes a triumphal fanfare of trumpets and trombones punctuates the off-stage "Evvivas" of the Cypriot population. Desdemona tries to comfort him, but he curses her—a terrifying moment underlined in the orchestra by a shake for cornets and trumpets. The scene empties and Otello and Iago are left alone.

Otello rapidly grows delirious, shouting for the handkerchief and disjointedly repeating Iago's insinuations, until he becomes convulsive and faints away—and—in Shakespeare's words, "is fallen into an epilepsy".

Iago remarks with satisfaction that his poison is beginning to work. The fanfares and jubilant cries of the populace start up again behind the scenes; Iago stands over Otello's senseless body and asks, "Chi può vietar che questa fronte prema col mio tallone?" ("Who can prevent me pressing my heel into this forehead?"):

Ex *419*

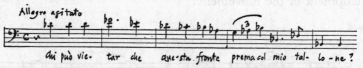

Whether this wonderfully characteristic phrase is a deliberate echo or not, it is difficult to say, but it has a strong affinity with the first evil words uttered by Iago in the opera, when during the storm in Act I he turns to Roderigo and prays that Otello's ship will sink:

Ex *420*

The fanfares continue and the back-stage male chorus, now much nearer, acclaims Otello and cries glory to the Lion of Venice. Iago, standing erect, listens and then points triumphantly at the motionless body of Otello and with a terrible sarcasm, coloured with unison trills in the low register of the two clarinets, the four bassoons, violas and violoncellos, snarls: "There is the Lion!"

With a last burst of "viva Otello!" and a *ff* echo of the first trumpet calls the act ends with a curtain that has no counterpart in Shakespeare's play. It is purely Boito's invention and with Verdi's music must rank as one of the most masterly strokes of pure theatre in the history of opera.

ACT IV

Scene: Desdemona's bed-chamber. A bed, a prie-dieu, a table, a looking glass, some chairs. A lamp hangs burning before the picture of the Madonna, which is above the prie-dieu. There is a door on the right, a lighted candle on the table. It is night.

Before the curtain rises there is an orchestral introduction for wood-wind and one horn—a passage of extreme sadness and heavy with a sense of foreboding, in which the cor anglais plays a leading part. The first six bars of the orchestral prelude introduce three phrases which are important in the action that follows; the first is for the cor anglais; the second for three flutes in unison in their low register; the third is the hollow, sinister sound of bare fifths in the *chalumeau* register of the two clarinets heard already in *Rigoletto* and *Don Carlos*:

Ex *421*

Desdemona is preparing for bed where, she tells Emilia, she has been ordered by Otello to wait. She delivers the words in a flat matter-of-fact voice, punctuated by the stark, knell-like fifths of the clarinets. Desdemona asks her lady-in-waiting to lay out her white bridal garment, and then in passionate tones as Emilia makes the bed, tells her:

> If I do die before thee, prithee, shroud me
> In one of those same sheets.

Emilia begs her to put such ideas out of her head, but Desdemona replies that she is sad. The clarinets play their ominous fifths again. Seating herself mechanically in front of the looking glass Desdemona relates how her mother had a maid called Barbara, who was in love but was deserted by her lover and sang "a song of 'Willow' ". The song haunts her tonight, she says, and as Emilia undoes her hair she sings it.

The Willow Song is prefaced by a short passage for woodwind which serves as an interlude between the verses. The opening phrase of the song itself is that of the cor anglais tune in Ex *421* which began the act. There are three verses in all, none of them identical, but their sequence is interrupted first by Desdemona bidding Emilia to make haste lest Otello arrive; then by Desdemona taking a ring from her finger and giving it to Emilia to put away; and finally by Desdemona thinking she hears the sound of wailing outside and a knock on the door, which Emilia reassures her is only the wind. The invention is endless, from the simple "willow, willow, willow," phrase itself with its affecting fall of a minor third, always sung unaccompanied "like a voice in the distance", its last phrase echoed far away by the cor anglais, to the inspired hovering between major and minor harmonies.

The orchestration of the episode is masterly; it is original, simple, and its effect achieved with an astonishing economy of means—such as the *pp* F sharp sustained by the piccolo and cor anglais three octaves apart, the low-register shakes for the flutes (the flute writing throughout this scene is as imaginative and skilful as it was in *Aida*), and the voicing of the woodwind chord with a solo double bass on the fundamental note as Desdemona sings "Cantiamo", so unexpectedly in the major, to lead into the three final *pianissimo* cries of "Salce!"

When she has ended her song Desdemona bids Emilia farewell and to the sound of four repeated and wonderfully-scored chords of F sharp major, says goodnight. The scoring of these chords is again quite astonishingly simple—two flutes in unison on their low F sharp, the cor anglais an octave lower, the second clarinet on the C sharp below that with the first clarinet on A sharp a sixth above, second and fourth bassoons on their low F sharp with the first and third bassoons on the C sharp above, the violins double the notes of the flutes and first clarinet, violas and violoncellos *divisi* play their low F sharps and C sharps.

Although the double basses supply a short pizzicato F sharp on the first beat of each bar (supported by a *ppp* beat on the bass drum) the low C sharp held by the violoncellos gives the sound the character of a second inversion of the chord of F sharp major—that is, of the so-called six-four chord of which C sharp is the bass note—and the effect is most unusual.

As Emilia turns to leave, Desdemona cries out a passionate farewell and embraces her in one of the most heart-rending phrases in all music—Verdi's final expression of the tears and anguish of a brokenhearted woman which we first heard in *Il trovatore* (Ex 116):

Ex 422

Andante mosso

con passione

Ah! E- milia, Emilia, ad- dio, E-mi-lia, ad- di - - o!

Emilia leaves and the music dies down slowly in a sequence in which the phrase for three flutes in Ex 421 (bars 4 and 5) is repeated and varied, played first by the three flutes, oboe and first clarinet in unison and then, in a register that goes below that of the flutes and oboe, by cor anglais and solo horn in unison.*

The first of these sequences is accompanied by a long descending chromatic passage played *pp* by the four bassoons in unison with the violoncellos (tremolo) and double basses, the second by a similar passage *più piano* for two bassoons in octaves, with violoncellos and double basses as before. This short orchestral postlude to Desdemona's parting from Emilia is a further stage in Verdi's inspired creation of increasing tension and also of that increasing silence which now dominates the scene to an almost unbearable degree. The half-dozen bars for muted strings (no basses) which are heard as Desdemona kneels before the picture of the Madonna seem scarcely louder than thought and are a superb example of Verdi's uncanny gift, only ever approached by Puccini, of making the representation of silence by musical means more convincing and dramatic than silence itself.

In a *sotto voce* monotone Desdemona recites (in Italian) the first slightly modified lines of the Ave Maria; she then beseeches the Virgin to pray for the sinner, for the innocent, for all "who bow their heads beneath outrage and misfortune"—

Ex *423*

Her prayer, which ends with the words from the Ave Maria, "Pray for us now and in the hour of our death", is accompanied by muted strings (no basses) in a sequence of that beautiful and smooth part-writing for the instruments which was so characteristic of Verdi's later operas. In the course of a *pp* coda which takes violins and violas into the higher positions, Desdemona remains kneeling, resting her head on the *prie-dieu* and repeating the Ave Maria, of which only the first and last words are audible—"Ave Maria . . . in the hour of our death". With a final *dolcissimo* "Ave!" ending on her high A flat (one of the most difficult moments in the whole

---

* The second oboe, who does not double cor anglais, has been silent since the start of the act—in case, I imagine, the work is played in theatres where there is no such luxury as an independent cor anglais player and the part has to be doubled after all.

soprano repertoire) and an "Amen" in the same monotone in which she began her prayer, Desdemona rises to her feet and lies down on the bed.

There now occurs a classic passage for muted double basses alone. It accompanies the entrance of Otello, and like many of my contemporaries I had read about it and seen it in print in Richard Strauss' edition of Berlioz' treatise on orchestration, where it was presented as a supreme example of writing for the instrument, long before I first heard it in the opera house.* When at last I heard it played in its full theatrical context the effect was beyond anything I could have imagined and I was not surprised to learn that the whole passage, twenty-six bars long, had been encored at the Scala première of the opera:

Ex 424

In Verdi's day the number of four-stringed double basses in the orchestra capable of playing the first six bars was limited; at the seventh bar the words "tutti un po' marcato" appear in the score to show that the music was now within the compass of the three-stringed instruments without a low E as well.

Played by anybody but really first-rate bass players the passage can be a miserable experience for performer and listener, for it exposes the slightest suggestion of inaccurate intonation in a merciless manner. The only relief—and it is the relief of punctuation not support—comes from the brief phrase played twice by violas and once by second violins, followed each time by a sinister distant *ppp* beat of the bass drum which Boito likened to "shovelfuls of earth being dropped into a grave". It is a sequence of quite terrifying dramatic suspense, which the stage action is timed to follow carefully.

"At the first note," run the stage directions, "Otello is seen standing on the threshold of a secret door. He comes forward and lays a scimitar on the table. He stands before the candle wondering whether to blow it out or not. He looks at Desdemona, then puts out the candle." With a gesture of fury, which he makes as the double

* Strauss' quotation gave us the passage in its context of two whole pages of full score—for most of us the first sight we had ever had of anything but a vocal score of Verdi's opera.

basses reach their final bar of agitated semiquavers, Otello goes towards the bed. He stops. Then he draws back the bed-curtains and
looks for a long time on the sleeping Desdemona—an action he performs as the cor anglais and a solo bassoon in unison, against a sustained *ppp* tremolo chord of A minor played by violins and violas,
twice play a short, poignant minor phrase (which seems to derive
from the first three bars of the double bass solo—Ex 424) and leads
to a repetition of the theme first heard in the Love Duet at the end
of Act I (Ex 398):

Ex 425

Otello kisses Desdemona three times as she lies asleep (the kisses
are shown in the score to coincide with the second, fourth and sixth
bars of the Love Theme). At the third kiss she awakens. In the scene
that follows the orchestral comment is dominated by the staccato
semiquaver figure which punctuated the double bass passage
(twelfth and thirteenth bars of Ex 424); when it is first heard at this
later point the bars have been lengthened from 4/4 to 3/2 time and
the bass drum note has been translated into an ominous unison C
across two octaves played by three trombones, the trumpets and
cornet.

Otello asks Desdemona if she has said her prayers—

> If you bethink yourself of any crime
> Unreconcil'd as yet to heaven and grace,
> Solicit for it straight.

Gradually Desdemona realizes that Otello means to kill her; she
loves Cassio, he says; and tells her about the handkerchief. Desdemona denies this and asks that Cassio should be allowed to speak;
Otello replies that Cassio is dead. Desdemona's cry of despair that
she is lost and Cassio betrayed angers Otello still further. His rage
grows and as the agitated semiquaver figure develops into a climax
he smothers her. There are three loud knocks at the door, but Otello
doesn't hear them as he stands staring at Desdemona's inert body
and murmurs, "Calma come la tomba"—Shakespeare's "Still as the
grave".

Otello comes to himself when the knocking is repeated and Emilia
is heard urgently demanding to come in. Otello opens the door and
she tells him that Cassio has killed Roderigo in a duel. From the bed
the dying Desdemona is heard murmuring faintly that she is innocent

and tells Emilia that no one is responsible for her death but herself. With her last breath, in a phrase full of heart-breaking pathos, Desdemona begs to be commended to her lord and bids Emilia farewell.

A short passage of rapid unaccompanied dialogue follows *a tempo prestissimo*, much of it sung by both singers on one note, in which Otello cries that Desdemona is a liar; he killed her because she was Cassio's mistress; Emilia has only to ask Iago. Emilia is appalled by Otello's stupidity, shakes herself free of his threatening grasp and runs to the door to shout for help. Lodovico, Cassio and Iago enter. Emilia tells her husband to give the lie to Otello's story. Did he believe Desdemona was unfaithful? Iago replies that he believed her guilty, and Otello tells how she gave the handkerchief to Cassio. Emilia, defying Iago's attempt to silence her, relates how Iago took the handkerchief from her by force; Cassio adds that he found it at his lodging.

At this moment Montano enters, with armed followers, and pointing to Iago announces that in his dying moments Roderigo told him of Iago's plot—a neater device but less admissible as evidence than the letter found on Roderigo's body in Shakespeare's play. Otello turns to Iago and tells him to refute the charge, but with a cry of refusal Iago flees, pursued by some of Montano's followers.

Boito's modification of Shakespeare's play at this point is an admirable theatrical stroke: by suppressing Iago's murder of Emilia and allowing Iago to escape—at any rate temporarily—without any reference to the torture which Shakespeare tells us he is to suffer— we are spared an irrelevant corpse on the scene and rid of a character whose fate does not concern us. Iago has done his work; his absence now enables us to concentrate better on its full, final effect.

As Iago rushes from the room Otello snatches his sword from the table to kill him, but Lodovico holds him back. "Do you dare?" Otello cries. They are the last words Otello speaks in anger, emphasized by an orchestral *fortissimo* which subsides into a series of richly-scored semibreve chords played *ppp* by the whole orchestra as a knell-like accompaniment to Otello's solemn, monotone assurance to the silent onlookers that they need not fear him—"Niun mi tema":

> Be not afraid, though you do see me weapon'd;
> Here is my journey's end. . . .

After a last, full-voiced "Oh! Gloria!" accompanied by a sustained chord for the entire wind of the orchestra which quickly dies down from *ff* to a dead *pp* thump of bass drum and double bass pizzicato, Otello murmurs, "Otello fu" ("Otello was") and drops his sword. He goes over to the bed and looks at Desdemona; and in a phrase which Francis Toye regarded with reason as "the most

beautiful, the most moving passage of the opera", cries to the dead
Desdemona—"E tu ; come sei pallida ! e stanca, e muta e bella . . ."
—"And thou—how pale, and weary, how silent and beautiful !"—

Ex *426*

"In this single line of music," says Toye, "half sung, half sobbed,
without accompaniment of any kind [until the fourth bar], lies the
kernel of the whole tragedy." The passage is followed by another
accompanied by strings and the *ppp* throbbing of timpani, in which
Otello sings a brief and pathetic sequence founded by Boito on two
memorable phrases in the play—"O ill-starr'd wench", and "Cold,
cold, my girl ! Even like thy chastity". It ends, after a rather surprising, cadenza-like couple of bars for the three flutes marked "pp
dolcissimo—sempre pianissimo", with another agonizing unaccompanied phrase : Otello's "Desdemona ! Desdemona ! Ah ! morta !
morta ! morta !"

Suddenly the music flares up from a sinister sequence of chords
played by the trombones in their low register as Otello furtively
draws a hidden dagger and stabs himself. The brief *ff* outburst by
the whole orchestra dies down to an echo of the elegiac theme of Ex
425, now with a clarinet added to the cor anglais and bassoon unison.
Otello falls on Desdemona, with

> I kiss'd thee ere I kill'd thee; no way but this,
> Killing myself to die upon a kiss.

—paraphrased by Boito to match the rhyme of the words heard in
the Love Duet at the end of Act I (Ex 398). The echo of that theme
now, as Otello dies, is heart-rending in its poignant reference to the
happiness and splendour of a love now so tragically destroyed.

The curtain falls, on a characteristically simple and moving
sequence of descending whole-note chords over a pedal E—C major,
A minor, F major—which resolves in a final chord of E major to
which almost every instrument in the orchestra (with the exception
of one cornet, two of the trombones and two of the horns) contributes the lowest E, G sharp or B in its range. The orchestration of
these last few bars is a superb example of "voicing" which all students
and many contemporary composers might study to their advantage.

There is little doubt, I think, that *Otello* is Verdi's greatest opera,
though it is only during the last thirty years or so that its greatness

has come to be recognized by the ordinary opera-going public. For too long it suffered from being thought "different" from the Verdi everybody knew—largely, of course, because it was reputed to be "Wagnerian", even though as long ago as 1901 Bernard Shaw pointed out in an obituary essay on Verdi that "the critic who can find Wagner in *Otello* must surely be related to the gentleman who accused Bach of putting forth the accompaniment to Gounod's 'Ave Maria' as a prelude of his own composition".

If we have to accept *Otello* as "different" at all, it is because it is pure, hundred-per-cent Verdi without a bar that is not stamped with the composer's unmistakable *melodic* individuality. Even those few passages marked "Recit.", which in earlier Verdi operas still contained conventional phrases (as in the recitative before "Celeste Aida" for instance) which might have been written by Cimarosa or Pergolesi, Rossini or Donizetti, are in *Otello* entirely personal, the final perfection of that declamatory style the composer had been developing over the years—the transformation of recitative into dramatic melody. Rather oddly Verdi himself did not seem to be altogether conscious of the change he had made—or if he was, did not trust his singers to respect it—for in the angry unaccompanied exchange between Emilia and Otello in the last act, where great dramatic effect is made by the characters abusing each other in phrases on the same note, he specifically instructs the singers to omit all appoggiaturas, in a passage which, as it happened, is not even marked "Recit.".

Whether marked "Recit." or not, the intensity and originality of the dialogue passages alone are characteristic of an opera which is constructed with the precision and workmanship of a Rolls-Royce, where the foreign language of Boito's libretto and the foreign medium of Verdi's music combine to re-create Shakespeare with such uncanny and instinctive certainty that the opera itself acquires its own unmistakable Shakespearian quality. Some of the set pieces of the play inevitably had to be jettisoned by Boito, but if we are denied Shakespeare's poetry we are more than compensated by the poetry of Verdi's music with its peculiar power to touch the heart more deeply than words.

There is nothing, for there could be nothing, in Shakespeare's *Othello* as heart-breakingly moving as the return of the theme from the Love Duet in the last moments of Verdi's opera. The lyrical opportunities in *Otello* are in fact supplied by Boito more often than by Shakespeare, who, though he provided the Willow Song, left it to Boito to conceive the Love Duet, and the Ave Maria, both of which add to the drama in a way Shakespeare might have wished he had thought of himself. This is especially true of the inspired use of the Ave Maria to create the suspense of impending tragedy with its terrifying reiteration of "Pray for us now, and in the hour of our death".

The speed, directness and inevitability of the action of the opera are natural obstacles to the indulgent inclusion of conventional "numbers", but where they were possible and relevant either to the action or as moments of contrast and repose, Verdi did not hesitate to make the most of them. Here again Boito's ingenuity and "nose" for situations, or even stray remarks, in Shakespeare's text which would give him a Cue for Song had the touch of genius about them.

We have seen that by throwing overboard Shakespeare's "And let the canakin clink, clink" in favour of the Brindisi, the drinking song in *Otello* sounds not as if Iago was singing a song "learned in England, where indeed they are most potent in potting", but one he had made up himself. The idea for what is perhaps the most exquisite near-irrelevance in the opera—the episode in Act I of the "Fuoco di gioia"—Boito found, as we have seen, in four words proclaimed by the Herald in his short solo scene in Act II, Scene 2 of the play, where in the course of the proclamation enjoining the people of Cyprus to celebrate his victory, Othello bids some to dance, "some to make bonfires". Boito's quick perception of how these words could be translated into a visual and musical interlude needed to change the mood and tempo of the action after the exhausting experience of the opening storm, was a brilliant stroke.

In *Otello* Verdi's delineation of character reached its highest level. Harmonically and melodically there is little in the opera that has not been heard before *somewhere* in Verdi. The difference is that in *Otello* a supreme concentration of a great many familiar elements is presented in unfamiliar proportions. What is brand new is the quality and nature of the characterization. Verdi had characterized jealousy before, but never jealousy like Iago's or Otello's; he had written love duets by the dozen before, but never one that expressed true love like that of Otello and Desdemona in Act I; he had depicted human decline and lingering death, but the subtle musical picture of the gradual degeneration, the inexorable wrecking of a man's reason and the destruction of his soul which fills the last three acts of *Otello* was—and has remained—something without parallel in opera.

Like *Don Giovanni* Verdi's *Otello* is an opera in which there is scarcely a side of human experience that is not touched on—love, hatred, happiness, grief, courage, humiliation, remorse, cruelty, jealousy, hypocrisy, laughter, tears, devotion, frustration, gullibility, anger, drunkenness, and death by duel, murder and suicide—all are expressed with the sympathy and insight of a composer whose understanding of human beings was never surpassed even by Mozart. "Shakespeare himself", concluded Francis Toye in his study of *Otello*, "did not do, could not have done, better."

FALSTAFF

(*Property of G. Ricordi and Co.*)

Lyric comedy in three acts. Libretto by Arrigo Boito—"taken from *The Merry Wives of Windsor* and from several passages of *Henry IV* relating to the character of Falstaff". First performed at La Scala, Milan, 9th February, 1893. First performance in England: Covent Garden, 19th May, 1894. First performance in the United States: Metropolitan Opera House, New York, 4th February, 1895.

IT WOULD have been reasonable to suppose that with *Otello* Verdi had earned the right to retire after nearly fifty years as an opera composer. He was close on seventy-four and had written what was undoubtedly his masterpiece. Boito, on the other hand, having once —and so successfully—lured Verdi back into the opera house, was determined not to let him return to the operatic inactivity that had filled the years between *Aida* in 1871 and *Otello* in 1887.

Exactly how and when Boito first came to suggest *Falstaff* to Verdi is not known for certain, but there is no doubt that the idea made an immediate appeal to the composer. What might pardonably be regarded as an unparalleled long-shot came off. Boito's suggestion was more than a gamble, however; it was a stroke of genius based on a rare psychological understanding of the mood the composer was in once *Otello* had been launched, and the knowledge that, in spite of the disastrous failure of his only comic opera, *Un giorno di regno* (1840), the idea of writing another comedy had engaged him for years.

When the news finally broke in 1890 that he was at work on *Falstaff* (strictly for his own amusement—"mi diverto", he said), Verdi declared that he had wanted to write a comic opera for forty years and that he had known Shakespeare's *Merry Wives of Windsor* for fifty, implying by this that it was only Boito's provision at long last of "a lyrical comedy unlike any other" which had finally removed all the "ifs" and "buts" which had stood in the way of realizing his long-standing dream of an opera based on the comedy by the playwright he referred to as "il Gran-poeta".

During this almost Wagnerian forty-year-period of gestation, however, the subject of an actual Falstaff opera was raised only once —by a rumour which Verdi immediately and flatly denied. This was in 1868, a year after he had finished *Don Carlos*. On the other hand, in the years between that opera and *Aida* in 1871 various other projects arose from time to time. In 1869, for instance, we know Verdi gave some thought to Molière's comedy *Tartuffe*, but discarded the idea without recorded comment; also that in the same year he considered the possibilities of another French comedy, *Froufrou* by Halévy and Meilhac, but that this, too, was rejected because although he regarded the first three acts as *stupendi* the last two he thought were commonplace, in spite of their theatrical effectiveness.*

After this no more was heard about a comic opera for another ten years when, in 1879, an article appeared in the *Gazzetta musicale*, edited by Verdi's publisher Giulio Ricordi, drawing attention to a remark made by Rossini in 1847 that Verdi was incapable of writing an *opera buffa*. This caused Verdi, half-indignantly, half-jokingly, to write to Ricordi protesting strongly against words likely to create an intolerable prejudice in the public mind at the very moment when "after twenty years' search for a comic opera libretto . . . I have practically found one". Verdi continued that if he should be tempted to write a comic opera Ricordi need have no fear: he would ruin some other publisher instead.

What the subject of the libretto was that Verdi had "practically found" nobody knows; it may even have been a pure invention, brought about by the injury to Verdi's sometimes over-sensitive feelings. True or not, the news certainly disturbed Giulio Ricordi, who had thought Verdi busily at work on *Otello*. However, the question of a comic opera does not seem to have arisen again until after *Otello* had been performed in 1887, when Verdi was reported to be seriously considering the idea, suggested by the Mayor of Milan, of an opera on Don Quixote.

The next figure to come on the scene was the original Iago of *Otello*, the French baritone Victor Maurel, to whom in the late eighties Verdi is said to have confessed that the idea of a lyrical comedy taken from Shakespeare had long fascinated him. Maurel, always eager for a new Verdi role, helpfully sent the composer a version of *The Taming of the Shrew* which had been made for Coquelin the Elder. Verdi returned the manuscript saying it was superb and that he envied the musician whose lot it would be to compose it; but as far as he was concerned it was too late. It was not until nearly two years later that Verdi explained to Maurel why it had been too late: "Boito and I had planned a lyrical comedy, now almost finished." Which is how Maurel came to be Verdi's first Falstaff instead of his first Petruchio.

Verdi's decision to compose *Falstaff* was made in the course of a

* It seems a pity that Verdi could not have teamed up with the authors of *Froufrou* in some way, for Halévy and Meilhac, either severally or in concert, were responsible not only for the librettos of *Carmen* and *Manon*, but of Offenbach's *Belle Hélène*, *Orpheus in the Underworld* and *La Vie Parisienne*, as well as having written the original play later transformed into Johann Strauss's *Fledermaus*.

few days in July 1889, though there was a critical moment of misgiving when, after greeting Boito's suggestion with enthusiasm one
day, he wrote full of fear that he was too old and too tired the next.
Boito in reply would have none of this; he brushed aside all Verdi's
arguments about age, health, hard work for composer and librettist
alike as not being valid obstacles to a new work.

Boito did not believe that writing a comic opera would tire the
composer. Writing a tragedy caused real suffering to the writer,
because the mind was afflicted by a sadness which affected the health
of the nerves. But the fun and laughter of comedy stimulated both
mind and body—"a smile adds a thread to the web of life".

Verdi's great desire to work was an undeniable proof of health and
strength to Boito, and the fact that he had wanted a good theme for a
comic opera all his life was a sure indication that a vein of artistic
gaiety existed in the composer's brain. "Instinct", said Boito, "is a
good counsellor." There was only one way better than finishing with
Otello, Boito went on, and that was to finish triumphantly with
Falstaff. "After having expressed the tears and lamentations of the
human heart," said Boito, "to finish with an immense explosion of
hilarity! That would be really amazing!"

After its many years of speculation about Verdi's intentions concerning a comic opera the public suffered another period of frustrating curiosity while the composer was actually known to be composing
Falstaff. He took nearly three years over its composition (longer than
he had taken for *Rigoletto*, *Il trovatore* and *La traviata* put together),
and in an infuriating manner seemed to regard the whole thing as a
purely personal affair, giving, on the one hand, no indication of
when, or even if, it would be finished, and on the other reserving the
right, if and when the time came, to withdraw the opera completely
and permanently, after the dress rehearsal if he felt so inclined.

Verdi's work on the score of *Falstaff* was leisurely and spasmodic,
interrupted sometimes by stretches of three months of inactivity
caused by ill-health, or delayed by the purely physical shortcomings
of old age, such as poor eyesight and the simple lack of manual
strength to do the orchestration. There are several touching instances
in the autograph score of Verdi having put the manuscript aside
and, on resuming work after the interruption, repeating the previous
couple of bars by mistake so that they had to be crossed out. But even
when at last the score was finished and rehearsals had begun at La
Scala, Verdi did not cease to change and modify details in the
music—including in one case an important alteration in the tune of
Fenton's *sonetto* in the second scene of Act III. More changes were
made for the performance of the work in Rome a few weeks after
the Milan première, while by the time *Falstaff* reached a third Italian
city, Venice in May 1893, Verdi had rewritten quite a lot of the

ensemble which leads to the discovery of the young lovers behind the screen in Act II, and the magical scene following Quickly's departure from the inn which ends the first scene of Act III.

Probably no universally recognized masterpiece in the history of opera was ever so widely, immediately, and rapturously acclaimed on its first appearance as *Falstaff*. One of the loudest notes in the general critical chorus which greeted it was one of admiration and astonishment that the composer of *Rigoletto* and *Il trovatore* should have written this entrancing comedy almost as a tremendous inspired and entirely unpredictable afterthought. Among the few who did not join in this chorus, however, was Bernard Shaw who drew attention to many earlier instances of Verdi's gift for dramatic humour—the ironic humour of Iago, the grim humour of Sparafucile, the agonized humour of Rigoletto, the befuddled humour of Cassio in the Brindisi, to say nothing of the comedy in *Un ballo in maschera* (Shaw somehow forgot the comic figure of Fra Melitone in *La forza del destino*).

Apart from Shaw's examples of that characteristic sense of musical humour which Verdi exploited to its fullest extent in *Falstaff*, there seem to me to be two equally important elements that had long been regularly recurrent features of his operas: Verdi's gaiety and lyrical charm. But whereas both these elements had formerly been used to create dramatic contrast—with ungay situations in *La traviata*, *Rigoletto*, *La forza del destino* and *Un ballo in maschera*, for instance, and uncharming events in *Aida* and *Otello*—in *Falstaff* they existed in their own rights, as it were. In other words, it was not a "new" Verdi who wrote *Falstaff*, but a composer who, as he had already done in *Otello*, was using familiar ingredients assembled in a different way and used in unfamiliar proportions.

CHARACTERS IN ORDER OF SINGING

DR CAIUS, *a French physician*	*Tenor*
SIR JOHN FALSTAFF	*Baritone*
BARDOLPH } *followers of Falstaff*	*Tenor*
PISTOL }	*Bass*
MRS MEG PAGE	*Mezzo-soprano*
MRS ALICE FORD	*Soprano*
MISTRESS QUICKLY	*Mezzo-soprano*
NANNETTA, *daughter of Alice Ford*	*Soprano*
FENTON	*Tenor*
FORD, *husband of Alice*	*Baritone*

Landlord of the Garter Inn; Robin, Falstaff's page; citizens; Ford's servants; Maskers disguised as spirits, fairies, witches, etc.

Scene: Windsor   Time: During the reign of Henry IV of England

16

CHARACTERS IN ORDER OF SINGING

DR CAIUS, *a French physician* . . . . Tenor

SIR JOHN FALSTAFF . . . . . Baritone

BARDOLPH ⎱ *followers of Falstaff* . . . Tenor
PISTOL ⎰ Bass

MRS MEG PAGE . . . . . Mezzo-soprano

MRS ALICE FORD . . . . . Soprano

MISTRESS QUICKLY . . . . Mezzo-soprano

NANNETTA, *daughter of Alice Ford* . . . Soprano

FENTON . . . . Tenor

FORD, *husband of Alice* . . . . . Baritone

Landlord of the Garter Inn; Robin, Falstaff's page; Ford's page; citizens; Ford's servants; Maskers disguised as spirits, fairies, witches, etc.

Scene: Windsor   Time: During the reign of Henry IV of England

ACT I

PART ONE

Scene: A Room in the Garter Inn. A table. A big armchair. A bench. On the table are the remains of breakfast, several bottles and a glass, an inkstand, pens, paper, a lighted candle. A broom leaning against the wall. There is a way out at the back, and a door on the left.

The curtain rises almost at once on *Falstaff* as it does on *Otello*—this time with a great *ff* guffaw in the orchestra to tell us what manner of opera this is and to introduce another of those opening themes which, as in *Otello*, Verdi uses as a recurrent theme in the scene that follows and then discards for good:

Ex 427

Dr Caius bursts into the room where Sir John Falstaff sits drinking with his followers, Bardolph and Pistol. Dr Caius shouts menacingly at Falstaff who takes no notice of the interruption but calls to the landlord to bring another bottle of sherry. Dr Caius accuses him of breaking into his house and beating his servants. Falstaff calmly admits that he did just that, but warns Dr Caius that he would be well advised to do nothing about it. Dr Caius now turns on Bardolph and Pistol and complains that they made him drunk the previous night and emptied his pockets. Falstaff, assuming the role of referee, examines all sides of the argument; Dr Caius' accusations are flatly denied by the two ruffians (Pistol engages in a private slanging match with the plaintiff) and Falstaff dismisses the case.

Punctuated by a series of repeated explosive staccato notes in the trombones Dr Caius swears solemnly that if ever he gets drunk again in a tavern it will be "in honest, civil, godly company"—words which come from Shakespeare's *Merry Wives of Windsor* where, however, they are not spoken by Dr Caius but by Slender. Boito, in tightening up Shakespeare's sprawling, untidy comedy, eliminated not only Slender but Justice Shallow as well, and in their absence made Dr Caius the victim of the misfortunes they suffered at the hands of Falstaff and his minions. It was Shallow whose house was broken into and Slender who was robbed while drunk.

As Dr Caius makes his resolution we hear the last suggestion of the opening theme (Ex 427) which has served something of a dual purpose—as an expression of Falstaff's boisterousness and of Dr Caius' spluttering indignation. Dr Caius leaves and is accompanied to the door by Pistol who sings a long Amen in what seems to be G major, echoed at a distance of two beats by Bardolph who sings in A minor— a passage of discordant bitonality which Falstaff finds most unpleasant and interrupts, reminding Bardolph and Pistol of the maxim that stealing must be done "with charm and at the right time". They are rotten artists, he adds.

An attempted reprise of the Amen by his two followers is silenced by Falstaff who studies the bill brought to him by the landlord with the last bottle of sherry. He reads it out: "Six chickens: six shillings; thirty jugs of sherry: two pounds; three turkeys; two pheasants; one anchovy." This is another of Boito's adaptations of Shakespeare—in this case, the use of an idea taken from *Henry IV, Part I*, where in the second act Prince Hal tells Peto to search the pockets of Falstaff who is "fast asleep behind the arras and snorting like a horse". Peto discovers a bill for food and drink, which includes, as the Prince remarks, "but one halfpenny-worth of bread to this intolerable deal of sack!" In Verdi's opera there is not even a ha'porth of bread on the reckoning.

Falstaff throws Bardolph his purse and tells him to see what he can find in it. The purse contains "one mark, one mark, one penny".* Falstaff addresses Bardolph:

Ex 428

* Boito was not the first foreigner to be thrown by the mysteries of English currency. A mark was a money of account—that is, not a coin but a sum, like the guinea today, and was worth 13s. 4d. Which sounds as if Falstaff's purse contained 26s. 9d.; but obviously it didn't, for Falstaff complains that he has no money left: Bardolph and Pistol cost him ten guineas a week. Certainly the "everlasting bonfire light" of Bardolph's nose has lit the way at night and saved money in lanterns and lamp oil; but, Falstaff points out (we are still in *Henry IV, Part I*), the wine Bardolph has drunk "would have bought me lights as good cheap at the dearest chandler's in Europe".

—an oddly gentle and attractive passage which is so incongruously lyrical about Bardolph's nose ("naso ardentissimo") that one suspects that Verdi, having thought of a charming tune at that point, was determined to use it.

That Verdi could use these eight bars and then forget them for good and all is maddeningly characteristic of the lavishness of invention in this opera—and incidentally, the sort of thing which makes *Falstaff* the most difficult of his operas to analyse and quote from. The gentle mood lasts only eight bars, however, when it is followed by Falstaff's gruff protest at the cost of feeding the "purple fungus" on Bardolph's nose for thirty years (as Shakespeare put it: "I have maintained that salamander of yours with fire any time this two-and-thirty years").

Falstaff calls loudly for another bottle of wine, and turning to Bardolph and Pistol warns them that they are eating up his substance; if he grew thin he would no longer be himself, nobody would love him—a gloomy picture coloured by a highly original passage of orchestration in which, over a *pp* semiquaver ostinato in the second violins, this sombre tune in the lowest register of the violoncellos—

Ex *429*

—is doubled by the piccolo four octaves higher. It is a remarkable and unexpected sound.

The tempo changes to Maestoso and Falstaff sings the praises of his paunch, accompanied by a solemn fanfare-like unison of clarinets, bassoons, horns and bass trombone, and the acclamation of Bardolph and Pistol who salute the "Immenso Falstaff! Enorme Falstaff!" for all the world as though they were singing of "Immenso Fthà!" in *Aida*.

Talk now turns to more urgent matters. Falstaff intends to start a love affair with two women in Windsor; they are married to rich merchants, they have the keys to their husbands' money boxes and they are both, he says, greatly attracted to him. The first is Alice, the beautiful wife of Ford; she has the glance of a star, the neck of a swan, lips like a laughing flower, and she has smiled at him.

Ex *430*

Falstaff's recital of her charms and graces is made to a ravishing four-note phrase in the orchestra (Ex 430) which Verdi repeats in one unexpected key after another with enchanting effect.

Falstaff goes on to tell Bardolph and Pistol about the other woman—Mrs Meg Page, who, however, does not inspire the same sort of lyrical music as Alice Ford. Taking two letters from the table he gives one to Bardolph to deliver to Meg Page, the other to Pistol for Alice Ford. Pistol refuses; he is no Pandarus. Bardolph refuses; his honour forbids him. Falstaff calls his page, Robin, and sends him out with the letters—an exquisitely light-fingered Allegro presto passage of dialogue and exit-music which starts out as a fugue but doesn't last long enough to end as one. Turning to Bardolph and Pistol, Falstaff delivers a stern discourse on honour.

How dare they talk of honour? They are nothing but thieves and sewers of ignominy! With their shifty looks and sneering laughter, what do they know of honour? Falstaff abuses his companions roundly in a fine and forceful passage of declamation, for this scene is not an aria but the musical counterpart of the prose he speaks in the Shakespeare plays. Those who know *Henry IV, Part I*, however, will recognize that so far what is often called the Honour Monologue is all Boito's own work, a variation on the theme before the original theme has been heard, as it were. When we do at last recognize the Shakespearian theme, with its typical question-and-negative-answer examination of the nature of honour (context and dramatic situation are, of course, quite different in *Henry IV*), we find that here too Boito has decorated and elaborated most ingeniously—and magnificently "in character". In place of Shakespeare's first question, "Can honour set to a leg?", we have the endearing "Can honour fill your empty belly?", which Verdi sets to the captivating little phrase:

Ex 431

Each question Falstaff asks (and we get some of the original *Henry IV* questions in due course) is answered by an emphatic "No" on the note of D, sung to the dull thud of concurrence of a unison D by clarinet in its lowest register, by a bassoon doubling the same note, and a couple of solo double basses playing pizzicato, the first bass an octave lower than the second and asked by the composer to lower his fourth string by a tone in order to do so.

Since honour is no surgeon and cannot replace a shin, or a foot, a finger or a hair, what is it? asks Falstaff. A word. And what is there in that word? Air that floats away—to a couple of thistledown phrases for two flutes and a piccolo. (Verdi's use of the piccolo in *Falstaff* is without parallel; he exploits all the instrument's possibilities in all its moods—perky, lyrical, loud, soft, mysterious, pensive and subdued. After hearing Toscanini's performance of the opera, with its miraculous clarity and detail, I was not surprised to find that there seem to be only about forty-one bars all told—and all but seven of those in the last scene of the opera—when the piccolo player puts aside the instrument to double third flute.)

Falstaff finishes his discourse convinced that honour is a useless thing—"Therefore I'll none of it." His conclusion is underlined by a broad *fortissimo* orchestral version of the fragmentary theme of Ex 431. He then turns on Bardolph and Pistol, lays about them with the broom and drives them out of the Garter Inn for a pair of thieves. The curtain falls with the tune of Ex 431 transformed into a brilliantly-scored coda in the C major in which the scene began.

PART TWO

Scene: In Ford's Garden. Ford's house in on the left. In the centre of the scene there are groups of trees.

Perhaps the prize example of Verdi's melodic prodigality in *Falstaff* is the passage for woodwind and horns which introduces this second scene:

Ex 432

This wonderfully exuberant, bubbling tune (in which the piccolo inevitably plays a star part) has an immediate and irresistible effect on the hearer, arousing expectancy, creating good humour, and setting the mood of the scene it introduces in a masterly way. But once we have been shown the tune Verdi whisks it away and we never meet it again except for a moment in a subtly altered form as the curtain falls at the end of the act.

If the tune itself disappears its gaiety and sparkle remain behind to introduce us to the laughter and high spirits of the Merry Wives themselves. Meg and Mistress Quickly enter from the right, and go

towards Ford's house. On the step they meet Alice Ford and Nannetta, who are coming out.*

Alice and Meg have each received a letter from Falstaff; except
for the names the contents are identical. They exchange letters and
Meg reads out loud the letter addressed to Alice. Or rather, Meg
sings what she reads, for as far as I know this is the first time in his
life Verdi ever set a letter to a tune instead of having the singer read
it out in a normal speaking voice, or at best recite its contents on
one note. The accompaniment as Meg reads Alice's letter, and Alice
reads Meg's, is intriguing and not a little unexpected, for it consists
mostly of a cor anglais solo which rambles amiably round the voice:

Ex 433

After the vivacity and laughter of the music that has gone before,
the rather lugubrious tones of the cor anglais is almost the last sound
one would expect to hear. Alice and Meg match their letters word
for word to the joy of Nannetta and Mistress Quickly, who read
over their shoulders ("all of them with their noses in the letters" the
stage directions run). The most lyrical passages in the letter are given
to Alice to sing, and she delivers the final purple paragraph—"And
your face shall shine upon me like a star, like a star on the immensity"
—to a long phrase which Verdi indicates to be sung "con carica-
tura"; no amount of caricature, however, can deprive this passage
of its infectious tunefulness which—caricature or not—Alice is
nevertheless instructed to sing "dolcissimo":

Ex 434

e il viso tuo su me risplende - rà come una stel - -la come una stel-la sull'immen-si- tà

Perhaps through absent-mindedness Verdi wrote the last word of
the phrase as "eternità" in the manuscript score, where it was

* Nannetta is no longer "Sweet Ann Page", but has been changed by Boito into
Ford's daughter. Page is another of the many characters in Shakespeare's play who
are left out of the opera, and the translation of Ann into two other people's
daughter is a device that succeeds admirably in tightening up the action—even
though it means that in consequence Ford has to suffer Page's frustrations as
well as his own.

crossed out and corrected to "immensità"—a word which my Italian dictionary describes as "(*poet.*)" and was obviously chosen by Boito for this very reason.

At the end of Alice's lyrical flourish the four women dissolve into laughter. The letter finishes with, "Answer to your cavalier, John Falstaff, Knight"—words which are read by Alice in the traditional monotone (*senza misura* and *parlato*) reserved for sung, as distinct from spoken, letter-reading in most Italian operas.

The women decide that Falstaff must be taught a sharp lesson and made a fool of. The fact that they are unanimous in their intention doesn't prevent them expressing their opinions independently and simultaneously—so independently, indeed, that only twice in the course of sixteen lines of verse is there any unanimity of rhyme between Alice and the three companions who all address her at once. The quartet is a brief and sparkling episode:

Ex 435

There is always some controversy about whether this episode (eighteen bars altogether) should or should not be accompanied. In Verdi's manuscript the original accompaniment for two oboes and two clarinets playing *ppp* was crossed out by the composer, obviously as a result of finding that the four women at the Scala première were able to keep in tune without an instrumental prop. Very often, however, the passage is performed *with* the accompaniment; this is because the oboe and clarinet parts are printed in scores without any typographical indication that they are optional and to be used only in case of emergency.

In the notes to the 1964 RCA recording of the opera we are told that "in conformity with the original score of Verdi, which Maestro Solti consulted during the recording in Rome, these instruments are deleted". Mr Solti was quite right, of course. Equally if he had chosen to follow the printed score he wouldn't have been wrong either. Verdi always hoped the quartet could be sung unaccompanied, but he didn't necessarily expect it. When Edoardo Mascheroni, who conducted the première of *Falstaff*, went to Venice for the first performance of the opera there three months later, Verdi wrote to him: "If you believe it is useful to add the instruments in the quartet, do so—provided they can't be heard. But take out the B's from the oboes [Verdi quoted the octaves in the first bar of the quartet—Ex 435]. The low B is too clumsy a sound in the oboes."

16*

I have mentioned this question of the accompanied or unaccompanied quartet to show that, like all great composers, Verdi was always ready to admit that circumstances can alter cases. What he wrote in his manuscript was *not* his last word on the subject, and I think this sort of thing should be borne in mind before we overdo the modern tendency to treat composers' manuscripts as gospel all the time.

As soon as they have finished their conversation the women leave the scene in a group; they are visible among the trees in the background from time to time during the action immediately following, but without being aware that the men are there when Mr Ford enters with Dr Caius, Fenton, Bardolph and Pistol. Like his wife before him, Ford is addressed by all his companions at once. The same two-in-a-bar of the women's quartet is maintained by the men's ensemble; the tempo doesn't change, only the time from 6/8 to 2/2:

Ex *436*

There is no question of an optional accompaniment to this tune which is started off by Dr Caius, and continued by Bardolph, Fenton and Pistol. Horns and bassoons add a masculine gruffness to the men's voices before other instruments join in. The subject of the conversation is again Falstaff, but this time without a single syllable of communal rhyming at any point. The simultaneous chatter of the men may not seem a very practical way of telling Ford of Falstaff's iniquitous character and monstrous plans, but what we hear is only a repetition of views and information already given to Ford off stage.

For his own benefit (as well as ours) Ford bids Bardolph and Pistol repeat their story. They do so, protesting how, for reasons of honour, they refused to deliver Falstaff's letter to Alice and warning Ford that the horns of cuckoldry are already hanging over his head—a warning delivered to an ominous orchestral sequence filled with the dark tones of clarinets and violas, bassoons and violoncellos in their lower registers, and deep sustained notes in the bass trombone and double basses.

Ford's jealousy is successfully aroused and he vows to keep his eyes open. The women come back for a moment, and as Ford and his companions leave in one direction they go off in the other—all except Nannetta and Fenton, who stay behind for the first of those enchanting little love scenes which Boito described so beautifully to Verdi when they first discussed *Falstaff*. He told the composer that this love between Nannetta and Fenton must appear suddenly at very frequent intervals; in all the scenes in which they took part they would keep on kissing stealthily in corners, astutely, boldly, without letting themselves be discovered, with fresh little phrases and brief, rapid little dialogues, from the beginning to the end of the comedy. It would be a most lively, joyful love, continued Boito, always being disturbed and interrupted and always ready to start up again. "I don't know how to explain myself," said Boito. "I should like, as one sprinkles sugar on a tart, to sprinkle the whole comedy with this gay love, without collecting it together at one point."

It is natural to think of these scenes as duets, but in fact Nannetta and Fenton scarcely sing together at all. They are in reality a series of short, hurried conversations between lovers set to tunes which begin, continue, and eventually—a little reluctantly and infuriatingly soon—come to an end. From the first note the mood and character of the young lovers are unmistakable; there is a charm and innocence and eagerness in the music which is quite impossible to analyse. Like young love itself, it just seems to happen:

The accompaniment to this first encounter is exquisitely scored—a richly harmonized sequence for muted strings and occasional solo wind which Francis Toye felt was harmonized "à la Wagner" but which I prefer to call à la Verdi of Aida, where there are a dozen precedents for this lovely string writing in Falstaff.

The lovers separate and move away in different directions as they hear people approaching; the smooth lyrical flow of the strings is interrupted by a short series of feathery triplet figures taken one way by the solo woodwind and the other way by the strings. Fenton, hidden among the trees, calls to Nannetta: "The mouth that is kissed is never unlucky." Nannetta answers: "Instead it revives like the moon itself":

Ex 438

Nannetta's high A flat is sustained against an entirely magical coda played *pp* by the muted strings (*ppp* for the violoncellos). It is one of the most entrancingly beautiful moments in all opera.

Alice, Meg and Mistress Quickly return to the scene full of plans and a determination in their hearts which is vigorously echoed in the orchestra. Alice proposes writing a letter to Falstaff, but Nannetta (who joins her companions' huddle without anybody apparently noticing that she hasn't been there all the time) suggests that it would be better to make a personal approach. This is unanimously agreed and it is arranged to send Mistress Quickly to Falstaff with an invitation from Alice.

The women's joyful anticipation of the punishment that lies ahead for Falstaff is interrupted when Quickly catches sight of Fenton moving in the background. "Somebody's spying on us," says Meg, and she leaves hurriedly with Alice and Mistress Quickly. Nannetta stays behind, and she is joined by her lover in another hurried little love scene. This time the tune is in the clarinets, decorated by a flute and strings, and a series of miraculously delicate orchestral touches from the piccolo and two trumpets playing *ppp*. Once more Nannetta and Fenton are interrupted by people approaching, and the music breaks off. Fenton goes off in one direction singing, "Bocca baciata non perde ventura" ("The mouth that is kissed is never unlucky") to be answered from the distance by Nannetta's closing phrase in Ex 438. This time, however, Fenton also sings as the strings play their ravishing epilogue under Nannetta's sustained A flat.

The disturbance on this occasion is caused by the return of Dr Caius, Bardolph, Ford and Pistol, who are joined by Fenton. With the connivance of Bardolph and Pistol, Ford has arranged to call on Falstaff under an assumed name to find out exactly what is going on and to lay a trap for him.

Alice, Nannetta, Meg and Mistress Quickly return, and when the men begin to repeat the tune, but not necessarily all the words, of their earlier ensemble (Ex 436), they join in with their 6/8 quartet (Ex 435) and we have both groups singing simultaneously. Fenton soliloquizes about Nannetta, singing a broad tune all of his own as a lyrical countermelody to the rest of the ensemble; he is supported in this by four horns in unison with him.

Verdi's display of counterpoint and the 3-against-4 conflict of rhythm combine to make this passage an intriguing technical *tour de force*. I feel, however, that a thought should be spared for the selfless Boito who composed no fewer than nine different sets of words for this ensemble—one set for each singer—scarcely one syllable of which can be clearly heard by the audience. But the total effect, thanks to Verdi's music, is what Boito obviously intended: the effect of nine people all chattering at once, eight of them on a single common topic.

The men leave the scene; the women make their last-minute plans, joyfully anticipating how Falstaff's belly will swell with pride and then explode. Verdi imitates the pricking and deflation of what Alice calls "that terrible and puffed-up paunch" with a shattering, rapid descending chromatic scale for bassoons and trombones in unison. There is a sudden quietness and Alice echoes the rich tune of Falstaff's purple passage (Ex 434), but changing the first words to "But my face shall shine upon him".

Alice's companions join her to sing the end of the phrase in unison and amid general laughter the four women separate and leave the scene. The curtain falls to a fully orchestral and shortened ff version of the 6/8 which began the scene, but with the tempo now speeded up from the original Allegro vivace to Vivace. It is a brilliant, irresistible pay-off.

ACT II

PART ONE

Scene: The interior of the Garter Inn as in the first act.

A short boisterous orchestral passage precedes the rise of the curtain, and like the tune that opens the opera, it sets the pattern of the music in the first stages of the action that follows. A *fortissimo* unison for oboes, clarinets, bassoons, horns, trumpets, three trombones and strings is followed by a unison phrase for strings only:

Ex *439*

Falstaff is discovered stretched out in his big armchair, in his usual place drinking his sherry. Bardolph and Pistol come forward from the door on the left and beating their breasts protest in a solemn unison that they are penitent and contrite (like their Amen at the exit of Dr Caius in Act I, this too has a grotesquely ecclesiastic character). They also announce in the same tone of voice that they are returning to Falstaff's service. Bardolph then tells Falstaff that there is a woman outside who is waiting to see him. Falstaff bids him show her in; Bardolph hurries out and returns immediately with Mistress Quickly, who makes her entry with the immortal greeting, accompanied by ludicrously solemn strings, and dropping a deep curtsy, "Reverenza!":

Ex *440*

This is perhaps Verdi's greatest moment in the whole opera of music which is funny in itself; it is a superb synthesis in five notes of the whole situation, revealing unmistakably to the audience that

494

Mistress Quickly's show of humility and respect is phoney, but avoiding any exaggeration that could make Falstaff suspicious.

"Quik", as Verdi kept calling her in his manuscript score, approaches Falstaff "with great respect and circumspection", saying that if his Grace pleases there is something she would like to tell him secretly. Falstaff sends Bardolph and Pistol packing; Mistress Quickly makes another deep curtsy and hesitatingly, *a bassa voce*, mentions the name of Alice Ford. Falstaff gets up out of his chair and goes eagerly towards Mistress Quickly.

"Oh dear!" she sighs. "Poor lady! You are a great seducer."

"I know," replies Falstaff simply. "Continue."

Mistress Quickly reports that Alice is in a "great agitation of love" for him, that she has received his letter (for which she thanks him), and that her husband is always away from home "from two until three"—a time which is expressed in the unforgettable phrase, "Dalle due alle tre . . .":

Ex *441*

Boito's alteration of Shakespeare at this point was a brilliant stroke. In the play Mistress Quickly tells Falstaff that Alice "gives you to notify that her husband will be absence from his house between ten and eleven". Translated as "dalle dieci alle undici" Shakespeare's "between ten and eleven" would never have begun to make the neat, unfailing impact of "dalle due alle tre". Indeed, short of Ford being away from home for four hours to enable his wife to extend her invitation "dalle due alle sei" there is no period in twenty-four Italian hours that even Verdi could have set to music with the same inimitable effect as "dalle due alle tre". The phrase sticks in Falstaff's mind immediately and he repeats it to himself as Mistress Quickly continues her heart-rending story of the unhappy Alice Ford and "the frampold life" she leads with her jealous husband.

Falstaff tells Quickly to assure Mistress Ford that he is impatiently waiting for the hour; he will not fail in his duty—a resolution which is followed by a delicious *ppp* echo of "dalle due alle tre" first in the violins and then two octaves lower in the violoncellos.

Mistress Quickly has more to say, however, and with a well-feigned air of sorrow delivers a message from Meg Page, who, while greeting Falstaff *amorosamente*, regrets to say that her husband is very seldom away from home. "Poor lady!" laments Mistress Quickly, "a lily of candour and faith! You bewitch them all!"

Witchcraft, Falstaff replies, has nothing to do with it—just a personal fascination. . . . He asks Mistress Quickly if the two women know about each other. She tells him to have no fear; women are born deceitful. Falstaff gives her a coin, and dismissing her with a that's-for-your-trouble-my-good-woman gesture bids her greet the two ladies for him. Mistress Quickly curtsies, leaving the strings to play the cadence of "Reverenza!" as she goes out.

Greatly excited, Falstaff cries, "Alice is mine!" and the whole orchestra shares his elation with the robust comment:

Ex 442

Falstaff meditates on his success with a slow and splendidly self-satisfied four-in-a-bar: "Va, vecchio John, va per la tua via"—"Old Jack, go thy ways. I'll make more of thy old body than I have done." The measured tread of Old Jack's progress is coloured with a special dignity by the *pp* beats of two trumpets, two trombones and timpani. A return to the boisterous tutti of Ex 442 is followed by the entrance of Bardolph, who announces breathlessly that there is a certain Master Fontana outside who very much wants to make Falstaff's acquaintance and offers a demijohn of Cyprus wine for his breakfast (was Falstaff's "morning draught of sack" only Xeres-type Empire wine from Cyprus after all?).

"Welcome to the fountain that spills forth such liquor!" says Falstaff—which is the neat Italian translation of Shakespeare's original "Such Brooks are welcome to me that o'er-flow such liquor". The change of "Brook" into "Fontana" not only does no harm to the pun, but "Fontana", like "Brook" in England, is a familiar surname in Italy, which "Ruscello", the literal equivalent of "brook", is not.

Falstaff sends Bardolph to show in Master Fontana, and for a brief moment reflects on "vecchio John". Bardolph returns with Master Fontana, who proves to be Ford in disguise. Pistol follows carrying a demijohn. Bardolph and Pistol remain in the background. In his hand Ford holds a small bag. He bows deeply and goes towards Falstaff, who returns the salute.

Ford, effusive and "sempre complimentoso", apologizes for coming with so little ceremony. Falstaff replies that he is very welcome. Ford explains that he is a man of substance, accustomed to spend and scatter his wealth as he pleases—a piece of information that causes Falstaff to shake him warmly by the hand: "Good Master Fontana, I desire more acquaintance of you." Ford says he would like to talk to Falstaff in confidence; Bardolph and Pistol, who have been enjoying their eavesdropping, are dismissed, and Falstaff prepares to listen.

There is a popular proverb, Ford says, that money opens all doors. Falstaff agrees: "Money is a good soldier, and will on", and trumpets and trombones back him up with a discreet fanfare. Accompanied by a series of jingling noises from the triangle and woodwind in the orchestra, Ford invites Falstaff to help him with a bag of coins too heavy for one man to carry. Falstaff takes the bag from him and puts it on the table, saying that he doesn't know what he has done to deserve this visit. Ford begins: "There is a gentlewoman in this town, her husband's name is Ford"—"C'è a Windsor una dama . . .":

Ex 443

In tones of utter sadness Ford tells how he loves Alice, and she doesn't love him; how he writes to her, and she doesn't answer; how he looks at her, and she ignores him; how he looks for her, and she hides from him. He has showered her with gifts and treasure, but it has all been in vain. He is left on the steps outside, neglected and dry-mouthed, singing a madrigal. In Shakespeare's play Ford quotes his madrigal; in the opera, obviously knowing the words and music well, and accompanied by some characteristically perky piccolo passages, Falstaff takes Ford's mention of it in a florid cadence as a cue to sing it himself:

> Love like a shadow flies when substance love pursues;
> Pursuing that that flies and flying what pursues—

Ex 444

Ford contributes a phrase or two from time to time, imitating Falstaff as he does so. It is a madrigal, he says, that he has learned at great cost. "That is the fatal destiny of the miserable lover," comments Falstaff. Ford sings a few bars of his madrigal but is interrupted by Falstaff who asks him whether Alice has ever given him any reason for hope. "No," replies Ford. "Then why", asks Falstaff, "confide in me?"

Because, says Ford, Falstaff is a gentleman, a soldier, a man of the world. He hands Falstaff the bag of money, telling him to spend it and squander it, to be rich and happy. (The triangle contributes a sparkling roll throughout the orchestra's jingling background to these words, and there is some unexpectedly light-hearted scoring for the three trumpets.) In exchange for the money Ford asks only one thing: that Falstaff shall conquer Alice. This strikes Falstaff as a strange request, but, Ford explains, once the citadel of Alice's obstinate chastity has been breached his chance will come too, for one lapse leads to another, and then . . . What does Falstaff think?

Falstaff announces that first of all he will accept the bag of money, and then (on his honour as a knight) assures Master Fontana that he shall possess Ford's wife. In fact, continues Falstaff, things are pretty well advanced already. "Within half an hour she will be in my arms," he says.

"Who?" shouts Ford.

"Alice," replies Falstaff, *con calma*. "She sent a messenger to tell me that her boor of a husband will be absent—from two until three," and like a Charlie Chaplin gag one can see coming a mile off (Charlie's dive into the shallow water in *Modern Times*, for instance) the return of the phrase "dalle due alle tre" makes an hilarious impact by its expected unexpectedness.

Ford asks Falstaff if he knows Alice's husband. "May the devil take him!" replies Falstaff, evading a direct answer, since it is obvious to him, to Ford, and to us, that he cannot know him, although Shakespeare has him say, "I know him not."

"Ford is a boor and a beast," Falstaff tells Fontana, "and I shall cuckold him for you well and truly"—"Te lo cornifico netto, netto!":

Ex 445

This little theme assumes an unexpected musical importance later in the scene. Meanwhile, Falstaff rolls it round his tongue and it serves as a coda to his exit-music when, telling Ford to wait for him while he goes to make himself beautiful, he takes the bag of money and leaves the room.

Left alone, Ford cannot believe what he has heard. Is it a dream or reality? There are cuckold's horns growing from his head. Is he dreaming? The monologue becomes as angry and dramatic, as vehement and unhumorous as almost anything Verdi ever wrote, and a masterly essay in the declamatory style he perfected in his later works.

It is only the words and the situation, and the setting of a traditionally comic subject like cuckoldry in highly serious musical surroundings which remind us that we are not listening in a mixed-up
nightmare to Iago's voice expressing Otello's thoughts of jealousy.
As Francis Toye put it, "one is inclined to guess that in setting the
words, Verdi found his old instincts taking the bit between their
teeth and had to pull them up with a jerk from time to time". As it is,
the notes of Falstaff's confident "Te lo cornifico" (Ex 445) lose their
skittishness and are used by Verdi in Ford's monologue to build up
dramatic tension which is scarcely out of place in the company of
such familiar excerpts from Verdi's vocabulary as the evil unison
trills and the characteristic downward leap of an octave so strongly
associated with Iago in *Otello* (for example, in the Brindisi—Ex 391).

There are momentary echoes, too, of *Don Carlos*, when the horns,
well known as musical symbols of cuckoldry since Mozart's *Figaro*,
remind us of Philip's "Dormirò sol nel manto mio regal" (Ex 323 on
p 355), at the words, "L'ora è fissata" ("The hour is fixed . . ."):

Even the suggestion (*pp legg. e stacc.*) of "dalle due alle tre" with
which the bassoon and violoncellos punctuate the gloomy horn
phrases does not dispel these echoes altogether, for there are still
ominous *pp* notes held in the trumpets which intensify the incongruously sinister atmosphere of this passage.

There is altogether, indeed, more declamation than obvious
melody in a scene remarkable for the bitterness and irony of words
which have been neatly fused by Boito from two different points in
Shakespeare's play, where Ford visits Falstaff incognito not once but
twice, and on each occasion is left to soliloquize in a desperate state
of turmoil and jealousy. Boito has taken passages from both speeches,
beginning his text for Verdi with, "Is this a vision? is this a dream?
do I sleep? Master Ford awake! awake, Master Ford!", which ends
Act III of *The Merry Wives of Windsor*, and continuing with several
passages from the soliloquy at the end of Act II, Scene 2, though not
necessarily in the order in which Ford says them in that speech.
(Shakespeare's opening, "What a damned Epicurean rascal is this!"
is heard in the opera towards the end of the monologue, for instance.)

The lines about Ford's rather trusting a Fleming with his butter,
Parson Hugh the Welshman with his cheese, an Irishman with his
aqua-vitae bottle, or a thief to walk his ambling gelding than his
wife to herself, undergo an understandable geographical change in

Italian and it becomes a question of trusting his beer to a German, his horse to a thieving Dutchman and his aqua-vitae to a Turk.

The monologue ends with Ford in a fierce and determined mood, which, whether feigned or genuine, the music at any rate would have us believe is sincere enough to make the greatest possible contrast with the delicious comedy and the complete change of situation and atmosphere into which the tension unwinds with the return of Falstaff, dressed up to the nines in a new doublet, hat and cane. Falstaff's entrance is accompanied by a violin tune of a charm and elegance without precedent in Verdi's operas—unless it can be traced to some of the music in *Un ballo in maschera*:

Ex *447*

Falstaff asks Ford if he would like to accompany him for a step or two. Ford replies that he will see him on his way. They start to go out; at the door there is a great deal of bowing and making of *complimentosi* gestures as each refuses to take precedence over the other. The scene, a delightful invention of Boito's and making a wonderful curtain, ends with Ford and Falstaff going out together arm in arm. The curtain falls with a *ff* repetition of the exultant tutti that followed Falstaff's "Alice is mine!" (Ex 442).

PART TWO

Scene : A Room in Ford's House. There is a big window at the back. There is a door on the left, a door on the right, and another door towards the upstage right hand corner which gives on to the stairs. There is another staircase in the upstage left hand corner. The garden can be seen through the big window which is wide open. There is a folded screen leaning against the left hand wall beside a huge fireplace. Against the right hand wall there is a chest of drawers. There are also a small table with flowers on it, a seat locker, and against the walls a big chair and several high-backed ones. There is a lute on the big chair.

As neither Verdi's manuscript nor my copy of the orchestral score

Ex *448*

gives any indication when the curtain should rise we must suppose it rises at once with the wonderfully mischievous, conspiratorial passage in thirds and sixths for the first and second violins in Ex 448.

Alice and Meg enter, followed almost at once by Mistress Quickly, and a moment later by Nannetta, who stands sadly apart from the others. Mistress Quickly reports the success of her mission. She went to the Garter, she says, where Sir John deigned to grant her audience. She assumes his *voce grossa* and in the same vocal register as he sang it, mimics his pompous "buon giorno, buona donna" and then caricatures her own obsequious "Reverenza!" She goes on to describe how Falstaff swallowed her story whole and now believes that both Alice and Meg are infatuated with him—a little passage of narrative in which the voice part is piquantly doubled by a solo oboe and a piccolo two octaves higher.

Falstaff, Mistress Quickly concludes, will be coming to Ford's house shortly—"dalle due alle tre". As it is already two o'clock Alice calls to her servants to bring in the laundry basket, explaining to Quickly that everything has already been prepared. Alice notices suddenly that Nannetta is crying instead of enjoying the fun and she asks what is the matter. With the oboe and strings expressing her tears in another of those characteristic weeping phrases Verdi used all his life—and now uses for the last time in opera, though the last time of all was in the Stabat Mater written in 1898—Nannetta answers that her father wants her to marry Dr Caius; she would rather be stoned to death. Her mother and the other women comfort her with promises to help and Nannetta cheers up.

The servants bring in the laundry basket and Alice assumes the part of *metteuse en scène*, directing her companions in the placing of props for the comedy that is being prepared—a chair here, the lute there, the opened screen between basket and fireplace. The operation does not take long and is accompanied by a return of the opening passage for strings (Ex 448) broken up from time to time into three-bar phrases to create an intriguing atmosphere of conspiracy and suspense.

When everything is to her satisfaction Alice announces that in a moment the comedy will begin, and there follows a scene which must surely be the most indispensable luxury in all opera: a luxury because it serves no dramatic purpose and indispensable because without it we would miss some of the most bewitching music Verdi ever wrote. This is the brief, sparkling, scherzo-like movement (Ex 449)

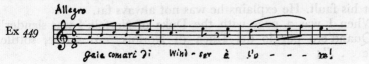

begun by Alice—"Gaie comari di Windsor è l'ora . . ." ("Merry wives of Windsor, the time has come . . .").

Alice's opening solo is a sustained thirty-two-bar passage of immense charm and grace which, when she has sung it, she follows with final instructions to her companions. Meg is a little nervous, but Alice reassures her; she will whistle if she is in any danger. Meanwhile, Mistress Quickly has gone to the window to keep a look-out; she waits there long enough to allow Meg and Nannetta to add their voices to Alice's for a short bubbling coda, and announces that Falstaff has been sighted. Meg, Nannetta and Mistress Quickly disperse to a couple of bars of exit music which is full of breathless excitement and anticipation, while Alice settles down and plays the lute.

The lute is imitated by a guitar played behind the scenes. (The manuscript incidentally shows the guitar writing to be much fuller than it appears in my study score. Verdi spreads his chords over five or even all six strings of the instrument where the printed part uses only four.) Falstaff enters *con vivacità*, and finding Alice's lute infectious begins to warble, finally breaking into a snatch of song: "At last I have plucked thee, O radiant flower." Falstaff cuts his singing short, however, and grabbing Alice by the waist (the original Italian is *busto*, but we can hardly translate it as bust, corset or stays) proclaims that he can now die happy; he will have lived enough after this hour of love.

Alice's reaction is skilfully coy and coquettish, and when Falstaff confesses that he wishes Ford were dead (Boito modifies Shakespeare's brusque, "I would thy husband were dead", to the more euphemistic, "I wish Master Ford would pass on to a better life"), she protests that she would make him "a pitiful Lady". She would be worthy of a king, insists Falstaff, and in a comically awkward passage sung in unison with two bassoons at their least romantic, he imagines her decorated with his coat-of-arms, displaying the beauty of her bosom framed in jewels. Verdi continues to make use of the bassoons' comic qualities in a busy staccato figure in the accompaniment to Falstaff's glowing picture of Alice as more splendidly radiant than any rainbow.

Modestly and *con grazia*, and accompanied by the woodwind which has dominated the dialogue so far, Alice declares that costly jewels do not become her; all she needs is "a plain kerchief", a buckle at her waist and a flower in her hair.

Falstaff tries to kiss her, but she steps away saying that he is being sinful. Falstaff says it is no sin to follow a vocation; he loves her, it is not his fault. He explains he was not always fat.

"When I was a page with the Duke of Norfolk I was slender" —"Quand'ero paggio del Duca di Norfolk, ero sottile, sottile, sottile . . .":

Ex *450*

This miraculous little scene (it lasts barely thirty seconds) is perhaps the most surprising and captivating conception of the whole opera. It has an irresistible charm and intimacy, a breath-taking spontaneity which have no precedent in Verdi's music unless one can accept a distant melodic resemblance to the first few bars of Iago's "Questa è una ragna" (Ex 415). On consideration, perhaps the true precedent is to be found in the whole spirit and air of those pages of *Falstaff* we have already heard. "Quand'ero paggio" is set solidly in the exhilarating tradition the composer established so firmly on Page 1 of the opera.

The idea was entirely Boito's, of course, for not only is there nothing in Shakespeare's play that remotely resembles it, but nowhere in *The Merry Wives of Windsor* is Falstaff the sympathetic, rather endearing, character he suddenly becomes at this point in the opera. With "Quand'ero paggio", in other words, Falstaff ceases to be a buffoon and is a human being with the power to move us, and not for the last time.

The difficulties of the English language and its usage caused Boito to commit only two solecisms in the libretto of *Falstaff*—a truly remarkable achievement especially since the first of them, found in the words of this little ditty, was deliberate anyway. (The second solecism, which does not occur until the last scene of the opera, could have been just carelessness, as we shall see.) Everywhere else in the libretto Boito was most particular about the accentuation of English proper names, but when he came to the word "Norfolk" he put the accent on the second syllable.

"The first syllable should be accented," he wrote to Verdi, "as in 'Windsor' and 'Falstaff'." He said he was breaking the rule "that no word in all the English language has an accent on the last syllable" because in this particular case he had several times tried to correct it, but whenever he altered the accent he spoilt the verse, and he preferred of the two evils to get the accent wrong.*

Verdi accepted the explanation of Boito's solecism as reasonable

---

* Boito must have been referring to proper names only when he said that no "word" in all the English language had an accent on the last syllable. Among English verbs alone—like attend, defy, proclaim, degrade, promote, revolve—there are dozens of bisyllables with this accent, of course, but place names and proper names can be another matter.

and wrote the word in his score as "Norfolth"—"th" or "k", it was presumably all the same in the exotic world of English orthography.

The orchestral accompaniment to "Quand'ero paggio" is as featherweight as one would expect from the context, and a salutary example for all in the art of scoring so that every *pp* word is audible in a theatre the size of La Scala.

Alice accuses Falstaff of mocking her; he is deceiving her and really loves Meg. Falstaff denies this vehemently; he can't stand Meg's face. Alice is his only love; he seizes her passionately and tries to kiss her, but is disturbed by the approach of Mistress Quickly who enters in a state of well-feigned agitation to tell Alice in a series of breathless, broken sentences that Mistress Meg is outside and wants to see her urgently. Quickly's words spark off a busy *moto perpetuo* in the orchestra which carries the action along with an irresistible unison semiquaver figure launched by violas, violoncellos and double basses:

Ex 451

Falstaff, in a panic, hides behind the screen. Quickly signals Meg to come in, and leaves. Meg, most convincingly *agitatissima*, tells Alice that she must fly: Ford is on his way in a furious state. "Speak louder!" Alice whispers. Meg pitches her voice a fourth higher so that Falstaff can hear clearly how Ford is coming to cut the throat of the lover his wife is hiding in the house. Meg's recital of Ford's bloodthirsty intentions is interrupted by the return of Mistress Quickly, now genuinely agitated and frightened (*paventatissima*). Ford really *is* coming; he is in the garden with a crowd of followers. Quickly's alarm is accompanied by another semiquaver figure played *più mosso*:

Ex 452

This passage, fifteen bars long and first heard in the second violins, is the basis of another *moto perpetuo*. It is taken over in E major by the first violins, followed by the violas in G major. These string sequences are marked in Verdi's manuscript to be played legato, four semi-quavers to each bow; the decision to play them *staccatissimo* must presumably have been made by the composer at rehearsal. If not, and the idea was a later, unauthorized addition, then it raises yet another nice point in the whole argument of whether the composer's original, untouched manuscript is to be accepted without question or not. One has only to imagine these passages played according to the manuscript to recognize that they would not make half the effect they do when played according to the printed score.

Mistress Quickly's words, followed by Ford's threatening shout off stage of "Scoundrel!" ("Malandrino!"), cause general panic. Falstaff comes out of his hiding place in an attempt to escape, but on hearing Ford's voice, retreats behind the screen which Alice now arranges so that he is completely hidden.

Ford enters, shouting to his followers to shut all the doors and bar the staircases. Dr Caius and Fenton come running in, followed by Bardolph and Pistol; Ford sends them off in different directions to search the house. Alice faces her husband: "Have you gone out of your mind? What are you doing?" Ford doesn't reply, but catching sight of the laundry basket, suspects that Falstaff is concealed in it. He rummages among the dirty linen, which he throws all over the floor, and finds nothing. Proclaiming that they must look under the bed, in the oven, in the well, in the bath, under the roof, in the cellar, Ford storms out to join his companions.

The scurrying *staccatissimo* now gradually merges into an echo of the two-semiquaver figure of Ex 451, and in the comparaitve quiet that now follows Meg suggests Falstaff should hide in the basket. Alice is doubtful; he is too fat. Falstaff, however, comes out from behind his screen and insists that he can. Alice goes out to call the menservants. Falstaff climbs into the basket, protesting to Meg that he loves her and her only, and begging her to save him. He squeezes himself into the basket with difficulty and Meg and Quickly cover him with the dirty linen.

While Meg and Quickly are busy with the basket Nannetta and Fenton steal in to snatch a hurried moment together. This time we do not hear the music associated with them before; but the mood is much the same—a brief lyrical Allegro 3/4 accompanied by wood-wind and horns and punctuated by scattered phrases in the strings, reminding us with the first four notes of Ex 452 sometimes legato, sometimes staccato, that the hurly-burly is not over, only temporarily interrupted. The lovers hide behind the screen whose presence they bless gratefully in a final unison cadence.

The hurly-burly returns with a vengeance as the tune of Ex 452, which has been hanging over the Nannetta–Fenton scene like a distant storm cloud, bursts forth with all the *ff* fury of a wood-wind and-strings unison across five octaves aided and accentuated by the brass. The reason for this sudden thunder-clap is the loud off-stage hue-and-crying of Ford and Dr Caius who enter, followed by Bardolph and Pistol. After this short outburst the theme reverts to its quiet, first form, in the violins to begin with, then in the violoncellos and violas, as the hunt for Falstaff is stepped up. Cupboards and chests are forced open, the chimney is searched; Ford, blindly obsessed with his search, even looks inside a small drawer in the table. (For those who wish to praise or censure the modern producer for the inclusion of this bit of business it should be pointed out that it is in the original libretto.)

During a sudden lull in the uproar the sound of a kiss is heard from behind the screen where Nannetta and Fenton have been making love. The music stops dead in its tracks with two silent bars. Ford, noticing Alice's absence, is now convinced that she is behind the screen with Falstaff. Slowly and cautiously, and muttering bloodthirsty threats, he approaches the screen. The tempo drops to a stealthy Andante, the start of a superbly ingenious ensemble embracing three different plots simultaneously. While Ford is organizing his plan of campaign, directing his forces to their positions, Meg and Quickly push the stifling and protesting Falstaff deeper into the basket and pile dirty linen on to him. Behind the screen Nannetta and Fenton continue their love-making. The three-against-four rhythmical pattern of this ensemble (the number of voices increases with the entrance of Bardolph and Pistol and a chorus of male followers) is not unlike that of the nonet which ends Act I (see p 490, Exx 435–6). Once again the women (limited on this occasion to Meg and Quickly) carry on their conversation in a characteristic triple time against the men's solid, indignant four. Fenton, as before, keeps musically independent of the other men, but this time—since he is topographically tied to her—he takes Nannetta along with him in a series of long lyrical phrases.

Alice, unnoticed by her husband, returns to the scene quietly and helps push Falstaff down into his basket. The sequence ends with Fenton and Nannetta reaffirming their love for each other, Falstaff gasping for help, and Ford, with his companions, overturning the screen.

Ford is furious at his discovery of the two very confused young lovers and sends them packing. Nannetta runs away; Fenton goes out at the back. Bardolph and Pistol mistake him for Falstaff, all the men join in the chase once more and the women are left alone on the scene.

The hectic bustle of Ex 452 breaks out in a loud orchestral tutti, but dies down to *pp* as Alice calls for her menservants. Nannetta comes back, bringing with her four men and a small page boy. In a rapid monotone Alice instructs the servants to carry the basket to the window and empty its contents into the river. While the servants are struggling to lift the the basket, Alice sends the page boy to fetch her husband. After a mighty effort, reflected in the orchestra by a powerful sequence of heavy unison octaves, the servants succeed in carrying the basket to the window. A loud unison semitone shake by the four horns creates a sudden air of tension which is sustained as the shake is continued by two horns and finally dies away on one.

The tension is broken as basket and contents are pitched into the river and Ford returns in time to be taken by Alice to the window, to enjoy a spectacle which, as she anticipated, dispels all thoughts of jealousy. The curtain falls to "immense laughter" on the stage and a joyful C major flourish of trumpets in the orchestra.

ACT III

PART ONE

Scene : Outside the Garter Inn. On the right the inn with the sign and motto :
"Honni soit qui mal y pense". There is a bench by the big door. It is sunset.

Before the curtain rises the orchestra plays the nearest approach we
get in the opera to a full-blown instrumental prelude : it consists of a
superb building-up of the *moto perpetuo* figure of Ex 451 from an
agitated *ppp* in the double basses to a shattering *ff* in which the tune
is played by trumpets and trombones to the accompaniment of repeated semiquaver E's in unison by the rest of the orchestra, and lasts
slightly less than thirty seconds.

The curtain goes up to show Falstaff seated on the bench deep in
meditation. On occasions producers have been known to make Falstaff appear as if he had just climbed out of the Thames and they
have been sternly reprimanded by critics for doing so on the ground
that there is nothing in the libretto to justify this. Certainly there is
no specific indication in the libretto. On the other hand, the producer is entitled to presume from the simple course and timing of
events that Falstaff is still wet from his ducking. The plot has all the
speed and directness of action of the familiar one-day programme of
the other great comic operas; like *The Marriage of Figaro* and *Così fan
tutte*, like *The Barber of Seville*, the story of *Falstaff* is told within
twenty-four hours, beginning in the morning of Act I to the *due-alle-
tre* of Act II, from the sunset of this first scene of Act III to the midnight dénouement of the finale in the second.

Or so it seems. In fact, in the best Shakespearian manner, Boito
did not observe the classical unities in writing *Falstaff*. The action of
the opera takes place not within the traditional twenty-four hours,
but on two consecutive days—a deduction made from the use of a
single word uttered by Alice Ford towards the very end of the
second scene of Act I. In telling Mistress Quickly that she wants
Falstaff "to mew for love like a tomcat" Alice adds the word "domani". From this we must therefore conclude that the witching hour
dalle due alle tre when Falstaff is lured to Ford's house is on the
following day.

While this extends the action of the opera beyond the classical
time limit it still does not mean that Falstaff should not be costumed
as though he had quite recently clambered out of the Thames and

returned home to the Garter on the same day that was to be *domani*. It would be a legitimate fancy. Again, on the other hand, if we accept that the unity of time is not observed in the libretto there is no reason why this first scene of Act III should not take place two or three weeks later, by which time Falstaff's clothes would be dry; or he might even have changed into clean ones. Which he might well have done immediately after the washing basket disaster anyway, of course—unities or no unities. Nevertheless, Boito's libretto is so filled with the feeling of unity and rapid logical development that characterizes *Figaro*, *Così fan tutte* and *The Barber of Seville* that it still comes as a surprise to find that it achieves it without conforming to the laws. It is a cunning illusion.

Falstaff continues to sit in silence as the introductory music dies away. Then, on a sudden *ff* blast of a tutti chord and an angry solo passage running from top to bottom of the first violins, he thumps the table with his fist and shouts for the landlord. Almost immediately, however, Falstaff sinks back into his black mood, expressed at its blackest by the clarinets and four horns in unison in one octave, the bassoons and three trombones in unison an octave lower:

Ex 453

Falstaff growls at the "thieving, cheating, criminal world" around him; on the entry of the landlord he orders a glass of mulled wine—presumably as the first precaution against catching cold from his recent ducking (as he calls for "a glass" and not "another glass" he has obviously only just arrived at the Garter). The landlord takes the order and goes back into the inn. Falstaff resumes his indignant meditation on the way he has been treated—a knight tipped into the water with a load of dirty linen "as they do with cats and blind kittens". If his paunch had not buoyed him up, he would have drowned; as it is, he is full of water.

The black tones of Ex 453 are heard again, with the bass trombone now added in the octave below the trombones and bassoons. "An evil world," growls Falstaff. "There is no virtue left—everything is in decline", and with an air of resignation he echoes the slow, dignified address to himself that we heard in Act II (see p 496)—"Va, vecchio John"—"Go your ways; go your ways until you die and then all true manhood will disappear from the earth." This unexpected return of "Va, vecchio John" is a genuinely touching moment; after the angry grumbling that has made him a figure of fun we are on Falstaff's side again and we listen sympathetically to his lament that he is growing too fat and has grey hairs on his head. These last gloomy sentiments, incidentally, are underlined by a gloomy phrase in the strings—

Ex 454

—which has been said to be a deliberate quotation by Verdi of the so-called *Zauber-Motiv* or Magic motif from *Parsifal*. Whether this is so or not I do not know; the similarity is unmistakable, however, and while it may have been a coincidence, it may equally have been intentional—a private joke in a score which Verdi regarded as a strictly private matter.

The loud chord and brilliant violin passage that preceded Falstaff's call for the landlord, now bring the landlord back, bearing a large glass of mulled wine; he puts it on the table and returns indoors. Unbuttoning his waistcoat, Falstaff takes a deep draught of wine and recovers his spirits and feeling of well-being before our very eyes, as it were.

Good wine, he reflects, lights up the eyes and wits, and fills the body of man with a warming tingle that invades the whole world. As the wine flows through Falstaff's veins we hear the warming tingle in the orchestra—an astonishing crescendo from a single trill on a solo flute to a mighty trill by the whole orchestra. It is a spectacular display of orchestral invention that consists of a series of sustained trills heard first in the second flute, then in the third, then in the first. Two solo first, two solo second violins and two solo violas are now added; one oboe, one clarinet, one bassoon and two solo violoncellos join in, the violins are increased to four firsts, four seconds and the violas to three. Second oboe, second clarinet, two horns, then four horns come in; the four solo first and second violins are augmented to six with four violas and four violoncellos. The full body of strings is brought in with the entry of piccolo, second bassoon, the three trumpets and timpani and the final crescendo of trill is reached with the addition of the four trombones and the bass drum.

The climax is at once perhaps the most inspired and superbly comic anticlimax in all opera: the appearance of Mistress Quickly, who interrupts Falstaff "in his Bacchic flight" with her obsequious "Reverenza!"*

* The swiftness of the change of mood from the belly-warming trills to the entirely unexpected entrance of Mistress Quickly was achieved only by Verdi's second thoughts. The manuscript shows that he originally wrote a longer linking passage in which the first violins hummed and hah'd—musically speaking—for a couple of bars before coming to the point of Quickly's entrance.

"The beautiful Alice . . .", continues Mistress Quickly. "You and your beautiful Alice can go to the devil!" cries Falstaff angrily, recalling all the discomfort and indignities he has suffered. Mistress Quickly protests that Alice is innocent; it was the fault of those miserable menservants. Alice weeps and moans (oboes and clarinets confirm this), she invokes the saints—"Poor lady!"

While Quickly has been talking Alice, Meg, Nannetta, Ford, Dr Caius and Fenton have hidden behind a house on the left; one after the other they peek out for a moment and hide again. Quickly protests to Falstaff that Alice loves him, and gives him a letter from her. Falstaff reads it to himself; then he re-reads it aloud, in the traditional monotone of operatic letter-reading: "I shall await you in the Royal Park at midnight. You will come disguised as the Black Hunter to Herne's Oak."

Love, says Mistress Quickly, likes a mystery and Alice is taking advantage of a popular legend to see him again. As Quickly, in ominous tones, begins to tell him all about Herne and the Oak, Falstaff suggests they go into the Inn where the matter can be discussed better. Putting on her most "mysterious" voice, Mistress Quickly begins her story against equally "mysterious" sustained *ppp* notes by a solo horn and the piccolo, and enters the Inn with Falstaff. Before Quickly's voice fades in the distance, Alice takes over the story from the beginning again, imitating Quickly in a *voce grossa*, and, indeed, surpassing her in the melodramatic impact of her recital—though a great deal of this heightened effect is due to the addition of sinister thumps on the bass drum, and low notes in the horns, trumpets and trombones. Alice's performance is so eerie and realistic that she has to reassure Nannetta and Meg in her natural voice that it is only a children's fairy tale after all—"Fandonie che ai bamboli":

Ex 455

The perkiness of this tune is stressed by the piccolo which doubles the vocal line. The passage is rounded off by the three women—Alice, Nannetta and Meg—determined that their vendetta shall not fail. Alice resumes her story-telling in the same tone of voice as before, accompanied this time only by the horns to make a musical pun for her tale of the Black Hunter and the two long horns that grow on his head when he appears at midnight. Ford is delighted at the prospect of Falstaff's punishment, but is reminded by his wife that with his intolerable suspicions he is not so undeserving of punishment himself.

Alice now gets busy arranging the masquerade to take place at Herne's Oak. Nannetta shall be Queen of the Fairies, wearing a pure white dress and veil and a pink sash; Meg shall be the green Woodland Nymph, and Mistress Quickly a witch. Almost imperceptibly the atmosphere of the music has changed; evening is now falling, the scene darkens, and as the plot thickens (as they say), so an air of stealth and hushed conspiracy develops.

Alice goes on to say how she will dress a troop of small boys as elves and imps, little ghosts and devils—a whispered passage which parodies all Verdi's conspirators, footpads and soft-treading murderers:

Ex 456

Avrò con me lei put-ti che fingeran fol- letti E spiritelli e Diavo- letti E pipistrelli e farfa-relli

The brief unison cry of "tutti! tutti!" with which Nannetta, Meg and Fenton agree to Alice's plans shatters the stillness for a moment, and there is a short passage when Alice raises her voice and flies up to a top B in her excitement, but the mood is only momentarily interrupted and the slow-fade of twilight and air of conspiracy continue.

To a *pianissimo* echo by piccolo and first violins of the tune of Ex 456, Alice, Nannetta and Fenton begin to go off to the left, Meg to the right. As they go out Mistress Quickly comes out of the Inn, but seeing Ford and Dr Caius talking secretly together, she stops and listens. The men's conversation is accompanied by another conspiratorial figure, with a stealthy march-like tread derived from the rhythm of Ex 455:

Ex 457

Under his breath Ford is heard to tell Dr Caius not to worry: he shall marry Nannetta. Does Caius remember the disguise she is to wear? Then, continues Ford, when the revelry is over Caius and Nannetta are to come to him with their faces covered—Nannetta's by a veil, Caius's by a friar's cowl—and he will bless them as man and wife. Ford exposes his plan to the continued tramp of Ex 457, now given a more masculine character by bassoons and divided violas and violoncellos playing pizzicato. As Ford and Dr Caius leave the scene, Mistress Quickly, "making a sly gesture" in their direction, hurries off to tell Nannetta and Alice. She goes to the sound of what is perhaps the most magical harmonic sequence Verdi ever wrote:

Ex 458

With the tune in the piccolo and first violins, the harmony supplied by flutes and clarinets doubled by divided second violins and violas, the first sound of this phrase is breath-taking. The voices of Meg, Nannetta and Quickly die away off stage, and the street is empty. It is now night time; there is a *pp* echo in the violins of the delicate mischief of the tune of Ex 456 and a coda that evaporates into thin air with the highest D on their instruments. It is a wonderful curtain, which not only ends the scene superbly, but in an amazing way prepares us so thoroughly for the summer night scene that follows that the mood we are left in survives undisturbed by the distractions and audience chatter during the inevitable wait between scenes in the theatre. As Toscanini once said: the brief ending of this scene is already the prelude to the next. It is a unique moment.

PART TWO

Scene: Windsor Great Park. Herne's Oak stands in the centre. At the back, the banks of a ditch. The trees are thick with leaves and the shrubs are in flower. It is night, with moonlight that grows gradually brighter.

The magical atmosphere so miraculously created at the end of the previous scene is continued as the curtain rises to the sound of a horn in the distance. The instrument which, according to the score, plays behind the scenes to fulfil the stage direction that "the distant calls of the forest wardens are heard", is the unfamiliar horn in A flat-basso, though how often the characteristic, rather eerie tones of this instrument are heard and not those of the more usual horn in F in performances of *Falstaff* is another matter.

The horn calls—a wonderfully mysterious and evocative sound—are punctuated a couple of times by a brief echo in the woodwind of the opening bars of the young lover's music—Ex 437—which serves as an introduction to the entrance of Fenton.

17

The last of the horn calls dies away and for the first time since Act I, Scene 2, we hear the cor anglais which plays a prominent and imaginative part in the orchestral pages that follow. The exquisite love song that Fenton sings, and which Verdi called his *sonetto*, is not, in fact, a sonnet but the only aria in the opera (the Ford and Falstaff monologues are more properly rated as dramatic "scenes" than as arias)—and opens with a phrase that was the result of an intriguing second thought by Verdi. "Dal labbro il canto estasiato vola" ("My song of ecstasy flies from my lips"), as we now know it, begins with :

That is surely one of the most beautiful and spontaneous-sounding phrases in the whole opera. But when *Falstaff* first went into rehearsal the printed vocal score used by the cast showed the phrase as :

Those bars, which were among several that Verdi altered and modified in Fenton's aria during rehearsal, offer not only a fascinating but also a very rare glimpse of the composer at work. There is no trace of them in the manuscript of the full score as Verdi nearly always obliterated all signs of first thoughts of this kind when they affected melody or harmony. With alterations in the orchestration, on the other hand, he was content to cross out what he didn't want, often leaving the original version clearly legible. With the Fenton aria, however, the corrections were made in an already printed copy of the vocal score which was not subsequently destroyed as the alterations had to be incorporated in the revised edition.

Perhaps the most striking feature of the *sonetto* is the orchestral accompaniment full of original touches and delicate scoring for muted strings (with a solo double bass instructed to lower his E string to E flat) which is not so much a new phase in Verdi's writing for the orchestra as a development of the exquisite chamber-music orchestration first heard in *Aida*. Throughout the aria the cor anglais plays an intriguingly prominent part, providing the bass part for a sequence of *pp* shakes by three flutes and burbling away happily in a way that seems altogether peculiar to this opera. Instead of the familiar elegiac and pastoral sounds one normally associates with the instrument, in this scene of *Falstaff* the cor anglais has a wonderfully warm, nocturnal quality which is at once romantic and mysterious.

In this sequence also the harp makes its first appearance in the opera with a simple but arresting entrance to accompany Fenton's echo of "Bocca baciata non perde ventura" (Ex 438), now harmonized for the first time. From the distance Nannetta answers, "Anzi rinova come fa la luna", and enters dressed as the Queen of the Fairies. Fenton runs towards her but is held back by Alice, who suddenly appears bringing with her a black friar's cloak and a mask which she tells Fenton to put on. Fenton is understandably puzzled by what is going on, but does as he's told. All Alice will say is that Ford's plan to betray them must be scotched and turned against him in their favour.

The dressing-up of Fenton and the brief conversation that accompanies it (Nannetta remarks affectionately that he looks like a young fugitive from La Trappe) takes place to a delightfully light-fingered passage for strings, *leggero* and *pp*, punctuated by little four-note phrases in octaves tossed about by the woodwind which seem to have strayed into the score from the "Fuoco di gioia" movement in the first act of *Otello*—a fascinating example of the way Verdi, like Mozart, so often made the same music mean two different things.

In the course of this whispered movement the Merry Wives make their final plans. Mistress Quickly, who followed Alice, is disguised as a witch with a large hat and grey cloak, a stick and an ugly mask. She tells Alice that the "bride" will be the long-nosed thief who detests Dr Caius—in other words, Bardolph. Meg, masked and wearing green veils, joins them to say that the children who are to be the "imps" have been hidden along the ditch and that all is ready. Falstaff is heard approaching; the four women and Fenton leave the scene quickly.

Falstaff's entrance is preceded by a *ff* string phrase (first heard as a unison for violins and violas) which is repeated *ppp*, *fff*, *p* over a series of changing harmonies:

Ex *461*

There is something impressively ominous about this sequence which is not entirely dispelled by the grotesque appearance of Falstaff who arrives on the first stroke of midnight disguised as Herne the Hunter, with a stag's horns on his head, and wrapped in a voluminous cloak. The twelve strokes of Windsor bell are counted aloud by Falstaff in an ingeniously harmonized passage, where each F of the bell is struck to a different chord in the strings. The string phrase of Ex 461 is resumed, this time *ppp* and in unison, as Falstaff cautiously identifies Herne's Oak and calls on the heavens for aid—"Remember, Jove, thou wast a bull for thy Europa."

With the thought that love changes a man into a beast, Falstaff ceases to be so awestruck and reverts to his more familiar robust manner. Alice enters and to an exquisitely delicate orchestral accompaniment Falstaff makes love to her. Alice keeps him at arm's length with coy protests of "Sir John!" Falstaff grows more ardent but she warns him that she is being followed by Meg. "A double adventure! Let her come too!" cries Falstaff loudly. "Let me be quartered like a chamois at the table! Tear me in pieces!"—emphatic words underlined by a series of unison A's played *f* with rising grace notes by trumpets and trombones, who did the same thing during the storm scene in *Otello*.

Falstaff's fervent declarations of love are interrupted by shouts for help from Meg off stage. She makes a fleeting appearance without a mask, crying that the fairies are coming and runs away, followed by Alice who feigns terror and prays for forgiveness for her sins. The wretched Falstaff is left alone and flattens himself against the trunk of the oak, convinced that the devil will not have him damned. (Boito does not give us the whole of Shakespeare's "I think the devil will not have me damned, lest the oil that is in me should set hell on fire; he would never cross me thus".)

The atmosphere of a nocturne that began the scene and was briefly interrupted by Falstaff's wooing of Alice, now returns. Violins and violas hold a *ppp* tremolo chord and there comes an enchanted sound from an oboe, cor anglais and clarinet in unison—a kind of horn call but played by a horn unlike any heard before. It is an astonishing effect which punctuates Nannetta's call behind the scenes to the nymphs and elves, sylphs, dryads and sirens, who echo her words in the far distance. Falstaff, hearing voices, throws himself flat on the ground, murmuring, "They are the fairies; he that sees them shall die."

Nannetta can be seen through the trees. She is dressed as Queen of the Fairies and is attended by little girls representing White Fairies and Blue Fairies. Alice appears wearing a mask and accompanied by several fairies. She indicates where Falstaff is lying motionless on the ground. Nannetta enters with other fairies and does the same. The fairies are directed to their places, and Alice leaves quickly; Nannetta collects the fairies round her, telling them not to laugh and placing the little ones close to her, the bigger ones in a group on the left.

These preparations are accompanied by music whose delicacy and colour it is almost impossible to describe. Once again the orchestration has the texture of chamber music—muted strings, flutes and piccolo, three trombones with low unison E's played *ppp*, the harmonics of a solo violoncello doubling the harmonics of the harp.

When everything is ready Nannetta sings the Fairy Queen's song she was learning at the end of the previous scene—"Sul fil d'un soffio etesio" ("On the breath of the summer breeze . . ."):

Ex 462

The orchestral accompaniment is again of quite startling beauty and originality, starting out with first and second violins each divided in three parts—one half of the first violins playing sustained harmonics unmuted, the other half muted and divided in a semiquaver sextolet figure marked *stacc. e leggeriss.* which is doubled an octave lower by half the second violins, divided and muted, while the other desks contribute muted trills. The harp, having limbered up in the *sonetto*, now begins to play a more spectacular part, providing some telling single notes in harmonics (Verdi marked them in his manuscript to be played *ppppp*, but the printed score suggests that half the number of p's—*ppp*—would do), and later doubling—also in harmonics—the notes played by the bass clarinet in the course of this instrument's decoration of Nannetta's vocal line. The cor anglais also reappears, but in a more modest role than hitherto.

Nannetta's long opening phrase of fifteen bars is followed by a short movement in the same tempo but in four-time to accompany what is shown in the score as "Danzetta lenta e molle delle piccole Fate"—"A slow and gentle little dance of the small fairies":

Ex 463

This tune in the first violins is echoed *pp* in a simply-decorated form by flute and oboe in unison, doubled by the piccolo an octave higher. The *danzetta*, accompanied by a chorus of fairies singing in a near monotone, lasts only eight bars before Nannetta resumes the Fairy Queen's song. The second "verse" follows much the same orchestral and melodic course as the first, with a slight alteration of the tune in one bar, and a half-close which leads on to an extended cadence with the violins soaring in octaves over the voice. The *danzetta* comes back as the little fairies pick flowers and the others, singing softly in unison, slowly approach the oak tree. The harp is treated as a solo instrument in this passage, playing the tune of Ex 463 in octaves. The song ends with a final phrase from Nannetta that floats up to a high A and dies away.

Within the space of four bars the spell is now almost brutally broken. The plot gets going again and we are back in a world of action and reality. Or rather, in a world of a different kind of reality, for the most uncanny quality of the summer-night's music that lasts from the end of Act III, Scene 1, to the end of Nannetta's song, is that although we are told right from the start that the whole thing is a masquerade, that the characters are only *pretending* to be fairies, that the whole thing is play-acting within a play to fool Falstaff, the music transports us into a real enchanted forest where imps and elves and Fairy Queen are as real to us as they so obviously are to Falstaff. Verdi had never been at all happy with the supernatural, and he clearly didn't believe in fairies; but like the superb storyteller he was he could make *us* believe in them.

But where, with the brisk arrival on the scene of Bardolph, Pistol, Ford, Dr Caius, followed by Alice, Meg, Quickly and a chorus, the magic of Windsor Forest fades before our eyes and ears, it is still a reality to the gullible Falstaff. And little wonder, for Falstaff, one of the most gullible of all the gullible figures in which both comic and serious opera abounds, and already terrified by the unearthly beauty of the Fairy Queen's song, is confronted with an even more alarming and grotesque masquerade than the one he has just experienced.

First comes Bardolph, in a red cloak but without a mask, and wearing a monk's cowl pulled down over his face; and Pistol, dressed as a satyr. Next Dr Caius, wearing a grey cloak but no mask, and Fenton in the black monk's habit and mask we saw him put on earlier. Ford wears neither cloak nor mask. The women follow. Alice is now masked, Meg masked and disguised as the Green Nymph, and Mistress Quickly dressed as a witch. Bringing up the rear is a crowd of assorted citizens in "fantastic costumes" who form themselves into a group on the right of the stage. In the background other grotesquely masked characters carry various sort of lanterns.

The gentle tempo of the nocturne changes to a vigorous Prestissimo as the crowd enters and begins to torment the prostrate Falstaff. This new tempo becomes the pulse that beats throughout the rest of the opera; even the occasional slower interludes which occur give the impression (although they are not marked as such) of being "lo stesso movimento".

While Bardolph, with exaggerated magicianly gestures begins to perform a mock ritual of exorcism over Falstaff's body, Dr Caius moves about as if he were looking for somebody. Alice notices this and warns Nannetta who, protected by Alice and Quickly, moves off into the background where she is to remain in hiding with Fenton until Quickly calls for them.*

The rhythm changes to a fierce 6/8 (*lo stesso movimento*) as Bardolph continues his exorcism and summons elves, imps, bats, vampires and insects to prick and punch Falstaff. Little boys dressed as imps and devils appear on the scene from all directions and fling themselves on Falstaff. Some of them shake rattles, others have switches in their hands; many of them carry little red lanterns. The tenors and basses of the chorus, disguised as goblins and larger demons, take hold of Falstaff and roll him across the ground. With cries of "pizzica, pizzica" ("pinch him, pinch him") from Alice, Meg and Quickly, the children set on Falstaff, pinching his arms, his cheeks, beating his paunch with twigs and stinging him with nettles:

Ex 464

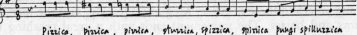

On closer inspection this famous "Pizzica" movement proves to be a most ingenious translation by Boito of the clear 6/8 rhythm of the last two lines of the fairies' song in the final scene of *The Merry Wives of Windsor*:

> Pinch him, and burn him, and turn him about,
> Till candles and starlight and moonshine be out.

In at least one respect, however, Boito improves on Shakespeare's original and that is in his use of the wonderfully vicious-sounding words that are spat out at the unhappy Falstaff:

* There is considerable disagreement between the various scores, librettos and the manuscript at this point about exactly who says what and who goes into hiding. According to Verdi's autograph Nannetta, Fenton and Alice go off and hide behind the trees; according to the 1913 edition of the printed miniature score, it is Nannetta, Fenton and Quickly. The RCA–Victor libretto of the 1964 recording states that Nannetta and Fenton disappear alone into the trees; the earlier Columbia libretto agrees with that but has Nannetta and Fenton protected not by Alice but by Meg. The people I'm really sorry for are the modern "producers" who have to satisfy their personal vanity by doing exactly the opposite of what composer and librettist intended. How can they find an opposite to do among that lot?

Cozzalo, aizzolo
dai piè al cocuzzolo!
Strozzalo, strizzalo!
Gli svampi l'uzzolo!
*Pizzica, pizzica, l'unghia rintuzzola!**

The orchestration of the accompaniment not unnaturally makes effective use of pizzicato, but the most sensational touch is the triangle played *pp* on the strong beats of the bar which adds a sudden unexpected, reassuring air of innocence to the pinching and punching. The same basically good-humoured lightness persists even when trumpets and trombones—*staccato* and *pp*—and cymbals are added. Not that Falstaff regards his treatment as altogether good-humoured and innocent, of course, but his cries of anguish are heard at such regular and formal intervals that they seem to be uttered more for the sake of a neat cadence than as expressions of great physical pain.

During all this the smallest imps dance around Falstaff, others climb on his back and perform little steps on it. Falstaff tries to defend himself but is unable to move.

The "pizzica" rhythm builds up, with the fairies adding their piping voices to those of Alice, Meg and Quickly, and the menacing tenors and basses. The movement ends with a great crashing tutti chord and the time (still *lo stesso movimento*) changes to 2/4 as Ford, Dr Caius, Pistol and Bardolph pull Falstaff up off the ground and make him kneel. They begin to recite a catalogue of abusive names —"Filthy wretch! Poltroon! Glutton! Big-Belly! Drunkard! Scoundrel!"—which Alice, Meg and Quickly extend with their own contributions in time and tune with a new orchestral figure faintly derived from the "pizzica" chorus and which Verdi uses ingeniously in the pages that follow:

Ex *465*

Bardolph grabs Mistress Quickly's stick and beats Falstaff; Pistol grabs the stick from Bardolph and beats Falstaff again. "Say you repent!" exclaim the men and women. "I repent!" cries Falstaff,

* Butt him and sting him
From his feet to his head!
Strangle him, squeeze him
Till all lust is gone.
Pinch him, pinch him till your fingernails are blunted!

but shows that he is still full of spirit (or rather that Bardolph is), when Bardolph leans over and with his face close to Falstaff's tells his master to reform his life. Falstaff's answer is, "You stink of aqua-vitae!"

Alice, Meg and Mistress Quickly now join in unison to sing what Verdi called "a sort of Litany". In a mock-religious unison they intone, "Domine, fallo casto" ("Lord make him chaste!") which is answered with a nice play on words by Falstaff who pleads that his abdomen may be spared—"Ma salvagli l'addomine":

Ex 466

Do-mine fal-lo ca - sto Fal: Ma sal-vagli L'ad-do-mi-ne

If the tune sounds vaguely familiar this may be because it is a gentle and delicious parody of two phrases from the composer's Requiem Mass, which when combined add up to something very like Verdi's "sort of Litany". The passages come respectively from the *Hostias* and the *Ingemisco*, which for the sake of easy comparison with the *Falstaff* tune I have translated into the key of A major:

Ex 467

The "Litany" phrase (Ex 466) is accompanied by a solemn wind consort of flutes and oboes playing the tune in unison, cor anglais, bass clarinet, bassoons and horns. It is played four times without alteration to the melody but with variation in the harmonies and the words sung by the three women. Falstaff's plea remains the same.

At each repetition of the tune the second bar is coloured by brief phrases of abuse by the four men to the rhythm of Ex 465, and the fourth bar by echoes of "pizzica" by the chorus of fairies.

At some angry unison demands by the men for an answer from Falstaff the tempo quickens, and with the rather unexpected and vigorous use of a distorted, but still recognizable, paraphrase of the first two bars of the "Litany", a simple sequence of almost classical "development" builds up to a vehement outburst by Bardolph, in the course of which his cowl falls off and he is recognized by Falstaff.

Rising from his knees Falstaff now turns on his tormentor (Bardolph has been particularly vindictive), and in a passage of superb

17*

invective chases after him. Falstaff's crescendo of abuse builds up in
the rhythm of Ex 465 and is a rare recital of epithets which sound
magnificent in Italian. A literal translation give some idea of the
richness of the imagery but little of its fierce effect: "Scarlet nose!
wattle nose! Pointed awl! Fire of resin! Salamander! *Ignis fatuus!*
Battered old halberd! Tailor's stick! Spit of hell! Dried herring!
Vampire! Basilisk! [*manigoldo*] Ruffian! Thief!"

Falstaff turns to the rest of the company: "I have spoken! And if I
lie may my sword belt cut me in half!" His words are greeted with a
general "bravo!" The rhythm of Ex 465 is taken up again as a *ppp*
figure in the orchestra and Falstaff, in a line that can have great
pathos in the theatre, sits down, asking for a little rest; he is tired.

Bardolph has meanwhile been approached by Mistress Quickly,
who whispers that she will hide him under a white veil; they disappear behind the trees in one direction. Dr Caius resumes his
search and leaves the scene in the opposite direction.

Ford turns to Falstaff and with an ironical bow asks who is the one
who wears the horns now. Alice and Meg come forward and taking
off their masks echo the question *ironicamente*. Falstaff is silent for a
moment; then he stretches out his hand to greet "Dear Signor
Fontana". Alice quickly puts him right: "This is Ford, my husband," she says, ending the phrase on a trill that few Alices can ever
treat us to. Before Falstaff can say anything Mistress Quickly returns
and makes her deep curtsy with "Cavaliero!" (to the familiar tune,
of course, of Ex 440), which Falstaff mimics with a disgusted
"Reverenza!"

This little skirmish, which ends with Falstaff and Quickly singing
the last couple of bars in an ambiguous unison, is perhaps the biggest
laugh created by purely musical means in the opera. No producer
can hope to extract more comedy from a phrase which is in itself
musically comic and which makes its greatest effect by its totally
unexpected timing. We have had Falstaff reacting with disgust at
Quickly's reappearance in Act II, Scene 2, when her "Reverenza!"
acts as a superb anticlimax to the great orchestral trill and Falstaff's
sense of well-being. Here, in the last scene, there is the final surprise
of Falstaff, as full of spirit as before, mocking Quickly as he acknow-
ledges defeat.

Mistress Quickly asks him how he could possibly have believed
that two women could be so dense and thick-headed as to give
themselves body and soul to the devil for the sake of a dirty fat old
man—"with that bald head", she says in unison with Meg, "and
with that weight!" sing Alice, Meg and Quickly in unison.

Falstaff admits, in a phrase that ends in a hee-hawing cadence
with unison support from oboes, bassoons and violas, that he is
beginning to see that he has been an ass. As he has already mas-

queraded as a stag and behaved like an ox (*bue* in Italian also means dunce), Falstaff is greeted joyfully as a rare monster. He retorts calmly that if it hadn't been for him there would never have been any joke to laugh at—a line accompanied with a feather-light couple of bars in the orchestra which echoes the airy view of honour as a mere word in the famous monologue in Act I. Boito at this point confirms our suspicions of what he has been wanting to say, by saying it—and quoting Falstaff's line in *Henry IV, Part II*: "I am not only witty in myself, but the cause that wit is in other men." This meets with general approval, except from Ford who swears by the gods that if Falstaff hadn't laughed he would have slaughtered him.*

Ford quickly recovers his temper and proposes that the masquerade should be crowned by the nuptials of the Fairy Queen. The ceremony begins to the music of a minuet-like movement of great charm:

Ex *468*

The tune is played on the G string of the first violins, doubled by three flutes in unison in the same register. Dr Caius, who wears a mask, and Bardolph, who is dressed as the Queen of the Fairies with his face covered by a veil, enter slowly hand in hand. They move to the centre of the scene where they are surrounded by fairies. At this point Alice asks that another couple of lovers might be allowed to take part in the nuptial ceremony, and presents Nannetta and Fenton. Nannetta wears a large blue veil which covers her completely; Fenton wears a mask and his monk's habit. Ford agrees to Alice's request; it shall be a double wedding.

Guided by Alice, the imps and elves carrying their lanterns go closer to Bardolph and Dr Caius. A small imp, carried in Alice's arms, raises his lantern close to Bardolph's face. Nannetta and Fenton, holding hands, stand a little apart from the central group. Calling on heaven to unite the couples in marriage, Ford orders the removal of masks and veils with a cry of "Apotheosis!" On Ford's command everybody unmasks or unveils; Quickly, who is standing behind him, snatches the veil from Bardolph's head.

Verdi wrote the word "Quadro" across the autograph score at this point, and the old-fashioned English theatrical equivalent

---

* This passage is badly mistranslated in the English version of the libretto accompanying the Geraint Evans RCA–Victor recording of 1964, where "Se non ridessi" is given as "if you hadn't come back". Even allowing for the confusion caused by the use of the perfect subjunctive of the verb *ridere*, to laugh, where on earth is Falstaff supposed to have come back from?

"tableau" certainly seems the apt word to describe the situation of laughter and consternation that has resulted. Dr Caius finds he has married Bardolph, Ford's surprise turns to fury when he discovers that the other couple are Fenton and his daughter. Alice, Meg and Quickly cry, "Vittoria!" and their "Evviva!" is supported by the chorus.

Alice goes over to her husband who, one might say, is still suffering from shock, and reminds him that man often falls into the nets woven by his own malice. Falstaff, with an ironical bow, asks "dear good Master Ford" to tell him who is the sucker *now*. "Him," replies Ford, pointing to Caius. "You," retorts Caius to Ford. "You two," insists Bardolph, pointing to Ford and Caius. "Those two," concurs Fenton, also pointing at them. "Us," says Caius, standing by Ford. "Both of them," exclaims Falstaff. "No," contradicts Alice, putting Falstaff with Ford and Caius, "all three of them!" A little figure constructed from the last four notes of the Allegretto phrase quoted as Ex 468, takes the orchestra through one or two gentle modulations while Alice tells her husband to look at the young lovers and their touching anxiety. Ford admits defeat with a good grace and gives Nannetta and Fenton his blessing.

(The validity of the marriages that Ford performs is extremely doubtful, of course. In Shakespeare's play the characters are legally married off stage during the Forest scene, so we are denied the hilarious dénouement of the opera and Boito's inspired comic touch of marrying Dr Caius to his arch-enemy Bardolph. The main thing with Boito's story, however, is that Ford has been made a fool of and he would find it very difficult to arrange a fully legal marriage between Dr Caius and Nannetta after what has happened. If we are really concerned with the way things happen in the libretto we can always accept the Forest "marriage" of Nannetta and Fenton as a symbol, with a proper religious ceremony to follow.)

There is a general "Evviva!" of approval at Ford's gesture. Falstaff proposes that they should have a chorus and end the scene, after which, adds Ford, they will all go and have supper with Falstaff—or as the libretto puts it, with "Sir Falstaff".

This sudden reference by Boito to "Sir Falstaff" in the very last moments of the opera is most puzzling. Until now his observance of the correct English manner of addressing or referring to a knight has been exemplary. So exemplary, indeed, that it is surprising to find how many Italian singers who have sung and heard the very words "Sir John" in *Falstaff* have failed to learn the lesson and will talk—like so many other foreigners—of "Sir Smith" when they meet a Sir John Smith in real life.

The assembled company in the opera, however, are not put out by Ford's lapse and his mention of supper for all with "Sir Falstaff" is greeted with another enthusiastic "Evviva!" And with little more ado Falstaff starts the fugue which ends the opera in the same key of C major that began it, pointing the moral that the whole world is a jest and that man was born a jester. Every mortal laughs at every other one, but he laughs best who laughs the last laugh of all:

Ex 469

The final fugue of *Falstaff* was Verdi's most cherished private joke. In the very early stages of work on the opera, before Boito had delivered the libretto of the first two acts, in fact, Verdi wrote to Boito that he was amusing himself by writing fugues ". . . and a *comic fugue* which would be in place in *Falstaff*! 'But how do you mean, a comic fugue? Why comic?' you'll say, I don't know *how* or *why*, but it's a *comic fugue*!"

From which one may suppose that the last pages of the score, "Tutto nel mondo è burla", was the first part of the opera to be written and that words were put to it later.

"Comic", although it is the most obvious English equivalent, is perhaps a rather misleading adjective, for the phrase Verdi used was *fuga buffa*, which certainly describes this finale inasmuch as it is clearly not a *fuga seria*. But it is not, I think, a fugue in which even the musician is expected to find only musical jokes, although he can enjoy endless little contrapuntal ingenuities and surprising moments like the sudden switch from C to E flat at one point.

One thing is certain, however: that this ending to the opera is absolutely dead right. Once having heard it, what other ending could one possibly imagine, anyway? What better coda could Verdi have written to this vast Scherzo with Lyrical Interludes which is *Falstaff*? And perhaps the most astonishing aspect of the whole thing is the complete absence of any hint of anticlimax. The fugue comes as a logical musical and dramatic rounding-off of the action in a way which is virtually without parallel in comic opera. There is nothing to equal it in Rossini, where last-act finales too often sound as if they were written (or taken over from other operas) merely because it was time the evening's entertainment came to an end. Even in *Così fan tutte* and *Figaro* Mozart's signing-off was more an exquisite formality, like the rhyming couplets at the end of a Shakespeare comedy, than a final comment made with the great explosion of musical laughter and good humour that brings down the curtain on Verdi's last and most exhilarating opera.

It happened that *Falstaff* was not only the first opera by Verdi I ever saw, but the first opera of any kind. I was taken to it as a boy during the holidays in Florence and heard the incomparable Mariano Stabile in the title role. Not unnaturally I imagined that Verdi always wrote music like that, so I was rather surprised when I heard *La traviata* a few days later to discover that a composer who could write such gay music was actually capable of moving one to tears. In other words, instead of being astonished by the unexpectedness of *Falstaff*, as everybody else had been, I was astonished by *La traviata*.

It was only as I grew older and more experienced that I began to see why *Falstaff* was universally regarded as an exceptional opera for Verdi to have written. But even now I think that the most astonishing aspect of *Falstaff* is not that it was written by a man of nearly eighty, but that it was written at all. A great deal is always made of Verdi's great age at the time he wrote *Falstaff*; no opera composer had ever written a masterpiece in his late seventies before. Naturally not, because no other great composer had ever lived that long—Mozart had died at thirty-five, Bellini at thirty-four, Donizetti at fifty; Rossini, though he died at seventy-six, had retired from dramatic composition at thirty-seven; Puccini died at sixty-five. Only Monteverdi, who died at seventy-six, lived to compose an opera in his seventies and he wrote his masterpiece, *L'incoronazione di Poppea*, the year before he died. Which suggests, if Monteverdi and Verdi are anything to go by, that if opera composers can live that long, their best work will normally be done in their seventies.

What has always struck me as most astonishing about *Falstaff* is its *improbability*; it was reasonable to expect that Verdi's last opera would be a worthy climax to his career, but not that it would take the form it did. However, improbability is an essential feature of all miracles and *Falstaff* has understandably come to be regarded as a miracle.

Verdi wrote *Falstaff* primarily to amuse himself; whether, if it had come to it, he would in fact have withheld it altogether from performance as he threatened, is doubtful I think. The theatre was too much in his blood for him ever to have considered the writing of *Falstaff* as a mere paper transaction, an academic exercise to be looked at or put away in a drawer; of all people he knew that opera has no life or purpose outside the opera house.

Nevertheless, because Verdi regarded it as an essentially private affair in some respects, there is something more than usually personal about *Falstaff*—as though we were listening to the reflections of an old man on the sort of music he would perhaps liked to have written more of, but somehow had never had time to, until the late evening of his life.

There was surely never a composer one had to make more excuses
and allowances for, slap down more often with more love and affection, knowing that it didn't matter, than Giuseppe Verdi. It is
almost as though one were in honour bound to do so just *because* one
loves him so much. Certainly few composers have had faults that—
like Verdi's—are as endearing and stimulating as their virtues. It is
possible, of course, that other people do not take the same attitude to
Verdi's lapses as I do, but to me these homeric noddings are characteristic of his unparalleled universality. In Verdi there is always
something for everybody. I know people who cannot bear Mozart
at any price, and there are some quite well-known musical figures in
our own country who publicly boast that they feel the same about
Puccini. But the case of the layman, the student, or the professional
who can find nothing in Verdi to please him is something I have
never encountered.

For those who do not like *Rigoletto*, *Il trovatore* or *La traviata* there
are *Aida*, *Otello* and *Falstaff*. For those who find *Aida*, *Otello* and *Falstaff* a little lacking in show-stopping high spots there are always
Rigoletto, *Il trovatore* and *La traviata*. But whether all or only some
Verdi operas appeal to the individual listener they have one great
element in common—Verdi's gift of characterization, of breathing
life and reality into his characters by musical means. There are
times when the hero is never anything more than a tenor, the baritone no more than a cardboard villain, but even when this happens
there is consolation in the composer's endless melodic invention and
his instinctive determination that there shall always be something to
sing.

From *Nabucco* to *Falstaff* Verdi's gallery of musical portraits is
filled with a wealth of rich and original studies, perhaps none of
them more lovingly and personally drawn than those of the fathers
in the operas. As I mentioned in the chapter on *Rigoletto* Vittorio Gui
once suggested that this was largely a consequence of Verdi's own
tragic experiences as a father in early life, when his young wife and
two children died within less than two years of each other.

This could well have been so, for there is in the portraits of Verdi's
fathers an unusually personal element of compassion and understanding which is different from anything else in the operas. Rigoletto, Philip of Spain, Simon Boccanegra, Amonasro, the elder
Germont, Macduff when he sings, "Ah, la paterna mano"—all are
affected by the sorrow and despair of unhappy fatherhood and have
a peculiar pathos.

Mother-love, on the other hand, is most meagrely touched on in
Verdi's operas. Alice Ford is a real mother; but Azucena is what, in
the jargon of the new school of criticism that believes sex was invented by Freud, would be described as a Mother Figure. She

seems to have all the devotion and selflessness of the real thing, and indeed both the Count di Luna and Manrico himself believe she is genuinely Manrico's mother, but she is not. Azucena stands apart from Verdi's heroines; she is a mezzo-soprano, she is old and ugly and unromantic; nobody falls in love with her; she is more than half dotty, but Verdi needs no Mad Scene to let us know it; and if she is not in the strictly conventional sense a heroine (for heroines are always sopranos and have tenors as lovers) she dominates *Il trovatore* far more than Leonora, the official heroine.

In Verdi's other operas, of course, the heroine-soprano is never faced with anything like the competition Leonora gets from Azucena in *Il trovatore*—at least, not from other women. Aida and Amneris are complementary, so are Elisabeth and Eboli in *Don Carlos*; in both cases the fate of the sad and unfortunate soprano heroine is almost matched by that of the sad and unfortunate mezzo-soprano villainess whose despair and defeat move the audience far beyond the slight, formal, sportsmanlike sympathy it normally feels for the loser in the average operatic contest of this kind.

Pathos, indeed, is the most powerful, recurrent element in Verdi's dramatic music, found perhaps more often in the principal women's roles than in the men's; sometimes, as in *La traviata*, it is relieved by a poignant gaiety, sometimes, as in *Falstaff*, it gives added point to comedy. But wherever it occurs, it has a peculiar, unmistakable reality. The tears and anguish of Aida and Amneris, Elisabeth and Eboli, of Violetta and Azucena, of Amelia in *Un ballo in maschera*, of the two Leonoras—in *Il trovatore* and *La forza del destino*—of the Jews in *Nabucco*, and the Scottish exiles in *Macbeth*, of Desdemona, the most tragic figure of them all, are the tears and anguish of intensely human figures.

Verdi's famous words in a letter to his friend Countess Clara Maffei in 1876, have often been quoted: "It may be a good thing to copy reality, but *to invent reality* is better, much better." What is less well known is the rest of the letter, prompted by his opinion of a comedy he had seen in Genoa. The letter continued:

> "The three words—*to invent reality*—look a little contradictory, but ask *Papà* [Shakespeare]. It could be that he, *Papà*, met one or two Falstaffs, but it would have been difficult to find so villainous a villain as Iago, and he could never have found such angels as Cordelia, Imogen, Desdemona, etc. etc., yet they are so real!
> "To copy reality is a fine thing, but it is photography, not painting."

In the extent of the reality he invented, the vast range of human experience he expressed in music, Verdi may have been equalled by Mozart, but he was never surpassed by him. The twelve operas discussed in this book represent less than half of his total output in this

form, but in their pages can be found almost every emotion and misfortune known to mankind. Love, hatred, laughter, tears, cruelty,
jealousy, loyalty, frustration, suicide, murder, death by fire and
poison, suffocation and unbelievable accident, death in battle and
duel, death from heart failure, consumption and being buried alive,
paternal love, devotion, pride, bigotry, religious consolation, grief,
courage, humiliation, vengeance, hypocrisy, illness, superstition,
nostalgia, poverty, patriotic fervour, drunkenness—the list of things
that happen to the characters in Verdi's operas is endless. So, too,
is the catalogue of scenes set by the orchestra, from the Sleepwalking
Scene in *Macbeth*, the storm in *Rigoletto*, the sickroom in *La traviata*,
to the poetry of the Nile Scene and Windsor Forest, the terror of the
tempest at sea in *Otello*, and numberless other masterly moments of
instantaneously-created atmosphere and colour in which all Verdi's
operas seem to abound.

"To invent reality is better, much better." Perhaps these words
should have appeared as a motto at the beginning of this book.
Certainly no others so clearly define the aims and achievements, or
provide the final explanation of the greatness of Giuseppe Verdi.

Ringmer,
Sussex,
1967

INDEX OF CONTEXTS

An "Index of Contexts" by which the reader may refer to the dramatic situation in which the more familiar items occur in Verdi's operas.

NABUCCO

MACBETH

RIGOLETTO

IL TROVATORE

LA TRAVIATA

DON CARLOS

AIDA

OTELLO

APPENDIX B

TWO VERDI LETTERS

The first was written by Verdi while he was in London in 1862 for the first performance of his cantata *Inno delle nazioni* ("Hymn of the Nations") composed for the opening of the London Exhibition of that year to words by Arrigo Boito. The Exhibition commissioners, among them the hostile director of the Covent Garden Opera, Michael Costa, rejected the cantata on the pretext that there was not enough time to rehearse it. The public indignation that followed was appeased by Col. Mapleson, who presented it at the rival opera house, Her Majesty's in the Haymarket.

The letter is addressed to Mr (later Sir) Julius Benedict (1804–1885), composer of *The Lily of Killarney*, and conductor of The Vocal Association who gave the first performance of Verdi's cantata.

A.L.s *1 page*   13 cm × 20·5 cm
                                                     Londra 21 Mag. 1862
                                                           ore 12
Car^{mo}. Benedict

Ricevo in questo momento un'invito in nome vostro dal segretario *The Vocal Association* d'assistare stassera alla repetizione della cantata; ma un preventivo impegno mi assenta oggi da Londra, nè so a qual ora sarò di ritorno. In ogni modo sono nelle vostre, e per consequenza in buonissime mani, e non v'è bisogno della mia assistenza.

Aveva domandato per domani una prova al Teatro, e se vi sarà, io pure v'assisterò.*

Co' miei più vivi ringraziamenti mi dico il vostro aff.

G. Verdi

Translation: London, 21st May, 1862, 12 o'clock. Dearest Benedict: I have just received an invitation in your name from the secretary of *The Vocal Association* to attend the rehearsal of the cantata this evening; but I have an engagement that will take me out of London today and I do not know what time I shall return. In any case I am in your, and consequently the best, hands, and there is no need for my presence.

I have asked for a rehearsal for tomorrow at the Theatre, and if it takes place I shall be there.

With my best thanks I am your affectionate

G. Verdi

The second letter is to an unidentified correspondent written when Verdi and his wife Giuseppina were in Paris for the first performance of *Aida* at the Opéra in 1880. The letter, written in French, is dated 27th February; the performance at the Opéra was on 22nd March (*Aida* had already been given in Italian at the Théâtre des Italiens in 1876 and in French at the same theatre in 1878).

The letter is written on three sides of a piece of folded writing paper headed with the engraved monogram "G.V.", the initials common to both Verdi and his wife. Giuseppina writes on pages 1 and 2, Verdi on the third page; the fourth page is blank. I have transcribed Giuseppina's part of the letter exactly as it was written without drawing attention to a whole series of *sic*'s to the missing accents in words like *présenté*, *précédée*, *préface*, *supérieurement* etc. and the mis-spelling of *remerciements*.

A.L.s *3 pages*   11·2 cm × 17·2 cm

Monsieur,

Verdi m'a presenté en votre nom cette traduction si vantée de Faust, precedé d'une magnifique preface, le tout dans une splendide édition! J'en suis toute confuse et reconnaissante! Quoique dans le plus mauvais français du monde, voulez vous me permetter, Monsieur, de vous adresser ces quelques mots, comme l'expression de mes doubles remerciments? Se rappeler de moi, *che vivo di luce riflessa*, c'est une manière superieurement delicate, pour témoigner à Verdi votre éstime et votre sympathie, comme homme et comme artiste.

[Page 2]

Merci pour lui et pour moi!

Je vous souhaite, Monsieur, de pourvoir bientôt quitter votre lit de douleur, pour rentrer sain de corps et d'esprit dans ce monde d'intelligences parmis lesquelles vous occupez une place si élevée!

Josephine Verdi

* "Aveva" is not a misprint for "avevo", nor a misreading of the manuscript, but Verdi's use of an old-fashioned grammatical form in which the third person singular was used for the first (see Ex 74).

Paris 27 Fevrier
1880

[Page 3]

Ma femme qui aime les livres est devenue toute rouge de plaisir, voyant
le magnifique volume que vous avez bien voulu lui offrir. Je ne sais
comment vous remercier de cette politesse, à laquelle j'y suis très
sensible. J'espère que vous voudrez bien me permettre de vous serrer la
main, assitôt que les occupations du théatre voudront bien me le
permettre.

Agréez en attendant avec mes remerciments l'expression de mes
souhaits pour votre prompte guérison.

                                              G. Verdi

Translation: Monsieur, Verdi has given me in your name this highly-praised translation
of *Faust*, preceded by a magnificent preface and all of it in a splendid edition! I am all
confused and grateful! Although in the worst French in the world will you permit me,
Monsieur, to address to you these few words as the expression of my double thanks. To
remember me, who live only in reflected light, is an extremely delicate way of showing
Verdi your esteem and your sympathy as man and artist. [Page 2] Thank you for him and
for me! I hope, Monsieur, you will soon be able to leave your bed of sickness to return
healthy in body and mind to that world of intelligent people among whom you occupy so
high a place! Josephine Verdi. Paris 27th February, 1880. [Page 3] My wife who loves
books grew quite flushed with pleasure on seeing the magnificent volume which you were
so kind as to send her. I do not know how to thank you for this kindness which touches
me very much. I hope you will allow me to shake your hand as soon as my theatrical
business permits me. Meanwhile please accept with my thanks my wishes for your rapid
recovery. G. Verdi

If anybody would like to look at the manuscript of these two letters
there are photostat copies of them (made for me by my friend Roy Law-
rence, who as a solicitor and Under-Sheriff of Sussex, has that sort of
machine in his office) in the Istituto di Studi Verdiani in Parma, where
they are busy rounding up the numberless Verdi letters which have never
appeared in print. But even they have so far been unable to identify the
mysterious and obviously eminent Monsieur who sent the translation of
Faust. I don't think Verdi ever thought of *Faust* as an operatic subject,
but I must admit I'd still like to know what this letter was all about.

GENERAL INDEX

INDEX OF VERDI'S ORCHESTRATION